Teaching Today

An Introduction to Education

Seventh Edition

David G. Armstrong

Late of The University of North Carolina at Greensboro

Kenneth T. Henson

The Citadel

Tom V. Savage

Santa Clara University

PEARSON

Merrill
Prentice Hall

Upper Saddle River, New Jersey
Columbus, Ohio

Library of Congress Cataloging-in-Publication Data

Armstrong, David G.
  Teaching today: an introduction to education/David G. Armstrong, Kenneth T. Henson,
Tom V. Savage— 7th ed.
    p. cm.
  Includes bibliographical references and indexes.
  ISBN 0–13–183782–6
  1. Teaching—United States. 2. Education—Study and teaching—United States.
  3. Teaching—Vocational guidance—United States. I. Henson, Kenneth T. II. Savage, Tom V. III. Title.

LB1775.2.A75 2005
371.102—dc22   2004044812

Vice President and Executive Publisher: Jeffery W. Johnston
Executive Editor: Debra A. Stollenwerk
Developmental Editors: Kimberly J. Lundy and Amy Nelson
Editorial Assistant: Mary Morrill
Production Editor: Kris Roach
Photo Coordinator: Sandy Schaefer
Production Coordination: Amy Gehl, Carlisle Publishers Services
Design Coordinator: Diane C. Lorenzo
Cover Designer: Jeff Vanik

Production Manager: Pamela D. Bennett
Director of Marketing: Ann Castel Davis
Marketing Manager: Darcy Betts Prybella
Marketing Coordinator: Tyra Poole

This book was set in Stempel Schneidler by Carlisle Communications, Ltd. It was printed and bound by Courier Kendallville, Inc. The cover was printed by The Lehigh Press, Inc.

Photo Credits: Anthony Magnacca/Merrill, pp. 2, 48, 69, 95, 104, 141, 183, 189, 196, 228, 233, 244, 247, 254, 262, 274, 284, 340, 354, 380; Kathy Kirtland/Merrill, p. 5; Anne Vega/Merrill, pp. 14, 160, 170, 175, 256; Scott Cunningham/Merrill, pp. 20, 32, 62, 117, 138, 144, 198, 204, 216, 293, 312, 343, 377, 386; Andy Brunk/Merrill, p. 36; U.S. National Education Association of the United States, p. 39; AP/Wide World Photos, p. 56; Michelle Bridwell/PhotoEdit, p. 75; Shirley Zeiberg/PH College, p. 86; Stephen Capra/PH College, p. 89; Barbara Schwartz/Merrill, pp. 112, 125; Corbis/Bettmann, pp. 118, 302, 318, 322; KS Studios/Merrill, p. 287; Courtesy of the Library of Congress, p. 324; David Young-Wolff/PhotoEdit, p. 359; Peter Stone/Black Star, p. 372.

Praxis™ is a registered trademark of Educational Testing Service (ETS). This book is not endorsed or approved by ETS.

Pearson Prentice Hall™ is a trademark of Pearson Education, Inc.
Pearson® is a registered trademark of Pearson plc
Prentice Hall® is a registered trademark of Pearson Education, Inc.
Merrill® is a registered trademark of Pearson Education, Inc.

Pearson Education Ltd.
Pearson Education Singapore Pte. Ltd.
Pearson Education Canada, Ltd.
Pearson Education—Japan

Pearson Educacion Australia Pty. Limited
Pearson Education North Asia Ltd.
Pearson Education de Mexico, S.A. de C.V.
Pearson Education Malaysia Pte. Ltd.

10 9 8 7 6 5 4 3 2 1
ISBN: 0-13-183782-6

Dedication

We would like to dedicate this edition of *Teaching Today* to David Grant Armstrong. Unfortunately, Dave passed away just days after completion of the manuscript for this edition. We have worked with Dave on various editions of *Teaching Today* for 25 years. He was not only a consummate professional, but a good personal friend. He had a great influence on educational practice throughout his many years in the profession. It is fitting that this edition will continue to expand his influence.

Kenneth T. Henson

Tom V. Savage

You may not have thought much about the diverse, potentially competing roles you will play out in the classroom. When you work with learners, you will be expected to establish an appropriate balance between

- Teaching young people to behave appropriately in groups while, at the same time, developing a personal relationship with each member of your class (Cuban, 2001);
- Promoting the value of individualism while, at the same time, encouraging commitment to the larger community's shared perspectives;
- Encouraging learners to master long-standing approaches to problems while, simultaneously, nurturing their abilities to engage reality in creative ways; and
- Presenting content that you deem to be essential and, at the same time, preparing learners for mandatory assessments that may focus on content that you consider less important.

How you navigate among these varying expectations will depend on your teaching situation, your academic background, and your personal values. Your responses may change over the course of your teaching career. Variations in your approaches will be driven by changes in learners, legislation, community expectations, and your store of personal knowledge.

Education demands smart, altruistic teachers. If school districts were to post notices to attract the kinds of people they want to hire, the signs might read: "Wanted: Teachers Who Lead." If you seek a career free from the confrontations of contemporary life, choose another line of work. As a teacher, you need to act as a proactive leader. Today teachers are becoming ever more involved in making decisions about budgets, school management, and other areas that go well beyond traditional concerns for instructional planning.

In preparing the seventh edition of *Teaching Today*, we have emphasized topics relevant to the world you will enter as a classroom teacher. In addition to basic information about these topics, you will find material designed to help you analyze, reflect, and decide. You can expand your understanding of these issues by going beyond the text to pursue information at a number of World Wide Web sites that we recommend. You also will find useful the extensive glossary of specialized terms that follows the final chapter.

You may live in a state that requires you to take the *Praxis II* examination as a qualification for a teaching certificate, credential, or license. (You will find detailed information about the Praxis exams in Chapter 1, "Education in an Age of Change.") At the end of each chapter, you will be invited to reflect on what you have learned and to think about how the content might help you prepare for the *Praxis II* examination.

In your effort to make content from this text part of your own professional-knowledge base, consider starting and maintaining a personal *initial-development portfolio*. An initial-development portfolio provides a means to record important new information, highlight key points you wish to remember, and reflect on ways to use this new content as you prepare for your teaching career. At the end of each chapter, you will be prompted to consider how newly introduced content might be incorporated into your initial-development portfolio. (You will find detailed information about initial-development portfolios in Chapter 1.)

The end-of-chapter materials related to preparing for *Praxis II* and your initial-development portfolio are reminders that, to derive maximum benefit from this text, you need to engage new information actively. The more you reflect on the content and integrate it into what you already know, the better the information will serve you. We hope your work with this text and the other experiences you encounter in your preparation program will enhance your ability to think carefully about educational issues and will help you grasp key characteristics of teaching and schooling.

ORGANIZATION OF THIS TEXT

Earlier editions of *Teaching Today* have been used both by undergraduate and graduate students. We prepared the book for use in introduction-to-education classes, introduction-to-teaching classes, foundations-of-education classes, school-curriculum classes, issues-in-education classes, and problems-in-education classes. This edition organizes content under four major headings. The title of each provides a context for the chapters it includes.

Part 1 is titled "The Profession." Chapter 1 focuses on the changing nature of the profession. To illustrate teachers' many responsibilities, there is a useful description of a teacher's typical day. Chapter 2 emphasizes the phases in a teacher's professional development, the use of teaching portfolios to document performance, and the important support roles that professional organizations play. The chapter also briefly introduces several nonteaching roles in education. Chapter 3 explores the impact of numerous reform initiatives and recent legislation that is changing the nature of what schools and teachers do.

Part 2 focuses on "Learners and Their Needs." Chapter 4 provides important descriptive information about characteristics of learners in today's schools. There is an emphasis on how certain learner variables may affect school performance. Chapter 5 explores issues associated with multiculturalism. Specific examples of programs that have served culturally diverse young people are introduced. Chapter 6 describes legal requirements and instructional approaches relevant to appropriately serving learners with special needs and gifted learners.

Part 3 centers on "Teaching and Assessing." Chapter 7 introduces curriculum orientations, state curriculum standards, and information related to the influence that standardized tests have on content selection. In addition, basic elementary and secondary curriculum patterns are described. Chapter 8 presents approaches associated with effective instruction. Content includes information related to active teaching, constructivist teaching, ways to achieve clarity of communication, and characteristics of good questions. This chapter also includes descriptions of teacher–learner observation instruments that can be used in the classroom. Chapter 9 focuses on the important issue of classroom management and discipline. Specific suggestions for an escalating series of teacher responses, varied according to the seriousness and frequency of the disruptive behavior, are included. Chapter 10 describes approaches to assessment, measurement, evaluation, and grading. In addition to more traditional approaches, there is extensive treatment of learner portfolios.

Part 4 focuses on "Shapers of Today's Educational World." Chapter 11 provides information that illustrates how varying philosophical perspectives affect attitudes toward specific curricula and instructional practices. The chapter also describes how attendance at specific schools, family attitudes, perspectives of certain religious and social organizations, and membership in certain ethnic and cultural groups influence patterns of learner behavior in the classroom. Chapter 12 traces important historical influences that have helped shape practices in today's schools. Information includes descriptions of European and non-European influences and important developments in the evolution of American education. Chapter 13 focuses on the important role technology plays in today's schools. Content includes information related to technology standards, technology's influence on behavior, and promises and challenges associated with the introduction of new technologies in today's schools. Chapter 14 explores learners' rights and responsibilities, and their legal implications for teachers. The chapter discusses several relevant court cases.

At the end of the book, you will find a complete glossary. It includes helpful definitions of all terms introduced in the text.

NEW TO THIS EDITION

- **Chapter 13: Influences of Technology.** This chapter illustrates the impact of technology on teaching today, how teachers can incorporate technology into their classroom practice, and how to make informed decisions about the use of technology in the classroom.
- **Reorganized chapters include:**
  - Profiles of Today's Learners (Chapter 4)
  - Responding to Diversity (Chapter 5)
  - Social and Philosophical Perspectives (Chapter 11)
  - Legal Issues Affecting Learners and Teachers (Chapter 14)
- Several useful and appealing new chapter additions to extend learning include:
  - **Preparing for Praxis** activities at the end of each chapter motivate students to take notes and organize materials in ways that will help them prepare for the *Praxis II* examinations.
  - **For Your Initial-Development Portfolio** encourages students to reflect on chapter content, consider its relevance for their own professional development, and organize materials for a portfolio that is consistent with INTASC standards.
  - **Profiling a Teacher** anecdotes that appear in several chapters bring students face to face with real-world challenges faced by classroom teachers today.
- **Web Extensions** prompt students to learn more about topics by selecting Web sites to search to find engaging supplementary information that will deepen their understanding of newly introduced text content.
- Extended coverage throughout the book of **curriculum standards, standardized testing, accountability,** and the **No Child Left Behind Act.**
- New content related to **violence in schools** in Chapter 4.
- Expanded coverage of **portfolios,** including **initial-development portfolios, teaching portfolios,** and **learner portfolios** featured in Chapter 2 and throughout the book.
- Increased attention to **constructivist teaching** in Chapter 8.
- Greatly expanded coverage of **non-European influences** on American education featured throughout Chapter 5.
- Updated content on important **legal issues** facing learners and teachers, as discussed throughout Chapter 14.
- Continued broad and updated coverage of **management and discipline** issues, as addressed in Chapter 9.
- Extensive coverage of issues related to **multicultural education** in Chapter 5.

SPECIAL FEATURES OF THIS TEXT

Features of the seventh edition of *Teaching Today* include the following:

- **Bulleted objectives** at the beginning of each chapter draw students' attention to important chapter content.
- **Graphic organizers** at the beginning of each chapter provide a convenient visual summary of chapter organization and content.
- Numerous **Web Extensions** (*NEW!*) appear in each chapter.
- The **Profiling a Teacher** (*NEW!*) features appear in several chapters.
- **Critical Incidents** in several chapters present students with opportunities to engage in higher-level thinking as they reflect on situations faced by today's teachers.
- **Boldfaced terms** (*NEW!*), each of which is defined in the end-of-text glossary, draw students' attention to the importance of the specialized vocabulary they will be using in their roles as professional educators.
- **Preparing for Praxis** (*NEW!*) activities appear at the end of each chapter.
- **For Your Initial-Development Portfolio** (*NEW!*) features are located at the end of each chapter and connected with INTASC standards.
- A **Companion Website,** located at http://www.prenhall.com/armstrong, provides students with access to a related message board, a chat room, links to additional websites and to other resources tied to the text's content.
- **Cartoons** that appear in selected chapters illustrate educational issues and help convey to students that, although education is serious business, it need not be grim.
- **Figures** in each chapter enrich content and provide additional opportunities for students to reflect on new information.
- **Video Viewpoints** tie chapter content to an accompanying ABC News video library that features important education-related news segments from ABC News programs.
- **Self-Tests** provide students with opportunities to check their understanding of newly introduced content by going to a module at the Companion Website (http://www.prenhall.com/armstrong).
- **Key Ideas in Summary** sections at the end of each chapter facilitate content review by drawing students' attention to important ideas.
- **Reflection** materials at the end of each chapter prompt students to engage in critical thinking about various issues that have been raised.
- **Field Experiences, Projects, and Enrichment** sections at the conclusion of the chapters provide opportunities for students to extend their understandings by engaging in appropriate application activities.
- **References** at the end of each chapter direct students to source materials used by the authors.
- A **glossary** at the end of the text helps students to cement their understanding of new terms.

USING THE TEXT

We believe that schoolteachers should take personal control over the instructional process. They should not feel obliged to follow the numerical order of chapters in their texts. Similarly, we encourage instructors who use this text to follow this logic and to assign students to read chapters in an order that makes sense in light of how they have designed their courses. We have written chapters in this book to be "freestanding." That is, no chapter has content that is prerequisite to that introduced in any other chapter.

SUPPLEMENTS TO THE TEXT

All supplements are available free of charge to instructors who adopt this text. To request any of the following supplements, contact your Prentice Hall representative or visit our Website at http://www.prenhall.com. (If you do not know how to contact your local sales representative, please call faculty services at 1–800–526–0485 for assistance.)

Instructor's Guide
The **Instructor's Guide** provides professors with a variety of useful resources, including chapter goals, chapter outlines, teaching approaches, and ideas for classroom activities, discussions, and assessment.

The guide also includes chapter self-assessment questions as well as Web extensions and Praxis case study activities.

Computerized Test Banks
Customizable **computerized test banks** are available for both Macintosh and PC users to use as they prepare classroom assessments.

Acetate Transparencies
A packet of **acetate transparencies** featuring figures and other important material from the text is available to augment lectures and other presentations related to chapter topics.

DISCOVER THE COMPANION WEBSITE ACCOMPANYING THIS BOOK

Web-Based Supplements:
The Prentice Hall Companion Website

The **Companion Website** for this text can be found at www.prenhall.com/armstrong. Technology is a constantly growing and changing aspect of our field that is creating a need for content and resources. To address this emerging need, Prentice Hall has developed an online learning environment for students and professors alike—Companion Websites—to support our textbooks.

In creating a Companion Website, our goal is to build on and enhance what the textbook already offers. For this reason, the content for each user-friendly website is organized by chapter and provides the professor and student with a variety of meaningful resources.

For the Professor—
The Companion Website provides teaching aides and resources for instructors using the text.

Professor Resources—This password-protected instructor resource includes downloadable copies of the following:

- **PowerPoint Presentations**—Detailed slide presentations for each chapter of the textbook

- **Instructor's Manual**—An electronic copy of the Instructor's Manual that includes chapter objectives, chapter outlines, and suggested activities.
- **Message Board**—Virtual bulletin board to post or respond to questions or comments from a national audience.

Every Companion Website Integrates **Syllabus Manager™,** an online syllabus creation and management utility.

- **Syllabus Manager™** provides you, the instructor, with an easy, step-by-step process to create and revise syllabi, with direct links into Companion Website and other online content without having to learn HTML.
- Students may logon to your syllabus during any study session. All they need to know is the web address for the Companion Website and the password you've assigned to your syllabus.
- After you have created a syllabus using **Syllabus Manager™,** students may enter the syllabus for their course section from any point in the Companion Website.
- Clicking on a date, the student is shown the list of activities for the assignment. The activities for each assignment are linked directly to actual content, saving time for students.
- Adding assignments consists of clicking on the desired due date, then filling in the details of the assignment—name of the assignment, instructions, and whether or not it is a one-time or repeating assignment.
- In addition, links to other activities can be created easily. If the activity is online, a URL can be entered in the space provided, and it will be linked automatically in the final syllabus.
- Your completed syllabus is hosted on our servers, allowing convenient updates from any computer on the Internet. Changes you make to your syllabus are immediately available to your students at their next logon.

For the Student—

The student portion of the Companion Website provides activities and resources that enhance and supplement chapter content:

- **Chapter Objectives**—Questions for the student to think about as they read the chapter.
- **Web Extensions**—Provides a topic or situation related to chapter content, includes a designated Web link or links, along with meaningful activities/questions.
- **Self-Assessment**—Includes multiple choice and true and false questions for each chapter complete with hints and automatic grading that provide immediate feedback for students.

After students submit their answers for the interactive self-quizzes, the Companion Website Results Reporter computes a percentage grade, provides a graphic representation of how many questions were answered correctly and incorrectly, and gives a question-by-question analysis of the quiz. Students are given the option to send their quiz to up to four e-mail addresses (professor, teaching assistant, study partner, etc.)

- **Praxis Case Study Exercises**—Case analysis modeled from the Praxis test that includes both essay and multiple-choice questions and tied to the text's features "Profiling a Teacher" and "Critical Incidents."
- **Message Board**—Virtual bulletin board to post or respond to questions or comments from a national audience.

To take advantage of the many available resources, please visit the *Teaching Today* Companion Website at

http://www.prenhall.com/armstrong

ACKNOWLEDGMENTS

Some fine people participated in the development of the seventh edition of *Teaching Today*. Jean Camp and Ada Vallecorsa made numerous helpful suggestions related to technology in today's schools. We also gratefully acknowledge the contributions of these other professionals who reviewed preliminary versions of the chapters: Dwight Allen, Old Dominion University; Donna Adair Breault, Illinois State University; Jean Camp, University of North Carolina at Greensboro; Debra J. Chandler, University of South Florida; Leigh Chiarelott, Bowling Green State University; Lydia Carol Gabbard, Eastern Kentucky University; Alan Garrett, Eastern New Mexico University; Fred H. Groves, University of Louisiana at Monroe; Melissa Marks, University of Pittsburgh at Greensburg; and Angelia J. Ridgway, University of Indianapolis.

In addition, we are especially grateful for the help of Debbie Stollenwerk, Kim Lundy, and Amy Nelson of Merrill/Prentice Hall, whose excellent suggestions greatly influenced our thinking about changes we have incorporated in this revision. Finally, we extend a special "thank you" to our spouses for their unwavering support while we were working on this project.

DGA

KTH

TVS

REFERENCE

Cuban, L. (2001). *Oversold & underused: Computers in the classroom.* Cambridge, MA: Harvard University Press.

EDUCATOR LEARNING CENTER: AN INVALUABLE ONLINE RESOURCE

Merrill Education and the Association for Supervision and Curriculum Development (ASCD) invite you to take advantage of a new online resource, one that provides access to the top research and proven strategies associated with ASCD and Merrill—the Educator Learning Center. At www.EducatorLearningCenter.com you will find resources that will enhance your students' understanding of course topics and of current educational issues, in addition to being invaluable for further research.

How the Educator Learning Center will help your students become better teachers With the combined resources of Merrill Education and ASCD, you and your students will find a wealth of tools and materials to better prepare them for the classroom.

Research
- More than 600 articles from the ASCD journal Educational Leadership discuss everyday issues faced by practicing teachers.
- A direct link on the site to Research Navigator™ gives students access to many of the leading education journals, as well as extensive content detailing the research process.
- Excerpts from Merrill Education texts give your students insights on important topics of instructional methods, diverse populations, assessment, classroom management, technology, and refining classroom practice.

Classroom Practice
- Hundreds of lesson plans and teaching strategies are categorized by content area and age range.
- Case studies and classroom video footage provide virtual field experience for student reflection.
- Computer simulations and other electronic tools keep your students abreast of today's classrooms and current technologies.

Look into the value of Educator Learning Center yourself

A four-month subscription to Educator Learning Center is $25 but is FREE when used in conjunction with this text. To obtain free passcodes for your students, simply contact your local Merrill/Prentice Hall sales representative, and your representative will give you a special ISBN to give your bookstore when ordering your textbooks. To preview the value of this website to you and your students, please go to www.EducatorLearningCenter.com and click on "Demo."

Contents in Brief

Contents

PART 2
Learners and Their Needs   *85*

PART 3

Teaching and Assessing   *169*

PART 4

Shapers of Today's Educational World   **283**

11   Social and Philosophical Perspectives   284

Note: Every effort has been made to provide accurate and current Internet information in this book. However, the Internet and information posted on it are constantly changing, and it is inevitable that some of the Internet addresses listed in this textbook will change.

Special Features

Critical Incidents

Preparing for Praxis

Profiling a Teacher

What Do You Think?

ABC News/Prentice Hall Video Library

The ABC News/Prentice Hall Video Library titled "Critical Issues in Education, Volume II" is created for use with *Teaching Today*, Seventh Edition. This video library challenges students to explore chapter topics through ABC News segments focusing on educational issues. *Video Viewpoints* features within each chapter offer a short summary of each episode and ask students to think about and respond to questions relating to the video and chapter content. The video segments described here are available to accompany this text.

Alternative Certification

This ABC News video segment discusses the issue of using alternative routes to certification in order to meet the teacher shortage. This segment focuses on short credential programs designed to attract second-career individuals into teaching. The merits of opening teaching to skilled individuals are also emphasized.

> Chapter 1, Page 22
> Running Time: 2:10

Providing a Quality Education for All Students

This ABC News video segment features Charles Best, a teacher who came from a privileged background and attended prestigious schools, but who chose to teach in the New York public schools. He then had an idea about finding funding for teacher ideas and created a Web site, www.donorschoose.org. This segment discusses a person's motivation to choose teaching as a career, as well as an innovative way to provide resources for teachers who need them the most.

> Chapter 2, Page 46
> Running Time: 19:47

Vouchers

This ABC News episode from *20/20* focuses on the issue of vouchers. The host clearly favors a voucher system and believes vouchers to be a key ingredient in school reform. He emphasizes the need for choice and the power of competition in bringing about change. However, this video segment also includes comments from those opposed to voucher systems. They contend that competition does not necessarily work in education and that voucher systems take needed money for change away from the schools that need it most.

> Chapter 3, Page 66
> Running Time: 9:40

What Are the Keys to Improving Achievement?

This ABC News special focuses on the Seed Charter School in Washington, D.C. The founders of this charter school believed it would take more than choice, the elimination of red tape, and a change of curriculum to improve student performance. The founders established a public boarding school for 40 students from troubled schools and difficult neighborhoods. This segment details the experiences of a few students in the school and illustrates the challenges of changing student attitudes and achievement.

> Chapter 4, Page 93
> Running Time: 23:34

How Do We Achieve Diversity?

This ABC News video segment focuses on the University of Michigan's point system for achieving diversity. The segment includes arguments about the importance of diversity in education and how to achieve diversity. Although the video segment is directed toward higher education, specifically the law school, the issue has implications for all levels of education.

> Chapter 5, Page 115
> Running Time: 6:44

Meeting the Needs of Exceptional Students

This ABC News video segment focuses on a special school for emotionally disturbed teens in Chicago. The segment reveals the deep turmoil in some students that interferes with their ability to succeed or even survive in a regular public school. The major focus is on one girl who suffers from severe depression.

> Chapter 6, Page 152
> Running Time: 19:20

High-Stakes Testing

This ABC News video segment discusses the issue of high-stakes testing. The focus is on Florida and the Florida Comprehensive Assessment Test that is required for promotion and graduation. The segment covers two sides of the issues: the need for high standards in order to prepare students for success in the world and the question of whether graduation or promotion should rest solely on the scores received on just one test.

> Chapter 7, Page 178
> Running Time: 19:45

How Much Homework Is Enough?

This ABC News segment focuses on the debate over how much homework should be assigned to young children. It cites a University of Michigan study that found the amount of time young children spend on homework has increased dramatically. Some parents are complaining that homework is taking away the opportunity for children to participate in other activities. Others state that too much homework is having a negative effect on children's motivation.

> Chapter 8, Page 215
> Running Time: 6:20

How Should Rules Be Enforced?

This ABC News segment focuses on enforcement of zero tolerance policies in schools. One instance is investigated where two 8-year-old boys were taken to police headquarters and suspended from school for a day for playing "cowboys and outlaws" using paper guns. In another instance, a high school mascot is prevented from having a paper spear as a part of his costume. The segment includes arguments from those who think the policy is appropriate for making schools safe. Others contend that there needs to be sensible enforcement, rather than literal and automatic responses to rules.

> Chapter 9, Page 248
> Running Time: 19:32

The Uses and Misuses of Standardized Tests

This ABC News segment focuses on the issue of using the SAT as a college admission requirement. It discusses the history of the SAT and points out that the use of the SAT might be the opposite of what was originally intended. Discussion centers on the recommendation of the chancellor of the University of California system to eliminate the SAT as an admission requirement after he visited an upscale private school and noted that they were preparing 12-year-old students for the SAT. Further investigation revealed a variation in scores based on ethnicity and a lack of data that indicated that high SAT scores actually predicted college success.

> Chapter 10, Page 258
> Running Time: 20:06

The Power of the Neighborhood School?

This ABC News video segment focuses on the issue of busing and neighborhood schools, particularly in Delray Beach, Florida. For years, African American students from Delray Beach were bused to achieve racial balance. However, there was a high dropout rate for those who were bused, and the parents did not feel like a part of the school community. With the assistance of a philanthropist, a new community school has been established that seems to be thriving. Throughout the segment, the issue of racial segregation and the landmark *Brown v. Board of Education* case emerge.

> Chapter 11, Page 293
> Running Time: 20:13

Revisiting History

This ABC News segment concerns the creation–evolution debate. The Kansas Board of Education discusses whether to drop the teaching of evolution and allow the inclusion of "intelligent design" as an alternative theory. The video includes numerous individuals speaking for and against the measure, and it highlights the issue of whether inclusion of intelligent design is appropriate because it is merely another scientific theory or if it is inappropriate because it is a religious belief.

> Chapter 12, Page 317
> Running Time: 19:43

What Is the Impact of Computers in the Classroom?

This ABC video segment focuses on the impact of computers in the classroom. It points out that school districts have increased dollar allocations for computers while reducing the budget for other things. However, research seems to indicate that computers have not had much impact on student achievement. One of the reasons given is that teachers have not been taught how to use computers in the classroom.

Chapter 13, Page 346

Running Time: 23:35

Cheating Teachers

This ABC News segment focuses on the issue of teachers helping students perform better on high-stakes tests. A teacher is interviewed who claims that her school principal told her to cheat to help students get higher test scores. The segment emphasizes the stress created for administrators and teachers when their salaries and even their jobs depend on students doing well on a high-stakes test.

Chapter 14, Page 390

Running Time: 20:02

What is the biggest of Computers in the Classroom?

Reading Teacher

Part 1

The Profession

CHAPTERS

1 Education in an Age of Change

2 Becoming a Professional Educator

3 Challenges of School Reform

1

Education in an Age of Change

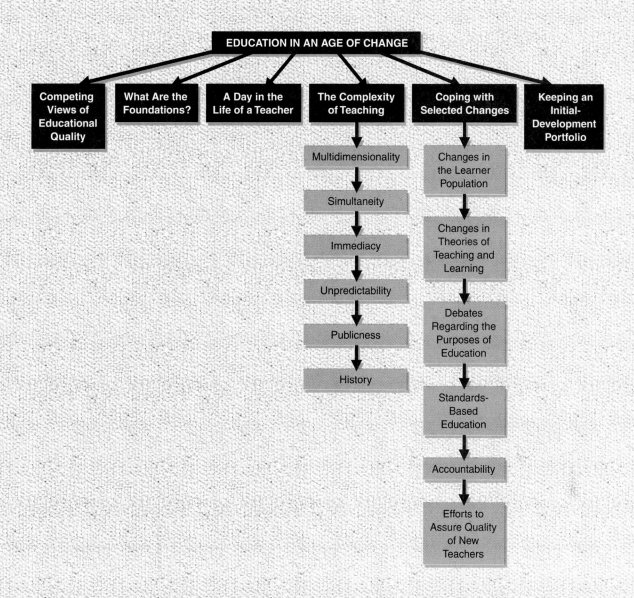

EDUCATION IN AN AGE OF CHANGE

- Competing Views of Educational Quality
- What Are the Foundations?
- A Day in the Life of a Teacher
- The Complexity of Teaching
  - Multidimensionality
  - Simultaneity
  - Immediacy
  - Unpredictability
  - Publicness
  - History
- Coping with Selected Changes
  - Changes in the Learner Population
  - Changes in Theories of Teaching and Learning
  - Debates Regarding the Purposes of Education
  - Standards-Based Education
  - Accountability
  - Efforts to Assure Quality of New Teachers
- Keeping an Initial-Development Portfolio

OBJECTIVES

This chapter will help you to

- identify basic foundational questions related to education.
- describe many of the realities teachers face each day.
- point out characteristics that add to the complexity of teachers' responsibilities.

- explain how changes related to characteristics of learners, knowledge about teaching and learning, views of education's purposes, curriculum standards, and demands for learner and teacher accountability affect teachers' work today.
- describe advantages of developing a professional-development portfolio.

3

COMPETING VIEWS OF EDUCATIONAL QUALITY

Congratulations on your decision to consider a career in teaching. You have made an initial commitment to our society's "essential" profession. Without education there would be no engineering, medicine, or law. The quality of education has a strong impact on our nation's social, economic, and political health. Because of its importance, everyone has a stake in its quality. As a result, you will find that nearly everyone has a view about what needs to be done to "make our schools better."

You will find that ideas about educational improvement vary enormously. As you analyze individual proposals, you will encounter many suggestions that are supported by compelling evidence and have great potential for enhancing the quality of learners' experiences in school. On the other hand, you are certain to encounter other prescriptions for improvement that, if implemented, might actually diminish the quality of school programs. One of your challenges as an educator will be to distinguish between school-improvement proposals with legitimate prospects to make schools better and more-dubious propositions with little potential to make positive changes.

WHAT ARE THE FOUNDATIONS?

Schools' characteristics derive in large measure from answers our society has made to important questions associated with the **foundations of education.** The foundations comprise the set of historical, philosophical, social, legal, and cultural assumptions that form a logical base for decisions about schools and schooling. As a preparation for making informed decisions about competing school-improvement ideas, you will find it useful to know something about questions associated with the foundations of education. Some examples that are associated with selected foundation categories follow:

- Social and philosophical foundations. *What is the good society, and how should education contribute to that society?* (Many debates about changes in education are really debates among people who have different views of what constitutes the good society. Debates about what should be taught and who should be taught are two areas of conflict in the social and philosophical foundations.)
- Historical foundations. *Where did current school practices and traditions come from, and are they still important?* (Current school practices did not come about because a group of experts sat down and worked from a blank slate. Historical developments have greatly influenced our educational system. Your task is to determine the extent to which these historical influences still have merit.)
- Political foundations. *Who has the power to decide priorities and to influence how schools operate?* (You will find that proposals for changes in the ways schools conduct their business are directed at the wrong audience. You and others interested in school reform need to know who has the power to make decisions that will result in desired modifications.)
- Curriculum foundations. *What is taught, and why is it taught?* The term **curriculum** is used to describe the overall framework for an instructional program. (You will find that much debate about the quality of education centers on what is taught in the schools. There is much consensus around the idea that the curriculum must keep up-to-date with technological changes. However, much more contention rages around other issues. Should more be required of learners at earlier ages? How much content about different cultures should be included? Should young people be allowed to learn in their primary language? Are some subjects "frills" that can be eliminated?)

- Instructional foundations. *What is good teaching?* The term **instruction** refers to teaching approaches that are used to help learners achieve the overall purposes that are outlined in the curriculum. (The issue of good teaching is central to any debate about education. You will find that not everybody defines "good teaching" in the same way. For example, some people want teachers to embrace findings of recent research into how the brain operates and processes information. Others favor approaches based on other research or theoretical perspectives. One issue you will need to confront concerns striking a balance between (a) requiring teachers to follow certain common instructional patterns and (b) allowing teachers flexibility to implement instructional approaches of their own choosing.)
- Legal foundations. *What are the legal and ethical rights and responsibilities of teachers and learners?* (In recent decades there has been much litigation relating to education. Proposals for change have to take into account legal principles that influence the actions of teachers and school administrators.)

Think about these questions as you progress through this text and continue your professional development. They are central to discussions about educational change. Understandings you develop related to these questions will help you better evaluate specific educational change proposals.

A DAY IN THE LIFE OF A TEACHER

What is teaching really like? You have spent thousands of hours as a learner in classrooms and you may have spent time observing teachers. As a result, you may think you have a clear grasp of the role of the teacher. However, it is probable that at this point in your professional development you still have a somewhat-restricted view of what teachers do. Some limitations of understanding result from the necessity of making inferences about what teachers do from your perspective as a learner or from your perspective as an outside visitor to the classroom.

Technology has had a profound effect on the many roles of teachers.

As a recipient of instructional services and as an observer, you have experienced only the visible actions of teachers as they communicated with their learners. The reality is that many excellent teachers are so good at what they do that they make teaching look easy to observers. They move smoothly through the curriculum, their learners are engaged in lessons, and few disruptions interfere with the instructional process. What you probably were not able to discern during your observations were (1) the thinking and the decision making involved in lesson preparation and (2) the teachers' prior efforts to understand the interests and motivations of individuals that resulted in lesson strategies that learners found meaningful. Often, too, good teachers make small, important, and sometimes-invisible-to-observers adjustments to changing classroom situations that keep learning on track. As a result, what you may have seen as a seamless, almost effortless activity actually involved a complex interplay of actions requiring application of sophisticated learner-understanding and interpersonal-communication skills.

The unobserved aspects of the public performance of good teachers may be only one of the surprises you will encounter as you start work in the profession. We have often heard former students comment, "There is so much I didn't know." Many people are surprised at how much time is taken up by activities that do not involve direct work with learners. Among them are responsibilities associated with

- Planning lessons,
- Record keeping and other administrative duties,
- Participating in special school events (back-to-school nights, parent–teacher meetings, athletic contests, school dances, graduation exercises, and so forth),
- Serving on various committees,
- Participating in professional group activities, and
- Communicating with parents or guardians.

The types of activities you will be involved with will vary according to the age level of your learners and the nature of your school and school district. What might be an issue in one place may not be an issue in another. For example, the special characteristics of your school may make it essential that you quickly come to an understanding of the political climate. This understanding might be less critical in another setting. If you teach at the secondary level, you may be expected to serve as an adviser or a sponsor for a school organization or to assist at athletic events. If you teach in an elementary school, you may spend time monitoring learners on the playground or in the lunchroom.

WEB EXTENSION I–I

National Survey Gauges Parent Perceptions of State-Mandated, Standardized Tests

The Web offers an excellent opportunity for you to extend your understanding and to find resources that can assist you in accomplishing your professional goals. A good place to start is the New Teacher page. This site provides specific information about a variety of topics such as finding a job, substitute teaching, and becoming a professional in the classroom.

http://www.new-teacher.com/

There are no ordinary days in teaching, and there are no typical schools. As a result, place-to-place and day-to-day differences make it difficult to describe the reality of a day in the life of a teacher. However, we thought it worthwhile to make the attempt. We observed a randomly chosen elementary teacher for a single day. (See "Profiling a Teacher: What Does a Teacher Do All Day?") We make no claim that this scenario generalizes to this teacher's other days or to other teachers in other settings. Our purpose is not to suggest that this day is typical. Rather, our intent is to prompt you to reflect on some aspects of teaching that you may not have considered.

PROFILING A TEACHER

WHAT DOES A TEACHER DO ALL DAY?

As you read through the following profile, think about these questions:

- How does this profile fit with your perceptions of a day in the life of a teacher?
- What might be some other activities in the daily life of a teacher that are not included in this profile?
- What is your reaction to what is required of a teacher?
- What differences would you expect in the typical day of a middle school teacher? Of a high school teacher?

J. D. SMITH'S DAY IN SCHOOL

Students in J. D. Smith's elementary school are expected to arrive by 8:30 A.M. However, the day for J. D. and the rest of the teachers begins much earlier because school regulations require teachers to be present no later than 8:00 A.M. Many teachers are in the building by 7:30 A.M. or earlier, working on room decorations, preparing lessons, making copies, taking care of administrative work, and preparing for the instructional day. On this morning J. D. spends time completing paperwork from the district personnel department relating to validation of summer-term courses he took at a local university.

J. D. learns that a parent has called the school. Her child is ill and will miss several days of school. J. D. has been asked to prepare assignments the parent can pick up and use with the child at home. The parent does not want her son to fall behind. Another surprise event this morning is the unexpected arrival of another parent. This parent is concerned about a youngster's progress, and J. D. and the parent spend some time discussing the situation. Phone calls from parents, unexpected arrivals, and other early-morning events are typical of what he encounters every morning. On some days, there are scheduled early-morning meetings of the entire faculty. What all this means is that there are few days when J. D. has uninterrupted time in the morning to work in the classroom.

We are visiting J. D. early in the fall. This is the time of the year when the district regularly holds its annual Back-to-School Night. During this event, each teacher gives parents an overview of the curriculum and teacher expectations. J. D. knows that his explanation will need to be repeated at least twice so that parents with more than one youngster can visit at least two classrooms. On the other hand, he will not have to engage in as much repetition as secondary school teachers, who have to make a presentation for every period of the day. J. D. is expected to pay close attention to the public relations' importance of

(continued)

the Back-to-School event, and extra time will have to be spent making the room attractive and stimulating. This morning, he spends what is left of his morning putting up samples of learner work on the bulletin boards.

The children arrive, and things begin to move quickly. During the first part of the morning, J. D. moves the class smoothly through the curriculum. Class members are generally on task, and things go well. Recess time arrives, and students quickly exit the classroom. J. D. gathers up material and books that have been used and puts them away. Then, after a quick check to make sure all material is ready for the rest of the morning, it is time for a quick trip to the lounge for a cup of coffee and conversation with other teachers.

Recess time passes quickly. J. D. and the other teachers position themselves outside their doors to monitor learners as they file back into each classroom. Several problems have occurred during recess. One of the girls has a skinned elbow that needs attention, so J. D. sends the youngster to the office. In times past, the school nurse would have handled this situation, but because of budget cuts, a nurse is available only one day a week. As a result, the school secretary calls the parents and gets permission to bandage the elbow.

J. D. also has to deal with a complaint brought by several children who claim that others were not behaving properly on the playground during recess. J. D. informs them that the matter will be addressed. These assurances satisfy them, and he quickly gets the class to work. As learners work independently, J. D. holds a brief conference with those involved in the recess incident. A warning and a firm tone of voice seem to achieve the desired outcome.

As the morning passes, some class members experience difficulty staying on task because their attention spans shorten. In response to this situation, J. D. moves around the classroom working with different groups and refocusing learners' attention on what they are supposed to be doing. Lunch comes as a welcome break.

The lunch period begins with a trip to the cafeteria. J. D. briefly enjoys light conversation and joking with other teachers. Then there is a trip to the mailbox, where he finds messages and announcements about Back-to-School Night that need to be sent home that afternoon. J. D. finishes the break by gathering equipment needed for this afternoon's science lesson. As usual, several items are missing. This discovery prompts a quick search and some adjustments to the original plan.

J. D. arrives back in the classroom before it is time for the class members to return. Materials left over from the morning are cleaned up. After spending a few minutes reviewing plans for the afternoon, he goes on to organize materials and to add a few notes to lesson plans as reminders of things that must be done tomorrow.

J. D. is still making preparations for the afternoon when the bell rings and learners line up outside the classroom. They are still excited from lunch and the few minutes they have spent on the playground. They are talking loudly. To calm them, J. D. instructs them to go quickly to their seats and sit quietly. Then, he takes a children's book from his desk and begins to read a few pages aloud. The story interests learners, and there are a few groans when the reading stops.

It is time for the next lesson. This lesson and those that follow go well, but the rest of the school day seems to pass slowly. The class is restless and less

attentive. J. D. knows this is a typical pattern, and many afternoon activities feature active learner participation in the hope that this will keep class members focused and involved. A few minutes before the dismissal bell, J. D. stops all instructional activities. He asks members of the class who have been assigned as workers to perform their duties. Books are placed in the bookshelves, papers are collected, and he takes time to make last-minute announcements and to give reminders about homework. J. D. distributes papers that must be sent home and dismisses the class.

Today J. D. has bus duty. After a hurried walk to the bus loading zone, he monitors the behavior of young people who ride buses and handles any problems that come up. Once all the buses have left, J. D. heads back to the classroom.

The first order of business is to gather the papers that need to be taken home and corrected. Next, he begins reviewing the sequence of lessons for the next day and jotting down reminders about what is to be done in the margins of the daily plan book. Then it is time to create, gather, and organize supplementary material that will be used. Some materials for tomorrow need work, and these are placed in the "take-home" bag. Over an hour has passed since the last child boarded the bus. Finally, J. D. locks the door and heads home, carrying papers to be graded and lessons to be planned.

THE COMPLEXITY OF TEACHING

As you review the day described, consider the variety of things to which J. D. had to attend. When you begin your career in the classroom, your duties will embrace much more than simply teaching lessons. You may find yourself emotionally stretched as you learn to cope with these many responsibilities. Walter Doyle (1986) suggests that the following features combine to make the role you will play as a teacher particularly complex:

- Multidimensionality
- Simultaneity
- Immediacy
- Unpredictability
- Publicness
- History

Multidimensionality

Multidimensionality refers to the idea that teachers' responsibilities range across a broad array of duties. When you teach, you have to know how to multitask. In addition to planning and delivering instruction, you have to diagnose learning difficulties, spot misconceptions, monitor learner progress, make on-the-spot adjustments, respond to unanticipated events, administer standardized tests, attend meetings, keep accurate records, relate to parents, work productively with colleagues, and create materials. You may well wonder, "How am I supposed to do all of these things and still teach?"

Perhaps the biggest challenge you will face as a teacher is responding adequately to young people in your classes who come to you with different backgrounds, motivations, aspirations, needs, abilities, and learning styles. Some of them will have the prerequisite skills and abilities to achieve success; some will not. Some learners will come from backgrounds that differ from your own. Some will come to school as cheerful, well-rested individuals, while others may be tired and angry. Although many young people you teach are likely to see you as a caring and supportive mentor, a few may see you as a threatening adult who cares little for the things they deem important.

Simultaneity

Simultaneity refers to the idea that many things happen at once in the classroom. When you stand before your learners, you need to watch for indications of comprehension, interest, and attention. You should listen carefully to answers to determine their relevance and to spot misconceptions and signs of confusion. While providing assistance to one learner, you must, at the same time, monitor the behavior of the rest of the class. You also need to devise ways to keep members of your class focused on your lesson when you must deal with an unexpected interruption such as a message from the office requiring you to provide an immediate written response. Over time, you will grow in your ability to prioritize and respond immediately to multiple stimuli.

Immediacy

The term **immediacy** refers to a classroom reality that features situations that require you as a teacher to respond at once. Often you will not have the luxury of placing things on hold until you have the time and energy to deal with them. The need to act quickly in complex situations places great stress on teachers. This kind of stress is likely to be particularly acute when you are new to the profession and inclined to worry about whether you have made appropriate decisions.

The immediacy character of the classroom requires you to develop good judgment. You cannot learn these kinds of decision-making skills from reading a book. However, you can prepare yourself by thinking about kinds of situations that might develop in the classroom and considering possible responses you might make. Henson (2004) labels this practice proactive teaching and provides activities to develop proactive skills. The process of simulating responses will help you develop higher levels of comfort when you are confronted with making real decisions in your own classroom.

Unpredictability

Unpredictability refers to teachers' challenges in working with learners whose reactions do not always follow consistent patterns and with situations that arise that may unexpectedly interfere with established routines. Neither you nor your learners are programmable computers who respond in consistent ways to similar situations. This reality contributes to making teaching both interesting and challenging. Individual learners and classes respond to the same stimuli in different ways. You will soon find out that a lesson that works well with one class may not be effective with learners in another.

Unpredictability results not just from differences among individual learners but from unexpected distractions and interruptions that occur when you are teaching. Unexpected visitors, a call over the intercom, a fire drill, a suddenly-ill member of your class, or an unusual change in the daily schedule are events that often intrude just as you are trying to make an important point in your lesson.

How should you respond to unpredictable events? The answer will vary depending on your personality, philosophical views, and general orientation to teaching. In other words, different teachers respond to similar situations in various ways. For example, one of your colleagues might interpret an unexpected learner response as an act of defiance, whereas you might see it as a manifestation of nothing more than a lack of understanding. There probably will be occasions when you will view unanticipated occurrences as frustrating disruptions and other occasions when you may see them as providing interesting, though unexpected, learning opportunities.

How should you respond to unpredictability? Do you need to have things follow a predictable pattern? Do you get upset if things do not always go as planned? You need to think about your answers to these questions. Although you need to work toward a classroom that runs smoothly, unpredictable events will happen and will upset the best of plans. You need to be ready for this reality. If you are uncomfortable in situations that feature unpredictability, you might want to consider a career other than teaching.

Publicness

Publicness refers to the idea that teaching is a profession that occurs in an arena that allows recipients of the instructional process to monitor every classroom action their instructor takes. When you teach, you are operating in an environment that allows your learners to observe your every move. Young people are keen observers, and it will not take them long to make personal decisions about what you are "really like." Your mannerisms, your enthusiasms, your biases, and your values will soon be public knowledge. Some members of your class will quickly learn what pleases you and what upsets you.

The particular character of your interaction with learners is strongly influenced by the interplay between your actions and your learners' interpretations of those actions. A ripple effect often follows your actions in the classroom. In other words, your actions will be observed and interpreted and have consequences beyond the immediate situation. For example, if you display great anger when a learner makes a mistake in class, you may find class members increasingly fearful of volunteering responses to your questions. If you teach in a middle school or high school, behaviors you have displayed in one class quickly become known and affect your relationships with other classes you teach.

History

The interaction you have with members of a class over a term or an entire year develops a **class history.** A class history is a kind of culture that is unique to each class of learners and results from an ongoing record of interaction between the teacher and learners. The manner in which you relate to learners, plan instruction, and react to unpredictable events creates this history.

Differences in particular class histories explain why apparently similar behaviors by different teachers do not always produce similar events. For example, you might find that a quiet word may stop inappropriate behavior, but another teacher using this approach may find that it fails to correct the situation. As you think about developing your own teaching style, you will not find it productive to simply mimic what you have observed a successful teacher doing. Your class members will have a history that may vary considerably from the history of learners of the teacher you are trying to emulate. As a result, your learners will have a different interpretation of your actions.

COPING WITH SELECTED CHANGES

Profound changes have affected our society in recent decades. It is hard to remember that just a few years ago personal computers, the World Wide Web, cell phones, and satellite television did not exist. Now, we find it hard to imagine life without them. These technological innovations have also changed educational practices. Because education is a part of society, changes in society influence changes in education. These changes are likely to continue, and as a future teacher, you need to be prepared to accommodate new realities that, over time, may significantly alter the ways in which you and your colleagues interact with learners.

Changes in the Learner Population

One of the most significant changes in society has been an increase in diversity. Because of population mobility and international interdependence, you are almost certain to be teaching in communities in which schools enroll young people from varied cultural and language backgrounds. Many adults and policy makers have not grasped the significance of this change. School leaders today struggle as they attempt to help the general public understand that the characteristics of learners in today's schools differ markedly from those enrolled just a decade or two ago.

Today's schools enroll many young people from homes in which the primary language spoken is not English. There are nearly 50 million children in the schools who are nonnative speakers of English and who are still working toward complete fluency in the language. This figure represents more than a 95 percent increase in such learners from those enrolled in academic year 1991–1992 (Padolsky, 2002). In some states, these young people comprise high percentages of the total school population. In California, for example, fully one fourth of the young people in grades K–12 are nonnative speakers of English. Other states with schools that enroll extremely high percentages of these learners are Texas, Florida, New York, Illinois, and Arizona (Kindler, 2002). As a teacher you will face tremendous challenges in creating an environment in which all learners can succeed and in which there is open communication between the school and parents or guardians of these young people.

© 1999 Randy Glasbergen.
www.glasbergen.com

"Friday night you stayed out until almost 9:00, yesterday you had cola instead of milk and this morning you forgot to floss. Your father and I are afraid you're getting too wild."

Attempts to respond to this diversity in the classroom have led to several important changes. Many schools have **bilingual education** programs, where learners are taught in their native language for at least a part of the day until they become proficient in English. There has been a major emphasis on **multicultural education,** a perspective that holds that school programs should present learners with instruction that honors and respects the contributions of many individual cultures to our nation and world.

James Banks (2001), a leading expert on multicultural education, points out that growing ethnic and cultural diversity requires rethinking school curricula. He believes that all learners should develop multicultural perspectives. Banks wants school curricula to accurately describe how different cultural groups have interacted with and influenced Western civilization.

Supporters of multicultural education have begun to exert a serious influence on educational practices. For example, you will find that many school textbooks now include multicultural content, and many states mandate the inclusion of multicultural content in the curriculum. Not everyone supports the idea that more multicultural perspectives should be included.

Critics of multicultural education worry that, at best, multicultural content replaces important substantive content in the curriculum or, at worst, it tears down the basic values of our national heritage and leads to national disunity (Schlesinger, 1995). They fear that traditional Western writers such as Shakespeare will be eliminated from the curriculum and the teaching of history will be distorted.

Bilingual education also has both supporters and critics. Advocates contend that learners' education should not be delayed until they acquire English proficiency. The Bilingual Education Act of 1968 was developed as a program to help nonnative speakers of English study school subjects in their home languages until they develop adequate proficiency in English. This arrangement allows young people to continue to master school subjects at the same time as their facility with English develops. The bilingual arrangement also is supported by research that supports the view that learning in one's primary language improves feelings of self-worth and helps develop an understanding of one's own culture (Macedo, 1995).

Critics contend that the effectiveness of bilingual education has not been validated (Ravitch, 1995). They believe that a common language promotes national unity. Some opponents of bilingual education also object to its high cost. Still other critics contend that allowing young people to learn in their home language delays their acquisition of English.

Some critics of bilingual education suggest that learners who come to school speaking home languages other than English should be enrolled in **total immersion** programs (Ravitch, 1995). Total immersion programs attempt to speed nonnative speakers' acquisition of English by involving them in instructional programs that surround them with English-language instructional programs. The controversy over bilingual education has sparked an effort to have English declared to be the official language of the United States. Some supporters of this idea would like to take money currently spent on bilingual education and reallocate it to pay for total immersion programs for learners.

Another type of diversity that has had an impact on the classroom is the increasing presence of learners with a range of mental and physical challenges in the classroom. **Inclusion** refers to a commitment to the view that learners, regardless of unique personal characteristics (disabilities, for example), not only have a legal right to services in the regular classroom but they are welcomed and wanted as members of these classes. For many years, the traditional practice was to separate these learners in special education classrooms. Today **special education teachers,** who have received special academic preparation related to teaching learners with varying disabilities, increasingly work with regular classroom teachers in designing and delivering instruction to these learners.

You will probably encounter learners in your classes whose first language is not English. Young people whose first language is not English are increasing as a percentage of the total school population.

WEB EXTENSION 1–2

Education Week on the Web

This is the home page for a Web version of a publication that provides weekly information about a variety of educational issues. It is a good way to keep current on contemporary issues and emerging trends.

http://www.edweek.org

Changes in Theories of Teaching and Learning

How individuals learn has been the subject of debate for centuries. There is still much that we do not know about the human brain and what causes learning to occur. We do know that the brain is incredibly complex. In recent years new insights into the brain and into the nature of what is termed "intelligence" have influenced educational practice. Today many teachers are implementing instructional programs that are strongly influenced by research related to (1) constructivism and (2) multiple intelligences.

Constructivism.   **Constructivism** is based on the principle that individuals cannot simply be given knowledge. Rather, individuals must create knowledge as they interact with the world around them. Their constructions of knowledge are rooted in their prior knowledge. Your learners' knowledge will grow as they compare new information with what they already know. The theory holds that the mind is constantly searching for patterns and attempting to resolve discrepancies. The social and cultural contexts within which learning takes place also heavily influence what is constructed or learned.

There are several important implications of constructivism. One is that the conditions that best facilitate learning are what might be described as learner-centered and problem-centered. This means that as a teacher you need to provide learners with complex, complete, "authentic" problems. Once this is done, guidance is provided to class members to help them gain the knowledge needed to solve the problems. This contrasts with more traditional approaches that introduce learners to small pieces of information that, in time, are put together into a whole.

For example, a traditional approach to teaching elementary children arithmetic emphasizes lessons requiring them to memorize multiplication tables. The expectation is that the information will prove useful at some future date when they need to apply these skills to solve problems that are important to them. By way of contrast, a constructivist approach to teaching multiplication tables might begin by presenting learners with a problem that requires multiplication skills in order to find a solution. You and class members together consider what learners need to know to solve the problem. You help class members note patterns and develop a generalization on how multiplication processes work. The idea is to teach multiplication in the context of "real" problems when your learners need this skill.

In the same vein, constructivist approaches to teaching topics such as punctuation and spelling are embedded with larger, story-writing activities that provide learners with a real need to know this kind of content. The general approach has led to a reading philosophy that is commonly referred to as **whole language** instruction, which features lessons in which reading, writing, speaking, and listening are taught as a single, integrated process. Youngsters in the earliest grades are urged to write stories and then read them to others. The focus is on encouraging learners to use language, to look for patterns, and to learn writing and spelling conventions as they are needed.

Storytelling is another activity that constructivist teachers use, and it works well with students of all ages and abilities. Former Virginia Teacher of the Year, Mary Bicouvaris (see Henson, 2004, p. 250) explains, "The smartest students love storytelling; the weakest ones worship it."

Another assumption of constructivism is that members of your class need to be actively engaged in the learning process. They must actively seek solutions to problems and share ideas. Because the social and cultural context is important, and because it is not likely that any one individual can find the solution working alone, often your learners will work in pairs or in teams. As a result, lessons built around constructivism principles may involve members of your class in considerable talking and movement.

Constructivism also has changed conceptions of **assessment,** the process of ascertaining what members of your class have learned. If you are teaching according to this perspective, you will be interested in assessment procedures that focus on how well class members can solve problems and that explain what they have discovered and learned. You will be less interested in traditional tests that often measure largely what learners remember about what they have been told.

As you may have already noted, these approaches differ from certain popular present-day assessment practices. The current emphasis on **accountability,** the idea that teachers and schools should be held directly responsible for teaching specific information to specific learners, has relied heavily on the use of **standardized tests.** Standardized tests are tests designed to measure the performance of a single learner as it compares to performances of other similar learners. The emphasis on standardized testing has forced many teachers to focus on small bits of information that might be tested and to use practices that run counter to constructivist learning. Accountability concerns also have led to the creation of some instructional approaches that are highly controlled. In these approaches, the role of the teacher is to follow a provided script. Constructivists argue that this type instruction does not take into account prior knowledge of learner differences and is based on the old idea that learning has to proceed in small, predictable steps.

Multiple Intelligences.   Another important change that has influenced education relates to conceptions of intelligence. Throughout history, there have been debates focusing on the nature of intelligence (Woolfolk, 2001). Traditionally, intelligence has been viewed as a single trait that can be measured by an **Intelligence Quotient** or **IQ test.** The IQ test assumes that if a person is smart in one area, he or she will be smart in other areas as well. People with higher IQ scores are assumed to have more of the "intelligence trait" and hence be able to achieve more success in challenging academic endeavors.

In recent years, there has been growing support for the idea that intelligence has many facets or that there are **multiple intelligences.** According to this view, intelligence is not a unitary trait but rather consists of a number of separate categories. A person may have different levels of ability in individual categories. That is, a person may be smart in terms of certain categories of intelligence and not so smart in terms of certain other categories. Most people are thought to have combinations of strengths rather than just a strength in one area and weakness in all others. Howard Gardner (1999), a leading authority in multiple intelligences, has identified at least nine distinct kinds of intelligence:

- Logical–mathematical intelligence—People with strengths in this area are good at seeking meaning through analytical processes that involve the use of abstract symbols.
- Linguistic intelligence—People with strengths in this area are especially adept at making sense of the world through language.
- Musical intelligence—People with strengths in this area have the capacity to communicate and create meaning that involves consideration of sound.
- Spatial intelligence—People with strengths in this area have facility in perceiving, transforming, and re-creating visual images that contribute to their understanding of their world.
- Bodily–kinesthetic intelligence—People with strengths in this area are good at using muscular and other body systems to respond to situations and to solve problems.
- Interpersonal intelligence—People with strengths in this area are particularly good at recognizing and responding to feelings and motivations of others.
- Intrapersonal intelligence—People with strengths in this area heavily weigh their own personal capacities and attitudes when determining which course of action to follow in a given situation.
- Naturalist intelligence—People with strengths in this area are especially good at making inferences based on classifications and analyses of features of the physical world.
- Existential intelligence—People with strengths in this area seek insights regarding ultimate issues such as the meaning of life and how their own existence does or should fit into this scheme.

Robert Sternberg (1990) is another theorist who has done work in the area of multiple intelligences. He has proposed a **triarchic theory of intelligence** that includes

- **Componential intelligence,**
- **Experiential intelligence,** and
- **Contextual intelligence.**

Componential intelligence refers to the ability to acquire information by separating the relevant from the irrelevant, thinking abstractly, and determining what needs to be done. *Experiential intelligence* involves the ability to cope with new experiences by formulating new ideas and combining unrelated facts to solve new problems. There are two major characteristics of experiential learning. They involve (1) having an insight or the ability to deal with novel situations and (2) having **automaticity,** the ability to quickly turn new solutions into routine procedures (Woolfolk, 2001). *Contextual intelligence* is characterized by an ability to adapt to new experiences and to solve problems in a specific situation or context.

Yet another dimension to the conception of multiple intelligence has been added by Daniel Goleman (1995). Goleman defined what he calls **emotional intelligence** as the ability to exercise self-control, remain persistent, and be self-motivating. Individuals with high levels of emotional intelligence have developed expertise in five key areas:

- Mood management—A person's ability to handle feelings in ways that are appropriate to and relevant for a situation.
- Self-awareness—A person's ability to know feelings he or she is sensing and to discriminate among them in meaningful ways.
- Self-motivation—A person's ability to organize feelings in ways that allow self-directed activity in behalf of a goal to go forward, even in the face of self-doubts and distracting temptations.
- Empathy—A person's ability to recognize verbal and nonverbal cues of others and to be sensitive to their feelings.
- Managing relationships—A person's ability to work productively with others to resolve conflicts, to maintain open lines of communication, and to negotiate compromises.

Multiple-intelligence theories have implications for you as a teacher. Perhaps the most important is the need to avoid labeling learners according to their IQ score. Scholars who have studied multiple intelligences point out that there are many ways an individual can be gifted. Another implication is that you need to vary your instructional program in ways that excite and challenge learners with strengths in varying kinds of intelligences. This reality means that you need to vary your modes of presentation. A lesson that is perfectly appropriate for a learner who has great strength in the area of linguistic intelligence may not well serve the needs of another learner who is weak in this area but strong in spatial intelligence.

Debates Regarding the Purposes of Education

As you struggle to do an excellent job in your classroom, one of the realities you will face is that people hold wildly different views regarding what schools and educators should be doing (Clincy, 1998). You will find that different individuals often give quite varied answers to questions such as

- What subjects should our schools emphasize?
- Should we be primarily concerned about preparing academically proficient individuals for higher education?
- Should we be producing individuals with marketable vocational skills?
- Should schools be addressing social justice issues?
- To what extent should schools address persistent social problems such as substance abuse and healthy living?
- To what extent should schools be developing moral and ethical character?
- Should there be standardized expectations for all learners, or should there be a focus on the development of the unique potential of individuals?
- What should the schools do to prepare individuals for their citizenship responsibilities?

School policy makers have always attempted to address all of these questions in a perspective on education that holds that school programs should be diverse and flexible enough to accommodate diverse individuals and emerging societal concerns. When there is a prominent health concern, such as AIDS, new programs are added to schools. When there is an increase in crime, there is an outcry for schools to spend more time on morality and character education. In times of national crisis, schools are criticized for not having enough focus on citizenship. When the economy dips, schools are accused of not producing skilled workers who can immediately enter the workplace as productive employees. Almost always, some parents are worried about whether their children will be prepared to gain admission to colleges and universities.

Because individuals have varying priorities, proposals to improve or reform education reflect a tremendous diversity. Throughout the history of American education there have always been voices criticizing the schools and calling for reform. For example, in the 1940s and 1950s, books such as *Crisis in Education: A Challenge to American Complacency* (Bell, 1949), *Educational Wastelands: The Retreat from Learning in our Public Schools* (Bestor, 1953), *The Diminished Mind: A Study of Planned Mediocrity in Our Public Schools* (Smith, 1954), and *Quackery in the Public School* (Lynd, 1953) leveled criticisms against the schools that in some ways are similar to those we continue to hear today. During the late 1950s and 1960s, American space failures following the 1957 appearance of *Sputnik*, an earth satellite launched by the former Soviet Union, were blamed on poor education, and a decade of pressure for school reform followed. In the 1970s the focus changed to a concern about potential damage that highly structured school programs might be doing to children. The view of schools as repressive, unimaginative places was reflected in widely read books, including *How Children Fail* (Holt, 1964), *Death at an Early Age* (Kozol, 1967), *Teaching as a Subversive Activity* (Postman & Weingartner, 1969), and *Crisis in the Classroom* (Silberman, 1970).

One thing you will discover is that many critics of the schools have little knowledge of the history of educational reform efforts. It is interesting to hear contemporary critics call for a return to the schools of the past, a suggestion that implies that nobody complained about the quality of the schools we had 10, 20, 30, or more years ago. As the list of titles introduced in the previous paragraph attests, the idea that there was a "golden age" just a few years ago when everybody agreed the schools were excellent simply is nonsense. There has never been a time in our educational history when everybody agreed our schools were performing appropriately.

Because people have varied views about which aspects of schooling are important, the evidence used to measure the success of schools varies according to purposes that are given priority. For example, in recent decades some groups have measured the success or failure of schools by using the scores of students taking college entrance exams such as the **Scholastic Achievement Test (SAT),** international tests of learner achievement, and most recently, standardized achievement tests. Obviously, these indicators of school success focus on just a few of the purposes of education. Some critics contend that these indicators are poor measures of many important educational goals.

Standards-Based Education

Frustrations of policy makers in having valid and reliable data upon which to judge the success of schools have led to support for **standards-based education.** Standards-based education is an attempt to develop clear, measurable descriptions of what learners should know and be able to do as a result of their education. These descriptions typically take the form of goals to reach or levels of proficiency to be attained (Noddings, 1997). Educational specialist Elliot Eisner (1999) notes that one basic motivation behind the standards-based movement is to hold schools accountable. Accountability is facilitated when there are common standards that allow schools, classrooms, teachers, and learners to be compared. Most states and many professional associations have spent considerable time and effort in defining standards.

There are several different types of standards. **Performance standards** relate to the identification of levels of proficiency that given groups of learners are expected to attain. For example, a performance standard in reading might state that all learners will attain a certain level of reading proficiency. **Content standards** describe what teachers are supposed to teach and what young people in their classrooms are expected to learn (Noddings, 1997).

Many national subject-matter groups have developed content standards for what they believe to be essential learning in their subjects. Many states also have developed academic content standards for most of the subjects commonly taught in their schools.

Proponents of clearly defined content standards believe that once standards are specified, measurements can be developed that will provide data that can be used to evaluate school performance and to guide the allocation of scarce resources. They argue that this information is important to provide the public with information relative to the excellence of their schools and teachers. It is assumed that this will prompt teachers to higher levels of performance and provide parents with more information that they can use in selecting schools for their children.

Not everyone agrees that standards-based education is a good idea. Elliot Eisner (1999), for example, suggests that this approach is based on a faulty understanding of the educational process. He argues that proponents of standards-based education inappropriately view schooling as something like a horse race or an educational Olympics that emphasizes competition among individuals rather than as an enterprise designed to develop the distinctive talents and abilities of individuals.

The focus on standards represents a fundamental shift in the traditional ways educational decisions have been made. It is a particular challenge to the tradition of local control. Local control has meant that curriculum decisions and school improvement efforts (1) have been made at the local community level and (2) have attempted to match improvement efforts with local priorities and interests (Stake, 1999). Standards applied across the entire nation or across an entire state effectively remove control from local school authorities. Robert Stake acknowledges that whole states and the entire nation do have a legitimate interest in what every child is learning. However, he argues that this does not mean that every child should learn exactly the same content.

Stake's concern raises this critical question: Who should determine the content standards for the schools? Should a group appointed by politicians such as the President, members of Congress, or governors determine them? Should the standards be decided by a group of business leaders or academic professors in higher education? Is the role of education to supply a trained workforce for industry, or should programs be designed with the expectation that all learners will qualify for admission to a college or university? At times in recent years, members of all of these groups have been involved in efforts to define educational content standards.

Efforts to establish standards have often led to divisive debates. For example, when national standards for history were proposed, there was widespread support for the project. However, once the original standards were published, many people, even those who had originally supported the project, quickly rejected them as too multicultural and unpatriotic. Hence, the seemingly logical and innocent idea of clearly defining expectations for learners quickly assumed political overtones.

In another instance, when science standards were proposed in California, a group of Nobel Prize winners in science criticized them and proposed their own set of standards.

Because of their high profile, the media disseminated their views widely, and a debate was under way. Critics pointed out that a Nobel Prize does not necessarily confer on the winner a store of validated knowledge about what is appropriate for young people to learn at different grade levels. Others attacked the Nobel Prize winners' assumption that every public school learner should master science content at a sophistication level necessary to qualify for admission to the most selective universities.

One of the most significant changes brought about by standards-based education has been a tremendous increase in the emphasis on testing in every subject and at every grade level (Stake, 1999). Much of this assessment consists of **high-stakes testing.** This means that the results of assessments have important consequences. Scores may strongly influence the promotion or retention of learners, the graduation of high school students, the evaluation and the salaries of teachers, and the levels of funding individual schools receive. Because low learner scores can have extremely negative effects, today teachers spend considerable time helping learners master content that will be assessed on high-stakes tests. In some schools where you might accept employment, you and your colleagues may sense pressure to "get test scores up." Such pressures have the potential to narrow the extent of the taught curriculum. In effect, the taught curriculum becomes the part of the adopted curriculum that is most likely to be emphasized by standardized-test makers. Some critics of standardized testing assert that this tendency has given anonymous test-makers more power over the content of the curriculum than they legitimately should have.

Accountability

The concept of accountability relates closely to standards-based education. Standards are developed to indicate what schools should be teaching and the level of performance that learners should be attaining. Accountability frequently is related to issues such as the financing and control of the schools. In many places, schools that do not demonstrate attainment of certain learner performance levels, usually measured by standardized tests, face certain consequences. For example, they may lose a portion of their funding, the

An increased emphasis on accountability has led to increased testing of students.

principals may be replaced, learners may be allowed to transfer to other schools, and the schools or districts may even be placed under state control. In some places, a tendency has developed for teacher evaluations to be based not on general observations of their classroom performance, but rather on their learners' test scores.

Accountability has developed in response to several concerns. One relates to education costs. Educational expenditures are a significant portion of any state budget. As education costs have increased, policy makers have demanded that schools be held responsible for spending the money in ways that result in improved learning.

In recent decades there has been an erosion of confidence in educators. The public has been bombarded in recent years with claims that the schools are failing. Although some data used to back up these assertions is suspect, the effect of sustained criticism of educators has been to erode many citizens' confidence in the schools. Increasingly, members of the public are demanding concrete evidence from educators to reassure them that schools are doing a good job of serving learners.

When considering debates regarding accountability, you need to separate the general concept of accountability from the issue of measurements that are used to make judgments about teachers and school programs. For example, few educators oppose the idea of accountability. When you begin teaching, you will find the majority of your colleagues are sincerely interested in using resources carefully and in working to assure that learners get the best education possible. Issues teachers have with accountability center not on the idea itself, but rather on what is used to determine whether educational services are as good as they should be. In particular, teachers argue against using standardized test scores as the only accountability measure.

One problem with using standardized test scores is that a judgment about a teacher's instructional effectiveness is based on what a learner does on a single day of standardized testing. This appears to many teachers to be entirely too limited a sample of the learner's levels of understanding to be taken as overall evidence of what he or she has learned. In addition, teachers critical of too much reliance on standardized tests point out that learners' scores depend on many variables other than the quality of instruction they receive. Further, many variables are beyond individual teacher's control. Some variables that may affect learners' test scores and that are not subject to teacher influence include

- The home language of individual learners (Learners who speak a language at home other than English sometimes have difficulty scoring well on standardized tests.)
- The income and educational levels of learners' families (Learners' home situations affect their school learning. There are huge differences in reading material found in individual learners' homes, levels of parental education and, hence, parental capacities to help with homework, noise levels in the home, and so forth. Scores on standardized tests are highly correlated with the socioeconomic status of parents. Therefore, they are probably a better indicator of parental status than teacher performance.)
- The quality of learning materials provided to supplement the teacher's instruction (Are there books available that are appropriate for the grade level? Is content of the adopted books consistent with content assessed on standardized tests?)
- The nature of the school's facilities (Is classroom lighting adequate? Are classrooms well insulated from outside noise? And so forth).

Even assuming none of the above differences existed, there are still problems associated with using learners' scores on tests as accountability measures. Critics point out that these tests are poorly suited to stand as academic-success indicators. Because so many learners take standardized tests, individual items must be presented in a form that allows for quick, mechanical correction. This tends to limit test content to fairly unsophisticated information that can be assessed using item formats that require learners to use less-complex thinking levels. They fail to challenge learners to use the sophisticated thinking processes they need to engage more-difficult content.

How might accountability data be gathered in ways that more appropriately respond to some difficulties associated with overuse of standardized test results? Some critics of present practices propose that data on such topics as school dropout and graduation rates, college acceptance rates, follow-up studies of graduates, teacher-turnover rates, school safety issues (such as the number of suspensions and discipline incidents), and other variables need to be considered in addition to test scores. The problem is that gathering this information can be time-consuming, difficult, and expensive.

In summary, you are certain to encounter continued discussions of concerns related to standards and accountability when you enter the profession. You and other professionals will face challenges as you seek to ensure that adopted standards are consistent with the purposes of education and that the measurements used for accountability purposes are valid and fair.

Efforts to Ensure Quality of New Teachers

The focus on standards has not been confined to the K–12 schools. In recent years, a broadened accountability interest has embraced development of standards for beginning teachers. Accompanying assessments seek to evaluate higher education programs based on how well their graduates meet those standards. In previous years, state authorities issued teaching certificates to newcomers based only on their completion of a prescribed sequence of college courses. Today most states are moving to performance-based systems that judge candidates' readiness in terms of their ability to perform in the classroom in ways consistent with adopted professional standards.

VIDEO VIEWPOINTS

Alternative Certification

WATCH: In this ABC News video segment, the issue of using alternative routes to certification in order to meet the teacher shortage is discussed. This segment focuses on very short credential programs designed to attract second-career individuals into teaching. The merits of opening teaching to skilled individuals is emphasized. Early in the tape, Bob Woodruff mentions that the struggle is to find quality teachers. What is not addressed in the segment is a definition of a quality teacher or what a person needs to know in order to be a qualified teacher. Other points that are not covered are the impact of poorly prepared individuals on the students and the high attrition rate of individuals who are poorly prepared for the complexities of the classroom.

THINK: Discuss with your classmates, or in your teaching journal, the following questions:

1. What is your definition of a quality teacher?
2. Can a person be prepared to teach successfully with just a few weeks of preparation?
3. What is the public perception of the importance and complexity of teaching that is communicated through the implementation of brief alternative-certification programs?

LINK: What are the requirements for obtaining a teaching credential in your state?

Complete this activity and submit your responses online in the Video Viewpoints module for this chapter of the Companion Website.

Interstate New Teacher Assessment and Support Consortium. More than 30 states participate in a consortium called the **Interstate New Teacher Assessment and Support Consortium (INTASC).** INTASC has identified 10 principles correlated to what beginning teachers should know and be able to do. Yours may be one of the many states that now use these principles as a basis for organizing teacher-preparation programs and for issuing teaching licenses. These principles, referred to as the **INTASC Model Core Standards,** follow (Interstate New Teacher Assessment and Support Consortium [INTASC], 1992):

Standard 1 (S1).	The teacher understands the central concepts, tools of inquiry, and structures of the discipline(s) he or she teaches and can create learning experiences that make these aspects of subject matter meaningful for students.
Standard 2 (S2).	The teacher understands how children learn and develop, and can provide learning opportunities that support their intellectual, social, and personal development.
Standard 3 (S3).	The teacher understands how students differ in their approaches to learning and creates instructional opportunities that are adapted to diverse learners.
Standard 4 (S4).	The teacher understands and uses a variety of instructional strategies to encourage students' development of critical thinking, problem solving, and performance skills.
Standard 5 (S5).	The teacher uses an understanding of individual and group motivation and behavior to create a learning environment that encourages positive social interaction, active engagement in learning, and self-motivation.
Standard 6 (S6).	The teacher uses knowledge of effective verbal, nonverbal, and media communication techniques to foster active inquiry, collaboration, and supportive interaction in the classroom.
Standard 7 (S7).	The teacher plans instruction based upon knowledge of subject matter, students, the community, and curriculum goals.
Standard 8 (S8).	The teacher understands and uses formal and informal assessment strategies to evaluate and ensure the continuous intellectual, social, and physical development of the learner.
Standard 9 (S9).	The teacher is a reflective practitioner who continually evaluates the effects of his/her choices and actions on others (students, parents, and other professionals in the learning community) and who actively seeks out opportunities to grow professionally.
Standard 10 (S10).	The teacher fosters relationships with school colleagues, parents, and agencies in the larger community to support students' learning and well-being.

As you continue through your teacher-preparation sequence, you will gain the knowledge and skills you need to meet these standards. From time to time, you may wish to review your own professional development in terms of your growing ability to understand and perform in ways consistent with the INTASC Model Core Standards.

WEB EXTENSION 1–3

INTASC Standards

More information about the INTASC standards and about content standards that have been developed for particular subjects can be accessed at the INTASC Web site.

http://www.ccsso.org/Projects/Interstate_New_Teacher_Assessment_and_Support_Consortium

Praxis Assessments for Beginning Teachers.   Educational Testing Service (ETS) developed the **Praxis series** of assessments to evaluate individuals preparing for careers in teaching at various points in their professional development. Many states and universities use results of these tests as a basis for making program-entry decisions; awarding **teaching certificates, licenses,** or **credentials** (documents making it legally possible for a person to teach in a state's schools); and determining whether beginners' levels of teaching performance are at an acceptable level. Currently, 35 states use some or all of the assessments as a credential requirement.

Praxis has three different assessment categories. **Praxis I** consists of academic skills assessments. These tests are used early in the academic careers of students who wish to pursue education careers. They seek to determine whether prospective teacher candidates have adequate reading, writing, and mathematics skills.

Praxis II assessments provide information about teacher candidates' knowledge of the subject(s), important pedagogical knowledge, and knowledge of important learning and teaching principles. In many places, teacher candidates must receive certain minimum scores before they will be issued teaching licenses, certificates, or credentials.

Praxis III is a classroom-performance assessment that usually takes place during the first year of teaching. Local assessors use nationally validated criteria to observe and make judgments about a teacher's performance. Results often are used to help newcomers to the profession prepare professional-improvement plans.

As you go through your professional development program, you may find it particularly useful to keep in mind some categories assessed by the Praxis II assessments. Because Praxis II assessments are used in a large majority of the states, at some point in your program you may be required to take these tests. Even if you are not required to do so, the Praxis II categories describe aspects of practice that are important for you to master as you work to become a professional educator.

Some of the topics covered in the Principles of Learning and Teaching Test include how learning occurs, learner motivation, learner diversity, different instructional approaches, planning instruction, effective communication, the role of the school in the community, debates on best teaching practices, major laws relating to learner and teacher rights, and personal reflection on teaching practices. To help you synthesize this information, at various points throughout this text you will be invited to reflect on what you have learned and to consider its relevance for some of the categories featured in the Praxis II assessments.

WEB EXTENSION 1–4

Investigating Praxis

More detailed information on the Praxis series of assessments and even sample questions can be found on their Web site.

http://www.ets.org/praxis

KEEPING AN INITIAL-DEVELOPMENT PORTFOLIO

The profession's complexity presents prospective teachers with daunting challenges. As you begin grappling with new content and difficult issues that you will face throughout your career, you may find it useful to develop a system that will help you establish priorities and make decisions. As you work with the material in this text and with information that will come to you from subsequent courses and from other sources, consider preparing a **portfolio.** A portfolio consists of organized information that helps the person who prepares it to synthesize what he or she knows in ways that allow for easy retrieval of information. Contents also reflect the developer's personal understandings, beliefs, and priorities. The **initial-development portfolio** is a portfolio type that focuses on information you gather that you believe will contribute to your development and potential effectiveness as a beginning teacher.

Components of initial-development portfolios vary. Many of them include features such as the following:

- An *introduction* that describes the basic purpose of the portfolio,
- A basic *table of contents* that identifies categories you will use to organize information,
- Individual *artifacts* or *pieces of critical information* that form the basic portfolio content,
- Your *reflections* about artifacts and pieces of information (For example, you may wish to comment about any discrepancies between new information and your prior beliefs or understandings about a given topic.), and
- *Summary comments* that tie together your reactions to broad categories of information.

As a prompt to developing an initial-development portfolio, you will find a section at the end of each chapter titled "For Your Initial-Development Portfolio." You will be encouraged to think about information presented in the chapter in terms of its possible relevance to one or more of the INTASC standards.

You may wish to use a portfolio system as you continue your development throughout your career. In Chapter 2, "Becoming a Professional Educator," you will be introduced to a format for maintaining a portfolio of this type.

 Critical Incident

Teaching to the Test

Maria is a first-year teacher. She wants to develop lessons that interest and motivate her students. Recently, her principal visited her classroom for an observation. Following the lesson, the principal said, "You had an interesting lesson and everybody in your class was engaged. However, you need to remember that test scores are very important here. Our parents expect us to post high test scores and we cannot afford to let them slip. We expect that all of the people in your classroom will do well on the test. If I were a parent and asked you how today's lesson ties to the testing program, what would you say?"

• • •

What are your reactions to the principal's comments? Should teachers be teaching to the test? Is there an inconsistency between having interesting lessons and meeting standards? How would you respond?

 To respond to this Critical Incident online, go to the Critical Incidents *module for this chapter of the* Companion Website.

- Because education is viewed as such an important societal institution, it is the subject of much debate and numerous proposals for change. Because there is no national consensus regarding the purposes of education, you are likely to find disagreements and inconsistency among proposals to improve the schools.
- School policies and practices are influenced by answers to important questions associated with the foundations of the education profession. These questions include those associated with (1) social and philosophical foundations, (2) historical foundations, (3) political foundations, (4) curriculum foundations, (5) instructional foundations, and (6) legal foundations.
- Teachers' responsibilities require them to discharge diverse responsibilities. These include (1) planning lessons, (2) maintaining records, (3) attending special school events, (4) working on committees, (5) participating in professional groups' activities, and (6) communicating with parents and guardians.
- The complexity of teaching relates to its *multidimensionality* (the idea that responsibilities range across a broad variety of duties), *simultaneity* (the need for teachers to work in an environment in which many things occur at the same time), *immediacy* (the necessity to respond at the same time to multiple events), *unpredictability* (the need to work in an environment in which learners' behaviors do not always follow consistent patterns), *publicness* (the need to work in an arena that is subject to constant monitoring by others), and *history* (the need to cope with classroom patterns or culture that have resulted from previous teacher–learner interactions).
- As a teacher today, you will confront challenges that change over time in important ways. These challenges require you to be flexible and to be willing to modify your teaching approaches in light of new conditions and situations.
- Instructional approaches tied to *constructivism* and *multiple intelligences* are examples of those you may encounter early in your career. Constructivism refers to the idea that people cannot simply be given new knowledge. For knowledge to become meaningful, they must create information through interactions that involve prior knowledge and knowledge that is presented to them for the first time. Multiple-intelligence theory holds that intelligence is not a unitary trait. Rather, there are various kinds of intelligences, and individuals are likely to be "smarter" in terms of some intelligence types than others.
- Over time, there have been numerous debates about what the appropriate purposes of schooling are. There has never been a time in our educational history when there has been a national consensus about what constitutes a good education. You may expect to encounter debates about what we need to do to "make schools better" throughout your career in the profession.
- Today, there is great interest in establishing public standards against which to measure learners' academic progress. These standards often are accompanied by testing programs that seek to assess how well young people are mastering the prescribed content. Increasingly, school leaders and teachers are being held accountable for learner performance on these tests. Some people argue that this trend irresponsibly forces teachers to "teach to the test."
- In recent years, legislators and others responsible for overseeing the schools have become greatly interested in the issue of teacher quality. The Interstate New Teacher Assessment and Support Consortium (INTASC) is an example of an entity created as a result of this interest. INTASC has developed a set of expectations for new teachers known as the *INTASC Model Core Standards*. These standards lay out knowledge and behavioral expectations for beginning teachers. Many colleges and universities use these standards as a framework for constructing their teacher-preparation programs.

- The *Praxis* series of assessments represents another response to the desire to assure that new teachers meet acceptable minimum standards of quality. Many states require all prospective teachers to take these tests. Individual Praxis tests are given at three points during a teacher's professional development sequence: (1) a basic understanding and skills test is given as a precondition to formal entry into the professional component of a teacher education program; (2) a test over subject matter and pedagogical knowledge is given as a prerequisite to awarding teacher certificates, licenses, or credentials; and (3) a classroom-performance assessment is given during a new teacher's first year in the classroom.
- You may wish to keep an *initial-development portfolio* as you go through your teacher-preparation program. The portfolio allows you to organize information, reflect on it, and make decisions about what important information you already know and what important information you need to obtain to adequately prepare yourself for the classroom.

Chapter 1 Self-Test

To review terms and concepts in this chapter, go to the Companion Website and take the Chapter 1 Self-Test. *Feedback for the self-test is immediate. You can keep track of your self-test scores yourself, or you can choose to submit your scores to your instructor via e-mail.*

Preparing for Praxis

To learn more about the Praxis test and complete this activity online, go to the Preparing for Praxis *module for this chapter of the Companion Website.*

You may be required to pass Educational Testing Service's Praxis II exam as you seek formal authorization to teach in the public schools. The *Principles of Learning and Teaching* component of Praxis II seeks to assess your knowledge about these topics: (1) Students as Learners, (2) Instruction and Assessment, (3) Communication Techniques, and (4) Profession and Community.

The introductory material in this chapter may be especially relevant as you prepare for questions related to the categories of Students as Learners and Profession and Community. Some content may also provide you with information related to other Praxis II categories. You may find it useful to prepare a chart for your own use similar to the one provided here. As you encounter information related to individual categories, you can enter it into the chart under the appropriate heading. A completed chart of this kind will be useful as you begin reviewing what you have learned in preparation for the Praxis II exam.

Students as Learners	Instruction and Assessment
• Student Development and the Learning Process	• Instructional Strategies
• Students as Diverse Learners	• Planning Instruction
• Student Motivation and the Learning Environment	• Assessment Strategies
Communication Techniques	**Profession and Community**
• Basic, Effective, Verbal and Nonverbal Communication Techniques	• The Reflective Practitioner
• Effect of Cultural and Gender Differences on Communications in the Classroom	• The Larger Community
• Types of Questions That Can Stimulate Discussion in Different Ways for Particular Purposes	

For Your Initial-Development Portfolio

To complete this activity and submit your response online, go to the For Your Initial-Development Portfolio *module for this chapter of the Companion Website.*

1. What materials and ideas that you learned in this chapter about the nature of teaching and the education field will you include as "evidence" in your portfolio? Select up to three separate items of information. Number them 1, 2, and 3.
2. Think about why you selected these materials. As you do so, consider these issues:
   - Specific uses you might make of this information as you plan, deliver, and assess the impact of your teaching,
   - The compatibility of the information with your own priorities and values,
   - Any contributions this information can make to your development as a teacher, and
   - Factors that led you to include this information as opposed to some alternatives you considered, but rejected.
3. Place a check in the chart here to indicate to which INTASC standard(s) each of your items of information relates.

INTASC Standard Number

ITEM OF EVIDENCE NUMBER	S1	S2	S3	S4	S5	S6	S7	S8	S9	S10
1										
2										
3										

4. Prepare a written reflection in which you analyze the decision-making process you followed. In your comments, mention the INTASC standard(s) to which your selected material relates.

Reflections

To respond to these questions online, go to the Reflections *module for this chapter of the Companion Website.*

1. In this chapter, you learned that many debates about education are rooted in different perceptions about what is a good society and how education should contribute to that society. What are your views of the good society? How does your view of the good society influence your views of what education ought to be?
2. Schools reflect society, and changes in society influence education. What do you see as two or three changes that are occurring in society that will have an important impact on schools and education? What impact do you think they will have? How do you propose to react to these changes?

3. Review material in the chapter dealing with *constructivism*. If you decided to embrace this approach, what would your lessons be like? What is your response to constructivism, and why do you feel this way? Do you recall any of your own teachers operating in ways that are consistent with this approach? What did they do that you liked or disliked?
4. Sometimes today's critics paint pictures of so-called "golden ages" when the schools were excellent and everybody was happy with our educational system. In this chapter you learned that, contrary to the pronouncements of these critics, there has never been a time when there has been an absence of debate about the quality of our educational system. During your career, you are virtually certain to encounter some

people who will tell you, "Our schools are much worse than they used to be." How will you respond to people who share this view?

5. The INTASC standards and Praxis examinations are becoming important components guiding the preparation and licensure of teachers. What is your reaction to them? How will you use information you now have about the INTASC standards and the Praxis examinations as you continue your preparation for classroom teaching?

Field Experiences, Projects, and Enrichment

1. Interview a teacher who has taught for at least 10 years. Select someone who teaches at a grade level and in a subject area you would like to teach. Ask this person to reflect on kinds of criticisms of teachers and schools he or she has heard over the years. What has been the general nature of this criticism? Have all critics complained about the same things? What remedies have been proposed? How have this teacher and his or her teaching colleagues dealt with these criticisms? Share responses with others in your class.

2. Observe a teacher and look for instances of *multidimensionality, unpredictability, simultaneity, immediacy*, and *history*. After your observation, ask the teacher what impact these have on planning and instructing. Which of these variables does the teacher think provided the most challenges during his or her first year of teaching? What advice does the teacher have for a newcomer to the profession who will be dealing with these challenges for the first time? Share your findings with others in your class.

3. In this chapter you read a brief explanation of *emotional intelligence*. Educators are becoming increasingly interested in this topic. To enrich your own understanding, use a good search engine such as Google (http://www.google.com), enter the search terms "emotional intelligence," and conduct an Internet search. You will find dozens of sites with good information. One you may particularly wish to visit is the EQ International Site on Emotions, Emotional Needs, and Emotional Intelligence at http://www.eqi.org. At this site, you can follow a link to a massive table of contents that includes topics such as conflict resolution, emotional awareness, emotional literacy, emotional intelligence, and emotional needs. Review information at one or more Internet sites. Then, prepare a short report for others in your class that will expand their understanding of emotional intelligence.

4. Research the state standards and state assessment programs for the grade level(s) and subject(s) you plan to teach. Your instructor will be able to help you locate this information. Many state departments of education put this information on their Web sites. Then, think about these questions: Did you find any surprises? Do you agree with them? Why or why not? To conclude the exercise, prepare a personal plan of action in which you outline some specific things you intend to do to gain the knowledge and expertise you will need to deal with any standards (and related tests) for which you do not feel your present preparation is adequate.

5. Take the 10 principles outlined by the INTASC standards and create an *Already Know/Want to Learn/Learned* chart. For each standard make three columns. At the top of the first, write "Know." At the top of the second column, write "Want to Learn." At the top of the third column, write "Learned." Begin by entering what you think you already know about the principle in the first column and what you want or need to learn about it in the second column. As you progress in your development, write what you learn about each principle in the third column. You may wish to keep this in a professional-development portfolio as documentation of what you have learned.

References

Banks, J. (2001). *An introduction to multicultural education* (3rd ed.). Boston: Allyn & Bacon.

Bell, B. I. (1949). *Crisis in education: A challenge to American complacency.* New York: Whittlesey House.

Bestor, A. (1953). *Educational wastelands: The retreat from learning in our public schools.* Urbana, IL: University of Illinois Press.

Bicouvaris, M. (2004). In K. T. Henson, *Constructivist teaching strategies for diverse middle-level classrooms.* Boston: Allyn & Bacon.

Clincy, E. (1998). The educationally challenged American school district. *Phi Delta Kappan, 80*(40), 272–277.

Doyle, W. (1986). Classroom organization and management. In M. Wittrock (Ed.), *Handbook of research on teaching* (3rd ed., pp. 392–431). New York: Macmillan.

Eisner, E. (1999). The uses and limits of performance assessment. *Phi Delta Kappan, 80*(9), 658–660.

Gardner, H. (1999). *Intelligence reframed: Multiple intelligences for the 21st century.* New York: Basic Books.

Goleman, D. (1995). *Emotional intelligence.* New York: Bantam Books.

Henson, K. T. (2004). *Constructivist teaching strategies for middle-level classrooms.* Boston: Allyn & Bacon.

Holt, J. (1964). *How children fail.* New York: Dell.

Interstate New Teacher Assessment and Support Consortium. (1992). *Model standard for beginning teacher licensing, assessment and development.* Washington, DC: Council of Chief State School Officers.

Kindler, A. L. (2002). *Survey of the states' limited English proficient students and available educational programs and services: 2000–2001 summary report.* Washington, DC: National Clearinghouse for English Language Acquisition & Language Instruction Educational Programs.

Kozol, J. (1967). *Death at an early age.* Boston: Houghton Mifflin.

Lynd, A. (1953). *Quackery in the public school.* Boston: Little, Brown.

Macedo, D. (1995). English only: The tongue tying of America. In J. Noll (Ed.), *Taking sides: Clashing views on controversial educational issues* (8th ed., pp. 249–258). Guilford, CT: Dushkin.

Noddings, N. (1997). Thinking about standards. *Phi Delta Kappan, 79*(3), 184–189.

Padolsky, D. (2002). *AskNCELA no. 8: How has the English language learner (ELL) population changed in recent years?* [http://www.ncela.gwu.edu/askncela/08leps.htm].

Postman, N., & Weingartner, C. (1969). *Teaching as a subversive activity.* New York: Delacourte.

Ravitch, D. (1995). Politicization and the schools: The case against bilingual education. In J. Noll (Ed.), *Taking sides: Clashing views on controversial educational issues* (8th ed., pp. 240–248). Guilford, CT: Dushkin.

Schlesinger, A. (1995). The disuniting of America. In J. Noll (Ed.), *Taking sides: Clashing views on controversial educational issues* (8th ed., pp. 227–236). Guilford, CT: Dushkin.

Silberman, C. E. (1970). *Crisis in the classroom.* New York: Random House.

Slavin, R. (2002). *Educational psychology: Theory and practice* (7th ed.). Boston: Allyn & Bacon.

Smith, M. (1954). *The diminished mind: A study of planned mediocrity in our public schools.* Chicago: Greenwood Press.

Stake, R. (1999). The goods on American education. *Phi Delta Kappan, 80*(9), 668–672.

Sternberg, R. (1990). *Metaphors of mind: Conceptions on the nature of intelligence.* New York: Cambridge University Press.

Woolfolk, A. (2001). *Educational Psychology* (8th ed.). Boston: Allyn & Bacon.

2

Becoming a Professional Educator

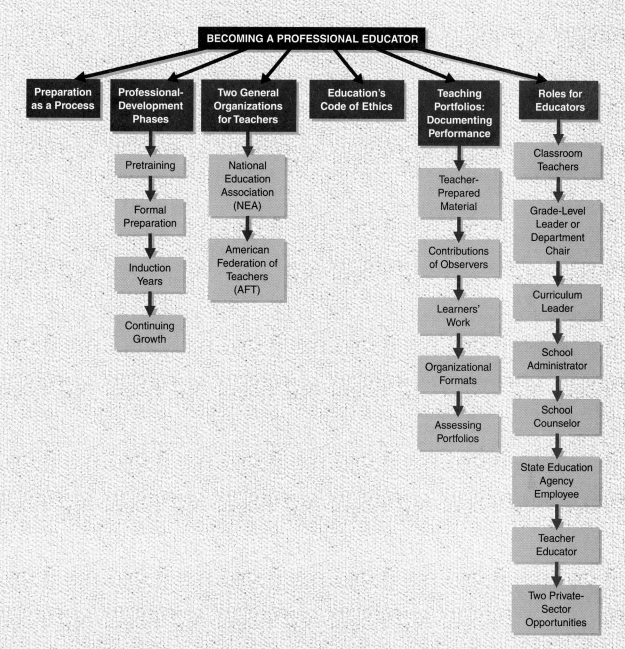

BECOMING A PROFESSIONAL EDUCATOR

- Preparation as a Process
- Professional-Development Phases
  - Pretraining
  - Formal Preparation
  - Induction Years
  - Continuing Growth
- Two General Organizations for Teachers
  - National Education Association (NEA)
  - American Federation of Teachers (AFT)
- Education's Code of Ethics
- Teaching Portfolios: Documenting Performance
  - Teacher-Prepared Material
  - Contributions of Observers
  - Learners' Work
  - Organizational Formats
  - Assessing Portfolios
- Roles for Educators
  - Classroom Teachers
  - Grade-Level Leader or Department Chair
  - Curriculum Leader
  - School Administrator
  - School Counselor
  - State Education Agency Employee
  - Teacher Educator
  - Two Private-Sector Opportunities

OBJECTIVES

This chapter will help you to

- explain why teacher preparation is better thought of as a career-long process rather than as a series of steps having a definite end.
- describe important phases in a typical teacher-development process.
- suggest ways that information from such national teacher organizations as the National Education Association and the American Federation of Teachers can help beginning teachers adjust to their new profession.
- describe some key provisions of the *Code of Ethics of the Education Profession*.
- explain benefits associated with the development of teaching portfolios, and describe components that these documents often include.
- point out examples of the variety of roles that are found within the education profession.

PREPARATION AS A PROCESS

Think about what the word *preparing* means in the phrase "preparing for teaching." When you learned to ride a bicycle, you reached a point when someone let you go and you could confidently ride. A profession does not work this way. You do not wake up one day shouting, "Eureka! I know all I need to know about this business." Professionalism is a deliberative, developmental experience. When you prepare for teaching, you develop a commitment to career-long growth (Steffy, Wolfe, Pasch, & Enz, 2000). Your initial preparation program helps you to start learning the kinds of things necessary to continue learning.

Members of individual professions share common values and perspectives. For example, there are ethical standards to which members of the teaching profession subscribe. A shared commitment to certain ethical practices, a concern for the development of the capacities of all learners who come to school, and a sense that education should be a high-priority concern for the entire society have led educators to band together in large and powerful organizations. These include the **National Education Association (NEA)** and the **American Federation of Teachers (AFT)**. These groups help set national and state education agendas.

In recent years, public discussion of education has focused increasingly on performance of both learners and teachers. As a new teacher, you will be entering a profession that attracts much public scrutiny, and it is likely that you will be asked to provide evidence that documents your performance. In many places, teachers are being asked to prepare teaching portfolios for this purpose.

As you begin work as an educator, you probably will be surprised by the diversity of the field. People who begin as classroom teachers have knowledge and skills that equip them to pursue many interesting career paths. Some of these options exist within formal education systems and related governmental agencies; some are in the private sector. These options provide you with a wonderful opportunity to find a role in education that fits you well.

PROFESSIONAL-DEVELOPMENT PHASES

Your professional development as a teacher did not begin when you entered your teacher-preparation program. The roots of your decision go all the way back to your personal set of prior experiences, your thoughts about them, and the decisions you made that ultimately resulted in your taking steps to pursue a program leading to a teaching certificate, license, or credential.

Though your teacher-preparation program will contribute to making you a professional, the preparatory process will continue throughout your career. As you think about entering the profession, you may find it helpful to know something about four important phases that characterize teachers' professional lives. They are

- the **pretraining phase,**
- the **formal-preparation phase,**
- the **induction-years phase,** and
- the **continuing-growth phase.**

Pretraining

Your personal experiences and the attitudes you developed before enrolling in any teacher-preparation courses reflect an influence of the pretraining phase of your professional development. Your attitudes probably derive in part to views that your family members hold.

In addition, your feelings about teaching may have been affected by teachers who taught you, your classmates, and other experiences you had when you were in elementary, middle, and high school. Influences of your own schooling experiences are to be expected, given that the typical high school graduate has spent more than 10,000 hours in K–12 classrooms.

Memories of your own school days may not be as helpful as you think. Schools and learners today vary tremendously. You may find that the schools you see during your preparation program are quite different from those you attended. The young people, too, may differ from those with whom you went to school, and you may find that some instructional techniques that your favorite teachers used (and that you liked) do not work well with other learners in other settings. You need to keep an open mind about what constitutes "good teaching" and recognize that practices that are enthusiastically received by learners in some places may not be appropriate for learners in others.

Formal Preparation

You are using this text, so you are probably in the formal-preparation phase of your professional development. Though there are some differences from institution to institution, there are common features in most teacher-preparation programs. In part, these common features have been developed in response to guidelines of state and national accrediting bodies such as the **National Council for Accreditation of Teacher Education (NCATE).** Preparation programs often have these three basic parts:

- Core studies,
- Teaching specialization(s)/academic major(s), and
- Professional education.

Core Studies.   In addition to the specific content areas you will be expected to teach, you are expected to be familiar with information that educated adults know. The **core-studies component** of teacher-preparation programs is designed to accommodate this need. Typically, core-studies requirements ask students to take a specified number of content courses from mathematics, the sciences, the liberal arts, and the fine arts. These courses tend to constitute about 30% to 40% of a typical bachelor's degree program.

Teaching Specializations/Academic Majors.   If you are preparing for a career in elementary schools, you will be expected to teach information from a variety of content areas. You may also have a particular **teaching specialization** such as reading or mathematics that you have studied in some depth as part of your preparation program.

Prospective middle school teachers may have teaching specializations or a formal **academic major,** and future senior high school teachers almost always have an academic major. If you are preparing to teach in high school, you probably intend to teach courses in your academic major, though often it is also possible for you to be assigned to teach at least a few courses in other subject areas. (Requirements related to teaching outside of the academic major vary greatly; however, a certain minimum number of college or university courses are often required.)

Professional Education.   The **professional-education component** of your preparation program seeks to give you the expertise needed to deliver instruction and manage learners. In recent years, there has been a trend toward having more of this component of the preparation program offered at field sites located in K–12 schools. Prospective teachers today spend much more time in the schools than was the case 10 or 20 years ago. The

One of the most important components of the professional development of teachers is opportunity to work with experienced teachers in student teaching.

goal is to smooth the transition from the world of the college or university to the world of the K–12 school. Many programs today provide opportunities for prospective teachers to engage in some supervised instruction of learners in the schools at various stages throughout their preparation program. Historically, preparation programs provided prospective teachers with virtually no direct contact with K–12 schools until student-teaching experience, a capstone experience that often did not occur until the term just before graduation.

You may have already had some experience teaching K–12 students as part of your own preparation program. If not, you probably will soon have an opportunity to do so. Successes you experience will be confidence builders. They can also broaden your appreciation of the many kinds of learners in the schools, and they can challenge your capacity for honoring and responding professionally to the diversity you probably will encounter. Work in the schools, particularly when it is approached seriously, can be a wonderful beginning to a successful teaching career.

Induction Years

The first years in teaching are sometimes called the **induction-years phase.** This term implies that no one assumes you will arrive on the job fully formed as a professional educator. It is another recognition that professionals are involved in a process of career-long development and that the early years are times of particularly intense learning. Much learning during the first few years of teaching centers on adapting to the special characteristics of the school—the learners, the surrounding community, the prescribed curriculum, the available resources, the interpersonal relationships among the teachers, and so forth.

Even new teachers from the finest preparation programs experience stress during the initial years of teaching. Beginners sometimes miss the support university supervisors and supervising teachers provided them during student teaching. Many school systems recognize this problem, and some respond by assigning experienced mentor teachers to work with newcomers. Some states now have laws requiring school districts to provide this kind of support to new teachers.

Much discussion about challenges facing newcomers to the profession used to focus on the first year of teaching. Today, there is recognition that beginners take several years to settle comfortably into their new roles. Increasingly, school leaders are thinking about ways to provide special assistance during the first 2 to 4 years of teachers' professional service. Some states permit teacher-education students to graduate, but they withhold teacher certification until the new teachers have experienced a successful year of supervised internship. Other states are planning to adopt this practice.

Continuing Growth

Professional development does not end with your induction into the profession. It is a career-long self-improvement process (Flowers, Mertens, & Mulhall, 2002). You will have a number of alternative professional-development approaches to pursue when you are in your continuing-growth phase. These include

- Staff-development opportunities,
- College and university courses, and
- Work associated with professional organizations.

Staff Development.   You may find yourself employed in one of the many school districts that organize extensive **staff-development** activities for teachers. Districts commit funds to these activities as part of their efforts to enhance the overall quality of instruction. The term **in-service education** often is applied to these efforts. These programs often feature special sessions to introduce new teaching techniques, well-known educational speakers, workshops to prepare materials or modify curricula, or "share" sessions in which participants exchange materials and ideas.

It is likely that you will be required to attend some staff-development sessions; others may be optional. In some districts, teachers receive staff-development credits, and when they have accumulated enough credits, they qualify for higher salaries.

Copyright 2002 by Randy Glasbergen.
www.glasbergen.com

BOOKS

"Yes, we have *Chicken Soup for the Math Teacher's Soul.*
The price is $475 ÷ 23 x .018² – Y³ + 4X ÷ $73.99999 + 2."

College and University Courses.   You may elect to take college and university courses to build your professional knowledge base. Many institutions offer night courses so teachers may take them during the school year. It is common for colleges and universities to have extensive summer-session offerings for teachers. You can often use college and university courses to fulfill requirements for an advanced degree. Frequently, school districts award increases in salaries to teachers who complete specified courses or fulfill advanced-degree requirements.

As you consider possible courses you might take during your early years in the classroom, think first about taking those that will help you meet specific challenges you might be facing in the classroom. You should focus on selecting courses that will directly help you with your work rather than those designed to meet advanced-degree requirements. You may be in the profession for a long time. There will be plenty of time to complete an advanced-degree program after you have addressed some more-pressing gaps in the knowledge you need to succeed in the classroom.

Involvement with Professional Groups.   You will find that many professional organizations sponsor meetings that include sessions designed to improve teachers' expertise. These groups often offer professional-development opportunities of various kinds, including workshops or more-formal sessions in which individual presenters share ideas. Some professional organizations focus on specific subject areas and specific categories of learners. Some examples you may wish to contact for further information include

- American Alliance for Health, Physical Education, Recreation, and Dance (AAHPERD)—http://www.aahperd.org/
- Council on Exceptional Children (CEC)—http://www.cec.sped.org
- International Reading Association (IRA)—http://www.reading.org
- International Society for Technology in Education (ISTE)—http://www.iste.org
- Music Teachers National Association (MTNA)—http://www.mtna.org
- National Art Education Association (NAEA)—http://www.naea-reston.org/
- National Association for Gifted Children—http://www.nagc.org/
- National Business Education Association (NBEA)—http://www.nbea.org/
- National Council for the Social Studies (NCSS)—http://www.ncss.org/
- National Council of Teachers of English (NCTE)—http://www.ncte.org/
- National Council of Teachers of Mathematics (NCTM)—http://www.nctm.org/
- National Middle School Association (NMSA)—http://www.nmsa.org/
- National Science Teachers Association (NSTA)—http://www.nsta.org/

Joining a professional group gives you an opportunity to meet people with shared interests. Members often get productive new ideas from even casual conversations with others in the group. Many professional organizations sponsor the publication of journals that feature excellent, practical how-to-do-it articles.

TWO GENERAL ORGANIZATIONS FOR TEACHERS

In addition to the many specialty organizations that serve teachers with particular grade-level or subject-area interests, two national organizations represent the more-general interests of the teaching profession. These organizations are

- The National Education Association (NEA) and
- The American Federation of Teachers (AFT).

These organizations perform many services for their members. They help explain teachers' work to the public at large. They engage in lobbying activities seeking legislation thought to advance the interest of their members and opposing legislation thought to have negative implications for teachers. They provide opportunities for classroom practitioners to keep abreast of new knowledge as it relates to their professional development and practice. They also often specify standards of appropriate or ethical practice.

National Education Association (NEA)

The NEA is the larger of the two major teachers' organizations. Though today the NEA does recognize the strike as one legitimate weapon that teachers can use as they seek improved conditions of practice and better salaries, in general the organization conceives of teachers as members of a learned profession such as law and medicine. Because these professionals have a long tradition of self-governance, the NEA has had a tradition of supporting policies that give teachers more control over their professional lives. This implies a role for teachers in such areas as preparation of new teachers, qualifications for hiring teachers, appropriate content of courses, selection of learning materials, and identification of instructional methods.

WEB EXTENSION 2–1

The National Education Association

You will find much information about the National Education Association (NEA) at the organization's Web site. Click on a link titled "For and About Members." This link will take you to a page that includes additional links to information of interest to future teachers, beginning teachers, support staff in the schools, retired teachers, and other groups. You will find information of potential interest to you as a prospective educator by following links titled "Beginning Teachers" and "Future Teachers." At this site, you can also find a listing of the NEA's mailing address should you wish to initiate correspondence with the group about a topic that interests you.

http://www.nea.org/

The National Education Association is the largest of the general organizations for teachers.

American Federation of Teachers (AFT)

The American Federation of Teachers (AFT), a union affiliated with the AFL-CIO, views teachers as occupying positions similar to those of employees of large corporations. The AFT points out that teachers, unlike professionals such as lawyers, rarely are self-employed. Nearly all of them work for institutions (school districts). This employment reality creates a situation in which many teachers work at sites distant from the lead administrators in their districts. In the view of the AFT, this creates a need for teachers to have a strong organization to counter the possibility that distant administrators may make decisions that disadvantage teachers and learners.

The AFT has long embraced the strike as a legitimate bargaining tool. It seeks negotiated decisions that maximize teachers' benefits and restrict arbitrary exercise of administrative power. Negotiated agreements tend to specify in considerable detail the responsibilities and rights of both teachers and administrators. When there are differences of interpretation related to these agreements, an arbitration system is followed that is similar to those used in traditional labor-management disputes.

WEB EXTENSION 2–2

The American Federation of Teachers

This site is the home page of the American Federation of Teachers (AFT). You will find information about a wide range of activities the group undertakes in support of its members. Click on the link titled "PreK–12 Teachers." This link will take you to a page that includes a link titled "Teachers." Click on this link to go to a page with information about becoming a teacher, staff-development opportunities for teachers, and ideas for working with learners in the classroom.

http://www.aft.org/

EDUCATION'S CODE OF ETHICS

More than professionals in many other fields, teachers are subjected to high levels of public scrutiny. There are several reasons for this. First of all, as a teacher you will work with children, who are widely acknowledged to be among the most vulnerable of "clients." Second, teachers are numerous, and they are represented in virtually every neighborhood in the country. Hence, when you join the profession, you will be a member of an especially visible group of professionals. Finally, when you teach you will perform your duties in environments that are familiar to most of the adult population. This circumstance means that many people in your community will have strong ideas about what constitutes right and appropriate teacher behavior.

Because of their own concerns about what constitutes appropriate practice and because of public demands that teachers meet high behavioral standards, national organizations of teachers have long been interested in promoting ethical practices. In response to this concern, the Representatives Assembly of the National Education Association adopted a **Code of Ethics of the Education Profession** in 1975. (See Figure 2.1.)

WHAT DO YOU THINK?

Teachers' Strikes

Should teachers go on strike? This question often leads to heated exchanges between supporters and opponents of strikes. People opposed to strikes often argue that they undermine teachers' images. They fear that strikes will alienate middle- and upper-class citizens who traditionally have been among public education's strongest supporters. Disgust with strikes could lead these citizens to oppose needed funding for the schools.

Supporters of strikes often observe that people in general are simply unaware of the pressures teachers face. For example, they point to obligations many state legislatures have placed on teachers to raise learners' achievement levels in the absence of new commitments of state revenues to help them get the job done. Proponents of strikes contend that people may "talk a good line" about the need to improve schools, but little real action is likely without pressure such as can be exerted by a strike.

What Do You Think?

1. Do strike actions threaten teachers' credibility with parents and other influential members of the community? Why or why not?
2. Should the question of whether or not teachers should strike be answered "yes" in some instances and "no" in others? If so, under what circumstances might strikes be appropriate? Under what conditions might they be inappropriate?
3. Have you or any of your family members been involved in a strike, particularly one involving schools? If so, what were the reactions of various groups of people who had a stake in the outcome?
4. How do you personally feel about strikes by teachers? Have you had personal experiences that have led you to your position on this issue?

 To respond to these questions online go to the What Do You Think? *module for this chapter of the Companion Website.*

Preamble

The educator, believing in the worth and dignity of each human being, recognizes the supreme importance of the pursuit of truth, devotion to excellence, and the nurture of the democratic principles. Essential to these goals is the protection of freedom to learn and to teach and the guarantee of equal educational opportunity for all. The educator accepts the responsibility to adhere to the highest ethical standards.

The educator recognizes the magnitude of the responsibility inherent in the teaching process. The desire for the respect and confidence of one's colleagues, of students, of parents, and of the members of the community provides the incentive to attain and maintain the highest possible degree of ethical conduct. The Code of Ethics of the Education Profession indicates the aspiration of all educators and provides standards by which to judge conduct.

The remedies specified by the NEA and/or its affiliates for the violation of any provision of this Code shall be exclusive and no such provision shall be enforceable in any form other than the one specifically designated by the NEA or its affiliates.

(continued)

FIGURE 2.1 Code of Ethics of the Education Profession

Adopted by the NEA 1975 Representative Assembly. Reprinted with the permission of the National Education Association.

PRINCIPLE I

Commitment to the Student

The educator strives to help each student realize his or her potential as a worthy and effective member of society. The educator therefore works to stimulate the spirit of inquiry, the acquisition of knowledge and understanding, and the thoughtful formulation of worthy goals.

In fulfillment of the obligation to the student, the educator—

1. Shall not unreasonably restrain the student from independent action in the pursuit of learning.
2. Shall not unreasonably deny the student's access to varying points of view.
3. Shall not deliberately suppress or distort subject matter relevant to the student's progress.
4. Shall make reasonable effort to protect the student from conditions harmful to learning or to health and safety.
5. Shall not intentionally expose the student to embarrassment or disparagement.
6. Shall not on the basis of race, color, creed, sex, national origin, marital status, political or religious beliefs, family, social or cultural background, or sexual orientation, unfairly—
   a. Exclude any student from participation in any program
   b. Deny benefits to any student
   c. Grant any advantage to any student
7. Shall not use professional relationships with students for private advantage.
8. Shall not disclose information about students obtained in the course of professional service unless disclosure serves a compelling professional purpose or is required by law.

PRINCIPLE II

Commitment to the Profession

The education profession is vested by the public with a trust and responsibility requiring the highest ideals of professional service.

In the belief that the quality of the services of the education profession directly influences the nation and its citizens, the educator shall exert every effort to raise professional standards, to promote a climate that encourages the exercise of professional judgment, to achieve conditions that attract persons worthy of the trust to careers in education, and to assist in preventing the practice of the profession by unqualified persons.

In fulfillment of the obligation to the profession, the educator—

1. Shall not in an application for a professional position deliberately make a false statement or fail to disclose a material fact related to competency and qualifications.
2. Shall not misrepresent his/her professional qualifications.
3. Shall not assist any entry into the profession of a person known to be unqualified in respect to character, education, or other relevant attribute.
4. Shall not knowingly make a false statement concerning the qualifications of a candidate for a professional position.
5. Shall not assist a noneducator in the unauthorized practice of teaching.
6. Shall not disclose information about colleagues obtained in the course of professional service unless disclosure serves a compelling professional purpose or is required by law.
7. Shall not knowingly make false or malicious statements about a colleague.
8. Shall not accept any gratuity, gift, or favor that might impair or appear to influence professional decisions or action.

FIGURE 2.1 Continued

TEACHING PORTFOLIOS: DOCUMENTING PERFORMANCE

In Chapter 1, "Education in an Age of Change," you learned about features of an *initial-development portfolio*. Today increasing numbers of teachers also regularly keep **teaching portfolios** to document their performance and as aids to professional development. Portfolios of this type seek to document accomplishments and to record reflections gathered over a period of time and in a variety of situations (Hom, 1977). A teaching portfolio can give you a means of playing an active role in your own assessment (Tillman, Hart, & Ferguson, 2002). Hence, they act to increase your awareness of your cumulative growth needs as well as of the successes you have enjoyed when working with learners in the classroom.

If you decide to maintain a teaching portfolio, some key components you need to include are examples of instructional units you have developed, tests you have prepared, assignments you have made, and other materials you have devised. You probably will also wish to include samples of papers, projects, and other work prepared by members of your class. You will also add information and comments made by people who have observed your work and have prepared formal assessments of your teaching. Typically, your portfolio will also include some of your own written reflections. Material in this section of the portfolio gives you an opportunity to think about what went well (and why) and to consider possible modifications to what you might do if you find yourself not satisfied with certain aspects of the instructional actions you are reviewing.

Not all teaching portfolios organize information into the same set of categories. Often, however, there will be examples of

- Teacher-prepared material,
- Contributions of observers, and
- Learners' work.

Teacher-Prepared Material

If you are putting together a teaching portfolio, you will use the "teacher-prepared" section to state your own views about characteristics of good teaching. You will probably describe the learners with whom you work and some contextual constraints that affect your performance (e.g., local and state regulations, kinds of materials available, and problems associated with facilities). You may also wish to refer to specific learning objectives you are using to guide your instruction.

You may also choose to mention your preferred instructional and evaluation methodologies. This part of the portfolio is an appropriate place to display examples of instructional units, tests, and lesson plans. You may want to include examples of below-average, average, and above-average work that has been graded. These materials showcase your ability to differentiate among learners whose performances reflect varying achievement levels. You can also include information related to specific actions you have taken to deal with exceptional students and with others with special learning characteristics and needs. Finally, you will want to include reflections about the adequacy of your instructional performance.

Contributions of Observers

You may teach in a school where principals or other administrators regularly evaluate you. It is possible, too, that your school may use a **peer-evaluation system,** in which teachers observe and evaluate lessons taught by other teachers. You will want to include in your portfolio all information you receive that relates to formal evaluations of your classroom performance. Opinions and other reactions from learners and comments from parents, if available, represent other desirable categories of information.

Learners' Work

You also will want to include some evidence related to how well young people you teach have performed on learning assessments, such as class records of learners' scores on quizzes and examinations. In addition, depending on the age level of your learners and the subject(s) you teach, you may find it useful to add learner essays, models, term papers, and completed projects.

Organizational Formats

Several schemes for organizing portfolios have been adopted. An approach developed by James Green and Sheryl Smyser (1996) features five basic categories:

- **Personal background.** In this section, you provide details about your educational and professional experiences, with special reference to your current teaching responsibilities.
- **Context information.** In this section, you discuss the physical characteristics of the classroom, the specific nature of your learners, the adequacy of instructional materials, and other environmental factors that may affect how you teach and how members of your class learn.
- **Instruction-related information.** In this section, you include information about your lesson plans and unit plans and provide examples of materials and instructional aids you have developed. This part of the portfolio gives you an opportunity to include comments and reflections about the adequacy of your instructional approaches, especially about how those approaches have influenced what your students have learned.
- **Responses to special needs of individuals.** This section gives you an opportunity to describe actions taken to individualize instruction to meet specific student needs. Here you will include examples of differentiated assignments, varied learning materials, and alternative assessment procedures.
- **Contributions to the overall mission of the school.** This section allows you to display evidence that demonstrates how your actions have contributed to improving the teaching and learning environment of the entire school. You might include information such as professional-development objectives and plans for meeting them and committee work focusing on schoolwide and communitywide educational-reform issues.

Assessing Portfolios

Similar kinds of information do not appear in every portfolio. Hence, to some degree, assessment procedures need to be tailored to the specific portfolio that is being evaluated. One of the challenges in assessing portfolios concerns the issue of consistency or reliability. Guidelines should allow different reviewers to apply a similar standard in assessing a given portfolio. For example, if reviewers are expected to assign portfolios a rating of "unsatisfactory," "satisfactory," or "outstanding," these terms need to be clearly defined so that different raters will apply them in the same way. This need is often accomplished through the development of a **scoring rubric.** The scoring rubric specifies in considerable detail how a portfolio would look when assigned one of the available rating points. See Figure 2.2 for an example.

The developer of this *scoring rubric* prepared it for use with teaching portfolios focusing on teachers' use of a specified set of one state's mandated "advanced technology competencies." Note how the scoring rubric helps define the three rating points: "Needs Work," "Satisfactory," and "Exemplary."

Needs Work	The portfolio fails to include data in support of each identified competency. Examples that are provided fail to make a compelling case that the associated competency has been mastered. Teacher reflections, where present, are written in vague, general terms that fail to address specific issues and problems associated with mastering the required competencies. The organizational scheme is not clear or, alternatively, it has not been consistently implemented throughout the portfolio.
Satisfactory	The portfolio exhibits examples that address all advanced technology competencies. These examples display evidence sufficient to support that mastery of essential features/components of each competency has occurred. A clear organizational scheme is evident, and it is executed consistently throughout the portfolio. Reflections focus clearly on complexities associated with mastering competencies, though some of them reflect deeper, more-reasoned consideration than others.
Exemplary	The portfolio exhibits strong and overwhelming evidence that each advanced technology competency has been mastered. A rich array of pertinent evidence is presented to support the mastery claim for each competency. Examples provided are multiple, varied, and appropriate. A clear organizational scheme is evident, and it is executed carefully throughout with no "thin" sections. Reflections respecting all competencies evidence a solid grasp of issues and careful, rational analyses of problems and, perhaps, unexpected "easy stretches" associated with the mastery of each.

FIGURE 2.2   Example of a Scoring Rubric for Portfolio Assessment

Using an appropriate scoring rubric, the portfolio reviewer looks for behaviors that reflect the teacher's expectations, noting any behaviors that are at odds with them. For example, a reviewer might look at what the teacher has described as key features of "good teaching" as a backdrop for considering evidence in the portfolio. Are materials presented in the portfolio consistent with the stated vision of good teaching? Does the provided information support the view that practices were consistent with stated priorities?

You will find that teacher evaluation based on portfolios has important advantages over traditional schemes that depend on data gathered from one or two classroom observations. By gathering information from multiple sources over a considerable period, you can build a portfolio that has the potential to provide a much more comprehensive picture of your classroom performance than could be attained through only one or two classroom visits by an outside observer.

ROLES FOR EDUCATORS

Approximately one of every six Americans is a learner in a public school. School systems employ millions of people to serve the needs of these young people. People employed in the schools work in diverse environments, and they perform varied functions. When you think about the education profession today, you refer not just to teachers but to people playing all of the roles that must be discharged as part of our society's effort to help young people grow toward productive and personally satisfying patterns of adult living.

Classroom Teachers

Teachers are by far the largest single category of employees in the schools. In the United States today, slightly more than 3 million people are employed as teachers in the public schools. By 2011, this number is expected to grow to approximately 3.6 million (Hussar, 2002).

Because initial-preparation programs for educators focus primarily on helping prospective newcomers get ready for roles in the classroom, you probably already know that teachers are the key players in schools. Their professional expertise unites important subject-area knowledge, planning and organizational skills, and abilities to motivate learners. They develop their capacity to respond to individual learner needs. Over time, they become skilled in articulating and defending their teaching practices to parents, interested community members, political leaders, and others.

Soon you may belong to a **teaching team.** A teaching team consists of a group of teachers who draw on one another's strengths and insights to prepare programs and to deliver instruction that is responsive to learners' needs. Teaming requires teachers to have good collaboration skills as well as sound backgrounds in their subject fields and in various teaching methodologies.

Teachers also function as leaders who are charged with making changes and adjustments to improve the quality of the learning environment (Lambert, 2002). To maintain a sharp professional edge, you will want to keep up with new knowledge related to effective teaching techniques and developmental aspects of learners, and new knowledge related to your subject(s). Developing a pattern of regular reading of professional journals can help you keep up-to-date. As noted previously, you will find that active participation in professional groups can be a useful part of your continuing-education agenda.

VIDEO VIEWPOINTS

Providing a Quality Education for All Students

WATCH: In this *Nightline: Up Close* video segment, Michel Martin interviews a teacher, Charles Best, who came from a privileged background, attended prestigious schools, and chose to become a teacher in the New York public schools. Charles Best then had an idea about finding funding for teacher ideas and created a Web site: www.donorschoose.org. This segment includes a discussion of the motivation of a person to choose teaching, as well as an innovative way to provide resources for teachers who most need them.

THINK: Discuss with your classmates, or in your teaching journal, the following questions:
1. What do the interviewer's questions infer about the status of teaching in the United States?
2. What does this segment indicate regarding equal educational opportunities for all students?
3. What are some of the other things that motivate people to become teachers?
4. What are the lessons that could be learned from the experiences of donorschoose.org?

LINK: Can you think of some other ideas that could be creative ways of addressing educational issues?

Complete this activity and submit your responses online in the Video Viewpoints module for this chapter of the Companion Website.

WEB EXTENSION 2–3

Phi Delta Kappa and Kappa Delta Pi

Phi Delta Kappa and Kappa Delta Pi are international honorary societies in education. Each organization publishes materials designed to help new teachers make a smooth entry into their new profession. Information related to Phi Delta Kappa is available at:

http://www.pdkintl.org

Go to this Web address and click first on "Professional Development." This will take you to a page with other links. Click on the one titled "New Teacher Connection." At the New Teacher Connection page you will be able to access an advice column for new teachers, ideas new teachers have found useful in their classrooms, and information about working with challenging learners. Information related to Kappa Delta Pi is available at:

http://www.kdp.org

Go to this Web address. Click on "KDP Store." This will take you to a page with other links. Click on "subscriptions." At the subscriptions page, you will find ordering information for a number of Kappa Delta Pi publications. You might be especially interested in subscribing to New Teacher Advocate. This inexpensive newsletter features helpful tips and inspirational reflections for new teachers.

Grade-Level Leader or Department Chair

Many elementary schools have **grade-level chairs** with responsibilities for leading all teachers in the building who teach the same grade. In many middle schools and high schools, a person serving as the **department chair** plays a similar role. In high schools, this individual exercises leadership in a specific subject area (for example, English, social studies, mathematics, or science). In middle schools, most teaching teams are interdisciplinary. Duties vary, but grade-level leaders often engage in such activities as ordering supplies, evaluating new faculty, coordinating staff-development opportunities, and disseminating information about school policies. In general, grade-level leaders and department chairs act as liaisons between school administrators and other teachers.

Typically, grade-level leaders and department chairs are selected from among the most experienced teachers. They have credibility both with their teaching colleagues and with school administrators. In some schools, grade-level leaders and department chairs teach a reduced load to allow them time to perform other assigned duties. They may receive extra salary, and they often work more days each year than regular classroom teachers.

Curriculum Leader

The position of **curriculum leader** may also be titled **curriculum director, curriculum supervisor,** or **curriculum coordinator.** By whatever title it is known, this position features leadership in such areas as curriculum planning, in-service planning, and instructional-support planning. If you work in small school districts, you may find that a single curriculum leader has responsibilities for several subject areas and grade levels and may even continue to teach part-time. If you are a member of the teaching staff in a larger district, individual curriculum leaders may be responsible for only a few grade levels or a

Staff development opportunities that occur on the school site are an important component of professional development.

single secondary-level subject area. In larger school districts, curriculum leaders often do not teach. In many districts, curriculum leaders have offices in the central administrative headquarters of the school district where they work.

Curriculum leaders are professionals who are familiar with up-to-date trends in the grade-level areas and/or subject areas for which they are responsible. They are in a position to influence the nature of the instructional program throughout the district in their areas of responsibility. Many curriculum leaders hold advanced degrees, work a longer school year than teachers, and receive higher salaries.

School Administrator

Traditionally, school administrators have started their careers as classroom teachers. A few school districts around the country have begun to appoint school administrators who have had prior leadership experience in business or the military services. Administrative positions often require holders to have completed a master's degree and to have met other specified administrative certification, licensure, or credentialing requirements.

Administrative positions exist both at the school level and at the central district administrative level. Typical administrative positions at the school level are assistant principal and principal. Examples of positions often found at the central administrative headquarters of a school district include director of personnel, assistant superintendent, and superintendent.

Over the past two decades, administrators' roles have increasingly involved providing instructional leadership. Pressures on administrators to increase learners' achievement have acted to make instruction-related concerns high on administrators' lists of professional priorities. To accomplish this purpose, successful administrators work hard to create a culture in their schools that makes it easy for teachers to enjoy working together and to engage in teaching practices that foster improved learner performance (Fullan, 2002).

More traditional duties of administrators include preparing budgets, developing schedules, preparing paperwork for state and federal authorities, and evaluating teachers and other staff members. They also function as official representatives of the schools to the community. Consequently, they must have good public relations skills. School administrators usually work a longer school year than teachers and are also paid higher salaries.

School Counselor

Some school counselors begin their careers as classroom teachers. There is debate within the professional community of counselors about whether school counselors should have had classroom teaching experience before becoming counselors. Those who support the idea argue that such experience gives the counselor a better understanding of what learners have experienced in their classrooms. Others argue that teaching is basically a controlling function and that counselors who have been teachers may not be able to change their roles from that of a controller to that of a listener and a facilitator.

Most states require counselors to complete academic course work beyond the bachelor's degree. Many prospective counselors enroll in master's degree programs with a school-counseling emphasis. In addition to personal and academic counseling, school counselors also are expected to perform a number of administrative tasks. Sometimes counselors are responsible for establishing the master teaching schedule for a school, and they are often in charge of all standardized testing. They must spend considerable time attending special meetings.

Counselors usually work a longer school year than teachers, and they are paid more. Time available for working with individual students often is surprisingly limited.

State Education Agency Employee

All states have education departments or agencies largely staffed by professionals with backgrounds in education. State education agencies hire people with a variety of backgrounds for diverse purposes. For example, subject-area specialists coordinate curriculum guidelines and in-service training throughout the state for teachers in specific subjects (for example, English, social studies, music, science, mathematics, vocational education, or physical education). Typically, state education agencies also have assessment specialists who coordinate statewide testing programs. In addition, they usually staff teacher-certification or licensure specialists who work with colleges and universities to ensure that teacher-preparation programs are consistent with state regulations.

Many state education agency employees have had considerable prior experience working in the schools. Large numbers have at least a master's degree, and many have doctoral degrees. Often state agency employees have to travel to meetings at various locations throughout the state they serve. Usually, these employees are on the job 12 months of the year and are paid salaries that are higher than those of classroom teachers.

Teacher Educator

Successful teachers sometimes seek opportunities to share their expertise with future teachers. One way for them to do this is to become a teacher educator. Teacher educators are former teachers. They have assumed new responsibilities as instructors of and academic mentors for people preparing for careers as classroom teachers. Most teacher educators are faculty members of colleges and universities, though a few are employed by large school districts. Almost always, teacher educators hold doctoral degrees.

The role of the teacher educator is varied and complex. Although exemplary teaching contributes to success as a faculty member in teacher education, still more is necessary. As university faculty members, teacher educators must demonstrate initiative in improving preparation programs, stay current on findings of researchers, conduct research, and write for publication. In addition, they must seek opportunities to make presentations at regional and national meetings, maintain good working relations with other departments and with the schools, serve on many committees, maintain good links with state education agencies, and counsel students. All of these obligations require processing of massive quantities of paperwork.

Teacher educators typically are employed for nine months a year. Many of them have opportunities to work during the summer months as well. Salaries are not particularly high; in fact, some beginning teacher educators are paid less than some experienced public school classroom teachers. Although beginning salaries of teacher educators tend to be modest, top salaries for experienced teacher educators are higher than those paid to classroom teachers.

Two Private-Sector Opportunities

For a variety of reasons, some teachers decide to leave the classroom after just a few years. If you decide to leave teaching, will your teacher-preparation be of any value? Yes it will. There are employment options outside of the public schools for individuals with backgrounds in teaching.

Publishers of textbooks and other instructional materials hire people with backgrounds in education to work both as editors and salespeople. The expertise they bring from their background in the classroom helps firms ensure that materials they develop and market are appropriately designed. In addition, there is an important added element of credibility when the salesperson talking to a teacher who is a prospective buyer can say that he or she has been a classroom teacher.

Large firms, some of which have large training divisions, also employ people with backgrounds in education in their employee training programs. The term **human resource development,** often abbreviated **HRD,** frequently is used to describe the corporate training function. If you are interested in education and training in the private sector, go to your library and find a publication called *Training and Development*. It is the official journal of the **American Society for Training and Development (ASTD),** a professional organization for educators in private industries.

Critical Incident

Two Offers, One Problem

"Guess what, Letitia. I've got two—count 'em—two job offers, and my life is just the pits." One week following student teaching and graduation, Linda Norton was sharing a private moment with her longtime friend, Letitia Carlisle.

"Did I hear you right, Linda," said Letitia. "You've got two job offers, and that's a problem?! I'm tempted to say 'be still my heart' and 'send some of that agony my way.' So what's going on? Where's the negative that's escaping my notice?"

Linda smiled briefly and said, "I know I should be excited, happy, all those good things. I mean, we've talked before about how great it would be to finally be out of school and actually doing what we've been preparing for. The deal is, though, that these two job offers are quite different. And everybody's giving me different advice."

"Different how?" asked Letitia.

"Well, one of them is for a math opening in a middle school. That fits pretty well with my math background, and I did enjoy my student teaching with a group of sixth graders. The other one is from this electronics company. They want me to work in their training division helping newcomers who need to sharpen up their basic math skills. The thing is, this job pays $7,000 more a year to start than the teaching job."

"So, what's the problem? You could afford payments on a good car with that extra $7,000, couldn't you?" asked Letitia.

Linda nodded and replied, "That's true. But there are some other things to think about. For example, the teacher who worked with me during student teaching is really distressed that I may not end up working with kids in the school. He tells me that good math teachers are scarce and that I could be one of the best. He said I should consider all the kids whose lives I could help over the years if I stayed in the classroom."

"So you're feeling a bit guilty? Is that the situation?" asked Letitia.

"You've got it," acknowledged Linda. "The 'go to work as a teacher' argument is being counterbalanced by my mother's attitude. She says women have always been underpaid and underappreciated. If an employer out there is willing to pay me more, I should go for it. Besides, she says, a private company that can pay a higher starting salary probably can pay me more money in the future than I'll ever earn as a teacher."

Letitia sat quietly thinking for a minute. Then, leaning closer to her friend, she counseled, "Okay, Linda, you've told me what a couple of other people think you should do. But, it's your life and your career. What do *you* want to do?"

"I'm trying to tell you that that's the problem," Linda replied, her face showing some strain. "I flat out don't know. I come to the point of making a decision, and then I feel guilty about not making the other choice. Then, I convince myself to take the other job and feel guilty all over again. It would be nice if somewhere along the line somebody gave us a book titled *The Guide to Making Great Choices for Happy and Fulfilled Living*."

"That would be terrific," agreed Letitia. "But, I suppose you can't defer your choice until some publisher brings out this much-needed volume. So, what are you going to do?"

• • •

What is Linda really worried about? She says she feels guilty. What is the source of this guilt? Has she considered the advantages and disadvantages associated with each choice? How accurate is the information she has received from the teacher and from her mother? Are there other people she should consult? Are there other sources of information she should consider? How would you respond to her dilemma?

 To respond to this Critical Incident online, go to the Critical Incidents *module for this chapter of the Companion Website.*

Key Ideas in Summary

- The phrase "preparing for teaching" does not suggest that the process of preparation has a definite ending point. Rather, it implies that preparation is a career-long process of professional growth and adaptation.

- Teachers' professional development features four important phases. These include (1) the *pretraining phase*, (2) the *formal-preparation phase*, (3) the *induction-years phase*, and (4) the *continuing-growth phase*.

- The pretraining phase of teachers' development essentially represents a time when their attitudes and predispositions toward teaching are shaped by influences of families and of other life experiences. These experiences often give prospective teachers a set of expectations about teachers and their work that may constitute a limited view of what teachers do.

- The formal-preparation phase of teachers' professional development divides into three parts. *Core studies* include academic content that educated adults are expected to know, regardless of their college or university major. The *teaching specialization(s)/academic major(s)* component embraces content of the academic major (in the case of prospective secondary teachers) or academic content of the several school subjects they will teach (in the case of prospective elementary teachers). The *professional-education* component consists of preparation experiences related to instruction, evaluation, and management of school learners.

- The *induction years*, the first years of fully licensed classroom teaching, present important challenges to many teachers. During this period, teachers learn to adapt to the particular characteristics of their learners and to the special characteristics of their schools and communities.

- During the *continuing-growth phase* of a teacher's career, there are many opportunities for continued professional development. Among them are (1) staff-development opportunities sponsored by local school districts and local, state, and national professional associations; (2) college and university courses; and (3) possibilities for involvement with local, state, and national units of major professional groups.

- Two large national organizations represent the general interests of the teaching profession. The largest of these is the *National Education Association (NEA)*. Another important general organization for teachers is the *American Federation of Teachers (AFT)*, a group that is affiliated with organized labor.

- Teachers are expected to reflect patterns of behavior characterized by high ethical standards. The National Education Association has developed a *Code of Ethics of the Education Profession*. It obligates teachers to certain patterns of behavior with respect to their learners and with respect to the teaching profession.

- In recent years, there has been growing interest in the use of *teaching portfolios* to document teachers' accomplishments. Teaching portfolios attempt to gather evidence that attests to teachers' effectiveness and performance over time and in a variety of situations. Teaching portfolios often include examples of teacher-prepared materials, comments of people who have observed the teacher's work, and samples of work produced by the teacher's learners.

- There are many roles within the profession of education. People with initial preparation for classroom teaching may find themselves employed at some point in their careers in roles such as: (1) classroom teachers, (2) grade-level or department chairs, (3) curriculum leaders, (4) school administrators, (5) school counselors, (6) state education agency employees, (7) teacher educators, (8) textbook editors or salespersons, or (9) trainers in business or industry.

Chapter 2 Self-Test

 To review terms and concepts in this chapter, go to the Companion Website and take the Chapter 2 Self-Test. Feedback for the self-test is immediate. You can keep track of your self-test scores yourself, or you can choose to submit your scores to your instructor via e-mail.

Preparing for Praxis

 To learn more about the Praxis test and complete this activity online, go to the Preparing for Praxis *module for this chapter of the Companion Website.*

You may be required to pass Educational Testing Service's Praxis II exam as you seek formal authorization to teach in the public schools. The *Principles of Learning and Teaching* component of Praxis II seeks to assess your knowledge about these topics: (1) Students as Learners, (2) Instruction and Assessment, (3) Communication Techniques, and (4) Profession and Community. Material presented in this chapter potentially relates to several of these categories.

You may find it useful to prepare a chart for your own use similar to the one provided here. As you encounter information related to individual categories, you can enter it into the chart under the appropriate heading. A completed chart of this kind will be useful as you begin reviewing what you have learned in preparation for taking the Praxis II exam.

Students as Learners	Instruction and Assessment
• Student Development and the Learning Process	• Instructional Strategies
• Students as Diverse Learners	• Planning Instruction
• Student Motivation and the Learning Environment	• Assessment Strategies
Communication Techniques	**Profession and Community**
• Basic, Effective, Verbal and Nonverbal Communication Techniques	• The Reflective Practitioner
• Effect of Cultural and Gender Differences on Communications in the Classroom	• The Larger Community
• Types of Questions That Can Stimulate Discussion in Different Ways for Particular Purposes	

For Your Initial-Development Portfolio

 To complete this activity and submit your response online, go to the For Your Initial-Development Portfolio *module for this chapter of the Companion Website.*

1. What materials and ideas that you learned in this chapter about *becoming a professional educator* might you include as "evidence" in your portfolio? Select up to three separate items of information. Number them 1, 2, and 3.
2. Think about why you selected these materials. As you do so, consider these issues:
   - Specific uses you might make of this information as you plan, deliver, and assess the impact of your teaching,
   - The compatibility of the information with your own priorities and values,
   - Any contributions this information can make to your development as a teacher, and

- Factors that led you to include this information, as opposed to some alternatives you considered, but rejected.
3. Place a check in this chart to indicate the INTASC standard(s) to which each of your items of information relates.

INTASC Standard Number

ITEM OF EVIDENCE NUMBER	S1	S2	S3	S4	S5	S6	S7	S8	S9	S10
1										
2										
3										

4. Prepare a written reflection in which you analyze the decision-making process you followed. In your comments, mention the INTASC standard(s) to which your selected material relates.

Reflections

To respond to these questions online, go to the Reflections *module for this chapter of the Companion Website.*

1. In this chapter, you learned that pretraining influences of families and prior experiences of prospective teachers often give them certain attitudes and perspectives on the education profession. Such influences may have influenced your own views. For example, think about how you would answer these questions:
   - What do good teachers do?
   - What is the ideal school like?
   - What kind of behaviors do you expect to characterize learners you will teach?

   Now, take time to think about where you acquired these perspectives. How sure are you that the ideas you now have represent an accurate picture of the teaching profession? How might you test the adequacy and accuracy of some of your present impressions?

2. Are there general concerns that teachers share regardless of (a) where they teach in the country, (b) the nature of their learners, or (c) the subjects they teach? Or, are situation-to-situation differences so profound that it makes little sense to talk about national patterns? Given your responses to these questions, what value do you attach to membership in national organizations for teachers such as the National Education Association and the American Federation of Teachers?

3. Review the *Code of Ethics of the Education Profession*. (See Figure 2.1). Look carefully at Principle I, "Commitment to the Student." Which three of these commitments do you think will present you with the greatest challenges? What actions can you begin taking now to help you to meet these obligations?

4. Suppose you were asked to prepare a *teaching portfolio* that, among other things, had to include information related to how well people in your class were mastering content associated with your state's required curriculum. What kind of information might you include? What would you like to see in a *scoring rubric* designed to assess the quality of your portfolio?

5. Review information presented in the chapter about roles other than classroom teaching that are potentially open to individuals who have completed teacher-preparation programs. (Some of these roles require additional academic preparation.) Which of these roles interest you? What do you find appealing about them? Are your views based on extensive knowledge about the real day-to-day work of people in these roles, or are your opinions based only on general impressions about what they do? How might you go about learning more about these roles and about specific steps you might need to take to qualify for them?

Field Experiences, Projects, and Enrichment

1. Interview a teacher who has been in the profession for at least 15 years. Ask this person to describe his or her preparation for teaching and any in-service or other developmental activities he or she has experienced over the years. Make a report to your class on this topic: "The Professional Life Space of a Teacher: One Person's Experience."

2. Contact an administrator in the central office of a local school district who has responsibilities for staff development. (Your course instructor may be able to suggest the name of an appropriate person.) Try to obtain information about (1) the kind of in-service development the school district expects of its teachers and (2) the kind of in-service opportunities the school district provides to its teachers. Report your findings to others in your class.

3. Some people argue that teachers should have higher ethical standards than the population as a whole. Others suggest that this kind of a standard ensures that only atypical people will serve in the classrooms and that such individuals will be unrealistic models for young people. Organize a class debate on the issue, "Resolved That Teachers Must Be More Ethical Than Typical Citizens."

4. Many teachers today keep teaching portfolios. In this chapter, you learned about some design features that characterize many teaching portfolios. To broaden your understandings of teaching portfolios, enter the term "teaching portfolios" into a good Web search engine such as Google (http://www.google.com). Follow several of the links, and use the information you find as the basis for a report that features these basic categories:
   - Design formats,
   - Kinds of evidence included,
   - The nature of teachers' reflective commentary, and
   - Your own reactions to the information. (Include specific references to ideas you have learned that you will use in your own teaching portfolios.)

5. Many large corporations have large employee-education staffs. The American Society for Training and Development is a professional organization to which many of them belong. Look at several issues of this group's journal, *Training and Development*. How would you compare and contrast articles from *Training and Development* with those appearing in journals that are directed at audiences of school teachers? (Your instructor may be able to suggest some journals you should review.) Present your findings in the form of a short paper.

References

Flowers, N., Mertens, S. B., & Mulhall, P. F. (2002). Four important lessons about teacher professional development. *Middle School Journal, 33*(5), 57–61.

Fullan, M. (2002). The change leader. *Phi Delta Kappan, 59*(8), 12–20.

Green, J. E., & Smyser, S. O. (1996). *The teaching portfolio.* Lancaster, PA: Technomic.

Hom, A. (1977). *The power of teacher portfolios for professional development.* New York: National Teacher Policy Institute. [www.teachnet.org/TNPI/research/growth/hom.htm]

Hussar, W. J. (2002). *Projections of education statistics to 2011.* Washington, DC: National Center for Education Statistics.

Lambert, L. (2002). A framework for shared leadership. *Educational Leadership, 59*(8), 37–40.

Steffy, B. E., Wolfe, M. P., Pasch, S. H., & Enz, B. J. (2000). *Life cycle of the career teacher.* Thousand Oaks, CA: Corwin Press.

Tillman, B. A., Hart, P. M., & Ferguson, S. M. (2002). Using student portfolios with the NMSA/NCATE Guidelines and Praxis III Framework. *Middle School Journal, 33*(5), 14–19.

3

Challenges of School Reform

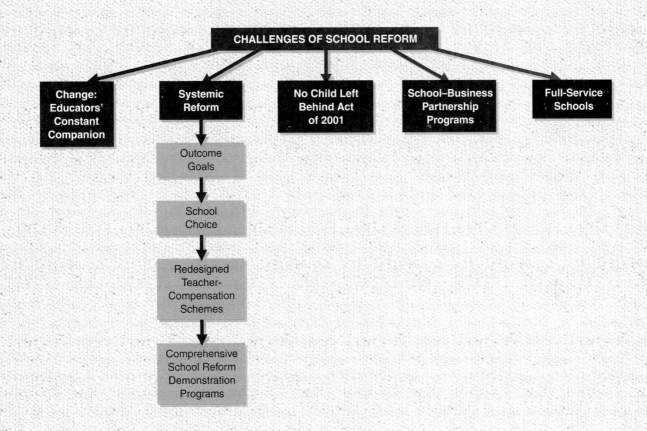

OBJECTIVES

This chapter will help you to

- recognize that change will be a constant feature of your professional life as a teacher.
- describe characteristics of *systemic reform*.
- cite examples and describe features of selected approaches to providing parents, guardians, and learners with *school choice*.
- explain how the *No Child Left Behind Act of 2001* acts to influence schools and school practices.
- describe examples of approaches to change teacher-compensation plans.
- explain purposes of *school–business partnerships*.
- describe characteristics of *full-service schools*.

CHANGE: EDUCATORS' CONSTANT COMPANION

How do you react to change? Do you desire stability? What is it about the role of teacher that you find attractive? You need to think about these questions as you consider a career in education. As you seek answers, you may discover that schools are evolving in some ways that are different from what you experienced during your own elementary, middle, and high school years. You need to be comfortable with a professional environment that continues to alter in response to changing social and political environments.

At least in the near future, the rate of change is not likely to slow. Modifications in schools and school practices are a reflection of larger societal changes. Schools do not stand apart from society but are influenced by the ebb and flow of events and changes in the larger community. For example, the increasingly diverse cultural and ethnic makeup of our nation's population of young people has tremendous implications for education. Across the nation, more and more schools include learners from a variety of cultures, ethnicities, and languages. When you enter the profession, you will find that members of your class bring with them a wide spectrum of backgrounds and abilities.

Technology is another factor that fuels changes in schools. New digital wonders present new opportunities and provide tools you can use to organize your instruction and interact with learners. These technological marvels also bring you face-to-face with important moral and ethical issues. For example, young people from more-affluent families are much more likely to have computers in their homes than learners from less-affluent families. If school-based instruction depends more and more on access to computer technology, does this situation give an unfair advantage to members of your class from more economically advantaged families? If so, should public money be spent to purchase additional computers so learners from impoverished families can check them out and take them home? These questions continue to be debated.

The accelerating rate of social change and a growing public awareness of the need for our schools to prepare young people to accommodate new conditions have attracted the attention of political leaders. During the past several decades, more and more elected officials have discovered that education is a political issue that resonates with the public. As a result, they have been quick to enter into debates centered on education and to propose legislation that purports to improve the schools.

The increasing politicization of educational issues raises important value-laden questions that you and other citizens must answer in the years ahead. They include:

- What should be the purposes of education in a democratic society?
- Who should control education?
- What should young people learn at school?
- What characteristics should "good" teachers have?

You may find that specific agendas drive answers to these questions suggested by certain individuals and groups. As a professional, you need to be a "player" in discussions related to changes in school policies and practices. To prepare yourself for this kind of proactive involvement, you need to develop (1) sound understandings of issues that have prompted suggestions for change, (2) an appreciation of the particular interests that will be served when a change is implemented, and (3) a commitment to proposals that are consistent with your own professional values.

SYSTEMIC REFORM

As you learned in Chapter 1, suggestions that schools need to be changed or reformed have been with us for many years. The most recent wave of change and reform proposals began with the publication of *A Nation at Risk: The Imperative for Educational Reform* (National Commission on Excellence in Education, 1983). This document detailed potential threats to the nation that might follow declines in test scores and increases in dropout rates. The report concluded:

> "We report to the American people that while we can take justifiable pride in what our schools and colleges have historically accomplished and contributed to the United States and the well-being of its people, the educational foundations of our society are presently being eroded by a rising tide of mediocrity that threatens our very future as a Nation and a people." (p. 10)

The report perpetuated the myth that the schools of the past were excellent but now they are poor. Looking back over two decades, it is quite clear that the report's alarmist rhetoric was at odds with reality. The threats that were cited in the report have not materialized, and today the United States stands as the world's dominant economic and political power. Educational programs that our schools provide have contributed to our country's continued development.

Although data have failed to confirm many of the conclusions of *A Nation at Risk,* the report's recommendations continue to influence public perceptions and debates about education policy. Many people, including policy makers, persist in seeing American public schools as failures. Although large numbers of individuals hold this attitude about schools in the nation as a whole, they often have higher opinions of their local schools. For example, polls of public attitudes toward schools report that most parents rate their local school quite high, but schools in general much lower.

If history is a guide, you will find debates about improving education to be a feature of your professional world throughout your career. You will find that many discussions focus on arguments between people who hold competing ideas regarding school practices and educational purposes. See Figure 3.1 for two very different sets of ideas. As you look at these lists, you might think about differences in proposals for school improvement that people committed to list "A" and list "B" would recommend.

As you may recall from Chapter 1, reform efforts calling for accountability and standardized testing have been among those having the most widespread influence on school practices. Over the past 20 years, school authorities have faced increasing pressure to make public learners' scores on required tests. Supporters of this kind of disclosure take the position that wide dissemination of scores introduces an element of competition into the educational enterprise that acts to improve teachers' and schools' levels of performance.

This argument presumes that low test scores are reliable indicators of "problem schools." Critics challenge this assumption. Scores, they argue, tell the public nothing about the conditions that led to them. The reality is that poor levels of learner performance on tests may have multiple causes. A comprehensive attempt to understand why learners may not have done well requires answers to questions such as these:

- Is there evidence that teaching was appropriate?
- Were learners exposed to a curriculum that varied markedly from what was tested?
- Were the teachers qualified to teach the tested material?

- Does the school have a safe environment?
- Did learners have access to high-quality instructional materials?
- Did learners have opportunities to do schoolwork in supportive home and family environments?
- Were families or support agencies adequately meeting learners' nutritional needs?
- Were learners healthy, particularly on the day they took the test?
- Were the tests given to excited youngsters on the last school day before a holiday?

When you have answers to these questions, you are in a position to work with others to take needed remedial action. When all you have to work with are numbers representing learners' scores, you lack information you need to change conditions that will improve achievement levels (Popham, 2003). If you do not reflect on critical variables that may have influenced the test scores of people in your class, there is a danger that any changes you make will be narrowly focused and will not be responsive to all difficulties learners face. You may make changes that waste valuable resources and that fail to address the multiple causes of problems.

List A	List B
• Educational achievement is promoted by high standards, competition, and comparative assessments of students, teachers, and schools.	• Educational achievement is enhanced by conditions of cooperation, trust, confidence, and support among and between teachers and learners.
• Competition stimulates individuals to higher levels of individual achievement.	• Cooperation provides the nurturance and support that stimulate individual achievement.
• Standardized test scores should document learner achievement and should be used as a basis for making decisions about teaching and learning.	• Assessment should be a collaborative effort between students and teachers to understand student learning and open possibilities for student growth.
• Performance standards and frequent assessments ensure high-quality outcomes.	• Improved organizational processes ensure high-quality organizational outcomes.
• Curriculum is constructed around a common core of knowledge that reflects a common cultural heritage.	• Curriculum is constructed around diverse knowledge that reflects a pluralistic heritage.
• Society uses education to maintain the stability of social, economic, and political order.	• Society uses education to contribute to the improvement, growth, and transformation of the social order.
• The test of the education system is its ability to prepare individuals for their role in society.	• The test of an education system is the extent to which it helps all children access the benefits of society.
• The purpose of education is to reward merit and allow individuals to progress through the system on the basis of their ability and talent.	• The purpose of schooling is to help all children achieve their potential.
• Additional resource investments in public education will not increase performance and are not necessary to bring about educational reform.	• Additional resource investments in education will increase system performance and sustain change.

FIGURE 3.1   Competing Ideas About School Practices and Purposes

Real improvement of instruction and of school programs results from responses that attack a number of clearly identified problem areas at the same time. These comprehensive solutions may include changes related to (1) administrative arrangements, (2) the nature of instructional materials, (3) the degree of support provided by learners' families, (4) the degree to which teachers are free to select instructional approaches that are well-suited to their learners' needs, and (5) the general nature of the classroom and school environment. The term that is applied to efforts to respond proactively to multiple problems is **systemic reform.** Some responses associated with systemic reform have generated support for efforts to

- Promote greater use of outcome goals,
- Support the idea of school choice,
- Redesign teacher responsibility and compensation schemes, and
- Implement federal Comprehensive School Reform Demonstration programs.

WEB EXTENSION 3–1

CPRE—Consortium for Policy Research in Education

The Consortium for Policy Research in Education (CPRE) is a group that links policy researchers from the University of Pennsylvania, Harvard University, Stanford University, the University of Michigan, and the University of Wisconsin-Madison. At this site, you will find a link labeled "publications." If you click on this link, you will be taken to an extensive list of reports and articles, many of which deal with issues related to systemic reform.

http://www.cpre.org/

Outcome Goals

Today, many education reformers support establishing **outcome goals.** Goals of this type emphasize the results or effects of instruction. For example, one outcome goal for primary-grades arithmetic might reference the learners' need to master basic operations and numbers facts.

The trend in support of outcome goals represents a shift away from a focus on **input goals.** Input goals relate to individual components of the school program that, collectively, are thought to produce desirable outcomes. For example, an input goal related to primary-grades mathematics might refer to the need to have an up-to-date arithmetic text available for each child to use.

In the past, comparisons among schools focused heavily on input goals. Sometimes school-to-school comparisons were made on the basis of evidence such as the number of computers in the classrooms, the percentage of teachers with advanced degrees, and the availability of recently published texts and other instructional materials. Input information says little about what learners are gaining from their experiences in school programs. For example, if a school had a large up-to-date library, an observer using input goals might conclude this was a "good" school. An observer who was committed to looking at outcome measures might say, "Wait a minute. What evidence is there that learners are profiting from the library and everything else going on in this building?"

You may be tempted to conclude that inputs are unimportant. This is not the case. Adequate resources, such as qualified teachers and up-to-date texts, are important if learning is to take place. However, your focus should be on the impact these collective resources have on learners. In brief, high-quality inputs are a necessary but not a sufficient condition for educational excellence.

In recent years, there have been numerous efforts to identify high-quality learning outcomes for all subject areas. For example, excellent work of this kind has been done by national subject-area specialty organizations such as the **National Council of Teachers of English (NCTE),** the **National Council of Teachers of Mathematics (NCTM),** the **National Council for the Social Studies (NCSS),** and the **National Science Teachers Association (NSTA).** Increasingly, commercial publishers are incorporating outcome standards developed by these groups in texts, software, and other learning materials. These standards also are influencing content of teacher-preparation programs.

Another trend in efforts to reform schools is the new importance attached to **rigorous assessment** procedures. Rigorous assessments require learners to demonstrate sophisticated thinking skills. They stand in contrast to forced-choice techniques such as true–false and matching tests that often do not assess higher-order learning. One approach to evaluating learners' performances that is now attracting much interest is **authentic assessment** (Spady, 1994; Wiggins, 1989).

Authentic assessment requires learners to demonstrate what they have learned in a way that has much in common with how a proficient adult might deal with this content. In a traditional class, you might ask learners to write an essay about possible consequences of locating a new factory close to a residential neighborhood. In authentic assessment, you might ask members of your class to provide documentation and testimony to a committee playing the role of a zoning board (and you might actually invite a zoning board member or two to participate in the exercise).

Advocates view authentic assessment as a more-valid approach for holding teachers and schools accountable for the attainment of worthwhile educational standards than standardized tests. Detractors contend that authentic assessments rely too much on teacher judgments and are therefore too subjective. In addition, they do not provide data that can be used to compare students; therefore, they do not facilitate accountability. (For more information about authentic assessment, see Chapter 10, "Assessing Learning.")

In recent years, there has been broad public support for the idea of using results of standardized tests as a measure of educational quality (Lewis, 2001). Outcome measures

School choice options provide students and parents the opportunity to attend schools that have the types of programs they desire.

of this type are part of a category you will often see referred to as *high-stakes tests.* This description refers to the significant consequences of scores on these tests for learners, teachers, and schools. For example, scores can (1) influence learners' chances to be admitted to certain colleges and universities, (2) affect a teacher's employment status or salary, and (3) reflect either positively or negatively on a school's overall reputation.

The bottom line for you as you think about outcome assessment is that you and your colleagues will be expected to present evidence that the young people you teach are learning. Your school is unlikely to be labeled "good" or "successful" based only on your claim that you have exemplary resources, bright and cheery classrooms, and teachers who have advanced degrees. In essence, the public demands answers to two key questions: (1) What have the young people learned? and (2) What evidence have you to support this claim?

School Choice

Historically, most children have attended schools located within a particular **attendance zone.** Such a zone, prescribed by local school districts, typically requires learners to attend schools within certain areas of their community. In the case of elementary schools, the authorized buildings often are located in neighborhoods close to learners' homes. Learners must meet very special sets of conditions to win permission to attend a school outside of their normal attendance zone.

School choice supporters challenge the traditional attendance-zone arrangement. They see school choice as an approach to improving educational quality. Proponents of school choice view schooling as a product. The product will be made better when the "producers" (i.e., individual schools) compete for "clients" (i.e., learners) in a free and competitive marketplace. When such a scheme is in place, poor schools will lose learners and the state funds that accompany them. As a result, they will have an incentive to make their programs better. If they succeed, they will experience enrollment gains. If they fail, the schools may be closed.

Proponents of school choice also argue that this approach has excellent potential to respond well to diverse learner needs. It is difficult for a single school to develop programs that are responsive to the special characteristics of all the young people it enrolls. School choice allows parents and learners to consider many different schools and to select one that they believe represents a best fit with the priorities of each family. These factors have the potential to increase both student and parent satisfaction with schools and to prevent some of these problems.

In summary, among advantages claimed for school choice are the following:

- School-choice policies have the potential to allow learners from low-income families to avoid mediocre, overcrowded inner-city schools.
- Families' interest in education may increase because they play an active role in selecting the schools their children attend.
- Competition among schools to attract learners may improve the quality of all schools.
- Children attending schools that have been selected from among several alternatives potentially will find themselves in learning environments better matched to their needs than schools within their traditional mandatory-attendance areas. (Wells, 1990)

Not everyone agrees that school choice is a good idea. Critics challenge the idea that schools that lose enrollment will improve. Schools that lose learners also lose the state support money that is associated with enrollment. Hence, the "poor" schools will be expected to make themselves more effective, but they will have less money to do so than they had at the time they were perceived to not be doing a good job. Critics of school-choice plans argue that setting a higher standard at the same time as support money decreases makes little sense.

Opponents also argue that school choice is not truly an option for all parents and guardians. Only affluent parents and guardians find it possible to transport their children to distant schools lying far outside normal attendance-zone areas. Parents and guardians with fewer resources depend on having schools that are either fairly close to their homes or accessible by their children as a result of well-established school bus routes. The difficulty of getting children to out-of-area schools does not make school choice a real option for many families.

Critics of school choice also wonder about the impact of such an approach on teachers' decisions about where to accept employment. Many conditions affect learners' academic performance (condition of the building, availability of up-to-date instructional resources, noise levels in and around the school, and so forth). When a school-choice program is in place and individual schools face the threat of losing learners and state financial support, teachers may avoid accepting employment in buildings where, for various reasons, learners' performance levels on standardized tests have not been as high as those of learners in other schools. The possibility is very real that school-choice programs may establish a system of teacher incentives that cause them to not serve those learners who are most in need of effective instruction.

Voucher Plans.   **Voucher plans** represent one approach to implementing school choice. In a voucher plan, parents and guardians receive tax money that they can use to pay for the education of their children at a school of their choice. Suppose a state pays individual schools $7,500 per year for each child in attendance. In a voucher system, a parent or guardian would receive a voucher in this amount for each school-aged child in the household. Once the parent or guardian decides which school the child will attend, this voucher is turned over to officials at that school. The officials deposit the money in the school's account and use it as part of the school's instructional and operational budget. This arrangement forces schools to compete for students and, in theory, would reward those schools doing well by attracting more students.

The voucher idea has been the focus of intense debate for several years. Much of the debate centers on different assumptions about the role of schools in a democratic society characterized by great diversity. Educational-policy researcher Henry Levin (2002) points out that schools have a dual role of providing both private and public benefits.

The private benefits are related to the rights of parents to rear their children in a manner that they see fit. Because schools play an important role in child rearing, parents should be able to choose schools that best meet their philosophical, religious, and political lifestyles.

One important public benefit concerns schooling as a promoter of social cohesion. Society needs to reproduce the institutions of a free society. An effort must be made to provide learners with the knowledge, behavior, and values that will enable them to participate in the social and political institutions that provide the foundation for a pluralistic democratic society. Hence, the state has an interest in reducing social and ethnic stratification and in making sure that all students have a common set of educational experiences.

Supporters of vouchers argue that they provide a way to help parents and their children seek an appropriate balance between education's private and public benefits. Proponents also argue that decisions people make when confronted with competing alternatives are superior and more satisfying to them than decisions employees of bureaucracies make for them. In addition, they point out that for real competition to exist, alternatives available to parents should include both public and private schools.

Another argument advanced by supporters is that vouchers will prompt the development of alternative educational opportunities for learners from less-affluent families who currently are trapped in low-performing schools. Vouchers, they argue, will accord less-affluent parents the same privileges of choice that have long been available to more-affluent families.

Critics argue that there are important negatives associated with vouchers. Voucher plans have the potential to lead parents and guardians to focus on issues other than the quality of a school's academic programs. Some choices they make may lead to an increased stratification of society along social class, political, and religious lines. For example, some parents or guardians may decide to send their sons and daughters to a particular school because of the makeup of the learner population or the availability of religious instruction. Such decisions represent choices based on criteria other than instructional-program quality.

In order to make good choices, parents and guardians need good information. Because variables other than qualities of school programs can affect learners' standardized test scores, it is questionable that such scores represent high-quality indicators of school achievement. Yet, when parents and guardians inquire about the relative quality of programs at individual schools, supporters of vouchers often respond, "look at test scores."

Opponents of vouchers question the assumption that a voucher system will result in alternative schools springing up to serve the needs of learners from low-income families. As evidence, they point to a voucher system in Milwaukee. The dollar value of vouchers offered to parents and guardians for each learner was higher than the amount the Milwaukee Public Schools received to support the instruction of each enrolled student. In spite of the dollars for which new, alternative schools could compete, few new schools appeared to take advantage of this opportunity to serve students from less-affluent families (Carnoy, 2000).

Voucher opponents point out that, in places where vouchers have been tried, religious schools, usually Catholic, are the dominant choices. This raises constitutional issues relating to subsidization of religious training. In an important 2002 U.S. Supreme Court decision, the Court upheld the constitutionality of vouchers given by the Cleveland Scholarship and Tutoring Program. The Court said that program was neutral with respect to religion because it simply provided a wider range of options to the existing choice options in a failing school district (Levin, 2002).

Critics of vouchers raise concerns related to fairness, particularly in situations in which vouchers can be used to pay for educational services provided by private schools. Private schools can select the learners they admit. If they choose to do so, they can admit only the most able learners and turn away young people who need special kinds of educational services. Opponents argue that if use of vouchers to pay for private-school educational services becomes widespread, over time public schools will be left with disproportionately high enrollments of learners with disabilities.

In summary, there have been numerous attempts to promote vouchers. The jury is still out on their effectiveness and impact on society. Supporters argue that vouchers have the potential to put in place a much-needed system of competition among schools that, over time, will improve the quality of programming throughout our educational system. Opponents argue that, instead of improving the schools, widespread use of vouchers may undermine social cohesion, interfere with issues related to church–state separation, and divert resources in ways that would make less-advantaged learners worse off than they are today.

VIDEO VIEWPOINTS

Vouchers

WATCH: This *20/20* episode focuses on the issue of vouchers. John Stossel, the host, clearly favors a voucher system and believes vouchers to be a key ingredient in school reform. He emphasizes the need for choice and the power of competition in bringing about change. Included, however, are some comments from those opposed to voucher systems. They contend that competition does not necessarily work in education and that voucher systems take needed money for change away from the schools that need it most.

THINK: Discuss with your classmates or in your teaching journal the following questions:

1. Do you think that competition is a key element in bringing about change in schools? Why or why not?
2. Do you think vouchers are the best way of bringing about choice? Why or why not?
3. In addition to the points made in the video segment, what are some other issues surrounding vouchers that should be discussed?

LINK: What is the current status of vouchers and other choice programs?

Complete this activity and submit your responses online in the Video Viewpoints *module for this chapter of the* Companion Website.

WEB EXTENSION 3–2

Education Week on the Web

Education Week, a leading publisher of articles related to education, maintains this site. You will find a link labeled "archives." If you click on the link, you will be taken to a search engine. Enter the term "vouchers" in the search engine. You will be presented with an extensive list of articles from recent issues of *Education Week* that relate to vouchers. You can read them online.

http://www.edweek.org/

Charter Schools.   Another approach to providing school choice is reflected in the movement to establish **charter schools.** Charter schools are semiautonomous public schools that can be founded by a variety of groups such as teachers, parents, or independent operators. A charter school may be an existing public school or an entirely new entity. One of the major issues facing many new charter schools is that of finding acceptable space.

Typically, chartering agencies that are associated with an arm of government approve applications to establish charter schools. Mechanisms for dealing with this process vary from place to place. For example, in some states the local school board must approve applications. However, in Arizona there is a state board for charter schools that approves applications. In Indianapolis, the mayor approves charters. In some instances, institutions of higher education have been given the authority to approve them.

One of the rationales behind charter schools is that many of the problems faced by public schools result from excessive regulation. Charter schools usually are exempted from many state regulations in order to provide more flexibility of operation and management. For example, about half of the charter schools are free to hire teachers who lack a teaching certificate, and they are free from contractual obligations that local districts have with teacher associations.

The first charter school opened in Minnesota in 1992. By 2002, 39 states had approved charter schools involving over 2,000 schools enrolling more than 500,000 students (Education Commission of the States, 2003). Growth has been rapid and is likely to continue because of widespread political support. For example, the U.S. Department of Education has established a **Charter School Demonstration Program** that is designed to generate and disseminate knowledge about how effective charter schools operate.

Most charter schools operate elementary and middle school programs. High school programs are less common. The Education Commission of the States (2003) has gathered statistical information about charter schools. About 70% of the charter schools have racial and ethnic populations similar to those in the surrounding school district. Overall, about 53% of the learners are ethnic minorities, and 47% are white. About 6% of the students are limited-English-proficient students. The most active charter-school state is Arizona, with over 400 charter schools.

Charter-school proponents make some of the same arguments as those favoring voucher plans. They contend that providing competition and freeing charter schools from regulatory burdens will allow them to develop outstanding instructional programs that will become models for other schools to emulate.

Proponents argue that charter schools are cost-effective. They claim this is true because charter schools do not have to put up with the bureaucratic inefficiencies characterizing typical public schools. Supporters contend that absence of excessive regulations acts to lure outstanding teachers to charter schools who are unhappy with paperwork and other administrative constraints imposed by state and school-district regulations. In charter schools, these teachers face few limits on their abilities to introduce exciting and innovative instructional approaches.

Opponents point to negatives associated with this approach. They claim that charter schools have the potential to divert money away from public schools. Charter schools draw money from the same sources as existing schools. When charter schools are created, unless there are unusual infusions of additional money to support operation of all publicly funded schools, the charter schools will consume dollars that will decrease amounts available to other schools. Hence, any improvements in education achieved at a charter school may come at the expense of a decrease in quality at other schools.

Other charter-school opponents argue that supporters of these schools exaggerate problems that bureaucratic constraints create for traditional public schools. They contend that, in spite of governmental and school-district regulations, numerous public schools have developed highly innovative programs and instructional practices. These schools have done so without having to ask for the regulatory relief that has been given to charter schools.

Some critics of charter schools acknowledge that, at times, state and school-district regulations can inhibit schools' abilities to develop more-effective programs. However, they doubt that establishing regulations-free charter schools is the answer. They argue that if regulations are undesirable, efforts should be directed to changing the regulations for all schools, not just charter schools. Changes of this kind would open the door for widespread innovation and improvement.

Because large numbers of charter schools have been operating for over a decade, studies are beginning to provide information regarding their effectiveness. On the positive side, parents and guardians, learners, and teachers involved with charter schools rate these schools higher than parents and guardians, learners, and teachers involved with traditional public schools. However, the charter-school participants have been found to be somewhat less satisfied with facilities and support than are those associated with regular public schools (Bulkey & Fisler, 2002).

The data on the academic achievement of charter schools are mixed. In one study focusing on Michigan schools, researchers found that learners in charter schools had lower average test scores than learners in regular public schools in their school district (Horn & Miron, 1999). In general, no definitive information yet exists that supports the contention that there are important achievement differences between learners taught in charter schools and in traditional public schools (Good & Braden, 2000).

Researchers have identified several concerns about the operation of charter schools (Good & Braden, 2000). One hope of charter-school supporters has been that these schools will serve as models for innovation and change, and that new approaches established in these schools will spread to other public schools. To date, there is little evidence that charter schools are serving as important educational-innovation centers. Researchers Good and Braden found that (1) in California, 85% of charter schools were using a traditional approach to instruction; (2) in Michigan, studies revealed virtually no innovation in that state's charter schools; and (3) in Arizona, little was occurring in the charter schools that could be classified as new or powerful.

Have charter schools reduced administrative bureaucracies and devoted more resources to support teaching? Critics point out that many have not done so (Good & Braden, 2000). Some charter schools spend more money on administration, maintenance, and operations and less per student on instruction than noncharter public schools. Indeed, some charter schools may be overfunded when compared with traditional public schools (Nelson, 1997). This situation can occur because charter schools do not have the same high costs as traditional schools that enroll many more at-risk and special-needs learners.

Large numbers of charter schools do not succeed. In one large-scale study of the survival rate of charter schools, investigators found that, of an original total of 2,874 schools, 194 had closed and 77 others had been reconstituted as traditional schools within the host district (Looney, 2002). Most failures appear to have occurred because of mismanagement, fiscal instability, and bankruptcy rather than as a result of evidence relating to poor learner performance (Good & Braden, 2000).

In summary, after a decade of growth there is little evidence to support a claim that charter schools, as a whole, have yet delivered on their promises. To be sure, there are some excellent charter schools. In many places, the charter-school movement continues to enjoy strong political support. Two key questions probably will remain central to the continuing debate about charter schools:

- Is the fundamental idea of charter schools flawed, and should this approach to educational reform and improvement be abandoned?
- Are problems associated with charter schools the result of poor implementation of an idea that basically is sound?

WEB EXTENSION 3–3

U.S. Charter Schools

The Center for Education Reform maintains this site. It includes excellent links to information focusing on topics such as (a) starting and running a charter school, (b) state information and contacts regarding charter schools, (c) profiles of individual charter schools, and (d) general resources and information sources regarding charter schools.

http://www.uscharterschools.org/

School reforms have prompted an increased need for teacher planning and collaboration.

Open-Enrollment Plans.   **Open-enrollment plans** vary from voucher plans in that they do not issue tax funds directly to parents or guardians. They also differ from charter schools in that they simply let parents or guardians choose an existing school for their child to attend. Most open-enrollment plans limit learners' choices to schools within a given school district. A few allow learners to cross district lines.

Sometimes open-enrollment plans are described as **controlled-choice plans.** Even though these plans are designed to honor parents' and guardians' preferences in assigning learners to individual schools, other factors are considered. School district administrators retain final control over assignment of learners to particular schools. Typically there are provisions that allow administrators to maintain acceptable racial balances in individual schools. In addition, most districts develop plans that allow people who live within the attendance boundaries of each school first choice. Thus, many excellent neighborhood schools have few slots available for learners who live outside the traditional attendance area.

Supporters believe that open-enrollment policies encourage parents and guardians to look carefully at the quality of academic programs in individual schools. The premise is that they will choose to send their children to those schools that they believe provide better learning experiences. Critics point out that, in districts with open-enrollment policies, parents and guardians often choose schools for reasons unrelated to the quality of educational programs. They contend that school-choice decisions are made for reasons such as the proximity of a school to parents' or guardians' workplace or because prospects are higher for their child to play a varsity sport at school "A" as opposed to school "B."

Magnet Schools.   **Magnet schools** represent another approach to school choice. Usually magnet schools have a specific theme for which they are especially well-known. For example, there may be a magnet school specializing in the sciences or one specializing in the performing arts. In addition to serving the special interests of learners they enroll, magnet schools also provide urban school districts with a means of achieving acceptable levels of racial integration. Integration occurs because magnet schools, unlike schools that draw learners from neighborhoods that may not have racially mixed populations, enroll learners from all residential areas in a district. This feature has led many large cities to establish magnet schools. For example, Houston, Chicago, Boston, New York, and Philadelphia have had them for many years.

Magnet schools provide outstanding learning experiences for many of the learners they enroll. They do create certain problems, however. The issue of transportation is a particular concern. Some critics allege that lack of transportation for learners from economically impoverished families makes it easier for learners from more-affluent families to attend magnet schools. In response to this difficulty, many districts with magnet schools provide transportation subsidies of some kind to learners from low-income families.

Admission to many magnet schools usually requires learners to have established a record of excellent academic performance at the schools they previously attended. As a result, some opponents of magnet schools argue that these schools remove the best learners from other schools and, thereby, reduce the overall talent pool in these buildings. Some critics also allege that magnet schools receive higher levels of financial support than other schools. As a result, learners in non-magnet schools may receive a level of educational services that is lower than it would be in the absence of magnet schools.

Redesigned Teacher-Compensation Schemes

Salaries you are offered may well play a part in your decision to commit to a long-term career as a teacher. Educational-improvement proponents agree that outstanding school programs depend on the ability of the schools to attract and keep high-quality teachers. Existing **teacher-salary schedules** (school-district documents that indicate what teachers in various categories are paid) normally are designed in ways that pay teachers based on their number of years of teaching experience and the number of advanced college credits and degrees beyond the bachelor's degree they have earned. Policy makers have been reluctant to simply add money to these existing salary schedules. Consistent with growing interest in accountability, new proposals for compensation assign a higher priority to measures of teacher performance.

Knowledge- and Skills-Based Pay.   The **knowledge- and skills-based pay (KSBP)** proposal would reward teachers for acquiring knowledge and skills needed for them to successfully teach a standards-based curriculum (Odden, 2001). In this scheme, a teacher's performance would be documented through meeting a series of professional benchmarks. These benchmarks refer to expected standards for teachers related to a series of tests, various performance tasks, and other indicators. The plan calls for schools to receive bonuses if learners meet certain achievement targets. Individual teachers' salaries would be based on (1) measures associated with their own professional growth and (2) their school's success in qualifying for a bonus based on learners' achievement.

Merit Pay.   The knowledge- and skills-based compensation plan has characteristics associated with a general category of proposals that seek to use teaching effectiveness as a basis for paying teachers. The general term applied to these proposals is **merit pay.** If a merit pay proposal were in place in a school district where you were employed, a portion of your annual raises would be determined by evidence related to the academic performance of your learners.

There has been more talk than implementation of merit pay proposals. One problem they have faced relates to difficulties associated with identifying and measuring meritorious performance. In order for merit pay to work as designed, salary increases must be tied to behaviors related to effective teaching and not other variables such as personality, appearance, or teachers' philosophical agreement with their raters. Defining the components of effective teaching and gathering data to support decisions regarding those who should receive merit is time-consuming and expensive. In recent decades, states such as Georgia, Florida, Texas, Tennessee, and Louisiana have all attempted this task. All have experienced great difficulty.

Despite these problems, there continues to be widespread interest in merit pay proposals, particularly among people who favor using learners' scores on standardized tests as measures of teacher effectiveness. Proponents argue that using standardized test scores to assess individual teachers makes sense because (1) such tests increasingly are tied to important content associated with mandated state curriculum standards and (2) such tests represent a common standard that can be applied to all teachers at a given grade level or within a particular subject area. Further, these plans can encourage healthy competition among teachers, a condition that can stimulate all of them to do their best work.

Opponents of merit pay strongly challenge the appropriateness of this approach. They point out that much of the research in the private sector actually indicates that merit pay systems rarely work as incentives to improve the quality of work of the people who are evaluated (Holt, 2001). Further, the idea that higher salaries should be associated with higher test scores assumes that potential financial gain is a highly-significant motivator for teachers. Critics of this view argue that few individuals choose a teaching career because of issues associated with salary. They are driven by other motives, including a strong personal commitment to serve others.

Critics of merit pay point out that what your learners take away from your instruction is attributable to variables that go beyond your actions in the classroom. Elements such as your school's safety record, social environment, and emotional climate; the health of your learners; the socioeconomic status of their families; the support of their parents and guardians; and the availability of adequate resources all play important roles in the achievement of students. These multiple influences suggest that merit pay systems, alone, have little potential to improve education because, as a teacher, you do not have control over many of the critical elements that influence your learners' achievement.

The idea that promoting competition among teachers will result in improved instructional programs is also questioned. This claim runs counter even to findings in industry that collaboration and shared ownership in work activities produce better results than highly-competitive work environments (Holt, 2001).

Comprehensive School Reform Demonstration Programs

Traditionally, federal programs to improve education have been designed to support limited-purpose programs. For example, federal monies have been allocated to support special education programs, mathematics programs, certain literacy programs, and programs for learners in districts with high levels of poverty. These "add-on" programs have not sought simultaneous improvement of an entire school. Because of concerns that these narrowly focused agendas were not greatly affecting the overall quality of schools, Congress passed Public Law 105-78 (1997), which established the **Comprehensive School Reform Demonstration (CSRD)** program.

CSRD focuses on schoolwide reform. It is designed to help schools improve their entire operation. It calls for changes in basic academics, professional development of teachers, levels of involvement of parents and guardians, use of analyses of local needs, and use of research-based ideas for improvement. CSRD encourages school districts to develop programs that will allow all learners to meet challenging academic standards. Program funds flow from the federal governments to the states. State-level authorities pass on funds to individual school districts. In turn, local school districts allocate the money to eligible schools. States must meet certain criteria to qualify for the funds.

To be eligible for CSRD funds, a school must have a plan for comprehensive school reform that includes each of the following nine components:

- Effective, research-based methods and strategies;
- Comprehensive design with aligned components (with the intent of meeting the needs of *all* enrolled learners);
- Professional development (for teachers and staff members);
- Measurable goals and benchmarks;
- Support within the school (to include a strong commitment of faculty, administrators, and staff);
- Parental and community involvement;
- External technical support and assistance (available from an outside group with experience in supporting school reforms);
- Evaluation strategies; and
- Coordination of resources (suggestions for how money from various sources will be used to support the comprehensive improvement program). (Comprehensive School Reform Demonstration Program, 1998)

The intent of CSRD to pay for reforms that will benefit all learners in a school represents a shift in the nature of federal support for school-improvement initiatives. In the past, much federal money was targeted at specific subgroups within the total school population.

NO CHILD LEFT BEHIND ACT OF 2001

In recent years, people concerned about making schools better have increasingly looked for improvements that would not only improve average levels of learner performance but would also ensure that learners in each subgroup of the school population are well served. As you know, an improved average by no means guarantees that all learners are doing better. Such a result is possible when sufficient numbers of learners score high enough on achievement tests to overcome scores of others who may be performing at about the same level (or even somewhat worse) than they were before. Critics of basing judgments related to school improvement on averages have been especially concerned that many proposed changes may not well serve young people from racial, language, and cultural minorities.

Certain provisions of an important piece of federal legislation, the **No Child Left Behind Act of 2001** (Public Law 107-110, 2002), reflect this concern. School districts now are required to measure more than "average" learner achievement. The law requires additional documentation that adequate progress is being made by learners from ethnic minorities, from homes in which English is not the first language, from economically impoverished backgrounds, and by learners with disabilities. These provisions may well exert a strong influence on your professional world in the years ahead.

The No Child Left Behind Act features *accountability* as a basic principle. It requires every state to adopt standards that describe what students should learn at each grade level. Each school district and school is expected to make adequate yearly progress toward meeting state standards, and yearly "report cards" must be issued for individual schools. Within 12 years, all learners must reach the level of proficiency as defined by their state. Districts and schools that do not make progress will be required to take corrective actions and may face negative consequences if problems persist.

One of the purposes of stringent accountability is to provide data that parents and guardians can use to make choices and exercise their options. If a school does not meet its academic growth target for two consecutive years, parents and guardians have the right to transfer their child to a successful public school. School districts must pay for learners' transportation to the new school. If a school fails to meet adequate yearly progress goals for three consecutive years, parents and guardians of disadvantaged learners have the right to supplemental educational services at the expense of the school district.

Some provisions of the No Child Left Behind Act have important implications for you and your teaching colleagues. The law requires school districts to assign a "highly qualified" teacher in every classroom in which an academic core subject is taught. Academic core subjects are defined as English, reading or language arts, mathematics, science, foreign languages, civics and government, economics, the arts, history, and geography. A "highly qualified" teacher is defined as a person who has obtained full state certification or has passed the state teacher licensing examination, holds the minimum of a bachelor's degree, and has demonstrated subject-area competence in each of the academic areas in which he or she teaches.

This provision has the potential to create problems for school districts. For example, there are several areas of the secondary curriculum in which smaller schools often do not offer enough course sections to hire a teacher to teach only one subject. In the past, a person who had a valid teaching certificate in a related area, such as history, and who had some background in geography might be asked to teach one or two geography classes. That this approach will no longer be a legal option for school administrators responsible for staffing of courses raises concern. One result may be a reduction in the variety of courses small secondary schools can offer.

This discussion has introduced only a few changes you may encounter in the schools as a result of passage of the No Child Left Behind Act. As you progress through your preparation program, you will want to find out how your state has defined a highly qualified teacher and what you will need to do to be designated as one. Your course instructor should be able to help you obtain this information.

WEB EXTENSION 3–4

No Child Left Behind

The No Child Left Behind Act of 2001 is so important that the U.S. Department of Education has developed a Web site that focuses exclusively on information related to this legislation. At this site you will find detailed material related to the act's provisions, background material for parents, news related to implementation efforts, and other information with ties to this key reform legislation.

http://www.nclb.gov/

SCHOOL–BUSINESS PARTNERSHIP PROGRAMS

Because our entire society benefits when learners have productive experiences in school, many outside our profession have a keen interest in what goes on in the schools. This interest has led to efforts to establish partnerships of various kinds between public schools and other agencies and organizations. For example, many colleges and universities around the country now link with specific schools for the purpose of helping them develop academic programs that will adequately prepare graduates for the demands of higher education. In some places, social agencies have established ties with schools that are designed to make their services more readily available to learners. (More information about this kind of cooperative activity is introduced in the next section, which focuses on full-service schools.) In recent years, corporations and businesses of all kinds have actively sought to establish formal **school–business partnerships.**

Establishment of **tech-prep programs** throughout the country has been one important effect of businesses' interest in the schools. Tech-prep programs developed in response to fears that many efforts to reform schools were promoting academic experiences having little practical value to students once they left school. Tech-prep programs for the most part are 2 + 2 models, which means that they focus on the last two years of high school and two additional years of training, most often in community and junior colleges.

The intent of tech-prep programs is to provide rigorous, integrated experiences that will smooth the transition from school to the world of the contributing adult citizen. To this end, the **Carl D. Perkins Vocational and Applied Technology Act** of 1990 (http://www.ed.gov/offices/DVAE/CTE/legis.html) defines tech-prep as a program that

- Leads to an associate degree or two-year certificate;
- Provides technical preparation in at least one field of engineering technology, applied science, mechanical, industrial, or practical art or trade, or agriculture, health, or business;
- Builds student competence in mathematics, science, and communication (including applied academics) through a sequential course of study; and
- Leads to placement in employment.

The U.S. Department of Education's Office of Vocational and Adult Education distributes money to support tech-prep initiatives through its **Tech-Prep Demonstration Program.** Applicants must be consortiums consisting of representatives of (1) grades K–12 schools, (2) colleges offering two-year associate degrees, and (3) a business. Among other things, funded programs have to describe

- How the proposed 2 + 2 program will be implemented,
- How the instruction will meet or exceed high quality standards set by the state,
- The quality of the alignment between the first two and second two years of the four-year sequence, and
- The plan's ability to attract students. (Tech-Prep Demonstration Program, 2003)

Proliferation of programs designed to foster school programs that help students make a smooth transition to the workplace led to passage of the federal **School-to-Work Opportunities Act** in 1994 (http://www.ncrel.org/sdrs/areas/issues/envrnmnt/stw/sw3swopp.htm). This act provides grants to states and communities to develop systems and partnerships designed to better prepare young people for additional education and careers. The intent is for students to experience the workplace as an active learning environment and to ensure that they see relationships between what they experience in school and what they will need to know to earn a living. The focus is on working with learners throughout the entire span of their K–12 school years.

WEB EXTENSION 3–5

The National Centers for Career and Technical Education

The National Centers for Career and Technical Education are located at the University of Minnesota, Twin Cities, and The Ohio State University. At this Web site, you will find excellent resources that focus on topics related to career and technical education. You can locate descriptions of effective programs, useful publications, standards related to career and technical education, and links to many additional materials.

http://www.nccte.com/

Business interest in school programs has taken many forms other than supporting legislation such as the Carl D. Perkins Act and the School-to-Work Opportunities Act. In some cases, schools have been helped in somewhat indirect ways. For example, companies have initiated child-care services and programs for employees, encouraging them to play active roles in their children's education. Often these initiatives have offered employees flexible work schedules to enable parents or guardians to visit schools during the day.

Other school–business partnerships have been much more ambitious and have encouraged partnerships as a way of improving entire school systems. One of the most notable efforts has occurred in Kentucky, where leaders of The Business Roundtable, which

This man's company has established a partnership with the local school district. The program allows him to spend several hours each week working with learners in his daughter's school.

is a national group including chief executive officers of 200 of the nation's largest corporations, have encouraged their branches in individual states to join with local schools to improve instructional quality and to better prepare young people for the world of work. You can locate many examples of these school–business partnerships by using a search engine such as Google (http://www.google.com) and entering the terms "business round-table" and "school-business partnerships."

In New York, the Long Island Works Coalition has established a school–business partnership for the purpose of ensuring a future workforce that possesses the educational background that local-area employers require. The program links employers, educators, parents, and learners. An important part of the program's agenda is identifying and closing gaps between business-skill needs and educational programs. Initiatives of this program include internship fairs that bring together local school students and employers that offer internship opportunities, an electronic-postcard system that provides information to school learners about career events and opportunities in the local area, "workforce summits" that bring together education and business leaders to discuss future workforce needs, and conferences for high school students that seek to encourage them to master important technology skills (Long Island Works Coalition, 2003).

In Wisconsin, learners of the Milwaukee Public Schools instituted a systemwide school-to-work emphasis. Elements of this approach are found in curricula at every grade from kindergarten through Grade 12. For example, children in early childhood programs engage in activities that are designed to develop their problem-solving abilities. Elementary children receive basic training in various aspects of the world of work and have lessons involving classroom businesses. Middle school learners have out-of-school experiences with organizations and businesses in the city. High school students have opportunities to become involved in a variety of apprenticeship programs (*System-Wide School-to-Work Transition and Parental Choice,* 1999).

In New York City, the Chamber of Commerce has established a Department of Education and Workforce Development. The department's Partnership for Leadership program has established a way for school principals to seek out and receive assistance from experienced leaders in the business community. The Summer Jobs program provides opportunities for public-school students to gain work experience and learn skills that will help them obtain positions when they leave the school system (*Education and Workforce Development,* 1999).

In Alaska, the Anchorage School Business Partnership program has operated successfully since 1991. This sophisticated cooperative effort now involves almost 70% of the school district's schools and features nearly 200 separate partnership arrangements. The nature of business–school partnership varies greatly from activity to activity. In some cases, an individual business arranges for a single employee to work closely with a designated school. In others, large corporations have many employees working with large numbers of individual schools and their staffs. Some examples of collaborative activities include mentorships, internships for learners, on-the-job training opportunities, and donations of various kinds from participating businesses to support particular school projects (Anchorage School District, 2002).

Interest in business–school partnerships is increasing. However, as you continue to learn about these programs, you will find that they have critics as well as supporters. Some people who are skeptical about school–business partnerships fear that some businesses are not as interested in helping children as they are in promoting their own products. Supporters counter that schools can develop guidelines to prevent this sort of thing from happening and that it is in the interest of educators to encourage an interest in public education among people outside of the profession. Discussions about this issue continue.

FULL-SERVICE SCHOOLS

Individual **human-support-service professions** that serve our nation's education, health, legal, and social-support needs have developed huge bodies of sophisticated knowledge over the past half-century. Training of specialists in these professions has never been better. What has not happened, however, is the coordination of these professions in ways that build on the strengths of each and that bring their diverse understandings to bear on common problems. This is particularly true in public education. Difficulties children face cannot neatly be sorted into categories labeled educational problems, health problems, legal problems, and social problems. What children experience as individuals are difficulties that cross all of these lines.

Full-service schools are beginning to emerge. These schools attempt to bring all human-support activities together under one roof. The need to do this was recognized over 20 years ago when the Bicentennial Commission of the American Association of Colleges of Teacher Education devoted fully 40 pages to the need to link education and human services (Howsam, Corrigan, Denemark, & Nash, 1976). In the middle 1990s, the Children's Defense Fund in its publication *The State of America's Children Yearbook* (1994) highlighted the intractability of problems facing our young people and the need to engage multiple human-services professions in the effort to solve them.

Many full-service schools have been established to help learners from economically or educationally impoverished backgrounds. There is evidence that some families in these circumstances are unable to take advantage of some of the support services various social agencies provide. When these services are gathered together in one place—the school—access becomes more user-friendly. Full-service schools are in operation in many parts of the country. Their programs vary, but they always feature the provision of services to learners and their families that go beyond schools' traditional obligation to provide curriculum-related services. They often feature collaborations with professionals from specialties outside of education and from community agencies to provide support services that may include:

- After-school care for learners,
- Medical and dental examinations conducted at the school,
- Adult education for parents and guardians,
- Family-support services provided by social workers,
- Legal services,
- Drug-and-alcohol-abuse prevention programs,
- Counseling services for learners and their families, and
- Emergency-treatment and crisis-reaction services. (Warger, 2000)

Some critics of full-service schools argue that they represent an attempt to charge the schools with solving every social ill. Opponents add that, although the efforts are well-intentioned, expecting schools to deliver counseling, medical, and other kinds of support services to learners and their families has the potential to divert resources from schools' important instructional function. Other opponents argue that full-service schools irresponsibly take responsibilities that properly belong to families and put them in the hands of outsiders.

WEB EXTENSION 3–6

Research on Full-Service Schools and Students with Disabilities

Learners with disabilities often need special support services that go beyond those they receive at school. Full-service schools provide some of these. In this *ERIC Digest,* author Cynthia Warger summarizes findings of research studies that have examined the impact of full-service school programs on learners with disabilities.

http://www.ericfacility.net/ericdigests/ed458749.html

Supporters of full-service schools say that services provided at full-service schools by noneducators often are not paid for out of the education budget. Governments already pay for social workers, health specialists, and other specialists to work with families who need these services and who cannot pay for them with their own funds. Full-service schools simply move some of these professionals to school buildings, where learners and their families can easily access their expertise.

Proponents of full-service schools argue that such plans do not diminish the importance of families in learners' lives. Families play important roles in determining what goes on in full-service schools. Learners who are enrolled often would not be able to access many provided services if they were not available at the school site.

At the present time, many national organizations representing the interests of different human-support services advocate expanding the number of full-service schools. Any growth in their numbers will have implications for training of future social service professionals.

If your own preparation program is typical, when you begin teaching you will have been introduced to information about such issues as learning styles, instructional design, psychological development of young people, classroom management, assessment of learners, and administrative arrangements of schools. You may have had little exposure to content related to public health, social work, law enforcement, and other areas that have always been discharged by social service professionals working in other settings. More attention to this kind of preparation will be needed if full-service schools become more common.

Critical Incident

Is My Subject Now a Frill?

My name is Sook-ja Kim. I'm about eight months through my second year of teaching at Centennial Middle School. I direct the school orchestra and teach orchestra classes. For the most part, I've had a great experience.

Last month, I took my students on a two-day trip to the state orchestra competition. We went to the state capital, about 100 miles away. The students raised money for the trip, and we had plenty of parents along to help. These kids had really worked hard for this contest experience, and I was absolutely thrilled when we received a "1" rating, the highest awarded.

As soon as the award ceremony was over, I hurried back to the hotel and called my principal. She was delighted at the good news. Centennial's orchestra had never before received such a high rating. In fact, the principal was so excited that she immediately called the superintendent, who has been concerned for some time that our district's music program has not been as strong as it should be. The news about our 1 rating was very welcome.

A few days after I returned to school, I got a nice letter of congratulation from the superintendent. The letter included an invitation for me to attend a school board meeting, where I was to receive public thanks for the honor brought to the district by our orchestra's high rating.

On the evening of the school board meeting, it was fairly late when the board president asked me to stand. He and other board members said some very nice words about what had been accomplished by the Centennial orchestra kids. I appreciated hearing nice comments about how much the district appreciated what I had accomplished in just two years. At the conclusion of these remarks, each member of the school board came over to shake my hand. I felt I had arrived at some kind of professional pinnacle.

The next item on the agenda was an open forum for citizens' comments. The first speaker deflated my fine feelings in a hurry. He said that the school district was spending too much money on frivolous, nonacademic subjects such as music. He indicated that the two days my orchestra kids had spent participating in the state contest had robbed them of two days of serious instruction in English and mathematics. He said this kind of thing provided just one more reason to support an effort he and a group of citizens were mounting to replace the present school board with people would emphasize what he called *serious* academics.

I left the meeting feeling depressed. I've worked so hard this year, but now I know that there are people in town who think my entire function is unnecessary. I have a really bad taste in my mouth about this. I just don't know what I'm going to do.

• • •

Are some subjects in the curriculum more important than others? Do you think that schools spend too much time and effort on activities outside the core academic subjects?
What do you think are the essential subjects that should be included in the school curriculum? How would you defend the importance of the subject you plan to teach?

 To respond to this Critical Incident online, go to the Critical Incidents *module for this chapter of the Companion Website.*

Key Ideas in Summary

- Change is afoot in education. As a prospective teacher, you need to become familiar with school-reform initiatives and join the national discussion related to these issues. By becoming involved, you can influence the direction of changes. If you do not, people whose views you do not share may influence the nature of your work environment in ways that dismay you.
- Because problems of schools are so complex, many critics of present practices are convinced that the only successful reforms will be those that will attack many variables at the same time. This effort is known as *systemic reform*. Many systemic-reform efforts emphasize outcomes of education rather than inputs, school choice, and redesigned teacher-compensation schemes.
- *School choice* implies that parents or guardians and learners should be able to select a school from among a number of alternatives. This approach represents a change from usual arrangements that assign learners to specific schools based on their home addresses.
- One approach to school choice is represented in the *voucher plan*. When a voucher plan is in operation, parents and guardians essentially receive a voucher (a kind of check) from state authorities representing the total number of dollars required to support instruction for each child in the family. The voucher can be "spent" only at a school. Parents or guardians select the school they wish their child to attend and give the voucher to administrators at this school. School authorities add the value of the voucher to the funds they have available to support their educational programs.

- The *charter school* represents another approach to school choice. Charter schools are semiautonomous public schools that are freed from many state regulations. A charter school can be established at an existing public school or established as a new school. Individuals interested in establishing such a school provide a plan to an authorized chartering agency. The plan spells out what the school will do and how success will be measured.

- *Magnet schools* and *open enrollment plans* are examples of other attempts to provide parents and guardians with school choice. Magnet schools typically have a theme (for example science education) where programs are especially strong. Parents and guardians from across an entire school district seek entry to magnet schools for their children regardless of where they live. Open-enrollment plans are arrangements that allow parents and guardians to disregard traditional school-attendance boundaries and enroll their children in any school in the school district. Ordinarily, some restrictions are set to prevent too many learners from crowding into just a few schools.

- The *No Child Left Behind Act of 2001* requires public schools in all states to make important changes. This legislation requires annual testing of all learners in several subjects in Grades 3 through 8. It also requires schools to give annual report cards that detail each learner's progress, and it allows parents to move their child to another school if a school fails to meet achievement targets. In addition, the law requires a "qualified teacher" in every classroom. A qualified teacher is someone who has passed a rigorous subject-matter examination and who has met all state certification requirements.

- Today, many school-improvement initiatives feature proposals to change teacher-compensation plans. These generally call for moving away from traditional compensation arrangements that reward teachers based on a combination of (1) university degrees and accumulated academic credit hours and (2) years of classroom experiences. Newer proposals favor basing teacher salaries on evidence related to academic achievement of the learners that individual teachers instruct.

- Many businesses and corporations wish to play a part in improving the quality of public education. Private-sector support has been an important factor helping the spread of *tech-prep* programs that seek to integrate training during the last two years of high school and the first two years in a post-high school institution—typically a community or junior college. In addition to their support of tech-prep programs, many businesses have joined with schools in *school–business partnership* programs. These range from efforts to improve the quality of education within an entire state to efforts centered on a single school.

- Individuals from many professions are involved in important human-support-service activities. In addition to education, these include professionals trained in health care, social welfare, law, and law enforcement. There is a trend to bring these professional services together in schools. Interest in this approach has led to the establishment of full-service schools. In these schools, people from a variety of human-service professions are available to provide comprehensive support services for learners and their families.

Chapter 3 Self-Test

 To review terms and concepts in this chapter, go to the Companion Website and take the Chapter 3 Self-Test. Feedback for the self-test is immediate. You can keep track of your self-test scores yourself, or you can submit your scores to your instructor via e-mail.

Preparing for Praxis

 To learn more about the Praxis test and complete this activity online, go to the Preparing for Praxis *module for this chapter of the Companion Website.*

You may be required to pass Educational Testing Service's Praxis II exam as you seek formal authorization to teach in the public schools. The *Principles of Learning and Teaching* component of Praxis II seeks to assess your knowledge about these topics: (1) Students as Learners, (2) Instruction and Assessment, (3) Communication Techniques, and (4) Profession and Community.

Information presented in this chapter may be especially relevant to you as you prepare for questions related to the category of Profession and Community. Some content may also deal with issues having logical ties to other Praxis II categories. You may find it useful to prepare a chart similar to the one provided here. As you encounter information related to individual categories, you can enter it into the chart under the appropriate heading. This completed chart will be useful as you begin preparing for the Praxis II exam.

Students as Learners	Instruction and Assessment
• Student Development and the Learning Process	• Instructional Strategies
• Students as Diverse Learners	• Planning Instruction
• Student Motivation and the Learning Environment	• Assessment Strategies
Communication Techniques	**Profession and Community**
• Basic, Effective, Verbal and Nonverbal Communication Techniques	• The Reflective Practitioner
• Effect of Cultural and Gender Differences on Communications in the Classroom	• The Larger Community
• Types of Questions That Can Stimulate Discussion in Different Ways for Particular Purposes	

For Your Initial-Development Portfolio

 To complete this activity and submit your response online, go to the For Your Initial-Development Portfolio *module for this chapter of the Companion Website.*

1. What materials and ideas from this chapter about *challenges of school reform* will you include as "evidence" in your portfolio? Select up to three separate items of information. Number them 1, 2, and 3.
2. Think about why you selected these materials. As you do so, consider these issues:
   - Specific uses you might make of this information as you plan, deliver, and assess the impact of your teaching
   - The compatibility of the information with your own priorities and values
   - Any contributions this information can make to your development as a teacher
   - Factors that led you to include this information, as opposed to some alternatives you considered but rejected

3. Place a check in the chart here to indicate the INTASC standard(s) to which each of your items of information relates. (You may wish to refer to Chapter 1 for more-detailed information about INTASC.)

INTASC Standard Number

ITEM OF EVIDENCE NUMBER		S1	S2	S3	S4	S5	S6	S7	S8	S9	S10
	1										
	2										
	3										

4. Prepare a written reflection in which you analyze the decision-making process you followed. In your comments, mention the INTASC standard(s) to which your selected material relates.

Reflections

 To respond to these questions online, go to the Reflections *module for this chapter of the* Companion Website.

1. Supporters of *systemic reform* argue that, to achieve meaningful school improvement, multiple variables must be attacked simultaneously. Others argue that making multiple changes at the same time is so difficult that, in the end, no modifications to present practices will occur. They contend that incremental improvement that is achieved by addressing one problem at a time, in the long run, has more potential to improve schools than do all-encompassing systemic-reform initiatives. What are your own reactions to these arguments, and why do you take your position?

2. Suppose all school districts in the United States adopted *voucher plans*. What changes would there be in how schools operate? What problems might you and your teaching colleagues face? What challenges would confront your school's administrators? What positives do you see associated with this policy? What negatives? Would such a policy improve our schools? Why or why not?

3. Suppose you and a group of colleagues decided to establish a *charter school*. What problems of traditional public schools would you attempt to overcome? How might your freedom to ignore certain requirements your state imposes on

most schools allow you to serve your learners well? You would have to present a plan to a chartering agency and win this agency's support for your ideas. Among other things, you would have to include a description of variables you would consider and procedures you would use to determine your school's effectiveness. What are some ideas you might include in your plan?

4. Most teacher-compensation plans base salaries on (1) teachers' university degrees and academic credits and (2) teachers' years of experience in the classroom. In this chapter, you learned about *merit pay* and other approaches to teacher compensation that deviate from typical practices. What kind of compensation plan might you devise that would both attract and hold teachers in the profession and satisfy the public that teachers' salaries are connected in some way to what young people learn? What difficulties might you encounter in implementing such a plan?

5. Full-service schools attempt to bring together at one place a range of educational, health, legal, and social-welfare services. Professionals from these human-support-service organizations work cooperatively to help learners and their families. Supporters argue that making these services available at a school site allows learners and families to access them easily. Detractors contend

that providing noninstructional services at schools diverts schools from their primary mission of teaching learners. Opponents also argue that full-service-school staffing costs may divert funds to support services that are unrelated to instructing young people. What are your own reactions to full-service schools, and why do you feel this way?

Field Experiences, Projects, and Enrichment

1. In a few places around the country, local citizens have lost so much faith in the abilities of public school officials to manage local school programs that they have turned over operation of their schools to private corporations or to a local university. The term *contract school* sometimes is applied to a school that has been placed under the authority of this kind of external contracting agency. In essence, the private corporation or university contracts with the local citizens to improve the quality of educational services. Read about how these arrangements have worked out. Prepare a report to share with others in your class.

2. Most states have legislation allowing the establishment of charter schools. If your state has or is considering such legislation, find out what requirements must be met to establish a charter school. If your state legislature has not considered this issue, gather information about the situation in a neighboring state. Prepare a short paper in which you make reference to such issues as (1) the kinds of groups that can request authority to establish a charter school, (2) the limitations on the numbers of charter schools that can be established, and (3) the provisions relating to funding of charter schools.

3. Though there are important national trends related to educational change, you will also find that some calls for modifications in schools and school programs center around issues that may loom large in some communities while being virtually nonexistent in others. An interesting example involves the theory of evolution. In many parts of the country, this issue is never raised. In others, it is an issue that only occasionally prompts local interest. In still others, it is a subject of great concern, and school board meetings often are punctuated by comments of school patrons who have conflicting views on this issue. You may be interested in learning more about the nature of this debate. Using a search engine such as Google (http://www.google.com), conduct several searches. Enter these terms as you seek links to relevant information: "Evolution debate" and "Intelligent Design." Prepare a report for your class based on your findings.

4. The *No Child Left Behind Act of 2001* imposes important obligations on local schools and school districts. Interview an administrator from a local school district. Ask about changes the school district has made in response to this legislation and about any difficulties the district has faced in doing so. Share your findings with others in your class.

5. The activities that various *school–business partnerships* support vary greatly from place to place. To gain some idea of the scope of these activities, use a search engine such as Google (http://www.google.com) and enter the term "school-business partnership." Go to a selection of the identified links, and look for information related to the nature of activities that various partnerships support. Prepare a bulleted list of these activities, and make copies to share with others in your class.

References

Anchorage School District. (2002). *School business partnership report, 2001–2002*. ASD Memorandum No. 15 (2002–2003). Anchorage, AK: Author.

Bulkey, K., & Fisler, J. (2002). A decade of charter schools: From theory to practice. *Consortium for Policy Research in Education Policy Briefs*. Philadelphia: University of Pennsylvania (RB-35).

Carnoy, M. (2000). School choice or is it privatization? *Educational Researcher, 79*(7), 15–20.

Children's Defense Fund. (1994). *The state of America's children yearbook 1994: Leave no child behind.* Washington, DC: Author.

Comprehensive School Reform Demonstration Program. (1998). *Guidance on the comprehensive school reform demonstration program U.S. Department of Education.* [http://www.nwrel.org/csrdp/about.html]

Education and Workforce Development. (1999). [http://www.public policy.com/educat.html]

Education Commission of the States. (2004). *Charter Schools.* [http://www.ecs.org/ecsmain.asp?page=/html/issues.asp?]

Good, T. L., & Braden, J. S. (2000). Charter schools: Another reform failure or a worthwhile investment? *Phi Delta Kappan, 81*(10), 745–750.

Holt, M. (2001). Performance pay for teachers: The standards movement's last stand? *Phi Delta Kappan, 83*(4), 312–317.

Horn, J., & Miron, G. (1999). *Evaluation of the Michigan public school academy initiative.* Kalamazoo: Western Michigan University.

Howsam, R. B., Corrigan, D. C., Denemark, G. W., & Nash, R. J. (1976). *Educating a profession: Relating to human services education.* Washington, DC: American Association of Colleges for Teacher Education.

Levin, H. M. (2002). A comprehensive framework for evaluating educational vouchers. *Educational Evaluation and Policy Analysis, 24*(3) 159–174.

Lewis, A. C. (September, 2001). Heads in the sand. *Phi Delta Kappan, 83*(1) 4–5.

Long Island Works Coalition. (2003). *Long Island works coalition.* Long Island, NY: Author. [http://www.liworks.org/about.cfm]

Looney, M. (2002). *Charter schools today: Changing the face of American education.* Washington, DC: Center for Education Reform.

National Commission on Excellence in Education. (1983). *A nation at risk: The imperative for educational reform.* Washington, DC: U.S. Department of Education.

Nelson, F. H. (1997). *How much thirty thousand charter schools cost.* Paper presented at the annual meeting of the American Educational Finance Association, Jacksonville, FL.

Odden, A. (2001). The new school finance. *Phi Delta Kappan, 83*(1), 85–91.

Popham, W. J. (2003). The seductive allure of data. *Educational Leadership, 60*(5), 48–51.

Public Law 105-78. (1997, November 13). An act making appropriations for the Departments of Labor, Health and Human Services, and Education, and related agencies for the fiscal year ending September 30, 1998, and for other purposes. *Statutes at Large* (111 Stat. 1467).

Public Law 107-110. (2002, January 8). No Child Left Behind Act of 2001. *Statutes at Large* (115 Stat. 1425).

Spady, W. G. (1994). Choosing outcomes of significance. *Educational Leadership, 51*(6), 18–22.

System-Wide School-to-Work Transition and Parental Choice. (1999). [http://www.aypf.org/tripreports/1995/tr101995.htm]

Tech-Prep Demonstration Program. (2003, January 24). *Federal Register, 68*(16), 3517–3520.

Warger, C. (2000). *Research on full-service schools and students with disabilities.* (ERIC Document Reproduction Service No. ED 182 465).

Wells, A. S. (1990, March). *Public school choice: Issues and concerns for urban educators. ERIC/CUE Digest,* No. 63. (ERIC Clearinghouse on Urban Education No. ED 322275).

Wiggins, G. (1989). A true test: Toward more authentic and equitable measurement. *Phi Delta Kappan, 70*(9), 703–713.

Part 2

Learners and Their Needs

CHAPTERS

4

Profiles of Today's Learners

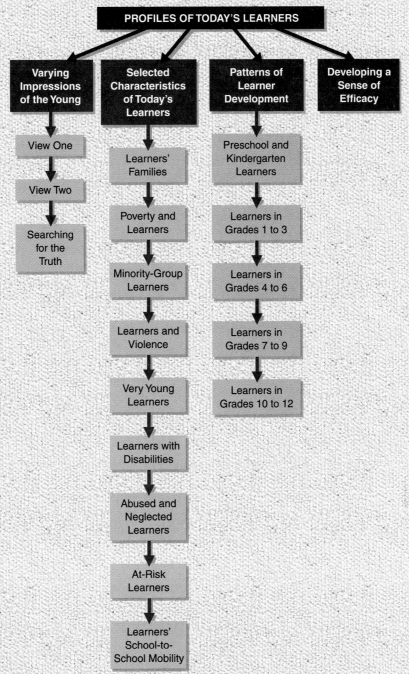

PROFILES OF TODAY'S LEARNERS

- Varying Impressions of the Young
  - View One
  - View Two
  - Searching for the Truth

- Selected Characteristics of Today's Learners
  - Learners' Families
  - Poverty and Learners
  - Minority-Group Learners
  - Learners and Violence
  - Very Young Learners
  - Learners with Disabilities
  - Abused and Neglected Learners
  - At-Risk Learners
  - Learners' School-to-School Mobility

- Patterns of Learner Development
  - Preschool and Kindergarten Learners
  - Learners in Grades 1 to 3
  - Learners in Grades 4 to 6
  - Learners in Grades 7 to 9
  - Learners in Grades 10 to 12

- Developing a Sense of Efficacy

OBJECTIVES

This chapter will help you to

- explain that young people in the schools reflect great diversity and, at the same time, share certain common characteristics.
- identify selected characteristics of learners likely to be present in many elementary, middle, and high school classrooms.
- describe how your teaching practices may be influenced by the diversity reflected in your classes.
- cite examples of age- and development-related characteristics of young people that you might expect to see at different grade levels.
- describe some teacher characteristics that seem to be associated with learner success at different grade levels.
- explain why it is important for you to help learners develop a sense of self-efficacy.

87

VARYING IMPRESSIONS OF THE YOUNG

How do you see today's young people? If you pose this question to others, you probably will get a variety of answers. Some responses may reflect patterns such as those included in these two views.

View One

Drug abuse is rampant among young people today. Use of such drugs as alcohol, marijuana, amphetamines, LSD, and cocaine is up dramatically from levels of 15 years ago.

Disinterest in school among young people is reflected in their eagerness to accept part-time employment. Too many students in high school work an excessive number of hours while they are going to school. More high school students work more than 20 hours a week now than did students who were in high school 20 years ago.

The kinds of institutions that are important to adults are little prized by young people. For example, organized religion and public schools are not held in high esteem. On the other hand, young people place great faith in what they see on television.

Young people tend to reject traditional role models. Parents and teachers are not held in particularly high regard. Heroes of young people tend to be musicians and well-known film and television stars. Occupational roles that young people see as important for a "good society" deviate markedly from those chosen by adults. Young people place little stock in the importance of teachers and scientists as opposed to rock musicians.

View Two

Educators and others continue to be concerned about drug use in our society. On a positive note, there is evidence that the numbers of children and young people who report using tobacco are going down. In recent years, the percentage of young people who have used marijuana is much lower than it was in the middle 1970s. There has also been a downward trend in young people's illicit use of cocaine.

Many young people in high school have part-time jobs. However, the number of students who work 20 or more hours a week has gone down over the past 20 years. The 20-hours-per-week figure is important because young people who work more than 20 hours a week tend to experience fatigue that negatively affects their performance at school.

Institutions viewed as important by children and young people are not greatly different from those prized by adults. For example, they hold organized religion and public schools in high esteem, and they don't hold television in particularly high regard.

Children and young people, when asked to identify role models who are important to them, cite parents and teachers as people they particularly admire, not rock musicians. When asked to comment on the importance of various groups to maintaining a "good society," young people rate school teachers and scientists high and rock musicians low.

Searching for the Truth

Did you find one of these views to be more credible than the other? If you chose View One, your selection would have been consistent with impressions that many members of the general public have about young people today. This view is consistent with much of what we see on television and read in the newspapers. The emphasis on problems of young people helps focus proper attention on issues that deserve public attention. On the other hand, it can also give people a distorted picture of the characteristics of typical learners in today's schools.

Research evidence often fails to confirm widely held popular attitudes. Though many people you ask might believe otherwise, the picture of children and young people provided in View Two is more consistent with the best evidence we now have (Carskadon, 1999; National Center for Education Statistics, 2002b, Naylor, 1999; & U.S. Department of Health and Human Services, 2001).

Though the attitudes of young people on many key issues do not seem to deviate markedly from those of many adults, we need to keep in mind that the data represent averages of a huge group. With almost 50 million young people in the schools (National Center for Education Statistics, 2002b), many different perspectives are represented. This is a particularly critical point for those of us who work in the public schools.

As a teacher, you will fulfill your responsibilities at a workplace that brings together a cross section of our entire population. Many attitudes and perspectives that characterize the general population are sure to be represented in your classroom. This diversity will add spice (and occasionally great challenge) to your teaching days.

SELECTED CHARACTERISTICS OF TODAY'S LEARNERS

The diversity of learners always impresses visitors who have not been in a school for a long time. As a teacher, you will be challenged to recognize and respond to common characteristics of young people. At the same time, you will have to adjust your instruction to meet unique needs of individual learners.

Learners' Families

Television programs sometimes promote an image of a "typical" American family that includes a father who is employed, a mother who stays in the family's well-appointed suburban home, and two well-scrubbed children who romp endlessly with the family's

Many students ride buses to attend schools outside their neighborhood. For some students this causes a fear of the unknown.

	Attended a General School Meeting	Attended Scheduled Meeting with Teacher	Attended a School Event	Acted as a Volunteer or Served on a Committee
Child in Grades K–5	84.6	87.5	70.4	47.6
Child in Grades 6–8	79.6	70.4	65.7	29.1
Child in Grades 9–12	67.3	51.3	57.3	25.6

FIGURE 4.1   Differences in Percentages of Parent/Guardian Involvement in School-Related Activities by Grade Level of Their Children

Source: The Condition of Education, 2001 (p. 175), by the National Center for Education Statistics, 2001, Washington, DC: NCES.

shaggy dog. This image, in all its dimensions, never was typical. The U.S. Census Bureau (2001) has published data indicating that this picture is far from present-day realities. For example, fewer than one-fourth of school-aged young people live in homes headed by a live-in mother and father. Large numbers today live with a single parent, another relative, or a guardian. An especially high number of young people come from homes in which no male is permanently present. Of children in this latter group, many live with a single female.

Families vary greatly in terms of their active involvement in young people's educational experiences. Parents and guardians from higher-income households are more likely to have some active contact with their children's schools. Educational levels of parents and guardians tend to influence their interest in education. On average, adults with more education are more involved with their children's schools (National Center for Education Statistics, 2001). As Figure 4.1 shows, family members tend to be more involved (1) in activities that require relatively modest commitments of their time and (2) when their children are in the elementary rather than the middle school or high school grades.

Current family and employment statistics indicate that large numbers of school-children spend many hours with babysitters and at day care centers. The kind of generation-to-generation communication that went on in traditional families happens less frequently today. As a result, we in the schools often provide social and personal information to learners that, in years gone by, was passed on by parents. Increasingly, the dividing line separating responsibilities of the home and the school is blurring.

Poverty and Learners

Poverty continues to be a depressing national problem. Approximately one-fourth of our nation's children live in poverty (Futrell, Gomez, & Bedden, 2003). This poverty rate is among the highest in all developed nations (Thomas & Brainbridge, 2002). During the first year of the new millennium, the number of poor increased by 1.3 million to 32.9 million

(National Center for Education Statistics, 2001). Rates of poverty vary greatly from ethnic group to ethnic group. Households that include minority children of high school age that are headed by a female and in which no male is present are especially likely to be economically impoverished. Percentages of Americans younger-than 18 living in poverty have generally increased over the past 25 years.

For many reasons, children from economically deprived homes often do not do well in school. Disadvantaged learners have difficulty with cognitive development, vocabulary, and reading (Thomas & Bainbridge, 2002). Too many of these learners are assigned to special education classes because of cognitive and developmental deficiencies. Many of these problems result because of mothers' inability to pay for quality prenatal care. Also, poor children often do not receive adequate diets, which may affect their performance in school.

Many of the economically impoverished learners you teach will come from homes that lack personal computers. Large numbers of poor families cannot afford newspaper and magazine subscriptions. Poor children are not nearly as likely to observe their parents reading as are children from more-affluent homes. Because these learners seldom see their parents or guardians reading, you may find that some of them fail to understand the importance you attach to helping them acquire sophisticated reading skills. Failure of these learners to develop good reading proficiencies in the early grades often begins a cycle of failure that leads to poor academic performance in later school years.

Present trends suggest that you will be dealing with significant numbers of students from economically impoverished backgrounds during your years in the profession (Doorey & Harter, 2003). Helping these learners succeed requires you to plan instructional programs that take into account their special needs.

WEB EXTENSION 4–1

U.S. Census Bureau

The U.S. Census Bureau gathers information related to many characteristics and conditions of people in the United States, including poverty. At this site, you will find a search engine that invites you to supply a keyword. If you type in the word "poverty," you will be presented with a number of links to data tables and other information sets that provide useful information about poverty among different groups.

http://factfinder.census.gov/servlet/BasicFactsServlet

Minority-Group Learners

Minority-group children are becoming a larger proportion of the total school population. At the beginning of the 21st century, they accounted for nearly 40% of all young people in school, an increase of 17% since 1972 (National Center for Education Statistics, 2002a). About 17% of the nation's schoolchildren are African American, and about 17% are of Latino heritage. Latinos are the fastest growing minority group in the schools today. Learners from Asian or Pacific Islander, Native American, and other racial and ethnic groups comprise about 5% of the total school enrollment (National Center for Education Statistics, 2002a).

Distribution of students from minority groups is not uniform across the country. In the South, African Americans account for 26% of the total school enrollment, whereas in the West, Latinos comprise about 32% of the total (National Center for Education Statistics, 2002a).

Minority-group students, with the exception of some of Asian heritage, often have not adapted well to school programs. This pattern is especially pronounced among Latinos. For example, data published in 2002 revealed that nearly 28% of Latinos between the ages of 16 and 24 had dropped out of school before high school graduation. Though this percentage has declined in recent years, it still is well above the 2002 figures for African Americans (about 13%) and whites (about 7%) (National Center for Education Statistics, 2002a).

Educators today are concerned about the **achievement gap** between white students and those from many minority groups, including African Americans and Latinos. Scores of these minorities have lagged behind those of whites, though the gap between white and African American learners has narrowed in recent years (National Center for Education Statistics, 2002a). Educators today are working hard to understand factors that contribute to these achievement differences and to develop responses that will better serve the needs of African Americans and Latinos. Given (1) our profession's commitment to serve all learners well and (2) the reality that students from minority backgrounds are a growing percentage of the school population, you probably will be involved in efforts to design programs to reduce the achievement gap.

Learners and Violence

If young people you teach do not feel safe, their ability to learn will be impaired. In recent years, incidents such as the mass shooting at Columbine High School in Colorado and other disturbing incidents have raised serious questions about learners' safety at school. Although school violence continues to be a problem, you need to keep the issue in perspective. In general, schools are quite safe places. A student is almost twice as likely to be a victim of a serious crime away from school than at school (DeVoe et al., 2002).

Efforts to reduce the violent incidents in schools are beginning to have a positive effect. For example, between 1995 and 2000, there was a decline in the number of students who reported being victimized at school (DeVoe et al., 2002). Despite this positive trend, school violence continues to be a matter of great concern that educators, community leaders, law enforcement officials, and members of other groups continue to address.

Involvement in a physical fight without a weapon is the most common kind of physical violence young people experience at school. In 2001, U.S. schools reported nearly 188,000 such incidents. Middle school and high school students are much more likely to experience this problem than are elementary school students (National Center for Education Statistics, 2002a).

As you learn more about school violence, you will discover that learners in schools with certain characteristics have a higher likelihood of being victimized than learners in other schools. For example, more schools in the West report serious crimes occurring in and around their buildings than schools in the Northeast, Southeast, or Central United States. Schools in inner cities experience more problems than schools in suburban areas, small towns, or rural areas. Interestingly, poverty does *not* seem to be a variable associated with incidents of serious school violence. High-poverty and low-poverty schools report about the same percentage of episodes of violence on students (DeVoe et al., 2002). See Figure 4.2 for additional information about schools with varying characteristics and their reported violence.

Enrollment	Percentage of Minority Enrollment	Instructional Level
Fewer than 300: 17% *300 to 999:* 26% *1,000 or more:* 67%	*Less than 5%:* 6% *5 to 19%:* 11% *20 to 49%:* 11% *50% or more:* 15%	*Elementary School:* 4% *Middle School:* 19% *High School:* 21%

FIGURE 4.2   Percentages of Schools Reporting Serious Crimes Inside or Around Their Buildings

Source: *Digest of Education Statistics—2001* (pp. 165–166), by the National Center for Education Statistics, 2002, Washington, DC: NCES.

Certain characteristics associated with a school's climate and culture have been found to be associated with violence and antisocial behavior. Among them are

- Overcrowding;
- Poor design and use of school space;
- Lack of firm, yet caring, disciplinary procedures;
- Learner alienation;
- Multicultural insensitivity;
- Teacher and peer rejection of at-risk learners; and
- Student resentment of school routines. (*How Can We Prevent Violence in Our Schools?*, 2000)

VIDEO VIEWPOINTS

What Are the Keys to Improving Achievement?

WATCH: This *Nightline* special focuses on the Seed Charter School in Washington, D.C. The founders of this charter school believed that it would take more than choice, the elimination of red tape, and a change of curriculum to improve student performance. They believed that nothing short of changing the environment would work. They established a public boarding school for 40 students coming from troubled schools and difficult neighborhoods.

This segment details the experiences of several of the students and illustrates the challenges of changing student attitudes and achievement.

THINK: Discuss with your classmates, or in your teaching journal, the following questions:

1. What do you see as the critical variables that need to be addressed if fundamental change is to occur?
2. What do you see as the implications of this program for reform efforts focused on improving student achievement?
3. What do you think can be done if it is impossible to change the environment?

LINK: How might reform efforts focus on cooperation between schools and other social agencies?

   Complete this activity and submit your responses online in the Video Viewpoints module for this chapter of the Companion Website.

WEB EXTENSION 4–2

National Center for Children Exposed to Violence

The National Center for Children Exposed to Violence brings together a vast array of information related to the general issue of violence and children. At this site, you will find statistical information, a comprehensive online library, lists of publications, examples of programs that have been established to deal with this problem, and links to a large number of useful Web sites.

http://www.nccev.org/

Very Young Learners

As you drive around neighborhoods close to elementary schools today, you are likely to see large numbers of day care facilities. Their growth is a reflection in the tremendous increase over the past 30 years in the numbers of female parents and guardians who have or who are actively looking for full-time employment outside the home. A side effect of this trend has been an increasing interest in enrolling young children in educational programs. Because of the expense and uneven quality of private day care operations, public schools have been under pressure to expand programs available to 3- and 4-year-old children.

Growth of these programs has been dramatic. In 1970, for example, only about 13% of 3-year-olds and about 28% of 4-year-olds were in formal educational programs. In 1970, almost three times as many of the enrolled 3- and 4-year-olds attended private nursery schools as attended public nursery schools. By 2000, more than 39% of 3-year-olds and nearly 65% of 4-year-olds participated in formal educational programs. More than 40% of 3-year-olds and over 50% of 4-year-olds attended publicly supported nursery schools (National Center for Education Statistics, 2002b).

Expansion of school programs for young learners has prompted much debate. Supporters cite research suggesting that early childhood programs can help young children to develop positive self-images and abilities to work productively and harmoniously with others. Critics argue that expansion of early childhood programs imposes obligations on schools that properly should be discharged in the home by parents and guardians. Forces supporting expansion of school programs seem to be carrying the day, as economic pressures continue to encourage female heads of families with young children to seek out-of-the-home employment. The years ahead probably will witness an even greater expansion of school programs for very young learners.

WEB EXTENSION 4–3

NAEYC—National Association for the Education of Young Children

The National Association for the Education of Young Children (NAEYC) is the largest national professional organization for educators and others who are dedicated to providing high-quality programs for young children in the schools. At this site, you will find links related to program standards, program accreditation, policy discussions, and other issues related to educating young learners.

http://www.naeyc.org

Preschool children have great curiosity and high energy.

Learners with Disabilities

In the past, learners with disabilities were often kept away from other school children in the schools. This practice was justified by the claim that such students needed training that was unavailable to them in the regular classroom. Since the mid-1970s, however, this situation has changed. The **Education for All Handicapped Children Act (Public Law 94-142)** of 1975 (renamed in 1990 the **Individuals with Disabilities Education Act**) required schools, to the extent possible, to teach learners with disabilities in traditional classrooms.

In part, this federal legislation was the result of concerns that the past practice of isolating learners with disabilities was tending to stigmatize them as less than real learners. Now, during a typical day, you will have students with a wide variety of disabilities in your classroom.

The National Center for Education Statistics (2002b) reports that programs for the disabled are directed at learners who comprise about 13% of the total school population. By far the largest group in this category, representing about 46% of the total, are young people classified as having "specific learning disabilities." Other major groups within this total and the percentages they represent are

- Learners with speech impairments: 17.4%
- Learners with some degree of mental retardation: 9.7%
- Learners suffering from severe emotional disturbance: 7.6% (National Center for Education Statistics, 2002b; p. 66)

For more detailed information about learners with disabilities, see Chapter 6, "Meeting the Needs of Exceptional Learners."

Abused and Neglected Learners

You may be surprised to learn that more children aged 4 and younger die each year from child abuse and neglect than from any other single cause (Childabuse.com, 2001). Problems of abused and neglected children have attracted public interest for years. As a teacher, you will have a legal obligation to report any injury to a learner that appears to be nonaccidental. You will not be doing anything unusual. Responsible governmental agencies receive around 3 million child abuse reports each year, many of them from teachers (Childabuse.com).

Suspected abuse is handled in most communities by **Child Protective Services (CPS).** This organization usually operates within a state or county agency, which might be known as the Department of Social Services, the Department of Human Resources, the Department of Social Welfare, the Department of Public Welfare, or some other name. Here are the types of abuse and typical behaviors of victims.

- **Physical Abuse.** Signs of physical abuse may include bruises, welts, burns, bite marks, and other unusual marks on the body; or the learner may be having what seem to be too many accidental injuries at home. Some behavioral indicators of physical abuse include:
  - Learner is hard to get along with and may frequently be in trouble.
  - Learner has bruises, abrasions, lacerations, or swellings that appear not to have been caused accidentally.
  - Learner is unusually shy or too eager to please.
  - Learner is frequently late or absent or comes to school too early and seems reluctant to go home.
  - Learner's body shows evidence of bite marks or pinches.
  - Learner shies away from physical contact with adults.
  - Learner seems frightened of parents.
  - Learner may seek affection from any adult.
- **Neglect.** Learners who have been neglected at home may show up at school dirty. They may not have any lunch money. They may need glasses and dental care. Their clothing may be unkempt, or they may wear clothes that are inappropriate given prevailing weather conditions. Some of these young people may beg food from their classmates. Examples of other indicators include:
  - Learner has a behavior pattern reflecting poor supervision at home.
  - Learner frequently falls asleep in class.
  - Learner has a medical condition that is not receiving attention.
- **Emotional Abuse.** Often, emotional abuse is reflected in extreme or excessive behavior patterns. Emotionally abused young people may be too compliant and passive; on the other hand, they may be very aggressive. Here are some other behavioral indicators of possible emotional abuse:
  - Behavior is either too adult-like or too immature, given the learner's age.
  - Learner is behind in physical, emotional, and intellectual development.
- **Sexual Abuse.** One indicator of this condition is that a learner's underclothing is torn, stained, or bloody. Or, the learner may experience pain or itching in the genital area. Other behavioral indicators of sexual abuse include:
  - Learner is very withdrawn, or learner engages in fantasy-like or baby-like behavior.

- Learner has poor relationships with other children.
- Learner engages in delinquent acts or runs away from home.
- Learner says he or she has been sexually assaulted.

Many groups in our society are interested in doing something to reduce child abuse and neglection. They recognize that teachers can play an important part by recognizing potential abuse and reporting it to authorities. You can easily access information related to this important issue by using a search engine such as Google (http://www.google.com) and typing in the words "child abuse and neglect."

WEB EXTENSION 4–4:

National Clearinghouse on Child Abuse and Neglect Information

The National Clearinghouse on Child Abuse and Neglect is a service of the Children's Bureau, a program that is part of the U.S. Department of Health and Human Services' Administration for Children and Families. At this site, you will find numerous useful links to information about child abuse and neglect. These links give you access to materials that include those that focus on (1) relevant statistics, (2) preventative measures, (3) applicable laws, and (4) publications.

http://www.calib.com/nccanch

At-Risk Learners

Particular personal and situational backgrounds of some young people inhibit their success at school. Experts have identified a number of **risk factors,** or characteristics of learners who do not perform well at school.

These include:

- Living with only one parent,
- Being a child of a single parent,
- Having parents who failed to complete high school,
- Living in a low-income household,
- Living in high-growth states,
- Having poorly developed academic skills (not necessarily low intelligence),
- Having low self-esteem, and
- Speaking English as a second language. (Druian & Butler, 2001)

Recent research reveals that schools that well serve at-risk learners have important characteristics associated with (1) school leadership, (2) **school climate** (i.e., the general school atmosphere within which instruction, learning, and person-to-person interactions occur), and (3) classroom instructional and management practices (Druian & Butler, 2001). Principals in these schools work to focus the entire school on the importance of providing high-quality instructional services to *all* learners. The climate features an expectation that all enrolled young people will learn; a safe, orderly environment; and well-established and fairly administered rules that govern learners' conduct. Teachers use clear objectives to focus their instruction, deliver information using a variety of methods, and frequently monitor and evaluate learner progress toward mastery of the established objectives (Druian & Butler, 2001).

Learners' School-to-School Mobility

How probable is it that you will be teaching exactly the same learners at the end of the school year as at the beginning? Perhaps not as much as you might suppose. More than half of all learners make at least one school change (from one elementary school to another elementary school, from one middle school to another middle school, or from one high school to another high school) during their K–12 school years. From 15 to 18% of all school-age children move from one school to another during a given school year (Rumberger, 2002).

A surprisingly large number—30 to 40%—of these school-to-school moves are not caused by a change in residence by parents or guardians. Other reasons include:

- Overcrowding in a learner's previous school
- Legislation related to class-size reduction that may force a learner to change schools
- An expulsion policy that may require a learner to leave a former school
- Legislation that, under certain conditions, allows parents and guardians to move their child from one school to another (Rumberger, 2002)

Many studies report that learners who move from school to school more than three times do not perform as well academically and tend to have more behavior problems in school than less-frequent school changers (Rumberger, 2002). Young people who change schools frequently have lower rates of high school graduation than learners who change schools rarely or not at all.

As an educator, you have a general professional interest in promoting the development of individual learners by encouraging them to remain in school. As a classroom teacher, you must be prepared to deal with class rosters that will not remain stable throughout the school year. You must develop ways to smooth the transition of new learners into the general flow of your classroom activity. In addition to taking steps to introduce these young people to other class members and to otherwise make them welcome, you have to ascertain their levels of understanding of the topics and subjects you teach.

To the extent possible, you should try to learn about newcomers' past enrollment history. It will be especially useful to find out what these young people were studying in their previous school. In addition to checking records that may have come to your school from the learner's previous building, you may find it useful to conduct a personal interview with the learner and, if possible, with his or her parents or guardians. When you have gathered this background information, you may find it necessary to develop learning materials for this student that vary from those you are using with others in your class to provide information needed for success.

PATTERNS OF LEARNER DEVELOPMENT

Ideas about how children develop influence ideas about how they should be educated. To be responsible, you need to base your instructional procedures on up-to-date knowledge about human development, not on outdated views. As you think about this issue, you might be interested in knowing that some perspectives that were very much in vogue at one time seem bizarre to us today.

According to one early view, children were mindless creatures who were incapable of feeling or knowing anything. Interesting ideas about education flowed logically from this idea. For example, supporters of this view tended to dismiss proposals to spend money on early childhood education because they saw formal education for very young children as pointless. Adults' roles were limited to meeting children's physical needs and to keeping them out of mischief.

In the past, others saw children as essentially miniature adults. Aside from their small size, children were believed to have adult characteristics, lacking only knowledge and experience. If these could be provided, it was assumed that children would be able to discharge adult roles at a very early age. Learning materials designed for use by adults were seen as perfectly appropriate for children. If children failed to learn, this failure was attributed to their laziness. The tradition of punishing children for failing to learn comes out of this view of childhood.

Still another historical perspective maintained that children came into the world totally lacking any personalities of their own. They were simply animated clay or putty awaiting appropriate "modeling" by adults. There was an assumption that young people, when appropriately guided, would turn into good citizens. In the schools, this view resulted in educational practices that were planned and delivered exclusively by adults. Children's interests were considered to be of little importance.

Most of these views from history have not stood up well to the rigors of modern scholarship. Today, we know that each child has unique qualities and that these qualities affect how individual children react to school. Though teaching might be simpler if young people were so many "lumps of clay," that is just not how it is. As a professional educator, your success in large measure depends on your recognition of diversity as an expected feature of your workplace.

WEB EXTENSION 4–5

Society for the History of Children and Youth

The Society for the History of Children and Youth maintains this Web site. On this page, click on a link titled "H-Childhood." This will take you to a page titled "H-Childhood: History of Children and Youth." Here you will find a useful link to reviews of recent publications that focus on the history of children. You will also be able to access discussion logs that focus on topics dealing with historical perspectives on children and adolescents.

http://academic.mu.edu/shcy/

As you think about this reality, consider the physical characteristics of young people in a typical eighth-grade classroom. On a visit, you might be struck by the differences in the appearances of the young people. Some of them are small and immature; others are as large and as physically well-developed as juniors and seniors in high school. Some of the boys may even sport mustaches (much to the envy of their less physically mature classmates). Differences in learners' rates of physical development present problems related not only to their ability to perform physical tasks, but also to their psychological development.

Preschool and Kindergarten Learners

Preschool- and kindergarten-age children are extremely active. They have quite good control of their bodies, and they seem to enjoy activity for its own sake. Because of their frequent bursts of activity, these children need regular rest periods. When rest periods are not provided, they may become irritable. Emotional outbursts often result when overtired children in this age group encounter even minor frustrations.

At this age, children's large-muscle coordination is better developed than their small-muscle coordination. As a result, tasks that require small-muscle control can be frustrating.

WHAT DO
YOU THINK?

DENYING THE IMPORTANCE OF LEARNERS' INDIVIDUAL CHARACTERISTICS

Children have not always been viewed as we see them today. At some times in the past, they were believed to have no individual identities at all. When society held this view of young people, the teacher's job was assumed to be directed at molding young people in ways that would reproduce the abilities and attitudes of adults. In her novel *The Prime of Miss Jean Brodie* (Philadelphia: Lippincott, 1962), Muriel Spark describes a teacher who tried to do this and the unanticipated results of her approach. You might like to read this book.

WHAT DO YOU THINK?

1. Did you have teachers who were insensitive to individual differences of learners? How did people in your classes feel about these teachers?
2. In what ways did these teachers' approaches to teaching differ from those of teachers who seemed more sensitive to special needs of individual learners?
3. How effective were these insensitive teachers in transmitting information to learners in their classes?

 To respond to these questions online, go to the What Do You Think? *module for this chapter of the Companion Website.*

Many children in this group have trouble managing shoestrings, buttons, and other fine-motor tasks that older children find easy. Some children in this age group may not yet have fully developed eyes and eye muscles. They may experience difficulty in focusing on small objects and in completing tasks that require good hand–eye coordination.

Boys in this age group tend to be slightly larger in size than girls, but girls are more advanced by almost any other measure that is applied. This is particularly true in the area of fine-motor-skill development. At this age, girls tend to display much better coordination than boys.

If you teach this age group, you have to be patient and able to tolerate a lot of activity in the classroom. You must understand that there are certain things these children simply cannot do. Be prepared to spend time tying shoes, mopping up paint spills, and buttoning coats, and learn to do these things with a smile. Children need a lot of affection at this time of their lives.

Learners in Grades 1 to 3

The high need for physical activity that characterizes kindergarten children carries through the first year or two of the primary grades. The large muscles still tend to be more fully developed than the small muscles. This large-muscle development gives these children a tremendous confidence in their ability to accomplish certain physical tasks. Many youngsters in this age group develop more confidence in their physical abilities than is warranted. The accident rate among primary-grades children is very high.

The early primary grades are difficult for many young people. Large numbers of them have a high need for activity. This need persists at a time when school programs begin to expect more "in-seat" learning, a clear break from the almost nonstop activity routine of many kindergarten classrooms. When there is too much forced sitting, youngsters in this age group may develop nervous habits such as pencil chewing, fingernail biting, and general fidgeting. These behaviors represent attempts of the body to compensate for the lack of the physical activity that it needs.

Typically, handwriting is introduced during this period. Learning how to perform this task can be a trying experience for late-maturing children, who may still have very poor control over their small muscles. If you are teaching in the primary grades, you need to be very sensitive in your comments to children regarding their first efforts at cursive writing. If small-muscle development is inadequate, no amount of admonishment from you will lead to improved writing skills.

Children's eyes do not fully develop until they are about 8 years old. Hence, many children in the primary grades experience difficulty when asked to focus on small print or small objects. This situation has important implications because serious reading instruction ordinarily begins in Grade 1. You need to understand that difficulties experienced by some of your charges may be due to inadequate eye development. Some class members may not yet be able to maintain a focus on objects as small as printed words.

When teachers are sensitive to their needs, slow-developing children generally have little difficulty in catching up to their classmates as their physical development accelerates. However, if you are insensitive to differences in rates of individual development and attribute problems of physically slow-developing learners to laziness, these children may conclude that they cannot succeed. When learners develop this kind of self-image, they often stop trying. A pattern of failure established early in learners' education can follow them through their remaining years in school.

Primary-grades children have a high need for praise and recognition. They want to please the teacher and do well in school. When you give them positive recognition, they tend to blossom. A positive adjustment to school during these years often sets a pattern for success that persists as they continue their education.

Learners in Grades 4 to 6

In grades 4 to 6, most girls and a few boys experience a tremendous growth spurt. It is not uncommon for 11-year-old girls to be taller and heavier than 11-year-old boys. Many girls reach puberty during this period and, especially toward the end of this time, they tend to become very interested in boys. In contrast, many boys, even at the end of this period of their lives, have little interest in girls.

Friendships tend to divide along sex lines: Boys tend to associate with boys, and girls tend to associate with girls. There is considerable competition between boys and girls. Insults are a common feature of interactions between groups of boys and groups of girls.

Learners' fine-motor control is generally quite good by this time. Many of them develop an interest in applying their new abilities to "make their fingers do what they're supposed to do" by getting involved in crafts, model building, piano playing, and other activities demanding fine-muscle control.

Youngsters in grades 4 through 6 pose different challenges for teachers than primary-grade children. There is an especially acute need for you to pay attention to your role as motivator. You also must be prepared to deal with these learners' emerging sense of independence.

Many young people in this age group tend to be perfectionists. Frequently, they set unrealistically high standards for themselves. When they fail to perform up to these standards, they may suffer extreme feelings of guilt. You need to be sensitive to these feelings and devise ways of letting these children know that they are developing in a satisfactory way.

Many teachers of this age group derive great pleasure observing their students' increased sophistication. Learners' interests broaden tremendously during these years. Some of them become voracious readers, some develop a great deal of technical expertise about computers, and others develop a surprising depth of knowledge about a wide range of additional topics. At the same time, these children still retain an engaging air of innocence and trust. They tend to be extremely loyal to teachers they like.

However, misbehavior problems are more prevalent here than in the primary grades. At this time of life, young people increasingly begin to look to their **peer group** (individuals who are similar in age and interests) rather than to adults for guidance regarding what is appropriate behavior. This tendency may occasionally challenge you. For example, you may come to school one day and discover that the peer group has decreed that "reading is boring." Given this dictum, you will face a difficult challenge motivating class members during the reading period. You have to become an expert in group dynamics and a keen observer of individual friendships within your classroom. Armed with such insights, you can often act to prevent the peer group from taking a negative position on important academic issues.

You need a healthy dose of patience when working with this age group. These children often find some school assignments to be frustrating and difficult, and you need to provide them with positive support. Learners make many mistakes. You need to be sympathetic and allow students the freedom to make and learn from their errors. At the same time, you have to maintain a reasonable and firm set of expectations. In this kind of atmosphere, children can make tremendous personal strides during these years.

Learners in Grades 7 to 9

Many educators consider young people in grades 7 to 9 to be difficult to teach, and there is evidence that a certain kind of teacher is needed to be successful. If you work with this age group, one of your challenges is to respond appropriately to these learners' incredible diversity. You will encounter variations in their maturity levels and often great day-to-day differences in the patterns of behavior of a single student. A particular eighth grader at one moment may be the very image of sophistication and at the next display a pattern of behavior that differs little from that of a fourth grader. Learners at this time of their lives swing crazily back and forth between adult and very childish behavior.

During these years, most girls complete their growth spurt. For boys, growth may continue to the end of this age range or even later. Nearly all individuals of both sexes attain puberty by the end of this period, and these young people often worry about the physical and psychological changes they are experiencing. Many wonder whether they are developing properly. Some young people become extremely self-conscious during this time of their lives, sometimes feeling as though their every action is being observed and evaluated. For many young people, their middle school/junior high school years are a highly uncomfortable time.

If you work with this age group, your prospects for success will increase if you are sensitive to the psychological changes that these young people are experiencing. You need to develop some tolerance for these students' occasionally loud, emotional outbursts. The range of development reflected among individual learners is huge, and developmental changes often are stressful. Indeed, this is the least stable period in a young person's life. In general, you need to be flexible and to develop the ability to respond appropriately to the sometimes wildly varying emotional, intellectual, and behavioral patterns you will observe in your classroom. If you are a person who likes variety and who can cope eagerly with young people whose day-to-day behaviors may be unpredictable,

© 1996 Randy Glasbergen.
www.glasbergen.com

**"At your age, Tommy, a boy's body goes through
changes that are not always easy to understand."**

you may be among the middle school teachers who find work with these youngsters to
be satisfying and stimulating (Henson, 2004). Teachers with these traits come to school
looking forward to new, unexpected adventures every day that they teach.

WEB EXTENSION 4–6

National Middle School Association

The National Middle School Association (NMSA) is the nation's leading professional association for educators and others who are interested in promoting high-quality educational
services for young adolescents. Click on the link labeled "Services/Resources." You will be
taken to a list of links that include (1) the home page of *Middle School Journal*, NMSA's official publication; (2) information related to school curricula for early adolescents; and (3) an
extensive listing of additional Web links to sites featuring information related to working with
early adolescents.

http://www.nmsa.org/

Learners in Grades 10 to 12

One important issue for young people during their high school years is their search for
personal identity (Erikson, 1982). They are trying to find personal selves that are distinct
from those of their parents. They ask themselves questions such as "Who am I?" "Will I
be successful?" and "Will I be accepted?" In their attempts to establish their personal
identities, these students often experiment with behaviors that they believe will show
the world that they are independent. They seek to become rulers of their environment.
At the same time, they desperately look for evidence that others are accepting them as
individuals.

David Elkind (1981), a leading developmental-learning theorist, suggests that young people may experience problems as they begin to develop the ability to engage in thinking processes involving abstract reasoning. With their newfound ability to think in more-sophisticated ways, a number of adolescents concern themselves with abstract notions of self and personal identity. It may be that some adolescents who have developed the ability to view their own identity as an abstract idea are unable to distinguish between what they think about themselves and what others think about them. Elkind proposes that this view sometimes takes the form of either (1) an **imaginary audience** or (2) a **personal fable.**

Adolescent behavior in response to an *imaginary audience* results when adolescents fail to distinguish between their own thoughts about themselves and those others hold. When this happens, they tend to view themselves as perpetually "on stage." They are certain that everybody is carefully scrutinizing their every move. The imaginary-audience concept explains much about the behavior of young people in this age group. Shyness, for example, is a logical result of their feeling that any mistake made in public will be noticed and criticized. The slavish attention to fashion trends results from an expectation that deviations from the expected norm will be noticed and commented on negatively.

In explaining the *personal fable,* Elkind (1981) notes that adolescents often become disoriented by the many physical and emotional changes they experience. At the same time, many of them find these changes to be utterly fascinating. Some of them believe that their new feelings are so unusual that no one else has ever experienced them before, especially not parents or teachers. They may believe that they are living out a one-of-a-kind life

Learners in grades 10–12 are often dealing with many issues in their lives and the challenge for teachers is to keep them focused on academic tasks.

story. Sometimes they keep diaries that are written out of a conviction that future generations will be intensely interested in their unique feelings and experiences.

As students in this age group have more and more life experiences, they test the validity of the imaginary audience and the personal fable against reality. In time, the imaginary audience gives way to the real audience, and the personal fable is adjusted as young people's interactions with others reveal that many others have experienced similar feelings and have had similar opinions.

If you teach in a high school, you will find that your students are capable of quite abstract thinking. At the same time, you will notice that young people in your classes have characteristics that separate them from college and university students and from older adult learners. For example, you are likely to observe that some students have emotional needs that require your attention. You need to strike a balance between your concern for students' psychological development and your commitment to provide them with a respectable grounding in the academic subject(s) you teach.

The task of motivating this group of learners has become increasingly challenging. Since 1983, the percentage of 12th graders who consider their schoolwork as meaningful has decreased from 40 percent to 21 percent (Scherer, 2002). One third of 12th graders skip at least one day of class each week. Although most American high school students do not give school their best efforts, a Public Agenda poll reported that 8 in 10 students are upbeat about their education (Public Agenda Online, 2002). This information suggests that you will find it helpful to learn individual interests of your students and use this information to prepare lessons that, to the extent possible, build on existing student enthusiasms.

DEVELOPING A SENSE OF EFFICACY

In this chapter, you have learned about a selection of learner characteristics. Though you need to be aware of these differences, you also should keep in mind that you will find some commonalities among the young people you teach. For example, all learners want to feel good about themselves. They want to believe that they are worthy human beings as well as capable learners. You want to help them develop a **sense of efficacy,** a belief that their existence "matters" and that they are capable of making important contributions to their world.

In your effort to promote feelings of worth and competence, you also need to think about your own professional sense of efficacy. As you continue professional preparation, you need to reflect on the actions you want to take to promote learners' development. Questions such as the following may help you think about your present strengths and weaknesses and about actions you might take to give you confidence and competence as you begin your career in the classroom:

- What are the special characteristics of learners I expect to teach?
- Which of these characteristics am I prepared to respond to in ways that will enhance students' personal growth and their mastery of important academic content?
- Is my knowledge of instructional approaches broad enough for me to respond to the needs of the learners I expect to teach? If not, how can I fill in any gaps?
- What is my level of comfort with day-to-day differences in learners' patterns of behavior? Are my ideas on this issue fixed? If so, what does this information tell me about the kinds of learners I would be best suited to teach?

Critical Incident

Should Ms. Stearns Take Advantage of Her Special Knowledge?

Laura Stearns is in her mid-50s. She has been an enthusiastic eighth-grade mathematics teacher at Drake Middle School (formerly Drake Junior High School) for 30 years. She is a high-spirited professional who looks forward to going to work each day. She tells her friends that she "gets pumped up" by her contact with the 13-year-olds who bounce and shove their way into her classroom each period of the day.

Laura has always taken a sincere personal interest in her students. She feels that her own experience in raising her two children (now both adults, college graduates, and working in other cities) helps her to empathize with what young people go through during the difficult middle/junior high school years. She is not at all pleased by one problem that has become increasingly serious at her school. With each passing year, more and more of the girls are getting pregnant.

In her role as sponsor of the pep club, Laura overhears lots of casual student conversations. Students also tend to confide in her. She has commented to her friends that "parents of my kids would blush if they knew what their kids tell me about what goes on at home." Recently, Laura learned that Beth McFarland, one of her outstanding math students, has been getting a lot of attention from a boy who is a junior in high school. Beth talks about the boy constantly and gives other evidence of having developed a very strong emotional attachment to him. Laura suspects that an intimate physical relationship is about to develop. She hopes that it has not yet happened.

Beth comes from a family with strong middle-class values. Both parents are deeply committed to their church. In Laura's view, neither parent has any idea about the kinds of social pressures that students in present-day middle schools face. Their view of the world is very much the one that was depicted on the old "Brady Bunch" television program.

Laura is quite certain that any talks Beth has had with her parents about sex have been highly circumspect. She is positive that Beth's mother would be incredulous at the suggestion that her daughter might be about to engage in an intimate physical relationship with a high school boy.

As a professional educator, Laura Stearns is outraged at the waste of human capital that results when young girls get pregnant and, sometimes, end up quitting school. As a parent, she senses the pain that might come to Beth's parents should she become pregnant. And, as a realist, Laura recognizes that, despite these negative consequences, pregnancy (or even AIDS) looms as a real possibility for Beth unless something is done *now*.

• • •

What is Laura's view of the problem? What past experiences might have shaped her attitudes? In what ways might her view of Beth's likely future behavior differ from the view of Beth's parents? What might account for any differences in the ways Laura and Beth's parents might see the present situation playing itself out? What should Laura do? Should she talk to Beth's parents? If she does, will they believe her? Will they think her comments an unconscionable intrusion on the family's privacy? Should she take it upon herself to provide birth control information to Beth? Should she counsel Beth about the need to avoid a physical relationship? Should she involve the school counseling staff? Should other teachers or administrators be brought into the picture? What kinds of actions can be taken that will resolve the problem and still maintain confidentiality? What do you think the most probable result will be?

To respond to this Critical Incident online, go to the Critical Incidents *module for this chapter of the Companion Website.*

Key Ideas in Summary

- Learners in today's schools are diverse. Abilities, attitudes, and perspectives characterizing our entire national population are represented in school classrooms. Though these difference are important, you will also find that young people from varying backgrounds share certain common characteristics.

- Families of typical learners by no means match the traditional family stereotype of an employed father, a mother who stayed at home, and two children. A single parent or guardian, often a female, now heads many families. Because so many parents and guardians work, many more children today spend much of their out-of-school time in day care centers or with babysitters. Learners' parents and guardians are more likely to be involved with their children's school if (1) they have attained high levels of education, (2) they have higher incomes, and (3) they have children in elementary schools, as compared with middle or high schools.

- Large numbers of schoolchildren come from families with annual incomes below the federal poverty level. The poverty rate among schoolchildren's families in the United States is higher than that in other developed nations. More African American and Latino children come from poor families than do white children. Children from economically impoverished homes often do not perform well in school.

- With each passing year, minority-group children comprise a larger percentage of the total school population. African American and Latino children represent the largest minority groups in the schools. The makeup of the minority population of schools varies greatly from state to state and from school district to school district within individual states.

- Though violence in schools is an important problem, you need to keep in mind that learners are almost twice as likely to be victims of serious crimes at sites away from their school. The kind of violence a given learner is most likely to experience in school is involvement in a physical fight without a weapon. Middle school and high school learners are more likely to be the victims of violence at school than are elementary school learners. Serious crimes against learners are more common in schools with extremely large enrollments.

- Over the past quarter century, there has been a great increase in the numbers of 3- and 4-year-olds enrolled in school programs. In part, this trend has been spurred by the tendency for more and more mothers to hold down full-time jobs outside the home. There also have been concerns about the quality and the expense of programs offered by private day care facilities. Today, about 40% of our nation's 3-year-olds and about 65% of our nation's 4-year-olds are enrolled in formal educational programs.

- About 13% of learners in the schools are eligible for programs directed toward the disabled. These learners have widely varied characteristics. In regular classes you teach, you are most likely to encounter learners classified as having "specific learning disabilities." Other large groups within this population are the speech-impaired and mentally-retarded learners.

- Every state has laws requiring teachers to file reports with the appropriate authorities when they observe injuries to children that appear to be non-accidental. Episodes of child abuse appear to be on the increase. Among categories of abuse are (1) physical abuse, (2) neglect, (3) emotional abuse, and (4) sexual abuse. Teachers are expected to know behavioral indicators of possible abuse.

- Many individuals who do not perform well at school have certain characteristics that place them *at risk*. Individual characteristics that often interfere with learners' adjustment to and success at school include (1) living with only one parent, (2) being a child of a single parent, (3) having parents who dropped out of high school, (4) living in a low-income household, (5) living in a high-growth state, (6) having poorly developed basic skills (but not necessarily low intelligence), (7) having low self-esteem, and (8) speaking English as a second language.

- Over half of all learners make at least one elementary–to–elementary, middle school–to–middle school, or high school–to–high school change during their K–12 school years. In any one year, 15% to 18% of school-age children change schools. There is evidence that learners who make three or more school changes do not do as well in school as learners making fewer school changes. Today, educators are working to develop ways to smooth the transition of school changers to their new schools.

- Children's general characteristics vary enormously as they progress through the school program. For example, preschool and kindergarten children tend to require high levels of physical activity. Learners in grades 1 to 3 still have underdeveloped fine-motor control, and they are often frustrated by tasks requiring them to manipulate small objects and do detailed work with their hands. In grades 4 to 6, girls are often physically larger than boys. For the most part, friendships among learners in these grade levels do not cross sex lines. There are tremendous differences in the physical development of individual learners in grades 7 to 9. These differences sometimes cause great personal anxieties on the part of these young people. During grades 10 to 12, many students are engaged in a search for personal identity. By this time in their development, many young people are able to deal with quite-abstract levels of thinking.

- As a teacher, you will confront learners who have widely varying personal characteristics. One of your purposes is to help each learner you serve develop a *sense of efficacy*, a feeling that he or she is a worthy and capable human being. As an instructional leader, you also need to think about your own sense of efficacy. In pursuit of this purpose you should reflect on the kinds of expertise you need to help learners you teach, sources of information that may help you, and specific actions you can take to acquire the knowledge you will need to operate as a secure, confident, and competent professional.

Chapter 4 Self-Test

To review terms and concepts in this chapter, go to the Companion Website and take the Chapter 4 Self-Test. *Feedback for the self-test is immediate. You can keep track of your self-test scores yourself, or you can submit your scores to your instructor via e-mail.*

Preparing for Praxis

To learn more about the Praxis test and complete this activity online, go to the Preparing for Praxis *module for this chapter of the Companion Website.*

You may be required to pass Educational Testing Service's Praxis II exam as you seek formal authorization to teach in the public schools. The *Principles of Learning and Teaching* component of Praxis II seeks to assess your knowledge about these topics: (1) Students as Learners, (2) Instruction and Assessment, (3) Communication Techniques, and (4) Profession and Community.

Information presented in this chapter may be especially relevant as you prepare for questions related to the category of Students as Learners. Some content may also deal with issues having logical ties to other Praxis II categories. You may find it useful to prepare a chart similar to the one provided here. As you encounter information related to individual categories, you can enter it into the chart. A completed chart of this kind will be useful as you begin reviewing what you have learned in preparation for taking the Praxis II exam.

Students as Learners	Instruction and Assessment
• Student Development and the Learning Process	• Instructional Strategies
• Students as Diverse Learners	• Planning Instruction
• Student Motivation and the Learning Environment	• Assessment Strategies
Communication Techniques	**Profession and Community**
• Basic, Effective, Verbal and Nonverbal Communication Techniques	• The Reflective Practitioner
• Effect of Cultural and Gender Differences on Communications in the Classroom	• The Larger Community
• Types of Questions That Can Stimulate Discussion in Different Ways for Particular Purposes	

For Your Initial-Development Portfolio

 To complete this activity and submit your response online, go to the For Your Initial-Development Portfolio *module for this chapter of the Companion Website.*

1. What materials and ideas that you learned in this chapter about *profiles of today's learners* will you include as "evidence" in your portfolio? Select up to three separate items of information. Number them 1, 2, and 3.
2. Think about why you selected these materials. As you do so, consider these issues:
   • Specific uses you might make of this information as you plan, deliver, and assess the impact of your teaching
   • The compatibility of the information with your own priorities and values
   • Any contributions this information can make to your development as a teacher
   • Factors that led you to include this information, as opposed to some alternatives you considered but rejected
3. Place a check in the chart here to indicate the INTASC standard(s) to which each item of information relates. (You may wish to refer to Chapter 1 for more-detailed information about INTASC.)

INTASC Standard Number

ITEM OF EVIDENCE NUMBER	S1	S2	S3	S4	S5	S6	S7	S8	S9	S10
1										
2										
3										

4. Prepare a written reflection in which you analyze the decision-making process you followed. In your comments, mention the INTASC standard(s) to which your selected material relates.

Reflections

To respond to these questions online, go to the Reflections *module for this chapter of the* Companion Website.

1. What are some popular ideas about what young people consider to be important? What are your own views? How do the opinions of others and those you hold square with studies that have been made of their attitudes? How do you account for any discrepancies?

2. You will find that large numbers of your learners' parents and guardians hold down full-time jobs, so many of the young people you teach may spend a considerable amount of each day in day care centers. As a result of heavy work obligations, some of your parents and guardians may not have spent adequate time teaching their children about "appropriate" patterns of behavior. To what extent should you feel obligated to deal with this situation by spending time in your classes teaching basic social skills and acceptable behavior patterns to your students? How would you allocate time between this kind of teaching and the teaching of traditional academic content?

3. For the past quarter century, there has been an increase in the percentage of Americans under the age of 18 who live in poverty. What are your speculations regarding why this trend has developed? Based on your own understanding of present social trends, do you expect the poverty rate among children and young people to increase or decrease over the next decade? Why?

4. Review the general characteristics of learners in different grades. Did any of these descriptions surprise you? If so, which ones, and why? As you assess your own personality, which grade levels now most appeal to you as you think about your future as a classroom teacher? What led you to select your preferred group?

5. One of your major tasks as a teacher will be to promote a strong *sense of efficacy* in each of the young people you teach. You also need to develop your own professional sense of efficacy. As you assess your present level of development, how do you see your strengths and weaknesses? Specifically, what are some things you can do to turn these weaknesses into strengths and gain the confidence and competence you will need when you begin your teaching career?

Field Experiences, Projects, and Enrichment

1. Interview two or more teachers at a grade level you would like to teach (and in your subject area(s) if you are interested in secondary-school teaching). Ask them to comment about the family life of learners in their classroom. In particular, seek information about economic status, family values, and the extent to which there is support in the home for what learners are expected to do at school. Also, inquire about problems associated with helping learners who transfer into the class in the middle of the school year. Share your findings with others in your class as part of a general discussion on the nature of learners in the schools.

2. Invite a school administrator to visit your class to speak about issues associated with (1) school violence and (2) abused and neglected children. Ask this person to comment on the frequency of problems. Inquire also about school-district regulations and applicable laws that require educators to take specific actions when problems occur.

3. Use a search engine such as Google (http://www.google.com) and resources in your library to identify articles that describe school programs that have proved to be particularly effective in helping learners from minority groups achieve academic success. Prepare short synopses of four or five of these articles, and share this information with others in your class.

4. Invite a panel of three to five middle school and junior high school teachers to visit your class. Ask them to comment on some special challenges of working with learners in this age group and to identify aspects of working with these learners that they find particularly satisfying.

5. Interview a counselor who works in a school that serves the age group you hope to teach. Ask the counselor to describe issues that contribute to self-image problems of some of the young people in this school. Inquire about specific actions teachers can take to help these individuals develop a positive *sense of efficacy*. Share your findings with others in your class.

References

Carskadon, M. A. (1999). When worlds collide: Adolescent need for sleep versus societal demands. *Phi Delta Kappan, 80*(5), 348–353.

Childabuse.com. (2001). *Child abuse statistics*. [http://www.childabuse.com/newsletter/stat0301.htm]

DeVoe, J. F., Peter, K., Kaufman, P., Ruddy, S. A., Miller, A. K., Planty, M., Snyder, T. D., Duhart, D. T., & Rand, M. R. (2002). *Indicators of school crime and safety*. Washington, DC: U.S. Departments of Education and Justice.

Doorey, N., & Harter, B. (2003). From court order to community commitment. *Educational Leadership, 60*(4), 22–25.

Druian, G., & Butler, J. A. (2001). *Effective schooling practices and at-risk youth: What the research shows* (School Improvement Research Series). Portland, OR: Northwest Regional Educational Laboratory.

Elkind, D. (1981). *Children and adolescents: Interpretive essays on Jean Piaget* (3rd ed.). New York: Oxford University Press.

Erikson, E. H. (1982). *The life cycle completed: A review*. New York: Norton.

Futrell, M., Gomez, J., & Bedden, D. (2003). Teaching the children of a new America: The challenge of diversity. *Phi Delta Kappan, 84*(5), 381–385.

Henson, K. T. (2004). *Constructivist methods for teaching in diverse middle level classrooms*. Boston: Allyn & Bacon.

How can we prevent violence in our schools? (2000). Educational Resources Information Center (Parent Brochure). [http://www.eric.ed.gov/resources/parent/prevent. html]

National Center for Education Statistics. (2001). *The condition of education 2001*. Washington, DC: Author.

National Center for Education Statistics. (2002a). *The condition of education 2002*. Washington, DC: Author.

National Center for Education Statistics. (2002b). *Digest of education statistics 2001*. Washington, DC: Author.

Naylor, C. (1999). How does working part-time influence secondary students' achievement and impact on their overall well-being? *BCTF Research Report*. [http://www.bctf.ca/ResearchReports/99ei02/report.html]

Public Agenda Online. (2002). Available at [http://www.publicagenda.org/issues]

Rumberger, R. W. (2002, June). *Student mobility and academic achievement*. Urbana-Champaign, IL: ERIC/EECE Publications—Digests. [http://ericeece.org/pubs/digests/2002/rumberger02.html]

Scherer, M. (2002). Perspectives: Who cares? And who wants to know? *Educational Leadership, 60*(1), 5.

Thomas, M. D., & Bainbridge, W. L. (2002). No child left behind: Facts and fallacies. *Phi Delta Kappan, 84*(5), 781–782.

U.S. Census Bureau. (2001, June). *America's families and living arrangements*. Washington, DC: Author.

U.S. Department of Health and Human Services. (2001). *Highlights—2001 National household survey on drug abuse (MHSDA)*. Washington, DC: Author.

Responding to Diversity

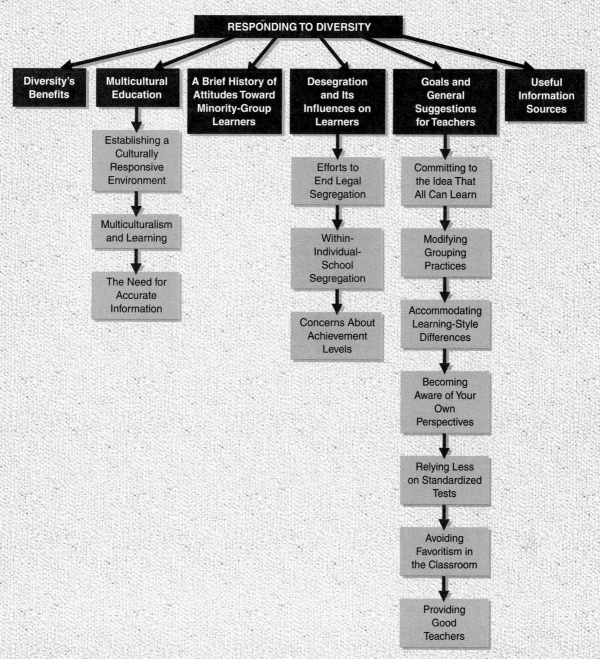

RESPONDING TO DIVERSITY

- Diversity's Benefits
- Multicultural Education
  - Establishing a Culturally Responsive Environment
  - Multiculturalism and Learning
  - The Need for Accurate Information
- A Brief History of Attitudes Toward Minority-Group Learners
- Desegration and Its Influences on Learners
  - Efforts to End Legal Segregation
  - Within-Individual-School Segregation
  - Concerns About Achievement Levels
- Goals and General Suggestions for Teachers
  - Committing to the Idea That All Can Learn
  - Modifying Grouping Practices
  - Accommodating Learning-Style Differences
  - Becoming Aware of Your Own Perspectives
  - Relying Less on Standardized Tests
  - Avoiding Favoritism in the Classroom
  - Providing Good Teachers
- Useful Information Sources

OBJECTIVES

This chapter will help you to

- identify a rationale for paying particular attention to school experiences of minority-group and female learners.
- recognize the changing demographic characteristics of school learners and describe some implications of these differences for what you do in the classroom.
- point out examples of within-individual-school segregation patterns that have persisted despite attempts to eliminate them.

- describe how some school programs have used race, ethnicity, and gender as criteria for determining which educational experiences to provide to certain categories of learners.
- recognize the growing disparity between demographic characteristics of teachers and learners.
- identify sources of materials and programs that will help you better understand multicultural and gender-equity issues.

DIVERSITY'S BENEFITS

Do you find variety to be an energizing force? Do you enjoy meeting people whose perspectives and backgrounds differ from your own? If so, you will find that the makeup of the school learner population fits well with your preferences. In today's classrooms, you will encounter young people from incredibly varied social, cultural, and ethnic backgrounds. The learner population is even more diverse than the general population.

For over a century, our country has sought to make public education available to nearly all young people. Now you can count on having learners in your classes who represent a mix of genders; racial and ethnic backgrounds; religious preferences; home-language backgrounds; economic-status levels; motivational levels; and physical, emotional, and intellectual conditions.

For many years, multicultural, multilingual immigrants have comprised a substantial portion of our total population. In the past, newcomers to our country were expected to abandon languages other than English and give up many other aspects of the cultures they brought with them from foreign lands. The expectation was that American culture would function as a "melting pot" that, over time, would erase traces of immigrants' former cultures. This expectation never was realized. Imported cultural influences and traditions continue to influence the thinking and behavioral patterns of newcomers and their descendants, even after many years of residency in the United States.

WEB EXTENSION 5–1

National Clearinghouse for English Language Acquisition and Language Instruction Educational Programs

The National Clearinghouse for English Language Acquisition and Language Instruction Educational Programs maintains this site. You will find much information you can use in planning instruction for learners who are not native speakers of English. The site also provides links to other relevant information sources.

http://www.ncela.gwu.edu/

Today, it is more accurate to describe our society as a "mosaic" rather than as a unitary culture brought about because of the action of an American melting pot. Members of our society take pride in their identities as members of certain racial, ethnic, economic, social, or religious groups. Individuals' group affiliations help them define their identities as human beings.

If you acknowledge the wisdom of learning about others with different backgrounds and welcome these differences as legitimate parts of our diverse national family, you have attitudes that are consistent with present social realities. You may not be aware that our country currently is experiencing one of the highest rates of immigration in its history (Garcia, 2002). Today, approximately 1 of every 13 people residing in the United States is foreign born, as compared with of 1 of 20 in 1950. Immigrants' countries of origin are somewhat different than the countries that supplied large numbers of immigrants in the past. In one recent year, most newcomers to the United States came from Mexico. The next four largest home countries were the Philippines, China, Vietnam, and India (Garcia, 2002).

To take advantage of the potential that diversity offers, you need to establish a general classroom atmosphere and an instructional program that encourage young people to see diversity in your class (and in our society) as a positive characteristic. For example, if you encourage young people to reach out to others who differ from themselves, you will have class members who may come to appreciate the abilities of your special-needs learners. Others may be rewarded and enriched by helping some of their classmates who are not native speakers of English become more proficient. Your efforts to maximize each learner's potential will have implications for issues that go beyond ethnic, cultural, social, and economic characteristics.

You also must think carefully about the issue of gender, particularly as applied to female learners. Today's adult females are as likely to be employed as adult males. For this reason, you must recognize that both females and males deserve the best possible educational experiences. All young people need rigorous preparation for the world they will enter as adults (Clinchy, 1993). Female learners have not always had the same educational opportunities as those provided to males.

Today's school programs recognize that human capital is a precious resource. You need to work hard to develop the talents of females, individuals with disabilities, members of ethnic and cultural minorities, and learners from other groups. When you succeed, our society benefits as young people leave school as confident, competent young adults who are prepared to assume positions of responsibility and leadership.

VIDEO VIEWPOINTS

How Do We Achieve Diversity?

WATCH: This Good Morning America video segment focuses on the University of Michigan's point system for achieving diversity. The segment includes arguments about the importance of diversity in education and, if it is important, how to achieve it. Although the video segment is directed toward higher education (specifically, the law school), the issue has implications for all levels of education.

THINK: Discuss with your classmates, or in your teaching journal, the following questions:

1. Do you agree with the basic premise that diversity in education is inherently important?
2. If a well-rounded education should include individuals from a variety of backgrounds, how can this be done in K–12 schools?
3. What do you see as the elements of a fair policy for achieving diversity in education?

LINK: How does this issue of giving credit to diversity candidates relate to other issues, such as equal educational opportunities for all students?

 Complete this activity and submit your responses online in the Video Viewpoints *module for this chapter of the* Companion Website.

MULTICULTURAL EDUCATION

Authorities on multicultural education often point out that the term means different things to different people (Gay, 1994; Gorski, 2000). For example, Geneva Gay identified as many as 13 independent definitions of the term *multicultural education* that appeared frequently in professional writings. Multicultural-education specialists James A. Banks and Cherry A. McGee Banks (2001) propose a definition that embraces many elements found in different descriptions of the term. In their view, multicultural education is education that promotes educational equity for all learners.

Establishing a Culturally Responsive Environment

In working with learners from diverse backgrounds, you will find it useful to establish a **culturally responsive environment** in your classroom. A culturally responsive environment is one that is comfortable for learners and their teacher and that enables learners to make acceptable academic progress. In culturally responsive environments, all students have similar opportunities to learn (Powell, McLaughlin, Savage, & Zehm, 2001). In these environments you will find

- An openness and sensitivity to learners' knowledge, experience, values, and tastes
- Alteration of instruction and selection of alternative texts, novels, and other reading materials that meet learners' academic needs
- Alternative discussion formats that encourage learner engagement and accept students' native discourse patterns
- Acknowledgement of the legitimacy of the cultural heritages of different ethnic groups
- Development of ethnic and cultural pride. (Brown, 2002)

Here are some statistics that may help you understand the importance of establishing a culturally responsive environment in your own classroom:

- About 1,000 learners from foreign countries enter our schools for the first time every day (Preissle & Rong, 1998).
- Nearly one-fifth of Americans live in households in which a language other than English is spoken (Garcia, 2002).
- Increased stratification of society has led to a social environment in which new immigrants are more, not less likely to live in environments that are segregated from whites (Garcia, 2002).
- Projections for 2026 indicate that the learner population will be approximately 70% Latino and nonwhite (Garcia, 2002).

These statistics suggest that in the decades ahead it will be virtually impossible for public- or private-school educators to teach in classrooms that are not culturally and ethnically varied. You need to adopt a view of education that assumes a diverse body of learners as a "given." You will find it especially helpful to study the special characteristics and backgrounds of your students. By aligning your reactions and instructional practices to this information, you will increase the chances that your interactions with class members will be positive and productive (Nieto, 1999).

WEB EXTENSION 5–2

Fostering Intercultural Harmony in Schools: Research Finding

The Northwest Regional Educational Laboratory, as part of ERIC's School Improvement Research Series, maintains this site. As the title suggests, you will find research-based information related to practices that have been found to be effective in promoting racial harmony in schools.

http://www.nwrel.org/scpd/sirs/8/topsyn7.html

Today's schools enroll young people from diverse racial and cultural groups.

Multiculturalism and Learning

What is the impact of culture on learning? Many educators fail to appreciate that the way they teach reflects the influence of their own cultural groups (Wlodkowski & Ginsberg, 1995). Think about your own situation. As you matured, you developed certain expectations about learning that are based on your own experiences. For example, you now may have particular assumptions related to how learners should participate in the classroom and define their personal success. You probably also have specific ideas about what motivates young people and how they should interact with others.

People growing up in different cultures often have different views regarding the kinds of behaviors that are right or suitable. Teachers sometimes experience difficulty when their expectations of learners differ from patterns of behaviors that some class members have learned at home. When these inconsistencies exist, some students may find themselves torn between two sets of authority figures. On the one hand, they know they should do what you want because you are their teacher. On the other hand, they have been taught to value worldviews they have acquired as part of their family and cultural communities.

The disconnect between teachers' perspectives and the perspectives of many of their learners is becoming more serious. While the vast majority of teachers continue to be drawn from the white middle class, students in the nation's classrooms reflect more racial, ethnic, and linguistic diversity with each passing year. For example, in the 1999–2000 school year, over 86% of the public- and private-school teachers and administrators were white. However, projections indicate that by 2026 the nonwhite, Latino enrollment in grades K–12 will rise to 70% (Garcia, 2002).

Exposure to inconsistencies between their teachers' cultural backgrounds and their own often causes significant problems for many learners from minority groups when they come to school. The resultant anxieties can often interfere with their learning. In response to this situation, you need to be proactive in your efforts to become familiar with the special worldview that each student brings to the classroom. This knowledge will enable you to modify your practices in ways that do not send inconsistent messages to these learners. You can develop and deliver a culturally responsive instructional program that will enable all your students to succeed.

The Need for Accurate Information

To plan instruction that responds appropriately to the needs of all class members, you need accurate information about their individual backgrounds. If you have an inadequate grasp of this kind of information, your teaching approaches may fail because they rest on faulty assumptions. For example, a teacher who believes that boys are "just naturally" not good at reading and writing may hold male learners to lower standards of performance than female learners on tasks requiring them to read and write. Assumptions that certain kinds of learners have innate inadequacies can have serious negative influences on what these young people take away from their experiences at school.

You will be well served if you take time to study your class members *as individuals* and avoid making assumptions about what they can and cannot do based on their membership in a particular group. This approach properly recognizes that there are enormous differences among people within groups. For example, values and perspectives of African Americans in rural areas often have little in common with those of African Americans in the nation's inner cities. There is by no means a common worldview that characterizes all urban African Americans or one that is common to all rural African Americans.

Today, educators strive to ensure that opportunities in all subject areas are available to male and female learners alike. As this photo shows, some subjects, such as woodworking, were in the past considered to be "male;" others such as sewing and baking, were considered to be "female."

The nation's Latino population is extremely diverse. Some critics charge that there has been a tendency for school authorities to view all Latinos as linguistically at risk and to treat them as "culturally deficient and linguistically deprived foreigners" (Grant, 1990, p. 27). "This treatment helps to explain their high dropout rate, their underrepresentation in advanced courses, and their low rate of college attendance." Carl Grant also points out that only a minority of Latino learners have a first language other than English. Clearly, school programs that presume that all Latinos are nonnative speakers of English do them an injustice.

Developing school programs that reflect a genuine appreciation for issues associated with multicultural and gender equity requires you to be well informed. Your need to develop sensitivity to the special perspectives of the groups from which your learners come will increase as the nation's school population becomes more diverse.

A BRIEF HISTORY OF ATTITUDES TOWARD MINORITY-GROUP LEARNERS

Educators have long been aware that large numbers of learners from minority groups have not done well in school. An early explanation for this phenomenon was the **genetic-deficit view** (Armstrong & Savage, 2002). People who subscribed to this position believed that minority-group learners lacked the necessary intellectual tools to succeed in school. Individuals who accepted this premise were reluctant to divert school resources to improve instructional programs for children who, they believed, could not benefit from them.

By the 1960s, the genetic deficit position had given way to a **cultural-deficit view** (Erickson, 1987). Those who subscribed to this argument contended that poor school performance could be blamed on the failure of minority-group children's parents to provide an intellectually stimulating home atmosphere that prepared the learners for the expectations of the school. The cultural-deficit view seemed to allow schools a way out when confronted with statistics revealing high dropout rates and other evidence of mediocre levels of school performance on the part of minority-group learners because it placed blame on learners' homes rather than on the school.

Another explanation for schools' failure to adequately serve the needs of minority-group learners was the **communication-process position** (Erickson, 1987). According to this view, language patterns of minority-group learners differ substantially from those of their teachers and majority-group learners; hence, they are not capable of understanding much of classroom instruction. This communication failure accounts for their poor academic performance. This position has been attacked for failing to explain why some minority-group learners do extremely well in school.

In recent years, professional educators have downplayed explanations for difficulties of minority-group learners that shift the blame away from the schools. Increasingly, they argue that school programs too often have failed to plan seriously for the success of all learners (even though educators' rhetoric has espoused this intent for years). Because of this failure, many minority-group students and their parents have questioned whether school programs truly have been promoting the development of each child.

Today, working to establish programs that truly reflect the principle that "all students can learn" has become a hallmark of education-reform proposals (Henson, 2001). This commitment is reflected in the results of a survey that found that three-fourths of Americans think the schools should promote both a common cultural tradition and the diverse individual traditions of the nation's different population groups (Elam, Rose, & Gallup, 1994). This finding is consistent with the view that multicultural education should seek a unity that is enriched by diversity (Banks, 1995). As a teacher, your efforts to help all to learn are especially likely to bear fruit when your actions reflect an understanding that human culture is the product of the struggles of all humanity, not the possession of a single racial or ethnic group (Hilliard, 1991/1992).

WEB EXTENSION 5–3

Educating Teachers for Diversity

If you are looking for an excellent overview of issues related to preparing teachers to respond to diversity in their classrooms, this is a site you should visit. In addition to general information about this important topic, you will find a lengthy list of organizations that you can contact for further assistance. Postal addresses, telephone numbers, and Web addresses are included.

http://www.ncrel.org/sdrs/areas/issues/educatrs/presrvce/pe300.htm

DESEGREGATION AND ITS INFLUENCES ON LEARNERS

For many years, educators found it difficult to promote the development of intercultural and interracial sensitivities in the schools because many schools were racially segregated. Over time, discussions about fostering better communication among learners from different racial and cultural backgrounds have tended to sort into three distinct categories (Simon-McWilliams, 1989):

- Concerns about ending legal segregation and following court-ordered plans to achieve integration
- Concerns about within-school segregation of minority-group learners and females
- Concerns about achievement levels of minority-group learners and females

Efforts to End Legal Segregation

The 1954 Supreme Court case *Brown v. Board of Education* established a legal guideline that led to the dismantling of segregated school systems. However, the effort to achieve a school system featuring a cross section of learners from a wide variety of ethnic and racial backgrounds has been only moderately successful. A key 1974 Supreme Court decision in the case of *Milliken v. Bradley* held that courts lacked authority to order busing between districts for the purpose of achieving racial balance in schools. This ruling meant that busing was authorized as an option only within the boundaries of individual school districts.

In districts with homogeneous populations, the *Milliken v. Bradley* restriction made it difficult for school authorities to organize schools that reflect a broad ethnic and racial diversity. For example, the nation's inner cities are becoming increasingly African American and Latino, while the suburbs remain predominantly white. As a result, a large number of inner-city schools are overwhelmingly African American, Latino, or a combination of both. Similarly, many suburban schools are overwhelmingly white.

Today, many learners attend schools with others who are much like themselves. As a result, they have few opportunities to interact with young people from other cultural and ethnic backgrounds. There is concern that some of the recent efforts to reform education by allowing more school choice as a result of voucher plans or charter-school plans will lead to even more socioeconomic, ability-level, religious, and ethnic segregation of learners. Some school reformers even want to segregate learners by gender. Efforts to "make schools better" that decrease the diversity of the student population in individual schools are of concern to educators who believe that learners and our society benefit when schools enroll young people from varied backgrounds. As a teacher, you will want to think carefully about any so-called "improvement" initiatives that contain features that may decrease diversity in your classroom.

Within-Individual-School Segregation

As school districts have attempted to achieve learner populations that include a healthy mix of young people from different cultural and ethnic groups, actions of school authorities in some places have created segregated classes within individual schools that, when viewed as a whole, enroll diverse groups of learners. Such segregation occurs when learners from Group A are assigned to courses that tend to differ from those to which learners from Group B, Group C, and Group D are assigned. **Within-individual-school segregation** of students along cultural, racial, and even gender lines is particularly serious at the secondary-school level. College preparatory courses in many high schools enroll disproportionately high percentages of white students. Remedial courses, on the other hand, frequently have much higher percentages of minority-group students enrolled than these students' numbers within the total school population would warrant.

Professionals who are concerned about the issue of within-individual-school segregation are not satisfied with a simple count of the number of learners from various ethnic and racial groups who are enrolled in a given school. They want evidence that there are efforts to serve all students in ways that will maximize their individual development. Further, they argue that learners will not develop multicultural sensitivity and an acceptance for diversity if particular classes within individual schools segregate the learner population.

Concerns About Achievement Levels

The issue of achievement levels ties closely to concerns about within-individual-school segregation. If academic expectations in classes to which certain groups of learners have been assigned are not high, it should be no surprise when these learners fare poorly on achievement tests. Examinations of student scores on various achievement tests over the past 50 years reveal a consistent pattern. These scores show an achievement gap between white learners and learners from certain minority groups (Hertert & Teague, 2003).

Although there appeared to be some progress in narrowing the achievement gap from the early 1970s to about 1988, in recent years the gap has widened again (Hertert & Teague, 2003). The existence of an achievement gap suggests that the benefits of schooling are not equally accorded to all groups of learners. For example, children from less-affluent families perform significantly below more economically advantaged classmates. The percentage of poor students scoring "below basic" on the **National Assessment of Educational Progress (NAEP)** is more than twice as high as it is for more-advantaged students. The National Assessment of Educational Progress, which is administered by the U.S. Department of Education, involves periodic testing of the nation's learners to determine what they know about various school subjects. The percentage of impoverished students scoring at the "proficient" level on these tests tends to be about one-third of that of the more-advantaged students (Hertert & Teague, 2003). Although poverty is spread throughout the population, it is especially high among families with very young children headed by single women in the African American and Latino populations.

Generally, more benefits accrue to learners the longer they stay in school. Ideally, there should be no difference in the dropout rates associated with race or ethnicity. However, this is not the case. Eugene Garcia (2002) points out that many studies have found that children from nonmainstream backgrounds experience a disproportionate number of problems during their school years. For example, learners from poor families are nearly twice as likely to be held back a grade than learners from more economically advantaged homes. They also are more than three times as likely to be school dropouts. Latino youths have the highest national dropout rate, followed by African Americans and then whites. On the positive side, dropout rates have improved over time for all racial and ethnic groups. For example, the dropout rate for African American children today is about half of what it was in the 1970s.

Regrettably, the dropout rate of Latino learners, though improved over levels in previous decades, remains extremely high. Because Latinos are the nation's most rapidly growing minority group, these figures greatly concern educators. Unless educators do a better job of preparing Latino learners, an ever-larger percentage of our population is going to be ill-prepared to contribute to a society that increasingly requires an educated workforce.

As you think about these figures, you cannot assume that learners' race and ethnicity alone explain these patterns. The reality is that African American and Latino learners are overrepresented in other groups whose levels of school achievement fall below national averages. For example, investigators have found the following to be true of the general population of African American learners (Sable, 1998):

When compared with white learners, African American learners are more likely to

- Live in poverty,
- Live in single-parent households, and
- Live in urban areas.

There are similar patterns that help explain performance differences between Latino and white learners. Consider these points:

- From the middle 1980s through the end of the 1990s, the likelihood that a Latino child would be living in poverty with a single parent increased.
- Latino 3- and 4-year-olds are less likely to participate in preprimary education and in early literacy activities than are white 3- and 4-year-olds. (Sable & Stennett, 1998)

Though performance levels of African American and Latino learners continue to lag behind those of white learners, there has been progress in addressing this concern. As you may know, parents greatly influence what their children learn. The active involvement of parents of African American learners in their children's education has increased in recent years. Today, much higher percentages of African American high school students enroll in advanced courses than they did in the 1980s. Performance gaps between African American and white learners' scores in reading, mathematics, and science also have narrowed over time (Sable, 1998).

The intensity of Latino learners' parents' involvement in their children's schools has also increased in recent years. Today, more Latino children are taking rigorous high school courses, particularly advanced-placement courses, than they did in the past. Many of these young people are using this rigorous high school preparation to qualify for admission to selective college and university degree programs. For example, Latino high school graduates who go on to colleges and universities now are more likely than white students to pursue degrees in computer and information sciences (Sable & Stennett, 1998).

Traditionally, female achievement in mathematics and the sciences has lagged behind that of males. Female students outnumber male students in the total population of university students. However, fewer females than males go on to pursue advanced degrees in mathematics and the sciences. One explanation for this pattern is that many females who go on to college and university did not receive adequate high school preparation in mathematics and the sciences.

Some specialists who have examined this situation contend that too many public schools have failed to make serious efforts to develop female learners' abilities in mathematics because they have assumed that females lack an aptitude for this kind of content (Chipman & Thomas, 1987). Some research has demonstrated very minor gender-related differences in males and females in terms of their abilities to deal with spatial abstractions. However, Susan Chipman and Veronica Thomas argue that there has never been any established connection between the kinds of spatial abilities for which there are slight gender differences and the ability to master the kinds of mathematics that schools teach. Despite this reality, a mythology has developed that females are not good at mathematics. Hence, at least in some schools, female students have not been challenged to take advanced mathematics courses and advanced science courses that require a good grounding in mathematics.

Until this myth of female quantitative inadequacy is finally put to rest everywhere, many females will be disadvantaged when they seek admission to college and university curricula that require students to have strong backgrounds in mathematics. A continuation of the pattern of female underenrollment in advanced high school mathematics and science courses has the potential to keep many females from well-paid technical employment. This reality represents a personal economic loss to these females as individuals. More importantly, it represents a loss of potential talent that, if properly developed, could benefit our entire society.

WHAT DO YOU THINK?

IMPROVING GIRLS' ACHIEVEMENT—ARE SINGLE-GENDER SCHOOLS THE ANSWER?

Researchers have found that girls sometimes do not perform as well as they should when they are enrolled with boys in typical coeducation classes. For example, there is evidence that girls do not participate as frequently as boys unless a class has a female majority as well as a female teacher.

In recent years, some parents have responded to this situation by seeking support for single-gender schools. In New York City, for example, many private girls' schools have been established (Lewin, 1999). In addition, there has been an especially high level of interest in enrolling female children in all-girl kindergartens.

WHAT DO YOU THINK?

1. How would your own school experiences have differed if you had attended a single-gender school?
2. What advantages and disadvantages do you see for single-gender schools?
3. Will the effort to establish single-gender schools detract from efforts to ensure that female learners are appropriately supported and challenged in coeducational schools? Why or why not?

 To respond to these questions online, go to the What Do You Think? *module for this chapter of the* Companion Website.

GOALS AND GENERAL SUGGESTIONS FOR TEACHERS

Many individuals and professional groups seek to improve school programs in ways that will better serve the needs of ethnic and cultural minorities and females. There is a growing recognition that the nation can ill afford to do anything less than fully develop the talents of all its young people. With each passing year, the number of jobs open to high school graduates decreases, and the number requiring at least a bachelor's degree goes up. Even though there has been some improvement in this situation, the high school dropout rate of minority-group learners raises serious concerns. If present trends continue, people with less than a high school education are going to find it difficult to secure employment.

Many recommendations have been made regarding what educators should do to respond to multicultural and equity needs (Armstrong & Savage, 2002; Banks, 1995; Brown, 2002; Nieto, 1999; Sleeter & Grant, 2002). Several suggestions are discussed in the sections that follow.

Committing to the Idea That All Can Learn

If you sincerely believe that young people from all ethnic and cultural groups can learn, and you work to make this happen, their chance for academic success will be improved. Your assumptions about learners influence your expectations regarding what they can do. If you expect much from everyone, you should not be surprised when most of your students do well. In contrast, inadequately challenged learners usually achieve below their capacities. Many drop out of school before graduating from high school. If you want the learners you teach to complete the entire school program and leave the school system ready for college, a university, or the workplace, you must have faith in the capacity of all of them to learn. Your belief in them is a prerequisite to the confidence and academic background they need to succeed.

Modifying Grouping Practices

Grouping practices in many schools disadvantage many ethnic- and cultural-minority learners. Young people who are shunted into a low-ability group early in their school years fall further behind their peers with each passing year.

Sometimes, ability grouping results in the creation of entire classes of learners who are thought to be in a given category. For example, a high school may have a freshman English class specifically designated for low-ability students. This kind of grouping can undermine learners' confidence in their own abilities. In addition, the content to which they are exposed often is less rigorous than that introduced in so-called regular classes, thus impairing their preparation for more advanced work.

There also can be drawbacks to grouping arrangements made within an individual class. You need to be especially cautious about grouping learners into high-ability, intermediate-ability, and low-ability groups. This approach sometimes results in the assignment of disproportionate numbers of learners from cultural and ethnic minorities to so-called "low-ability" groups. If this happens in your own class, you may find yourself open to charges that your sorting mechanism is based not on a true measure of ability but rather on an assumption that learners from certain minority groups are less academically able than others. In general, within-class groups function more positively when there is no attempt to standardize the ability levels of members within each group and when learners in each group constitute a representative racial, cultural, and gender sample of the entire class.

*Accomodating diversity requires that teachers use different methods to accommodate
different learning styles.*

Accommodating Learning-Style Differences

Individuals' **learning styles** vary. The term *learning style* refers to a person's preferred
mode of mastering new information. Researchers have found that learners' cultural backgrounds influence their preferences for given instructional styles (Sleeter & Grant, 2002).
This conclusion suggests that you need to plan lessons that allow individual learners to approach content in different ways. Some young people profit from opportunities to touch
and manipulate objects. Others do just fine when they are asked to read new information.
Still others respond well to opportunities to work with photographs, charts, or other
graphic representations of data. The tendency for individuals to change their preferred
learning styles as they mature complicates your instructional-planning decisions (Sternberg, 1994). Periodically, you need to reevaluate your assumptions about the preferred
learning styles of the young people you teach.

WEB EXTENSION 5–4

Learning Styles and Multiple Intelligence

At this site, you will find a useful definition of *learning styles*. There are also descriptions of
teaching approaches that are well suited to young people with varying learning styles, including visual learners, auditory learners, and kinesthetic learners.

http://www.Ldpride.net/learningstyles.MI.htm

Becoming Aware of Your Own Perspectives

Because majority-group perspectives are so pervasive, teachers who are white often fail to recognize the extent to which their own worldviews have been conditioned by their membership in the majority. The reality is that all ethnic and cultural groups, including the white majority, have certain established assumptions about "how the world is" and about what constitutes proper behavior.

If you have not taken time to think about your own assumptions about reality, you may make the mistake of assuming that everybody shares your basic views. This kind of thinking can create problems when you work with learners from ethnic and cultural backgrounds whose fundamental perspectives may differ from your own. For example, if you have not learned anything about the traditional culture of Thailand, you might be surprised at the negative reaction a Thai child might have to a light touch on the head. Your intent may be to convey concern and friendship, but to a child raised in a Thai home, the gesture may be interpreted as an offensive invasion of privacy.

Relying Less on Standardized Tests

In recent years, the producers of standardized tests have enjoyed prosperous times. Standardized tests report learner scores in terms of how they compare with expected scores of similar kinds of learners. Legislators throughout the nation who clamor for information about the quality of public school programs often are attracted to standardized test scores as a source of evidence they can use to identify good, mediocre, and poor schools. These tests summarize tremendous amounts of information in numerical form, and they allow easy school-to-school comparisons. In addition, the public finds these numerical ratings easy to understand.

At best, standardized tests provide an extremely limited view of an individual learner's capabilities. Many of these tests probe only very-low-level mental processes; few can assess higher-level thinking skills. The emphasis placed on test scores in some places creates great pressures for teachers to "teach to the test." This has the potential to trivialize the kinds of content addressed in the classroom. For example, if you find yourself teaching in a school district that places an excessive emphasis on standardized-test results, you may be tempted to de-emphasize the importance of developing your learners' higher-level thinking skills.

Standardized tests pose particular problems for young people from ethnic and cultural minorities. Critics contend that standardized tests deny minority-group learners opportunities to continue their education beyond the high school level. They also point out that a system that limits the continued academic development of the fastest-growing component of the total school population makes little sense. Instead, they argue, assessment techniques are needed that foster the maximum development of minority-group learners' talents. Further, these assessment techniques should encourage the development of sophisticated thinking abilities, not simply reinforce the recall-level thinking needed for most of today's standardized tests.

Ideally, assessment procedures should take into account background characteristics that typify many minority-group learners. This means the vocabulary of assessment instruments needs to be responsive to the learners' environments. In addition, opportunities these learners have had outside of school should be considered. (For example, how many poor inner-city children have computers at home? How many have traveled extensively? How many of their families subscribe to a large number of periodicals?) For additional information about testing in the schools, see Chapter 10, "Assessing Learning."

Avoiding Favoritism in the Classroom

Teachers are human. When you begin teaching, you will find you have better relationships with some learners than with others. In the classroom, however, professionalism requires you to make an effort to encourage each learner's development. It is particularly important for your students to believe that they will not be singled out in any kind of negative way because of their ethnicity, race, or gender.

You need to strive for equity in your relationships with learners. Episodes of misbehavior must be treated similarly, regardless of who the offender is. You also need to provide encouragement to all who perform well. You must remember that all of your students need to know they will be treated fairly. Your credibility depends on this perception. When your learners believe you are not being fair, their motivation declines and academic performance deteriorates. As a result, you will likely find yourself dealing with more discipline problems.

Providing Good Teachers

There is no doubt that the central ingredient in improving the education of diverse students is a good teacher. However, it is often the case that learners who most need quality teachers do not get them. This problem is pronounced in many schools that enroll large numbers of learners from minority groups.

Many minority-group learners are served in schools in which working conditions for teachers are not as good as they should be and where teachers' salaries are low. Large numbers of schools that offer up-to-date facilities and high salaries are located in affluent suburbs. These schools tend to have much-less-diverse learner populations than schools in older neighborhoods and in inner cities. The result is that schools enrolling highly diverse populations of learners often experience more difficulty in recruiting and retaining good teachers than do schools with less-diverse learner populations. When compared with teachers in schools with majority white learner populations, teachers in predominantly minority schools tend to be less experienced, more likely to be teaching out of their fields, and more likely to holding **emergency teaching certificates.** An emergency teaching certificate is a document that enables a holder to accept a teaching position even though he or she has not met all normally required qualifications.

One consequence of the emphasis on standardized tests is its tendency to influence teachers to seek employment in schools where test scores are already high. When teachers recognize that part of their performance evaluation will be based on how well their learners do on these tests, they have reason to think about the nature of the students they will be teaching when considering alternative employment options. When standardized test scores are used as a measure of teacher effectiveness, prospective teachers have few incentives to seek positions in schools that are located in less-affluent neighborhoods or communities and that enroll highly diverse learner populations. The dilemma of responding to political leaders and a general public that continue to favor widespread standardized testing while, at the same time, developing incentives to attract high-quality teachers to less-affluent schools with highly diverse learner populations continues to challenge educators. You and your colleagues will continue to confront this issue in the years ahead.

USEFUL INFORMATION SOURCES

There are many places on the World Wide Web where you can find information related to cultural, ethnic, and gender-equity. To access some of this material, simply type the phrase "multicultural education" into a search engine such as Google (http://www.google.com).

Today, much excellent print material is also available. Professional periodicals regularly publish articles with helpful ideas that you can use in the classroom. Some excellent books are also available. We particularly recommend these three titles:

- James A. Banks and Cherry A. McGee Banks (Eds.). (2001). *Handbook of Research on Multicultural Education*. San Francisco: Jossey-Bass.
- James A. Banks and Cherry A. McGee Banks (Eds.). (2002). *Multicultural Education: Issues and Perspectives* (4th ed.). New York: John Wiley & Sons.
- Christine E. Sleeter and Carl A. Grant. (2002). *Making Choices for Multicultural Education: Five Approaches to Race, Class, and Gender*, 4th edition. New York: John Wiley & Sons.

Calendars with references to dates and events of interest to many different ethnic groups are available at several Web sites. To locate them, simply type the phrase "multicultural calendar" into a search engine such as Google (http://www.google.com). You will find an especially good one at this URL:

- http://www.kidlink.org/KIDPROJ/MCC/ (At this site, you will be able to locate information about multicultural holidays by month of the year, by holiday, by country, or by name of the author that supplied the information. You also are invited to submit unlisted holidays you know about for possible inclusion in future multicultural calendar editions.)

The following four places are examples of sources of other material you can use to prepare lessons with a multicultural focus. Go to their Web sites or write letters asking about materials for classroom teachers and learners. If you contact these groups, be sure to indicate the grade levels of learners for whom you might be preparing lessons.

The Balch Institute for Ethnic Studies. 1300 Locust Street, Philadelphia, PA 19107.
Web site: http://www.hsp.org
Phone: (215) 732–6200

Center for Migration Studies of New York, Inc. 209 Flagg Place, Staten Island, NY 10304–1199
Web site: http://cmsny.org/
Phone: (718) 351–8800

Immigration History Research Center. University of Minnesota, College of Liberal Arts, 311 Andersen Library, 222 21st Avenue S., Minneapolis, MN 55455–0439.
Web site: http://www1.umn.edu/ihrc/index.htm#menu
Phone: (612) 625–4800

Institute of Texan Cultures. 801 South Bowie Street, San Antonio, TX 78205
Web site: http://www.texancultures.utsa.edu/public/index.htm
Phone: (210) 458–2300

There are also information sources for materials with a gender-equity focus. Some examples include the following:

UNICEF Education Initiatives: Girls' Education. UNICEF House, 3 United Nations Plaza, New York, NY 10017.
Web site: http://www.unicef.org/girls education/index.htm
Phone: (212) 326–7000.

Population Reference Bureau, Inc. 1875 Connecticut Avenue NW, Suite 520,
    Washington, DC 20009–5728
Web site: http://www.prb.org/
Phone: (202) 328–3927

Arthur and Elizabeth Schlesinger Library on the History of Women in America.
    3 James Street, Cambridge, MA 02138
Web site: http://www.radcliffe.edu/schles/
Phone: (617) 495–8647

The National Women's History Project. 3343 Industrial Dr., Suite 4, Santa Rosa, CA 95403
Web site: http://www.nwhp.org/
Phone: (707) 636–2888

United Nations Development Fund for Women (UNIFEM). 304 East 45th Street,
    15th Floor, New York, NY 10017
Web site: http://www.unifem.org/
Phone: (212) 906–6400

Critical Incident

Defending a Comprehensive Multicultural Education Program

While carefully balancing her cup of coffee, Cheri Leblanc took a seat in the chair next to the desk of Victor Birdsong, Elmwood Senior High School's vice principal for curriculum. Victor hung up the phone as he finished a call and looked up at Cheri, the school's highly respected head of the English department.

"I need some advice, Vic."

Victor nodded, smiled, and said, "How may I help?"

"It's about the schoolwide curriculum committee you've had me chair—the one planning a new, comprehensive multicultural program."

"Oh yes," Victor replied. "That's the one with representatives from each department, some students, some parents, and a few community members. I thought you'd finished your work and were about to make your recommendation."

"That's just the difficulty. We are finished with our work. We've been at it for over a year now, and most of us think we've come up with a great plan. Members recommended the program by a vote of 16 to 4. Although it would have been nice to have everybody on board, given the controversial nature of the subject, I thought a 4-to-1 margin was as close to consensus as we'd ever get."

Victor reacted with a puzzled frown. "Tell me more. You've come to a decision that just about everybody supports, and there's still a problem?"

"Yes, there is," Cheri continued. "The four who voted against it absolutely refuse to accept the results of the vote. They plan to go the school board meeting tonight to express their dismay with our decision. They think they can convince the board to intervene and block implementation of the plan."

Victor's shoulders slumped at this news. "That's all we need—a public fight pitting one group of committee members against another. As a start, help me understand the specifics of the new plan."

Cheri pulled notes from a folder. Briefly, she scanned them looking for a summary she had written. "All right, Vic, here it is in a nutshell. If you think of the overall plan as a pie, we have three major slices or pieces: the curriculum piece, the learner-success piece, and the social-action piece."

"Tell me a little about each," said Vic as he reached for a yellow note pad and a pen. "I'll take a few notes."

"Fine. Let me begin with the curriculum piece. This part of the program features changes in the subject-matter content we teach. These changes will ensure that we provide good information about the contributions of people from many different ethnic, cultural, and language groups."

"The second major slice of the pie," Cheri continued, "is the individual-learner piece. This commits us to working closely with students from all groups to ensure that they are achieving academic success. In part, this will require us to see whether there are any differences associated with ethnic, cultural, or language backgrounds of students and how students are doing in specific subject areas. If we uncover problems, we want to develop instructional approaches that will eliminate them."

Victor wrote a few comments on his notepad, looked up, and asked, "And the third piece?"

"The third piece, Vic, focuses on what we call social action. We propose providing lessons to students to encourage them to examine both legal and informal practices that sometimes have disadvantaged certain categories of people. For example, we know that sometimes people living in particular neighborhoods have had difficulty getting housing loans. We're not trying to create revolutionaries here. Our purpose is just to sensitize students to the idea of fairness and to encourage them to participate actively in the political process to support efforts to promote equity."

Victor wrote a few additional notes. He continued looking down at his notepad. Satisfied that he had captured the essential points Cheri had made, he said, "Let's move on to the concerns of the four people who plan to speak at the school board meeting. Is there a particular one of these three pieces they object to?"

Cheri shook her head. "Vic, at first I thought there was something specific that was bothering them. If that were the case, I thought we might win their support by fine-tuning or even eliminating something. When we pressed them for details, it became evident that they oppose the whole idea of a multicultural curriculum."

Victor looked pensive. "Cheri, that surprises me, given the changes in the makeup of the student population in recent years. The professional journals also have had article after article on the need for school programs that are attuned to perspectives of different groups. What exactly is it that these four don't like?"

"In general, their argument is that multicultural programs are unpatriotic," responded Cheri. "They believe that school programs should work harder at bringing people together. Several of them pointed out in our meetings that anyone who walks through our cafeteria at noon will see clusters of African Americans, clusters of Latinos, and clusters of students from other groups. They say students identify too much with 'their own kind' and that our multicultural programs, by emphasizing these differences, will make the problem worse. I think all of them would be more comfortable with something we might call the 'Americanism curriculum' that would emphasize those things members of different groups have in common rather than those things that separate them."

• • •

What are some values implied by the multicultural curriculum proposed by Cheri Leblanc's committee? How have members perceived any problems that should be addressed? What specific remedies have they proposed? What values are suggested by the positions taken by the four people who refused to endorse the curriculum committee's proposal? What things are important to these four, and what would they have the school do to address their priorities? What advice do you think Victor Birdsong will give to Cheri Leblanc? How do you think the school board will react to the positions taken by the four members who want to speak against the new multicultural curriculum? What would you do next if you were Cheri Leblanc?

To respond to this Critical Incident online, go to the Critical Incidents *module for this chapter of the Companion Website.*

Key Ideas in Summary

- The learner population is becoming increasingly diverse in terms of its cultural and ethnic makeup. This reality challenges you to provide instruction that appropriately fits the background of each child you teach. The more that lessons respect and respond to these differences, the higher the probability that learners will achieve success at school. Academic success breeds self-confidence and leads to positive attitudes toward schooling.

- Diversity is one of our national strengths. The varied experiences and backgrounds of our people enable them to bring multiple perspectives to bear on vexing problems. Your challenge in the classroom is to help young people develop pride in their own backgrounds while acquiring a commitment to democratic decision-making—a process that requires them to work productively and positively with people whose worldviews may differ from their own.

- Multicultural education seeks to provide equity for all learners. It does this by drawing on insights from history and the social and behavioral sciences, and especially from ethnic studies and women's studies. In working with learners from diverse backgrounds, you will find it useful to establish a *culturally responsive environment* in your classroom. Such an environment creates an important zone of comfort for both you and your students.

- Today, most new teachers are white and come to the profession from middle-class backgrounds. This background suggests that few have backgrounds consistent with the highly diverse array of cultures represented among learners in the schools. As a result, today's teachers and the young people they teach may have differing views regarding what constitutes appropriate behavior. As a teacher, you need to take time to learn about the backgrounds of all your students. Armed with this kind of information, you can develop patterns of interaction and instructional programs that respond logically to these learners' backgrounds.

- In working with learners from diverse groups, you need to avoid the mistake of assuming that all young people from a particular racial, ethnic, or home-language group share similar views and values. Perspectives of African Americans living in rural areas often vary greatly from African Americans living in central cities. Many people of Latino heritage do not speak Spanish as their first language. The bottom line is that you need to focus on characteristics of individuals, not on reputed (and often inaccurately reported) characteristics of the large groups to which they belong.

- In the early and middle years of the twentieth century, many learners from ethnic and cultural minorities were viewed as having a *genetic deficit* that accounted for their low levels of academic achievement. Later, this explanation gave way to a *cultural-deficit* view that attributed poor school performance to a failure of the learner's home environment to support school learning. The genetic-deficit and cultural-deficit positions are now generally rejected. It is recognized that the failure of many minority-group children to learn is due to the failure of schools to provide programs responsive to their needs.

- The case of *Brown v. Board of Education* (1954) led to the dismantling of segregated school systems. A subsequent decision, *Milliken v. Bradley* (1974), held that courts did not have a right to order busing across district lines for the purpose of integrating schools. As a result, schools in many places continue to enroll disproportionately large numbers of learners from certain cultural and ethnic groups because the groups are very heavily represented within the boundaries of their given school district. Many inner-city school districts, for example, have populations that are largely African American or Latino. There are not enough white learners in these districts to supply a high percentage of such learners to any school, even when districts bus to achieve a racial balance.

- There are many concerns today about *within-individual-school segregation.* Many college-preparatory programs in high schools enroll higher percentages of white students than are represented in the overall student body, while learners from ethnic and cultural minorities are overrepresented in special-education classes. Segregation by gender has also been observed. For example, the overwhelming majority of learners in high school physical science classes are male.

- Standardized achievement scores of African American and Latino learners have continually lagged behind those of white students. Dropout rates are also higher for African Americans and Latinos than for whites. In recent years, the dropout rate for African American learners has improved; however, the rate for Latinos remains far too high.

- In responding to needs of minority-group learners and females, you need to operate on the basis of accurate information. For example, the idea that female learners are less capable of mastering mathematics than males persists in many places despite contrary evidence. Generalizations regarding Latinos sometimes hint at their probable difficulty with English because it is not their native language. In fact, English is the first language for a majority of Latino learners.

- Recommendations for improving the quality of educational services for ethnic- and cultural-minority learners include (1) committing to the idea that everyone can learn, (2) modifying grouping practices, (3 accommodating learning-style differences, (4) making certain that teachers are aware of their own perspectives, (5) relying less on standardized tests, (6) ensuring that teachers avoid favoritism in the classroom, and (7) assigning good teachers to work with minority-group learners.

Chapter 5 Self-Test

 To review terms and concepts in this chapter, go to the Companion Website and take the Chapter 5 Self-Test. *Feedback for the self-test is immediate. You can keep track of your self-test scores yourself, or you can submit them to your instructor via e-mail.*

Preparing for Praxis

 To learn more about the Praxis test and complete this activity online, go to the Preparing for Praxis *module for this chapter of the Companion Website.*

You may be required to pass Educational Testing Service's Praxis II exam as you seek formal authorization to teach in the public schools. The *Principles of Learning and Teaching* component of Praxis II seeks to assess your knowledge about these topics: (1) Students as Learners, (2) Instruction and Assessment, (3) Communication Techniques, and (4) Profession and Community.

Material in this chapter may be especially relevant because there is a great interest in teachers being prepared to provide high-quality instruction to learners from all of the groups that make up today's school population. You may well find Praxis questions related to diversity associated with all of the four major Praxis categories.

As you prepare for the examination, you may find it useful to record notes in a chart similar to the one provided here. As you encounter information related to individual categories, enter it into the chart under the appropriate heading. You will find a completed chart of this kind helpful as you begin studying for the Praxis II exam.

Students as Learners	Instruction and Assessment
• Student Development and the Learning Process	• Instructional Strategies
• Students as Diverse Learners	• Planning Instruction
• Student Motivation and the Learning Environment	• Assessment Strategies
Communication Techniques	• **Profession and Community**
• Basic, Effective, Verbal and Nonverbal Communication Techniques	• The Reflective Practitioner
• Effect of Cultural and Gender Differences on Communications in the Classroom	• The Larger Community
• Types of Questions That Can Stimulate Discussion in Different Ways for Particular Purposes	

For Your Initial-Development Portfolio

 To complete this activity and submit your response online, go to the For Your Initial-Development Portfolio *module for this chapter of the Companion Website.*

1. What materials and ideas in this chapter about diversity will you include as "evidence" in your portfolio? Select up to three separate items of information. Number them 1, 2, and 3.
2. Think about why you selected these materials. As you do so, consider these issues:
   - Specific uses you might make of this information as you plan, deliver, and assess the impact of your teaching
   - The compatibility of the information with your own priorities and values
   - Any contributions this information can make to your development as a teacher
   - Factors that led you to include this information, as opposed to some alternatives you considered but rejected

3. Place a check in the chart here to indicate to which INTASC standard(s) each of your items of information relates.

INTASC Standard Number

ITEM OF EVIDENCE NUMBER	S1	S2	S3	S4	S5	S6	S7	S8	S9	S10
1										
2										
3										

4. Prepare a written reflection in which you analyze the decision-making process you followed. In your comments, mention the INTASC standard(s) to which your selected material relates.

Reflections

To respond to these questions online, go to the Reflections *module for this chapter of the Companion Website.*

1. In this chapter, you learned that individuals' backgrounds affect their beliefs and attitudes. Think about your own views regarding "how learners should behave." Where did your attitudes come from? Were there some specific people who influenced you to adopt your views? How do you think characteristics of these people match up with characteristics of individuals who are likely to influence young people you will teach?

2. Classrooms today include learners from a wide range of cultural, ethnic, social, and economic backgrounds. As a result, teachers find themselves challenged to help learners develop positive self-concepts by encouraging their pride in the groups to which they belong. At the same time, teachers also must promote a common commitment to universal democratic values that cut across all groups in our society. What difficulties do you see in trying to focus on the importance of individual–group perspectives while also seeking to promote a common commitment to society-wide shared values?

3. There is evidence that learners who are taught in *culturally responsive environments* do well in school. What difficulties do you envision as you attempt to establish such an environment in the classrooms in which you teach? How will you go about overcoming these challenges?

4. Some critics of using standardized-test results to evaluate teachers' effectiveness assert that such policies encourage teachers to avoid accepting employment in schools that enroll large numbers of learners from groups that traditionally do not score well on tests of this type. Are there incentives that might be put in place to encourage more teachers to seek employment in schools that enroll exceptionally diverse learner populations? If so, what are they, and what would it take to implement your ideas?

5. In this chapter, you learned about challenges teachers face in developing instructional experiences that are responsive to the needs of the diverse learners found in today's classrooms. Think about a plan you might develop in preparation for working with classes that enroll large numbers of learners from backgrounds that differ from your own. What will your plan feature, and why do you think these ideas will work?

Field Experiences, Projects, and Enrichment

1. If possible, arrange to visit some classes that include a mix of learners from different ethnic and cultural backgrounds. Observe participation patterns. How frequently do learners from minority groups volunteer to answer questions? How often are they called upon? (You may wish to identify other questions that will help you to pinpoint the degree to which minority-group learners are actively involved in lessons.) Share your findings with others in your class, and respond to these questions as a group:
   - Were minority-group learners as involved in lessons as majority-group learners?
   - What specific patterns did you note?
   - What might account for these patterns?
2. Some school districts provide special training for white teachers to sensitize them to perspectives of learners from ethnic, cultural, and language minorities. Interview local school administrators about programs that may have been implemented in their schools. Alternatively, consult professional journals for descriptions of such programs. Prepare a short paper for your course instructor in which you describe either one or two local programs or several programs that have been outlined in journal articles.
3. Organize a panel discussion focusing on this question: "Do school programs today do a good job of serving female learners?" Find relevant materials from Web sites, journal articles, and other relevant sources. Allow time for other class members to ask questions and make comments.
4. Read about successful attempts to improve the achievement levels of minority-group learners. Get together with four or five other classmates who have been working on the same task. Organize a symposium to present to your class on the topic "Hope for Learners from Ethnic and Cultural Minorities: Practical Examples from Real Schools."

References

Armstrong, D. G., & Savage, T. V. (2002). *Teaching in the secondary school* (5th ed.). Upper Saddle River, NJ: Merrill/Prentice Hall.

Banks, J. A. (1995). Multicultural education: Development, dimensions, and challenges. In J. Noll (Ed.), *Taking sides: Clashing views on controversial educational issues* (8th ed.) (pp. 94–98). Guilford, CT: Dushkin.

Banks, J. A., & Banks, C. A. M. (Eds.). (2001). *Handbook of research on multicultural education.* San Francisco: Jossey-Bass.

Banks, J. A., & Banks, C. A. M. (Eds.). (2002). *Multicultural education: Issues and Perspectives* (4th ed.). New York: John Wiley & Sons.

Brown, D. F. (2002). *Becoming a successful urban teacher.* Portsmouth, NH: Heinemann. Brown v. Board of Education, 347 U.S. 483 (1954).

Chipman, S. F., & Thomas, V. G. (1987). The participation of women and minorities in mathematical, scientific, and technical fields. In E. Z. Rothkopf (Ed.), *Review of educational research* (Vol. 14, pp. 387–430). Washington, DC: American Educational Research Association.

Clinchy, E. (1993). Needed: A Clinton crusade for quality and equality. *Educational Leadership, 74*(8), 605–612.

Elam, S. M., Rose, L. C., & Gallup, G. M. (1994). The 26th annual Phi Delta Kappa/Gallup poll of the public's attitudes toward the public schools. *Phi Delta Kappan, 76*(1), 41–56.

Erickson, F. (1987). Transformation and school success: The politics and culture of educational achievement. *Anthropology and Education Quarterly, 18*(4), 335–356.

Garcia, E. (2002). *Student cultural diversity* (3rd ed.). Boston: Houghton Mifflin.

Gay, G. (1994). *A synthesis of scholarship in multicultural education.* [http://www.ncrel.org/sdrs/areas/issues/leadership/le0gay.htm]

Gorski, P. (2000). *The challenge of defining a single " multicultural education."* [http://www.mhhe.com/socscience/ education/multi/define.html]

Grant, C. A. (1990). Desegregation, racial attitudes, and intergroup contact: A discussion of change. *Phi Delta Kappan, 72*(1), 25–32.

Henson, K. T. (2001). *Curriculum planning: Integrating multiculturalism, and motivism, and education reform* (2nd ed.) New York: McGraw-Hill. Reprinted in 2003 by Waveland Press. Long Grove, IL.

Hertert, L., & Teague, J. (2003). *Narrowing the achievement gap*. Palo Alto, CA: EdSource.

Hilliard, J. (1991/1992). Why must we pluralize the curriculum? *Educational Leadership, 49*(4), 12–13.

Lewin, T. (1999, April 11). Amid concerns about equity, parents are turning to girls' schools. *New York Times*. [http://www.nytimes.com/library/_national/regional/041199ny-girls-schools.html]

Milliken v. Bradley, 418 U.S. 717 (1974).

Nieto, S. (1999). *The light in their eyes: Creating multicultural learning communities*. New York: Teachers College Press.

Powell, R. R., McLaughlin, H. J., Savage, T. V., & Zehm, S. (2001). *Classroom management: Perspectives on the social curriculum*. Upper Saddle River, NJ: Merrill/Prentice Hall.

Preissle, J., & Rong, X. L. (1998). *Educating immigrant students: What we need to know to meet the challenges*. Thousand Oaks, CA: Corwin Press.

Sable, S. (1998). Issue in focus: The educational progress of black students. In R. Pratt (Ed.), *The condition of education, 1998*. Washington, DC: National Center for Education Statistics. [http://nces.ed.gov/pubs98/condition98/c98003.html]

Sable, S., & Stennett, J. (1998). Issue in focus: The educational progress of Latino students. In R. Pratt (Ed.), *The condition of education, 1998*. Washington, DC: National Center for Education Statistics. [http://nces.ed.gov/programs/coe]

Simon-McWilliams, E. (Ed.). (1989). *Resegregation of public schools: The third generation*. Portland, OR: Network of Regional Desegregation Assistance Centers and Northwest Regional Educational Laboratory.

Sleeter, C. E., & Grant, C. A. (2002). *Making choices for multicultural education: Five approaches to race, class, and gender* (4th ed.). New York: John Wiley & Sons.

Sternberg, R. J. (1994). Allowing for thinking styles. *Educational Leadership, 52*(3), 36–40.

Wlodkowski, R. J., & Ginsberg, M. B. (1995). *Diversity and motivation: Culturally responsive teaching*. San Francisco: Jossey-Bass.

6

Meeting the Needs of Exceptional Learners

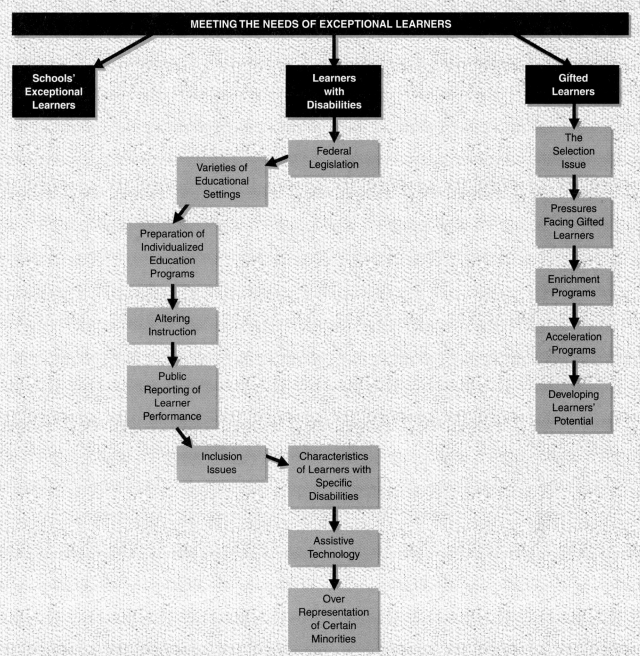

OBJECTIVES

This chapter will help you to

- describe federally legislated principles for working with learners with disabilities.
- identify characteristics of learners with different kinds of disabilities and describe some recommended instructional responses to these learners' needs.
- explain issues associated with overrepresentation of certain minorities among individuals with disabilities.

- describe characteristics of gifted learners.
- differentiate between the *enrichment* and *acceleration* approaches to meeting the needs of gifted learners.
- point out examples of specific teacher actions that have been found to promote development of gifted learners.

SCHOOLS' EXCEPTIONAL LEARNERS

Exceptional learners have characteristics that differentiate them from the general population of young people (Savage & Armstrong, 2004). Learners with disabilities and gifted learners are among the exceptional learners you will be teaching. They share many of the characteristics of other schoolchildren. Some are tall, and some are short. Some are extremely bright, and some find learning difficult. Some have positive attitudes about school, and some do not enjoy being at school at all. There is as much diversity among exceptional learners as there is among the total school population.

When you work with these young people, in addition to appreciating important learner-to-learner differences, you also need to know about common characteristics that many individuals within exceptional-learners groups share. This chapter introduces some of these characteristics and describes approaches for working with learners who have certain disabilities and learners who are gifted.

WEB EXTENSION 6–1

ERIC Clearinghouse on Disabilities and Gifted Education

To extend your understanding of topics and issues introduced in this chapter, you may wish to visit the Web site maintained by the ERIC Clearinghouse on Disabilities and Gifted Education. At this site, you will find excellent links to research related to the education of learners with disabilities and gifted learners, information about relevant federal legislation, sources of information for parents, fact sheets, and links to other online resources.

http://www.eric.ed.gov

LEARNERS WITH DISABILITIES

For many years, most classroom teachers had little contact with learners with disabilities. These young people were segregated from other learners and taught in special classrooms. This approach failed to meet the needs of large numbers of students. For example, in the late 1970s, one million children with disabilities did not attend school at all (National Education Association, 1999). Today, this situation is much different. Most learners with disabilities spend all or part of each day in regular classrooms. Today, public schools provide federally mandated services to more than 5.5 million young people with disabilities (U.S. Department of Education, 2001). Because fully 95% of classrooms enroll one or more learners with disabilities, you are certain to be working with such young people when you begin teaching (National Center for Education Statistics, 2002).

Federal Legislation

The change in views regarding the desirability of serving most learners in special education classrooms that kept them apart from learners enrolled in traditional classrooms came about from a recognition that the schools were not serving these young people well. These concerns prompted passage of important federal legislation that sought to respond to problems such as these:

- High school graduation rates for learners with disabilities are only about one third as high as for so-called "normal" learners (National Council on Disability, 2000b).

Assistive technology has allowed schools to better respond to the needs of students with special needs.

- Fully 70% of incarcerated youth are young people with disabilities (Burrell & Warboys, 2000).
- Learning-disabled girls who drop out of school become unwed mothers at a much higher rate than their nondisabled peers (IDEA '97: General Information, 2001).
- Many young people with disabilities are excluded from curriculum and assessments used with their nondisabled classmates. As a result, their possibilities of performing to higher standards of excellence are limited (IDEA '97: General Information, 2001).

Federal mandates for providing certain kinds of services to learners with disabilities appeared first in the Education for All Handicapped Children Act, passed in 1975. Sometimes this important legislation is referred to as **Public Law 94-142.** In 1990, Congress modified the law and renamed it the Individuals with Disabilities Education Act. Educators often refer to this legislation by its acronym, **IDEA.** This legislation is regularly updated. For example, some recent updates require schools to take advantage of new technologies that can facilitate learning of young people with disabilities.

Other relevant federal legislation includes the 1992 **Americans with Disabilities Act**. The act, which was patterned after earlier legislation (Section 504 of the Vocational Rehabilitation Act), extends the civil rights of individuals with disabilities to include (a) private-sector employment, (b) all public services, (c) transportation, and (d) telecommunications. The now nearly universal access ramps found in businesses, on city street corners, and in schools and universities are one clear result of this legislation.

Collectively, recent federal legislation and accompanying guidelines that deal with learners with disabilities require schools to observe six key principles as they provide service:

- The adoption of a policy of **zero rejects.** This means that schools must enroll every child, regardless of the nature of his or her disability.

- A commitment to **nondiscriminatory testing.** Schools must use multiple indicators to determine whether a learner has a disability and whether special services are needed. This requirement resulted from concerns that too many children from minority groups were being included among those with identified disabilities.
- The provision of an **appropriate education.** This principle commits schools to devise educational programs that are responsive to the unique educational needs of each learner with a disability. For example, schools must develop and implement an **Individualized Education Program,** often referred to as an **IEP,** for each learner with a disability. As a classroom teacher, you will be responsible for participating in the development of IEPs for young people in your classes.
- An agreement to provide instruction for each learner with a disability in the **least-restrictive environment.** This principle requires school districts, to the extent possible, to enable learners with disabilities to take advantage of school experiences in ways that do not restrict or limit their access to experiences provided to so-called "normal" learners.
- The protection of learners' rights. In making decisions regarding programs and placements of learners with disabilities, schools agree to recognize **due process** rights of young people and their parents/guardians.
- The inclusion of parents and guardians in planning. Educational plans for children with disabilities must be made with **parent/guardian participation.** Schools must provide parents/guardians opportunities to play substantive roles in making decisions about educational experiences planned for their sons and daughters with identified disabilities.
- A commitment to inclusion. Public schools must go beyond **mainstreaming** and adopt inclusion. *Mainstreaming* implies that a learner with a disability who spends part of the school day in a regular classroom also spends part (sometimes a majority) of his or her time in a separate, self-contained special education classroom. *Inclusion* refers to a policy of providing students with disabilities an education within a regular-school classroom in which special aids, supports, and instructional accommodations are made to respond to their needs.

WEB EXTENSION 6–2

OSEP—Office of Special Education Programs

The U.S. Department of Education's Office of Special Education Programs (OSEP) provides leadership and support to help states and local school districts provide appropriate educational services to individuals with disabilities who are between 3 and 31 years of age. You will find information about legislation related to serving these people, special projects, research and statistics, and links to additional resources you might wish to consult as you learn more about working with students with disabilities.

http://www.ed.gov/about/offices/list/osers/osep/index.html

Varieties of Educational Settings

Though you will have some learners with disabilities in your classroom, not all of them will be there for the entire school day. Some young people with disabilities have conditions that will result in their spending part or all of their instructional days in settings other than the traditional classroom.

In general, seven distinct educational environments are used with learners with disabilities. Most learners will spend part of each day in regular classrooms. Some will spend the rest of each day in a resource room, where specialists can provide educational services uniquely suited to their needs.

About one fourth of learners with disabilities spend all day as members of a **special class** taught by a teacher who works exclusively with these young people. A few learners with disabilities are educated in **separate public-school facilities** (facilities operated by a school district away from a regular school), **separate private-school facilities** (facilities operated by private entities that are away from a regular school), **publicly supported residential facilities** (school-district facilities away from regular schools where learners live and are taught), **private residential settings** (facilities away from a regular school that are operated by private entities where learners live and are taught), or **homebound** or **hospital settings** (homes or medical facilities where learners live and are taught) (National Center for Education Statistics, 2001).

As a regular classroom teacher, you are more likely to see learners with some disabilities more frequently than learners with others. For example, many young people with speech and language impairments spend the vast majority of their school time in regular classrooms. On the other hand, learners who have serious emotional disturbances typically spend the majority of their school days in other educational settings (National Center for Education Statistics, 2001). See the chart in Figure 6.1 for more information related to how young people with different kinds of disabilities divide their time between regular school classrooms and other instructional settings.

Instructional Setting / Learner Disability	Speech and Language Impairments	Visual Impairments	Orthopedic Impairments	Attention Deficit Disorder and Specific Learning Disabilities	Hearing Impairments	Serious Emotional Disturbance
In Regular Classroom 79 to 100% of the School Day	87.8%	48.1%	46.6%	43.8%	38.8%	24.9%
In Regular Classroom 40 to 78% of the School Day	7.3%	20.1%	21.3%	39.3%	19.9%	23.3%
In Setting Outside of Regular Classroom for 60% or More of the School Day	4.9%	31.8%	32.1%	16.9%	42.2%	51.8%

FIGURE 6.1   Likelihood That Young People with Certain Disabilities Will Spend Their Instructional Time in a Regular Classroom or in Another Instructional Setting

Source: Table 54, *Digest of Education Statistics, 2001* (p. 67), 2001, Washington, DC: National Center for Education Statistics.

Preparation of Individualized Education Programs

Federal regulations require that an Individualized Education Program (IEP) be established for each child with disabilities. IEPs must be developed at a meeting that is scheduled shortly after the learner's condition is verified. Participants must include the learner's regular teacher, one or both parents/guardians, and a representative of the school district other than the teacher. School counselors often serve as the nonteacher representative of the school district. The child may be present, when appropriate. There are certain conditions that sometimes also require the presence of additional members of the IEP planning group.

Discussion during the meeting centers on examination and development of the following information:

- The learner's present educational attainment level
- Special services/modifications needed to facilitate the learner's educational development
- Goals the learner is expected to achieve in one year
- Objectives, benchmarks, and evaluation procedures that will be used to measure the learner's progress toward established goals
- Identification of the least restrictive environment required to serve the learner's needs

The IEP team for each learner with a disability meets at least once each year to discuss progress. During these meetings, members are free to establish new goals and describe revised educational services. Parents/guardians who disagree with decisions, if they are unable to convince others on the IEP team to make changes they desire, have the right to ask for additional testing of their child and to seek to resolve disagreements by invoking their due process rights and asking for an impartial hearing.

These school professionals are meeting with a parent to discuss preparation of an Individualized Educational Program for a learner with disabilities.

WEB EXTENSION 6–3

Links Related to the PACER Center

The PACER Center was established in 1977 by parents of children with disabilities as an organization to provide mutual support. The name PACER is formed from the first letters of the group's formal name, which is the Parent Advocacy Coalition for Educational Rights. At this site you will find a listing of links to outstanding sources of information about topics such as national disability agencies and organizations, parenting resources, parent training and information centers, and important legislative resources. You also will find Web addresses for Parent Training and Information Centers in each state. These groups provide information for parents/guardians of learning disabled children, including their rights and responsibilities associated with the development of Individualized Education Programs (IEPs).

http://www.pacer.org/national/relatedpacerlinks.htm

Altering Instruction

Special needs identified during IEP meetings for members of your class with identified disabilities may require you to change certain of your instructional practices to adjust them to these learners' characteristics. These changes will be of two basic types. Sometimes your response will take the form of an **accommodation.** An accommodation represents a change you make that allows a learner to complete the same assigned tasks as others in your class by changing such variables as

- The schedule you establish for individual parts of the task to be completed and turned in
- The time allowed for the work to be completed
- The setting where the work is accomplished
- The nature of presentations or responses you accept from the learner at various points during the learning process
- The nature of evidence you will accept to verify that learning has occurred.

At other times, changes you make will take the form of a **modification.** A modification involves your substitution of a task for learners with disabilities that varies in important ways from the task you assign to other class members. Changes may involve holding these learners to different standards of performance or assigning them a task that better responds to their unique educational needs, even though it varies substantially in character from work others in the class are doing.

The **Office of Special Education Programs (OSEP)** is the component of the U.S. Department of Education that oversees programs for learners with disabilities. OSEP funds several groups that seek to promote high-quality school programs for learners with disabilities. One of these is **Family Partnership for Education (FAPE).** See Figure 6.2 for examples of ideas adapted from those FAPE has developed for teachers who wish to accommodate and modify their instructional programs to better meet needs of learners with disabilities.

Giving Tests	• Go over directions orally. • Permit as much time as needed to finish tests. • Ask the learner to complete an independent project as an alternative test. • Provide typed test materials, not tests written in cursive. • Teach learners how to take tests (e.g., how to review and plan time for each section). • Allow take-home or open-book tests. • Provide a vocabulary list with definitions.
Making Assignments	• Shorten assignments to focus learners' attention on mastery of key concepts. • Shorten spelling tests to focus on mastering the most functional words. • Substitute alternatives for written assignments (clay models, posters, panoramas, collections, and so forth). • Specify and list exactly what the learner will need to learn to pass. Review this list frequently. • Modify expectations based on learner needs (for example, "When you have read this chapter, you should be able to list three reasons the Civil War started."). Give alternatives to long written reports (e.g., give an oral report, write several short reports, and so forth).
Providing Directions	• Use both oral and printed directions. • Give directions in small steps and in as few words as possible. • Number and sequence the steps in a task. • Ask learners to repeat directions for a task to check on understanding. • Provide visual aids. • Show an example of what a completed assignment might look like. • Stand near the learner when giving directions or presenting a lesson.
Grading	• Provide a partial grade based on individual progress or effort. • Use daily or frequent grading averaged into a grade for the term. • Weight daily work higher than tests for learners who perform poorly on tests. • Mark the correct answers rather than the incorrect answers. • Permit a learner to rework missed problems for a better grade. • Average grades between original and reworked assignments, or grade only the reworked assignment. • Use pass–fail or an alternative grading.

FIGURE 6.2   Ideas for Altering Practices to Serve Needs of Learners with Disabilities

Source: Adapted from "School Accommodations and Modifications" (October 31, 2001), FAPE Coordinating Office: PACER Center, Inc., 8161 Normandale Blvd., Minneapolis, MN 55437.

Public Reporting of Learner Performance

In times past, many school districts either excused learners with disabilities from taking standardized tests or withheld scores of these learners in their official reports. Supporters of inclusion, who played an important role in passing the Individuals with Disabilities Education Act, pointed out that forcing schools to administer and report test scores of learners with disabilities was important. In their view, this requirement would provide a strong incentive for schools to expose these young people to the same curriculum as their nondisabled peers.

The No Child Left Behind Act of 2001 (2002) adds important legislative support to the idea that schools should be accountable for improving the learning of young people with disabilities. This law requires school districts to provide information each year related to subgroups within the general school population, for example, learners with disabilities. The requirement was included in the legislation to ensure that poor achievement of learners in certain subgroups (for example, ethnic and racial minorities, economically disadvantaged learners) were not hidden when included in data reported for a school's entire student population. This development means that, as a classroom teacher, you are as accountable for the progress of learners with disabilities as for the achievement of all other learners in your classroom.

Inclusion Issues

The change in emphasis from mainstreaming to inclusion embraces more than a shift from serving learners with disabilities in regular classrooms for part of the school day and in other settings for the rest of the day to serving learners with disabilities almost exclusively within regular classrooms. An attitude change is also involved. In a nutshell, mainstreaming led schools to serve some learners with disabilities in regular classrooms because this change was *required*. The inclusion principle has led schools to meet almost all needs of learners with disabilities within regular classrooms because their presence there is *desired*.

Mainstreaming sought to break away from the tradition of teaching learners with disabilities in separate special education classrooms or in other settings that isolated them from contact with other students in regular classrooms. Backed by such legislation as the Education for All Handicapped Children Act, supporters of mainstreaming altered the way schools served learners with disabilities by insisting that these young people, to the extent feasible, spend at least part of their time in regular classrooms. In response to legal pressures, school leaders began to place these young people in classrooms because they were required to do so.

Supporters of inclusion believed that teachers in regular classrooms could provide all or nearly all instructional services for learners with disabilities. The Individuals with Disabilities Education Act and follow-up legislation have strongly endorsed this idea. Proponents believe that when learners with disabilities are taught in regular classrooms, their academic achievement improves and other young people without disabilities who are members of their classes also receive benefits. The idea is that, in a highly diverse society, young people gain when they come into contact with individuals whose personal characteristics differ from their own. This perspective underlies the National Institute for Urban School Improvement's sponsorship of National Inclusive Schools Week. This annual event gives schools, classrooms, families, and communities opportunities to celebrate how diversity enriches our lives.

Does the trend in recent years favoring inclusion suggest that you no longer will find people who challenge this approach? Not at all. Proponents and skeptics continue to argue the pros and cons. In addition, educational researchers continue to study issues and report findings associated with inclusion.

Examples of Arguments Supporting Inclusion.

Special education once was thought of as a separate place or a separate program. It is neither. Special education is a collection of services designed to meet the unique needs of individuals with disabilities. Regular classroom teachers, with appropriate support equipment, instructional materials, and information about the particular needs of individual learners, can effectively provide high-quality educational services to learners with disabilities who are enrolled in their classes. Evidence that regular classroom teachers can work successively with learners with disabilities is strong enough to support **full inclusion** programs that feature placement of all learners with disabilities in regular classrooms at all times regardless of the nature or severity of their disabilities.

Inclusion arrangements yield psychological benefits for learners with disabilities, who see themselves as part of the total group of young people who go to school, not as individuals who have been labeled as "different" and, hence, consigned to be taught in environments isolated from so-called "normal" learners. In addition, other young people in their classes develop an increased awareness of the diversity of the general population—a reality they will confront throughout their lives.

In traditional special education environments, young people with disabilities were taught in settings that bore little resemblance to the nondisabled world that confronted them once they left the classroom. They came into contact with few models to emulate who would help them deal with people and their expected behaviors outside of school. For example, in special education classrooms including only learners with behavior problems, the norm was for everyone to have a behavior problem. Such a circumstance often impeded adjustments of learners with disabilities to outside-the-classroom realities.

Examples of Arguments Opposing Inclusion.

Enthusiastic supporters of inclusion have an unrealistic view of difficulties regular classroom teachers face when working with learners with disabilities. The time required for teachers to manage special equipment, arrange furniture to accommodate individuals with certain difficulties, and handle young people who may have multiple disabilities detracts from time available for instruction. As a result, achievement levels of all class members may suffer.

In an ideal world, regular classroom teachers would have specialized equipment and varied curricular materials that are designed to be responsive to needs of learners with a variety of disabilities as well as so-called "normal" learners. The reality is far from this ideal. Typical classroom teachers lack the kind of support equipment and teaching materials needed to work effectively with all of their learners with disabilities and with others in their classroom. As a result, both learners with and learners without disabilities are being shortchanged.

In the past, preparation programs of teachers who worked in separate special education classrooms featured intensive study of learners with disabilities and their needs. The kind of instruction provided today to regular classroom teachers to help them work with these young people does not compare in intensity and quality with training given to specialists. As a result, the quality and appropriateness of instruction provided to learners with disabilities who are taught as members of regular classrooms often falls short of that they would receive if they were taught in special classrooms by experts with solid training in diagnosing and responding to the needs of learners with handicaps.

What Research Says About Inclusion.   Inclusion is too new for there to be extensive research findings regarding its long-term effects. Some existing studies have revealed the following:

Learners *with* disabilities taught in inclusive classrooms have

- Performed better on standardized tests (*Long-Term Effects of Inclusion*, 2003)
- Left these experiences with improved social and communication skills (*Long-Term Effects of Inclusion*, 2003)
- Increased their personal knowledge of the world (*Long-Term Effects of Inclusion*, 2003).

Learners *without* disabilities taught in inclusive classrooms have

- Developed attitudes associated with valuing individual differences (*Long-Term Effects of Inclusion*, 2003)
- Left this experience with enhanced self-esteem (*Long-Term Effects of Inclusion*, 2003).

An interesting additional finding is that low-achieving students who do not have disabilities have benefitted by being in inclusive classrooms. These positive results seem to have happened because they have been exposed to the review, practice, instructional clarity, and feedback their teachers have provided for members of the class who have disabilities (*Long-Term Effects of Inclusion*, 2003).

WEB EXTENSION 6–4

Council for Exceptional Children

This is the home page for the Council for Exceptional Children, which is the leading professional organization for educators with particular interests in the education of learners with disabilities. You will find links to a variety of topics associated with the education of exceptional children, including many that deal with inclusion.

http://www.cec.sped.org/

Characteristics of Learners with Specific Disabilities

The inclusion principle places an obligation on you, as a teacher, to not simply welcome these young people as regular class members but to provide them with the help they will require to succeed. This means that you must know how to help young people who will be challenged by physical and other personal conditions that differ from those of many other young people. You should devote part of your personal professional-development work toward preparing yourself to help these special learners.

One of your challenges will be to make these special students truly feel that they belong in your classroom. Learners with disabilities often report great differences in the degree to which they are welcomed (Williams, 1998). When they feel they are an integral part of a class, their motivation increases.

Perhaps the best thing you can do to make all class members feel they belong is to promote the idea that learners with disabilities are no different than other learners. If you take this approach, prospects are good that other students will pay little attention to their class-mates' disabilities and will accept them as members of your classroom community (Williams, 1998).

Learning about the nature of individual disabilities is a good way to begin developing the expertise needed to work effectively with learners with disabilities. However, you need to be careful in conclusions you draw as you begin this preparation. You must recognize that the general characteristics of individuals who have specific conditions are just that—*general*. Great diversity exists among learners in each category. Many learners also fall into several categories simultaneously. Hence, it is well to approach information about each category of disability with an appreciation of the within-category diversity and of the multiple-category membership of many individual learners.

In the following subsections, you will learn about conditions that will characterize some learners with disabilities who will be in your classes.

WHAT DO YOU THINK?

PREPARING OTHER LEARNERS TO ACCEPT THOSE WITH DISABILITIES

You are a seventh-grade teacher. Your principal has told you that, starting about the third week of school, you will have two new learners in your classroom. One requires the use of a wheelchair; the other walks with crutches and braces. Consider what you might do to prepare members of your class to welcome these newcomers.

WHAT DO YOU THINK?

1. What initial reactions do you expect from other members of the class?
2. Specifically, what will you do to welcome these newcomers?
3. What ideas do you have for encouraging present class members to make these new learners feel like a part of the group?

 To respond to these questions online, go to the What Do You Think? *module for this chapter of the Companion Website.*

Speech Impairments.   Learners with speech impairments are young people whose speech differs in significant ways from that of others in their age groups. They experience difficulties associated with making certain sounds, stuttering, and maintaining an appropriate vocal quality.

As a result of frustrations associated with speaking, you will find that many learners in this category have low self-images because they believe they are inferior or incompetent. One unhappy result of this situation is that school dropout rates are high for learners in this group.

Visual Impairments.   Individuals who are visually impaired or blind can compete well with other learners in regular classrooms if their communications skills are well developed. As a teacher, you must modify your instructional program appropriately. For example, when making assignments, you need to provide information orally to your visually impaired learners. Sometimes you will want to make audio recordings of both assignments and important lesson-related information.

Many blind learners use personal computers to communicate in writing with their teachers. Blind learners also often use **Braille.** Braille is a system of touch reading developed for blind people. It employs embossed dots that represent letters and words that trained users can read.

Young people in this category may have mobility problems. They will require time to master the new room arrangements and to develop a good level of comfort in moving from place to place.

Hearing Impairments. Hearing-impaired learners' most marked differences from so-called normal learners are their difficulties in producing speech and in acquiring language skills. They fall into two basic categories. Deaf learners have a hearing loss that is so serious that their ability to acquire a normal use of language is greatly impaired. Hard-of-hearing learners have significant hearing loss, but they still are able to acquire normal speech patterns.

Some learners with hearing impairments use hearing aids. You need to know how these work. It is especially important for you to become acquainted with how batteries are replaced. You may want to keep a supply of batteries in your desk. If you have these items on hand, you'll be able to do an immediate battery replacement and avoid the possibility that a learner will lose the benefit of a whole day's instruction.

Attention Deficit Disorder and Other Specific Learning Disabilities. **Attention Deficit Disorder (ADD)** and other specific learning disabilities include disorders characterized by impairments to one or more of the psychological processes associated with understanding and using language. Learners with these disabilities have problems in listening, thinking, speaking, writing, spelling, and calculating. Such labels as *perceptual handicap, dyslexia,* or *minimal brain dysfunction* sometimes are used to refer to these kinds of learning disabilities.

You will find that classmembers with learning disabilities often will find it hard to follow your directions. Sometimes they find it difficult to get started on an assignment. Often, they have a low tolerance for frustration. These problems are widespread. More than one-half of all young people who receive federally sponsored services for the learning disabled fall within this category (U.S. Department of Education, 2000, p. 20).

Orthopedic Impairments. It is difficult to generalize about learners who are orthopedically impaired. These young people may suffer from one (or more) of a number of conditions that interfere with their motor control. You need to learn the nature of each disability and its implications for the instructional process before you can pinpoint the specific needs of an individual learner. For example, some of these young people may lack the ability to tap keys on a computer keyboard. You need to think about alternative equipment and supports you can provide that will allow them to access computer-based information. Your thinking also must extend to identification of ways for learners with orthopedic limitations to show that they have mastered assigned content. For example, some of them may not be able to complete written exams or to stand up in front of a group to make an oral presentation.

Emotional Disturbance. Behaviors of emotionally disturbed learners deviate from the behaviors expected for learners in their age group. Their behavior patterns interfere with their development as individuals and with their ability to establish and maintain harmonious relationships with others. Characteristics of learners in this group vary. Some learners may be outspoken, defiant, and rude seekers of attention. Others may be withdrawn, quiet, and even fearful.

VIDEO VIEWPOINTS

Meeting the Needs of Exceptional Students

WATCH: This *Nightline* video segment focuses on a special school in Chicago for emotionally disturbed teens. The segment reveals the deep turmoil in some students that interferes with their ability to succeed or even survive in a regular public school. The major focus is on one girl who suffers from severe depression.

THINK: Discuss with your classmates, or in your teaching journal, the following questions:

1. The video states that one in eight adolescents suffers from depression and that it is the third leading cause of death among Americans aged 15 to 24. This means that high school teachers are likely to have at least a couple of students suffering from depression in each classroom. What can the teacher in a regular classroom do to meet the needs of these students?

2. In this segment the students often had trouble relating to other students. How can a teacher prepare other students for working with special-needs students included in the regular classroom?

3. Are there limits to the full inclusion of students with special needs in regular classrooms? What should be the determining factors?

LINK: What do you think you need to know to teach in an inclusive classroom?

Complete this activity and submit your responses online in the Video Viewpoints *module for this chapter of the* Companion Website.

Many of these young people find it almost impossible to make independent decisions. Their peers heavily influence them. Even though they tend to look to peers for guidance, often their peers do not particularly like them. Many of these unhappy learners sense themselves to be isolated from others of their own age, and many have low self-concepts. Many do not do well in school.

Mental Retardation.   Mental retardation is a term applied to people (1) whose intellectual development lags significantly behind that of their age mates and (2) whose potential for academic achievement has been found to be markedly lower than that of so-called normal people. Mental retardation has multiple causes and levels. Three general categories are used to describe these learners: *educable, trainable,* and *profoundly retarded.* Most learners who spend all or part of their school day in regular classrooms are in the educable category. This group includes those learners who are mentally retarded who deviate the least from the normal range of mental functioning.

Huge differences exist among individual learners within the educable category. In general, all levels can derive some benefits from exposure to the school program. Their IEPs and the specific instruction you give them should reflect their individual characteristics. One of your objectives in working with these young people is to help them develop more self-confidence. Many of them have had a history of school failure. As a result, when presented with a new assignment, they may feel defeated before they begin.

Over the years, professionals have identified promising instructional approaches for helping young people with various kinds of disabilities. Some examples of common recommendations are provided in Figure 6.3.

Learners with Conditions Associated with	Suggested Approaches in the Classroom
Speech Impairments	• Call on learners with speech impairments only when they have raised a hand or otherwise indicated a willingness to speak. • Praise these learners when they make a verbal contribution. • Make time for these learners to speak to you one-on-one. Such conversations give you opportunities to raise their morale and give them opportunities to verbalize concerns about schoolwork in a "safe" atmosphere where other class members won't ridicule their communication problems.
Visual Impairments	• Take care to communicate instructions slowly to visually impaired learners that you provide to others in written form. • If instructions are complex and lengthy, consider giving visually impaired learners an audio recording of the information you want them to have. They can play back the cassette later (repeating the process, if necessary) to get the details they need. • Realize that moving around the school and the classroom can be a problem for visually impaired learners. Allow them to explore areas of the classroom when they first join your class so they can develop a good mental picture of its layout. Consider asking them to come into the room at a time when other learners are absent so they can better learn locations of chairs, desks, tables, and other classroom furniture.
Hearing Impairments	• Some learners with hearing loss have been taught to read lips. You need to be sure you face these learners when you speak so they can see your lips moving. Also, do not move around. Lip readers find it difficult to follow someone who is in motion. • Some hearing-impaired learners may have mastered a sign language. At some point, you may find it useful to take a course in signing to help you communicate with these young people. • Write key points on an overhead transparency or on the board. With older learners, you may occasionally give a short lecture. When you do this, consider distributing a sheet to class members that contains an outline of your comments.
Attention Deficit Disorder and Other Specific Learning Disabilities	• Many learners with these conditions find noise to be extremely distracting. To the extent possible, make arrangements for them to complete their work under conditions in which noise is kept to a minimum. • Work that is self-paced is more appropriate for these learners; many will give up if they sense that brighter learners are setting a pace that is "too fast." • These learners need much structure in their lessons. Provide lesson features with high motivational appeal: things to touch, special textures, interesting colors, and so forth. • Many of these learners do better when they are taught in small groups and when direct-instruction approaches are used.

FIGURE 6.3 Instructional Ideas for Helping Learners with Various Kinds of Disabilities

Source: To Assure the Free Appropriate Public Education of All Children with Disabilities: Twenty-Third Annual Report to Congress on the Implementation of the Individuals with Disabilities Education Act (p. II-27), 2001, Washington, DC: U.S. Department of Education.

Orthopedic Impairments	• Recognize that some orthopedic impairments interfere with learners' abilities to complete assignments as rapidly as other learners. You may need to allow these learners more time to complete their work. • Some learners with orthopedic impairments use walkers, crutches, and other specialized aids. You need to arrange classroom furniture in ways that allow them to use this equipment. You also may need to allow these learners to leave your class a few minutes before others because often it takes them longer to go from place to place.
Emotional Disturbance	• Develop lessons that learners with severe emotional disturbance will see as giving them a "real chance" to succeed. • Reduce distractions as learners do their work. • Take extra care in giving directions. These learners must know exactly what they are to do, and they need to understand that you will insist that they follow the instructions you provide. • As opportunities arise, help these learners understand that there is a definite connection between their behaviors and the consequences flowing from these behaviors. Many of these learners approach school (and, indeed, life) with a belief that rewards and punishments are more the result of good luck and bad luck.
Mental Retardation	• Develop lessons that are short, direct, and to the point. • Introduce new material in short, sequential steps. • Avoid placing educable learners in highly competitive situations. • Build educable learners' confidence by reducing the number of tasks they are to do and by ensuring that they complete them.

FIGURE 6.3   Continued

Assistive Technology

Help provided to learners with disabilities enjoys a higher probability of success when multiple approaches are used. As a teacher, you will want to make accommodations and modifications to your programs as required by individual learner needs. You may have additional adult help in your classroom from a teacher's aide or from another teacher who helps several teachers in your building meet needs of learners with disabilities. Finally, you and other teachers in your school may have access to special technologies that have been developed to help learners with disabilities. Support for learners with disabilities that comes from **assistive technology** involves the use of individual pieces of equipment or complex systems of equipment that are used to maintain or improve the functional capabilities of learners with disabilities (National Council on Disability, 2000a). Assistive technologies of various kinds help learners with disabilities to organize their work, take notes, prepare written responses to assignments, access reference materials, and change information formats to meet their special learning needs. Some assistive technologies are low-tech; others are high-tech.

Examples of low-tech technologies that help learners with disabilities are pencils with special grips, writing paper with raised lines, and sign language. Examples of high-tech assistive technologies are devices that allow speech to be converted into writing and electronic gear that enables students to use a single switch to move a computer cursor or to input data into a computer program.

As school programs have become more dependent on learner access to computers and the Internet, concerned educators have worried about achievement deficits that might result if learners with disabilities cannot take advantage of these important educational tools. In recent years, huge advances in the development of assistive technologies allowing individuals with serious physical and health limitations to use single-switch systems and other new devices to work with computers. Educators and others interested in serving the needs of learners with disabilities have recognized the potential contributions these technologies can make to the educational development of these young people. One result of this interest has been adoption of new federal requirements for members of IEP planning groups to consider how adaptive technologies might be incorporated into their IEPs.

Much work is needed to provide each learner with a disability with the necessary assistive technologies. Costs of these technologies are high. In addition, many school leaders and teachers do not know how to integrate newer assistive technologies into existing school programs. Given the federal government's interest in expanding school use of assistive technologies and the growing volume of support from educational professionals who have studied this issue, it is likely that you and your learners with disabilities will rely on more larger numbers of these technologies in the years ahead.

Some intriguing trends are developing that may affect how future technological advances will be used to help learners with disabilities. For a long time, these technologies have tended to be used to provide special assistance to individuals to help them accommodate to existing kinds of instructional materials. Sometimes this approach has been referred to as "fixing the learner" (*Special Education News*, 2000). In the future, new technologies may be embedded within instructional materials and programs so that learners with various characteristics (including disabilities) can access them according to their own needs. For more information about using technology for the purpose of "fixing instructional materials and programs," see Chapter 13, "Influences of Technology," about work being done at the Center for Applied Technology.

WEB EXTENSION 6–5

Computer and Web Resources for People with Disabilities

The Alliance for Technology Access is an organization dedicated to helping people with disabilities take advantage of new technologies. At this site, you will find information about the group's book, *Computer and Web Resources for People with Disabilities*. The book provides (1) true-life stories of individuals with disabilities who are extending their capacity through the use of special technologies; (2) extensive descriptions of many newly available assistive technologies; and (3) lists of organizations, publishers, and online sources of additional background materials. When you go to this site, on the left side of the page you will see the major heading "ATA Resources." Under this you will see the subordinate heading "Read Book." If you click on Read Book, you will be taken to a table of contents and clickable links that will allow you to read the entire book online if you wish to do so. You may be particularly interested in information in Part II, "The Technology Toolbox." You will find descriptions of assistive technologies that are available to today's learners with disabilities.

http://www.ataccess.org/resources/atabook/default.html

Overrepresentation of Certain Minorities

For many years, educators have worried about the overrepresentation of young people from certain minority groups among schoolchildren who have been designated as learners with disabilities. This is especially true for African Americans. In a recent school year, African Americans accounted for 14.5% of the national school population, but they made

	American Indian/ Alaska Native	Asian/ Pacific Islander	African American (Non-Latino)	Latino	White (Non-Latino)
Percentage of Total Population of Young People, Ages 6 Through 21, Who Have Been Identified as *Learners with Disabilities*	1.3	1.8	20.3	13.7	62.9
Percentage of Total Number of Young People, Ages 6 Through 21, in the *General Population*	1.0	3.8	14.5	16.2	64.5

FIGURE 6.4   Comparison of Percentages of Minorities, Ages 6 through 21, in (1) the Learners-with-Disabilities Population and (2) the General Population

Source: To assure the free appropriate Public Education of All Children with Disabilities: Twenty-Third Annual Report to Congress on the Implementation of the Individuals with Disabilities Education Act (p. II-27), 2001, Washington, DC: U.S. Department of Education.

up 20.3% of the population of learners with disabilities. See Figure 6.4 for more statistics related to this issue.

This discrepancy reveals some startling differences between the likelihoods that African Americans and white (non-Latino) learners will be identified as having certain disabilities. For example, in 1998–1999, African American learners were

- 2.9 times as likely as white students to be labeled mentally retarded (U.S. Department of Education, 2000)
- 1.9 times as likely to be labeled emotionally disturbed (U.S. Department of Education, 2000)
- 1.3 times as likely to be labeled as having a learning disability (U.S. Department of Education, 2000).

The federal government and other groups and individuals are concerned about these patterns. There are suspicions that many African American learners have been erroneously identified as candidates for special education services. In an attempt to determine why such mistakes occur, educators have begun to look at the characteristics of individual schools where there is no discrepancy between the percentages of specific groups within the total school population and the percentages of young people from these groups who have been designated as learners with disabilities. One finding is that there is no overrepresentation of African Americans in the learners-with-disabilities populations of schools in which the entire school community—teachers, principals, parents/guardians, and others—holds high expectations for *all* students, regardless of the particular ethic, racial, social, or economic groups to which they belong (*Addressing Over-Representation of African American Students in Special Education*, 2002).

In schools where these conditions are lacking, teachers and administrators may be failing to differentiate their instruction in ways that promote success among all school groups.

Frustrations about their inability to help learners from certain groups may lead some teachers to assume something is wrong with the learners rather than with their instruction. It is feared that these attitudes may lead some teachers to inappropriately recommend young people for programs designed for learners with disabilities.

To combat this possibility, organizations such as the Council for Special Education and the National Alliance of Black School Educators recommend that schools adopt a **prereferral intervention process** (*Addressing Over-Representation of African American Students in Special Education,* 2002). Instead of immediately referring "problem" learners to groups that will conduct formal screening to determine their eligibility for services for learning disabled learners, the prereferral intervention process first seeks to determine whether something might be done to improve the nature and quality of instruction they are receiving. The hope is that the prereferral process will result in assistance to regular classroom teachers that helps them provide instruction more responsive to needs of individual learners and, as a result, decrease their desire to refer so many people from certain minority groups to screening for classification as learners with disabilities.

Concerns about overrepresentation of certain minority groups in special education programs have vexed educators for three decades. Though professionals are beginning to better understand the dimensions of the problem and to consider some promising remedies, you can be sure that you and your colleagues will continue to work with this issue in the years ahead.

GIFTED LEARNERS

For three decades the federal government has been interested in programs for gifted learners. As long ago as 1972, Congress established the **Office of Gifted and Talented.** Public Law 91-230 (*United States Statutes at Large,* 1971, p. 153) defined "gifted learners" as "children who have outstanding intellectual ability or creative talent, the development of which requires special activities or services not ordinarily provided by local education agencies." In 1974, with the passage of Public Law 93-380, more federal attention focused on gifted learners. This legislation allocated federal funds to local and state agencies to improve gifted-and-talented programs. The **Jacob K. Javits Gifted and Talented Students Education Act of 1994** provided additional federal support for these programs. This legislation authorized the U.S. Department of Education to award grants, provide leadership, and sponsor a national research center focusing on the educational needs of gifted and talented learners.

WEB EXTENSION 6–6

The National Research Center on the Gifted and Talented

This is the home page of The National Research Center on the Gifted and Talented (NRCG/T), which a well-known leader in gifted education, Dr. Joseph S. Renzulli, directs at the University of Connecticut. At this site you will find highly useful lists of downloadable online resources that focus on school programs and instruction for gifted learners. The information is wide-ranging, including topics such as the selection of program participants and assistance to parents/guardians of gifted learners.

http://www.gifted.uconn.edu/nrcgt.html

The Selection Issue

If you become involved in programs for gifted learners, you will discover that controversy often surrounds selection of participants. In years past, educators relied almost exclusively on standardized test scores to identify gifted learners. Today, much broader criteria are used, including information about applicants' special psychomotor abilities and creative talents. The guidelines schools use often also include features that are designed to ensure that selection procedures do not disadvantage applicants from ethnic and cultural minorities.

In the 1970s, when federal legislation first prompted large numbers of schools to offer special programs for gifted learners, selection procedures assumed that only a tiny fraction of the total school population would qualify. Some authorities took the position that these programs should be limited to no more than about 3% of the total school population (Mitchell & Erickson, 1978). Over the years, practical political pressures have led to a great expansion in the numbers of learners who are eligible to participate in these programs.

Special school programs such as those designed for gifted students channel money away from programs for the general population of learners. School boards find it difficult to allocate funds to programs that serve extremely small numbers of learners. Hence, there has been a political incentive for people interested in expanding programs for gifted learners to increase enrollment sizes. As more students are served, the potential number of program supporters also increases, and school boards become more likely to allocate program-support funds. At the present time, programs for gifted learners in only a few states serve fewer than 6% of enrolled learners. Some states' programs enroll more than 14% of the total student population (National Center for Education Statistics, 2001; p. 67).

Pressures Facing Gifted Learners

As you work with gifted learners, be aware of the effects your efforts have on their relationships with their classmates. For example, sometimes, you will find other learners encouraging their gifted peers to "do less." Occasionally, gifted learners, in an effort to maintain positive relationships with others in a class, may succumb to these pressures. When this happens, you may find gifted learners asking you to ease up on assignments. You need to recognize these requests as indications that these bright learners are unsure of their acceptance by fellow class members. In response, you should think of actions you might take to point out to all members of your classes that your rigorous expectations are not designed as punishment but, instead, represent learning opportunities that are in the long-term best interests of all.

In addition, parents and guardians and, regrettably, some teachers may pressure gifted learners to perform flawlessly. If these learners feel they must be perfect, they may develop unrealistic self-expectations and frustration. You must understand the damage excessive pressure can do to gifted learners and work to help them focus on their strengths and their accomplishments, not their shortcomings. It is important for these bright young people to understand that everyone has strengths and weaknesses and that it is no sign of personal failure to be less than perfect in some areas.

Enrichment Programs

Enrichment programs represent one of the two basic approaches schools use to serve gifted learners. These programs seek to provide learning experiences for gifted young people that are in addition to or go beyond those given other learners. They feature

PROFILING A TEACHER

LOOKING AFTER LEARNERS' INTERESTS—PUBLIC VIEWS AND PRIVATE STATEMENTS OF PARENTS/GUARDIANS

You probably have often heard statements such as these:

- "School programs should be designed to help every child succeed. Young people in the schools belong to the whole community, and we all have an interest in providing them with a high-quality education."
- "School programs should ensure that no child is left behind."
- "Schools should operate on the assumption that every child can learn."

As you read this profile, think about these questions:

- What comments might Rodney Lasalle make about these statements in light of his years of experience as a teacher?
- How might you begin preparing to talk to parents/guardians of (1) learners with disabilities and (2) gifted learners so they will understand that you are working hard to serve the best interests of their children?

WHAT PARENTS REALLY WANT

Rodney Lasalle has taught biology, mostly to high school sophomores and juniors, for over 20 years. He has routinely had learners with disabilities in his classes, and he has worked hard to make program modifications and other changes to accommodate their needs. At the same time, many gifted students have been enrolled in his classes. In keeping with his school district's policy, he has used an enrichment approach to provide these talented young people with challenging and motivating instructional experiences.

Over the years, Rodney has had opportunities to visit with parents/guardians of many of his students. In thinking about these conversations, he has concluded that the attitudes of parents/guardians operate on two levels: public and private.

In a public setting, parents/guardians have typically said something like this: "We want the schools to be as good as they can be for everybody." Rodney sees this comment as an example of noncontroversial, mainstream thinking. Few parents/guardians sense they will be criticized for expressing such a view.

Rodney has found that parents/guardians often express quite different opinions when they speak to him privately. If their child has a learning disability, they want assurances that Rodney is working hard to meet this learner's needs and that the school district is providing him with the resources necessary to accomplish this purpose. Similarly, parents/guardians of gifted learners want to know that their children are receiving instruction that is sufficiently complex, challenging, and motivating. They, too, want to know that sufficient school-district resources are allocated to support programming for these talented learners.

The conclusion Rodney has drawn from years of meetings with parents/guardians is that, although they are committed in a general sense to providing a good education for all, their passions are directed at ensuring that their own children are well served. He has found that in conversations with parents/guardians he has needed to emphasize that efforts to serve the broad spectrum of learners are not diverting needed resources and teacher attention away from the special needs of their children. Rodney finds that general comments about helping "all of the students" are acceptable, but that what parents/guardians really want is an answer to these questions: "Are you doing all you can to help my son or daughter? Is the school district providing you with the resources you need to provide this kind of assistance?"

experiences that challenge gifted students to maximize their considerable abilities. At the same time, enrichment programs try to maintain continuous contact between gifted and nongifted learners by keeping them together in regular classes and by moving them through the K–12 instructional program at the same rate. This means, for example, that gifted learners will take U.S. history at the same time as their nongifted peers. But it also means that the specific learning experiences provided for them in the context of the U.S. history course will be different and more challenging than those to which nongifted learners are exposed.

If you are involved in an enrichment program, you will need to make a conscious attempt to ensure that what you ask gifted learners to do truly differs from what you require of other learners. It is not appropriate for you to simply introduce them earlier to material that they would ordinarily encounter further along in the school program. If you do this, problems will result in subsequent years for both gifted learners and their teachers. For example, if gifted learners have been taught the regular Grade 12 English material in Grade 10, they may find themselves being retaught what they have already learned when they reach Grade 12.

The guarantee that enrichment programs for gifted students will truly be different is important for another reason as well. Because gifted learners are able to progress through traditional material more rapidly than nongifted learners, it may be tempting for you simply to ask them to do *more* of the same. For example, while nongifted learners might be asked to do 10 mathematics problems, you might think about requiring your gifted learners to do 15. If you do this, you are sending a message that says giftedness is a burden rather than a blessing. Your gifted students may conclude that you have decided to punish them for their special abilities.

Gifted and talented students often are characterized by high degrees of creativity and sophisticated thinking.

The enrichment approach is the most popular one for responding to the needs of gifted learners. It enjoys wide support from parents, guardians, and administrators, and it is consistent with a view of the school as a place where all kinds of learners come together. It also conforms to a widely held feeling that there are benefits in keeping learners of approximately the same age together as they progress through school. Finally, enrichment programs are relatively easy for school leaders to implement.

For a discussion of some issues associated with enrichment, see the Critical Incident titled "A Gifted Learner with a Behavior Problem."

Acceleration Programs

Acceleration programs represent a second category of responses to the needs of gifted learners. These programs increase the pace at which gifted learners complete their schooling. For example, in an accelerated program, a gifted learner might complete the entire high school program in just two years. There is no attempt to keep gifted learners in classes with nongifted learners in the same age group. Supporters of acceleration programs reject the idea that there is something useful or inherently beneficial in keeping learners in a given grade for an entire academic year. They also see no particular need to keep them in classes with learners of approximately the same age. They believe that giftedness is best developed when bright learners are as intellectually challenged as possible. Often this means moving these learners into classes with older learners, where more-advanced content is taught.

There are two types of acceleration: *subject-matter acceleration* and *grade-level acceleration*. Subject-matter acceleration allows gifted learners to take courses earlier than would be typical. For example, a sixth grader might be enrolled in a ninth-grade algebra class. Grade-level acceleration occurs when a learner is allowed to skip an entire grade and enroll as a regular member of a class of older learners. For example, a bright third-grader might be accelerated to become a member of a fifth-grade class.

Some critics of accelerated programs argue that they may interfere with the social adjustment of gifted learners. For example, how is a bright 11-year-old who is accelerated to Grade 10 going to deal with the male–female social relationships typical at the high school level? How is a 14-year-old college graduate going to fare in a work environment that may restrict hiring to people who are several years older?

The percentage of gifted learners who are in accelerated programs is small compared with the percentage enrolled in enrichment programs. Enrichment programs have been much easier to sell to education policy makers. Enrichment is simply more consistent with traditional patterns and assumptions than acceleration.

Developing Learners' Potential

Robert J. Sternberg and Todd I. Lubart (1991), who are recognized authorities in education of the gifted, have identified several things you can do as a teacher to encourage creativity among your gifted learners. First of all, you can provide opportunities for these young people to engage in responsible risk taking, something that has been identified as an essential ingredient of mature thinking (Ellington, 1999).

Some traditional classroom practices definitely do not encourage risk taking. For example, consider the results of a teacher's award of a low grade to a learner who turns in a drawing rather than an essay when asked to present reactions to a short story. A bright student soon "learns" that risk taking, particularly creative risk taking, doesn't pay. The message for you as a teacher is that you must think about what kinds of signals you send learners. If the signals are negative when they engage in risk taking, they will soon learn that risk taking is a behavior to be avoided. On the other hand, if you send positive signals when learners respond creatively and unexpectedly, you create a safe, encouraging environment that tells them that risk taking has some value.

It is also important to take special steps to help gifted learners understand how the knowledge they will be acquiring can be used. Gifted learners need to see that new information is important to them personally and that it can be used to help them perform innovative and creative tasks (Sternberg & Lubart, 1991).

You also need to think about organizational steps that will make it easier for you to differentiate assignments so that your gifted learners will be challenged to do work commensurate with their interests and abilities. Susan Winebrenner and Barbara Devlin (2001), who are specialists in the education of gifted learners, suggest that you organize your class into groups of three to five learners each, according to their ability levels. If you include all of your gifted students in one group, then you can assign them work that differs in kind, sophistication, and intensity from work you give to others. Of course, this arrangement also allows you to differentiate assignments for others according to the needs, interests, and aptitudes of learners in each group.

Gifted learners need assistance in defining problems of their own. You also need to help them consider ways in which assignments are relevant to their own interests and personal lives. This kind of personalization helps to stimulate the creative powers of gifted learners. When these bright young people play a role in identifying a problem or goal, they tend to develop a stronger sense of purpose. This commitment, in turn, often will result in their generating responses that fully utilize their considerable intellectual and creative resources.

WEB EXTENSION 6–7

National Association for Gifted Children

This is the home page of the National Association for Gifted Children (NAGC), an organization of parents, teachers, community leaders, and other professionals interested in providing gifted children with educational experiences appropriate to their talents. At this site, you will find a variety of information for teachers and parents. NAGC publishes a quarterly, *Gifted Child*. You can download abstracts of articles at this site.

http://www.nagc.org

Critical Incident

A Gifted Learner with a Behavior Problem

Mario is an extraordinarily bright fifth grader. He ranks in the 99th percentile in every category on his school district's standardized tests. He reads novels and other materials that rarely interest his peers. He spends hours each evening visiting sites on the World Wide Web. Though Mario's academic potential is high, his school performance is not good.

Mario does his work when pressed, but he rushes through his assignments. His answers, though usually technically correct, reflect sloppy work habits and an absence of serious thought. Mario's agenda seems to be to do his own work quickly so he will have time to bother others while they are doing theirs.

His teacher, Lorena McPhee, has tried to deal with this situation by asking Mario to do more than others in the class. He complains that this represents unfair treatment, and he has publicly challenged Ms. McPhee about both the regular assignments and the proposed extra work. In Mario's words, all of these things are "bogus" attempts to keep him occupied, quiet, and out of the way of others in the class.

• • •

What thoughts do you have about Mario's behavior? What might motivate him to act as he does? How do you think others in the class see Mario? How do you think Mario sees himself? What options does Ms. McPhee have? What do you see as the strengths and weaknesses of each option? If you were Ms McPhee, what would you do next?

 To respond to this Critical Incident online, go to the Critical Incidents *module for this chapter of the Companion Website.*

Key Ideas in Summary

- *Exceptional learners* have characteristics that differentiate them from typical school learners. Learners with disabilities and learners who are gifted are among groups of exceptional learners in today's schools. Differences among exceptional learners are as great as those among the total student population of the school.
- Before the passage of relevant federal legislation, teachers in traditional classrooms had little daily contact with exceptional learners. When a school served these young people, they were assigned to special classrooms and taught by teachers who worked with them exclusively. The Individuals with Disabilities Education Act (IDEA) and other federal laws today require schools, to the extent possible, to provide services to learners with disabilities in regular classrooms where they sit alongside their nondisabled peers.
- Federal legislation requires teams of individuals, including the student's regular teacher, one or more parents/guardians, and representatives of the school district in addition to the teacher, to develop an *Individualized Education Program (IEP)* for each disabled learner. Among other things, an IEP outlines goals the learner is expected to achieve in one year, establishes benchmarks and evaluation procedures to be followed, and describes special services and instructional modifications to be provided.
- Teachers who deal with learners with disabilities work to modify their instructions in two basic ways. *Accommodations* they make involve changes that allow learners with disabilities to complete tasks similar to those assigned to others in the class by changing variables related to work deadlines, the time allowed to complete assignments, where work will take place, and the nature of responses that will be taken as evidence that learning has occurred. *Modifications* represent changes teachers make to meet needs of learners with disabilities that provide them with a substitute task that varies in important ways from the one assigned to other learners.
- Today, legislation such as the *No Child Left Behind Act* requires schools to report achievement levels of subgroups and achievement levels of the entire school population. These subgroups include learners with disabilities. This means that performance levels of learners with disabilities are held up to public scrutiny.

- *Inclusion* embraces the idea that learners with disabilities, to the extent possible, should receive instructional services in regular school classrooms. Supporters argue that with appropriate personnel assistance, technological aids, and teacher training, almost all learners, regardless of the nature of their disabilities, can be effectively accommodated in regular classrooms. Some critics argue that funds are insufficient to provide teachers with the help they need to work effectively with these learners and, at the same time, serve the needs of other learners. Debates about the appropriateness of the inclusion approach continue unabated.

- Learners with disabilities are characterized by many kinds of conditions. Some of them have multiple disabilities. Disabilities you may observe among learners in your classrooms include speech impairments, visual impairments, hearing impairments, attention deficit disorder (ADD) and other specific learning disabilities, orthopedic impairments, emotional disturbance, and mental retardation.

- Today developments in the area of *assistive technology* are helping learners with disabilities to cope better with school environments. Assistive technology uses individual pieces of equipment or complex systems of equipment to help maintain or improve the functional capability of learners with disabilities.

- Educators continue to be concerned about the overrepresentation of certain minority groups among the population of schoolchildren who have been labeled as learners with disabilities. For example, the percentage of African Americans within this group is much higher than the percentage of African Americans within the general school population. There are suspicions that not enough effort is being expended to alter instructional approaches to meet the needs of these young people and that, when teachers sense they are experiencing difficulties, they have moved too quickly to classify them as learners with disabilities. Efforts are under way to do a better job of screening learners who are being considered for classification as disabled. The intent is to ensure that the percentage from an individual group in the population of learners with disabilities is close to its percentage in the general school population.

- Gifted learners have outstanding intellectual or creative abilities that require nurturing by special school programs that go beyond those provided for nongifted young people. Learners are selected for special school programs by multiple criteria that often include test scores, information about special creative and psychomotor abilities, and recommendations of teachers and counselors. Some gifted learners experience self-image problems. One common difficulty results when, in response to parental and sometimes teacher pressures, they set impossibly high performance standards for themselves.

- Programs for gifted learners are of two basic types. *Enrichment programs* keep learners in their regular age-group classes and courses, but they provide special learning experiences that are designed to develop these students' special capabilities. *Acceleration programs* are designed to increase the rate at which gifted students pass through the school program. This objective is accomplished by allowing them to skip grades and enroll in courses with older learners. Enrichment is by far the more popular of the two approaches.

- It is important that school programs do not inadvertently punish gifted learners by requiring them to do more of the same kind of work that is required of nongifted learners. Rather, programs should be designed to encourage risk taking and creative endeavors. Further, they should help gifted learners understand how the new knowledge being taught will be particularly useful to them as individuals. Finally, gifted learners should help identify the problems they will solve and redefine problems selected by teachers so the problems will be more relevant to their own needs and interests.

Chapter 6 Self-Test

 To review terms and concepts in this chapter, go to the Companion Website and take the Chapter 6 Self-Test. *Feedback for the self-test is immediate. You can keep track of your self-test scores yourself, or you can submit your scores to your instructor via e-mail.*

Preparing for Praxis

 To learn more about the Praxis test and complete this activity online, go to the Preparing for Praxis *module for this chapter of the Companion Website.*

You may be required to pass Educational Testing Service's Praxis II exam as you seek formal authorization to teach in the public schools. The *Principles of Learning and Teaching* component of Praxis II seeks to assess your knowledge about these topics: (1) Students as Learners, (2) Instruction and Assessment, (3) Communication Techniques, and (4) Profession and Community.

This chapter may be especially relevant as you prepare for questions related to the categories of Students as Learners and Instruction and Assessment. Some content may also provide information related to other Praxis II categories. You may find it useful to prepare a chart for your own use similar to the one provided here. As you encounter information related to individual categories, you can enter it into the chart. You will find a completed chart of this kind helpful as you prepare to take the Praxis II exam.

Students as Learners	Instruction and Assessment
• Student Development and the Learning Process	• Instructional Strategies
• Students as Diverse Learners	• Planning Instruction
• Student Motivation and the Learning Environment	• Assessment Strategies
Communication Techniques	**Profession and Community**
• Basic, Effective, Verbal and Nonverbal Communication Techniques	• The Reflective Practitioner
• Effect of Cultural and Gender Differences on Communications in the Classroom	• The Larger Community
• Types of Questions That Can Stimulate Discussion in Different Ways for Particular Purposes	

For Your Initial-Development Portfolio

 To complete this activity and submit your response online, go to the For Your Initial-Development Portfolio *module for this chapter of the Companion Website.*

1. What materials and ideas that you learned in this chapter about needs of special learners will you include as "evidence" in your portfolio? Select up to three separate items of information. Number them 1, 2, and 3.
2. Think about why you selected these materials. As you do so, consider these issues:
   • Specific uses you might make of this information as you plan, deliver, and assess the impact of your teaching

- The compatibility of the information with your own priorities and values
- Any contributions this information can make to your development as a teacher
- Factors that led you to include this information, as opposed to some alternatives you considered but rejected

3. Place a check in the chart here to indicate to which INTASC standard(s) each of your items of information relates.

INTASC Standard Number

ITEM OF EVIDENCE NUMBER	S1	S2	S3	S4	S5	S6	S7	S8	S9	S10
1										
2										
3										

4. Prepare a written reflection in which you analyze the decision-making process you followed. In your comments, mention the INTASC standard(s) to which your selected material relates.

Reflections

To respond to these questions online, go to the Reflections *module for this chapter at the Companion Website.*

1. In this chapter, you learned about federal legislation to improve educational programming for learners with disabilities. As you may know, when we look at American education, the federal government is, in terms of providing financial support for schools, only a small player. Though there is much rhetoric from federal officials about "improving our schools," the reality is that states and local communities pay over 90% of the bill for education. Requiring and paying for services for learners with disabilities seems to be an exception to this general pattern. Why do you think the federal government has played such an active role in promoting and supporting services for learners with disabilities?

2. Parent/guardian constituency groups who demand more educational services for young people who fall within a given category often pressure school boards. In many communities, support groups for both learners with disabilities and gifted learners are active. How should school district leaders, who have limited financial resources at their disposal, deal with pressures from groups seeking improved programming for certain categories of learners when, at the same time, these leaders are responsible for providing a high-quality education to all school learners?

3. In this chapter, you learned about many kinds of disabilities that may be present among some students you will be teaching. At this point, are you more comfortable with what you know about responding to the needs of learners with certain kinds of conditions than with others? How might you increase your understandings of conditions that are less familiar to you?

4. Suppose a policy change suddenly required school districts to use *acceleration* as the only approach for providing educational programming for gifted learners. This might result in high school teachers having two or three learners in their classes who were 10 or 11 years old. What special challenges might including these much-younger learners pose for teachers, and how might they accommodate their presence? Do not restrict your thinking to just social interactions between these learners and other students. Consider physical arrangements in classrooms, sizes of desks and chairs, and other environmental challenges these younger learners might confront.

5. By definition, gifted learners are highly intelligent young people who, in the normal course of events, do not find the traditional academic

content of school programs to be a daunting challenge. Some critics of special school programs for gifted learners argue that these learners are already "advantaged." Because of their high intelligence, few will have difficulty completing graduation requirements and qualifying for admission to colleges and universities. Why, then, should school budgets divert more money to these young people who, absent this kind of help, are certain to "make it"? It would be better, these critics suggest, to spend money on less-able learners to provide them with the tools they will need either to compete effectively in the job market or to cope with college and university work. How compelling do you find this argument? Explain your answer.

Field Experiences, Projects, and Enrichment

1. Invite to your class a director of special education or another official from a local school district who is responsible for overseeing programs for learners with disabilities. Ask this person to describe the kinds of federal and state regulations that must be observed, and ask how decisions are made about learning experiences to be provided to each child who is served. If possible, ask to see a copy of a typical IEP.

2. Interview two or more classroom teachers who teach a grade level you intend to teach. Ask them about special things they do to provide instruction for exceptional learners. What kind of special training or assistance do they get from the district to help them with these young people? How do they react to working with these learners? Share your findings with the class in the form of a brief oral report.

3. Prepare a collection of professional journal articles that focus on practical things you might do in your classroom to meet the needs of learners with disabilities who are regular members of your classes. Organize a symposium with several others in your class on the topic "Practical Approaches to Developing a Successful Full-Inclusion Classroom." Draw content from your article collection.

4. Visit a class for gifted learners. (Your course instructor may be able to provide some assistance.) What kinds of instructional techniques do you see being used? Are learners asked to do things that are truly different from what goes on in regular classes? Are you able to form impressions of how learners feel about being in the class? Share your findings with your instructor in the form of a brief reaction paper.

5. Prepare a list of Web sites that feature information that might be useful to you in providing enrichment experiences for gifted learners. For each site, give a title, its URL, a brief description of contents, and why the site information might improve your understanding of gifted learners.

References

Addressing Over-Representation of African American Students in Special Education. (2002). Arlington, VA: Council for Exceptional Children, and Washington, DC: National Alliance of Black Educators.

Burrell, S., & Warboys, L. (2000, July). Special education and the juvenile justice system. *Juvenile Justice Bulletin.* [http:www.ncjrs.org/html/ojjdp/2000_6_5/contents.html]

Ellington, J. E. (1999). In K. T. Henson & B. F. Eller, *Educational Psychology for Effective Teaching.* Belmont, CA: Wadsworth.

IDEA '97: General Information. (2001). [http://www.ed.gov/offices/OSERS/IDEA/overview.html]

Long-term effects of inclusion. (2003, November). Arlington, VA: ERIC Clearinghouse on Disabilities and Gifted Education. [http://ericec.org/faq/i-long.html]

Mitchell, P. B., & Erickson, D. K. (1978). The education of gifted and talented children: A status report. *Exceptional Children.* 45(1), 12–16.

National Center for Education Statistics. (2001). *Digest of Education Statistics, 2001.* Washington, DC: Author.

National Center for Education Statistics. (2002). *Percent of public schools with students with various disabilities, and of those, percent with special hardware and special software for these students, by type of disability and by school characteristics: 2001.* Washington, DC: Author. [http://nces.ed.gov/pubs2002/internet/table12.asp]

National Council on Disability. (2000a). *Federal policy barriers to assistive technology.* Washington, DC: Author.

National Council on Disability. (2000b). *Transition and post-school outcomes for youth with disabilities: Closing the gaps to post-secondary education and employment.* Washington, DC: Author.

National Education Association. (1999, May). Inclusion confusion. *NEAToday Online.* [http://www.nea.org/neatoday/9905/cover.html]

No Child Left Behind Act of 2001, Public Law 107-110, 115 Stat. 1425 (2002).

Savage, T. V., & Armstrong, D. G. (2004). *Effective teaching in elementary social studies.* (5th ed.). Upper Saddle River, NJ: Merrill/Prentice Hall.

Special Education News. (2000, Oct 5). CAST director sees technology changing fundamental notion of students. [http://www.specialednews.com/technology/technews/CASTfuture100500.html]

Sternberg, R. J., & Lubart, T. I. (1991). Creating creative minds. *Phi Delta Kappan, 72*(8), 608–14.

United States Statutes at Large. (1971). 91st Congress, 1970–1971 (Vol. 84, Part 1). Washington, DC: U.S. Government Printing Office.

U.S. Department of Education. (2000). *To assure the free appropriate public education of all children with disabilities: Twenty-second annual report to Congress on the implementation of the Individuals with Disabilities Education Act.* Washington, DC: Author.

U.S. Department of Education. (2001). *To assure the free appropriate public education of all children with disabilities: Twenty-third annual report to Congress on the implementation of the Individuals with Disabilities Education Act.* Washington, DC: Author.

Williams, L. J. (1998). *Membership in inclusive classrooms: Middle school students' perceptions.* Unpublished doctoral dissertation, University of Arizona, Tucson.

Winebrenner, S., & Devlin, B. (2001). Cluster grouping of gifted students: How to provide full-time services on a part-time budget: Update 2001. (ERIC EC Digest No. E607). Alexandria, VA: ERIC Clearinghouse on Disabilities and Gifted Children.

Part 3

Teaching and Assessing

CHAPTERS

CHAPTER

7

The Curriculum

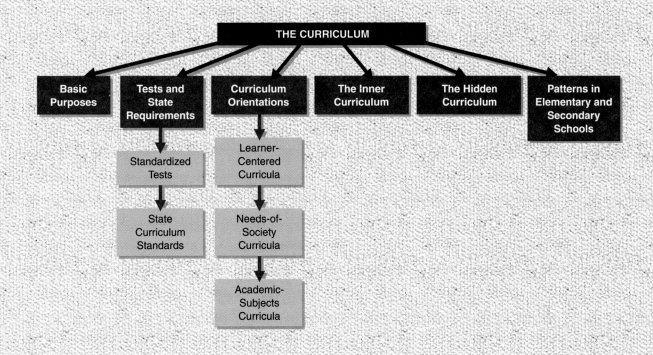

OBJECTIVES

This chapter will help you to

- describe the basic purposes of the *curriculum*.
- explain how topics you choose to emphasize in the classroom may be influenced by *standardized tests* and *state curriculum standards*.
- distinguish among *learner-centered*, *needs-of-society*, and *academic-subjects* curricula.
- point out how the *inner curriculum* shapes what learners will take away from your units and lessons.
- suggest ways in which the *hidden curriculum* sends messages to school learners.
- describe typical content patterns in elementary and secondary schools.

BASIC PURPOSES

One of the challenges you and your colleagues will face is striking a reasoned balance between the huge volume of content that potentially *could* be taught and the actual selection of content that *should* be taught. No matter how well prepared and well intentioned you are, you can never teach it all. For one thing, "teaching it all" suggests that there are repositories somewhere that contain every scrap of information about your subject. Obviously this is not true. In addition, your personal background probably makes you much better equipped to teach certain content. The priorities of your community will suggest that some content related to your subject will garner more local support than others. Your students' backgrounds also will place some practical limits on the information they can absorb. In short, many influences impose limits on the kinds of information you can include in your courses.

Identifying and organizing the basic content components in school programs are the domains of curriculum. The term originates from a Latin word that refers to a track for running. Over the years, the term has come to mean a running sequence of learning experiences. In a modern school setting, the curriculum reflects decisions that relate to

- Selecting specific elements of content to include in instructional programs,
- Establishing priorities among these content elements, and
- Identifying recommended sequences that allow content to be introduced to learners in ways that facilitate learning. (Armstrong, 2003)

Quite often, you will hear both the term *curriculum* and the term instruction used in discussions that focus on plans for school programs. Curriculum issues are those that relate to the characteristics of an overall plan for learning. Instruction deals with the specific means of achieving that plan.

TESTS AND STATE REQUIREMENTS

When you begin teaching, standardized tests and **state curriculum standards** will exert important influences on decisions you make about what content to include in your units and lessons. Standardized tests report individuals' scores and how they compare with expected scores of similar kinds of learners. State curriculum standards identify elements of content that must be included in programs taught at specific grades and in specific courses.

Standardized Tests

You probably took many standardized tests during your own days in public-school classrooms. Measurement professionals develop these test and first administer them to selected samples of learners (for example, sixth graders studying mathematics). Scores of individuals in these sample groups are used to establish **norms,** which are expected scores for learners with characteristics similar to the young people in the samples. When subsequent classes of students take these tests, their individual scores are compared with the norms.

For many years, although standardized-test scores interested educators who used them as a variable of concern when thinking about improving school programs, the general public paid little attention to them. In 1983, the National Commission on Excellence in Education published *A Nation at Risk*. This report suggested that indifference to the schools had led to serious deterioration in program quality and that our country had ". . . in effect been committing an act of unthinking, unilateral educational disarmament," (p. 5). *A*

Nation at Risk and the numerous educational reforms that have followed established educational improvement as a high-priority public concern.

One result of this national focus on education has been an increased public demand for data regarding what learners are taking away from their school experiences. Standardized-test scores have emerged as an information source citizens increasingly use to make judgments about the relative quality of individual school districts, individual schools, and even individual teachers and administrators. This interest has prompted a huge expansion in the numbers of standardized tests learners take. Today, American schools administer standardized tests more frequently than any other country in the world (Kohn, 2000).

The Case for Standardized Tests.   Supporters of standardized tests claim their extensive use in schools provides important benefits to the public at large, to teachers and administrators, and to students. Some arguments made in defense of standardized tests include:

- Standardized tests help the general public make judgments about the quality of individual schools and school districts. Scores allow for school-district-to-school-district and school-to-school comparisons based on a common standard.
- Standardized tests give school administrators and teachers a way to focus their instruction. Content featured in standardized tests removes ambiguity from the instructional planning process and allows educators to design instructional programs focused on the important content featured in standardized tests.
- Standardized tests facilitate student learning. This positive benefit occurs because the tests encourage teachers to provide well-organized, tightly focused learning experiences that center on limited, but important, content that is featured in the tests.
- Standardized tests allow for meaningful comparisons of the effectiveness of individual teachers. Scores of similar kinds of learners can be examined and used to identify "effective" and "ineffective" teachers. This information is useful to general public and to school leaders, who can help individual teachers whose effectiveness falls short.

WEB EXTENSION 7–1

Parents' Perceptions of Standardized Tests

At this site you will find survey highlights of parents' perceptions of and reactions to standardized tests. The American Society for Supervision and Curriculum Development (ASCD) commissioned the survey. Results indicate that many parents are unsure about the content featured on mandated state tests. You will find information here that may prove useful in discussing standardized tests with parents.

http://www.ascd.org/educationnews/pr/sylvan.html

The Case Against Standardized Tests.   As you examine discussions of standardized tests, you will find that much controversy swirls around this issue. The following are among points that some critics of standardized tests often make:

- Learners' standardized-test scores are based on their performance on the day (or days) that a test is given. There are questions about whether a given learner's performance at a particular time represents an adequate sample of the individual's level of understanding (Armstrong, 2003).

- Variables, including family income and parents' levels of education, often exert a stronger influence on learners' scores than the quality of teaching they receive (U.S. Department of Education, 2001). Hence, it makes little sense to use standardized-test scores to make comparisons among schools and teachers.
- Though it may be possible to identify groups of learners who have largely similar characteristics, there is no assurance that learning resources, buildings' physical facilities, and other variables that may affect learners' performances on tests can be equated. As a result, the assumption that test scores represent legitimate comparisons among similar groups of learners is open to question.
- The same standardized test may be given to thousands of learners. As a result, these tests must be designed in ways that allow for quick, electronic scoring. This reality results in tests that feature mostly forced-choice items such as multiple-choice, matching, and true–false questions. Test items of these kinds are ill suited to assessing more sophisticated levels of learner thinking, such as the abilities to compare/contrast, analyze, and synthesize. The emphasis these tests place on lower levels of thinking encourages teachers to focus instruction on memory-and-recall kinds of learning rather than on more-challenging instruction designed to nurture the development of more-sophisticated thinking processes.

WEB EXTENSION 7–2

Fair Test

The National Center for Fair & Open Testing maintains this site. This group is particularly concerned about biases that can be embedded within standardized tests that may work to the disadvantage of learners from certain racial, cultural, and income groups. You will find links to numerous additional sites that feature information challenging the wisdom of schools' decisions to make extensive use of standardized tests.

http://www.fairtest.org

Standardized Tests and Teachers.   Though questions about standardized tests continue to be debated, one reality you will face in the classroom is that school administrators, parents, and members of the general public will pay attention to the standardized test scores of your learners. In some parts of the country, high scores bring extra money and other rewards to schools, teachers, and administrators, and low scores can lead to negative results—even to loss of jobs. Interest in standardized-test scores will be an important influence as you identify elements of content to emphasize in your units and lessons. You and your teaching colleagues quite probably will spend time talking about the contents of standardized tests and discussing ways to shape your teaching programs to help your learners score well.

State Curriculum Standards

State curriculum standards specify kinds of content, and sometimes particular learning experiences, that schools are required to provide to learners in individual subjects in elementary schools and to students in individual courses in middle schools and high schools.

This teacher evaluates a proposed new text by comparing its content to his state's curriculum standards.

The rise of state curriculum standards, in part, resulted from more-intensive interest in standardized tests. As standardized tests grew in number and as more and more people started to use them to make district-to-district, school-to-school, and educator-to-educator comparisons, some critics pointed out a problem with place-to-place program consistency. Though learners in different places might take a similar test, there were few guarantees that the content they had been exposed to in their classes was similar. Without an assurance that teachers in multiple locations were introducing learners to the same content, differences in levels of performance on standardized tests could as easily be attributed to varying contents of lessons and units as to varying qualities of teacher performance.

By the early 1990s, many content-specialty organizations had become concerned that the quality of the school programs related to their subject areas was not as good as it should be. Many of these organizations began developing curriculum standards that laid out the content to be treated in individual elementary grades and in middle school and high school courses and that, in some cases, gave extensive suggestions for introducing these topics to learners. (See Figure 7.1 for some examples.) In 1995, Diane Ravitch, a former U.S. assistant secretary of Education, published *National Standards in American Education: A Citizen's Guide*. In this book, she argued that "standards are created because they improve the activity of life" (p. 89).

Large numbers of states used arguments in Ravitch's book as a rationale for establishing state curriculum standards. Many of these standards drew heavily on the work of content-specialty organizations such as the National Council of Teachers of Mathematics, the National Science Teachers Association, the National Council of Teachers of English, and the National Council for the Social Studies. Enthusiasm for state curriculum standards continued into the early 21st century. Today, the federal No Child Left Behind Act (2002)

Standards developed by content-specialty organizations often have influenced state curriculum standards. You may be interested in looking at the following standards. Each was developed by a major national content-specialty organization.

- *Standards for the English Language Arts* (1996). Urbana, IL: National Council of Teachers of English, and Newark, DE: International Reading Association.

  Web sites: National Council of Teachers of English—**http://www.ncte.org**

  International Reading Association—**http://www.reading.org/**

- *Principles and Standards for School Mathematics* (2000). Reston, VA: National Council of Teachers of Mathematics.

  Web site: **http://www.nctm.org/**

- *National Science Education Standards* (1996). Washington, DC: National Academy Press.

  Web site: National Science Teachers Association—**http://www.nsta.org/**

- *Expectations of Excellence: Curriculum Standards for Social Studies* (1994). Washington, DC: National Council for the Social Studies.

  Web site: **http://www.ncss.org /**

You will find links to these documents at the Web sites maintained by these organizations.

FIGURE 7.1   Standards Developed by Content-Specialty Organizations

requires every state to develop and assess learner performance related to a rigorous set of curriculum standards.

The Case for State Curriculum Standards.   Defenders of state curriculum standards contend that these important guidelines will improve the quality of education in the schools. Research findings support this view (Suter, 2000). The following examples are representative of the kinds of benefits supporters contend result when states adopt curriculum standards:

- Standards facilitate school-to-school comparisons. Standards make this possible because they require different schools to meet a common set of content standards.
- Standards provide targets that standardized-test developers can use. Because standards require that all schools teach the mandated content, their presence helps ensure that content assessed by standardized tests is content actually taught.
- Standards make it easier for learners to keep pace with an instructional program when they move from school to school. Because all schools in a state are required to emphasize similar kinds of content within individual grade levels and courses, the possibilities that learners moving to new schools will encounter totally unfamiliar kinds of academic programs are reduced.
- Standards promote educational equity. Because all students in a state, by law, must be exposed to content embedded in state curriculum standards, all children will experience the rigorous content the standards require.
- Specification of content in state curriculum standards results from a beneficial collection of widely dispersed content. Curriculum-development expertise is unevenly distributed across a state. Absent state-level standards, this condition

means that some school districts will have outstanding curricular programs whereas others will have much-less-distinguished programs. Preparation of standards draws together the best talents of the state and puts into law their decisions, which will benefit all school districts and students.

The Case Against State Curriculum Standards.   Not everyone agrees that the spread of state curriculum standards has been a desirable development. Critics sometimes raise these issues:

- There has been a long tradition of local control of education in the United States. The movement to establish state curriculum standards moves control of academic programs out of local school districts and militates against local school districts' efforts to provide instruction that is well fitted to the needs of young people in individual communities.
- Many state standards include content components that borrow heavily from standards developed by national content-specialty organizations. Individuals in these groups tend to exaggerate the importance of their subject areas and to insist that learners deal with more-sophisticated kinds of content than typical citizens need. Too often standards assume that all students are headed for futures as academic specialists in fields such as science, mathematics, English, and social studies.
- State curriculum standards include content that may not be representative of the field but that, rather, represents a biased perspective of pressure groups whose influence was felt by state-level decision makers when contents of standards were being developed and debated. Often well-organized pressure groups representing fringe-group opinions have influenced decisions that are contrary to what majority, mainstream opinion might desire.
- Though state standards are supposed to identify contents that measurement specialists should use when constructing related standardized tests, standardized-test development takes time. Requirements states impose on schools to implement state curriculum standards mean that, in many cases, the content taught to learners will not match the content of existing standardized tests. Because of time required to develop standardized tests, old, inappropriate tests may have to be used for years after classroom-content emphases have changed in light of mandates associated with curriculum standards.

State Curriculum Standards and Teachers.   State curriculum standards obligate teachers to introduce learners to content that is mandated for individual grade levels and courses. These requirements will limit what topics you cover. In preparation for teaching, you will want to become familiar with curriculum standards in your state as they apply to the grade level or subject area you want to teach. Many states now make these standards available through links at Web sites maintained by the state department of education. Your instructor also will be able to suggest other places to locate this information.

State curriculum standards provide general guidelines that will affect your choice of lesson and unit content; however, you probably will not find the content mandates to be excessively constraining. You still will have opportunities to introduce other content that you deem important, based on your learners' interests and backgrounds and the nature of your own professional preparation. You also will find few mandates regarding how content is to be introduced. In the main, decisions related to instructional procedures will be yours alone.

VIDEO VIEWPOINTS

High-Stakes Testing

WATCH: This *Nightline* video segment discusses the issue of high-stakes testing. The focus is on Florida and the Florida Comprehensive Assessment Test that is required for promotion and graduation. The segment covers both sides of the issue, illustrating the need for high standards to prepare students for success in the world and the issue of whether graduation or promotion should rest solely on the scores received on just one test.

THINK: Discuss with your classmates, or in your teaching journal, the following questions:

1. What is your response to the question of using one criterion, performance on a test, to make promotion and graduation decisions?
2. It seems clear that these types of tests are determining the curriculum of the schools. What do you see as the possible problems with that approach?
3. What are some of the issues surrounding the use of high-stakes tests that are not discussed in this video segment?

LINK: How does the debate regarding high-stakes testing relate to other factors such as equal educational opportunities and labeling of students?

Complete this activity and submit your responses online in the Video Viewpoints *module for this chapter of the Companion Website.*

WEB EXTENSION 7–3

Products—Standards

Mid-continent Research for Education Laboratory, better known as McREL, is a private, non-profit organization that promotes improved education through research, product development, and service. McREL professionals have been national leaders in researching educational standards and in disseminating information related to policies associated with the standards movement. At this Web page you will find links to numerous articles dealing with educational standards' issues.

http://www.mcrel.org/products/standards/index.asp

CURRICULUM ORIENTATIONS

Even though state curriculum standards and standardized testing programs influence curriculum decisions, school program leaders in individual districts still exercise much discretion over the exact configuration of programs. As a result, there still are place-to-place variations in the kinds of decisions school officials make regarding (1) specific content elements to include in instructional programs, (2) priorities assigned to individual program components, and (3) recommended sequences of learning experiences. Even within individual school districts, people may have differences of opinion about curriculum decisions that have been made. For example, when you begin teaching, you probably will find members of your faculty occasionally engaged in spirited discussions about which curricular patterns give learners "the best" kinds of academic experiences.

Opinions differ because people have different values and, as a result, individuals have varied ideas about what educational priorities should be. For example, some people favor a **learner-centered orientation** that emphasizes individual interests and needs more than subject-matter content. Those who subscribe to this position see personal development as the most important obligation of the school. For further discussion of learner-centered education see Henson (2003) and Henson (2004).

Others believe that schools should adopt curricula reflecting a **needs-of-society orientation** that features content and programs that will produce young people who can move smoothly into the workplace. Many supporters of this view worry that learner-centered programs may not provide young people with useful employment skills.

Still others reject both the learner-centered and needs-of-society approaches. They fear that learner-centered programs lack intellectual rigor. They also like to point out that the needs of society change frequently and, hence, do not provide dependable guidelines for planning and organizing school learning experiences. Individuals with these views frequently champion curricula built around an **academic-subjects orientation.** Programs associated with this point of view place heavy emphases on traditional school subjects such as English, history, and mathematics.

If you examine school programs today, you will find some that are consistent with all three of these basic orientations. Partisans of each position are sincere in believing their view to be the best or the most responsible. Differences in priorities reflected in these positions underscore the difficulties that policy makers face when they make decisions about what must be taught. Whatever approaches they take are likely to be applauded by some people and attacked by others.

Learner-Centered Curricula

The 18th-century philosopher Jean-Jacques Rousseau championed the idea that instructional programs should focus on individual learner needs. As he studied the world, Rousseau concluded that human civilization was corrupt. He rejected the idea that learners should be educated to meet the needs of society. In his view, this would result in an irresponsible transmission of corrupt social values from generation to generation.

Rousseau contended that children are born good and that whatever evil comes to characterize them later in life is imposed by society's negative influences. To remedy this situation, Rousseau wanted schools that would protect children from society and that would allow children's naturally good instincts to unfold with a minimum of disruption.

According to Rousseau, people pass through four distinct growth phases on the way to maturity. From birth to age 5, perceptual skills and muscle coordination develop. At this stage, Rousseau recommended that educators protect children from social restraints and allow them to experience directly the consequences of their own actions.

During the next stage, ages 5 through 12, Rousseau recommended that there be no formal education. Children at this stage of their lives should simply be allowed to do what comes naturally. Rousseau felt that personal experience alone was a sufficient teacher for young people in this age group.

Rousseau argued that education should become a formal enterprise for the first time only when children were in the next stage, ages 12 to 15. During this time, children should be exposed to teachers who would make learning opportunities available to them. Instruction should not be heavy-handed or prescriptive. Teachers should function primarily as motivators, and their roles should be to stimulate learners' curiosity so they will want to study such subjects as astronomy, geography, and agriculture.

Rousseau saw the final stage of development occurring between the ages of 15 and 20. During this time, he believed that individuals develop refined human-relations skills, an appreciation of beauty, and a sense of personal and religious values. He thought young people in this age group should be encouraged, but certainly not forced, to study such subjects as religion and ethics.

Rousseau's ideas influenced many more-recent supporters of the needs-of-learners orientation to curriculum. For example, the logic behind many proposals that seek to "humanize" school programs are indebted to Rousseau's thinking. Perhaps the best-known American believer in learners-centered education was the eminent American educational philosopher John Dewey. Dewey believed that the curriculum should be constructed out of the actual experience and curiosity of the child. However, he did not reject inclusion of traditional subject matter. Dewey believed that this academic content should always be organized in such a way that it related to learners' life experiences. Present-day supporters of needs-of-learner education often argue that the need for this orientation is becoming more compelling as students become increasingly ethnically, linguistically, and culturally diverse (Polakow, 1999).

The Case for Learner-Centered Curricula.   An important strength of needs-of-learners programs is their placement of concern for individual learners as the heart of the planning process. Such programs remind educators of their responsibility to serve young people and provide experiences that will help them to live rich and fulfilling lives.

Learning experiences associated with this orientation have the potential to break down artificial barriers among subject areas. For example, when you use the interests of young people as the basis for planning and organizing courses, you are able to draw specific information from a wide selection of academic specialties. This approach frees knowledge from its artificial compartmentalization into the traditional disciplines. It can also support your efforts to develop highly motivating learning environments.

The Case Against Learner-Centered Curricula.   Critics of curricula based on learners' needs often focus on the issue of efficiency. Efforts undertaken to diagnose and respond to students' special needs require excessive time; hence, curricula designed around needs of individual learners are not cost-effective. Doubters also believe that all learners should master some common content, regardless of their levels of initial interest.

Another major concern is that learners may be poor judges of their own real needs and will opt for academic experiences that are shallow. If, as a teacher, you pander to poor decisions of immature learners, the net result may be graduates who are ill equipped for the demands of living in a complex, technological society.

WEB EXTENSION 7–4

SERN—Sudbury Education Resource Network

Sudbury model schools base their philosophy and practices on the learner-centered orientation developed at the Sudbury Valley School in Massachusetts. Core ideas include freedom, democracy, trust, and responsibility. Learners in Sudbury schools direct their own educational experiences. At this site, you will find general information about ideas supporting practices in Sudbury schools and links to pages maintained by individual schools that are committed to this mode of education.

http://www.sudburynetwork.org/modelIntroduction.htm

Needs-of-Society Curricula

According to W. H. Schubert (1986), schools ". . . fulfill social needs. Societies ostensibly establish schools to help further their goals and promote their values in successive generations" (p. 217). Curricula developed from a needs-of-society perspective tend to fall into one of two categories: those taking a **problems approach** and those focusing on **citizenship development.**

School programs that emphasize the problems approach are designed to help learners develop skills and insights relevant to solving pressing social problems. Supporters contend that the schools are institutions charged with ensuring social survival. To accomplish this objective, school programs should introduce young people to problems that challenge our social order. This should prepare them to become citizens who will confront problems and work for solutions.

Proponents of citizenship development point out that adults in our society need certain basic skills in order to make a contribution. Programs consistent with this emphasis place a high priority on teaching topics that emphasize information learners will find useful in their adult years. Vocational education is assigned a high priority. Some partisans of this view are suspicious of school experiences that do not have a clear relationship to what young people will be encountering when they enter the employment market.

The citizenship-development approach has appealed to many pragmatically oriented Americans. Frequently, attacks on so-called frills in school programs are reflections of the concerns of people who want schools to concentrate more heavily on providing learning experiences more clearly relevant to their future careers.

The Case for Needs-of-Society Curricula.
Content of school programs associated with this perspective draws information from a variety of academic subjects. This arrangement challenges the assumption that knowledge must be compartmentalized into artificial categories labeled history, English, mathematics, physics, or something else. Needs-of-society curricula help young people integrate knowledge from a variety of sources as they use it to make sense of the world as it really is.

Supporters also point to the motivational advantages of organizing programs around reality. For example, if a class you are teaching is oriented toward a career that interests its members, their motivation will be high. Students who are interested in aviation probably will find it easier to master mathematics in the context of studying to become a pilot than by plodding through a traditional mathematics textbook, page by page. Reinstein (1998) found that an assignment requiring learners to interview someone in the community who used high-level math skills did more to stimulate their interest in mathematics than any action a school might take.

The Case Against Needs-of-Society Curricula.
A major problem of the needs-of-society emphasis is the difficulty you face as a teacher in identifying which needs to address in school programs. There is a danger that needs will be identified in haste and that programs will be excessively narrow in scope and nonsubstantive in content.

The rapidity with which needs change also poses difficulties. Some problems fade away; new ones emerge. Over time, technical changes alter job requirements tremendously. When educators view needs too narrowly, there is a danger that instruction will provide learners with information that will be obsolete by the time they leave school. Poorly conceived programs may also produce school graduates who lack the flexibility required for them to adapt easily to changing conditions.

Some critics of programs organized around needs of society contend that they encourage young people to make career choices too early in their school years. Learners who express a personal interest based on a whim or enthusiasm of the moment may find themselves tracked into a set of courses relevant for only a limited number of career options. It may prove difficult for them to switch to another preparation sequence when their interests change.

Needs-of-society programs that focus heavily on social problems sometimes draw criticism from parents and other community members. They may argue that this kind of instruction imposes what they believe to be inappropriate values or perspectives. These concerns have made school authorities in some places hesitant to organize school programs around a social-problems emphasis.

Academic-Subjects Curricula

Throughout history, one of the most common ways to organize the curriculum has been to divide it along the lines of academic subjects. Even educational leaders in ancient Rome organized knowledge into subjects based on the assumption that there are disciplines (or bodies of knowledge) that group together elements of content that are related in some natural way. Supporters of this approach believed that young people would find it easier to learn if knowledge were organized into academic subjects such as mathematics or music.

Many people who support the importance of using academic subjects as frameworks for school programs believe that scholars in individual disciplines have developed reliable, responsible, and precise ways of knowing about the world. They contend that you, as a teacher, should insist that learners master certain kinds of information. Proponents of this approach allege that mastering content that is organized into individual academic subjects gives young people the intellectual tools they need to control their own destinies. English, history, science, and mathematics are among subjects that many people believe are essential areas of content that must be introduced to all learners. Often state laws mandate inclusion of information from these subjects in K–12 school programs.

Exactly which subjects are *musts* for learners has been the subject of considerable debate. Perhaps not surprisingly, scholars in each subject have found compelling reasons for placing a very heavy emphasis on their own specializations. Mathematicians bemoan the public's lack of mathematical literacy; geographers decry the public's lack of geographic literacy; economists despair over the public's lack of economic literacy; and on and on. Conflicts among supporters of different academic subjects have become familiar events in state capitals throughout the nation, as legislators have called on expert witnesses to help them define the essential elements of a "basic education."

Some people suggest that teachers should not place too much emphasis on learners mastering factual content associated with each subject. Instead, educational programs should introduce learners to the organizational features of each discipline. Supporters of this **structure-of-the-disciplines emphasis** suggests that students would be best served by programs that taught them how individual disciplines are organized and how specialists in each discipline ask and answer questions. The idea is to develop learners' thinking abilities and engage them in activities that, to the extent possible, parallel problem-solving procedures used by professional academic scholars in each subject area.

Great interest in the structure of the disciplines developed after the former Soviet Union launched the earth satellite *Sputnik* in 1957. Some enthusiasm for this approach continued through the 1960s and into the early 1970s. An underlying theme was that learners who became thoroughly familiar with the structures of the academic disciplines during their school years would enter college ready to do more-advanced work.

Beginning in the 1970s, concerns about the Vietnam War, treatment of minorities at home, and other social issues eroded support for a strong structure-of-the-disciplines emphasis. Mandates for academic programs emphasizing equity and fairness dominated much of the educational debate in the 1970s.

In the 1980s, there was renewed interest in programs with a traditional academic-subject focus, but the reform reports of the 1980s tended to promote school programs that sought to familiarize learners with the findings of academic specialists, not with the structures of their disciplines. Concerns about the nation's relative intellectual and economic competitiveness prompted critics to call for school programs that would produce graduates who were well grounded in academics, particularly in content associated with mathematics and the sciences.

During the 1980s and 1990s and continuing the into first decade of the 21st century, some critics of school practices expressed doubts about whether teachers had adequate preparation in the academic subjects they were teaching. In response to these concerns, many teacher-preparation programs have extended the length of their programs. Others, while continuing to offer traditional four-year teacher certification schedules, have increased content requirements in the fields students have been preparing to teach.

The Case for Academic-Subjects Curricula. Individual subjects tend to organize content that contains many common elements. For example, mathematics courses of all kinds have much more common content than you would find in a course that blends English and physics. Supporters of the academic-subject-matter orientation believe that this curriculum pattern helps limit the scope of content you teach and encourages its presentation in logical ways. These conditions make it easier for learners to master material and to perform well on tests and other achievement measures.

As the most traditional form of organizing school programs, this pattern enjoys respectability because of its long familiarity to parents and other patrons of the school.

Working with other teachers in planning the curriculum can be a professionally and personally rewarding activity.

School programs organized in this way provide an aura of stability and continuity that many people find attractive. As a teacher, instruction oriented around academic disciplines involves you with subjects organized roughly along the lines you encountered when you took college and university courses. Administrators generally feel confident in explaining this kind of organizational pattern to parents.

The vast majority of school textbooks are organized on the assumption that they will be used in programs based on traditional academic subjects. For example, there are separate books for classes in mathematics, English, and biology. Textbooks that represent a fusion of content from several academic disciplines are less common. Even with today's Internet, the textbook continues to be a widely used instructional resource, and it acts as an influence to support an academic-subject-matter orientation throughout the school program.

Today, there is great interest in holding schools and teachers accountable for their performance. As noted earlier, people today often use standardized-test scores as evidence to suggest one school is "better," "about the same," or "inferior" to other schools. For the most part, standardized tests are organized around traditional academic subjects. Hence, school curricula that reflect an academic-subject-matter organizational pattern may deliver information to learners in ways similar to how it appears on standardized tests.

The Case Against Academic-Subjects Curricula.

Even though individual academic subjects have a certain internal consistency, it is by no means clear that the world is organized into history, mathematics, English, biology, and other separate subjects. The young people you will teach do not encounter a reality that is neatly sliced and filed into individual disciplines, so some critics of the academic-subject-matter orientation suggest that the school curriculum should be more interdisciplinary. That is, individual courses should be organized in a way that allows content to be drawn from many sources.

Other critics argue that dividing school programs into packages associated with academic disciplines inhibits transfer and integration of knowledge. For instance, some of your learners may produce flawless prose in their English classes but in other classes turn in papers with many mistakes, assuming the attitude: "This is history. We aren't supposed to write perfect papers here. That's for English. Here we learn names and dates."

Some learners complain that the learning experiences they encounter in the traditional academic subjects are irrelevant. For example, a student studying algebra may ask, "Why should I study this stuff? What good is it?" Although content from algebra certainly does have some important links to real life, many learners fail to make the connection between the content of the course and the demands of life beyond the school.

Broad-Fields Curriculum.

An approach that seeks to respond to certain criticisms of curricula that have been organized around academic subjects is the **broad-fields curriculum.** In this scheme, two or more traditional subjects are combined into a broad area. These areas sometimes center on large themes such as industrialism or evolution. As a teacher, you can use these themes to prepare lessons that draw on knowledge from several subject areas. This approach has been promoted as a means of breaking down barriers that separate knowledge into individual academic disciplines. Thompson and Gregg (1997) warn that attempts to break down the discipline barriers often fail because teachers have been trained to separate content into individual disciplines. As a result, they find it difficult to meld together content from several subjects into a new, broad-fields "whole." However, when teachers succeed in doing this, resulting programs are said to have important benefits for learners. Among other things, broad-fields instruction has the potential to enhance young people's abilities to transfer what they have learned to new situations.

PROFILING A TEACHER

A Curriculum-Change Proposal Confronts Practical Realities

Tradition is a powerful force in support of maintaining content features of existing school curricula. Important pressures constrain the decisions of school administrators and teachers who wish to make changes that might better serve learners' needs and interests. This profile points out the kinds of challenges you might confront should you decide to make important content changes in your instructional program.

As you read this profile, think about these questions:

- What values lie behind Sondra McPhee's proposal?
- What values lie behind Dr. Gutierrez's reaction?
- What might Sondra, perhaps acting cooperatively with Dr. Gutierrez, do to change the pressures acting to thwart her desire to make changes to the eighth-grade U.S. history program?

Some Forces That Shape Curricula

Sondra McPhee teaches U.S. history to eighth graders. Recently, in an effort to identify approaches that might interest more of her students in history, she has been doing research on the Web to learn about approaches other teachers have found effective with this age group. This background work led her to information about oral history, and she became convinced this approach was exactly what she needed to motivate her students. Her study led her to the conclusion that she needed to focus more on historical content that was more immediate to students' own lives. She took several weeks to plan a revised U.S. history program, then she sent a memorandum to the school principal, Dr. Viola Gutierrez, to explain changes she planned to implement.

In her memorandum, Ms. McPhee said the revised version would include much more information about lives of young people in early America, including clothing styles and the recreational activities people pursued. To make room for this new content, she would reduce emphases on such traditional topics as profiles of national leaders, elections, economic developments, and foreign affairs. She defended these changes on the grounds that her students would see the replacement topics as relevant and that researchers had found oral-history lessons to be good student motivators.

Dr. Gutierrez, a cautious administrator, initially was noncommittal, but she told Sondra she would think about her ideas. Three weeks later, Sondra found a note in her box from Dr. Gutierrez, asking her to come in during her planning period to talk about the oral-history proposal.

Dr. Gutierrez expressed appreciation to Sondra for her willingness to innovate and for her professionalism in searching out pertinent research literature to support her case. However, the principal added that she was denying permission for the oral-history project. She explained that the state U.S. history test for eighth graders focused on many of the topics Sondra wished to eliminate and included few, if any, items related to the topics she wanted to add.

Dr. Gutierrez also emphasized that few parents had experienced an oral-history approach when they were in school, and many of them might be skeptical of the technique. It was her experience that most parents seemed to prefer

(continued)

courses focusing on traditional topics featured in textbooks. If an oral-history project were started, particularly one featuring changed content, some influential parents might view the change as an effort to "water down" the history program.

Finally, Dr. Gutierrez pointed out that the administrators at the district's high school continued to be concerned about the lack of subject-matter preparation junior high school graduates had when they entered Grade 9. She indicated that the school simply couldn't take a chance that an oral-history program would make students appear to be even less prepared for high school than they currently were.

The broad-fields approach is not without its problems. One major difficulty is that many educators do not possess a breadth of knowledge in multiple academic disciplines. Few college and university courses that prepare teachers are organized according to a broad-fields approach. If this has been true of your own academic preparation, you may find it a real challenge to identify and use relevant content from a wide variety of sources. Efforts to blend content from several disciplines can also lead to trivialized treatment of important subject matter (Harrison, 1990).

WHAT DO YOU THINK?

RELATIVE ATTRACTIVENESS OF DIFFERENT TEACHING ASSIGNMENTS

Assume you are a newly certified teacher who is faced with the task of deciding which of two job offers to accept. Salaries and general working conditions are about the same in each school, and in both positions you will be expected to teach five classes a day.

The instructional program in one school has been organized according to a traditional academic-subjects orientation. In the other, content has been organized around broad-fields themes. Your assignments in each school are depicted in the following chart:

	School One	**School Two**
Period 1	American history	challenges of citizenship
Period 2	American history	challenges of citizenship
Period 3	world history	(planning period)
Period 4	(planning period)	militarism and democracy
Period 5	world history	environmental challenges
Period 6	world geography	militarism and democracy

WHAT DO YOU THINK?

1. In general, would you prefer School One or School Two?
2. For which teaching assignments do you have the better college or university preparation? Why do you think so?
3. In which situation do you think you would experience the most difficulty in locating appropriate instructional materials? Why?
4. How do you think learners would react to the courses in the two schools?

 To respond to these questions online, go to the What Do You Think? *module for this chapter of the Companion Website.*

THE INNER CURRICULUM

The orientation of your curriculum stands as just one influence on what members of your classes will take away from their school experiences. What they learn also will be influenced by their individual characteristics. Human beings seek to "make sense" out of new situations they confront. Past experiences help shape these understandings.

Curriculum specialists R. Murray Thomas and Dale L. Brubaker (2000) use the term **inner curriculum** to describe the nature of learning that occurs within individuals as they process new information in light of their own past experiences. Because members of your classes may come from diverse language, cultural, ethnic, and economic backgrounds, they probably will interpret information included within the formal school curriculum in different and highly individualistic ways.

Processes associated with the inner curriculum lead to the conclusion that the formal curriculum structure acts as a framework and stimulus that you will use to provide lessons to students that they will interpret in light of their own experiences. These experiences sometimes will lead learners to develop conclusions that are surprising or, at least, somewhat inconsistent with your expectations. There are positives and negatives associated with this reality. On the one hand, operation of the inner curriculum ensures that your learners will not passively take in new information in an unquestioning way. They will interpret content in terms of their own experiences, and this process, over time, will help them to develop sophisticated thinking capabilities. On the other hand, the filtering and interpreting associated with the inner curriculum challenge you to learn as much as you can about the personal background of each student. This information can help you understand how each member of your class is likely to react to and "make sense of" what you teach.

WEB EXTENSION 7–5

Association for Supervision and Curriculum Development

The Association for Supervision and Curriculum Development (ASCD) is the nation's largest organization for professionals interested in school curricula. This site is the organization's home page. You will find links to publications, professional development opportunities, discussions of policy issues, and other information related to content and organization of school programs. The association publishes a fine journal titled *Educational Leadership*. You can access many articles from this journal online.

http://www.ascd.org/

THE HIDDEN CURRICULUM

At school, young people learn more than the topics introduced in the formal, written curriculum. They are also influenced by their exposure to what experts have described as the **hidden curriculum**. The hidden curriculum includes things in the school setting that send our learners messages regarding what they ought to be doing and even how they should be thinking.

Gail McCutcheon (1988), who has studied the hidden curriculum, points out that much of its content is "transmitted through the everyday, normal goings-on in schools" (p. 191). Patterns vary from school to school and are influenced by administrators, teachers, parents, and guardians (Henson, 2001).

Your actions as a teacher will help shape the hidden curriculum in your own school. What you do signals to learners what you consider important. If you are unconscious of your hidden-curriculum actions, you may not realize that you are sending unintended messages to members of your class. For example, suppose you are teaching social studies at the high school level. You might have made a point of telling students that they should read articles on the front page of the newspaper every day because good citizens keep up on current events. If your students see you during morning, lunch, or after-school breaks reading only the sports section, they may well conclude that you are insincere. You may say the hard news on the front page is important, but they see that you really only pay attention to sports. The "lesson" these students take away from this experience is part of the hidden curriculum. In the case of this social studies example, this kind of learning has little to do with either the formal, prescribed curriculum or with what you believe to be your real academic intentions.

Some authorities who have studied the hidden curriculum fear that it sometimes sends messages to learners that are inconsistent with the values of their own cultural or social group. For example, curriculum experts Michael Apple and Landon Beyer (1988) note that the hidden curriculum in many schools emphasizes deference to authority and an attitude that competence in school subjects will result in high status and lucrative jobs for graduates. Many learners find these perspectives inconsistent with the attitudes of their parents, families, and friends, and hence they may reject the entire school program as irrelevant.

Most authorities agree that the hidden curriculum influences learners' attitudes toward the school program. There is a consensus that teachers need to be sensitive to all the messages that learners may be getting from both the school program and the general school environment. What learners take away from exposure to the hidden curriculum can influence their attitudes toward teachers and the academic offerings of the school in important ways.

PATTERNS IN ELEMENTARY AND SECONDARY SCHOOLS

Although there are place-to-place differences, basic programs offered in the nation's elementary, middle, junior high, and senior high schools feature many similarities. Guidelines governing general categories of information to be taught are often included in state regulations governing education, especially in state curriculum standards.

Most elementary school programs include instruction in these areas:

- Reading and language arts
- Mathematics
- Social studies
- Science
- Health
- Physical education
- Fine arts

In elementary schools, it is common for reading instruction to occur at the beginning of the day. Reading is considered to be a critically important subject, and many educators believe that students should be exposed to its instruction when they are well rested and ready to learn.

The amount of time devoted to each subject area in elementary schools varies from place to place. In some parts of the country, there are strict state regulations mandating that minimum amounts of time be devoted each day to certain high-priority areas of the curriculum. In other areas, no such guidelines exist, and time-allocation decisions are left to

Allowing students to work together and select their own material to read is an example of learner-centered curriculum.

local districts, principals, and individual teachers. Because proficiency in reading is a key to academic success in so many other areas, most elementary school teachers devote considerable time to reading instruction. Some unfavorable comparisons of U.S. learners' proficiency in mathematics and science when compared with learners in other countries have tended to prompt more emphases on these subjects in elementary school programs. Increasingly, too, elementary schools are providing basic instruction in computers.

Middle school and junior high school programs feature many of the same subjects taught in elementary schools. However, particularly in grades 7 and 8, options for students with different interests and abilities are available. For example, several mathematics courses may be taught. Some students may take algebra, others may choose a less rigorous course, and still others may enroll in a more challenging class.

State and local high school graduation requirements largely drive the programs at the senior high school level. These requirements vary somewhat from place to place, but patterns tend to converge around a set that prescribes a minimum number of years or semesters of high school instruction in English/language arts, mathematics, science, and physical education. Many places now require specified levels of computer literacy. However, large numbers of electives are also available to high school students.

Many school-reform reports have recommended that more work be required for high school graduation in certain so-called basic subjects such as English, mathematics, social studies, and science. Over the past 20 years, larger numbers of students have been enrolling in these courses. However, this trend does not reveal much about the nature of the content that learners encounter in these courses. At best, displays of curricular programs provide a sketchy outline of what goes on in schools. When you begin teaching, you will find that the real school program is the one shaped by the actions of you and your colleagues as you work with learners assigned to your classrooms.

Today's explosion of knowledge, ready access to information via technology, and improved understandings of how individuals learn suggest a need for continuous curriculum evaluation and revision. Content that was considered indispensable in the past may have to be replaced with newer content. In time, even the basic patterns of school curricula you remember from your own school days will be forced to give way to new patterns that respond to changes in knowledge, technology, and insights into the learning process.

There is evidence that such changes will not come easily. Tradition exerts a powerful force, and schools have proved to be among the most change-resistant of our institutions (Armstrong, 2003; Callan, 1998; Renzulli, 1998). However, despite these difficulties, pressures on schools to modify programs in light of new conditions continue to mount. It is probable that curricula you encounter early in your teaching career will vary markedly from those that will seem commonplace in your later years in the profession.

Key Ideas in Summary

- The term *curriculum* refers to the selection and organization of content and learning experiences. Because different people use varying criteria in making decisions about selection and organization of content, there are important place-to-place variations in elementary and secondary school curricula. Curriculum is different from *instruction,* which deals with specific means of achieving the general plan described in a particular curriculum.
- *Standardized tests* are used to compare scores of students in a given classroom or school with expected scores, or *norms,* of students with similar characteristics. Schools in the United States administer more standardized tests each year than do schools in any other country. Increasingly, members of the general public use scores on standardized tests as a basis for making judgments about school districts, schools, teachers, and administrators. This trend pressures teachers to cover content included in standardized tests.
- *State curriculum standards* specify kinds of content, and sometimes particular learning experiences, that schools are required to provide to learners in individual subjects in elementary schools and to students in individual courses in middle schools and high schools. Standards developed by content-specialty organizations such as those focusing on English, social studies, science, and mathematics have influenced some state curriculum standards. Increasingly, standardized tests are being developed that tie to information referenced in state standards.
- *Learner-centered curricula* are based on the idea that individual learner interests and needs should drive preparation of instructional programs. Jean-Jacques Rousseau was an early proponent of this perspective. In this approach, learners are placed at the center of the planning process. These curricula are alleged to motivate learners and to avoid unnecessary fragmentation of content. Critics argue that it is impractical to prepare separate academic experiences for each learner's needs and interests. They are also concerned about whether learners are the best judges of their own and society's needs.
- *Needs-of-society curricula* seek to produce learners capable of maintaining and extending broad social goals. These curricula sort into two basic types: Some programs use a *problems approach* to help learners recognize and respond to important issues, and others center on *citizenship development.* Many of the latter emphasize providing young people with the kinds of skills they will need to make a living. Supporters of these programs suggest that they promote learners' levels of interest because the content is highly relevant to their own lives. Critics suggest that identification of so-called problems may bring teachers into unproductive conflicts with parents and other community members who have different perspectives on these issues. These critics also maintain that vocationally oriented programs may not be responsive to rapid changes in the job market, and school programs may be providing learners with training expe-

riences that will not match up well with the needs of the employment market they will enter when they leave school.

- *Academic-subjects curricula* organize school programs along the lines of academic disciplines such as mathematics, history, and English. This approach is based on the assumption that material contained within an individual discipline shares certain similarities. These commonalities, it is alleged, make it easier for learners to master the material. Critics point out that the real world is not divided into separate academic disciplines, and they also note that division of content into packages associated with separate subjects fragments learning and makes it difficult for young people to transfer information to situations beyond the setting in which it was learned.
- There have been two general approaches to preparing academic-subjects curricula. The most common of these has featured the development of learning experiences designed to teach learners the findings of subject-matter specialists. A second approach favors familiarizing learners with the *structure of the disciplines*. Programs designed in this way seek to introduce young people to the processes that professionals in the disciplines use as they study data and arrive at conclusions.
- *Broad-fields curricula* attempt to respond to some criticisms that have been made of programs organized around traditional academic disciplines. Broad-fields approaches combine two or more traditional subjects into a single broad area or theme. This theme is used as a basis for planning, and programs are developed that draw content from several disciplines. Supporters promote broad-fields curricula on the basis of their capacity for helping learners break down boundaries between and among individual subjects. Problems with the approach include (1) a lack of instructional materials of an interdisciplinary nature and (2) the difficulty in finding individual teachers who have enough depth of knowledge in a variety of disciplines that they can draw materials responsibly from a wide selection of content areas.
- The *inner curriculum* influences what learners take away from their experiences in school. The inner curriculum involves an interaction between a learner's past experience and the new information the learner receives at school. Actual learning comes about as a result of the melding of these existing experiences and impressions and the new content.
- In addition to the kinds of learning experiences described in the formal school curriculum, the so-called *hidden curriculum* also influences what young people learn at school. It includes all aspects of the school settings that send learners messages about what they should be doing and even about what they should be thinking. Learners often refer to the hidden curriculum to see whether teachers' behaviors square with their statements. For example, if a high school teacher tells social studies students it is important for them to read articles on the front page of the newspaper each day but the students see this teacher only reading the sports page, the lesson learned may be that what is "really important" is news on the sports page, not news on the front page.
- Even though there are important place-to-place differences, certain common patterns are found in many elementary and secondary schools. Large numbers of elementary schools require learners to be exposed to instruction focusing on reading and language arts, mathematics, social studies, science, health, and physical education. Increasingly, elementary students are also being introduced to the use of computers. In secondary schools (particularly in senior high schools), learners have a number of electives from which to choose. However, they are usually still obligated to take a certain number of courses in such areas as English, social studies, mathematics, science, and physical education. Subjects and course offerings at individual schools are heavily influenced by state curriculum standards.

Chapter 7 Self-Test

To review terms and concepts in this chapter, go to the Companion Website and take the Chapter 7 Self-Test. Feedback for the self-test is immediate. You can keep track of your self-test scores yourself, or you can submit your scores to your instructor via e-mail.

Preparing for Praxis

To learn more about the Praxis test and complete this activity online, go to the Preparing for Praxis *module for this chapter of the Companion Website.*

You may be required to pass Educational Testing Service's Praxis II exam as you seek formal authorization to teach in the public schools. The *Principles of Learning and Teaching* component of Praxis II seeks to assess your knowledge about these topics: (1) Students as Learners, (2) Instruction and Assessment, (3) Communication Techniques, and (4) Profession and Community.

Curriculum-related content in this chapter may be especially relevant as you prepare for questions related to the category of Instruction and Assessment. Some content may also provide information with logical ties to other Praxis II categories. You may find it useful to prepare a chart for your own use similar to the one provided here. As you encounter information related to individual categories, you can enter it into the chart. A completed chart of this kind will be useful as you prepare to take the Praxis II exam.

Students as Learners	Instruction and Assessment
• Student Development and the Learning Process	• Instructional Strategies
• Students as Diverse Learners	• Planning Instruction
• Student Motivation and the Learning Environment	• Assessment Strategies
Communication Techniques	**Profession and Community**
• Basic, Effective, Verbal and Nonverbal Communication Techniques	• The Reflective Practitioner
• Effect of Cultural and Gender Differences on Communications in the Classroom	• The Larger Community
• Types of Questions That Can Stimulate Discussion in Different Ways for Particular Purposes	

For Your Initial-Development Portfolio

To complete this activity and submit your response online, go to the For Your Initial-Development Portfolio *module for this chapter of the Companion Website.*

1. What materials and ideas have you learned in this chapter about *curriculum* that you will include as "evidence" in your portfolio? Select up to three separate items of information. Number them 1, 2, and 3.
2. Think about why you selected these materials. As you do so, consider these issues:
   • Specific uses you might make of this information as you plan, deliver, and assess the impact of your teaching

- The compatibility of the information with your own priorities and values
- Any contributions this information can make to your development as a teacher
- Factors that led you to include this information, as opposed to some alternatives you considered but rejected

3. Place a check in the chart here to indicate the INTASC standard(s) to which each of your items of information relates. (You may wish to refer to Chapter 1 for more-detailed information about INTASC.)

INTASC Standard Number

ITEM OF EVIDENCE NUMBER	S1	S2	S3	S4	S5	S6	S7	S8	S9	S10
1										
2										
3										

4. Prepare a written reflection in which you analyze the decision-making process you followed. In your comments, mention the INTASC standard(s) to which your selected material relates.

Reflections

 To respond to these questions online, go to the Reflections *module for this chapter of the* Companion Website.

1. Review material in the chapter that deals with state curriculum standards. You may also wish to find additional information related to this topic. Given what you now know about state curriculum standards, how do you think they will affect the quality of educational programs in the schools? What will be the specific benefits? What might be some negatives associated with these standards? As you assess strengths and weaknesses of standards, what is your final assessment? Will they (a) improve education; (b) have little impact, negative or positive, on education; or (c) produce generally negative results?

2. Certain critics argue that our schools are doing a poor job of preparing young people for work in an increasingly technologically complex society. How do you react to this view? If you accept the validity of this contention, what specific changes would you make in the present grades K–12 school program?

3. Supporters of the needs-of-learners orientation point out that learners tend to be motivated by school programs based on this point of view. By implication, are they suggesting that programs developed from the perspectives of the academic-subject-matter orientation and needs-of-society orientation are less motivating? If you agree with these people, what do you think might be done to make school programs based on these orientations more interesting to learners?

4. Some educational-reform proposals recommend that students should take more courses in English, mathematics, science, and social studies as requirements for graduation. Does requiring students to take more courses ensure that they will necessarily know more about these subject areas? Why or why not?

5. Can you think of some examples of "learning" you took away from the *hidden curriculum* in one or more of the schools you attended? What was the nature of this information, and how did it differ from perspectives being promoted by the official school curriculum? What are some actions you might take as a teacher that will help prevent young people from taking away undesirable impressions from the hidden curriculum?

Field Experiences, Projects, and Enrichment

1. With the assistance of a school principal or your course instructor, locate in your library a list of subjects taught at two or more grade levels within a given school. From titles and descriptions of these subjects, decide whether they are based on a needs-of-learner orientation, an academic-subject-matter orientation, a needs-of-society orientation, or a combination of two or even all three of these perspectives. Prepare a written report that summarizes your findings.

2. Locate a copy of your state's curriculum standards. Many states post a link to their standards on the state department of education's Web site. Your library may have a copy, and copies are likely to be available in many of your local area schools. Your instructor may be able to suggest other places where you can locate the standards. Examine requirements related to either (a) a specific elementary school subject or grade level you would like to teach or (b) a specific middle school or high school course you would like to teach. How comfortable are you with the required content? Do you have an adequate background to teach all of the required topics? Are there some topics missing that, in your view, should be added? What are some things you can be doing during your teacher-preparation program to get ready to prepare lessons that are consistent with your state's curriculum standards? Respond to these questions in a paper titled: *Reactions to State Curriculum Standards and a Personal Plan for Preparing to Meet Them.*

3. Interview a school principal or a school district curriculum director about changes in local programs made in the last decade. Determine whether any of these changes were correlated with those suggested in national reform proposals or mandated by new state curriculum standards. Inquire also about connections between the district's curriculum and the focus of any standardized tests administered to the district's students. Share your findings with your classmates.

4. Interview several teachers within a single building who teach a subject or grade level that interests you. Ask them about state, district, or school requirements for learners who take this subject or who are enrolled at this grade level. Also ask whether these requirements are well suited to learners' needs. Finally, ask these teachers what specific changes in requirements for students they would recommend. Prepare an oral report of your findings to share with members of your class.

5. Join together with three or four others in your class to prepare a report on one of these topics:
   - What should a "good" elementary school program look like today?
   - What should a "good" middle school or junior high school program look like today?
   - What should a "good" senior high school program look like today?

   Present your conclusions in the form of a symposium and then use them as the basis for a short article. Consider sending it to the features editor of your local newspaper.

References

Apple, M. W., & Beyer, L. E. (1988). Social evaluation. In L. E. Beyer & M. W. Apple (Eds.), *The curriculum: Problems, politics, and possibilities* (pp. 33–49). Albany: State University of New York Press.

Armstrong, D. G. (2003). *Curriculum today.* Upper Saddle River, NJ: Merrill/Prentice Hall.

Callan, R. J. (1998). Giving students the (right) time of day. *Educational Leadership, 55*(4), 84–87.

Harrison, C. J. (1990). Concepts, operational definitions, and case studies in instruction. *Education,* 110, 502–505.

Henson, K. T. (2001). *Curriculum development for education reform* (2nd ed.). New York: McGraw-Hill. Reissued in 2003 by Waveland Press.

Henson, K. T. (Guest Ed.). *Education,* Vol. 124, No. 1 (Fall 2003).

Henson, K. T. (2004) Constructivist teaching strategies for diverse middle-level classrooms. Boston: Allyn & Bacon.

Kohn, A. (2000, September 27). *Standardized testing and its victims.* Education Week on the Web. [http://www.edweek.org/ew/ewstory.cfm?slug = 04kohn.h20]

McCutcheon, G. (1988). Curriculum and the work of teachers. In L. E. Beyer & M. W. Apple (Eds.), *The curriculum: Problems, politics, and possibilities* (pp. 191–203). Albany: State University of New York Press.

National Commission on Excellence in Education. (1983). *A nation at risk: The imperative for educational reform.* Washington, DC: U.S. Department of Education.

No Child Left Behind Act of 2001, Public Law 107-110, 115 Stat. 1425 (2002).

Polakow, V. (1999). A view from the field. In K. T. Henson & B. F. Eller (Eds.), *Educational Psychology for Effective Teaching.* Belmont, CA: Wadsworth.

Ravitch, D. (1995). *National standards in American education: A citizen's guide.* Washington, DC: Brookings Institution.

Reinstein, D. (1998). Crossing the economic divide. *Educational Leadership, 55*(4), 28–29.

Renzulli, J. S. (1998). A rising tide lifts all ships: Developing the gifts and talents of all students. *Phi Delta Kappan, 80*(2), 105–111.

Schubert, W. H. (1986). *Curriculum: Perspective, paradigm, and possibility.* New York: Macmillan.

Suter, L. E. (2000). Is student achievement immutable? Evidence from international studies on schooling and student achievement. *Review of Educational Research, 70*(4), 529–545.

Thomas, R. M., & Brubaker, D. L. (2000). *Theses and dissertations: A guide to planning, research, and writing.* Westport, CT: Bergin & Garvey.

Thompson, S., & Gregg, L. (1997). Reculturing middle schools for meaningful change. *Middle School Journal, 28*(5), 27–31.

U.S. Department of Education. (2001). *The nation's report card: Mathematics 2000.* Washington, DC: National Center for Education Statistics.

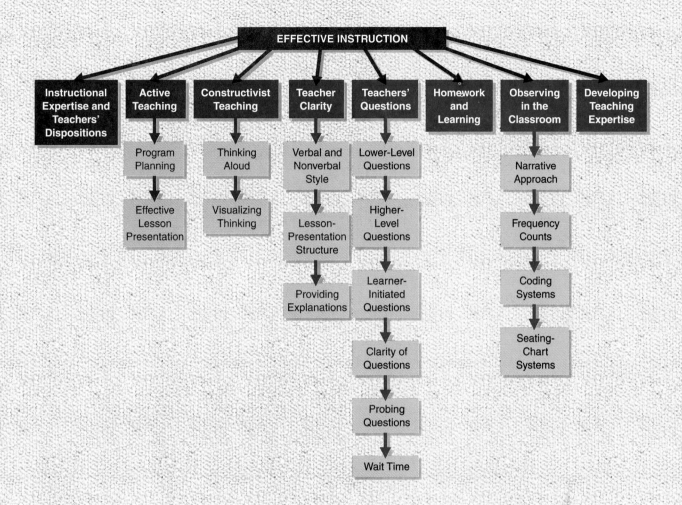

OBJECTIVES

This chapter will help you to

- explain why teachers' instructional role is so important and how *teachers' dispositions* influence their teaching.
- define the basic features of *active teaching* and *constructivist teaching*.
- point out characteristics of instructional practices that will enhance clarity and, hence, the likelihood that your learners will achieve academic success.
- explain characteristics of effective teacher-questioning practices.

- describe what you might do as a teacher to increase the probability that homework assignments will facilitate learners' mastery of new content.
- describe examples of techniques observers can use to gather and record information about classroom activities.
- recognize that your instructional proficiency will not be at its maximum potential when you complete your preparation program but will continue to improve as you gain classroom experience.

INSTRUCTIONAL EXPERTISE AND TEACHERS' DISPOSITIONS

Of all the things you do, your obligation to instruct will most clearly differentiate your work as a teacher from that performed by members of other professions. Teachers have long been judged on their instructional effectiveness, and rightfully so. "Of all the factors that affect academic performance, teachers have the most impact on their students' school experiences" (Parsley & Corcoran, 2003, p. 85). Concerns about instructional quality sometimes have led to speculation about whether a body of research-validated knowledge exists that adequately defines "effective" teaching.

Some people argue that there is such a body of knowledge and that future teachers should be trained to use it. Others scoff at this idea and believe that future teachers need no specialized training. They contend that good instruction will automatically result if prospective teachers have a good understanding of the subjects they teach. This position runs counter to a growing body of evidence that has identified categories of instructional behavior that are closely associated with enhanced learner achievement (Good & Brophy, 2000). These studies make a case in support of the idea that, as a teacher, you need more than a sound grasp of the subject(s) you teach. You also need to have expertise related to instructional design and delivery.

Most research on effective teaching has focused on teacher behaviors that relate to increasing learners' academic attainment. Instruction certainly also has other purposes. For example, as a teacher, you also have an interest in your learners' psychomotor development, social adjustment, and personal growth. You must attend to learners' affective needs because these simply cannot be separated from their cognitive needs (Henson & Eller, 1999). Ideally, you will create a classroom learning community in which you and your learners will enjoy helping each other create knowledge.

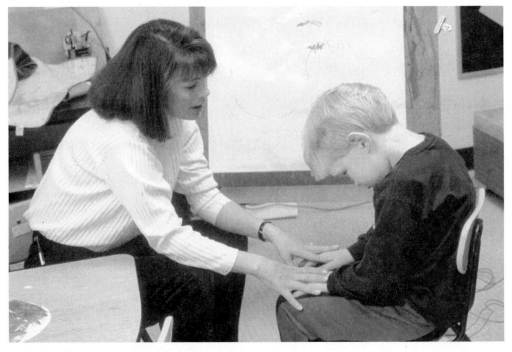

Researchers have found that learners' emotional needs cannot be separated from needs associated with content learning.

Individuals involved in teacher preparation increasingly are focusing on the issue of **teachers' dispositions.** Teachers' dispositions are the perceptions and attitudes that shape their behavior (Combs, 1962). As a teacher, you will be more effective when your disposition leads you to frame instruction in ways that allow learners to succeed academically, to develop appropriate social behaviors, and to become increasingly confident responders to sophisticated challenges. You will find it easier to achieve these ends if your beliefs include some of the following:

- Your learners are worthy individuals.
- Education is more than just preparation for work.
- Your relationships with your learners should be characterized by mutual respect.
- Diversity represents the strength of American education and American society.
- All students and teachers should be lifelong learners.
- Learners should feel competent and worthy.
- Lessons should encourage learners to become actively involved in creating their own knowledge.

A theme that runs through these examples of desirable dispositions is that learners are individuals. You have an obligation to respond to these differences in ways that help members of your class grow in self-esteem at the same time as they develop expertise in areas related to academic and social behaviors. As you think about how you might go about implementing instructional practices that respond to individual learners' needs, you may wish to consult teacher-effectiveness research.

You will find that research on teacher effectiveness differs from research in such areas as the physical sciences. It focuses on people who may have different personal backgrounds, motivations, and experiences. Findings of teacher-effectiveness research do not categorically assert that a specific procedure will work in a predictable way with every learner. Rather, this body of research seeks to identify principles that can guide you in making appropriate instructional decisions.

WEB EXTENSION 8–1

What Teachers Should Know and Be Able to Do

The National Board for Professional Teaching Standards (NBPTS) maintains this site. You will find a list of five propositions related to dispositions expected of effective teachers. Take time to read Proposition 5, "Teachers are members of learning communities." Are you comfortable with the kinds of attitudes teachers must have to operate effectively as learning-community members? You may also wish to look at material related to the other propositions.

http://www.nbpts.org/standards/know_do/conclusion.html

Then, in the Search For space, type in the word dispositions.

ACTIVE TEACHING

A growing body of research suggests that **active teaching** is associated with enhanced learner achievement (Good & Brophy, 2000). The term *active teaching* refers to situations when, as a teacher, you will directly lead the class and play such roles as

- Presenter of new information,
- Monitor of learner progress,

- Planner of opportunities for learners to apply content, and
- Reteacher of content (to learners who fail to learn the content when it is initially presented).

The active-teaching role contrasts with the view of the teacher as a general manager or facilitator of instruction who does not get directly involved in leading the class and personally overseeing learning activities. Program planning and providing effective lessons are two hallmarks of effective active teachers.

Program Planning

One of your professional duties as a teacher involves planning appropriate lessons and learning experiences for your students. These responsibilities include:

- Matching instruction to learners' characteristics
- Engaging in task analysis to identify appropriate beginning points for instruction
- Specifying learning intentions

Matching Programs to Learner Characteristics. To accomplish your intention of preparing and delivering instruction that is well suited to your learners, you must make two kinds of decisions. First, you must consider the difficulty level of the new material in light of your understanding of your learners' capabilities. If selected materials are too difficult and your expectations are beyond the current grasp of your students, frustration is unavoidable, and little learning will take place (Teddlie & Reynolds, 2000). On the other hand, if the learning materials you select are too easy, boredom and motivation problems may result.

Second, you need to match the program materials to learners' interests. This is not to suggest that you should introduce no content in which learners do not initially display a high level of interest. Rather, your task is to identify interest levels, and when they are found to be low, think about creative ways to generate greater learner interest and enthusiasm. Ideally, you will develop plans for lessons that will stimulate learners to want to acquire the new information. Successful planning of this kind requires you to know your learners well. Your strategy for each lesson should be right for the content selected for that lesson (Acheson & Gall, 1992), right for the learners, and right for you (Walker & Chance, 1994/1995).

Task Analysis. As you make judgments about content for a given group of learners, you need to engage in **task-analysis activities.** These require you to look at a proposed body of content that your learners are to master for the purposes of (1) breaking it into several smaller components or subtasks and (2) identifying a good beginning point for instruction. To determine whether learners have the needed prerequisite information, you identify what each subtask presumes learners know before they begin work on it. Figure 8.1 provides a step-by-step breakdown of task analysis.

Specifying Learning Intentions. After you determine which content is appropriate, you next specify **learning intentions.** A learning intention, sometimes called a **lesson objective,** identifies what learners should be able to do after they have mastered related content. Often, separate learning intentions are written for each of the subtasks identified during the task-analysis phase. Attainment of these learning intentions provides evidence you can use to judge whether members of your class have mastered the new material.

Task analysis consists of two parts: (1) identifying information learners will need to master specific content and (2) determining a logical beginning point for instruction.

Suppose you were planning a two- to three-week unit in a subject and at a grade level of your choice. List specific knowledge and skills needed to master this content.

Needed Knowledge: _____

_____

Needed Skills: _____

_____

Now, prepare a brief description of how you will begin instruction. To make this determination, you must find out how much of the needed knowledge and skills your learners already possess. Then you can identify the appropriate starting point.

FIGURE 8.1   Components of Task Analysis

Effective Lesson Presentation

When you function as an active teacher, you need to play a leadership role during all phases of instructional planning and implementation. This is particularly evident when you are actually presenting your lessons.

Stimulating and Maintaining Interest.   As you identify and select content, you need to pay particular heed to what motivates learners. **Motivational activities** stimulate and maintain learner interest in what you are teaching. This does not constrain you to selecting only material in which all learners have a high initial interest.

Because interests of individual learners vary, you need to think about a variety of approaches as you consider motivation (Rinne, 1998). Your challenge is to devise approaches that will motivate the largest possible number of students. Your motivational activities need to be embedded within your lessons. When this happens, motivation becomes an integral part of your behavior when students become actively engaged in new material. During the presentation-of-instruction phase, three distinct periods of motivation that must be considered are

- Motivation at the beginning of the learning sequence,
- Motivation during the learning sequence, and
- Motivation at the conclusion of the learning sequence.

The purpose of **initial motivation** is to engage learners' interest and to encourage them to want to learn the material. At this stage, you try to build on learners' general curiosity. Introducing something novel, unusual, or puzzling often works well. Members of your class need to understand how the new material connects to their own lives. What will mastering the content help them do or understand? Why should they commit themselves to mastering it? You need to be prepared to answer these kinds of questions during the first phase of motivation.

Within-the-lesson motivation helps sustain learners' interest levels. Learners are motivated by success. When they accomplish parts of a larger instructional task, you need to praise them for what they have done. This kind of support helps keep interest levels high. In general, motivation is facilitated when you maintain a positive classroom atmosphere that is free from threats and fear. Learners need to know that they have your solid support as they struggle with new content.

Your efforts directed toward promoting **end-of-the-instructional-sequence motivation** help learners to consolidate new information and reinforce their interest in what you are teaching. At this phase of a lesson, you should take particular care to point out to class members how much they have accomplished. A sense of achievement functions as an important motivator. Achievement during one instructional sequence makes it easier for learners to be motivated as they begin the next one.

WEB EXTENSION 8–2

Project-Based Education

At this Web site you will find a useful discussion of an approach to teaching that promotes learner motivation through the use of a teaching approach that requires young people to apply new knowledge as they complete assigned projects. You will find interesting descriptions of (1) class-motivated projects, (2) team-motivated projects, and (3) self-motivated projects.

http://www.motivation-tools.com/youth/project_education.html

Sequencing Lessons.   Over the years, many schemes have been proposed that relate to sequencing instruction. Centuries ago, the ancient Spartans developed a four-part sequence that required the teacher to follow these steps in presenting new material to learners:

- Introduce material to be learned.
- Ask learners to think about the material.
- Repeat the material again, and work with learners individually until they have it memorized.
- Listen to learners as they recite the material from memory. (Posner, 1987)

Copyright 1997 by Randy Glasbergen.

"Class, I've got a lot of material to cover, so to save time I won't be using vowels today. Nw lts bgn, pls pn t pg 122."

In the 19th century, the famous learning theorist Johann Herbart suggested a lesson cycle featuring these steps:

- Preparation for learning,
- Presentation of new information,
- Association (tying new information to old),
- Generalization, and
- Application. (Meyer, 1975)

Over the years, some school districts have recommended that teachers follow an instructional sequence suggested by Madeline Hunter and Douglas Russell (1977). The Hunter–Russell scheme includes these steps:

- Anticipatory set (focusing learners' attention on the instruction that is about to begin)
- Objective and purpose (helping learners understand what they will be able to do as a result of their exposure to the instruction)
- Instructional input (conveying information to learners)
- Modeling (providing learners with examples or demonstrations of competencies associated with the lesson)
- Checking for understanding (evaluating whether learners have the information needed to master the objective)
- Guided practice (monitoring learners as they work on tasks calling on them to apply the new information)
- Independent practice (assigning learners to work with new content under conditions in which they will not have direct teacher assistance available)

Other sequencing models have also been developed (e.g., Denton, Armstrong, & Savage, 1980; Posner, 1987) that share many common features. Most of them emphasize the importance of giving learners opportunities to apply new knowledge. Researchers have consistently found improved learning to be associated with instruction that allows learners to engage in application activities (Good & Brophy, 2000).

Pacing. **Pacing** refers to the rate at which you proceed through steps involved in teaching a particular lesson. Good active teaching requires you to provide lessons that move at a brisk pace and that are designed to promote high levels of learner success. You need to maintain a smooth, continuous developmental flow, avoiding any temptation to spend much time on certain points or matters that are not directly related to the central content. As the lesson develops, you need to ask questions and take other actions to ensure that members of your class are learning the material.

Within-Lesson Checks for Understanding. Active teaching demands the skillful use of **within-lesson checks for understanding.** These are pauses within your lessons when you ask brief questions to check for learner understanding. Research reveals that questions should be asked at regular intervals and addressed to a large number of class members (Good & Brophy, 2000). Within-lesson checks for understanding serve two basic purposes. First, they give you insights regarding learners' levels of understanding. Second, when learners know that you will be asking many people in the class to respond to questions about what they are learning, they stay alert. Learners realize that they need to pay attention because they know you might call on them at any time.

Monitoring. Your **monitoring** actions involve steps you take to keep yourself constantly apprised of how well members of your class are understanding your instruction

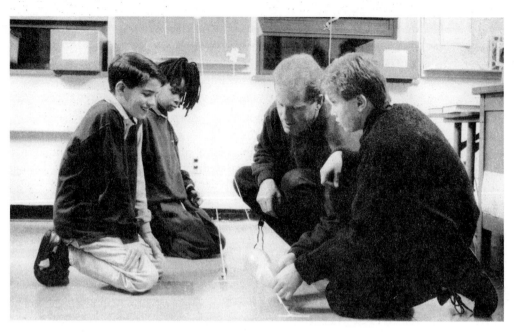

This middle school teacher monitors members of his class who are setting up a science experiment.

and the specific learning tasks you have assigned. In active teaching, your monitoring activities occur continuously throughout your lessons. It is particularly important after students engage in assignments that require them to use the new information. Effective monitoring cannot occur if you remain seated at your desk. You need to move about the classroom and check on learners' progress.

It is important to provide feedback both to learners who are performing the task correctly and to those who are experiencing difficulties. Successful performers need to know they are on the right track (Goodlad, 1984) and need to hear supportive comments from the teacher. Those learners who are having problems or who are not doing the work properly also need assistance. You must give them specific details regarding (1) what they are doing wrong and (2) how they can change what they are doing so they will experience success.

When, as a result of careful monitoring, you discover that many learners are not performing at an acceptable level, you need to halt the independent practice activity. At this point, you engage in **reteaching,** which is a renewed presentation of the material, perhaps using somewhat different and expanded examples. Reteaching serves to clear up misunderstandings and provide assistance to learners who failed to grasp the new content when you initially presented it. Successful reteaching is tightly focused, dealing with only those points that seem to be causing problems or confusion.

CONSTRUCTIVIST TEACHING

A growing body of research supports the effectiveness of instruction developed from a philosophical orientation known as constructivism (Henson, 2004). According to this view, young people are not passive responders to the world around them. Instead, they have an internal drive that causes them to draw together and interpret information they encounter. What they "learn" does not result from their exposure to new experiences but rather from the personal interpretations they make of these experiences. Teaching that proceeds in accordance with constructivist principles recognizes the active role young people play in developing their personal stores of knowledge. It also seeks to help them develop adequate **metacognitive powers.** These refer to their ability to become aware of their own thinking processes and to determine whether the processes they are using are appropriate given the problem they are seeking to resolve.

When you implement instruction consistent with contructivist principles, you present students with complete and authentic problems that include some elements of what they already know. You will involve your learners in quests that will help them identify patterns and discover discrepancies. You will provide them with opportunities to engage new content actively, interact with others in their attempts to arrive at new understandings, and engage in efforts to test and modify their perceptions in light of these experiences. Active engagement with content is a hallmark of these approaches (Parsley & Corcoran, 2003).

If you decide to use some constructivist techniques, you first must commit to the idea that you will not be presenting small bits of sequenced information in your lessons. What your learners take away from these lessons will depend in large measure on the intensity of their interest in the content. They are much more likely to actively engage situations or problems that are presented to them as a whole. In other words, they will react more enthusiastically to situations that are complete and authentic. Learners will master the basics as part of an effort to develop understandings of fully developed problems and circumstances.

When you teach, you need to focus clearly on your learners and how they are engaging the content. What members of your class take away from your lessons will depend as much on how they are personally involved with the new content as on the content's intrinsic nature. You want students to control their own behavior, take responsibility for their own learning, and construct their own knowledge and understanding.

Some approaches that are consistent with constructivist teaching are

- Thinking aloud
- Visualizing thinking

WEB EXTENSION 8–3

ASCD Tutorials: Constructivism

The Association for Supervision and Curriculum Development (ASCD), a large professional organization for school administrators and university professors interested in developing and managing high-quality instructional programs, sponsors this site. You will find an extensive tutorial here that defines *constructivism,* introduces examples of classroom applications of constructivist teaching, explores the relationship between constructivist teaching and assessment practices, and introduces other topics and issues with ties to the constructivist perspective.

http://webserver2.ascd.org/tutorials/tutorial2.cfm?ID=27&TITLE=Constructivism

Thinking Aloud

Thinking aloud is an instructional approach that seeks to help learners understand what kinds of thinking processes might be appropriate for them to use in completing an assigned task. Suppose you were interested in helping a group of high school students learn more about writing materials designed to appeal to the perspectives of a given group of readers. Your first assignment required class members to write a four-page paper containing as much descriptive information about your school as possible. As you begin preparing students for the next phase of this project, you might select one of the better papers you received. With permission from the writer, you might make copies of this paper, distribute it to class members, and have them look at it while you make these comments:

> In this paper, I told you to include as much descriptive information about our school as you could fit into four pages. Many of you did a good job on this assignment. I've asked Ian if he would mind our using his paper as a takeoff point for discussing the next assignment.
>
> The papers you wrote were not written for a specific audience. What I want you to do next is to prepare a new version of your papers. The new version will feature information that would appeal to a group of people with predictable interests, perspectives, or points of view. For example, suppose I told you that I wanted you to write a paper that would be interesting to a group of parents of middle school students who would be entering our high school for the first time next fall.
>
> If I had received this assignment, first I would think through kinds of information these parents might want to know. I would begin by making a bulleted list. My list might include items such as
>
> - What kind of help will my son/daughter receive in planning his/her course schedule?
> - Will teachers provide personal help for individual students?
> - How well will the school program prepare my son/daughter for college and university entrance or for employment immediately following graduation?
> - What procedures and policies does the school have to promote safety for students?
> - What supplies will my son or daughter be expected to purchase and bring to school?
> - What are the rules regarding leaving the school during the lunch hour?
> - What are the arrangements to help students who need medical assistance during the school day?
>
> In thinking about this audience, there is probably other information that might be of great interest to other audiences that would be less important to these parents. For example, they may not have great interest in detailed information about specific school clubs and organizations or the names of bands that typically play at school dances.
>
> Now, what I want you to do is rewrite your paper with a focus on one of these two possible reader audiences: (1) middle school students who will be coming to our school for the first time next fall or (2) a group of retirees, most of whom graduated from our school in the 1950s.
>
> As you proceed, consider following the same process I used to identify kinds of information that would be of particular interest to the group you select. Then use this information to prepare your revision.

Visualizing Thinking

Visualizing thinking is an instructional approach that helps learners use diagrams to examine the requirements of an assigned task, to consider the nature of thinking they will need to complete it, and to identify specific kinds of information they will need to finish it (Armstrong & Savage, 2002). For example, completed diagrams can help learners develop more-appropriate and more-efficient ways to respond to your assignments.

Suppose you asked members of your class to read the following selection from one of your texts:

The Rise and Decline of Manaus

We don't hear much about Manaus today. This Brazilian city, located almost a thousand miles inland from the mouth of the Amazon River, was one of the fastest growing cities in the world in the early 1900s. It is situated near the center of the vast Amazon rainforest, a place where thousands of wild rubber trees grow. In the early years of the 20th century, the fantastic growth in popularity of automobiles resulted in a huge demand for tire rubber.

Thousands of people flocked to Manaus, hoping to make their fortunes by becoming rubber barons. Many succeeded. Fabulous new homes sprung up overnight. Diamond merchants found a ready market for fine gemstones. Money from rubber supported construction of one of the world's most elegant opera houses. Manaus had electric streetcars well before they appeared in Boston.

The wealth of Manaus was short-lived. In the late 1870s, an Englishman, Henry Wickham, had taken thousands of seeds from rubber trees to England. He planted them in greenhouses. Some time later, he transplanted the small trees to plantations in the East Indies. These trees proved to be much more productive than those around Manaus. These trees also grew in rubber-tree-only plantation forests. In Brazil, wild trees were intermingled with other varieties. By the end of the second decade of the 20th century, the huge East Indian production of rubber had driven rubber prices to low levels. Manaus' glory days as a world rubber capital were at an end.

Because learners vary in their ability levels, you might decide to have some of them focus on aspects of this material that are different from aspects you assign to others. For example, you might ask some class members to keep this learning task in mind as they read the selection:

Outline the sequence of events reported in the selection from first to last, and describe what Henry Wickham did.

To help your learners focus on this task, you might provide them with a visual-thinking diagram something like the example in Figure 8.2. Once you have distributed copies of this diagram, you would tell students to take notes and list them under the appropriate headings. This organizational scheme will help them undertake learning activities that are relevant to the particulars of the assigned task. It provides members of your class with a mind-set or basic orientation to the assignment that will direct them toward information in the reading that ties to your assignment.

You may wish others in your class to wrestle with more-sophisticated issues raised in the Manaus selection. For example, you might have them pursue this alternative task:

Describe changes in the population of Manaus in the first two decades of the 20th century, and explain their causes.

This learning task demands more of learners than the one used in the Figure 8.2 example. It requires students not only to know certain facts but also to engage in some sophisticated cause-and-effect thinking. A visual-thinking diagram for this task needs to prompt

---

Assigned Task: *Outline the sequence of events reported in the selection from first to last, and describe what Henry Wickham did.*

Basic Sequence of Events   *Actions Taken by Henry Wickham*

_____   _____

_____   _____

_____   _____

_____   _____

_____   _____

FIGURE 8.2   An Example of a Simple Visual-Thinking Diagram

learners to approach the Manaus selection differently than the first task. To help learners do well on this more-sophisticated assignment, you might develop a visual-thinking diagram such as the one in Figure 8.3.

Note that the visual-thinking diagram in Figure 8.3 prompts learners to direct their reading to information that deals with content they will need to complete the assignment appropriately. The two examples of visual-thinking diagrams in Figures 8.2 and 8.3 underscore an important point. You cannot count on the presence of anything inherent within your assigned material that will orient your learners to your expectations. Without some guidance, individuals will establish priorities of their own, and though they may work hard to engage the assigned content, they may focus on information that is only marginally related to your instructional purposes. If you work with your class to develop visual-thinking diagrams before learners begin their work, you will find that much higher percentages of class members will focus on the content elements that you wish to emphasize.

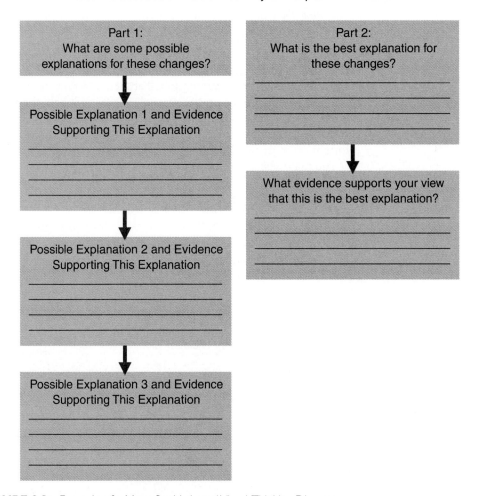

Assigned Task: *Describe changes in the population of Manaus in the first two decades of the 20th century and explain their causes.*

Part 1:
What are some possible explanations for these changes?

Possible Explanation 1 and Evidence Supporting This Explanation

Possible Explanation 2 and Evidence Supporting This Explanation

Possible Explanation 3 and Evidence Supporting This Explanation

Part 2:
What is the best explanation for these changes?

What evidence supports your view that this is the best explanation?

FIGURE 8.3   Example of a More-Sophisticated Visual-Thinking Diagram

TEACHER CLARITY

Research reveals that clarity is a defining characteristic of effective teachers. It involves several variables, including:

- The teacher's verbal and nonverbal style,
- The teacher's lesson-presentation structure, and
- The teacher's proficiency in providing cogent explanation.

Verbal and Nonverbal Style

Several issues play a part in defining a given presentation style. One of these involves **paralanguage.** Paralanguage includes those things that help shape what is conveyed by words that are spoken but that are not the words themselves. Elements of paralanguage include voice intonation, precision of articulation of words, and rate of speaking. Paralanguage, which also includes many of our nonverbal behaviors, has a great influence on how listeners hear and interpret what we say.

You acquire paralanguage as a natural overlay of language as you grow to maturity within your family, friendship groups, and community. There are important regional and cultural differences. When the paralanguage patterns of a speaker and listener differ, the listener may have difficulty understanding all that is being said.

For example, if you were brought up in a part of the country where speech rates and vowel sounds differ dramatically from those in the area where you are now teaching, you may find that the learners sometimes have difficulty grasping what you say. You must understand that communication problems sometimes result not from the level of difficulty of the words or message, but from the patterns of speech you use to deliver them.

Nonverbal behaviors involve gestures and other behaviors that do not require use of your voice. Nonverbal behaviors sometimes also get in the way of clear communication. This can happen when you send a nonverbal message that is not consistent with your spoken words. For example, suppose you scowled and shook a fist at a class while saying, "I'm really proud of the good work you're doing." Signals here are mixed; the nonverbal behaviors are hostile and threatening, but the verbal behavior is warm and supportive. The resulting message is confusing.

It is not unusual for people to be unaware of many of their nonverbal behaviors; yet, your varied nonverbal messages have a cumulative effect (Ornstein & Lasley, 2000). Because these behaviors are important, you need to develop some awareness of your nonverbal patterns. Class observers sometimes can help by providing feedback about what you are doing nonverbally to support your verbal instruction.

WEB EXTENSION 8-4

Components of Successful Classroom Communication: Use of Nonverbal Behavior

At this site, you will find explanations of categories of your nonverbal behavior that can influence how learners react to your instruction. You will find information related to such topics as (1) eye contact, (2) facial expressions, (3) body posture, (4) gestures, and (5) general movement patterns. Video clips that provide examples of good nonverbal practice accompany the text.

http://www.wmich.edu/celcisaw/1nvbehavior/componentstemplate.html

Lesson-Presentation Structure

The term **lesson-presentation structure** refers to the framework a teacher uses to organize and sequence delivery of learning experiences embedded within a given lesson. Good lesson-presentation structures make it easy for members of your class to learn. One feature of a good lesson-presentation structure is the **advance organizer.** An advance organizer is a label or term you present to learners that describes in a succinct way a large and important body of content you wish to cover. Advance organizers help learners sort out fragmented pieces of information and organize them under certain specified category labels. This process simplifies their learning task.

Consider the following example. Suppose you wanted a group of your high school students to study advertising. One purpose might be to help class members understand that some advertisers make claims that go beyond the evidence available to support them. You might begin with these instructions: "Look through any five magazines of your choice. By Wednesday, bring me three or four ads that you believe make untrue or unfair claims."

This assignment will bring students into contact with a huge volume of information. The task, as assigned, provides few guidelines for them to follow in deciding which ads might be better than others as examples of misleading advertising. The task you assigned would have been greatly simplified had you given students one or two advance organizers.

For example, you might have begun the class with an explanation and a discussion of the term *glittering generality*. You could have outlined the task by saying something such as, "Look through any five magazines of your choice. By Wednesday, bring me three or four ads that contain glittering generalities." This assignment provides learners with a good sense of direction by clearly communicating to them what they need to do to complete the task to your satisfaction.

A widely used type of advance organizer is the learning intention. You will recall that learning intentions clearly specify what learners should be able to grasp or do as a result of their exposure to teaching related to a particular lesson. Your learning intentions need not be complex. For example, you might say something as simple as, "When we've finished this lesson, you should be able to identify at least four main parts of a short story."

As lessons are being taught, you need to maintain **connected discourse.** This kind of verbal communication features smooth, point-by-point development of the content you are introducing. When your lesson is characterized by a high degree of connected discourse, it moves to its logical conclusion in a clear and systematic way. There are few digressions that take away from its main flow.

It is also important for you to take time to provide **internal summaries** as you teach your lessons. These are pause points that allow you and your learners to stop, take stock, and reflect upon what has been learned so far. Internal summaries allow you to clarify any misconceptions. When internal summaries are a regular feature of your teaching, learners tend to pay attention because they realize that you may stop from time to time to ask someone in the class to summarize what has been learned.

Your communication with learners also is enhanced when you use **marker expressions.** These are statements that underline or highlight something that has been said. You can use marker expressions to communicate the importance of certain kinds of information. Examples include statements such as

- Write this down.
- Pay close attention to this.
- Listen carefully to this explanation.

You can also "mark" the importance of specific content by changing your vocal intonation or volume.

A final aspect of lesson structuring is the **lesson summary** provided at the end of a lesson presentation. The summary is a recap of major ideas that have been covered that draws together what has been learned in a way that facilitates retention.

Providing Explanations

At various times during a lesson, you may be called on to explain something. You can do several things to enhance the clarity of your explanations. For example, you can help your learners grasp new information by taking particular care to define potentially confusing terms. Newcomers to teaching sometimes assume that learners know more than they really do.

Consider, for example, the case of a high school teacher who developed a marvelous presentation on the topic "Recent Political Trends." At the end of the teacher's lecture, a student cautiously raised a hand to ask, "What is a trend?" This teacher had not considered the possibility that some students would not be familiar with the word "trend."

Your explanations communicate best when they are free from ambiguous, vague, and imprecise terms. Some examples of phrasing you need to avoid include **terms of approximation,** such as kind of, sort of, and about. **Ambiguous designations,** such as somehow, somewhere, and someone, also often fail the clarity test. In addition, **probability statements,** such as frequently, generally, and often, do not mean the same thing to all learners.

TEACHERS' QUESTIONS

The view that to teach well is to question well has long had historic standing (DeGarmo, 1903). A large body of research supports the idea that effective teachers ask more questions than less-effective teachers. In one study, effective junior high school mathematics teachers were found to ask an average of 24 questions during a class period, whereas their less-effective counterparts asked an average of only 8.6 questions (Rosenshine & Stevens, 1986).

Interest in questioning encompasses more than the issue of the number of questions teachers ask. For example, many researchers have examined such issues as (1) the sophistication of the questions themselves, (2) the kinds of questions learners are prompted to ask their teachers, (3) the clarity of individual questions, (4) the use of questions to inquire more deeply about levels of learner understanding, and (5) the length of time teachers wait for responses after they ask questions.

Lower-Level Questions

Lower-level questions are appropriate when your purpose is to check learners' understanding of basic information. A productive pattern for this kind of questioning involves a three-part sequence:

1. You ask the question.
2. The learner responds to it.
3. You react to the learner's response.

Research suggests that your questions should be delivered at a brisk pace and that you should expect learners to respond quickly (Good & Brophy, 2000). This pattern allows you to ask a large number of recall questions in a short period of time. It also gives many members of your class an opportunity to respond. A fairly fast-paced pattern of questioning keeps learners alert and gives you opportunities to diagnose and respond to any misunderstandings revealed in answers from a cross section of class members.

Higher-Level Questions

If your aim is to stimulate more-sophisticated learner thinking, you will want to ask **higher-level questions** (Ramsey, Gabbard, Clawson, Lee, & Henson, 1990). Redfield and Rousseau's review of research related to questioning (1981) revealed that teachers' use of higher-level questions is associated with higher learner achievement. However, more-recent summaries of research reveal inconsistent results regarding the effects of higher-level questions on learner achievement (Good & Brophy, 2000).

For example, research has now established that asking higher-level questions, by itself, does not ensure academic success. Your learners must also have the knowledge base necessary to engage in complex thinking tasks. For a well-prepared high school class, a higher-level question such as, "How would you compare and contrast the late 19th-century foreign policies of France and the United Kingdom?" might produce some insightful responses from learners. On the other hand, if students who were asked this question lacked basic information about the 19th-century foreign policies of the two countries, responses probably would produce more wild guessing than sophisticated thought.

If you believe that members of your class have adequate background information to engage tasks requiring sophisticated patterns of thinking, you might consider following these guidelines when asking questions:

- Prepare many open-ended, probing questions about the material you teach.
- When questioning students, provide adequate time for learners to think about their responses before expecting answers.
- Consistently model the responses you expect by the way you answer students' questions.
- Teach and consistently incorporate into your questions words that have been shown to trip up at-risk students on standardized tests. (Bell, 2003)

Variables associated with the particular goals established for a specific lesson and variables related to the individual instructional context will help you determine whether you should use lower-level or higher-level questions in a particular situation (Good & Brophy, 2000). The impact of questions of various kinds on learners continues to be an area of interest to educational researchers.

Learner-Initiated Questions

Discussions about the effect of questions sometimes overlook the important category of learner-initiated questions. The questions your learners ask often reveal a great deal about the effectiveness of what you have taught. Questions that students ask also can cue you to some misconceptions they may have. Insights you gain from learner questions can be an invaluable aid as you plan lessons that are responsive to their instructional needs (Heckman, Confer, & Hakim, 1994).

Clarity of Questions

When you teach, you need to word your questions so that learners clearly understand what you are asking. Many questions that appear deceptively simple on the surface, upon closer examination, can be responded to in many ways. For example, a learner could logically answer the question, "Who was the first President of the United States?" with any of the following responses:

- A man
- A Virginian
- A general
- A person named George Washington

To avoid this situation, you should ask questions in ways that make it unnecessary for learners to guess about what you are really asking. For example, you could ask, "Can you give me the name of the first President of the United States?"

In addition, some research points out that it is unwise to begin a discussion with a series of questions. Cazden (1986) and Henson (2004) argue that it is better for you to give class members some general background information before asking questions. This practice establishes a context for the questions to follow and tends to associate with better learner answers.

One practice that can confuse students is asking a large question that contains two, three, or even more questions within it. Finding such questions confusing, learners are often puzzled about where to start their answers. Some of them deal with this dilemma by refusing to answer the question at all. It is better to ask one question at a time. Shorter questions are preferred (Good & Brophy, 2000). You also want to restrict vocabulary used in your questions to words that you know your learners understand.

Probing Questions

Good lessons that feature questioning require more than well-designed questions. You also must be prepared to attend carefully to what learners say and to respond appropriately. For example, you will want to use **probing questions** to dispute learners' judgments when they jump to premature conclusions about complex issues. Probing questions dispute assumptions and require members of your class to think more seriously and deeply about issues they are considering. Also, when learners use vague terminology in their responses, you should stop them and ask for clarification.

In summary, your reactions should convey to learners that you are carefully listening to their answers. Your actions signal to students that their responses are important and should be made thoughtfully.

Wait Time

The interval between when you ask a question and a learner responds is called **wait time.** Teachers have been found to wait an astonishingly short period before either answering their own questions, rephrasing their questions, or calling on different learners to respond. Rowe (1986) reported that, on average, teachers wait less than one second for learners to respond.

Abundant research supports the importance of the connection between the length of time teachers wait for responses after asking questions and learner achievement.

Achievement levels on tests demanding higher-level thinking have been found to be higher for students in classes where teachers wait at least three seconds for responses to questions (Tobin, 1987). Increasing wait time enables students to continue interacting with the information (Wormeli, 2002).

Efforts to increase teacher wait time have produced interesting results. When average wait time increases, teachers tend to ask a smaller number of total questions, but they increase the number of higher-level questions. When they wait longer, teachers make greater use of learners' answers in class discussions. Finally, when wait time increases, there often is a change in teachers' general attitudes about the capabilities of learners in their classes (Rowe, 1986). This attitude change appears to stem from a finding that, when average wait times are longer, learners who have not previously answered questions become more-active participants in discussions. These increased levels of involvement result in teachers' raising their estimations of these learners' abilities.

WEB EXTENSION 8–5

Effective Classroom Questioning

The University of Illinois maintains this site. Here you will find extensive information about classroom questioning. Topics included relate to (1) levels and kinds of questions, (2) planning questions, (3) teacher–learner interactions when a questioning technique is being used, and (4) assessing teachers' questioning skills.

http://www.oir.uiuc.edu/Did/docs/questioning.htm

HOMEWORK AND LEARNING

Researchers have found that the amount of homework teachers assign varies over time. Parents' desire for more (and less) homework runs in 30-year cycles, growing for 15 years and diminishing for the next 15 years (Cooper, 2001b). A national poll taken in 2000 reported that American parents were satisfied with the amount of homework being given (Public Agenda, 2000).

Performance on homework is one source of information you can use to determine what members of your class have taken away from a lesson or series of lessons. Researchers have concluded that sometimes homework facilitates learning, and sometimes it does not. In general, you will find it to have a more positive influence on what class members learn if you take time to explain your reasons for making a particular homework assignment (Cooper, 2001b).

Homework seems to have particular benefits for learners in specific age groups (Cooper, 2001b). Homework has the highest degree of impact on the achievement of high school students. Its benefit for middle school and junior high school students' achievement is only about half as great as that for senior high school students. Homework only marginally improves the achievement levels of elementary learners.

For junior high school and senior high school students, the length of homework assignments influences their effectiveness. Academic achievement for junior high school students tends to go up with length of homework assignments until a limit somewhere between one and two hours a night is reached. Longer homework assignments do not help these students learn. Senior high school students profit more from somewhat-longer homework assignments than do junior high school students. So, how can you use this

VIDEO VIEWPOINTS

How Much Homework Is Enough?

WATCH: This *Good Morning America* segment focuses on the debate over how much homework should be assigned to young children. It cites a University of Michigan study that found that the amount of time young children spend on homework has increased dramatically. Some parents are complaining that homework is taking away the opportunity for their children to participate in other activities. Others state that the impact is having a negative effect on the motivation of children. What is not discussed in the segment is the value of homework and the type of homework that is useful.

THINK: Discuss with your classmates, or in your teaching journal, the following questions:

1. What is the role of homework in learning?
2. Can too much homework be detrimental to learning? In what ways?
3. How would you go about determining how much homework to assign?
4. What could a teacher do to gain support from parents for homework policies?

LINK: Do you think that schools should consider other factors in the community, such as other activities, in making policies, or should the focus be entirely on what is educationally sound?

Complete this activity and submit your responses online in the Video Viewpoints *module for this chapter of the* Companion Website.

knowledge when you begin teaching your own classes? Cooper (2001a) offers the following guidelines:

- Use the 10-minute rule. Limit your homework assignments to 10 minutes multiplied by your grade level.
- Know what you expect students to gain from doing homework, and don't limit these goals to academics.
- Use homework as one of several instructional strategies.

WEB EXTENSION 8–6

Helping Your Students with Homework: A Guide for Teachers

The U.S. Department of Education sponsored preparation of this online publication. You will find important information about the general issue of homework. The "Tips for Getting Homework Done" section includes links to excellent ideas you can use to increase the probability that members of your class will complete and profit from your homework assignments.

http://www.ed.gov/pubs/HelpingStudents/

OBSERVING IN THE CLASSROOM

Effective teachers are those teachers whose students consistently reach high levels of academic and social success. (Henson 2004) You may want to know whether your patterns of classroom behavior are consistent with those researchers have found to be desirable. Some basic tools you can use to gather this kind of information include **event sampling** and **time sampling.**

This classroom observer is using an observational tool to gather information that will be shared later with the teacher. The teacher will use the information to make decisions about changes in procedures.

Event sampling requires the presence of an observer who records information about specific classroom events that might interest you. For example, an observer might wish to note what you do to motivate learners. In such a case, the observer would simply write down everything you do that relates to motivation during a lesson.

In *time sampling,* an observer records what is happening in the classroom at selected time intervals. For example, an observer could decide to take a sample once every 15 seconds. If you were lecturing at the end of the first 15-second interval, the observer would simply note "1—lecturing." If the lecture were still going on at the end of the next 15-second interval, the observer would write "2—lecturing." If you were asking a question at the end of the third 15-second interval, the observer would write "3—teacher question." This scheme provides a general profile of activity during a lesson. It tends to capture the flow of a lesson and can provide you with useful information for analysis.

Many different kinds of observational tools can be developed that are based on event sampling, time sampling, or a combination of the two. Some examples are introduced in the following subsections.

Narrative Approach

Observers using a **narrative approach,** sometimes referred to as **scripting,** try to capture information about what is happening in a classroom by rapidly writing down everything that is observed. Because much of what happens is verbal, narrative approaches focus heavily on what teachers and learners say.

A basic problem with an unstructured narrative approach is that so much happens in a classroom so quickly that it is impossible for everything to be recorded. What is recorded may reveal just a partial picture of what happened. To avoid this limitation, some observers prefer to use a more narrowly focused version, called **selective verbatim.**

In selective verbatim, an observer identifies a particular dimension of classroom verbal interaction as a focus. Then the observer records everything said that falls into this targeted category. Targeted categories might include such areas as "teacher questions," "motiva-

---

Focus: **Teacher Praise Statements**

Kind of lesson: **Arithmetic—Grade 5**

Time	Teacher Statements
9:02	Thank you for sitting down.
9:03	I appreciate that.
9:05	You have really been doing a good job on this unit.
9:09	Good answer.
9:10	Okay, good.
9:13	Good, I like that.
9:13	Right!
9:15	Good.
9:18	Juan, you used a good method to get the answer.
9:20	I'm glad you all started to work so promptly.

FIGURE 8.4 Example of a Selective-Verbatim Record

tional statements," "classroom-control statements," and "praise statements." Only the creativity and interests of the observer limit the focus for a selective-verbatim approach.

Suppose an observer is interested in the types of praise statements you make during a lesson. To gather information, the observer would write down everything you say when you are praising a learner. (Sometimes observers make an audio recording of the lesson so they can recheck the accuracy of what they wrote during the live observation.)

Results of a selective-verbatim observation are organized into a selective-verbatim record, which can provide data for a useful analysis. A series of questions is developed that can be answered by reference to this information. For example, if the focus of the observation were on praise behavior, the observer might develop questions such as

- Did the teacher use a variety of praise statements?
- How adequate was the quantity of praise statements?
- Were praise statements tied more to academic performance or to other kinds of learner behavior?
- Were more praise statements directed toward individuals or to the class as a whole?

An example of a selective-verbatim record is provided in Figure 8.4.

Frequency Counts

Frequency counts focus on the number of occurrences of desired and undesired behaviors. An observer identifies behavior categories before the observation begins. Frequency-count observations might focus on such categories as

- The number of teacher praise statements,
- The number of high-level teacher questions (demanding sophisticated thinking),
- The number of low-level teacher questions (demanding only simple recall of basic information),
- The number of classroom disruptions,
- The number of times individual learners visit learning centers, or
- The number of times learners made correct (or incorrect) responses to teacher questions.

Frequency-count systems are easy to use. A simple record is maintained of the number of times each selected focus behavior occurs. Tally marks are often used to indicate each occurrence.

Look at the example of a frequency-count system provided in Figure 8.5. Because frequency-count systems do not require much writing, it is possible for tallies to be made that relate to numerous behaviors. This example yields information that might help an observer identify some teacher behaviors that prompted learner involvement in the lesson.

Coding Systems

Coding systems require the use of codes or symbols that represent behaviors of interest to the observer. Symbols may vary in their complexity from a simple system of checks, minuses, and pluses to a complex scheme that assigns numbers to a wide array of individual behaviors. Usually, a record using the codes is made after a preestablished interval of time has passed, for example once every 20 seconds.

Having an entire coding scheme developed before a classroom observation begins is not necessary. Sometimes new codes can be added during the observation itself as interesting behaviors occur that were not included in the initial scheme. The ability to add new codes even during the observation gives needed flexibility.

Focus: **Teacher Statements and their Relationship to Learner Participation in a Discussion**

Directions: Tally each teacher behavior that has a positive impact on getting learners involved in the discussion. (These are found under the heading "Teacher Facilitating Moves.") Also tally each teacher behavior that has a negative impact on getting learners involved in the discussion. (These are found under the heading "Teacher Inhibiting Moves.") Tally learner responses that are correct and those that are incorrect. Also provide a tally for each time the teacher asks questions that fail to elicit a response. Finally, tally each time a learner initiates a question or a comment. (These are made under the heading "Learner Responses.")

Teacher Facilitating Moves
- Asks clear questions
- Asks for learner response (waits more than three seconds)
- Praises learner comment
- Uses learner comment in lesson
- Provides positive nonverbal reinforcement

Teacher Inhibiting Moves
- Asks ambiguous question
- Asks multiple questions
- Does not wait for learner response
- Criticizes learner response
- Sends negative nonverbal signals

Learner Responses
- Number of correct learner responses
- Number of incorrect learner responses
- Absence of any learner responses to question

FIGURE 8.5   Example of a Frequency-Count System

For example, suppose an observer began an observation with a very simple coding scheme in mind. It might feature only these two codes:

1. Indicates a learner who is working on the assigned task.
2. Indicates a learner who is not working on the assigned task.

During the actual observation, the observer might note that some learners were out of their seats, talking, or working on schoolwork other than the assigned task. The observer might decide to add specific codes to indicate these behaviors. (One way to do this would be to designate code 2a for "out of seat," code 2b for "talking," and code 2c for "other schoolwork." Code 2 would be reserved for all additional examples of learners who were not working on assigned tasks.) See Figure 8.6 for an example of an observation system using coding.

Focus: **Motivational Strategies**

Directions: During each five-minute time segment of the lesson, record the letters indicating the teacher's motivational strategies. Record letters in the sequence of their occurrence. If new motivational strategies are used that are not on the list, add them and give them a letter.

Motivational Strategy	**Record**
	5 min.
a. Used novelty	_____
b. Appeals to curiosity	_____
c. Provides concrete reinforcer	_____
d. Provides dramatic buildup	_____
e. Indicates importance of task	_____
	5 min.
f. Relates to learner needs, interests	_____
g. Provides encouragement	_____
h. Predicts success or enjoyment	_____
i. Warns about testing, grades	_____
j. Threatens punishment for noncompletion	_____
	5 min.
k. _____	_____
l. _____	_____
_____	_____
_____	_____
_____	_____
	5 min.
_____	_____
_____	_____
_____	_____
_____	_____
_____	_____

FIGURE 8.6 Example of a Coding-System Observation Scheme

Seating-Chart Systems

Observation systems involving the use of seating charts often are appropriate when the focus is on learner behaviors. Suppose you wanted to know which learners contributed to a discussion or which ones stayed on task during a seatwork assignment. A system might be devised that would record information about which learners you worked with during a given class period. **Seating-chart systems** also work well when you are curious about your location in the classroom during different parts of an instructional period.

In developing a seating-chart system, an observer begins by making a sketch of the classroom that includes the locations of individual learner seats. The observer may also want to record seat locations of males and females. This can be done by writing a small "m" for male and a small "f" for female on each seat represented in the chart.

Next, the observer develops a set of symbols to represent the various aspects of instruction that are to be emphasized. For example, a simple arrow pointing to a seat might indicate a teacher question to a particular learner, and a simple arrow pointing away from the seat might indicate a communication directed from a particular learner to the teacher. Numerals or letters can be designated to represent different kinds of individual learner behaviors at selected time intervals during the lesson. The location of the teacher at specific places in the room at different times could be indicated by a sequence of circled numbers (1 indicating the first location, 2 indicating the second, and so forth). Any symbols that work for the observer are acceptable. Look at the sample information provided in the chart featured in Figure 8.7.

Many interesting questions can be answered by examining data gathered from a completed chart of this kind. For example, by referring to information gathered through use of the scheme depicted in Figure 8.7, an observer might be able to answer questions such as

- How many learners were involved in the discussion?
- Were more males or females called on?
- Were learners seated on one side of the room called on more frequently?
- Did the teacher call more often on learners seated in the front than in the back of the room?
- How many learners who volunteered did the teacher fail to call on?

DEVELOPING TEACHING EXPERTISE

When you begin your career as a teacher, you will not have all the skills necessary to be as effective as you can be. Good teachers improve over time and progress through a series of developmental stages, from novice to expert (Steffy & Wolfe, 1997). Do not be excessively self-critical, and give yourself time to grow. Teachers who are more experienced and skilled will surround you and can play an invaluable role in your development (Halford, 1998)

Systematic growth will require your own efforts, and these will include, above all, a commitment to inquire into your own methodology. Continuing assessments of your instructional practices can provide information you can use to adapt your instruction to learners' needs.

Observation focus: Identifying discussion participants

Lesson topic: Review for a test

Directions: Each space in the chart below represents a learner seat. Sex of learners should be indicated by an *m* for males and an *f* for females. The following symbols are drawn in the box denoting the learner's seat and are used to indicate the first time the particular behavior is noted:

- A learner raises a hand to volunteer (indicated by a vertical line).

- A learner is recognized and makes a contribution (indicated by an arrow pointed away from the learner).

- The teacher calls on a learner (indicated by a down-pointing arrow).

- A learner is called but fails to respond (indicated by a zero drawn immediately below the down-pointing arrow indicating a teacher question).

- Repetitions of the same behavior are indicated by horizontal marks across the vertical ones. Note examples below:

This learner volunteered four times but was not called on.

This learner was called on and made a contribution twice.

This learner was called on three times.

Seating Chart with Sample Data

m **1**	m **2**	f **3**	m **4**	f **5**
m **6**	f **7**	m **8**	f **9**	m **10**
f **11**	m **12**	f **13**	m **14**	f **15**
f **16**	m **17**	m **18**	f **19**	m **20**
m **21**	f **22**	f **23**	f **24**	m **25**
f **26**	f **27**	m **28**	f **29**	f **30**

FIGURE 8.7 Example of a Seating-Chart Observation Scheme (with Sample Data)

Key Ideas in Summary

- Instruction is a key responsibility you will assume when you begin your career as a classroom teacher. In part, your effectiveness will be influenced by your *dispositions*. Dispositions are attitudes and perceptions that affect your behavior. Desirable dispositions promote behaviors that help learners grow academically, in self-esteem, and in their abilities to interact positively with others.
- When you engage in *active teaching*, you will assume such roles as (1) presenter of new information, (2) monitor of learner progress, (3) planner of opportunities for learners to apply what they have learned, and (4) reteacher of content to learners who need additional help in mastering material.
- Effective lessons feature actions you take to (1) stimulate and maintain learner interest, (2) present material systematically, (3) model expected behaviors and expected products of learning, (4) maintain an appropriate lesson pace, (5) ask questions skillfully, (6) provide opportunities for learners to practice what they have learned, and (7) monitor learners' progress.
- *Constructivist teaching* assumes that young people do not respond passively to the world around them. Instead, they are driven to interpret information they encounter. What they learn results not from the act of being exposed to new experiences but rather from their personal interpretations of these experiences.
- When you use a constructivist approach, you will be interested in developing learners' *metacognitive powers*. These include their abilities to develop a personal awareness of their own thinking processes and, as a result, to select thinking processes that are well suited to an assigned task. You may use techniques such as *thinking aloud* and *visualizing thinking* to help learners develop thinking patterns that will help them make sense of new information.
- Research has established the importance of clarity as a teacher variable associated with learner achievement. Among dimensions of clarity you need to consider are those related to (1) your verbal style, (2) your nonverbal style, (3) your lesson-presentation style, and (4) your ability to provide cogent explanations.
- Homework sometimes affects learners' levels of achievement, and sometimes it does not. Researchers have found that homework benefits high school students more than middle school students and high school students and middle school students more than elementary school learners.
- Many observation systems are available that can provide specific information about what happens in classrooms. Some of these approaches use time sampling, others use event sampling, and still others employ a combination of the two.

Chapter 8 Self-Test

 To review terms and concepts in this chapter, go to the Companion Website and take the Chapter 8 Self-Test. Feedback for the self-test is immediate. You can keep track of your self-test scores yourself, or you can submit them to your instructor via e-mail.

Preparing for Praxis

 To learn more about the Praxis test and complete this activity online, go to the Preparing for Praxis *module for this chapter of the Companion Website.*

You may be required to pass Educational Testing Service's Praxis II exam as you seek formal authorization to teach in the public schools. The *Principles of Learning and Teaching* component of Praxis II seeks to assess your knowledge about these topics: (1) Students as Learners, (2) Instruction and Assessment, (3) Communication Techniques, and (4) Profession and Community. Material presented in this chapter potentially relates to several of these categories.

You may find it useful to prepare a chart for your own use similar to the one provided here. As you encounter information related to individual categories, you can enter it into the chart. A completed chart will be useful as you prepare to take the Praxis II exam.

Students as Learners	Instruction and Assessment
• Student Development and the Learning Process	• Instructional Strategies
• Students as Diverse Learners	• Planning Instruction
• Student Motivation and the Learning Environment	• Assessment Strategies
Communication Techniques	**Profession and Community**
• Basic, Effective, Verbal and Nonverbal Communication Techniques	• The Reflective Practitioner
• Effect of Cultural and Gender Differences on Communications in the Classroom	• The Larger Community
• Types of Questions That Can Stimulate Discussion in Different Ways for Particular Purposes	

For Your Initial-Development Portfolio

 To complete this activity and submit your response online, go to the For Your Initial-Development Portfolio *module for this chapter of the Companion Website.*

1. What materials and ideas that you learned in this chapter about *effective teaching practices* might you include as "evidence" in your portfolio? Select up to three separate items of information. Number them 1, 2, and 3.
2. Think about why you selected these materials. As you do so, consider these issues:
   - Specific uses you might make of this information as you plan, deliver, and assess the impact of your teaching.
   - The compatibility of the information with your own priorities and values.
   - Any contributions this information can make to your development as a teacher.
   - Factors that led you to include this information, as opposed to some alternatives you considered but rejected.
3. Place a check in the chart here to indicate the INTASC standard(s) to which each of your items of information relates.

INTASC Standard Number

ITEM OF EVIDENCE NUMBER	S1	S2	S3	S4	S5	S6	S7	S8	S9	S10
1										
2										
3										

4. Prepare a written reflection in which you analyze the decision-making process you followed. In your comments, mention the INTASC standard(s) to which your selected material relates.

Reflections

 To respond to these questions online, go to the Reflections module for this chapter of the Companion Website.

1. Arguments continue to rage regarding what characterizes an "effective" teacher. Often these debates center on whether teachers should concentrate on mastering and transmitting their subjects or whether they should have major concerns about and responsibility for promoting learners' social development and growth in self-esteem. Proponents of an emphasis on academics sometimes contend that broadening teachers' responsibilities to other areas will divert their attention from content teaching and, as a result, learners will emerge from their school experiences lacking the knowledge and skills they need for effective citizenship. Opponents of this view contend that, when teachers fail to attend to all dimensions of learner development, young people will not benefit from academic instruction and, as a result, will emerge from schools lacking both subject-matter knowledge and needed personal and social skills. What is your reaction to these arguments? How would you define an "effective" teacher?

2. In the chapter, you learned that some authorities recommend that, when preparing lessons, you select content that is (1) right for the subject matter you are teaching, (2) right for the particular group of learners you are teaching, and (3) right for you. What difficulties might you face in attempting to meet these conditions? How might you go about overcoming them?

3. You will recall that *constructivist teaching* assumes that people have a strong internal drive that leads them to arrive at conclusions when they confront novel circumstances. This drive sometimes leads them to develop "information" that is inaccurate. Perhaps you can think of a time in your own life when you brought certain faulty assumptions to a situation or used an inappropriate kind of logic and arrived at a conclusion that, in light of insights you gained later, proved to be incorrect. Think about some lessons you will be teaching. Are there some that may lead learners with inadequate previous levels of understanding to arrive at mistaken conclusions? How might you go about preparing members of your class to use logic and thinking patterns that will help them avoid unfortunate mistakes?

4. Think about homework assignments you had to complete when you were a learner at the grade level you would like to teach. Were you expected to complete these assignments at home, or did your teachers give you time to complete at least some of the work during the school day? What was your reaction to these assignments? Did they help you master important content? As you think about your own role in the classroom, what characteristics will you include in your homework assignments, and why do you believe the ones you identify are important?

5. Today, observers have many tools they can use to gather information about what they see a teacher doing during an observation period. Though critics acknowledge that some observation tools are well designed and provide quite an

accurate picture of what the observer saw, nevertheless, they have concerns about these instruments. They argue that the presence of an observer always changes the conditions in a classroom. Learners know that someone who does not regularly belong in the room is there. Often, too, they know what this individual is doing. As a result, patterns of behavior may not be representative of what goes on when the observer is not present. Hence, results of the observation cannot be taken as valid indication of how the teacher and learners interact on days when the observer is not present. How do you react to this argument? Do you think information gathered by classroom observers can have value? Explain your answer.

Field Experiences, Projects, and Enrichment

1. Review ideas for gathering observational data. Select one category associated with a teacher's instructional behavior that interests you. Visit a classroom and gather data related to this category using an observation system of your own design. You may wish to consider a scheme based on a narrative approach, frequency count, coding system, or seating chart.

2. In recent years, specialists in the area of teacher effectiveness have become convinced that teacher dispositions play an important role in determining how they interact with learners and how learners react to their teachers' instructional practices. Seek out additional information about this topic by typing the words "teacher dispositions" into a good Internet search engine such as Google (http://www.google.com). You will find links to many sites with content related to this topic. Follow several of these links, and make notes regarding some key information that you uncover. Share your findings with others in your class.

3. Some of the research on teacher effectiveness has produced results that have surprised some people, particularly when the discovered information has challenged some popularly held beliefs. With your instructor's guidance, look up some research findings associated with teacher praise. Is teacher praise always good? Report your conclusions in the form of a short paper.

4. Identify a topic you would like to use as a focus for two lessons you would like to teach. Choose a grade level and subject area that interests you. For each lesson, assign class members to read some background information from the textbook or from another source. For your first lesson, you will expect learners to recall only basic information. For the second lesson, you will want students to engage in sophisticated thinking involving analysis of key issues. For each lesson, prepare a *visual-thinking* diagram that you might distribute to students to help guide their work with the assigned reading material. Ask your instructor to critique the two diagrams you prepare.

5. Interview an experienced teacher who teaches in a content area and at a grade level that interests you. Ask this teacher to comment on his or her homework practices. Ask questions related to (1) the frequency of homework assignments; (2) the approximate amount of time, on average, learners must commit to complete the typical assignment; (3) learners' attitudes toward homework assignments; and (4) what school policies, if any, relate to the issue of making regular homework assignments. Share this teacher's comments with others in your class.

References

Acheson, K. A., & Gall, M. (1992). *Techniques in the clinical supervision of teachers.* White Plains, NY: Longman.

Armstrong, D. G., & Savage, T. V. (2002). *Teaching in the secondary school: An introduction* (5th ed.). Upper Saddle River, NJ: Merrill/Prentice Hall.

Bell, L. I. (2003). "Strategies that close the gap." *Educational Leadership, 60*(4), 32–34.

Cazden, C. (1986). Classroom discourse. In M. Wittrock (Ed.), *Handbook of research on teaching* (3rd ed., pp. 432–463). New York: Macmillan.

Combs, A. (Ed.). (1962). *Perceiving, behaving, becoming.* Washington, DC: Association for Supervision and Curriculum Development.

Cooper, H. (2001a). The battle over homework: Common ground for administrators, teachers, and parents. Newbury Park, CA: Corwin Press.

Cooper, H. (2001b). Homework for all: In moderation. *Educational Leadership, 58*(7), 34–38.

DeGarmo, C. (1903). *Interest in education: The doctrine of interest and its concrete applications.* New York: Macmillan.

Denton, J. J., Armstrong, D. G., & Savage, T. V. (1980). Matching events of instruction to objectives. *Theory into Practice, 19*(1), 10–14.

Good, T. L., & Brophy, J. E. (2000). *Looking in classrooms* (8th ed.). New York: Longman.

Goodlad, J. A. (1984). *A place called school.* New York: McGraw-Hill.

Halford, J. M. (1998). Easing the way for new teachers. *Educational Leadership, 55*(5), 33–36.

Heckman, P. E., Confer, C. B., & Hakim, D. C. (1994). Planting seeds: Understanding through investigation. *Educational Leadership, 51*(5), 36–39.

Henson, K. T. (2004). Constructivist teaching strategies for diverse middle-level classrooms. Boston: Allyn & Bacon.

Henson, K. T., & Eller, B. F. (1999). *Educational psychology for effective teaching.* Belmont, CA: Wadsworth.

Hunter, M., & Russell, D. (1977). How can I plan more effective lessons? *Instructor, 87*(2), 74–75, 88.

Meyer, A. E. (1975). *Grandmasters of educational thought.* New York: McGraw-Hill.

Ornstein, A. C., & Lasley, T. J. (2000). *Strategies for effective teaching* (3rd ed.). New York: McGraw-Hill.

Parsley, K., & Corcoran, C. A. (2003). The classroom teacher's role in preventing school failure. *Kappa Delta Pi Record, 39*(2), 84–87.

Posner, R. S. (1987). Pacing and sequencing. In M. J. Dunken (Ed.), *The international encyclopedia of teaching and teacher education* (pp. 266–272). Oxford, England: Pergamon Press.

Public Agenda. (2000). *Playing their parts: What parents and teachers really mean by "parental involvement."* [http://www.publicagenda.org/specials/parent/parent.html]

Ramsey, I., Gabbard, C., Clawson, K., Lee, L., & Henson, K. T. (1990). Questioning: An effective teaching method. *The Clearing House, 63*(9), 420–422.

Redfield, D., & Rousseau, E. (1981). A meta-analysis of experimental research on teacher questioning behavior. *Review of Educational Research, 18*(2), 237–245.

Rinne, C. H. (1998). Motivating students is a percentage game. *Phi Delta Kappan, 79*(8), 620–628.

Rosenshine, B., & Stevens, R. (1986). Teaching functions. In M. Wittrock (Ed.), *Handbook of research on teaching* (3rd ed., pp. 376–391). New York: Macmillan.

Rowe, M. B. (1986). Wait time: Slowing down may be a way of speeding up. *Journal of Teacher Education*, 37(1), 43–50.

Steffy, B. E., & Wolfe, M. P. (1997). *The life cycle of the career teacher: Maintaining excellence for a lifetime.* West Lafayette, IN: Kappa Delta Pi Publications.

Teddlie, C., & Reynolds, D. (2000). *The international handbook of school effectiveness research.* New York: Falmer Press.

Tobin, K. (1987). The role of wait time in higher cognitive learning. *Review of Educational Research, 24*(1), 69–95.

Walker, V. N., & Chance, E. W. (1994/1995). National award winning teachers' exemplary instructional techniques and activities. *National Forum of Teacher Education Journal, 5*(1), 11–24.

Wormeli, R. (2002). Beating a path to the brain. *Middle Ground, 5*(5), 23–25.

9 *Classroom Management and Discipline*

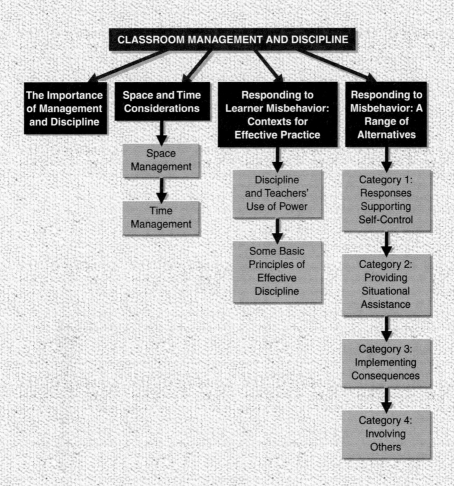

CLASSROOM MANAGEMENT AND DISCIPLINE

- The Importance of Management and Discipline
- Space and Time Considerations
  - Space Management
  - Time Management
- Responding to Learner Misbehavior: Contexts for Effective Practice
  - Discipline and Teachers' Use of Power
  - Some Basic Principles of Effective Discipline
- Responding to Misbehavior: A Range of Alternatives
  - Category 1: Responses Supporting Self-Control
  - Category 2: Providing Situational Assistance
  - Category 3: Implementing Consequences
  - Category 4: Involving Others

OBJECTIVES

This chapter will help you to

- point out the relationship between management and discipline.
- identify the importance of space and time management.
- define what needs to be considered when establishing the context for effective discipline.

- describe what negotiation means in relation to discipline.
- identify basic principles that you can follow when responding to inappropriate behavior.
- list a range of alternative responses you can choose from when addressing discipline problems.

THE IMPORTANCE OF MANAGEMENT AND DISCIPLINE

To succeed in the classroom, you need to know how to manage learners and respond appropriately to their behavior. An inability to control the classroom is a major reason for teacher failure and dismissal. A poll of public attitudes rated lack of discipline as one of the top problems facing today's schools (Rose & Gallup, 2002). Well-meaning people who want to help beginners often willingly share a number of "surefire" prescriptions for success, such as

- Plan your lessons thoroughly.
- Love the students.
- Be enthusiastic.
- Do not smile until Christmas.
- Start off tough.
- Let them know you are the boss.

Although some of these statements may contain an element of truth, they are inadequate for the complex task of managing the classroom, which clearly is one of the most challenging responsibilities that teachers face (Williams, Alley, & Henson, 1999). It is true that you do need to plan carefully, but even teachers who devote lots of time to planning lessons occasionally encounter discipline problems. Certainly, too, members of our profession who like young people and who approach life enthusiastically often do exceptionally well in the classroom. But these characteristics alone are no guarantee that classroom control and management problems will not surface from time to time.

The hard truth is that all teachers occasionally contend with problems associated with learner misbehavior. There are no simple solutions to this challenge. However, there are general principles you can follow to reduce the frequency of problem behavior.

Part of your work as a teacher involves helping young people learn appropriate behavior patterns. Because a well-managed classroom is an essential part of the climate required for academic learning, you have a responsibility both to establish sound management procedures and to teach academic content (Savage, 1999). The two roles complement one another; good teaching helps prevent management problems, and sound management provides a context within which good teaching can occur. There is evidence that suggests that as much as 80% of all discipline problems result from ineffective teaching (Brown, 1998).

Teacher-preparation programs often devote considerable time to acquainting prospective teachers with information related to good teaching. Classroom management, however, usually receives much less attention. This may be because some instructors view management and discipline as dependent on personality traits and problem-solving skills that are difficult to teach. It is true that personality traits such as common sense and the ability to think quickly are important in managing a classroom. However, much can be done to prepare *all* individuals to better manage their classrooms.

In this chapter, you will learn about important aspects of classroom management. One of these relates to how you can use good management procedures to prevent problems. Another focuses on the kinds of actions that are appropriate when you find it necessary to deal with inappropriate learner behaviors.

SPACE AND TIME CONSIDERATIONS

Successful classroom management requires you to understand the unique nature of the classroom and the role you play as the teacher. The classroom is a complex environment. Class members often vary greatly in their abilities, backgrounds, interests, maturity levels, and motivations, and they spend large blocks of time in close proximity. Events that take place in this type of an environment can be unpredictable.

Your responsibility is to take this mixture of individuals, provide them with appropriate materials, capture their interest, organize the space, and use the time so that learning occurs in ways that leaves class members feeling positive about the instructional experience. What motivates varies greatly from person to person, so you must seek ways to interest all learners. Some authorities have identified as many as 30 different categories of psychological motivators (Henson & Eller, 1999).

PROFILING A TEACHER

DEALING WITH A BRIGHT LEARNER WHO DOESN'T VALUE SCHOOL

As a teacher, you "get them all" in your classes. Some learners will almost always be highly interested in what you are doing. This interest may spring from their high level of enthusiasm either for you or your subject. Sometimes the interest comes as a result of efforts of parents and guardians to impress on their sons and daughters the importance of doing good work at school. Patterns of individual learner interest often reflect some inconsistencies. You will find some class members to be highly motivated on certain days and indifferent on others.

Even though you work hard to develop lessons that your learners will find interesting, you still will encounter occasional individuals whose behaviors communicate to you that they would rather not be bothered with what you are asking them to do. Some of these young people will challenge your classroom-management skills.

These challenges will come not only from low-ability learners. Sometimes extremely bright young people will develop nonacademic interests that are so compelling that they will lose their motivation to do good work at school. Consider the case of high school teacher Joe Silva's student, Todd Morrison. Joe recently made these comments about Todd. As you read them, think through how you might respond to these questions:

- How do you react to Mr. Silva's assessment of Todd?
- As you reflect on your own personality, how might you approach a situation similar to the one described here?

A MATTER OF ATTITUDE

"Todd isn't a bad kid. In fact, he's really bright. But in class he's become just a pain. He just talks, talks, talks. He interrupts others. He doesn't spend time on his homework, and his grades are not good . . . not nearly what they could be.

He works for his dad's software company. He lives and breathes computer code, and he's already created some software that's bringing in some big money. He thinks that hours spent in school are just a wasteful interlude that he has to endure before he can get back to his 'real life' at his dad's company. By the way, he thinks we teachers are a pretty sorry lot of folks. I think he believes we take low-paying teaching jobs because nobody else will have us. In any event, he just doesn't particularly care what we think of his behavior in class. He's a challenge."

While you try to deal imaginatively with academic content, you also have to be prepared to respond constructively to unanticipated and spontaneous events. Fortunately, there are things that you can do to make instruction flow more smoothly and reduce the number of potentially disruptive learner behaviors.

Researchers point out that you can diminish the probability that you will face serious behavior problems when you plan and implement a management strategy very early in the school year or even before school starts (Emmer, Evertson, & Anderson, 1980; Evertson, 1989). In this connection, researcher Carolyn Evertson (1989) points out that "solving managerial and organizational problems at the beginning of the year is essential in laying the groundwork for quality learning opportunities for students" (p. 90). If you follow this practice, you will bring into clearer focus your own ideas about how you want your classroom to operate and will be better able to communicate your views to learners.

WEB EXTENSION 9–1

Managing Inappropriate Behavior in the Classroom: ERIC Digest 408

At this site, you will find an ERIC Clearinghouse on Handicapped and Gifted Children publication that introduces general procedures for preventing misbehavior in the classroom. You will find guidelines for helping both individual learners and entire classes develop acceptable patterns of behavior.

http://www.ericfacility.net/ericdigests/ed371506.html

Space Management

Classroom management begins with your actions to organize and manage classroom space. Architects and psychologists have long emphasized the impact of space on human behavior. In fact, they have coined the term **behavioral setting** to explain this relationship. A behavioral setting is a space that influences the behavior of the individuals within that space. Consider a church, temple, or cathedral. These environments inspire awe in ways that reinforce quiet, respectful behaviors. When planning your classroom environment, you need to consider what you can do to communicate your behavioral expectations to your learners.

In thinking about this issue, consider your reactions to different environments. How do you feel in crowded spaces where others invade your space? What is your reaction to clutter or unappealing places? What happens when you are in places that are too hot or too cold? How are your motivation and learning affected by these variables? Individuals typically find that they are distracted, irritable, anxious, fatigued, and angry when they confront these conditions. These undesirable attitudes are not ones that you want to engender in learners.

When you plan problem prevention, you need to consider the attractiveness of the space, the degree of crowding, the comfort level of learners, the arrangement of materials and desks, and the location and availability of instructional materials. It makes sense to begin planning the physical layout of the classroom as early as possible, even several weeks before the beginning of the school year (Williams, Alley, & Henson, 1999).

Wall Space.   Constructive use of your classroom wall space will enhance the quality of the instructional environment. You can devote some of this space to motivational displays that stimulate learner interest in topics that you are covering in your lessons. You may also want to reserve some wall space for displaying learners' work. Such displays are particularly motivating for children in the elementary grades. You might use other wall areas to display schedules, important announcements, and classroom rules. Adding a little color to a wall, occasionally changing the displays, and keeping walls free of unnecessary clutter will enhance the overall appeal of your classroom environment.

Floor Space.   As you think about establishing an environment that will support and reinforce your instruction, you will find it useful to prepare a **classroom floor plan.** A plan of this type provides you with a visual representation of the distribution of desks, tables, and other classroom features that occupy floor space. You want to arrange learners' seats so that individuals do not feel overcrowded, can observe and hear you, and can see important information sources such as whiteboards and projection screens.

The nature of your planned instructional activities should strongly influence your spacing decisions. For example, you may need different configurations when your lessons feature (1) mostly whole-group instruction, (2) mostly small-group instruction, or (3) mostly learner work at individual activity centers or stations.

Whole-group instruction requires a physical arrangement that permits all members of your class to see you well. You want to arrange learners' desks to accommodate this need. Occasionally, you need to check on an individual learner's work or understanding during whole-group instruction. Consequently, the desks should be arranged so that there are aisles or spaces that permit you to move quickly from learner to learner.

In planning floor arrangements for small-group discussion, you need to arrange learning spaces in ways that allow you to monitor the whole class when you work with members of individual groups. If possible, seating spaces for the small group you are working with should be placed some distance from other learners. This arrangement diminishes the temptation for small-group members to talk to others in the class. It also helps reduce the general noise level and makes it easier for all learners to attend to their assigned tasks.

Organizing the classroom space so that teachers can monitor student work is an important component of classroom management.

You want to achieve two purposes in establishing locations for learning centers. First of all, you want to locate centers in areas of the classroom that are easily accessible to all class members. Second, you want to place them in ways that will minimize the possibility that learners who are not at these locations will be distracted by ongoing activities at the centers. Because projected media can be very distracting to others, you want to place centers that feature them out of the direct sight lines of learners who are not working there.

Traffic Patterns.   When you develop a plan to control traffic patterns in your classroom, begin by identifying parts of the room that are heavily used. These include such areas as doorways, places where learners' personal belongings and class materials are stored, book storage areas, and areas around map stands and other objects that rest on the floor. Spaces around these frequently visited parts of the classroom need to be kept obstruction-free. You also need to arrange learners' desks so that people going to and from these areas of the classroom can do so without disturbing others.

Teacher's Desk.   The location of your desk can have management consequences. You may recall from your own years in school that often the teacher's desk is located at the front and center of the room. This setup is a custom dictated by tradition rather than by sound management. A better choice is an unobtrusive place near the back of the room.

Locating your desk near the rear of the classroom has several advantages. This arrangement encourages you to stand up and move around the classroom, which often leads to more-careful monitoring of learners' work. Researchers have found that learners perceive teachers who circulate through a classroom and avoid sitting behind a desk to have "warmer" personalities than teachers who remain seated (Smith, 1987). A second advantage is that a rear-of-the-room desk location makes it impossible for you to teach from behind the desk. Teaching while sitting at the teacher's desk often gives learners the impression that you lack enthusiasm for what you are doing.

A third advantage is that it is normally easier to monitor learners' on-task behavior from the rear of the classroom. Students will not know when you are observing them. When individuals in your class feel you may be looking at them, they are much less likely to misbehave. Finally, a desk at the rear of the classroom makes it easier for you to have individual learner conferences at your desk without attracting the attention of everyone in the room. This arrangement minimizes the likelihood that large numbers of class members will pay more attention to what is going on at your desk than to their assigned tasks.

Equipment Storage.   Depending on the ages of your learners and the subjects you teach, your lessons may require the use of a lot of specialized equipment (computers, video projectors, special devices for learners with disabilities, and so forth). Storage space for equipment needs to be both secure and accessible. Although maintaining equipment in good operating order is a major headache for school officials, the possibilities for misuse or malicious damage decrease when your equipment is stored in a way that permits access only by authorized people. When possible, it is wise to secure equipment in cabinets or other areas that can be locked.

Time Management

Time management is one of your most important and difficult classroom tasks. When you teach, you have a limited amount of time to accomplish important educational goals. It is important that the time be used so that learners do not become bored because of wasted time or overwhelmed and frustrated because there is inadequate time. Researchers have found that in many classrooms, a high percentage of time is spent on noninstructional tasks (Smyth, 1987). Not surprisingly, research also reveals that learners in classes where teachers spend more time on instruction learn more (Berliner, 1984; Good & Brophy, 2000).

Time management requires you to (1) handle routine tasks in a quick and efficient manner, (2) act to ensure that class members get to work promptly, (3) present necessary information in a clear and concise manner, and (4) keep learners engaged in learning throughout the lesson.

Transitions. Many beginning teachers spend extensive periods of time planning lessons, but they give little thought to **transitions** within and between lessons. Transitions occur when there is a shift from one activity to another, and they offer the potential for much class time to be lost.

To avoid wasting time, you need to plan carefully for transition points. When materials are to be distributed or work returned during a transition point, you will find it useful to organize the material in advance. When this is done, materials can be distributed to learners quickly and efficiently. Sometimes transitions will require students to move from one part of an instructional area to another or from one room to another. Providing them with clear directions about how to make these changes and establishing a time frame within which the changes need to be made will save valuable time.

Beginning Class. Some teachers take too much time getting their classes started. Lessons that begin promptly engage learners' attention, eliminate potential off-task behavior that can lead to problems, and maximize instructional time. This means that you need to perform tasks associated with attendance-taking and other routine administrative duties quickly.

You may find it useful to establish a signal system that informs class members that it is time for learning. Some teachers who use such a system move to a special place in the front of the class and look out over the learners. Others use a particular command such as "all eyes up here." At the beginning of the school year, you can explain the specific signal system you want to use.

Do not start your lesson until all members of your class are paying attention. By insisting on quiet before you begin signals to learners that what you say is important and worth hearing. In addition, insisting on quiet saves your voice. If you attempt to begin a lesson while some learners are still engaged in private conversations, you will find it necessary to speak more loudly than normal. Speaking in this way may strain your voice. A vocal strain can leave you hoarse and uncomfortable.

Lesson Pacing. How you pace lessons has important behavior implications for learners. Your lessons should move briskly, but not so fast as to be confusing. Although a certain amount of repetition is necessary to highlight key points, excessive repetition leads to boredom. Learners often seek relief from boredom by engaging in inappropriate patterns of classroom behavior.

To determine an appropriate instructional pace, some teachers select a **reference group** in their class. The reference group includes four or five learners who represent a cross section of class members. You can watch the reference group to determine their reactions to what you are doing. Based on your observations of these class members, you can speed up, slow down, or maintain the present instructional pace.

In planning for pacing, decide what learners should do who finish assignments early. Have follow-up activities ready for your early finishers so that they can immediately make a transition into another productive activity. The follow-up activities you choose should not be "more of the same," which could lead bright learners to feel that they are being punished for finishing their work quickly. On the other hand, these follow-up experiences should not be so enticing that learners race through the assigned task to gain more time to work on them.

Providing Assistance.   While members of your class work on assignments, many of them will seek your assistance. You need to develop a system to avoid becoming frustrated as you try to help large numbers of individuals requiring special assistance. Frederic H. Jones (1979) suggests some guidelines you might wish to consider. In his research, he found that the average teacher spends much more time working with individual learners than is necessary. To decrease the total time spent with each person and, hence, increase the opportunities to help more individuals seeking assistance, consider adopting the following sequence:

1. First, you should build confidence by finding something the learner has done correctly and then follow up by praising the good work.
2. Second, you should provide a direct suggestion about what the learner should do next. (But you want to avoid doing the work for the learner.)
3. After completing the first two steps, you should move on quickly to the next learner. You may check back in a short while to make sure the first learner is still on task. However, you need to avoid getting trapped helping just one person or creating a sense of dependency so that individual learners depend on you to do most of the work and thinking for them.

Jones (1979) points out that this process will enable you to help a large number of learners in a relatively short time period. He recommends that, on average, you spend no more than 20 seconds at a time with a single learner.

Establishing Routines and Procedures.   You need to develop routines and procedures for handling recurring and predictable events. These regular patterns simplify the demands on your time so you can devote your attention to the exceptions or the unplanned and unpredictable events. During a typical day, you will experience hundreds of personal contacts with learners. Unless you develop a system for managing these contacts, your emotional reserves will be drained, and the likelihood of making management mistakes will increase. Consider developing routines and procedures related to the following:

- What learners are to do as soon as they enter the classroom,
- What learners should do when they have a personal problem to discuss with the teacher,
- What procedures are to be used in passing out and collecting materials,
- When and where pencils are to be sharpened,
- How daily attendance is to be taken, and
- What learners are to do when they need to leave the room.

Once you develop your set of routines and procedures, you need to explain them. When teaching younger children, you may want to include this information in a formal lesson. With more-mature learners, particularly those in secondary schools, usually a brief explanation of this information will suffice. Figure 9.1 provides you with an opportunity to think about routines and procedures you would like to follow in your own classroom.

Researchers have found that effective teachers are especially good at establishing rules and procedures (Doyle, 1986). Effective teachers not only establish rules and procedures, they systematically teach them to learners. The rules and procedures need to be written in clear, explicit language so that learners know when they are in compliance. Furthermore, the rules and procedures need to be written and developed as they are needed. It is best to establish the rules with the class; however, there are a few that you may feel are absolutely necessary in your classroom. Take some time to reflect on the rules and procedures you believe you will need as a teacher. The chart supplied will help you in that task.

	Rules and procedures related to classroom conduct	Rules and procedures related to academic work
Rules and procedures that need to be communicated at the beginning of the school year		
Rules and procedures that may be established later		

FIGURE 9.1 Establishing Rules and Procedures

RESPONDING TO LEARNER MISBEHAVIOR: CONTEXTS FOR EFFECTIVE PRACTICE

Even in classrooms in which lessons are exciting and teachers are good managers, learners occasionally misbehave. No universally applicable bag of tricks exists that, once mastered, allows you to respond effectively to learner behavior problems. You need to construct your own repertoire of actions after carefully considering your own attitudes and expectations. As you begin thinking through your own feelings, you might develop personal responses to these questions:

- What do you expect of students? Do you believe they are interested in learning?
- How do you see your role as a teacher? Do you believe it is wise to "lay down the law"?
- How do you think teachers establish good discipline in the classroom?
- What is your image of the ideal classroom?
- What is your image of young people today?
- What is the appropriate relationship between teachers and learners?
- Are you comfortable sharing power with members of your class?

Your answers will help you better understand your attitudes toward learners and your philosophy of teaching and learning. These perspectives will have a strong influence on how you view classroom management and how you will respond when problems arise.

Classroom management embraces all actions teachers take to maintain a smooth, focused flow of activity for the purpose of nurturing learners' academic and personal development. Some people conceive of classroom management as implying top-down control with a primary focus on maintaining teacher authority and learner obedience. According to this view, the role of the teacher is to manage and control, and the role of the learner is to submit and obey. Today, there is growing support for the idea that effective management is better conceived of as a process involving negotiation between teacher and learners (McLaughlin, 1994). According to this view, teachers should recognize the dignity of learners by giving them some power to decide what happens in the classroom (Henson, 2004). Individuals who subscribe to this position view the classroom as a community where cooperative learning, shared decision making, and group problem solving are the defining characteristics.

A growing body of research supports the management-as-negotiation point of view. Learners are likely to understand rules they helped make much better than rules handed to them by the teacher (Latham, 1998). Successful negotiation approaches require you to be honest with learners about those issues they can decide and those issues that you, as a teacher, will decide. Encouraging learner participation in establishing some classroom operating guidelines should begin with the first day of class (Vars, 1997).

Negotiation as a metaphor is consistent with a *constructivist approach* to learning. You will recall from Chapter 1, "Teaching in an Age of Change," that constructivism holds that learning occurs as individuals process information and construct their own meanings. Control forced on an individual from external sources such as a teacher does not provide conditions optimal for learning. This perspective suggests that you should strive for ways to help learners develop internal and personal commitments to desirable patterns of behavior. Some of the most important things young people take away from their years in school relate to experiences that have led to noncoercive self-discipline and self-control.

Negotiation does not mean abdicating responsibility; it means taking the needs of others into account. As the teacher, you are still in charge of the classroom, and you deserve respect from learners in your role as leader. How you exercise this leadership is critical to the success of negotiation as a management technique. What constitutes appropriate leadership will vary depending on individual circumstances. There will be times, for example, when serious disruptions require you to exercise unilateral power.

The case for negotiation as a technique is buttressed by a major purpose of classroom discipline (and of education, in general): teaching learners how to exercise self-control and responsibility. Individuals with a wealth of knowledge but no self-control are unlikely to become productive individuals contributing to the good of humankind. Learning self-control and the acceptance of responsibility are enhanced when individuals are treated with dignity and are given responsibility. As they experience the consequences of their actions, learners come to understand that they have the power to control negative outcomes by choosing behaviors that do not cause them to happen (McLaughlin, 1994).

Several elements are involved in classrooms featuring negotiation. First, the degree to which individuals have self-control and a sense of responsibility is related to how they perceive reality. Those who believe that their environment is warm, trusting, and positive are more likely to exercise self-control than those who believe their environment is cold, indifferent, and negative. Opening many aspects of the classroom to negotiation and looking at the classroom as a place where the needs, concerns, and interests of the learners are taken into account goes a long way toward creating this type of a classroom climate.

Second, giving young people opportunities to make choices helps them develop self-control and responsibility. Making decisions from among alternatives and living with the consequences are important growth experiences. Opportunities to choose provide learners with the feeling that they can exercise some personal control over their lives. People who have a sense that their personal actions and decisions count tend to act in more-responsible, controlled ways than individuals who lack these feelings.

Third, learners with positive self-concepts are more likely to develop patterns of self-control and personal responsibility than those with negative self-concepts. Self-concepts derive from interactions with others. Because you exercise some control over classroom interactions, you are in a position to influence the nature of the self-concept developed by each learner. A success-oriented classroom in which every effort is made to help each person experience some feelings of achievement encourages the development of positive self-concepts among the students.

Finally, learners who feel that they "belong" are likely to develop good self-control and a sense of personal responsibility. Pride in group membership is important to many young people. Providing learners with responsibility and remaining open to their concerns and interests, helps them feel a sense of ownership and pride in being a part of your class.

In summary, creating a context within which good discipline can take place requires you to think carefully about your "proper" role as a teacher and about what it means to teach. In particular, you need to consider how you will define and use your own authority. The following material outlines several different types of power and how they might be used in the classroom.

Discipline and Teachers' Use of Power

When learners misbehave, you have to do something to remedy the situation. The nature of teacher power and how it is used can influence general patterns of classroom behavior. Several types of power you can use include:

- Expert power,
- Referent power,
- Legitimate power,
- Reward power,
- Coercive power (French & Raven, 1959)

Expert Power.   **Expert power** is power that comes to a person as a result of possessing specialized knowledge. In general, people who are acknowledged experts in a given area exercise considerable influence over others. Their opinions are respected because they are thought to know a great deal about their specialties. This type of power is earned rather than demanded.

Referent Power.   **Referent power** is power that results from a warm, positive relationship. Individuals are willing to give another some power when they perceive that the other person is trustworthy. People accept advice they receive from those whom they like and respect. If you are to enjoy referent power as a teacher, learners must see you as someone they respect and trust . . . someone who cares about them. As is the case with expert power, referent power cannot be demanded. It must be earned through actions that demonstrate trust, caring, and concern for others.

Legitimate Power.   **Legitimate power** derives from the particular position a person holds. For example, city mayors can wield certain powers because of the office they hold. As a teacher you have some legitimate power because of the authority that school administrators and the school board have delegated to you. For example, you have the power to make certain decisions about how to teach and how to deal with learners' behavior.

Problems sometimes result because not all learners accept that you have legitimate power. This can cause difficulties if you begin teaching under the mistaken assumption that everyone in your class will respect your legitimate power. Some will not. What all this means is that you cannot rely on legitimate power alone to manage your classroom. You will be much more successful if you work to build your authority on expert power and referent power—powers that you will have to earn. When learners recognize your expert power and referent power, your legitimate authority will also be increased.

Reward Power.   **Reward power** comes to individuals as a result of their ability to provide something that another person wants. As a teacher, you are in a position to provide benefits to learners in the form of praise, grades, and privileges; hence, you have some reward power. However, this kind of power has limits. The number of rewards available is small. Further, some learners may not always see what you view as rewards as desirable. For example, a few of your students may not care what grades they receive. (There are such people in the schools.) These students may not find compelling your offer to award good grades in exchange for good performance.

The power to give rewards comes with your position as a teacher. It is not a type of power that you earn. It is an effective type of power as long as there are rewards to give that learners value. This type of authority may vanish quickly when the rewards are exhausted or are not desired. As with legitimate power, when you establish expert power and referent power as a base, rewards such as grades and praise become more powerful.

Coercive Power.   **Coercive power** is power that people wield because of their authority to administer punishment. If you rely heavily on coercive power, it is highly probable that members of your class will not see you as someone who is warm, caring, and positive. When you apply coercive power, many students may not see any compelling reason to adopt behavior patterns you favor. In some situations, you may find that although your exercise of coercive power suppresses one undesirable behavior, another undesirable behavior springs up to replace it.

In summary, expert power and referent power are the two types of power that are most important as you strive to develop positive working relationships with your learners. These two types of power are also most consistent with the negotiations view of classroom management. Young people are usually willing to accept leadership from teachers they perceive to be experts who are ethical, warm individuals.

The benefits of being seen as an expert underscore the importance of you being well-grounded in the subjects you teach. A solid grasp of content can give you the credibility needed to establish your expert power. At the same time, you need to establish positive classroom climates. When learners sense that you care about them personally and truly support them, you accrue valuable referent power.

WEB EXTENSION 9–2

Unit 5: Behavior Management

This Web page is part of a site the University of Nebraska at Lincoln maintains for the purpose of providing training for individuals who work as **paraeducators**. Paraeducators, sometimes also known as **paraprofessionals**, **teacher's aides**, or **teacher's assistants**, are individuals hired by school districts to work with and assist teachers in the classroom. At this site, you will find a number of online lessons that focus on various dimensions of classroom management. Information is as relevant for classroom teachers as for paraeducators.

http://para.unl.edu/para/Behavior/Intro.html

Some Basic Principles of Effective Discipline

Regardless of the number of preventive actions you take, sometimes you will have to deal with learner behavior problems. This is simply a part of being a teacher. Young people lack experience, and they sometimes make wrong choices. Here are some basic principles you can follow that will increase the probability that responses you make to incidents of inappropriate learner behavior will be effective:

- Preserve the dignity of the learner.
- Private correction is preferable to public correction.
- The causes of misbehavior must be addressed, not simply the misbehavior itself.
- Distinctions must be made between minor and major misbehavior problems.
- Learners must be helped to understand that they have chosen to misbehave and, therefore, have chosen to experience the consequences.
- Responses to misbehavior must be consistent and fair.

Preserving Learners' Dignity. When correcting misbehavior, you need to be careful that your comments do not diminish learners' self-worth. Such responses have the potential to lead to more discipline problems (Jones & Jones, 1986). Anything you do that assaults learners' dignity has the potential to lead to power conflicts. Frustrated members of your class may feel that their only recourse is to respond with assaults on your dignity. Older learners report that one of the reasons they misbehave is that they feel they have been "put down" by their teachers. You can avoid personal dignity difficulties by remembering that "teaching respect begins by giving respect" (Martin, 1997; p. 7).

Private Correction Versus Public Correction. One way you can diminish the likelihood that learners will feel that their self-worth has been attacked is to correct an individual's inappropriate behavior in a place where others cannot hear your comments. The verbal reprimand might take place outside of the classroom, for example. Private correction takes pressure off misbehaving young people. On the other hand, public reprimands often pressure them to take action to "save face" in front of their peers. Private correction also promotes better, more-personal contact between you and individual learners. The young people to whom you are speaking know that you are committing your full and undivided attention to the situation under discussion.

WEB EXTENSION 9–3

You Can Help Them All: Solutions for Handling 117 Misbehaviors

At this site, you will find useful information related to numerous categories of learner misbehavior. There are descriptions of (1) the nature of individuals who manifest specific kinds of inappropriate behavior, (2) the effects of these behaviors, (3) appropriate actions you can take as a teacher, and (4) common mistakes teachers make in responding to misbehavior.

http://www.disciplinehelp.com

Addressing the Causes, Not Just the Behavior. Effective behavior management requires a long-term perspective. Your responses should be geared not simply to stopping misbehavior when it occurs, but rather to changing conditions so that problem behaviors will not recur. You need to look for underlying causes of improper behavior and try to remove conditions that reinforce unacceptable patterns (Brophy, 1983).

Serious and persistent misbehavior is often a learner's way of asking for help. It attracts your attention and prompts you to act. Given this sequence, learners occasionally will behave in ways they know are unacceptable simply to attract your attention to a serious problem. You need to recognize that some misbehaving young people are desperately seeking supportive, adult assistance.

Distinguishing Between Major and Minor Problems.   Many incidents in schools result from learners' immaturity rather than from attempts to challenge authority. You need to be sensitive to the distinction between these minor behavioral lapses and those that represent more-serious challenges to your ability to function as an instructional leader. This means you must avoid overreactions that can build learner resentment and lead to more-serious misbehavior episodes.

Learners Choose to Misbehave and to Experience the Consequences.   You need to convey to members of your class that unpleasant consequences of misbehavior result from their own irresponsible behavioral choices, not from arbitrary and vindictive actions that you, as their teacher, have decided to take. Your objective is to help learners see the relationship between inappropriate behaviors and resultant consequences. To accomplish this, you need to make certain they understand what behaviors are unacceptable and what specific consequences will follow if they engage in these actions. Your purpose is to help students recognize that by choosing irresponsible behaviors, they are also choosing the consequences.

Consistent and Fair Responses.   The principle of consistent and fair responses implies that you must respond to all incidents of misbehavior. If you ignore some episodes, you signal to learners that there is nothing really wrong with these kinds of behaviors. When this happens, unacceptable patterns that begin as minor problems often escalate into major ones.

Consistency provides at least two key benefits. First, it communicates to learners that you are serious about discouraging a certain pattern of behavior. Second, it suggests to members of your class that you are fair. This perception is strengthened when you react similarly to a specified type of misbehavior regardless of which person in the class is involved.

RESPONDING TO MISBEHAVIOR: A RANGE OF ALTERNATIVES

Many beginning teachers do not know how to respond to misbehavior. As you prepare to handle this part of your teaching responsibility, you should develop a plan that identifies a range of actions that you can take in response to problems. Your intended range of actions should begin with appropriately mild responses to minor problems and escalate to include more-severe responses you can use to address more-serious difficulties. This kind of planning allows you to consider alternatives in an unhurried way. Following the plan provides some assurance that you are maintaining consistent and fair patterns of responses when dealing with incidents of misbehavior.

WEB EXTENSION 9–4

Discipline by Design: The Honor Level System

At this site, you will find a description of the Honor Level System, an approach to classroom management that many elementary, middle, and high schools now use. It features (1) a scheme for classifying learners in terms of their likelihood to misbehave and (2) a system of escalating teacher responses to persistent patterns of inappropriate behavior.

http://www.honorlevel.com

The subsections that follow list possible responses you might include in your plan in order of their severity. In following this design, you would choose options from the first several categories when minor problems arise and from categories farther down the list when more-serious problems occur.

Category 1: Responses Supporting Self-Control

One of your responsibilities is helping the young people you teach learn how to exert personal control over their behavior. When you succeed in communicating this kind of information, often members of your class, with your guidance, will replace an unacceptable behavior with an acceptable alternative. Your actions in this category are relatively unobtrusive. They are most appropriate for minor behavior problems.

Reinforcing Productive Behavior.   One of the most important things you can do to help learners develop self-control is to reinforce desirable patterns of behavior. You can accomplish this purpose by rewarding individuals and members of an entire class when they have behaved well. Rewards can take many forms. Verbal praise works well, and there may be special activities that class members particularly enjoy that function well as rewards. The specific rewards you use should vary with your students' interests. To be functional, a reward must be something that learners like. Simply because a reward appeals to you does not mean it will necessarily interest members of your class.

Using Nonverbal Signals to Indicate Disapproval.   To the extent possible, you want to handle minor episodes of misbehavior in ways that do not interrupt the flow of your lesson. **Nonverbal responses** involve gestures, eye movements, facial expressions, and other nonvocal responses that allow you to indicate to a learner that an inappropriate behavior has been noted (Grubaugh, 1989). Such responses tell learners that they are being given time to correct their behavior and avoid more-serious consequences.

Using Proximity Control.   **Proximity control** is control over learner behavior that occurs when the teacher's position in the classroom is close to that of an individual learner. Moving to the area of the classroom where minor problems occur often extinguishes the problem. Such action, known as proximity control, can eliminate a problem without disrupting the flow of the lesson.

Using a Learner's Name in the Context of a Lesson.   Using an individuals' name during a lesson informs learners that their inappropriate behavior has been noted. It works something like this. If you notice that John's attention is drifting during a discussion of explorers, you might say, "Now, if John were a member of the crew sailing for the New World, he would have made his plans and . . . ." The use of a learner's name will often result in a quick cessation of inappropriate behavior.

Redirecting Learner Attention.   Redirecting learner attention is something you will find particularly helpful if you are working with very young children. Sometimes this approach also is effective with older learners. To implement it, you need to watch class members carefully and redirect misbehaving learners to more-productive behavior. A few brief words from you that direct a learner's attention back to the assigned task often are all that is required.

Encouraging Learners to Take Personal Action.   Encouraging learners to take personal action when they are tempted to misbehave is implemented more frequently

Keeping students actively involved reduces discipline problems.

in elementary schools than in secondary schools. To implement this approach, you teach members of your class to take some specific action when they feel compelled to act inappropriately. The idea is to give them time (1) to reflect about what they are considering doing and (2) to reestablish their self-control. Sometimes young learners are taught to put their heads on their desks, clench their fists, or count to 10 when they sense themselves to be on the verge of misbehaving. These actions give the learners opportunities to relax and unwind before they do something that they might regret (Brophy, 1983).

In other classrooms, learners are urged to move to another part of the room and talk softly to themselves about the problem they are facing and possible responses they might make. This procedure works best when you have taken time to teach learners the process of coping with problems by thinking about them aloud (Camp & Bash, 1981).

Category 2: Providing Situational Assistance

Responses associated with providing situational assistance require you to intervene more directly than those in Category 1. When actions associated with Category 1 have not been effective, then you need to consider Category 2 options. These actions are a little more intrusive. In using them, you take assertive actions to help learners exercise self-control and responsibility. Your emphases are on preserving the dignity of the learners and dealing with the problems in a relatively private manner.

Taking Time for a Quiet Word.   To implement taking time out for a quiet word, you move toward the misbehaving learner. Remind the misbehaving learner about the kind of behavior you expect. Once you have delivered this message, you return quickly to teaching your lesson.

Providing a Rule Reminder. Providing a rule reminder represents a slight escalation from taking time for a quiet word. When a behavior problem occurs, you stop the lesson and speak to the misbehaving learner or learners in a voice loud enough for the whole class to hear. This is an example of a rule-reminder statement you might use: "Bill's group, what does our list of class rules say about not talking when someone is asking a question?"

Removing the Learner from the Situation. To implement removal of a misbehaving learner, you arrange for the offending individual to move. You might require that this person go to a different seat nearby or to another part of the room. Your instructions related to movement need to be brief, direct, and nonconfrontational: "Mary, please take your material and go to the empty table. Continue working there." You might also remove the offender to a time-out area. When you choose this approach, you need to implement the strategy quickly and quietly without displaying any anger. You can often avoid arguments by saying something like: "Please go to the time-out seat. We will talk later."

Responding with Clarity and Firmness. If previous techniques have failed to squelch inappropriate behavior, you need to consider more-intrusive actions. For example, you may find it necessary to address a learner by name, using a clear, direct, authoritative, no-nonsense tone of voice. In implementing this approach, you make eye contact with the learner you are addressing, and your demeanor takes on an I-mean-business character as you specify the behavior that must stop and describe the one that must replace it.

Arranging Conferences with Misbehaving Learners. The next step up your ladder of escalating set of responses requires you to schedule an individual conference with the offender. During the conference, you explain exactly what must be done to correct the behavior problem. Keep threats to a minimum. Typically, you identify the problem, share your feelings about it, and ask the learner what might be done to solve it.

Some conferences conclude with the preparation of a **behavior contract** that specifies what the learner will do. Behavior contracts often mention some good things that will result if the contract terms are met. Frequently, there also are references to consequences that will follow if the unacceptable pattern of behavior continues.

Asking Parents or Guardians for Help. When you begin your career as a teacher, you may feel apprehensive about talking to parents or guardians. Although you may fear these discussions, parents and guardians potentially are among your best allies. Most parents and guardians are concerned about the progress and behavior of their children, and they may be unaware that their children are misbehaving in school. Often a phone call to explain the unacceptable behavior will result in an excellent cooperative plan to solve the problem.

However, you need to understand that involving parents or guardians will not always lead to the desired result. The success of this approach may be influenced by variables such as the age level of the learner and the kind of relationship the learner has with his or her parents or guardians. When you contact a parent or guardian, you should emphasize your interest in working together to solve the problem. You want to avoid assigning blame for the learner's inappropriate behavior.

Category 3: Implementing Consequences

After responses in categories 1 and 2 have been tried with no success, or if the misbehavior is very serious, you need to take actions that will ensure that learners experience the consequences of their inappropriate actions. The consequences you impose will be most effective when they are appropriate to the nature of the offense.

Losing a Privilege.   Loss of a privilege functions as an effective punishment for some young people. The success of this approach depends on the kinds of privileges you have extended to your students. Depending on age levels, these privileges might vary from a classroom job (such as taking care of erasers) to promises of seats in favored sections at athletic events to opportunities to go on out-of-town field trips. To be effective, your students must genuinely value the privilege that you take away. If they do not, then your action is unlikely to influence their behavior.

Loss of a privilege is more apt to influence a more-appropriate pattern of learner behavior if the loss is not made permanent. When learners understand that you are willing to reinstate a lost privilege in exchange for better behavior, there is an incentive for them to adopt a more-acceptable pattern.

Providing for In-Class Isolation.   If you are teaching in an elementary school classroom, you may find that **in-class isolation** will motivate learners to adopt more-appropriate patterns of behavior. In-class isolation involves moving misbehaving individuals to a part of the classroom area where they cannot interact with other class members. To implement this approach, you designate a certain part of the classroom as an area where misbehaving learners are sent.

Sometimes you may allow people who have been sent to these isolated areas to continue working on assignments. At other times, you may ask them to reflect on the nature of their misbehavior and to think about their ideas for change. Occasionally, you may find it useful simply to tell an offending learner to go to this area of the classroom and sit quietly. Many younger children find the resultant boredom to be an undesirable consequence of their misbehavior.

Removing the Learner.   If serious misbehavior persists, you may find it necessary to remove a learner from your classroom. When this happens, you typically will begin by telling the learner to go to the office of the principal or a counselor. Your purpose is to send the learner to an area supervised by another professional. You must never send a learner to unsupervised areas such as hallways. If a learner were injured in such an unsupervised area, you, as the responsible teacher, might be liable for negligence.

Making Up Wasted Time.   When you feel that a learner has failed to make appropriate use of class time, you may find it useful to require the offending individual to make up the wasted time. Depending on the grade level, you may keep the learner in the room during recess or may require the individual to spend extra time in class either before or after school. Make sure that you do not inadvertently convert this kind of punishment to a reward. For example, some people in your class may enjoy chatting informally with you. If this happens during a making-up-wasted-time session, there will be little incentive for the learner to change the pattern of behavior that resulted in this consequence.

You will not always be able to insist that misbehaving learners make up wasted time. In some schools, many young people ride buses to and from school. If they are kept after school, they have no way to get home. You also may find it hard to keep high school students who have part-time jobs in the classroom after normal school hours.

WEB EXTENSION 9–5

LDOnLine

At this site you will find the home page of LDOnLine, a Web site that seeks to serve the needs of parents, teachers, and other professionals who are interested in promoting better educational experiences for young people with learning disabilities. At this site, you will find a section titled "Search LD Online." Type in the words "classroom management." You will be taken to a page with a huge number of links to articles and other information focusing on appropriate actions you can take to manage and control individuals in your classes who have learning disabilities.

http: www.ldonline.org

Category 4: Involving Others

Involving others is the category of last-resort options. When your measures have failed, you need to consider organizing a conference to discuss the situation. Participants might include parents or guardians, other educational professionals including administrators and counselors, and personnel from agencies outside the school system.

Involving Parents or Guardians. Before you schedule a formal conference, you should make an initial contact with parents or guardians to apprise them of the problem and seek their help in solving it. If a conference proves necessary, you must prepare for it carefully. For example, you will need to organize evidence to bring to the conference, including anecdotal records that document specific examples of problem behaviors and dates when they occurred. The best conferences feature a sharing of information and a communal effort to work out a proposed solution. You need to be particularly careful during this kind of a conference to avoid putting parents or guardians in a position of feeling that their own adequacy is being questioned.

A teacher meets with administrators, counselors, and other teachers to discuss possible ways of dealing with a learner who has become a severe discipline problem.

Arranging Conferences with Other Professionals.   As you think about involving others to help you resolve a particularly challenging learner behavior problem, you do not want to overlook one of your most valuable and easily accessible resources: your colleagues. According to Clark, Clark, and Irvin (1997, p. 55), collaborating with fellow teachers offers many advantages, such as

- Improved teacher attitudes
- Improved communications
- Higher morale, and
- Increased self-empowerment

At some point, you may find it worthwhile to bring together a group of professionals to discuss a learner's unacceptable behavior patterns. Principals, counselors, psychologists, social workers, and others might attend. In advance of the meeting, you need to give them documentation that will let them know exactly what the learner has been doing. Meetings of this kind often result in the development of a **corrective action plan.** For example, such a group might decide to place the learner in another class, temporarily suspend the learner from school, or assign the learner to a special counselor. The plan typically is implemented under the authority of the school principal. Usually, there are provisions requiring periodic reporting of results to the school principal or someone the principal designates to watch over the situation.

. . .

Thinking in advance about a sequence of responses you might take as you respond to misbehaviors ranging from minor to major will help you deal with many of the behavior problems you will encounter in the classroom. The vast majority of these problems can be corrected using actions chosen from categories 1, 2, and 3. A carefully constructed scheme that includes a set of systematically escalating responses will be of great value as you work to develop a positive and safe classroom environment for your learners.

VIDEO VIEWPOINTS

How Should Rules Be Enforced?

WATCH: This *Nightline* segment focuses on enforcement of zero-tolerance policies in schools. One instance is investigated in which two 8-year-old boys were taken to police headquarters and suspended from school for a day for playing "cowboys and outlaws" using paper guns. In another instance, a high school mascot is prevented from having a paper spear as a part of his costume. The segment includes some arguments from those who think the policy is appropriate for making schools safe. Others contend that sensible enforcement is needed instead of literal and automatic responses to rules.

THINK: Discuss with your classmates, or in your teaching journal, the following questions:

1. What is your position on this issue?
2. What do you think students learn about rules if they are enforced without discretion?
3. What would be a sensible rule that would protect students from threat yet would not lead to abuses?

LINK: This video segment illustrates how societal problems, such as violence in society, impact education. What are some other social concerns that may be impacting schools in negative ways?

 Complete this activity and submit your responses online in the Video Viewpoints module for this chapter of the Companion Website.

Critical Incident

Getting Tough

John Robbins is nearing the end of his first year of teaching seventh-grade history at Ride Middle School. The school is in a suburban area just outside a major Midwestern city. John took the teaching job in this school because of the location. He was sure that the parents would be supportive of education and that the students would be motivated. He expected fewer discipline problems here than he might encounter in a more "difficult" setting. However, this has not turned out to be the case. In fact, he is wondering if he is up to returning in the fall.

John started his first year upbeat and optimistic. He loved history and believed he could convey his enthusiasm to students by sharing the interesting anecdotes and insights he had obtained as a history major in college. He "just knew" he would relate well to students because he was much nearer their age than most teachers and could talk their language. He had had some difficulties in his student teaching, but he ascribed these problems to being in the classroom of another teacher and not having the freedom to do what he felt was best.

At the beginning of the year, John told his students that he wanted to make things enjoyable for them. He was sure that if he made the class fun and was friendly and open with the students, they would be motivated to work and cooperate with him. After a month, however, he realized that the class was getting out of control. The students did not want to listen and were only interested in playing around. He became angry and decided that it was time to clamp down. Perhaps, he thought, a teacher really should not smile until Christmas.

In an effort to regain control, John laid down the law to his students and established strict rules and punishments. Although this seemed to stop some undesirable behaviors, it also resulted in students becoming increasingly negative. More and more of them seemed to take every opportunity to test the limits of his rules. He found that being engaged in a constant test of wills with his students was not much fun.

As the year drew to a close, John felt that he had accomplished little. Many of his students were openly expressing a dislike of history and were asking why it is important to learn something about a "bunch of dead guys." John wondered if things were this bad in other schools. Maybe not. Perhaps he should try to get a job in a high school. Certainly other schools had students with more-mature attitudes who appreciated the value of learning something about history.

• • •

Do you think the problems would be easier at another grade? Do you think the problems are with John or with the students? Specifically, what does John perceive the problem to be? What do you think his students perceive the problem to be? What might have been the sources of the feelings of each?

What mistakes do you think John might have made? What suggestions would you give him? Do you worry about situations like this happening to you? What do you think you could do? How do you respond to the suggestion of not smiling until Christmas and being tough from the first day of school? What are the alternatives?

To respond to this Critical Incident online, go to the Critical Incidents *module for this chapter of the Companion Website.*

Key Ideas in Summary

- Conveying information and managing learners are among your most important responsibilities. Commiting time to planning your approaches to management and control will increase your prospects for success.
- *Space management* and *time management* are two areas of concern you face when developing a classroom-management plan. Among your space-management decisions will be those related to such issues as (1) use of wall space, (2) organization of floor space, (3) placement of furniture to facilitate ease of movement within the classroom, (4) placement of your own desk, and (5) equipment storage. Time management involves planning for (1) lesson transitions, (2) the start of lesson instruction, (3) lesson pacing, (4) assistance of individual learners, and (5) the establishment of routines to deal with normal occurrences.
- The purpose of your disciplinary procedures is to teach learners responsibility and self-control. As a beginning point, you need to take time to develop a set of behavioral expectations. You may find it convenient to lay out your views in terms of "rules and behaviors related to classroom conduct" and "rules and procedures related to academic work." You need to share this information with members of your class so they will have a clear understanding of your expectations.
- Successful classroom-management approaches often will be the result of a process that features some negotiation between you and students. You need to balance the negotiation process so that, on the one hand, you retain your legitimate authority to take charge of the classroom and, on the other hand, you promote "ownership" in adopted rules and regulations by incorporating some learners' ideas into your final set of guidelines.
- Several principles are related to appropriate teacher responses to misbehavior. You need to respect learners, deal with problems quietly and unobtrusively, distinguish between minor and major problems, and help learners grasp the connection between unacceptable behaviors and unpleasant consequences that come their way as a result.
- Several basic types of teacher power and authority have been identified. These include *expert power* (power that comes to a person as a result of his/her specialized knowledge), *referent power* (power that comes to an individual because of the warm, positive relationship he/she has with others), *legitimate power* (power that comes to an individual because of the position he/she holds), *reward power* (power that comes to an individual because he/she is in a position to provide something another person sees as desirable), and *coercive power* (power that comes to an individual because of his/her authority to administer punishment).
- Your efforts to prevent behavior problems in the classroom should be guarded by several important principles. In general, your actions should (1) preserve learners' dignity, (2) use private versus public correction, (3) address the causes of the misbehavior, not the misbehavior alone, (4) be guided by an appreciation of the difference between minor and major problems, (5) help learners understand that choosing misbehavior also means choosing the consequences that go along with misbehavior, and (6) be consistent and fair.
- In general, the plan you develop to minimize the number of unacceptable learner behaviors should feature a scaled set of responses ranging from less intrusive/less severe to more intrusive/more severe. You might organize these responses under categories designed to achieve three purposes: (1) supporting learner development of self-control, (2) providing situational assistance, and (3) implementing consequences involving others.

Chapter 9 Self-Test

 To review terms and concepts in this chapter, go to the Companion Website and take the Chapter 9 Self-Test. Feedback for the self-test is immediate. You can keep track of your self-test scores yourself, or you can submit them to your instructor via e-mail.

Preparing for Praxis

 To learn more about the Praxis test and complete this activity online, go to the Preparing for Praxis *module for this chapter of the Companion Website.*

You may be required to pass Educational Testing Service's Praxis II exam as you seek formal authorization to teach in the public schools. The *Principles of Learning and Teaching* component of Praxis II seeks to assess your knowledge about these topics: (1) Students as Learners, (2) Instruction and Assessment, (3) Communication Techniques, and (4) Profession and Community.

Information presented in this chapter may be especially relevant as you prepare for questions related to the category of "Students as Learners." Some content may also deal with issues having logical ties to other Praxis II categories. You may find it useful to prepare a chart for your own use similar to the one provided here. As you encounter information related to individual categories, you can enter it into the chart. A completed chart of this kind will be useful as you prepare to take the Praxis II exam.

Students as Learners	Instruction and Assessment
• Student Development and the Learning Process	• Instructional Strategies
• Students as Diverse Learners	• Planning Instruction
• Student Motivation and the Learning Environment	• Assessment Strategies
Communication Techniques	**Profession and Community**
• Basic, Effective, Verbal and Nonverbal Communication Techniques	• The Reflective Practitioner
• Effect of Cultural and Gender Differences on Communications in the Classroom	• The Larger Community
• Types of Questions That Can Stimulate Discussion in Different Ways for Particular Purposes	

For Your Initial-Development Portfolio

 To complete this activity and submit your response online, go to the For Your Initial-Development Portfolio *module for this chapter of the Companion Website.*

1. What materials and ideas that you learned in this chapter about *classroom management and discipline* will you include as "evidence" in your portfolio? Select up to three separate items of information. Number them 1, 2, and 3.
2. Think about why you selected these materials. As you do so, consider these issues:
   • Specific uses you might make of this information as you plan, deliver, and assess the impact of your teaching

- The compatibility of the information with your own priorities and values
- Any contributions this information can make to your development as a teacher
- Factors that led you to include this information, as opposed to some alternatives you considered but rejected

3. Place a check in the chart here to indicate the INTASC standard(s) to which each of your items of information relates. (You may wish to refer to Chapter 1 for more-detailed information about INTASC.)

INTASC Standard Number

ITEM OF EVIDENCE NUMBER	S1	S2	S3	S4	S5	S6	S7	S8	S9	S10
1										
2										
3										

4. Prepare a written reflection in which you analyze the decision-making process you followed. In your comments, mention the INTASC standard(s) to which your selected material relates.

Reflections

 To respond to these questions online, go to the Reflections module for this chapter of the Companion Website.

1. What is the rationale for constructing a well-developed plan for responding to classroom management and control challenges? In this chapter, you learned about some elements that you might wish to include in your plan. Which of these do you think will pose the most difficulties for you? How will you go about resolving them? Are there components that should be included that were not discussed in the chapter? If so, what are they, and why do you think they should be included?

2. Think about the subject(s) you will be teaching and the probable age levels of your learners. On some days you will want to deliver instruction to the whole group. On other days, you will divide the class into several groups. On still other days, you may have learners working on assignments that require you to move through the classroom to check on individual progress. Think about differences in how you would configure your classroom space for each of these purposes. How and when will you make the necessary changes? Keep in mind that you will want to minimize the time the process of making these changes takes away from your instructional time.

3. Given the subject(s) and learners you intend to teach, what kinds of classroom rules and regulations would you like to have? What is your rationale for wanting these guidelines? What actions will you take to encourage your learners to commit to these expectations?

4. If you agree that learners' support for classroom rules and regulations increases when they have some involvement in their development, how will you set these guidelines? What features of your negotiation process will ensure that you retain your legitimate authority as the classroom instructional leader while, at the same time, giving learners some ownership in the guideline-development process?

5. When it becomes necessary to involve others (for example, other teachers, administrators, parents, and guardians) in discussions related to a learner with a persistent pattern of inappropriate behavior, you need to provide these people with background information that describes the nature of the situation. Specifically, what kinds of information would you provide? Will the potential need for this kind of information prompt you to keep certain kinds of records? If so, describe them.

Field Experiences, Projects, and Enrichment

1. Observe a lesson and pay special attention to how the teacher uses available time. How much time is spent on tasks other than instruction? What suggestions can you offer to make the use of time more efficient?

2. Interview some teachers and ask them about the types of discipline problems they encounter most frequently. Consider which of the alternative responses you might use in responding to the common problems identified by the teachers.

3. Interview a principal or a school district official. Ask about common classroom management and discipline difficulties experienced by new teachers.

4. Interview several school learners about their reactions to discipline problems in the schools. Select learners who are in the same age group as those you hope to teach. What do they see as the major causes of discipline problems? How can you use an understanding of those causes to plan for the classroom?

5. Begin to develop your plan for discipline by thinking about the rules you will need in the classroom, the ways you will organize the classroom, and the types of responses you will use when confronting misbehavior. Share your ideas with your professor and ask for comments.

References

Berliner, D. C. (1984). The half-full glass: A review of research on teaching. In P. L. Hosford (Ed.), *Using what we know about teaching* (pp. 51–77). Alexandria, VA: Association for Supervision and Curriculum Development.

Brophy, J. (1983). Classroom organization and management. *The Elementary School Journal, 83*(4), 265–285.

Brown, T. (1998, July 7). *Effective school research and student behavior.* Southeast/South Central Educational Cooperative Fourth Retreat: Making a difference in student behavior, Lexington, KY.

Camp, B., & Bash, M. (1981). *Think aloud: Increasing social and cognitive skills: A problem solving program for children (small group program).* Champaign, IL: Research Press.

Clark, S. N., Clark, D. C., & Irvin, J. I. (1997). Collaborative decision making. *Middle School Journal, 28*(5), 54–56.

Doyle, W. (1986). Classroom organization and management. In M. C. Wittrock (Ed.), *Handbook of research on teaching* (3rd ed., pp. 392–431). New York: Macmillan.

Emmer, E. T., Evertson, C. M., & Anderson, L. (1980). Effective classroom management at the beginning of the school year. *Elementary School Journal, 80*(5), 219–231.

Evertson, C. M. (1989). Improving elementary classroom management: A school-based training program for beginning the year. *Journal of Educational Research, 83*(2), 82–90.

French, J. R. P., & Raven, B. H. (1959). The bases of social power. In D. Cartwright (Ed.), *Studies in social power* (pp. 118–149). Ann Arbor: University of Michigan Press.

Good, T. L., & Brophy, J. E. (2000). *Looking in classrooms* (8th ed.). New York: Longman.

Grubaugh, S. (1989). Nonverbal language techniques for better classroom management and discipline. *High School Journal, 73*(1), 34–40.

Henson, K. T. (2004) *Constructivist teaching strategies for diverse middle-level classrooms.* Boston: Allyn & Bacon.

Henson, K. T., & Eller, B. F. (1999). *Educational psychology for effective teaching.* Belmont, CA: Wadsworth.

Jones, F. H. (1979). The gentle art of classroom discipline. *National Elementary Principal, 58*(4), 26–32.

Jones, V. F., & Jones, L. S. (1986). *Comprehensive classroom management: Creating positive learning environments* (2nd ed.). Boston: Allyn & Bacon.

Latham, A. S. (1998). Rules and learning. *Educational Leadership, 56*(1), 104–105.

Martin, M. K. (1997). Connecting instruction and management in a student-centered classroom. *Middle School Journal, 28*(5), 3–9.

McLaughlin, H. J. (1994). From negation to negotiation: Moving away from the management metaphor. *Action in Teacher Education, 16*(1), 75–84.

Rose, L. C., & Gallup, A. M. (2002). The 34th annual Phi Delta Kappa /Gallup Poll of the public's attitudes toward the public school. *Phi Delta Kappan, 84*(1), 41–58.

Savage, T. V. (1999). *Developing self-control through classroom management and discipline* (2nd ed.). Boston: Allyn & Bacon.

Smith, H. A. (1987). Nonverbal communication. In M. J. Dunkin (Ed.), *The international encyclopedia of teaching and teacher education* (pp. 466–476). New York: Pergamon Press.

Smyth, W. J. (1987). Time. In M. J. Dunkin (Ed.), *The international encyclopedia of teaching and teacher education* (pp. 372–380). New York: Pergamon Press.

Vars, G. F. (1997). Student concerns and standards, too. *Middle School Journal, 28*(4), 44–49.

Williams, P., Alley, R., & Henson, K. T. (1999). *Managing secondary classrooms: Principles and strategies for effective discipline and instruction.* Boston: Allyn & Bacon.

10 *Assessing Learning*

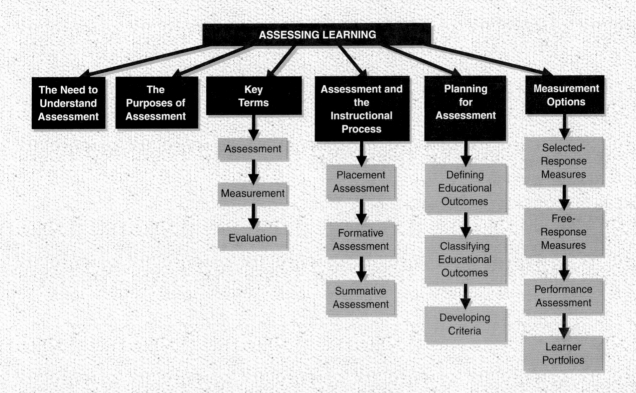

OBJECTIVES

This chapter will help you to

- explain the multiple roles of assessment in education.
- define commonly used assessment terms.
- point out the functions of *placement assessment, formative assessment,* and *summative assessment.*

- describe steps you might take as you plan a high-quality assessment program.
- describe characteristics of measurement options, including *selected-response measures, free-response measures, performance assessment,* and *portfolios.*

THE NEED TO UNDERSTAND ASSESSMENT

When you teach, you will make daily decisions about the progress of your learners and about the effectiveness of your instruction. These decisions must be based on sound evidence. In addition, you will have a professional stake in assessment because findings today are often used to inform the public about the quality of individual schools and the relative excellence of those who teach in particular buildings. Therefore, your performance evaluations and possibly your right to keep your job may depend on assessment. These realities strongly underscore the importance you should attach to becoming a sophisticated planner, interpreter, and user of assessment data.

THE PURPOSES OF ASSESSMENT

Assessment processes are used for more than determining learners' grades. They also function as accountability tools for evaluating both your performance and the overall effectiveness of your school. Results of assessment sometimes are offered to the public as indicators of the relative quality of teachers and instruction in each evaluated school.

Because collected information focuses on learner performance, you should understand how assessment processes affect your students. From the time learners first arrive at school, they desire indications of success. Data gathered from fair and appropriate assessment procedures can provide these affirmations. Evidence of success motivates learners to continue working and creates an expectation of future success (Stiggins, 1997).

Members of your class who are uncertain about their success may begin to doubt the value of their school experiences. These students may devalue what they do at school because they do not have a sense of accomplishment. Because of its potential to promote a negative view of schooling among learners, you need to view assessment as a component of the instructional process that you can use to reshape programs in ways that will enable students to succeed.

Increased emphasis on school accountability has led to more emphasis on school-wide planning for assessment.

When you think about teaching a given lesson, a variety of instructional approaches is available. Over time, attention to assessment data can help you decide techniques that are more effective with the kinds of young people you teach. As you seek to identify these successful instructional approaches, you need to keep track of how well individual techniques helped members of your class to learn material. If they have done well, you can logically conclude that your instructional approaches have been effective. On the other hand, if many people in your class have not performed adequately, you should consider alternative approaches to helping them master the content.

KEY TERMS

In casual conversations, several key assessment terms are used interchangeably. As a professional, you need to understand differences among them. A sound understanding of the meanings of these terms can help you identify sources of error, clarify issues, and make informed choices.

Assessment

Assessment refers to the purposeful collection of data from a variety of sources for the purpose of rendering a judgment (Gallagher, 1998). An **assessment plan** involves identification of data sources that are relevant to a specified set of learning outcomes. Useful information sources may include measurement tools such as tests, or they may draw on your observations of learners' in-class performances, abilities to complete projects according to specified guidelines, and abilities to succeed on tasks associated with daily assignments. Sometimes members of your class will know that they are being assessed. On other occasions, for example when you are watching groups of learners work on an in-class project, they may be less aware that you are assessing their work.

When developing an assessment plan, you should decide whether your plan is consistent with what you want learners to achieve. For example, if you are interested in promoting learner creativity, an assessment plan that places a heavy emphasis on the neat appearance of learners' work makes little sense. "Neatness" is not ordinarily considered a useful indicator of creativity. Instead, you should be looking for evidence that learners' work deviates markedly from the traditional or expected.

In addition to focusing on behaviors that make sense in light of what you want your young people to learn, your assessments need to be based on an adequate and fair sampling of behaviors that are of interest. How often was the behavior observed and under what conditions? Most coaches would not choose the starting lineup of a team based on one practice. Instead, they want numerous observations under various conditions in order to have a solid basis for making decisions.

Measurement

Measurement involves quantifying the presence or absence of a quality, trait, or attribute (Gallagher, 1998). For example, if you want to determine the height, width, or weight of an object, you measure it. Of course, the accuracy of this value depends on your using the right measurement tool. If you want to measure the length of something, you do not use an instrument designed to measure its weight. In addition, if you are interested in the size of a large object such as a football field, then you need a long tape measure rather than a ruler. If precision is needed, you need a tool more exact than a ruler or yardstick.

Unfortunately, when you are faced with a need to choose the right measurement tool for use in school, the decision often is not as obvious as when you are choosing something used to measure size or weight. To illustrate this point, consider something everybody has encountered—the test. Particular types of tests are appropriate for measuring different traits and abilities. When you teach, you want to select one that will provide useful information about the kind of learning you are interested in assessing.

VIDEO VIEWPOINTS

The Uses and Misuses of Standardized Tests

WATCH: This *Nightline* segment focuses on the issue of the uses of the SAT as a college admission requirement. The segment discusses some history of the SAT and points out that the current impact might be the opposite of what was originally intended. Much of the discussion centers on the recommendation of the chancellor of the University of California university system to eliminate the SAT as an admission requirement. He made this recommendation after visiting an upscale private school that was preparing 12-year-old students for the SAT. Further investigation revealed a variation in scores based on ethnicity and a lack of data indicating that high SAT scores actually predicted college success.

THINK: Discuss with your classmates, or in your teaching journal, the following questions:

1. What is the value of a standardized test such as the SAT?

2. Do you think that important and high-stakes decisions should be based on performance on a single test?

3. What evidence do you think would be appropriate for indicating that a person is ready for college?

LINK: What do you see as the social implications of basing admission decisions on a test that seems to be at least partly related to socioeconomic status?

 Complete this activity and submit your responses online in the Video Viewpoints module for this chapter of the Companion Website.

Sometimes nonspecialists are unaware that certain types of tests have particular (and often limited) uses. For example, the media often cite scores on the well-known Scholastic Achievement Test (SAT) as a valid measure of learner achievement and school quality. This is a mistake. First of all, the SAT is a voluntary test that is taken by approximately one half of the high school seniors in the nation. Thus, the scores reflect the characteristics only of students who choose to take the test rather than the characteristics of all high school seniors.

The SAT samples only a limited range of content. As you may know, the SAT is composed of two parts: a verbal section and a quantitative section. The verbal portion is designed to measure language usage and comprehension, and the quantitative part focuses on mathematical knowledge and comprehension. Because the SAT does not assess learning in *all* subject areas taught in the schools, it makes little sense to use results as an indicator of the overall quality of a given school or the teachers who work there. Despite this logic and despite SAT's own admission that such use of total SAT scores is invalid, incomplete, and unfair, some people continue to use the scores as an indicator of overall school or teacher quality (Berliner & Biddle, 1995).

In addition to thinking about appropriate uses of standardized tests such as the SAT, you need to consider what you are measuring when you construct your own tests. Poorly constructed teacher-made tests often focus on too narrow a sample of what learners have been taught. Sometimes they feature numerous poorly worded or even "trick" questions. When this happens, learners' scores are not good indicators of what they know or have learned.

Evaluation

Up to this point, we have discussed gathering data. Evaluation is the next step. **Evaluation** refers to making a judgment about the worth or value of something. For example, a physician may measure the height and weight of a child. The importance of this information is realized only when the physician makes judgments about whether the child is developing satisfactorily.

Your learners' scores on a test tell you little until you interpret them. To answer the question of whether achievement is satisfactory, you must make an evaluative judgment. To do so, you need clear criteria. The two common ways to establish criteria are norm referencing and criterion referencing.

WEB EXTENSION 10–1

American Evaluation Association

Here at the home page of the American Evaluation Association you will find a wide range of information on the general area of evaluation. There are lists of useful publications, notices about professional meetings focusing on evaluation-related issues, discussions of key issues confronting professional evaluators, and numerous links to additional information about evaluation.

http://www.eval.org/

Norm-Referenced Evaluation.   In **norm-referenced evaluation,** you make judgments about individual learners' levels of performance by comparing an individual's scores to scores of others. The usual way of establishing these norms, or expected scores, is by reference to scores that are distributed along a **bell-shaped curve.** This is a symmetrical curve derived from a mathematical formula. It is based on the assumption that any given trait or ability is found in the total population in a distribution that is similar to the bell curve. Most learners' scores will be grouped near the mean, or the average, and will decrease in frequency as one moves away from the mean in either direction. In other words, there will be a few people on each end of the distribution, with the numbers increasing toward the middle, or the mean.

Standardized tests are examples of norm-referenced tests. Developers of standardized tests first administer an initial version to a sample group. They plot these **raw scores** (scores based on the number of correct answers that have not been subjected to any kind of mathematical adjustment) on a distribution and apply the mathematical formula to establish what are commonly called norms, or **derived scores.** They attempt to include a sample of people who are representative of the total population of the United States so the norms or derived scores will approximate what one could expect if the test were actually given to the entire population.

For example, if it is reported that a given learner's score places him or her at the 50th percentile, this means that 50% of the comparison population performed at or below the score of this individual on this test. If the learner's score were at the 90th percentile, 90%

of the comparison population would have test results at or below this person's score. Usually when standardized tests are returned, both the raw score, which is the number the person actually got right, and the derived (standardized) score are given.

When you look at scores of class members on a standardized test, you need to ask several questions. How was the norm group selected? How should individuals' scores be interpreted? When were the norms established (Gronlund, 1998)? If you are to have confidence in the results, what you have to determine is whether the group used to standardize the test has characteristics that are similar to your own learners. If curricula and learning conditions of the **norming group**—the group whose scores are used to establish expected scores for individuals who take a standardized test—vary markedly from those of the tested group, results will not be valid.

There can be problems even when norm-referenced tests are well designed, up-to-date, and properly administered to learners with characteristics similar to the norming group. Much of the difficulty involves misinterpretation of the results. This situation has been spoofed in the reference to the mythical town of Lake Wobegon on the National Public Radio show, *Prairie Home Companion,* in which all children are described as "above average." It is statistically impossible for all children to be "above average."

Criterion-Referenced Evaluation.   When you use **criterion-referenced evaluation,** you make judgments based on how well the performance of each person in your class compares to a standard or a set of criteria rather than on how their scores compare to those of others (Gallagher, 1998). The standard established is set at a level appropriate to the type of knowledge or skill being assessed.

For example, if a company needs a worker who can carry 70-pound bags of fertilizer, the hiring officials are interested in whether people who apply for the job can carry this mandatory load. They are not interested in how this individual's load-carrying ability compares to a large group of people who might have been tested on their abilities to carry bags of different weights. Suppose in this large-group test, individuals had been tested on their ability to lift 40-pound bags. An applicant who could lift a 50-pound bag would look superior in comparison to this norming group. However, he or she would not succeed as an employee for a position requiring sufficient strength to lift 70-pound bags.

Both norm-referenced and criterion-referenced evaluation can be applied to the same assessment (Gronlund, 1998). Many standardized-testing companies report the norms and also learner performance in skill areas. For example, a math test may include how many addition, subtraction, multiplication, division, and word problems the learner scored correctly. In the classroom, this kind of information informs you that a particular learner, for example, did better than 90% of the learners in the class on the entire test (a norm-referenced conclusion) but failed to meet the minimum criterion for solving word problems (a criterion-referenced conclusion).

Two issues merit attention when you use criterion-referenced evaluation. First, you need to consider the appropriateness of what is being measured. It is sometimes tempting to focus only on what is easy to observe or measure. This is true because you may find it difficult to decide what to measure when your focus is on more-complex content. For example, if you are teaching geography, you will find it easier to construct tests focusing on use of latitude and longitude than on a more-complex geographic concept such as *diffusion of innovations*. Giving in to the temptation to use ease of measurement as a basis for constructing criterion-referenced tests can result in an inappropriate focus on less important, even trivial, content.

Another issue relates to setting the criterion. What should be the level of acceptable performance? If you set your standard too low, people in your class who have not really mastered the material may be incorrectly judged to have done so. On the other hand, if you set too high a standard, those who have mastered a great deal of new content may be judged to have failed.

Setting the criterion level in the classroom is largely a matter of professional judgment. You need to decide what is acceptable minimal performance, a determination that will vary depending on the nature of the intended learning. Some tasks such as basic reading and mathematics skills are so important for the future success of learners that a high standard of expected performance makes good sense. However, other types of outcomes will be much less critical for future success. In these situations, you will be justified in setting a lower criterion level.

WEB EXTENSION 10–2

CRESST

At this site you will find the home page of the National Center for Research on Evaluation, Standards, and Student Testing (CRESST). This group, an affiliate of the Graduate School of Education and Information Studies at UCLA, sponsors research on a variety of topics related to assessment. Here you will find links to research reports, monographs, newsletters, and other resources that focus on CRESST's areas of concern.

http://www.cresst.org

Grades.   Grades communicate the results of evaluation. They are of interest to learners, parents and guardians, employers, and higher-education admissions officers. Because people other than those in your classes may have an interest in the grades you award, you must be prepared to explain your grading system to others.

A system commonly used in the United States awards letter grades. A grade of *A* is supposed to indicate excellence, a grade of *C* is supposed to indicate average, and a grade of *F* is supposed to indicate failing. The letter grading system sometimes is used in conjunction with a norm-referenced system. When this system is used, a large group of learners clustered around the midpoint are given *C*s, a smaller number of learners are given *B*s or *D*s, and a few learners at each end of the distribution are awarded *A*s or *F*s.

You can also base grades on a criterion-referenced system. When this is done, you establish a separate standard that learners must meet to qualify for each grade. For example, you might indicate that all learners who accomplish 90% of the objectives of the course will get an *A,* those who master 80% will get a *B,* and so forth. Another criterion-referenced approach ties mastery of specific tasks to specific letter grades. In such an arrangement, you might define *C-level* performance as completion of certain critical tasks. To qualify for higher grades, members of your class would have to complete additional tasks successfully. You might develop separate lists of tasks that learners would need to complete for grades of *A* or *B*. This scheme would allow your learners to identify the level of mastery required for each grade and make decisions about which grade to work for. One interesting feature of criterion-referenced grading schemes is that they make it possible for all students to receive *any* grade; there is no mandatory distribution of *A*s, *B*s, *C*s, *D*s, and *F*s.

In general, you should judge the worth of a letter grading system or any alternative for reporting information related to learner performance on how well it communicates evaluation information to learners and to other interested parties. Critics of letter grades claim that they do not provide enough details and, therefore, are of limited value. For example, a letter grade may be an average or summary of several isolated performances and may mask the more-typical strengths and weaknesses of a learner. A grade may be based on elements of behavior bearing only a tenuous connection to learning of academic content. Some teachers consider variables such as behavior, work habits, and effort. In such cases, a learner who does well on academic tasks may receive a lower grade because of discipline problems.

WEB EXTENSION 10–3

Grading Students: ERIC/AE Digest

In this *ERIC Digest*, author Lawrence Cross explains a system for converting learner scores in a way that helps to establish equivalencies among scores from different tests learners take. You will find especially useful information about establishing cutoff points between individual pairs of grades (A and B, B and C, C and D, and so forth).

http://www.ericfacility.net/ericdigests/ed398239.html

Some critics argue that grading systems place too little emphasis on the individual learner. They argue that a better scheme would begin with assessment of each learner's abilities. According to this view, an individual learner's progress, as evidenced by grades, should be based on how much measurable growth is demonstrated by the learner between the beginning and end of the grading period. Such a system would have the desirable effect of focusing teachers' attention on the individual interests and characteristics of their learners (Tomlinson, 2001).

Although this perspective appeals strongly to people who want school programs to place a strong emphasis on serving special needs of individual learners, present-day interest in accountability testing presents difficulties for teachers and schools who might be interested in adopting this kind of approach. Opponents argue that grading individuals only against themselves denies the public an understanding of how well individual learners are doing when compared with their age mates within individual classes and schools and between schools and school districts.

This teacher is explaining grading criteria to members of the class.

Some critics of letter grades suggest that they should be replaced by extensive written comments prepared by the teacher. The idea is that written evaluations can communicate strengths and weaknesses of learners with more clarity than letter grades. Important constraints limit the practicality of this approach. Good written evaluations require long commitments of teacher time, and opponents of this approach argue that this time is better spent planning lessons and interacting with learners. In addition, the validity of a written evaluation, like a letter grade, depends on the quality of information that supports it. The worth of a written evaluation based on an inappropriate or excessively limited sample of learner behavior has no more value than a letter grade based on a similarly inadequate set of information.

ASSESSMENT AND THE INSTRUCTIONAL PROCESS

Assessment plays multiple roles in the instructional process. These include:

- Placement assessment,
- Formative assessment, and
- Summative assessment. (Gronlund, 1998)

Placement Assessment

Placement assessment addresses the question "Where do I begin?" You use placement assessment at the beginning of a new unit or course of study. Often it takes the form of a **pretest,** a test designed to provide information about what the learner may already know or think about content that is to be introduced.

Placement-assessment information helps you know what members of your class already understand before you present new content. This information provides a baseline you can use as you seek to determine what value has been added to learners' stores of understanding as a result of your teaching. Sometimes you will also want to use placement assessment to help you understand learners' attitudes toward content you are about to introduce. This information can give you insight into the kinds of motivational challenges you may face when you begin teaching the new material.

Formative Assessment

Formative assessment takes place as an instructional sequence is occurring. You use it to determine whether learners are making satisfactory progress and whether you need to modify your instructional approaches. Your formative-assessment procedures may include short quizzes covering limited amounts of content that you give at frequent intervals during your instructional sequence. You can also use daily or weekly work samples as sources of formative-assessment information.

You use formative assessment to make instructional adjustments that will improve the prospects that your students will learn (Gronlund, 1998; Tanner, 2001). You do not use the results to award grades. Information you get from formative assessment provides you with a kind of status-check on the quality of your teaching. If your formative assessments show that your learners are experiencing a high rate of success, you have some assurance that you are appropriately organizing and pacing your instruction. On the other hand, if you find a high rate of failure, this can signal a need to alter your teaching approaches in ways that are better suited to the particular needs of your learners.

If persistent problems occur and reteaching a subject seems to have little impact, you might want to consider a type of formative assessment called **diagnostic assessment** (Gronlund, 1998). The purpose of diagnostic assessment is to probe for specific causes of a failure. For example, if learners are making mistakes in responding to math problems, you might want to find out whether there is a consistent error pattern that reveals their lack of understanding of one of the basic computational procedures.

Summative Assessment

Summative assessment takes place at the conclusion of an instructional unit or sequence. The purposes are to determine which learners have accomplished the objectives and to provide you with information you can use to communicate to others what your students have learned. You will use results of summative assessment as a basis for assigning grades.

You need to plan your summative-assessment procedures at the same time as you plan your instructional units. Each learning outcome you identify needs to be accompanied by a description of your scheme for assessing learner performance. When you do this kind of planning, your summative assessment will adequately sample what has been taught. If you do not engage in careful planning for summative evaluation, there is a danger that your tests and other adopted assessment procedures will not adequately represent the content of your lessons.

The consequences of poor learner performance on summative assessments are serious. They can mean failure of a course or even failure of an entire grade. The importance of summative evaluations places an obligation on you to design them well. In addition, the high-stakes nature of these assessments emphasizes the importance of developing good formative-evaluation procedures. Formative-evaluation results can provide an early alert to learning problems, and they occur when there is still time for you to salvage an instructional situation that is not working. Corrective action in light of formative-assessment information can lead to instructional modifications that will help your learners master material and do well on your summative assessments.

PLANNING FOR ASSESSMENT

High-quality assessment requires considerable planning. You will experience problems if you wait until the last minute to develop tests and other evaluation procedures. Failure to plan for assessment often leads to ineffective programs.

Defining Educational Outcomes

Data you gather for use in assessment must have clear ties to your desired instructional outcomes. The first steps in planning for assessment involve (1) identifying important learning outcomes and (2) determining how they will be measured and evaluated. Ideally, assessment planning should take place at the same time as learning outcomes are determined. This helps you ensure that all key outcomes are assessed and evaluated. Later, when you review how learners performed, you will have confidence in the results.

Failure to spend the time needed to tie assessments clearly to the important learning outcomes you have identified may lead to focusing on tasks that are easy to measure rather than ones that are important. If this happens, your learners may conclude that they need to concentrate on the trivial and unimportant dimensions of a learning task.

Suppose you are teaching a high school social studies class and design a unit on the Civil War featuring learning outcomes that ask learners to give serious thought to causes and effects of the conflict. If you develop a last-minute test that does nothing more than ask learners to name selected Civil War generals, you send a message inconsistent with your intended learning outcomes. Members of your class will quickly conclude that the large "cause-and-effect" issues are unimportant and that, despite what you say in class, your *real* interest is having them memorize isolated facts.

Classifying Educational Outcomes

Educational outcomes vary in their complexity. Some outcomes require your learners to do little more than recall names, dates, or other facts. However, a sound instructional program also includes more-complex outcomes such as those that challenge learners to interpret, apply, and create. Identifying the level of complexity of educational outcomes provides you with guidance as you develop your assessment program. Some assessment procedures are useful when measuring less complex outcomes, and others are better suited to measuring more-complex outcomes.

The term **taxonomy** refers to a classification scheme. Several taxonomies that focus on educational outcomes have been developed (Bloom, Englehart, Furst, Hill, & Krathwohl, 1956; Krathwohl, Bloom, & Masia, 1964; Marzano, 2001). You may find taxonomies useful as aids when you plan instructional programs that feature a wide range of educational outcomes. Educational taxonomies generally emphasize three main domains of learning: the **cognitive domain,** the **affective domain,** and the **psychomotor domain.**

The *cognitive domain* includes a category of thinking associated with remembering and processing information. The *affective domain* includes attitudes, feelings, interests, and values. The *psychomotor domain* focuses on muscular coordination, manipulation, and motor skills.

A team of researchers headed by Benjamin Bloom developed the most popular cognitive taxonomy (Bloom, Englehart, Furst, Hill, & Krathwohl, 1956). Though it is popularly known as **Bloom's Taxonomy,** the full title is *Taxonomy of Educational Objectives: Handbook 1, Cognitive Domain.*

Bloom's Taxonomy is organized into six categories that are scaled according to their complexity. It begins with the relatively simple cognitive process of recall of factual information and moves to the more-complex cognitive processes of applying, analyzing, synthesizing, and evaluating. The six levels are as follows:

1. **Knowledge.** This category refers to the recall of specific items of information, such as recall of facts, procedures, methods, or even theories and principles. Many refer to this category as the "memory level" because it only demands the recall of information from stored memory.
2. **Comprehension.** This category requires a cognitive process that is a step beyond recall. It requires that learners not only recall specific items of information, but that they also reflect on their grasp of its meaning by interpreting, translating, or extrapolating. Many refer to this category when they say they want learners to "understand" the material.
3. **Application.** This category refers to the ability not only to understand material, but also to know how and when to apply the information to solve problems. Thus, when confronted with a problem, the learner is able to identify the needed information or principles and apply that information without being told what to do.

4. **Analysis.** This category refers to the ability to break complex information down into parts and to understand how the parts are related or organized. This level involves having learners understand the structure of complex information. It involves cognitive processes such as comparing and contrasting.
5. **Synthesis.** This category refers to the cognitive processes that we usually associate with creativity. Synthesis is the reverse of analysis. It requires putting parts together in some new or unique way and might involve such tasks as writing a composition or designing a science experiment to test a theory.
6. **Evaluation.** This category refers to judging something against a set of criteria. This means that one is not simply making a value judgment about the worth of something. Evaluation requires that judgments be based on specified criteria that might be provided by the teacher or, alternatively, be developed by the learner.

In using Bloom's Taxonomy to plan your assessment procedures, you start by looking at your knowledge-level learning outcomes. Next, you choose measurement approaches that can provide information about learners' abilities to store and recall specific bits of information. For example, you might choose true–false or matching tests because they are useful in measuring this kind of thinking and they are relatively easy to construct. For more-sophisticated kinds of learning outcomes (for example, those at the levels of application, analysis, and synthesis), you would need to choose different kinds of measurement tools because true–false and matching tests are not capable of assessing learners' abilities at these higher cognitive levels. For these learning outcomes, you might choose essay tests, learner-developed projects, or other suitable procedures.

Cognitive learning is only one dimension of education. Schools also seek to engender positive attitudes and values. You probably would feel terribly disappointed if young people at the end of the year scored well on tests of reading proficiency but left the school vowing "never to pick up another book." Interests in promoting positive attitudes toward learning reflects educators' concern for the affective domain. Because this domain includes the more-subjective area of attitudes and interests, the categories are not quite as precise as are those in the cognitive domain. However, they are helpful as guides for developing plans for instruction and assessment.

A team of researchers headed by David Krathwohl developed a taxonomy for the affective domain titled *Taxonomy of Educational Objectives: The Classification of Educational Goals. Handbook II: Affective Domain* (Krathwohl, Bloom, & Masia, 1964). This taxonomy, sometimes known as **Krathwohl's Taxonomy,** is organized into five categories on the basis of increased internalization of an attitude, interest, or value. The categories are as follows:

1. **Receiving.** The lowest level of internalization is that of showing an awareness of or being willing to receive other information or stimuli. This category indicates that little of value can take place if an individual is unwilling to attend to information. For example, a learner is not likely to develop a more-positive attitude toward reading if that person is unwilling to engage in a reading activity.
2. **Responding.** The next level moves a step beyond the passive reception of information or stimuli and requires that the person make some sort of a response. It might be a willingness to ask questions, seek more information, or participate in an activity.
3. **Valuing.** At this level the individual has begun to internalize the attitude, value, or interest so that he or she expresses an interest in or commitment to activities or positions. A person at this level might demonstrate a commitment by

choosing an activity when given a free choice. For example, he or she might freely choose to read a book or pursue a topic. Another indicator would be a willingness to take a stand or publicly associate with a belief or an activity.

4. **Organization.** At this level individuals start to integrate personal beliefs and attitudes and to establish a hierarchy. They begin to demonstrate priorities and use those priorities to make choices when confronted with decisions that involve conflicts between two or more of their values, beliefs, or commitments.

5. **Characterization.** At this level the attitudes, beliefs, and values have become so internalized that they become a way of life. Others can see the commitment of a person without being told because of the consistent choices and actions of the individual.

Assessments of behaviors in the affective domain cannot be performed with traditional tools such as paper-and-pencil tests. If you are interested in gathering information about affective behaviors of learners, you need to place them in situations that give them opportunities to receive new information and opportunities to begin internalizing an attitude or value. Internalization is a long-term growth process that requires measurement over time.

The psychomotor domain has not been as clearly defined as the cognitive and affective domains. Several attempts have been made to develop psychomotor taxonomies, but none has become as well entrenched as the Bloom and Krathwohl taxonomies.

Developing Criteria

There are some things that need to be considered either when you are in the process of designing an assessment plan or when you are evaluating an already existing assessment. The following questions suggest criteria or guidelines that will help you plan useful assessments.

- **Are the important outcomes assessed?** This question relates to the previous discussion. You need to make sure that what you assess is important and that every key learning outcome is included. You want to avoid making judgments about your learners or your instruction based on data that bear little or no relationship to what is important. You can avoid this problem by establishing close links between your intended learning outcomes and your assessment procedures.

- **Are the assessment procedures appropriate for the nature of the outcomes?** This guideline focuses on the issue of validity. **Validity** is concerned with the degree to which a measurement tool measures what it is supposed to measure. For example, a ruler is not a valid measurement tool for determining weight. A valid measurement tool will elicit the type of performance or behavior specified by the learning outcome. Any single measurement tool, such as a single paper-and-pencil test, will unlikely be valid for measuring all learning outcomes. Good assessment plans include a variety of measurement tools.

- **Are there sufficient samples of behavior to allow for a fair judgment?** The major issue posed by this question concerns the inappropriate judgments that sometimes result when only a limited sample of learner behavior is considered. The remedy is to provide learners with several opportunities to demonstrate their level of mastery of individual learning outcomes.

- **Do the measurement tools meet adequate technical standards?** This guideline focuses attention on the need to establish assessment procedures that are clear and of a high quality. Tests should be free from trick questions, and test items should be appropriately formatted and error free. Does the material meet an appropriate **reliability** standard? To meet this criterion, assessment tools must be designed in such a way that different evaluators will arrive at similar conclusions when making judgments about the performance of the same individual.

- **Is the assessment appropriate for the developmental level of the learners?** Assessment devices that are appropriate for secondary-level students often are not appropriate for primary-level learners. Some assessment procedures are not well suited for use with learners who have special needs. For example, a written examination that features complex instructions may cause severe problems for poor or slow readers. Their scores may be more a reflection of their inadequate reading skills than of their mastery of the content.

- **Are the assessment procedures free of bias?** Care needs to be taken to ensure that the assessment procedures do not conflict with cultural norms and beliefs. For example, timed tests may not be appropriate for those cultural groups that do not emphasize time or speed. When learner-produced projects are used as evidence that learning has occurred, young people from affluent homes with computers and other resources may be greatly advantaged compared with learners with fewer resources at their disposal.

- **How are the results of the assessment interpreted and used?** Clear criteria for evaluating the results of the assessment plan are essential. You should be able to use results to pinpoint specific strengths and weaknesses of individual learners. A good assessment plan will allow you to make detailed analyses of the performances of all your students. You want to be able to go beyond the ability to say, "Bobby is good in geography." If you have designed your assessment procedures well, you should be able to make statements such as, "Bobby can identify places on flat maps and globes using lines of latitude and longitude. He also has shown that he can identify names and locations of major ocean currents. He still needs to work on his ability to make analyses that require putting several kinds of information together at the same time. For example, he finds it difficult to predict what the climate at a given location on the globe might be when given its elevation, location on the continent, latitude, position relative to major bodies of water and mountain ranges, and situation with respect to prevailing winds."

MEASUREMENT OPTIONS

You can select from among numerous measurement tools as you gather data about learners' performance. You should select specific tools based on the type of learning you wish to assess and your intended uses of the gathered information.

Traditional measurement options sort into two broad categories: (1) standardized tests and (2) teacher-made assessment procedures of various kinds, including the traditional paper-and-pencil tests that have long been a feature of classroom life. Standardized tests have the advantage of being written by test-construction experts. Thus, they usually are free from serious design flaws. Individual test items typically have been carefully field-tested and, if needed, revised.

Strengths of standardized tests are counterbalanced by several problems. The issue of fairness, particularly as such tests relate to minority-group learners, continues to be debated (Armstrong, 2003; Ferguson, 1998). Such tests typically assess learner performance at a single point in time. Critics of standardized tests contend that a one-time-only snapshot of a learner's ability represents an inadequate measure of what that student knows. In addition, content emphasized in a standardized test may not match well with what you have been teaching, a circumstance that raises serious validity questions. It may be that learners scoring well on a standardized test have a good understanding of what you have been teaching, and it may be that learners scoring well on such a test have only a slight understanding of what you have been teaching. If there is not a tight connection between the content covered in the standardized tests and the content of your lessons, results simply are not a valid measure of what learners have taken away from your instructional program.

WEB EXTENSION 10–4

The National Center for Fair and Open Testing

The fairness of school testing processes is a widely debated issue. An advocacy group that is committed to eliminating abuses that sometimes have been associated with standardized testing maintains this site. You will find links to materials focusing on eliminating test biases that might negatively influence test takers because of their gender, race, class, and cultural characteristics.

http://www.fairtest.org/

On the other hand, tests you prepare yourself can be tightly fitted to what you have emphasized. The possibility of establishing congruence between what has been taught and what is tested is an advantage of teacher-made tests. The negative side concerns the fact that, to be valid measures of learner achievement, tests you devise must be well designed. Individual teacher tests do not get the kind of careful review to which new standardized tests are routinely subjected. This means that, as a teacher, you have to assume a lot of responsibility for designing test procedures carefully. When you do, you can get valid results that should allow you to draw confident conclusions both about performance levels of individual learners and about the effectiveness of the instructional approaches you have been using.

When you prepare traditional classroom tests, you can select from options that fall into one of the two basic categories of "selected-response measures" and "free-response measures."

Selected-Response Measures

Selected-response measures include those tests that require your learners to choose answers from several provided choices. They are not free to provide answers other than those represented on the test. Examples of tests in this category include two-response (for example, true–false, multiple-choice, and matching exams). Advantages of selected-response measurement tools include flexibility and efficiency (Stiggins, 1997). You will also find that they represent time-efficient choices because they are objectively and easily scored.

Two-Response Tests.   Selected-response measures that allow members of your class to select from two possible answers, one of which is correct, are called **two-response tests.** The most common assessment device of this type is the true–false test. Other choices in this category are yes–no, agree–disagree, supported–unsupported, cause-effect, and fact–opinion exams. You can use two-response tests to measure cognitive as well as affective outcomes. For example, agree–disagree items are useful in measuring attitudes and opinions.

Two-response assessments are popular because they are easy to construct. However, this ease of construction can create problems. If you prepare a true–false test in a hurry, the result may be a set of questions that focuses on trivial material with little connection to your priority learning outcomes. Creation of good two-response tests requires commitment of thought and time.

Because two-response items are easy to write and do not require a large response time, you can include a large number of items on a test. As a result, tests of this type permit you to sample a broad range of content. Generally speaking, more items and a broader sampling of content make for a more-valid measurement.

A disadvantage of two-response items is that they emphasize absolutes. For example, true–false responses indicate that something is always true or always false. This makes it more difficult to construct good items, can confuse learners, and can result in some heated arguments concerning correct responses.

Two-response items that measure complex outcomes are difficult to construct. You may prefer to use essays or other kinds of assessment approaches when seeking to evaluate learners' higher-level thinking skills. Some critics also dislike two-response items because they allow learners to guess at answers they do not know. Some attempts have been made to compensate for uneducated guessing by adding a correction space where learners must correct "false" items.

Multiple-Choice Tests.   **Multiple-choice tests** are the most widely used type of measurement tool (Gallagher, 1998). They require test takers to select an answer from among three or more alternatives. Individual test items include a **stem** that is often in the form of a question and three or more answer choices. One of the options is the correct or best choice, and the others are called **distractors.**

You can use multiple-choice tests to measure a variety of simple-to-complex outcomes. They represent one of the few selected-response tests that have the capacity to assess learners' higher-level thinking abilities. When this is your purpose, you typically begin by asking members of your class to complete a series of tasks before making a selection from among available answer alternatives. For example, you might ask them to work through a problem or apply a formula before selecting an answer from among a list of options.

One of the attractions of multiple-choice items is that, like two-response items, you can score them easily. Multiple-choice tests also are less susceptible to guessing than two-response items because learners must select from among three or more answer choices.

When you write multiple-choice items, your objective should be to provide distractors that are plausible choices that would be chosen by an individual who does not know the material. If this condition is not met, learners will easily eliminate the implausible distractors and select the correct answer, even if they really do not know the material.

As compared with two-response tests, multiple-choice tests can assess learners' abilities to deal with degrees of correctness or incorrectness. These tests allow you to tell your class to choose the "best answer." When constructing multiple-choice tests, you do include a number of alternative answers, several of which might be partially correct, but only one of which represents the "best" response.

Multiple-choice tests can measure a broad range of content in a relatively short period of time. In addition, if you develop your distractors carefully and pay close attention to kinds of mistaken choices specific learners make, you can get good information about the nature of misconceptions particular individuals in your class hold.

There are some disadvantages to using multiple-choice tests. First of all, preparation of good items is difficult and time-consuming. Time saved in scoring multiple-choice tests may be more than counterbalanced by the time required to construct good items. Like two-response tests, multiple-choice tests involve guessing and they lack the ability to enable students to express their ideas and feelings.

Matching Items.   The **matching test** is a variety of the multiple-choice test that has several special features. Individual items relate to a single topic. Further, all items in the set serve as distractors. For example, you might develop a matching item that asks members of your class to match selections of literature with their authors. The distractors would include all items in the long list of authors that you provide as part of the test. Matching tests usually consist of two lists. One list is the stimulus or the question; the second list includes possible responses.

You can use several formats when you prepare matching tests. One places the numbers or letters for items in a list next to the stimulus. Another option includes instructions that direct learners to draw a line connecting each stimulus item with the correct response on the distractor list. This design often is used with young children who have not learned to form letters. Still another arrangement provides a blank space before each item on the stimulus list, where learners are asked to write in the correct response from the distractor list.

Similar to other selected-response tests, matching tests are easy to score, so you can include a large number of items on a single test. To avoid making the test too easy, all items should relate to the same theme or class. If this is not done, you might end up with a test mixing together items focusing on such diverse topics as state capitals and mountain ranges. This arrangement makes it relatively simple for learners to eliminate some distractors (for example, all of the names of cities, if the stimulus relates to mountains) and mark correct responses even though, in fact, they may not know the content well.

One of the main disadvantages of matching tests is that they tend to focus on relationships. This restricts the range of content they can assess. In addition, matching tests are not well suited to assessing learners' abilities to perform tasks requiring the use of higher-level thinking skills.

Free-Response Measures

Free-response measures require learners to generate responses of their own rather than to select responses from a list of provided alternatives. The most common types of free-response measures are essay, short-answer, and oral tests. Free-response tests provide a stimulus that prompts learners to produce an extended written or oral response. For example, you may ask them to provide an explanation or interpretation, solve a problem, defend a position, or compare and contrast events.

Free-response tests have the technical capability to assess a broad range of thinking. Selected-response tests can usually be corrected more quickly than free-response tests. Further, selected-response tests are well suited to measuring learners' abilities to perform tasks demanding lower levels of cognitive thinking, such as knowledge and comprehension. For these reasons, free-response tests tend to be used most frequently to measure more-sophisticated learning that requires young people to perform at such levels as analysis, synthesis, and evaluation.

You can construct free-response items quickly, but good ones require serious thought. You need to write questions in ways that enable learners to understand exactly what you are asking them to do, the approximate length of the response you are expecting, and general categories of information you hope to see in their answers. Poorly written items such as "explain the causes of the Civil War" are too broad and poorly defined. Entire volumes have been written on this topic, and historians have long debated the roots of the conflict. An improved version might read something like this:

> In a response not to exceed two pages in length, describe (a) at least two political causes, (b) at least two economic causes, and (c) at least two social causes of the Civil War.

In addition to writing free-response items with clarity and precision, you also need to pay attention to how the response will be evaluated. Your correction task will be easier if the question includes references to some specific categories of information you want to see included (such as in the previous example). To help you maintain a consistent correction pattern, consider preparing a model response or a checklist that includes information you hope to see in learners' answers (Gallagher, 1998). Even when you have prepared this kind of a correction guideline, you should be open to considering the appropriateness of alternative answers that, though varying a bit from your own expectations, represent reasonable responses to your question.

Free-response tests have several disadvantages. One problem concerns scoring. Because you need to read and analyze each response, correction is time-consuming. Poor learner handwriting can slow down the correction process. Because a range of possible answers may be appropriate for many free-response questions, you sometimes have to make difficult decisions about when and when not to award credit for a given item. The possibility of multiple "right" answers also inclines some learners to complain when you judge their response inappropriate.

Another potential problem with scoring is that free-response items involve a number of different abilities such as writing, spelling, and handwriting. The tendency is to give more credit to those learners who have good writing or spelling skills. This is fine if your intended learning outcome refers to these skills. However, if you are interested in learners' thinking or problem-solving abilities, then your correction focus needs to remain on these abilities, not on writing and spelling.

Because scoring is somewhat subjective, your evaluation of individual responses can be influenced by such variables as (1) your mood or attitude when you score the answers, (2) your prior knowledge about individual learners' past levels of performance, and (3) the order in which you read the test papers. You need to make an effort to control the influence of these variables. For example, when possible, you might take time to read papers a second time and in a different order.

Another disadvantage of free-response items is that they sample a limited amount of material, which can lead to errors in judgment. For example, you might ask a question on a free-response test that happens to be one of the few things that the learner knows. You may mistakenly assume that this person has a good grasp of the entire range of content you have been treating based on his or her successful answer to the one question included on the test. Similarly, a single item might focus on one of the few areas you have covered that the learner does not know.

The problem of placing too much emphasis on a learner answer to one free-response question can be helped if you broaden the content sampled by providing a number of short-answer items. The downside of this approach is that you take away the opportunity to probe the depth of understanding that you can get by asking learners to provide extensive answers to just one or two questions.

Performance Assessment

Most traditional, paper-and-pencil types of measurements serve as surrogates or symbolic representations of learning. When you give a test, you do so based on a belief that the resulting score will tell you something about whether the learner has mastered the assessed content. This assumption may not always be true. For example, the test selected may not be based on an adequate sample of what the learner has learned. As a result, the score may be an invalid representation of mastery. In addition, successful learner performance on the test may not tell you very much about the ability a member of your class has to apply what has been learned outside of the artificial testing environment. In recent years, there has been a growing interest in assessing tasks in more-realistic and relevant ways. This type of assessment has been called **performance assessment,** authentic assessment, **direct assessment,** or **product assessment.**

You can use performance assessment to evaluate learner behaviors associated with such tasks as working with others, giving oral presentations, participating in discussions, playing a musical instrument, demonstrating physical education skills, conducting experiments, setting up equipment, and using computers.

Several factors should be considered when planning a performance-assessment approach. For example, you need to develop a sound understanding of the purpose of the assessment. Do you intend to capture a learner's "typical" performance, or are you more interested in the learner's "best" performance (Gallagher, 1998)? Assessing for different purposes requires different procedures. In addition to identifying purposes, you need to identify the outcomes that you wish to evaluate. This information will help you develop appropriate criteria for making valid judgments.

Developing the criteria for judging learner performance is an important step in your planning process. The criteria fulfill two key functions. First, they make public the guidelines you will follow in making judgments about individual learners. Second, they communicate your expectations to members of your class (Gallagher, 1998). Failure to develop clear criteria risks compromising the validity of your assessment. Criteria often are organized into *scoring rubrics.* These are sets of guidelines that provide clear definitions for kinds of performances and evidences required for specific ratings to be awarded. (For more information about scoring rubrics, review material in Chapter 2, "Becoming a Professional Educator.")

Checklists are also sometimes used to gather information related to learner performance. Completed checklists provide you with information about the presence or absence of targeted behaviors. You gather information by using a sheet with a list of focus behaviors and place a check mark by each one that occurs during the time you observe learners. **Rating scales** represent a somewhat more-sophisticated version of checklists. They enable you to make judgments about the quality of observed behaviors by using descriptors of rating points such as "unacceptable," "acceptable," "above average," and "greatly above average."

Learner Portfolios

A **learner portfolio** is a purposeful collection of products and performances that tells a story about a learner's effort, progress, or achievement. Learner-portfolio assessment is now a popular approach to evaluating learners' progress. If you want each member of your class to prepare a learner portfolio, you need to develop guidelines related to

- Categories of information to be included,
- Decision rules for selecting specific kinds items,

- Criteria for judging the material, and
- The learner's reflections on what he has experienced and learned. (Stiggins, 1997)

A learner portfolio may include results of performances on traditional selected-response and free-response tests as well as photos, sketches, visual displays, self-assessments, work samples, reflections on discussions, and other relevant materials. Ideally, each learner portfolio will provide as complete a picture or story as possible about the individual's development.

You can use learner portfolios to document growth of individuals over time. A sample of learner work products over a semester or a school year has the potential to provide much useful information to interested parties such as parents and guardians. Good learner portfolios yield a much more comprehensive picture of an individual's development than a report that focuses only on performance on traditional tests.

Because they can capture a rich array of material, learner portfolios can provide insight into areas that are normally overlooked, such as interests, abilities to persist when confronted with complex tasks, and self-concepts. In addition, you can involve members of your class directly in gathering information for their portfolios. This kind of activity helps them develop their organizational skills and encourages them to reflect on what they have learned.

There are good learner portfolios, and there are bad portfolios. Learner portfolios that have been put together in the absence of well-planned criteria may look nice, but the information they contain may be trivial, and inferences made on their contents are suspect. Some guidelines that can help you prepare high-quality learner portfolios follow:

- **Identify the purpose of the learner portfolio.** A portfolio is defined as a purposeful collection. It is not just a random storehouse. Keep in mind the

This learner discusses contents of his portfolio with his teacher. Teachers today often use learner portfolios as sources of evidence when they make judgments about the progress of individual members of their classes.

purposes you have in mind for your instruction. What is it that you are seeking to accomplish? Then consider the types of evidence you could use to reflect on the achievement of these important outcomes.

Next consider whether you want the portfolio to be a **working learner portfolio,** a **showcase learner portfolio,** or a **record-keeping learner portfolio** (Gallagher, 1998). A *working learner portfolio* includes items that show the individual's growth over time and reveals strengths as well as weaknesses. A *showcase learner portfolio* features only exhibits that reflect an individual's most notable accomplishments. A *record-keeping learner portfolio* is used to keep material that might be passed on to other teachers to help them understand the learner and design instruction to better meet the learner's needs.

- **Decide on the contents.** Because learner portfolios can contain a wide range of material, you need to exercise care to ensure that the portfolio's contents are useful. If this is not done, the end result may be examples that include much material that will be of little use when you attempt to evaluate learners' attainment of important outcomes. All items included in the learner portfolio should have a clear relationship to important outcomes. Stiggins (1997) suggests that the content should tell a story. A useful way to conceptualize a portfolio is to define a story line that you want to be able to follow. Guidelines can then be given to class members that will help them select representative material that best tells the story. It is important that enough items are included to enable you to make valid judgments.

- **Prepare cover sheets describing categories of individual items.** When students choose an item to include in their learner portfolios, they should be asked to assign the item to a particular category of information and to explain why they are including it. This helps evaluators and learners understand the importance and the meaning of the material. This is a useful step in making sure that learners reflect on their work and progress. If you provide students with cover sheets identifying categories of content to be included, they will have an easier time deciding what kinds of information to include and how to categorize individual materials.

- **Identify criteria to be used in scoring a learner portfolio.** Because so much material can be included in a portfolio and because items vary from portfolio to portfolio, evaluating a portfolio can be a challenge. To simplify this task and to avoid being influenced by extraneous variables such as attractiveness of presentation, you need to develop clear criteria to use as you review each portfolio. These criteria should be specific enough so that a group of individuals viewing a given learner portfolio will score it in the same way. As you consider scoring criteria, you should also think about how much weight you will give to specific entries. Some items will count more than others as you decide whether a learner has accomplished worthwhile learning outcomes. Deciding on how to weigh individual categories of information ahead of time will save you considerable frustration when it comes to actually reviewing learner portfolios and making decisions about the performances of members of your class.

In summary, portfolios can provide a rich array of information that will help you make sound judgments about individual learner performance. To be of use, they need to be carefully conceptualized and organized. If this is not the case, portfolios can become only a collection of items bearing little relationship to important learning outcomes.

Critical Incident

The "Evils" of Portfolio Assessment

"Estelle, I need help." As he spoke these words, Garth Peterson, a second-year U. S. history teacher at Edison High School, grabbed a stool and pulled it up to the desk where Estelle Garza, head of the social studies department, busily organized some papers. The digital clock that just this year had replaced the venerable Waltham read 9:45 P.M. The open house had just ended, and the last parent was leaving the building.

Ms. Garza tucked a final set of materials into a file folder and slowly looked over to Garth. "Another preconception out the window, Garth? An unhappy parent? Someone with a lurking suspicion that you're spending 'all your time' with the kids who 'aren't motivated' while denying your talents to their 'eminently qualified, dedicated, and hardworking' sons or daughters who are 'really going to amount to something?' So, what's up? I doubt you'll shock me."

"Estelle, it's about a parent, but the issue's not about my failure to give somebody a proper share of my time. It has to do with what I'm making the students do. To get to the point, Mrs. Hamlin, Stephanie's mom, is desperately anxious for Stephanie to get into an Ivy League school. She claims my evaluation procedures are insufficiently challenging and that I'm 'killing' Stephanie's chances to get the high SAT scores she'll need to impress the Ivy League admissions people."

Estelle gave Garth her noncommittal I'm-listening-and-keep-talking nod and said, "What's the nature of this precipitous fall from the heights of evaluative excellence we've all aspired to here at Edison? Come clean. What kinds of terrible things have you been up to?"

"Come on, Estelle, you know nobody's as concerned as I am that our people leave here with a solid grounding in history. The last thing I would do is back away from high academic standards. It's just that, what I see as a scheme to push the kids harder, Mrs. Hamlin sees as something fluffy, soft, and nonchallenging. It's depressing."

"Garth, *do* get to the point. Exactly what have you done?" Estelle looked wearily at her watch.

"I'm in trouble because of the 'p' word . . . *portfolios.* I'm having people in my class put a huge amount of effort into preparing portfolios. Incidentally these *do* include their grades on all the usual traditional kinds of tests. My people, including Stephanie, have done a great job putting materials together. They've written sophisticated reflections on what they have been doing and what they've learned. I think I'm pushing these students much harder than I did when my only evaluations were multiple-choice and essay tests."

"So what exactly is Mrs. Hamlin's worry?" asked Estelle, smiling and urging Garth to continue.

"I've had a hard time figuring that out. But sorting through everything she said, I think there are two or three things bothering her. First of all, she believes that taking traditional true–false, multiple-choice, and essay tests will be the best preparation for the SAT because those are the kinds of items Stephanie will encounter when she takes it. Her logic is that time spent doing the portfolios diverts Stephanie away from the task of developing good test-taking skills."

"OK, that's one concern. What else?"

"Here's another one," Garth replied. "Mrs. Hamlin worries about differences in portfolios prepared by individual students. She thinks this makes fair grading impossible because contents aren't the same. Stephanie has had good grades. These grades have come from her ability to score well on traditional tests. I think Mrs. Hamlin sees portfolio evaluation as a threat to Stephanie's final history grade . . . something that could lower her overall average and reduce the probability of her being admitted to a top university."

Estelle nodded. "Anything else?"

"One more thing. Mrs. Hamlin questions the value of having students spend time writing reflections on their own learning and including them in the portfolios. She says that high school students are too immature to engage in this kind of analysis. Again, I believe it comes back to her concern for SAT test scores. She's afraid that time spent on reflective writing takes time away from learning the 'facts' Stephanie should be working to master."

"Well, Garth," Estelle commented, "you seem to have a pretty good idea of what's bothering Mrs. Hamlin. What are you going to do now?"

• • •

Should Garth be worried about Mrs. Hamlin's comments? What do her concerns tell you about her values? What do we learn about those of Garth? Are differences in perspective between Garth and Mrs. Hamlin attributable to differences in their values? If you were faced with this situation, what would your next step be? Are there others who should be involved? If so, who are they, and what roles should they play?

To respond to this Critical Incident online, go to the Critical Incidents *module for this chapter of the Companion Website.*

Key Ideas in Summary

- Public concerns about the quality of the educational system establish a need for you to have a good understanding of assessment and assessment alternatives. A lack of knowledge about high-quality assessment procedures can lead you to collect flawed data and draw faulty conclusions about the performance of your learners. In addition, your teaching evaluations may be low if you fail to prepare your students for standardized tests.

- Assessment results provide information you can use to change your instructional practices in ways that lead to higher levels of learner motivation and achievement. You can make several important uses of assessment information. For example, you can use assessment results as the basis for adjusting instruction to learners' levels of readiness. You can also use this information as you plan an appropriate sequence of learning experiences for members of your class. As you teach, you can use periodic assessments as "reality checks" that will tell you if a lesson is appropriately designed or if you need to make some midcourse corrections. Finally, assessment results allow you to make summative evaluations at the conclusion of a block of instruction that will tell you what individual learners have taken away from their exposure to your instruction.

- *Assessment* refers to the broad process of collecting data from a variety of sources about what individuals have learned. *Measurement* refers to the process of quantifying the presence or absence of an attribute or quality. *Evaluation* is the process of making a judgment about what the data gathered through the various measurement and assessment processes means. *Grades* are communication devices you use to advise others of evaluation results.

- You typically will use one of two basic orientations as you make your evaluation decisions: (1) a *norm-referenced* approach or (2) a *criterion-referenced* approach. When you use a norm-referenced approach, you will compare the scores of individual learners against those of a group with similar characteristics. A criterion-referenced approach will enable you to compare scores of an individual learner against a standard or a set of criteria.

- Assessment activities comprise an integral part of your instructional responsibilities. You use *placement-assessment* information to help you determine an appropriate beginning point for instruction related to a new topic. For example, you may use a *pretest* as a means of determining learners' readiness for the new material. As instruction on a given topic goes forward, you will use *formative-assessment* techniques to periodically gather information that will tell you how well members of your class are learning the new material. You will use this information to modify your instructional program to accommodate class members' learning needs. You will use *summative assessments* to provide information about what knowledge and skills learners have acquired at the conclusion of a series of lessons or at the end of a school term.

- You need to make important decisions when you plan for assessment. Among other things, you need to (1) define your intended educational outcomes, (2) classify the educational outcomes you identify, and (3) develop criteria you will use as you make judgments related to the adequacy of learners' levels of achievement. Your plan should provide for adequate sampling of learner behavior or performance and include technically sound measurement tools that are appropriate for the outcomes being assessed. You also need to select fair and bias-free procedures.

- *Selected-response measures* are among the tools you may use to gather evaluation information about your learners. Measures of this type require your learners to choose answers from among several choices. Some examples are two-choice tests (for example, true–false tests), multiple-choice tests, and matching tests.

- *Free-response measures* require students to generate their own responses rather than to select answers from a list of provided alternatives. Some examples include essay tests, short-answer tests, and oral tests.

- *Performance assessments* require members of your class to demonstrate new learning in contexts that closely parallel real-world settings. This approach to assessment is known by varying labels, including *authentic assessment, direct assessment,* and *product assessment.* Sometimes you will use tools such as checklists and rating scales to gather information related to assessments of this type.

- You may be interested in having your learners organize information about what they have learned in the form of a *learner portfolio.* A learner portfolio is a purposeful collection of products and performances that includes information related to the learner's effort, progress, or achievement. You can use portfolios to document learning and growth of individuals over time.

Chapter 10 Self-Test

 To review terms and concepts in this chapter, go to the Companion Website and take the Chapter 10 Self-Test. Feedback for the self-test is immediate. You can keep track of your self-test scores yourself, or you can submit them to your instructor via e-mail.

Preparing for Praxis

To learn more about the Praxis test and complete this activity online, go to the Preparing for Praxis *module for this chapter of the Companion Website.*

You may be required to pass Educational Testing Service's Praxis II exam as you seek formal authorization to teach in the public schools. The *Principles of Learning and Teaching* component of Praxis II seeks to assess your knowledge about these topics: (1) Students as Learners, (2) Instruction and Assessment, (3) Communication Techniques, and (4) Profession and Community.

Information presented in this chapter may be especially relevant as you prepare for questions related to the category of Instruction and Assessment. Some content may also deal with issues having logical ties to other Praxis II categories. You may find it useful to prepare a chart similar to the one provided here. As you encounter information related to individual categories, you can enter it into the chart. A completed chart of this kind will be useful as you prepare to take the Praxis II exam.

Students as Learners	**Instruction and Assessment**
• Student Development and the Learning Process	• Instructional Strategies
• Students as Diverse Learners	• Planning Instruction
• Student Motivation and the Learning Environment	• Assessment Strategies
Communication Techniques	**Profession and Community**
• Basic, Effective, Verbal and Nonverbal Communication Techniques	• The Reflective Practitioner
• Effect of Cultural and Gender Differences on Communications in the Classroom	• The Larger Community
• Types of Questions That Can Stimulate Discussion in Different Ways for Particular Purposes	

For Your Initial-Development Portfolio

To complete this activity and activity and submit your response online, go to the For Your Initial-Development Portfolio *module for this chapter of the Companion Website.*

1. What materials and ideas that you learned in this chapter about *assessing learners* will you include as "evidence" in your portfolio? Select up to three separate items of information. Number them 1, 2, and 3.
2. Think about why you selected these materials. As you do so, consider these issues:
   - Specific uses you might make of this information as you plan, deliver, and assess the impact of your teaching
   - The compatibility of the information with your own priorities and values
   - Any contributions this information can make to your development as a teacher
   - Factors that led you to include this information, as opposed to some alternatives you considered but rejected

3. Place a check in the chart here to indicate the INTASC standard(s) to which each of your items of information relates. (You may wish to refer to Chapter 1 for more-detailed information about INTASC.)

INTASC Standard Number

ITEM OF EVIDENCE NUMBER	SI	S2	S3	S4	S5	S6	S7	S8	S9	S10
I										
2										
3										

4. Prepare a written reflection in which you analyze the decision-making process you followed. In your comments, mention the INTASC standard(s) to which your selected material relates.

Reflections

To respond to these questions online, go to the Reflections *module for this chapter of the* Companion Website.

1. Today, assessment results that focus on learners' academic achievement often are used to compare schools (and sometimes teachers) to determine their effectiveness. Some critics of this use of assessment data argue that using learners' scores to make comparisons between schools and teachers tends to drive teachers away from schools that most need their help. This result occurs because teachers naturally seek employment in schools where learners traditionally have done well on standardized tests. The net effect is to decrease the quality of educational services delivered to learners in schools where test scores traditionally have been low. What are your reactions to this argument? If you believe learner scores on achievement tests should not be used as a basis for making comparisons among schools and teachers, what approach should be used to make these judgments?

2. An editorialist in a local newspaper recently made these comments:

Despite additional money that has gone into the primary grades' reading program over the past five years, local pupils' scores continue to be unacceptably low. Fully 40% of our third graders scored below the national average. This simply is unacceptable. Community concern about reading was expressed to the school board five years ago when the issue of increased funding to improve reading instruction was debated. As a result, thousands of additional dollars were committed to fix the problem. The dismal test results are a painful disappointment given the actions, it had been hoped, this new money would support.

- Under what circumstances would it be appropriate to regard these tests results as "dismal"?
- Under what circumstances would it be appropriate to consider these tests as being "good" or even "excellent"?
- If you were to write a letter to the editor in response to these comments, what would you say?

3. *Placement assessment* involves steps designed to help you determine an appropriate beginning point for your instruction. You need to learn something about learners' prior levels of understanding and attitudes to get an appropriate answer to the where-do-I-start question. When you have worked for a time with a given class, your observation of individual learners and records of their past performance will be good sources of placement-assessment information. You face a somewhat different situation at the

beginning of the school year as you decide how to begin your initial lessons. What approaches might you take then to determine the appropriate instructional level?

4. The issue of grades and grading has long been a subject of debate within the education profession. Norm-referenced grading assumes that learners in your class have characteristics that are similar to the test group used to establish performance expectations. Criterion-referenced grading assumes that you have identified a preestablished standard of performance that has some grounding in reality. Grading based on individual improvement carries within it the possibility that you may give a high grade to a learner who has improved tremendously relative to where he or she began but who, even with this improvement, knows much less than others in your class. Preparing written comments about individual students instead of grades requires you to invest a huge block of time, particularly if you are

teaching in a middle school or high school where you may teach more than 100 students each day. Think about the subjects and learners you will be teaching. What approach to grading will you take, and why?

5. *Selected-response measures* allow you to assess a wide range of content on a single test. However, these assessment measures generally are not well suited to providing information about learners' abilities to engage in higher-level thinking. *Free-response measures* require learners to prepare fairly lengthy responses to individual questions. As a result, a single free-response test ordinarily cannot cover a wide range of content. On the other hand, tests of this type do allow you to engage learners' higher-level thinking skills. In preparing a large examination that might include a mixture of selected-response items and free-response items, how will you decide which elements of content will be assessed by each type?

Field Experiences, Projects, and Enrichment

1. Make a collection of newspaper and magazine articles that relate to assessment of learner achievement. What types of measures are mentioned? How are the results being used? Are there any criticisms of these procedures mentioned? If so, what are they, and who are the people who are making them? What consequences, if any, are reported for schools and teachers with learners whose scores are low?

2. Visit a local school. Identify the standardized tests that are used to measure learner achievement in the district. Interview teachers who must administer these tests. Ask them to describe strengths and weaknesses of these assessments. Gather information related to how these tests influence these teachers' instructional programs. Ask them whether they sense any pressure to improve learners' performances on these tests. If such pressure exists, does this represent a change from conditions in past years?

3. Identify some learning outcomes for a subject that interests you. Identify some examples of appropriate measurement tools for each of the outcomes. Describe your reasons for your selection of these approaches.

4. Gather some tests that either have been used or are suggested for use in the classroom (they may even be tests you have taken). Look at the included items. Do they provide an adequate sample of the content? Which outcomes are measured? Are the items clearly written? How might you improve these tests?

5. Enter the term *portfolio* into a search engine such as Google (http://www.google.com). Gather information about how portfolios for elementary, middle school, and senior high school learners are formatted. Prepare a report for your class in which you share some examples, paying particular attention to categories of information that are used and criteria that are employed to assess overall portfolio quality.

References

Armstrong, D. G. (2003). *Curriculum today*. Upper Saddle River, NJ: Merrill/Prentice Hall.

Berliner, D. C., & Biddle, B. J. (1995). *The manufactured crisis: Myth, fraud and the attack on America's public schools*. Reading, MA: Addison-Wesley.

Bloom, B. S., Englehart, M. D., Furst, E. J., Hill, W. H., & Krathwohl, D. R. (1956). *Taxonomy of educational objectives: Handbook 1, Cognitive domain*. New York: Mckay.

Ferguson, R. F. (1998). Can schools narrow the black–white test gap? In C. Jenks & M. Phillips (Eds.), *The black–white test core gap* (pp. 318–374). Washington, DC: Brookings Institution.

Gallagher, J. D. (1998). *Classroom assessment for teachers*. Upper Saddle River, NJ: Merrill.

Gronlund, N. E. (1998). *Assessment of student achievement* (6th ed.). Boston: Allyn & Bacon.

Krathwohl, D. R., Bloom, B. S., & Masia, B. B. (1964). *Taxonomy of educational objectives: Handbook II: Affective domain*. New York: Mckay.

Marzano, R. J. (2001). *Designing a new taxonomy of educational objectives*. Thousand Oaks, CA: Corwin Press.

Stiggins, R. J. (1997). *Student-centered classroom assessment* (2nd ed.). Upper Saddle River, NJ: Merrill.

Tanner, D. E. (2001). *Assessing academic achievement*. Boston: Allyn & Bacon.

Tomlinson, C. A. (2001). Grading for success. *Educational Leadership, 58*(6), 12–15.

Part 4

Shapers of Today's Educational World

CHAPTERS

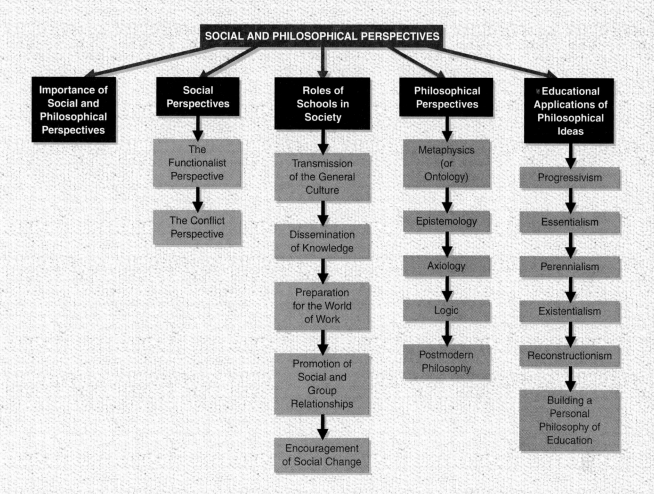

SOCIAL AND PHILOSOPHICAL PERSPECTIVES

Importance of Social and Philosophical Perspectives

Social Perspectives
- The Functionalist Perspective
- The Conflict Perspective

Roles of Schools in Society
- Transmission of the General Culture
- Dissemination of Knowledge
- Preparation for the World of Work
- Promotion of Social and Group Relationships
- Encouragement of Social Change

Philosophical Perspectives
- Metaphysics (or Ontology)
- Epistemology
- Axiology
- Logic
- Postmodern Philosophy

Educational Applications of Philosophical Ideas
- Progressivism
- Essentialism
- Perennialism
- Existentialism
- Reconstructionism
- Building a Personal Philosophy of Education

OBJECTIVES

This chapter will help you to

- identify the roles schools play as social institutions.
- differentiate between the *functionalist perspective* and the *conflict perspective.*
- explain how schools act to (1) transmit the general culture, (2) disseminate academic knowledge, (3) prepare learners for the world of work, (4) help learners to develop effective human-relationship skills, and (5) encourage social change.

- explain the general character of (1) *metaphysics,* or *ontology;* (2) *epistemology;* (3) *axiology;* (4) *logic;* and (5) *postmodern philosophy.*
- differentiate among educational applications of philosophical ideas, including (1) *progressivism,* (2) *essentialism,* (3) *perennialism,* (4) *existentialism,* and (5) *reconstructionism.*
- develop a personal philosophy of education.

IMPORTANCE OF SOCIAL AND PHILOSOPHICAL PERSPECTIVES

Education is one of the primary social institutions that, along with family, church, and government, exert major influences on society. It is an activity that is of interest to a broad spectrum of individuals. When you enter the education profession, one of the first things you will learn is that nearly everyone has an opinion about schools and teaching. You will make some decisions about what to teach, who to teach, and how to teach in response to complex and, sometimes, contradictory forces.

As a teacher, you need to understand the nature of the external pressures that seek to influence your decision making. In particular, you will find it useful to grasp the philosophical and social roots that underlie many proposals you encounter from individuals who push implementation of particular agendas that they think will "improve" the schools.

As you consider the sociological perspectives that underlie some school-improvement proposals, you need to answer questions such as these:

- What is the function of education in a pluralistic society?
- Whose interests are schools serving?
- Should schools focus primarily on helping learners adapt to the needs of society, or should they focus on helping them to improve and remake society?
- How do the schools interact with other social institutions?
- What roles do schools play in society?

As you consider the philosophical underpinnings of educational-reform suggestions, you will find it useful to answer questions such as the following:

- What is the nature of human beings? Are individuals inherently good or evil?
- What is truth and how is it determined?
- Does truth consist of a set of constant and unchanging principles?
- What is the nature of knowledge?
- What is worth knowing?
- What is right and what is wrong?
- What is the highest good?

SOCIAL PERSPECTIVES

The process of learning how to function in society is called **socialization.** Although parents and families are the primary socialization agents, schools also play an important part. You may have long understood that two primary roles of schools are to transmit societal expectations and to prepare citizens, but you may not have thought about *whose* culture schools should transmit. Different opinions regarding this issue generate heated debate.

Some people argue that the school's role is to transmit the dominant culture and to de-emphasize diversity. Proponents argue that everyone needs to learn a common heritage and adapt to the culture of the dominant group. Some partisans of this view adamantly oppose including multicultural perspectives in the curriculum. They see such content as interfering with the school's obligation to teach the dominant culture, provide learners with common values, and generate a kind of social glue that will hold our country together in future years.

Opponents argue that diversity enriches the school community and the curriculum. They contend that we live in a multicultural society and world. As a result, they believe that an understanding of diverse cultural perspectives is essential for young people who will live out their lives in a society and world that requires people from diverse cultural heritages

Teachers must work sensitively with learners from many cultural and ethnic groups.

to work together and get along. Supporters of cultural diversity also contend that there are sufficient commonalities among different cultures to accommodate the need to develop loyalties to the nation at the same time as diverse cultures are introduced to students.

Scholars who have studied how schools affect young people have worked from several perspectives. Two that you should know about are

- The **functionalist perspective** and
- The **conflict perspective.**

The Functionalist Perspective

Individuals who subscribe to the *functionalist perspective* see society as sharing a common set of values. Over time, these values have led to the development of institutions such as schools, families, governmental units, and religious bodies. Each of these institutions has a special responsibility or function. Functionalists believe these functions keep society going and promote **social cohesion.** Social cohesion is a sense of communal belonging and caring that binds together members of a society. Functionalists see existing arrangements that support this kind of social unity as appropriate and good. They believe that people share more common values than values that might lead to conflict and discord. Functionalists want the schools to preserve this harmonious social order and pass it on to future generations.

Families once took care of some functions that schools now discharge. An example is preparing young people for the world of work. Today, most work is performed away from the home. Skills employers need have become so specialized that parents are no longer able to train their children for their future vocational roles. Preparation for economic life has largely been turned over to specialists in the schools.

Talcott Parsons (1959), a leading American functionalist, saw the school as the social agency that had the basic responsibility for providing our society with trained workers. Functionalists assume that all learners have the ability to profit from the school's academic programs. They believe that individuals who later in life get the best jobs are learners who, by virtue of their individual abilities and effort, take full advantage of what the schools have to offer. There is an assumption that economic rewards are distributed on the basis of individual merit and that schools provide equal opportunities for all (Dougherty & Hammack, 1990).

Critics of this view argue against this meritocracy assumption. They point out that learners do not come to school and compete for jobs on a level playing field. Some of them come from affluent families in which education and specialized training are prized, encouragement and financial support are available for young people to pursue advanced levels of education, and abundant computer support, reading materials, and other learning resources are available at home. Other learners lack the advantages that enable affluent learners to take maximum advantage of opportunities that schools make available.

The Conflict Perspective

Supporters of the *conflict perspective* see schools as places where contending interest groups compete for educational advantages. They reject functionalism's premise that there is broad agreement about what the common values of our society are. They see society as a battleground where contesting groups strive for supremacy. Conflicts may be based on economic class or group status. Conflict "winners" succeed in having important educational resources dedicated to programs to serve their children.

Power and dominance are the key concepts of the conflict perspective. People who subscribe to this view contend that, in general, the schools have been structured to maintain the dominance of the groups who have the most power and who benefit most from the system. In assessing the potential worth of a proposed change, supporters of the conflict perspective look not for its potential to promote social cohesion but rather for information about which groups will gain power and benefits if the change is adopted.

Proponents of the conflict perspective fear that many school reforms represent self-serving efforts of powerful individuals and groups. For example, they sometimes oppose establishing accountability programs that reward schools that perform well on standardized tests. They take this position because many schools with learners who traditionally receive high scores on standardized tests are located in affluent neighborhoods. Conflict-perspective supporters see programs that provide additional funds to high-scoring schools as a ploy to direct more resources to schools serving advantaged young people and to decrease the financial support for schools serving needy learners living in less-affluent neighborhoods.

This group sometimes also questions proposals to establish new vocational courses in schools located in poorer neighborhoods. Adding such courses, they argue, signals an expectation that learners in these schools are destined for futures as workers rather than as highly educated managers and owners. What is going on, they argue, is an attempt of members of the managerial and ownership class to ensure a steady supply of workers whose aspirations do not require significant post–high school education or training.

• • •

People who subscribe to the functionalist and conflict perspectives look at efforts to change school programs in quite different ways. Functionalists see disagreements about present school programs as arguments within a basically harmonious family whose members are trying to define a common ground that all can support. Changes are adopted because they seem to have the potential to help the entire society. Functionalists ask two basic questions: (1) Is this change consistent with broadly held values? and (2) Is it designed to benefit all?

People who are committed to the conflict perspective look for potential winners and losers when they evaluate proposals to change school programs. They do not see discussions of change as part of an effort to achieve a societywide benefit. Instead, changes are viewed as a part of a recurring pattern of conflict between groups—a pattern that almost always results in individual decisions that benefit some groups more than others. A major objective of these proposals is to reveal the probable consequences of a proposed school policy or program change for members of individual groups.

WEB EXTENSION 11–1

International Studies in the Sociology of Education

Scholars in many countries focus on social and cultural influences on schools and schooling. The journal *International Studies in the Sociology of Education* is published in the United Kingdom. At this site, you will find articles written by scholars throughout the world that focus on topics related to social influences on education. You can read articles online.

http://www.triangle.co.uk/iss/

ROLES OF SCHOOLS IN SOCIETY

As important social institutions, schools play many roles, including the:

- Transmission of the general culture
- Dissemination of academic knowledge
- Preparation for the world of work
- Promotion of social and group relationships
- Encouragement of social change

Transmission of the General Culture

Schools transmit certain values, beliefs, and norms to learners. These perspectives have broad support in our society. But this does not mean that *all* individuals and groups in the community where you will teach subscribe to every value, belief, and norm that is explicitly or implicitly included in school programs. Disagreements about the extent of a school's responsibilities to shape learners' attitudes sometimes lead to acrimonious debates about the proper limits of educators' socialization responsibilities.

Part of the difficulty results because the school is only one of several influences on learners' values. Your learners' families also greatly influence their patterns of behavior and thinking. This is especially true of younger children, but families also continue to exercise some influence over older learners. Views of social organizations, churches, friends, and other groups also affect the perspectives of young people.

As an educator you will find yourself tugged between two competing realities. On the one hand, you will recognize a need to respond in different ways to learners coming to you from different family and cultural backgrounds. At the same time, you will sense some obligation to transmit certain common perspectives to all of your students. Seeking an

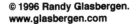

**"I'm lousy at spelling because of my older
relatives. They grew up listening to The
Beatles, Monkees, and Byrds!"**

appropriate balance between these two needs will be a professional challenge you will face throughout your career.

At times the socialization function of schools leads to concerns about schools infringing on the roles of other basic societal institutions. As a result, you can expect opposition from some parents and community members who believe that the school is improperly taking on responsibilities that other institutions should discharge.

The kinds of programs that sometimes prompt hostile parental reactions are those that relate to personal behavior, for example, sex education. Critics of instruction that deals with such personal issues often argue that this kind of teaching should be left to family members or to religious bodies.

Dissemination of Knowledge

When you start teaching, you will be obligated to transmit specialized knowledge, particularly academic knowledge, to learners. The quantity and sophistication of information needed by young people today goes beyond what most parents know. Experts in the schools are expected to draw on their specialized information and pass it along to students.

Time for teaching is limited. The quantity of available knowledge is vast. These two realities make it impossible for you to "teach everything." In practice, the adopted curriculum functions as a screen or filter that identifies the specific information you will be expected to teach. Because the curriculum is a general repository of what is presented to youngsters in schools, certain groups sometimes attack its contents because of their concerns about the adequacy or appropriateness of the included information. (For more information about the curriculum, review Chapter 7, "The Curriculum.")

Some ways of selecting and organizing content have persisted for so many years that you may find it difficult to imagine alternative ways to do them. For many years, the non-indigenous settlement and development of the United States has been described as a wave of migration from the Atlantic Coast to the Pacific Coast. Noting that Latinos have become our most numerous minority group, some parents and educators wonder about this traditional east-to-west presentation of U.S. history. They point out that this organizational scheme has made it difficult for writers of history texts to include much information about Latino contributions to the development of our country. This is true because the Latino population, generally, has occupied the country from south to north. Perhaps in the future more history curricula will present U.S. development from both perspectives.

Individuals looking at the role of schools in disseminating knowledge are also interested in other perspectives. They seek to identify characteristics of the *hidden curriculum,* which was discussed in Chapter 7. The hidden curriculum includes subtle messages sent to students as a result of how schools are organized and how learners are taught. Are they being socialized to accept authority? Are they taught to believe that certain occupations are more acceptable for males or females?

Another dimension of concern is what might be termed the **null curriculum.** The null curriculum includes "messages" that are communicated by what is not included in the curriculum. Are learners being socialized to think that the perspectives of some groups are unimportant because they are not included? Are they concluding that certain subjects and concepts are taboo because they are not discussed? Figure 11.1 examines this further.

WEB EXTENSION 11–2

Explicit, Implicit, and Null Curricula

At this site, you will find comments by educational theorist Elliot Eisner that will explain more about the null curriculum. Eisner argues that what educators leave out of the prescribed curriculum has a profound influence on what learners take away from their school experiences.

http://www.teachersmind.com/eisner.htm

Learners are taught many things in school that are not part of the official program of study. Much of what young people take away from their school experiences comes from their involvement in clubs, organizations, and other out-of-class activities.

Identify at least six things you "learned in school" outside of the formal curriculum that influenced your views of yourself, others, your role in society, gender roles, et cetera.

1. _____
2. _____
3. _____
4. _____
5. _____
6. _____

FIGURE 11.1   What Hidden Lessons Did You Learn in School?

Preparation for the World of Work

The economic existence of every society depends on the availability of people to perform necessary work. Individual jobs require different knowledge and skill levels. One of the school's functions is to prepare young people for the world of work. In a sense, the school functions as a sorting agency for future employers. As learners progress through their educational programs, they develop varying levels of expertise that help them qualify for some positions and eliminate them as serious contenders for positions that require different abilities and talents.

Some occupational roles carry with them more prestige and higher financial rewards than others. Most school programs that help young people prepare for these valued occupational roles are academically rigorous. For example, learners who want to pursue careers in engineering often enroll in challenging mathematics courses. In theory, the difficulty of some of these courses ensures that competent people will enter engineering curricula. It also means that the number of potential engineers will not be too large and that many individuals who are attracted to engineering early in their school years will switch to other career paths.

Controversy may accompany decisions you will make as a teacher when you advise individual learners to pursue courses of study that seem related to preparation for particular careers. For example, there may be suspicions that you are directing certain kinds of learners (perhaps those from economically impoverished households or from certain cultural and ethnic groups) away from courses of study needed by people interested in entering high-prestige occupations. You need to be careful that your recommendations about suggested courses or entire courses of study do not reflect unprofessional biases against certain categories of learners.

Promotion of Social and Group Relationships

Schools foster the development of learners' social and group skills. This occurs both by design and as a side effect of the special environment of the school setting. In schools, learners can acquire socially appropriate patterns of interpersonal relations. You will have learners from varied backgrounds in most of your classes. This mixture provides opportunities for your students to meet individuals who have backgrounds that differ from their own. Male and female relationships begin to flourish in schools as young people mature. Some school functions, such as dances, are designed to support socially acceptable ways of developing these friendships.

Having children from diverse backgrounds educated in the same schools enhances group relationships in society. A major issue over the past 50 years has been the promotion of diverse student populations. **School-busing policies** represent one approach to achieving within-building diversity. Busing seeks to achieve an appropriate mixture of learners in all schools by transporting learners from various groups to schools outside of their neighborhoods to achieve an appropriate racial, cultural, and ethnic mix in each building. Supporters of policies that seek to ensure diversity within individual schools argue that educating children of various socioeconomic and ethnic groups together promotes important social values such as tolerance and respect for diversity.

Opponents of diversity policies argue that efforts to achieve racial and ethnic mixes in individual buildings often take schools away from their primary responsibilities of transmitting important knowledge and skills to learners. These critics argue that parents and guardians of learners should have the right to select the schools their children attend based on the perceived excellence of their programs. They tend to support school-choice proposals, including charter-school and voucher plans that give parents and guardians considerable discretion in choosing schools. (For more information about voucher plans and charter schools, review the material in Chapter 3, "Challenges of School Reform.")

One function of the school is to help learners participate successfully as members of groups.

VIDEO VIEWPOINTS

The Power of the Neighborhood School?

WATCH: This *Nightline* video segment focuses on the issue of busing and neighborhood schools. The segment discusses the negative impact of busing in Delray Beach, Florida. For years, African American students from Delray Beach were *bused* to achieve racial balance. However, there was a high dropout rate for those who were bused and the parents did not feel like a part of the school community. With the assistance of a philanthropist, a new community school has been established that seems to be thriving. In a discussion of the school, Johnathon Kozol raises the issue of racial segregation and wonders if we are forgetting *Brown v. Board of Education*. He also contends improvement should be the responsibility of everyone and should not be left to the availability of philanthropic money.

THINK: Discuss with your classmates, or in your teaching journal, the following questions:
1. This segment illustrates a difficult choice between eliminating segregation in schools and facilitating academic achievement. How could both of these ends be achieved?
2. What do you see as the advantages of neighborhood schools?
3. What is the proper role of the state and of outside philanthropy in funding schools and bringing about change?

LINK: Should schools be a primary force in bringing about social change, or should schools basically be concerned with academic achievement?

 Complete this activity and submit your responses online in the Video Viewpoints module for this chapter of the Companion Website.

Encouragement of Social Change

Faith in "better education" as a curative agent is widespread. This view becomes especially popular at times when the public is concerned about serious social problems (Goslin, 1990). Few politicians miss opportunities to make clear their intentions to reduce the crime rate, defeat alcoholism, diminish the use of illegal drugs, or combat promiscuity and unwed motherhood through the institution of "sound educational programs."

The view that schools should function as powerful social-reform agents appeals to some educators. Others question this position. Critics point out that schools are part of the larger society that has produced the very problems they are charged with fixing. For this reason, they doubt that changes in school programs will do much unless there are also changes in our society as a whole.

Political leaders often attempt to place responsibility on schools for solving these social problems as the influences of other institutions such as churches and families diminish. Educators who believe that schools should solve social problems need to realize that there are some potential consequences. One is that time in school is a fixed quantity. Instructional time that must be committed to "solving" a particular problem means that time must be reduced elsewhere in the curriculum. What will be cut? In addition to issues related to time, school leaders who agree to modify the curriculum so that it better addresses a challenging problem may well be held accountable if and when educational efforts do not solve it.

Despite these drawbacks, the belief that education is a potent reform agent has wide support. Carefully designed programs can have positive results. For example, there is evidence that school programs that challenge learners to look seriously at problems that affect their own lives and actively connect with people trying to solve them increase their self-confidence (Boston, 1998/1999). Such programs also may lead young people to see a more-legitimate connection between what goes on in school and the "real world" where their parents and other adults live and work.

PHILOSOPHICAL PERSPECTIVES

Philosophical perspectives represent clusters of values and attitudes that individuals use to screen alternative action options and decide which ones to adopt. They influence educational decisions and practices. You may rarely have considered your own personal philosophy or how it affects your actions. Conscious thought about your beliefs can help you make more-purposeful and consistent decisions regarding what and how to teach.

What comes to your mind when you hear the term *philosophy*? You may get an image of an arcane subject that deals with issues far removed from the realm of the practical. Some of you may recall unpleasant experiences in undergraduate philosophy courses that required you to confront difficult abstractions. Frustrations in dealing with this kind of content may lurk behind some anxieties you may experience when, during a job interview, the representative of the school district asks, "What is your philosophy of education?"

Philosophy's reputation as a subject that is unconnected to the real world is undeserved. Your philosophical positions help explain your personal reactions to events you confront in your daily life. Philosophy explains your responses to such questions as

- Are people basically good or bad?
- What is right and what is wrong?
- How is truth determined?
- What is beauty?
- What is worth knowing?
- How should other people be treated?

Your living experiences have helped you to work out at least informal answers to these questions. In fact, your responses to many of them have become so automatic that you probably rarely think about them. Your reactions have become part of you because of your interactions with our society's customs and traditions. You assume that your patterns of behavior make sense and are natural responses to the world you live in. However, other people have different views and they also think their perspectives are the natural and logical ones. As you attempt to appreciate people's differing positions on educational issues, you need to know something about basic categories of philosophical questions. These categories are introduced in the sections that follow.

Metaphysics (or Ontology)

Metaphysics (sometimes known as **ontology**) focuses on the nature of reality. Metaphysics is defined as "realities lying beyond the physical or the material." It deals with questions that cannot be answered by reference to scientific investigation. Metaphysical questions are speculative. They focus on such issues as the nature of cause-and-effect relationships. Here are some examples:

- Do cause and effect exist in reality, or are they simply a creation of the mind?
- Is there a purpose to the universe, or is life basically meaningless?
- Are humans essentially spiritual beings, or are they creatures who exist in a particular time and space with no meaning beyond self?
- Is there a set of constant and unchanging principles that guides the operation of things and that, therefore, can be discovered?
- Is reality a constantly changing entity that is always relative, thus rendering any search for truth fruitless?

You may think that metaphysical questions are remote from the everyday world of the teacher, but they are not. Many serious debates and efforts to change the schools are based on alternative answers to these questions. For example, **theism** is a belief that one God created the universe. Meaning in life is found by serving this God and learning an established set of unchanging principles that God has provided to guide existence. Someone who accepts the premises of theism believes that the proper role of education is to help individuals in their search for their God and for these unchanging principles. In fact, some theists contend that there can be no real education that ignores their God. If such an education cannot be delivered in public schools, these theists argue that parents ought to be allowed to send their children to private schools where such content is a regular part of the program. Not surprisingly, there is widespread support for private schools and for school choice among theists.

There are others who are convinced that the primary purpose of education is to help learners achieve a well-adjusted or satisfying life. This implies that satisfaction or happiness is the answer to this important metaphysical question: What is the central purpose of life? People with this orientation contend that there is no subject matter worth knowing that is not of clear and pressing interest to the individual learner. They argue that schools should permit learners to determine what they will study and that, above all, schools should provide for learners' freedom and individual choice.

Many educational issues are divisive because people have arrived at different answers to basic metaphysical questions. If you are familiar with the nature of metaphysical questions—and more particularly with the reality that answers to such questions cannot be tested against scientific evidence—you will understand the assumptions supporting views about school practices that differ from your own. You will know when an argument is based on metaphysics (and cannot, therefore, be proved with scientific evidence) and when an argument is not based on metaphysics (and thus can be challenged or defended with this kind of information).

Epistemology

A second major category of philosophical theory is **epistemology.** Epistemological questions are concerned with the nature of knowledge. Because educators are interested in the discovery and transmission of knowledge, you should have a special interest in this category. Answers to epistemological questions provide a rationale for selecting material that is worth teaching and learning. They also suggest how information should be taught.

Two basic epistemological questions are

- What constitutes knowledge? and
- Is knowledge fixed or changing?

Some people maintain that there is no possibility of obtaining knowledge about ultimate reality. Others counter that it is possible to identify a set of principles that represents "true" knowledge. Still others argue that there are no principles that are true under all sets of conditions, but there is knowledge that is true in certain circumstances.

In the past, the dominant philosophical orientation to the mind and knowledge led most educators to help individuals acquire true knowledge of the world external to themselves (Soltis, 1981). However, the shift today is toward viewing knowledge as cultural and, therefore, as a human construction. This conception has important implications. It suggests that most knowledge is relative and that there are very few absolute truths.

If knowledge is a cultural construction, how do you judge which construction is correct? This concern leads to another fundamental epistemological question centering on ways of knowing and their reliability. How can you be sure that what you claim to know is true? Basically, the issue involves what you are willing to accept as a test of the truth of knowledge. Revelation, authority, intuition, the senses, reason, and experimentation represent some options that are open to you. Today, American culture has a bias favoring the position that knowledge comes from scientific experimentation. Indeed, among some people, this idea is so firmly rooted that they cannot imagine it being challenged. But even people who are extremely committed to scientific experimentations sometimes take actions based only on intuition. They do some things just because they "feel" they are right.

Many things you do as a teacher tie to your specific assumptions about how young people learn. Philosophical positions form the intellectual scaffolding for orientations to teaching and learning such as *constructivism*, which assumes that individual learners construct their own knowledge. Whether you embrace constructivism or any other orientation, you should consider what they presume about the nature of knowledge. For example, you might want to know that constructivism denies the existence of universal principles that all should know. (For more information about constructivism, review material in Chapter 1.)

How can you know what is right or appropriate for young people to learn? In thinking about this issue, you need to recognize that education has a responsibility not only to transmit knowledge, but also to help learners think about and critically test alternative knowledge claims. This implies that a central focus in education ought to be on critical and creative thinking.

This shift toward the view that knowledge is a cultural construction is reflected in many multicultural programs. James Banks (1994) includes knowledge construction as a key element in multicultural education. He states that it is important for all learners to understand that certain common experiences, perspectives, and values influence the knowledge construction of a given culture and that knowledge is dynamic and changing. He advocates making the classroom a forum for debates about different knowledge constructions.

People in many other cultures place a lower premium on scientific experimentation than we do. Because people in other parts of the world may have views about how knowledge is best acquired that differ from your own, you may sometimes find it difficult to understand the perspectives of members of other cultures. When your learners also lack such understandings, they may conclude that other cultures are strange or even funny. An important objective of the school program is to help them understand that they see the world through "cultural blinders" of their own. One of your tasks as a teacher is to help them recognize that there is nothing correct in any absolute sense in the way that they think knowledge is best acquired. Their opinions simply reflect how American culture has decided to view reality (Oliver & Gersham, 1989).

Content-of-the-curriculum arguments often are heated. These debates frequently stem from different philosophical views about the nature of knowledge, and they reflect diverse opinions about what should be central to the school instructional program. For example, some people believe the curriculum should feature the so-called classics of Western thought. Others favor a school program dedicated to developing learners' sophisticated thinking skills. Still others support school programs with heavy emphases on preparing learners for work.

When you teach, your approaches to introducing content will reveal many of your own answers to epistemological questions. For example, if you insist that learners master basic facts and principles, you will be operating on the assumption that there is such a thing as true knowledge. Some of your colleagues, on the other hand, may be more interested in teaching the processes of learning rather than specific content information. Their actions would signal their assumption that there are few, if any, ultimate truths learners need to master and that their time is best spent helping learners master problem-solving skills that can be applied to diverse situations.

Some school subjects feature instructional practices that derive from differing conclusions regarding the source of knowledge. For example, instruction in the humanities frequently assumes that knowledge results at least as much from intuition, feeling, and reason as from scientific experimentation. Critics who do not understand the appropriateness of an approach to truth through any process except scientific experimentation have sometimes labeled the humanities as **soft subjects;** that is, they are soft when compared with **hard subjects,** including sciences, that rely more heavily on scientific experimentation.

The labels "hard" and "soft" have nothing to do with the subjects' difficulty. Rather, they relate to the sources of knowledge deemed appropriate within each discipline. Debates over the worthiness of soft and hard subjects have important curricular implications. For example, people who believe that only scientifically verifiable knowledge is important tend to place a much heavier emphasis on the sciences than on the humanities. On the other hand, those advocating the cultural construction of knowledge point out that other modes of inquiry have a high status. For example, the methodologies used to assess the relative excellence of examples of art are very different from those used by the scientific community.

A comprehensive education includes learning experiences derived from different sources of knowledge and ways of knowing. As a teacher, you need to be open to helping young people view the world from different perspectives (Soltis, 1981).

Axiology

In the classroom, should you stress the acquisition of knowledge or the moral and character development of learners? Is there a particular standard of moral behavior that you should emphasize? Are there moral or ethical standards that you should follow? These questions relate to the area of **axiology.** Axiology focuses on questions about what "ought to be." The topics of morality, ethics, and aesthetics fall into this philosophical category. Some questions associated with axiology are

- How should life be lived?
- Does life have any meaning?
- What is the highest good?
- What is moral and immoral?
- What is beauty?

As a teacher, you should be interested in how your learners answer these questions. For example, the rate of suicide among young people suggests that many of them have concluded that life has no meaning (or at least not a meaning worth living for). In recent years, there have been a distressing number of incidents in which young people have taken others' lives with little apparent remorse. These events have led people to ask whether contemporary education has done an adequate job of addressing the basic questions of right and wrong that flow from axiology.

Drug problems in schools also tie to issues of the value and worth of life. Many people who use drugs are acting on the assumption that the highest good features seeking immediate pleasure and living for the moment. In traditional philosophy, such attitudes, collectively, are referred to as **hedonism.** Even though many learners would be unable to define this term, their actions suggest that hedonism is their basic philosophy of life.

Theists find life's purpose through religion. They believe there is an ultimate purpose to life and that every human being has a divine reason for being. In their view, the highest good is served when people strive to understand their God's will and meet God's expectations.

An important axiological question of a different kind concerns the nature of "right" conduct. How should a person behave? What is moral behavior? How does a person know when he or she is doing the right thing? In answering these questions, some argue that there are universal principles or guidelines that can be followed. For example, there are people who cite the Bible's Ten Commandments as an example of a universal guide to appropriate behavior. Others reject the idea that there are guidelines that fit every set of circumstances. They contend that appropriateness of behavior is situation-specific. An example of this point of view occurred during the late 1960s, when some people argued that the U.S. fight against Hitler during World War II was moral but that American participation in the Vietnam War was not.

Questions and issues related to axiology have important applications to education. For example, in recent years many politicians and others have promoted the goal of making American learners world leaders in math and science achievement. Is the competition between nations on standardized mathematics tests of such importance that significant resources should be devoted to achieve it? Why are science and mathematics specifically identified? Does this mean that they are the most important subjects? Should we not want to be first in the world in terms of an understanding of democratic processes or in treating all individuals humanely? Attention to these kinds of axiological questions can help clarify your thinking and assist you in making decisions about the purposes of education and the use of resources to support your priorities.

When you begin teaching, you will find yourself constantly confronted by axiological questions. Every decision about what to teach, how much time to spend on specific content, and how to teach reflects a value decision. Your views about the purposes of education or the highest good will affect your decisions. If you believe that the highest good is citizenship and the preservation of the state, then much of what you do will be directed toward helping learners become citizens. If you believe that the highest purpose is preparing individuals for a productive career, then much of your teaching will be slanted to providing vocational skills.

Another important application of axiology in the classroom will be reflected in the way you relate to learners. In establishing relationships with learners, you will find yourself guided by your sense of ethics. You may find yourself seeking answers to questions such as these:

- What is my moral responsibility toward those I teach?
- Should I ensure that all of my students have an opportunity for success, or should I devote most of my time to the academically talented, who are likely to benefit most from my efforts?
- Is my discipline plan fair and just, and does it communicate a sense of respect for the dignity of all humans?

When you were in school, you may have encountered teachers who viewed their work as nothing more than a job to be done as easily and quickly as possible. Such teachers probably had poorly developed senses of moral responsibility, and they may have had a marginal (or totally absent) commitment to a code of professional teaching ethics. You may also have had teachers who dealt with discipline problems in harsh and uncaring ways. Such insensitive treatment of young people is indicative of a more-general disrespect for the inherent dignity of human beings.

The content of the curriculum also relates to axiology. In the classroom, you will often be faced with the need to help learners make value choices. Many polls of public attitudes indicate that the public thinks that the teaching of values and morality is an important responsibility of education. Many Americans indicate a preference for more emphasis on these issues in schools. When it comes to values, educators face difficult questions. Consider your own answers to these examples:

- What values or virtues should be taught, and how should they be taught?
- If I choose to try to indoctrinate someone in a given value or virtue, what am I saying about the nature of values and morality?
- What statement am I making about what I value in terms of individual rights and freedoms?
- What does this indicate about my values and ethics as a teacher?

WEB EXTENSION 11-3

Philosophy of Education Society

This is the home page of the Philosophy of Education Society. You will find general information about the society and its publications, as well as links to other Internet sources of information about educational philosophy.

http://cuip.uchicago.edu/pes/

Logic

Logic, the science of exact thought, is a subfield of philosophy. Logic deals with the relationships among ideas and with the procedures used to differentiate between valid and fallacious thinking.

There are several reasons why you will find knowledge of logic useful. First, logic will help you communicate more effectively by encouraging a careful, systematic arrangement of your thoughts. Second, logic will assist you as you evaluate the consistency of learners' reasoning. Third, logic will contribute to your ability to assess the reliability of new information you encounter.

There are two basic types of logic: **deductive logic** and **inductive logic.** Deductive logic begins with a general conclusion and then elaborates on this conclusion by citing examples and particulars that logically flow from it. Inductive logic begins with particulars. Reasoning focuses on these particulars and then proceeds to a general conclusion that explains them.

The choice of a deductive or an inductive approach has implications for how you organize and present material. When you choose a deductive approach, you must take care to ensure that learners acquire a solid grasp of the major principle or idea before you move on to illustrate it through the use of examples. Teaching methods such as direct instruction, the use of advanced organizers, and the lecture method are basically deductive teaching approaches.

An inductive approach requires you to locate a large number of examples before instruction can begin. Further, you must select these examples with care. They must accurately represent the larger principle that you want learners to understand. Inquiry approaches and discovery learning are teaching strategies based on the inductive approach.

Postmodern Philosophy

Postmodern philosophy holds that people as individuals create knowledge in ways that free them from considering any boundaries, limits, or thought guidelines. The link between knowledge and "knower" is so tight that neither can be separated from the other. Postmodernists reject traditional philosophical questions and theories (Jacobsen, 1999). For example, they contend that metaphysical questions are meaningless and that there is no need for this category of philosophical inquiry. They also believe that epistemological questions regarding the nature of knowledge that are considered in isolation from the nature of learners are inappropriate. How people make sense of the world depends on the contexts within which they live their lives, including their social setting and their personal histories (Thayer-Bacon & Bacon, 1998).

A key principle associated with postmodern thought is that there is no one central scholarly tradition, such as the Western European one, that is "right." For postmodernists, reality shifts constantly and is very individual. As a result, postmodernism focuses on the self and on how people in a community or culture construct reality.

Postmodernism has implications for the curriculum. Postmodernists reject the idea that a fixed curriculum of "truth" should be transmitted to all. Instead, they believe the curriculum should vary according to the concerns and priorities of individual learners. Because of the huge variety of people and conditions today's learners will encounter during their lives, this perspective supports the expansion of the multicultural and multidimensional aspects of the curriculum. In particular, postmodernists argue that your learners' experiences in schools should not be drawn exclusively from the traditions of Western European culture. Your lessons should help them develop ways of questioning the motives of authorities to make sure that political agendas are not being pushed under the name of "truth." The understanding that knowledge is related to values and culture means that young people should encounter alternative interpretations of events and of reality.

Postmodernists question the heavy reliance American society has placed on science in the search for knowledge. They see stories, narratives, myths, and legends as legitimate knowledge sources. These information sources have resulted from dialogues among members of human communities. Postmodernists argue that learners need to join this dialogue and to encounter literature, music, art, and the humanities as they search for understanding and meaning in their own lives.

Not everyone subscribes to positions taken by the postmodernists. For example, in many places state-level authorities prescribe content of the curriculum, which is a trend more consistent with a "constituted-authority-knows-best" view than with postmodernism. However, even if you find yourself at odds with many positions of the postmodernists, their views may prompt you to question beliefs that underlie your own instructional approaches and the established curriculum.

EDUCATIONAL APPLICATIONS OF PHILOSOPHICAL IDEAS

Education-related systems of philosophy address basic philosophical questions and their applications to education. You will find that these systems can help you clarify your beliefs about what the goals of education ought to be, what individuals should be taught, and what methods should be used to teach them. They can also help you construct a personal philosophy.

No single system has been "proved" to be true. For one person, a given alternative may appear to be based on solid assumptions and sound arguments, whereas someone else may view it as weak and poorly reasoned. As you read about the systems, you need to consider the assumptions and arguments associated with each one and consider which ones you see as strong or weak. This exercise will be valuable as you consider educational programs and educational changes.

Progressivism

Progressivism, as applied to education, derives from the work of John Dewey (1902, 1910, 1916, 1938) and in the spirit of progress that characterized the close of the 19th century and the early years of the 20th century. Progressivism emphasizes change as the essence of reality. It views knowledge as something tentative that may explain present reality adequately but has no claim to being true forever. Progressives see a world that features continuously changing realities.

Progressives consider an educated person to be someone who has the insights needed to adapt to change. Dewey viewed scientific problem solving as the proper way to think and the scientific method as the most effective teaching approach (Gutek, 1997). Dewey opposed the pattern of formal education in his day that featured memorization of abstract information and ideas. He thought that this approach inappropriately separated schools from the realities of society (Gutek, 1997).

Dewey and the progressives emphasized that schools should teach learners how to solve problems and inquire about their natural and social environments. Laboratory or experimental methods were favored instructional approaches, and there was strong support for field trips to places around the community that would help young people relate learning to broad social, political, and economic issues (Gutek, 1997).

Progressives reject the idea that there are large numbers of unchanging truths that must be taught. For them, knowledge that is of value is knowledge that can help people think about and respond to problems associated with their need to adjust to change. Human beings are seen as basically good. Progressives believe that people who are free to choose generally will select a course of action that is best for them. Applied to schools, this perspective suggests that your learners should be given some choices regarding what and how they will study. Some principles of education that are consistent with progressivism include the following:

- Direct experience with the environment is the best stimulus for learning.
- Reliance on authoritarian textbooks and methods of teaching is inappropriate for the education of free people.
- Teachers should be instructional managers who establish the learning environment, ask stimulating questions, and guide learners' interests in productive directions.
- Individuals need to learn how to inquire about their environment.
- Schools should not be isolated from the social world outside of the school.

Dewey did not object to the introduction of new content to learners; however, he believed that the content should be presented so that learners' interests were stimulated through an interaction with the environment. He wanted subject matter to be organized in ways that would take advantage of learners' enthusiasms. By using learners' interests as

John Dewey, one of the giants of American educational thought, developed much of the intellectual foundation for progressivism.

a point of reference, Dewey believed that teachers could impart valuable problem-solving skills to members of their classes.

Some educators understood or adopted only parts of Dewey's philosophy. Extreme examples of these practices seriously distorted Dewey's views and led to educational practices of dubious significance. Some educators irresponsibly reduced Dewey's thinking to a simplistic, "the experience is the thing" slogan, which suggested that involving learners in enjoyable classroom activities was all right even in the absence of evidence that they were directed at promoting serious new learning. Irresponsible classroom practices stemming from an inaccurate understanding of Dewey's work contributed to the development of some suspicions about the entire approach of the progressives.

In addition to a concern about an overemphasis on "experience," some individuals objected to Dewey's work on the grounds that his ideas promoted dangerous "relativism." They believed that enduring bodies of knowledge and truth exist and that Dewey's ideas were contrary to Judeo-Christian beliefs (Gutek, 1997). These critics argued that certain truths and values are universally applicable and valid and that teachers should deliver this fixed body of content to learners.

Criticisms of progressivism, particularly since the end of World War II, have reduced the number of educators who actively support this perspective. However, even today many of the principles and approaches that educators take for granted have roots that trace to the philosophy of Dewey and the progressives. For example, the practice of requiring learners to solve problems and engage in experiments, as opposed to memorizing conclusions of others, clearly traces to the work of Dewey and his followers.

Essentialism

Essentialism, which owes much to the work of William C. Bagley (1941), began as a reaction against some of the more-extreme variants of progressivism. This philosophical system is based on several important propositions. First, the school program should not be diluted by trivial and nonessential courses. Second, many perspectives of the progressives threaten the academic rigor of American education. Third, schools should not lose sight of their fundamental purpose: the provision of sound practical and intellectual training.

Essentialists hold that a certain core of knowledge and skills should be taught to all learners. This common core includes content elements that are essential for preparing a person to function as a productive adult in society. For example, the basic subjects of reading, writing, and arithmetic should form the main body of content taught at the elementary level. At the secondary level, science, mathematics, English, and history should be among the core requirements. Essentialists perceive serious knowledge as residing primarily in the sciences and the technical fields. They favor vocational subjects because they meet the important criterion of practicality and usefulness.

Essentialists believe the arts and humanities are fine for personal pleasure, but they argue that content related to these subjects is not what learners need to prepare them for "useful" adulthood. Many essentialists view these subjects as frills and, when budgets are tight, suggest that they should be the first courses cut. Essentialists believe that the schools should not waste time dealing with topics that are of little practical utility.

Essentialists contend that the teacher's most important job is to impart information to learners. For their part, learners are expected to learn and retain this factual information. Teacher-centered techniques such as the lecture are favored, as are any new technologies that are thought to promote quick and efficient transmittal of new information.

Essentialists fear that individuals who are left to their own devices will not develop the habits and knowledge necessary for them to become good people. Therefore, the authority of the teacher, hard work, and discipline are important values. Because essentialists believe that character development is important and that teachers instruct by example, they are convinced that the character and habits of the teacher must be above reproach.

Essentialism reflects the hard-work and can-do spirit of Americans. The essentialist view traces to the earliest days of our country. Recall, for example, that Benjamin Franklin was interested in making the school a "more practical" place. Essentialism is a perspective that continues to exert great influence over practices in American schools.

Perennialism

Perennialism views truth as unchanging, or perennial. Perennialists such as Mortimer Adler (1982), Arthur Bestor (1955), and Robert Hutchins (1936) have argued that education should focus on the search for and dissemination of these unchanging principles. Although perennialists grant that changing times bring surface-level alterations to the problems people face, they believe that the real substance of life remains unaltered over time. Furthermore, they contend that the experiences of human beings through the centuries have established which truths are worth knowing.

Perennialists believe that Western society lost its way several centuries ago. They decry what they see as a trend to rely too much on experimental science and technology—a development they fear diverts learners' attention away from enduring truths. Perennialists argue that the growing status of scientific experimentation has led to a denial of the power and importance of human reason.

Perennialists favor schools that develop the intellect of all learners and prepare them for life. This preparation is best accomplished when individuals master the truths discovered through the centuries. Such wisdom is seen as important regardless of the career or vocation a person ultimately chooses to follow.

Because perennialists view knowledge as consisting of unified and unchanging principles, they condemn essentialists' emphasis on so-called "practical" information. The perennialist points out that what the essentialist considers "essential" is constantly changing. Therefore, a school program focused on the essentials runs the risk of teaching learners information that, in time, will have little relevance for their lives.

Perennialists are particularly vocal in their opposition to vocational training in the schools. They believe that vocational education represents a sellout of the educational purposes of the school to the narrow interests of business and government. This concern is directed not only at public schools, but also at colleges and universities.

Perennialists believe that higher education has entirely inappropriate emphases on developing learners' research skills and on preparing them for future careers. In their view, such courses interfere with a more-proper focus on a "genuine education" that emphasizes mastery of lasting truths. Many perennialists would like to ban research and practical training from colleges and universities and turn these responsibilities over to technical institutes.

Perennialists share with essentialists the idea that the primary goal of education is to develop the intellect. In the perennialists' view, however, learners should pursue truth for its own sake, not because it happens to be useful for some vocation. This pursuit of truth can best be accomplished through the study of the great literary works of civilization. Courses in the humanities and literature are particularly favored because they deal with universal issues and themes that are as contemporary today as when they were written.

WEB EXTENSION 11–4

Philosophy of Education from Wikipedia

At this site, you will find a general discussion of the historical roots of present-day education-related philosophies. You will find more details about information introduced in this chapter, as well as links to other philosophical orientations, including humanism and maturationism.

http://en.wikipedia.org/wiki/Philosophy_of_education

Existentialism

Existentialism, a philosophical position of relatively recent origin, is difficult to characterize in general terms. Many individuals associated with the existentialist position reject the view that existentialism is an all-embracing philosophical system with widely-agreed-upon tenets. However, one theme running through most descriptions of existentialism is that people come into this world facing only one ultimate constraint: the inevitability of their own death. In all other areas they should have freedom to make choices and identify their own reasons for existing. Existentialism suggests that people do not fit into any grand design of God or nature. There is no logic in the events of the world. People are born into a world devoid of any universal meanings. Each person has an individual responsibility to define truth, beauty, right, and wrong. Education should challenge people to create personal meanings of their own design (Morris, 1966).

Existentialism has influenced education less than the other basic philosophies. In part, this may be true because schools, as institutions designed to provide at least some common experiences to learners, promote goals that are inconsistent with the existentialists' commitment to personal freedom. Today's emphases on accountability and on measuring common educational outcomes across schools are contrary to the tenets of existentialism.

Though there are not many examples of schools that carefully follow existential principles, some do exist, including schools that follow the **Sudbury Model.** Sudbury-model schools place great emphasis on the value of personal freedom and give learners great responsibility for shaping their own learning experiences. These schools work hard to engender in learners a commitment to mutual trust, personal responsibility, and democratic decision making (Armstrong, 2003). The intent is to help young people explore the world and seek their own meaning and to avoid imposing on them the interpretations of others.

Reconstructionism

Reconstructionists, similar to perennialists, believe that society has lost its way. A classic work laying out this basic position is George Counts' 1932 book, *Dare the Schools Build a New Social Order?* Whereas perennialists seek answers from the past, reconstructionists propose to build a new kind of society. They believe that schools should serve as an important catalyst in the effort to improve the human condition through reform. For reconstructionists, education should lead people to view all elements of society critically. Graduates should be people who are in control of their own destinies and capable of promoting social reform.

Reconstructionists favor curricula that emphasize creating a world of economic abundance, equality, fairness, and democratic decision making. They see this social reconstruction as necessary for the survival of humankind. The school program should teach learners to analyze all aspects of life and to question rather than accept the pronouncements of those who hold political power. The reconstructionist curriculum draws heavily on insights from the behavioral sciences, which reconstructionists believe can be used as the basis for creating a society in which individuals can attain their fullest potentials.

Reconstructionists want teachers to see their roles as raisers of issues and guiders of learners to relevant resources, not as transmitters of knowledge. Young people should be actively engaged in the learning process. Ideally, the classroom should reflect the values of equality and social justice.

Building a Personal Philosophy of Education

When you are interviewed for a teaching position, you may be asked "What is your educational philosophy?" Why do you think interviewers so often ask this question, and why is it important ?

Before you respond, take some time to consider the purposes of books like this text and of the professors who assign them. You might conclude that authors and professors seek to provide you with a knowledge base you can apply when you begin to teach. However, what you take away from your encounters with your texts and your professors depends on your **personal filter.** An individual's personal filter screens and influences information in ways that are consistent with prior learning, attitudes, and values. These prior experiences affect how you react to, interpret, and assimilate new information.

Your personal filter is an expression of your philosophy of education. It exercises a profound influence on your judgments and attitudes. It is for this reason that many employers ask What is your philosophy of education? They want to know how your beliefs correspond with the goals and purposes of the school district and the community.

Your culture, your socioeconomic background, and your experiences in school are factors that influence your personal philosophy. You might not have reflected consciously on many of your fundamental convictions. Take time to do so. This philosophic self-understanding will contribute to your development as a teacher.

As you think about your own philosophy, review the questions raised in this chapter. Reexamine the different philosophical systems. Identify those positions and ideas that you think are strong or reasonable and those you think are weak and not so reasonable. How sound are your arguments for the positions with which you agree? What merit can you find in those positions with which you disagree? What points do they make that you consider valid? You may find that there is no one system that you agree with totally and that each system has elements that make sense to you. If so, you have what is termed an **eclectic philosophy,** one that includes elements of different philosophical systems.

Once you have identified the basic elements of your personal philosophy, think about their implications. What does your philosophy mean in terms of the content that you consider important? How will it affect how you treat learners? How does it relate to the methods that you will use with your students?

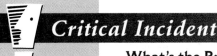

Critical Incident

What's the Problem?

Roberto Lopez teaches sixth grade in an inner-city school. He believes that young people need to be actively involved in their own education and that they are most interested in learning when they have a voice in deciding what to study. Roberto's instructional program is built around his students' questions and interests. He helps members of his class identify important problems that people face in the real world. Then he helps them learn what they need to know to understand the problems and to think about possible solutions. Often his lessons integrate content from many subject areas.

This afternoon, the school principal, Ms. Fifer, observed Roberto's teaching. After the observation, she and Roberto had a conference that left him upset and confused.

Ms. Fifer told Roberto that although she is impressed with the rapport he has with the students and the ease with which he relates to them, she is concerned about what he is teaching. She believes Roberto is straying too far from the prescribed curriculum. Ms. Fifer pointed out that the adopted curriculum includes key knowledge that the students need to master. She explained that if students fail to learn this information, they will not do well on the state tests. Low student scores will lead to serious problems. Some parents will be angry, the school board will be upset, and the published ratings of the school will suffer.

Ms. Fifer also said Roberto's sixth graders are too uninformed to deal meaningfully with the problems he is asking them to consider. She suggested that the student discussions she heard largely represented a sharing of ignorance and opinions with too few facts to support their ideas. To be able to handle this sort of activity, the students must first acquire a firm understanding of basic information. She added that lessons based on the adopted textbook will give learners information they can use to discuss issues in a more-responsible way. At the end of the conference, the principal summarized her feelings by telling Roberto that his actions are denying students access to the textbook-based knowledge they need to discuss issues based on fact and to score well on mandated standardized tests.

Roberto left the meeting very confused. He had believed that he was doing an excellent job. Now, he has been told that he is being irresponsible and is on the verge of harming his students. Roberto finds this hard to accept. He has seen the enthusiasm of the students, and he believes that one of the most important goals of education is to help individuals learn how to make our society better. He is not sure what he should do next.

• • •

What do you see as the source of the problem between Roberto and Ms. Fifer? What philosophical orientation does Roberto appear to have? What philosophical orientation does Ms. Fifer have? What do you see as the strong points in both of their arguments? What are their basic differences in fundamental values? What do you think ought to be done now? What does this situation suggest to you as you begin to think about seeking a teaching position?

 To respond to this Critical Incident online, go to the Critical Incidents *module for this chapter of the Companion Website.*

Key Ideas in Summary

- External pressures of various kinds influence decisions that affect our educational system. Differing sociological and philosophical perspectives account for some variance in views regarding the nature of good and effective schools.

- Supporters of the *functionalist perspective* see society as sharing a common set of values. These values have led to the establishment of institutions such as families, schools, and religious bodies. The best school programs are those that act to maintain these institutions in ways that preserve present social arrangements because they well serve the interests of all.

- Supporters of the *conflict perspective* view education through the lenses of power and dominance. They see two groups: winners and losers. They view reform proposals as struggles between groups for power and dominance. They see educational change not as a compromise between well-meaning groups but rather as a power struggle.

- As social institutions, schools play many roles. Among them are their roles as (1) transmitters of general culture, (2) disseminators of academic knowledge, (3) developers of individuals for the world of work, (4) promoters of social and group relationships, and (5) encouragers of social change.

- Many of the debates and disagreements about schools and the direction they should take are disagreements in philosophy. *Philosophical perspectives* represent clusters of values and attitudes that individuals use to assess varying action options and decide which ones to adopt. As a teacher, conscious thought about your own philosophical perspectives can help you make more-focused and consistent decisions regarding what and how to teach.

- Important categories of ideas that are addressed in philosophical systems are *metaphysics, epistemology, axiology,* and *logic.* Metaphysics focuses on the nature of reality. Epistemology concerns the nature of knowledge. Axiology deals with issues of values and ethics. Logic addresses the relationships among ideas and what differentiates valid from fallacious thinking.

- *Postmodern philosophy* holds that people as individuals create knowledge in ways that free them from considering any boundaries, limits, or thought guidelines. Postmodernists reject traditional philosophical questions and issues, such as those associated with metaphysics. They believe that the link between knowledge and "knower" is so tight that neither can be separated from the other.

- *Education-related systems of philosophy* address basic philosophical questions and their applications to education. *Progressivism* holds that schools should give students tools they need to cope successfully with ever-changing realities. Supporters of *essentialism* want schools to provide sound practical and intellectual training that is not diluted by courses that will not prepare young people for citizenship responsibilities and the world of work. Advocates of *perennialism* believe there are certain unchanging truths and these truths should be the focus of the school program. Supporters of *existentialism* believe that, in the end, learners face the ultimate constraint of their own death and that in response to this situation they should be free to make choices that help them identify their own reasons for living. *Reconstructionism* takes the position that society today is unjust and inhumane and school programs should help students appreciate the need for social reform.

- When you interview for a teaching position, you may be asked to describe your personal philosophy of education. Interviewers know that teachers' philosophies vary and that different philosophical perspectives lead them to make different decisions. Taking time to identify elements of your own philosophy will help you better articulate your educational priorities and understand your rationale for making decisions.

Chapter 11 Self-Test

To review terms and concepts in this chapter, go to the Companion Website and take the Chapter 11 Self-Test. Feedback for the self-test is immediate. You can keep track of your self-test scores, or you can submit them to your instructor via e-mail.

Preparing for Praxis

To learn more about the Praxis test and complete this activity online, go to the Preparing for Praxis *module for this chapter of the Companion Website.*

You may be required to pass Educational Testing Service's Praxis II exam as you seek formal authorization to teach in the public schools. The *Principles of Learning and Teaching* component of Praxis II seeks to assess your knowledge about these topics: (1) Students as Learners, (2) Instruction and Assessment, (3) Communication Techniques, and (4) Profession and Community.

Material in this chapter may be especially relevant as you prepare for questions related to the category of Profession and Community. Some content may also provide you with information related to other Praxis II categories. You may find it useful to prepare a chart similar to the one found here. As you encounter information related to individual categories, you can enter it into the chart. You will find a completed chart of this kind helpful as you prepare to take the Praxis II exam.

Students as Learners	Instruction and Assessment
• Student Development and the Learning Process	• Instructional Strategies
• Students as Diverse Learners	• Planning Instruction
• Student Motivation and the Learning Environment	• Assessment Strategies
Communication Techniques	**Profession and Community**
• Basic, Effective, Verbal and Nonverbal Communication Techniques	• The Reflective Practitioner
• Effect of Cultural and Gender Differences on Communications in the Classroom	• The Larger Community
• Types of Questions That Can Stimulate Discussion in Different Ways for Particular Purposes	

For Your Initial-Development Portfolio

To complete this activity and submit your response online, go to the For Your Initial-Development Portfolio *module for this chapter of the Companion Website.*

1. What materials and ideas in this chapter about social and philosophical perspectives will you include as "evidence" in your portfolio? Select up to three separate items of information. Number them 1, 2, and 3.
2. Think about why you selected these materials. As you do so, consider these issues:
   - Specific uses you might make of this information as you plan, deliver, and assess the impact of your teaching
   - The compatibility of the information with your own priorities and values
   - Any contributions this information can make to your development as a teacher
   - Factors that led you to include this information, as opposed to some alternatives you considered but rejected

3. Place a check in the chart here to indicate to which INTASC standard(s) each of your items of information relate.

INTASC Standard Number

ITEM OF EVIDENCE NUMBER	S1	S2	S3	S4	S5	S6	S7	S8	S9	S10
1										
2										
3										

4. Prepare a written reflection in which you analyze the decision-making process you followed. In your comments, mention the INTASC standard(s) to which your selected material relates.

Reflections

 To respond to these questions online, go to the Reflections *module for this chapter of the Companion Website.*

1. Think through your own views regarding school reforms. Are change ideas you favor more associated with the functionalist position or with the conflict position? Or, do you find some of your positions associated with functionalism and others with the conflict point of view? How were your opinions formed? Did they result from personal experiences you had when you were an elementary, middle school, or high school student, or did they result from other causes?

2. In this chapter you learned that roles of schools include (1) transmitting the general culture, (2) disseminating academic knowledge, (3) preparing young people for the world of work, (4) promoting social and group relationships, and (5) encouraging social change. Suppose you were asked to order these functions in terms of their importance. What would your ranking be, and how would you defend it?

3. Many multicultural programs seek to help learners understand that experiences people have within a given culture prompt them to construct their stores of knowledge. Supporters of these programs sometimes argue that exposing learners to alternative ways that people in varying cultures construct

knowledge makes them more accepting of people who differ from themselves. Some critics argue that these programs divert students away from the perspectives of their own culture and that, as a result, they learn imperfectly the values and priorities needed to function successfully in their own society. Think about these differing views. How do you react to each, and why?

4. In this chapter, you learned about several education-related systems of philosophy, including progressivism, essentialism, perennialism, existentialism, and reconstructionism. If you surveyed programs and practices in today's schools, you probably would find more schools basing their actions on ideas associated with essentialism than on progressivism, perennialism, existentialism, or reconstructionism. Why do you suppose this pattern prevails? Is this is a situation you favor, or would you prefer more emphasis on one of the other systems of philosophy?

5. As you begin thinking about your own educational philosophy, what kinds of information will you consider? How will you use material introduced in this chapter to help you articulate your philosophy? Specifically, what points will you make if an interviewer asks you to explain your philosophy of education and to provide examples of how it might guide decisions you would make in the classroom?

Field Experiences, Projects, and Enrichment

1. Choose and research a school-improvement idea, for example, vouchers. (For more information about vouchers, see Chapter 3, "Challenges of School Reform.") Use the functionalist and

conflict perspectives to evaluate the proposal. Will it benefit all? Is it designed to help students assume their role in society? Does it benefit certain groups? Who will gain power and who will lose power?

2. Organize a classroom debate on this topic: "Resolved That Advanced Placement Courses Irresponsibly Direct Scarce Tax Dollars to Benefit Categories of Students Who Do Not Need This Kind of Special Help." Assign one small group of people to argue the pro case and another small group to argue the con case. Conduct research on such issues as the costs of these programs and the nature of students who take and benefit from them. When both teams are prepared, conduct the debate in your class, and engage other class members in a debriefing discussion.

3. Interview some teachers and administrators about conflicts or protests they get from parents and others regarding the school curriculum, school responsibilities, and the conflict of school with other societal institutions. How do these differences reflect varied conceptions of (1) roles

of the school that should be regarded as having a high priority and (2) educational philosophies? Share your findings with others in your class.

4. Review state and local school policies and curriculum. You may find it useful to look at any statewide curriculum standards that exist in your state. Most state departments of education make this material available on their Web sites. Your instructor may direct you toward other sources. Examine the guidelines to identify elements of philosophical positions in each. Do not be surprised if you find that multiple positions are represented in various places throughout these materials. Which ones seem to predominate? Why do you think this pattern has emerged?

5. Reflect on some components you think will be part of your evolving personal philosophy of education. What do your positions suggest about characteristics of schools and classrooms that you will find attractive as workplaces? In light of this information, what are some questions about individual schools that you might ask when interviewing for a teaching position?

References

Adler, M. (1982). *The Paideia proposal*. New York: Macmillan.

Armstrong, D. G. (2003). *Curriculum today*. Upper Saddle River, NJ: Merrill/Prentice Hall.

Bagley, W. (1941). The case for essentialism in education. *National Education Association Journal, 30*(7), 202–220.

Banks, J. (1994). *Multiethnic education* (3rd ed.). Boston: Allyn & Bacon.

Bestor, A. (1955). *The restoration of learning*. New York: Knopf.

Boston, B. O. (1998/1999). If the water is nasty, fix it. *Educational Technology, 56*(4), 66–69.

Counts, G. (1932). *Dare the schools build a new social order?* New York: John Day.

Dewey, J. (1902). *The child and the curriculum*. Chicago: University of Chicago Press.

Dewey, J. (1910). *How we think*. Boston: D. C. Heath.

Dewey, J. (1916). *Democracy and education*. New York: Macmillan.

Dewey, J. (1938). *Experience and education*. New York: Macmillan.

Dougherty, K. J., & Hammack, F. M. (1990). *Education and society: A reader*. San Diego, CA: Harcourt Brace Jovanovich.

Goslin, D. A. (1990). The functions of the school in modern society. In K. J. Dougherty & F. M. Hammack (Eds.),

Education and society: A reader (pp. 29–38). San Diego, CA: Harcourt Brace Jovanovich.

Gutek, G. L. (1997). *Historical and philosophical foundations of education: A biographical introduction*, (2nd ed.) Upper Saddle River, NJ: Merrill/Prentice Hall.

Hutchins, R. (1936). *The higher learning in America*. New Haven: Yale University Press.

Jacobsen, D. A. (1999). *Philosophy in classroom teaching: Bridging the gap*. Upper Saddle River, NJ: Merrill/Prentice Hall.

Morris, V. (1966). *Existentialism in education*. New York: Harper and Row.

Oliver, D., & Gersham, K. (1989). *Education, modernity, and fractured meaning*. Albany: State University of New York Press.

Parsons, T. (1959). School class as a social system: Some of its functions in American society. *Harvard Educational Review, 49*, 297–318.

Soltis, J. (1981). Education and the concept of knowledge. In J. Soltis (Ed.), *Philosophy and education: Eightieth yearbook of the National Society for the Study of Education*. Chicago: University of Chicago Press.

Thayer-Bacon, B. J., and Bacon, C. S. (1998). *Philosophy applied to education: Nurturing a democratic community in the classroom*. Upper Saddle River, NJ: Merrill/Prentice Hall.

12 *Historical Influences*

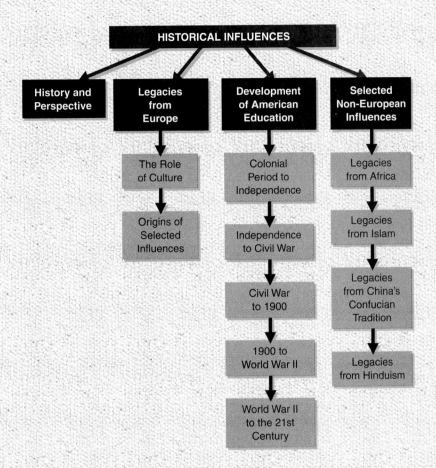

OBJECTIVES

This chapter will help you to

- recognize that historians' perspectives affect written history.
- explain why some critics argue that American education has not always developed in ways that have advantaged *all* learners.
- cite examples of practices in today's schools derived from European precedents.

- identify patterns of American education as they developed in the colonial period and years of the early republic.
- summarize key 19th-century developments that helped shape today's American education.
- describe important developments in the evolution of 20th-century American education.
- explain that personal histories of learners coming from certain cultural traditions can affect their attitudes toward school.

HISTORY AND PERSPECTIVE

When you read historical accounts, you get more than a simple recitation of past events. The material also embeds the historian's beliefs, biases, and values. For example, if you read many accounts of the development of American education, you will recognize that writers have followed a tradition of presuming that today's educational system, although not perfect, is better than it has ever been. This assumption underlies historical writing that often portrays ". . . past developments in education, especially public education, as continuous progress, beneficial to all" (Gordon & Szreter, 1989, p. 8).

When you encounter this idea, you are getting a perspective that reflects many of the biases of the majority of Americans, who are white and of European descent. People with this point of view accept both the general "goodness" of the basic organization of education in this country and the legitimacy of the majority political power that has developed and maintained many long-standing school practices.

Few deny that our schools derive many practices from Europe. There is more debate today about how well these traditional models have served *all* learners. In particular, you will find that contemporary historical scholarship increasingly questions whether schools have adequately responded to the special needs of young people from ethnic and cultural minorities.

You will find analysis of this issue to be tricky. It is not that American educators for many years have failed to embrace the idea of serving all children. Rather, it is a question of how much their practices have benefited young people from different groups. In general, school practices have provided more benefits to learners when they have been consistent with the priorities and values learners bring with them from home. Children from the majority white culture often have found the school world to be a logical extension of the values and perspectives prized in their own families. On the other hand, young people from ethnic and cultural minorities have sometimes found a jarring discontinuity between the expectations of their parents and families and the expectations of the school.

Even though you will find schools today more sensitive to this problem than they have been in the past, many learners from ethnic and cultural minorities still do not do as well in school as their white-majority classmates. Increasingly, educators are coming to understand that "no child should have to go through the painful dilemma of choosing between family and school and of what inevitably becomes a choice between belonging and succeeding" (Nieto, 1992, p. xxv). For example, efforts are under way to examine curricular materials to weed out negative stereotypes that can undermine the sense of self-worth for learners from certain groups. Think about how Native American youngsters must have felt not many years ago when the only textbook references to them mentioned "savages" who were introduced as obstacles to European development and progress.

Educational historians point out that sensitivity to ethnic and cultural differences is new. Throughout the 19th century and well into the 20th, individuals responsible for schools and school programs largely supported the idea that the majority-white European-based culture was the "true" American culture; it was the task of all learners to conform to its perspectives. "Good" schools were not designed to respond to cultural differences. They were supposed to root them out and turn children from minority groups into "real" Americans (Coleman, 1993). As an example of this point of view, consider this statement from the 1888 annual report for a special residential school for Native Americans in which the school's superintendent lamented the negative influences on the school's children when, occasionally, they had to be allowed to go home to visit their families:

"Children leaving even the best training schools for their homes, like the swine, return to their wallowing filth and barbarism." (Commissioner of Indian Affairs, 1888)

As you might imagine, when such attitudes prevailed, there was little support for the idea that school programs should be responsive to learners' ethnic and cultural differences. Schools *could* have modified some practices to accommodate cultural and ethnic differences years ago. For example, public schools could have adapted some existing educational models that were well suited to serving children from Native American groups. There were also educational legacies from Africa, Asia, and the Hispanic world that might have been considered. Such models *were* known. Regrettably, for decades educational leaders considered them irrelevant. As a result, for many years American education developed under the assumption that "proper" and "correct" education derived from European practices (Reagan, 2000).

The sections of this chapter that follow are not intended to suggest that modeling American education on European practices was the only course that could have been taken or even that it was the most appropriate. The reality simply is that the structure of today's educational enterprise finds its roots in traditions from Europe. Material focusing on European antecedents of prevailing American school practices is designed to familiarize you with an educational history that for many years failed to recognize the legitimacy of the perspectives of non-European groups.

As you may know, school populations today are more ethnically and culturally diverse than they have ever been (Armstrong, 2003). As a result, educators are working hard to develop school programs that are responsive to the needs of all. These reforms are being inserted into an American school system that historically did not hold responding to cultural diversity as a high priority. You can better understand challenges that accompany these change efforts if you are familiar with the historical developments that have shaped the American system.

LEGACIES FROM EUROPE

Some things you encounter in life are so common that you may find it hard to imagine a world in which they were absent. For example, do you ever really think about why a red light at an intersection tells you to stop or why a green light gives you permission to proceed? Why red, and why green? There is no reason that blue and brown could not have been the colors used to control the flow of traffic. Only long-standing tradition reinforces the nearly universal acceptance of red and green as stop and go signals.

The Role of Culture

Culture shapes our assumptions about the realities that guide our lives. Some of the things you do would appear strangely bizarre to individuals brought up in other traditions. People most frequently appreciate this point when they find themselves cut off temporarily from their own cultural group and surrounded by people who have different assumptions about how life should be lived.

Not many years ago, one of the authors found himself alone in a small community on the east coast of Korea. He witnessed women carefully examining live snakes in cages before purchasing one or two to take home to prepare for the evening meal. Next to the live-snake store there was a shop selling decorative lacquerware. In the center of the room, a large roasted pig rested atop a table. The pig's mouth was propped open to accommodate a large quantity of paper currency that had been stuffed between its teeth. To American eyes, housewives calmly purchasing live snakes for supper and a knickknack shop featuring a roasted pig with a mouthful of money might seem unusual. To the residents of this small village, these events were just unremarkable features of their everyday lives.

Many school practices are so familiar that you may find it hard to imagine different ways of doing things. Many of your assumptions about schools and schooling reflect long-standing cultural choices. For example, chances are you've never worried excessively about any of the following characteristics of American education:

- The idea that content should be organized under major categories or headings
- The idea that knowledge should be divided among individual subjects
- The idea that teaching should occur in a setting that brings young people together in groups for instructional purposes
- The idea that schools should be organized into a sequence of grades
- The idea that as many people as possible should be educated
- The idea that teachers should consider individual differences when planning instruction
- The idea that schools should help learners develop rational thinking processes
- The idea that teachers should have some kind of specialized training
- The idea that schooling should be a preparation for responsible citizenship
- The idea that schooling should provide young people with some understandings and skills needed in the adult workplace

Where did these ideas come from? For the most part, they evolved over the centuries from educational practices in Europe. The thinkers of ancient Greece, for example, developed the idea that knowledge could be organized into categories and that logical, rational thinking processes were important. The emphasis on education for citizenship likewise has roots in the concern of the ancient Athenians about producing adult citizens who could participate in democratic decision making.

Origins of Selected Influences

The ancient Romans wanted young people to receive a practical education that would provide them with "useful" knowledge. This perspective is one that many present-day Americans share. The Romans, too, argued about whether students should be harshly punished or whether gentler, more-sensitive approaches made better sense.

The Middle Ages witnessed the development of important work that divided knowledge into individual subject areas. The tradition of churches taking responsibility for secular education also traces to this period. American parochial schools continue this legacy.

Today's concern for universal education is a continuation of a trend that became pronounced during the Reformation. At this time, many church leaders believed that the Bible was the repository of all wisdom; hence, it was desirable for all to learn to read so they might have access to its truths. Later, during the Renaissance, a growing emphasis on the worth and the importance of the individual evolved. Our schools' concern for meeting individual differences developed from this perspective.

WEB EXTENSION 12–1

What Every Schoolboy Knows

At this site you will find topics dealing with education in Elizabethan England. There is information about differences in education for girls and boys and for children from different classes in English society. There is an interesting description of subjects a son of a noble might have been taught during each hour of the instructional day.

http://renaissance.dm.net/compendium/54.html

VIDEO VIEWPOINTS

Revisiting History

WATCH: This *Nightline* segment concerns the creation-evolution debate. The specific focus is on the decision of the Kansas Board of Education to drop teaching of evolution and allow the inclusion of "intelligent design" as an alternative theory. The tape includes numerous individuals speaking for and against the measure and highlights the issue of whether or not this is appropriate because it is merely another scientific theory or if it is inappropriate because it is a religious belief.

THINK: Discuss with your classmates, or in your teaching journal, the following questions:
1. Is this really an issue of separation of church and state or about alternative scientific theories?
2. Do you think it is important to separate education and religion? Why?
3. What does the history of education reveal to us about the separation of church and state?

LINK: What are the implications of this issue for the development of curriculum?

Complete this activity and submit your responses online in the Video Viewpoints module for this chapter of the Companion Website.

In the early 17th century, the work of **Francis Bacon** (1561–1626) helped to establish the idea that truth could be challenged and modified through observation and careful weighing of evidence. This provided the foundation for the modern scientific method, something that continues to be enormously important in today's schools. Another person who had a great influence on the development of education in Europe and, later, the United States, was **John Amos Comenius** (1592–1670). Comenius promoted the ideas of organizing learning into sequential, graded schools and of viewing education as something that should prepare people for happy lives.

The famous 18th-century educator **Johann Heinrich Pestalozzi** (1746–1827) suggested that education should take place in a caring atmosphere and should function as an agent to improve society. The view that education could promote social improvement was considered radical in Pestalozzi's time; today it has become an article of faith among many Americans. No matter what intractable social problem is garnering headlines at a given moment, one predictable response to the problem is that more education is needed. Pestalozzi would have agreed. Pestalozzi also introduced the idea that teachers should be provided with special training.

During the 19th century, a wave of interest in many aspects of education swept across Europe. One result was that, by the end of the century, mandatory public schooling had been adopted as public policy throughout much of the continent. **Friedrich Froebel** (1782–1852), who is regarded as the "father of the kindergarten," worked hard to convince people that they should support efforts to provide young children with well-planned educational experiences. The 19th-century educator **Johann Friedrich Herbart** (1776–1841) developed a standardized format for lesson planning. Lesson plans you will use probably will include many features initially introduced in Herbart's design. The 19th century also witnessed a tremendous growth of interest in the importance of the psychology of learning.

As you read the section that follows, bear in mind that European settlers of North America brought many European educational perspectives with them. Because the population of today's schools is becoming more culturally diverse, you will find that many people are debating the appropriateness of some of these Europe-based models. Should there

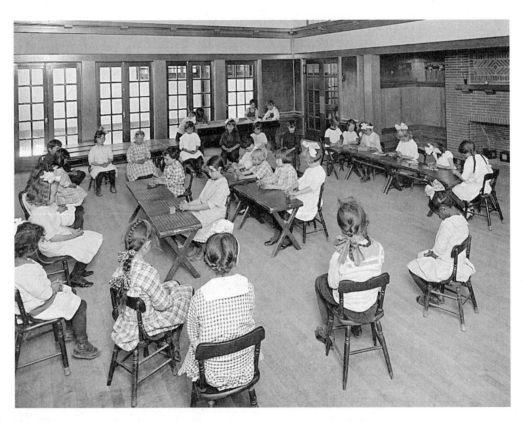

Friedrich Froebel is remembered as the "father of the kindergarten." This early kindergarten is an example of many that were established as a result of his work.

be changes in our schools to better meet the needs of more-diverse learners? Or can most existing practices be modified? These are questions that will confront you as you begin your professional career.

DEVELOPMENT OF AMERICAN EDUCATION

If you review American educational history, you will discover that, at different times, people have had a range of expectations regarding what schools should emphasize. Varying expectations have led to divergent views regarding the characteristics of a good school. Educational policymakers have responded in different ways to these key questions:

- What is the most important purpose of education?
- Who is to be educated?
- What are learners expected to take away from their educational experiences?
- How are learners to be educated?

An understanding of how responses to these questions have changed over time will help you better understand conflicting views represented in today's debates about educational policies and practices.

Colonial Period to Independence

The New England Colonies. Some familiarity with conditions in 16th- and 17th-century England will help you understand the nature of American education as it developed in New England during the colonial period. In England during this period, there was little room for open discussion of alternatives to the established church, the Church of England. Because it was the official church of the English government, governmental officials considered people who espoused religious views in opposition to those of the Church of England to be disloyal not only to the church, but also to the state. In effect, the Church of England was seen as the religious arm of the government. Religious dissenters received harsh treatment. Governmental officials saw such people as potential threats to the power of the crown.

Political problems in England for groups such as the Puritans, who wanted to reform the policies of the Church of England, led them to consider moving to the New World. They also feared remaining in England and exposing their children to what they considered to be the religious errors of the Church of England. The Puritans who settled in New England sought to establish a church and government different from those they had left behind. Their belief that their own church and government were more consistent with the Bible's teachings had important educational implications.

The Puritans saw the Bible as the source of all wisdom. As a result, they placed a high priority on developing an educational system that would enable large numbers of people to read "God's Holy Word." The Bible, as the Puritans interpreted it, outlined a specific type of preferred government for both church and state. This contrasted importantly with practices in England, where authority in the Church of England was highly centralized and few decisions were left to the discretion of members of individual churches. The Puritans determined that local church congregations should exercise both moral and political power. Their churches in Massachusetts reflected this pattern. These beliefs also helped establish the view that **local control** should be the principle followed in determining which authorities should control civil and religious affairs. The view that education should be locally controlled evolved out of this historical tradition.

Concern for education in Massachusetts was demonstrated in the **Massachusetts School Law of 1642.** This law charged local magistrates with the responsibility of ensuring that parents would not neglect the education of their children. Although the law itself did not provide for the establishment of schools, it did require that children attend schools. The law represented the first attempt in America to make school attendance compulsory. Reflecting the local-control tradition, this law placed responsibility for enforcement at the local, rather than the state, level.

The famous **"Old Deluder Satan Act" of 1647** extended educational requirements of the Massachusetts School Law of 1642. The name by which the law is popularly known derives from wording in the act that promoted education as a buffer against Satan's wiles. The law required every town of 50 or more families to hire a teacher of reading or writing. The teacher was to be paid by either the community or parents of the learners. This act represented an early legislative attempt to establish the principle of public responsibility for education.

During the 17th century, concern for publicly supported education referred only to the very basic education of young children; few learners attended secondary schools. However, small numbers of secondary schools did come into being during this time. One of the most famous was the **Boston Latin Grammar School,** founded in 1635. This school had a specific purpose: preparation of boys for Harvard. The curriculum consisted of difficult academic subjects, including Latin, Greek, and theology.

The Middle Colonies.   Most Puritan settlers of New England came from an area in eastern England known as East Anglia, where opposition to the Church of England was strongest. Many of these Puritan settlers came to the New World from 1629 to 1641 (Fischer, 1989). People who settled the middle colonies of New York, New Jersey, Delaware, and Pennsylvania, however, came from different parts of England than the Puritans, and they were a more-diverse group. These immigrants came mostly from the northern Midlands of England and Wales. Some of these settlers were descendants of the Dutch and Swedes who originally occupied parts of New York. Many English Quakers came to the New World between 1675 and 1725, and a majority of them settled in Pennsylvania. People originally from the north of England, Scotland, and Ireland settled western and frontier areas of the middle colonies during a period extending approximately from 1717 to 1775 (Fischer).

Not surprisingly, given the mixed origins of the population, patterns of schooling in the middle colonies were varied. For example, merchants in New York sponsored private schools that emphasized commercial subjects thought necessary for young people who would pursue business and trade. In contrast, the Pennsylvania Quakers maintained schools that were open to all children. These Quaker schools were notable for their willingness to recognize the educational needs and rights of African Americans, Native Americans, and other groups who usually were not encouraged (and often not allowed) to go to school.

Benjamin Franklin was among the first to give American education a practical orientation. In his 1749 work ***Proposals Relating to the Youth of Pennsylvania,*** Franklin proposed a new kind of school, oriented to the "real" world, that would be free of all religious ties. Two years later, he established the **Franklin Academy,** an institution that was nonsectarian and offered such practical subjects as mathematics, astronomy, navigation, and bookkeeping. By the end of the Revolutionary War, the Franklin Academy had replaced the Boston Latin Grammar School as the most important secondary school in America. Students at the Franklin Academy had the right to make some choices about their courses of study, thus setting the pattern of elective courses common in high schools today.

For all its strengths, relatively few learners attended the Franklin Academy. It was a private school, and tuition was beyond the means of most families. However, the establishment of the Franklin Academy directed a great deal of attention to the importance of secondary education. This interest was reflected in the subsequent establishment of many other private **academies.**

The private academies popularized the idea that secondary education had something important to offer, and they laid the foundation for public support of secondary schools. Collectively, the academies helped establish the following important precedents for American education:

- American education would have a strong orientation toward the practical rather than the purely intellectual or theoretical.
- American education would be nonsectarian.
- American education would feature diverse course offerings.

The Southern Colonies.   A revolution in England in the late 1640s resulted in victory for the side supporting Parliament and the Puritans against the king and the established Church of England. King Charles I was executed. For a dozen years England existed as a Puritan-controlled commonwealth, governed for much of this time by Oliver Cromwell as Lord Protector. This was an especially dangerous period for large landowners, members of the nobility, and others who had supported King Charles and wanted the monarchy restored (something that was finally achieved in 1660, when Charles II assumed the throne).

Because of dangers in England, many supporters of the king's cause migrated to the New World, often settling in the southern colonies of Maryland, Virginia, North Carolina, South Carolina, and Georgia. Large numbers of these settlers came from the southwestern part of England, an area different from both the East Anglican homeland of the Puritans and the northern Midland, northern English, Scottish, and Irish homelands of most of those who settled the middle colonies (Fischer, 1989).

Settlements in the southern colonies were distributed along rivers. There were few towns, and most families were separated by considerable distances. Under these conditions, it was difficult to gather sufficient numbers of children in one place to establish schools. Wealthy families hired tutors for their children. People in these colonies continued to identify strongly with upper-class English values. Many sent their sons to England to be educated in English schools. Education in these colonies was generally restricted to children of wealthy landowners; little schooling was available for children from less-affluent families.

WEB EXTENSION 12–2

Colonial Period

At this site you will find numerous links to topics associated with education during colonial times, including Puritan theology and its influences on education, hornbooks, the dame school, the *New England Primer*, the role of apprenticeship in education, the Latin Grammar School, and educational practices in the three major groupings of colonies (New England, middle, and southern). Included also, are photographs and other visual depictions of selected items of interest.

http://www.nd.edu/%7Erbarger/www7/colonial.html

Independence to the Civil War

For the first years of the United States' existence as an independent country, few educational innovations were introduced. The nation faced challenges such as defending its independent status from outside threats, settling the nation, and providing workers for growing industries. There was more interest in getting young people into the workforce than in providing them with extensive education. Schooling beyond rudimentary elementary instruction was generally available only to children of families who were able to pay for this privilege and who did not need the income that a young person could generate. Proposals for an educational system that was universal and free were just beginning to be discussed.

Developments in Secondary Education.   In the early 19th century, only a few students attended secondary schools. The most popular secondary school continued to be the academy, which responded well to an American educational bias in favor of preparing learners for practical problem solving and work rather than for a life of scholarship. Many new academies were established during the first half of the century. By 1850, when the number of academies reached its peak, over 6,000 were in operation (Barry, 1961).

Although the academies had good reputations, they had an important drawback. Overwhelmingly, they were private tuition-charging institutions. This limited their enrollment because only young people from relatively well off families could attend. Gradually, people became convinced that larger numbers of young people than were being accommodated by the private academies could profit from secondary-level education. This recognition led to support for a new institution: the public high school.

The first public high school, the **Boston English Classical School,** was established in 1821. The school's courses closely paralleled the practical curriculum of most academies. The idea of public high schools did not catch on quickly, however. In 1860, there were only 40 public high schools in the entire country (Barry, 1961), but by 1900 they outnumbered the academies.

The Work of Horace Mann.   During the 1820s, a leading figure in the development of American education, **Horace Mann** (1796–1859), began to make his views known. Mann, elected to the Massachusetts legislature in 1827, was an eloquent speaker who took up the cause of the **common school,** one for the average American. Mann's mission was to convince taxpayers that it was in their own interest to support the establishment of a system of public education. He pointed out that public schools would graduate students whose skills would ultimately improve living standards for all. In Mann's view, the school was a springboard for opportunity. It was an institution capable of equalizing differences among people from different social classes.

Mann's arguments were persuasive. In 1837, Massachusetts established a State Board of Education. Horace Mann gave up his career in politics to become its first secretary. In time, Mann's views attracted the attention of people throughout the entire country.

In addition to his interest in encouraging people to support public schools, Mann also recognized the importance of improving teachers' qualifications. In response to this concern, the nation's first **normal school** (an institution specifically designed to prepare people for careers as teachers) was established in 1839. In the beginning, normal schools provided only one or two years of formal education. Their importance is the precedent they set for formalizing the education of future teachers.

*Horace Mann helped convince American taxpayers
that it was in their best interests to support public schools.*

Prompted by Mann's work, public schools began to be established throughout the country. By 1860, 50.6% of the nation's children were enrolled in public school programs (U.S. Department of Commerce, 1975). A majority of states had formalized the development of free school systems, including elementary schools, secondary schools, and public universities. In 1867, a National Department of Education was established as part of the federal government. By the late 1860s, many of the basic patterns of American education were in place. That these patterns continue is a tribute to the vision, patience, and political skills of Horace Mann.

Civil War to 1900

The post–Civil War years witnessed unparalleled industrial growth. Technological innovations reduced the need for unskilled labor. The resulting demand for workers with knowledge needed in the workplace intensified interest in vocational education.

Huge numbers of immigrants entered the United States during this period. These people required both useful work skills and an orientation to the values of their new country. These needs placed new demands on educators, and there was a great increase in the number of schools. The schools were eager to "Americanize" newcomers, and many immigrant learners were exposed to school programs that made light of their native cultures and languages. There can be no doubt that American public schools exacted a psychological toll on many immigrant children.

To finance public schools, the famous **Kalamazoo case** (*Stuart v. School District No. 1 of the Village of Kalamazoo,* 1874) ruled that the state legislature had the right to pass laws levying taxes for the support of *both* elementary and secondary schools. This ruling established a legal precedent for public funding of secondary schools. As a result, secondary school enrollments increased as school districts began building many more high schools. Because of a widespread desire to provide older learners with "useful" educational experiences, many secondary schools broadened their curricula to include more practical, work-related subjects.

Organizational activity among teachers increased during this period. Prior to 1900, organizations that were the forerunners of today's American Federation of Teachers and National Education Association were established (see Chapter 2 for more information about these groups). Reports of such groups as the NEA's Committee of Ten (1892) and the Committee on College Entrance Requirements (1900) began to influence public school curricula. In the last decade of the 19th century, these groups acknowledged that schools should provide some services to learners with varied academic and career goals. However, they continued to assert that the primary purpose of high schools was to prepare students for college and university study. This orientation represented a temporary reversal of a century-long trend to view secondary education as a provider of more-practical kinds of learning experiences.

1900 to World War II

Toward the end of the 19th century, educators recognized that many learners who were entering high schools were having difficulty doing the required work. As numbers of high school students increased, this problem stimulated much discussion about what might be done to ease learners' transitions from elementary schools to high schools. A new kind of institution, the **junior high school**, was proposed as a solution.

Interiors of many schools in the late 19th century were very plain. Note the total absence of decoration in this classroom.

The first junior high school was established in Berkeley, California, in 1909. The Berkeley school district developed a 6–3–3 plan of school organization that, in time, came to be widely copied elsewhere (Popper, 1967). The first six grades comprised the elementary program, the next three grades the junior high school program, and the final three years the senior high school program.

The number of public schools and of learners attending them increased tremendously during the first four decades of the 20th century. Schooling became almost universal during this period. In 1900, only 50.5% of young people ages to 20 were in school, but by 1940, 74.8% of this age group were enrolled (U.S. Department of Commerce, 1975). Given the tremendous growth in the total U.S. population between 1900 and 1940, these figures indicate that millions more children were served by schools in 1940 than in 1900. Teacher-preparation requirements also were evolving across the country. See Figure 12.1 for more information.

Contributions of John Dewey.   An individual who had a tremendous influence on education during this period was **John Dewey** (1859–1952). Dewey viewed education as a process through which young people are brought to fully participate in society. He saw its primary goal to be the promotion of individual growth and development. Hence, schools should not set out to serve the goals of society (e.g., turning out electrical engineers if the society is short of them) at the cost of overlooking the unique needs of individual learners. Schools, Dewey contended, should produce secure human beings who are committed to their own continuing self-education.

Horace Mann was a strong believer in normal schools, institutions specifically designed to prepare teachers. The first normal school was established in 1839. Even though many people supported the logic of providing special training for teachers and certifying them before they were allowed to work, these innovations were slow to be adopted. Stringent certification requirements did not become universal until the 1930s and 1940s.

All states had normal schools by 1900, but few required teachers to be graduates of these institutions. The state with the strictest regulations regarding teachers' entry into the profession was Massachusetts, which required them to have a high school diploma and two years of formal teacher training. Every other state had less-stringent requirements.

As late as 1921, only four states required prospective teachers to have completed formal training programs. Fourteen states allowed people to earn a teaching credential with no more training than four years of high school, and some required only an eighth-grade education. Also in 1921, thirteen states had *no* official academic requirements for awarding a teaching credential (Bowen, 1981).

FIGURE 12.1   Certifying Teachers: An Innovation That Was Slow to Take Root

Dewey believed that every learner actively attempts to explore and understand the environment. Because of this drive, learners need to be provided with intellectual tools they can use to make sound judgments when they encounter novel situations. For this reason, Dewey argued that it was more important for young people to master systematic thinking processes than to learn specific items of information. Thinking processes can be applied universally, but specific information often has little value beyond the context in which it is learned.

Dewey was especially concerned that learners master the **scientific problem-solving** method. This systematic approach features (1) identifying of a problem, (2) gathering of information relevant to its solution, (3) developing of a tentative solution, and (4) testing of the solution in light of additional evidence. Dewey believed that young people who become familiar with this method of dealing with novel situations gain confidence in their abilities to develop good responses to dilemmas they will face throughout their lives. Dewey's work continues to influence educational thought and practice. Interest in teaching problem-solving techniques and a commitment to responding to individual differences still feature prominently in American schools today.

The Testing Movement.   Present-day schools also continue to be influenced by an early 20th-century testing movement that was developed in France. Education in France became compulsory in 1904. At that time, a special commission was established there to identify young people who might benefit from regular instruction in public schools and those who would be better off in special classes. In 1905, to help with this identification, Alfred Binet and his associates developed a test, called the **intelligence quotient (IQ) test,** that was designed to predict learners' likelihood of success in regular-school classrooms. Soon educators from other countries, including the United States, were seeking information about ways to measure intelligence. You may find it interesting that a test designed to predict school success was viewed almost immediately as a test of intelligence. The presumption was that the school program had been designed so that the most intelligent would do the best. (Today, this idea is debated. Some people, for example, argue that the "most intelligent" learners resist school rules and procedures and do not do well.)

The testing movement in the United States grew during World War I. The military needed a way to identify individuals well suited to a variety of necessary tasks. Intelligence tests were prepared to provide information that could be used to classify individuals by intelligence. At the time these tests were developed, few people doubted that the scores represented highly reliable measures of intelligence.

Some of the first intelligence tests were given to European immigrants. Immigrants from Western Europe did better than immigrants from Eastern Europe. (This was hardly a surprising development because most tests were developed by western Europeans or Americans trained by western Europeans.) There is some evidence that laws passed by Congress restricting the numbers of immigrants from Eastern Europe resulted from dissemination of these score differences. This might be one of the first examples of a **cultural bias** that can be embedded within tests of this sort. A test with a cultural bias is one that includes features that make it more likely for people from certain cultural groups to receive higher scores than people from other cultural groups.

During and after World War I, many educators embraced the testing movement. Educators began to counsel learners and direct them to individual courses on the basis of their IQ scores. There is evidence that some teachers' patterns of interaction with learners were affected by their perception of these learners' intelligence as defined by IQ scores.

In recent years, the use of intelligence tests, particularly paper-and-pencil group intelligence tests has been challenged. African Americans, Latinos, and other minorities have objected to the cultural biases that are embedded in certain intelligence tests. Other critics have argued that a factor as broad and diffuse as intelligence cannot possibly be measured by a single test. The debate about intelligence testing continues. Although there is not a consensus on this issue, it is fair to say that educators increasingly hesitate to predict the educational futures of young people on the basis of a single measure such as an IQ score.

The Cardinal Principles.   As special circumstances and needs associated with the war expanded interest in the testing movement during World War I, people also became concerned about education's more-general purposes. In particular, the last year of war, 1918, was a landmark one for education. In this year, the National Education Association's Commission on the Reorganization of Secondary Education identified seven specific goals. These seven goals came to be known as secondary education's **Cardinal Principles:**

- Health
- Command of fundamental processes
- Worthy home membership
- Vocational preparation
- Citizenship
- Worthy use of leisure time
- Ethical character

These principles laid the groundwork for the **comprehensive high school.** People supporting comprehensive high schools believed that the high school program should feature educational experiences broad enough to promote student development in all seven areas delineated in the Cardinal Principles. This perspective represented a huge change from the traditional view of the high school as an institution designed to prepare students for colleges and universities. In time, publication of the Cardinal Principles led many high schools to expand their course offerings. By no means, however, did all high schools give equal emphasis to each of the many subjects that came to be offered; in many, considerable attention (critics would say too much attention) continued to be given to college and university preparatory courses.

The Progressive Movement.   Changes in the schools wrought by both attention to the Cardinal Principles and actions taken by groups looking for a more-practical emphasis in the curriculum suggested that more and more people had come to see education as a necessity for all young people. Compulsory-attendance laws became common during the first two decades of the 20th century. Increasingly, learners were being required to stay in school until they turned 16.

In the 1920s and 1930s, the influence of those who also wanted schools to respond humanely to the needs and interests of individual learners was strong. The term **progressive education movement** has been applied to the general program of people who sought these goals. Supporters of the progressive education movement drew inspiration from John Dewey's work. The installation of counseling programs in schools, for example, which developed at an especially rapid rate during the 1930s, represented a logical extension of Dewey's concern for individual development.

World War II to the 21st Century

After World War II, the progressive education movement developed into a loosely knit group of people who supported school practices that came to be known as **life-adjustment education**. In some of its more extreme forms, life-adjustment education seemed to encourage learners to do whatever they pleased. Systematic attention to intellectual rigor or subject matter was avoided. Opponents of such programs suggested that schools that failed to provide young people with needed understandings and skills shortchanged learners. These critics attracted many supporters, and by the middle 1950s, support for life-adjustment education had greatly diminished.

Responding to International Challenges.   Rarely can change in education (or, indeed, in other social institutions) be attributed to a single event. But in the fall of 1957, the former Soviet Union's launch of the first earth satellite, **Sputnik,** so changed the public's perception of education's role that many subsequent alterations in school curricula can be traced back to this single, seminal event. *Sputnik* shocked the nation by challenging America's presumed technological supremacy. People looking for an explanation of why the Soviet Union was first with such an accomplishment placed much blame on public education. Large audiences listened sympathetically to critics who told them that American schools had gone soft and that instruction in subject-matter content compared unfavorably with that provided to learners in other countries. Instruction in the sciences was identified as a particularly weak area of the curriculum.

Reacting to pressures to "do something" about the schools, the federal government passed the **National Defense Education Act** in 1958. This legislation provided federal funds to improve the quality of education. Large-scale curriculum-reform projects were launched, first in mathematics and the sciences and later in the social sciences. Special summer workshops designed to upgrade teachers' skills were held on college campuses across the nation. Massive effort was underway to improve the quality of textbooks and other instructional materials. People carried high hopes that this revolution in American school programming could be carried to a successful conclusion.

Although the curriculum-reform movement of the 1960s produced important changes, these modifications fell well short of the expectations of many supporters of the National Defense Education Act. Teachers who attended summer programs funded by this legislation became proficient in the use of new techniques and materials, but only a small minority of all teachers participated. Teachers who had not had training in the use of new programs and materials often were ill at ease with many of the new programs. A majority of teachers continued doing things much as they had always done them.

Another problem involved the new instructional materials themselves. Subject experts who had little experience working with learners in public schools developed many of them. Consequently, some of the new materials were written at reading levels that were too difficult for many learners. Also, the issue of motivation was ignored. Many young people simply were not interested in the content of the new programs.

Probably the changing national culture of the 1960s did more than anything else to subvert those changes being pushed by people who wanted to introduce more "intellectual rigor" into school programs. There was growing discontent over official governmental policies toward fighting in Vietnam and minorities were frustrated in the nation's large cities, so the ground was not fertile for changes that appeared to critics to be efforts to push "establishment" values on the young. Increasingly, young people questioned the relevance of school curricula that seemed to favor esoteric intellectual subjects rather than topics of more immediate personal concern.

Advent of the Middle School.   After World War II, concerns increased about the junior high school. Many people had originally hoped that junior high schools would be particularly sensitive to the emotional and developmental needs of early adolescents. Over time, however, a majority of junior high schools became academic preparatory institutions for the high schools. In reaction to this trend the **middle school** has become tremendously popular.

The middle school movement first attracted large numbers of supporters during the 1960s. This interest continued throughout the 1970s, 1980s, and on into the 1990s. Individual middle schools often have one of several different grade-level organizational patterns. Generally, a middle school has three to five grades, and it almost always includes grades 6 and 7 (Lounsbury & Vars, 1978). The National Middle School Association and other supporters of middle schools emphasize programs that are sensitive to the special characteristics of learners in the 10- to 15-year-old age group. For example, middle school proponents tend to (1) support interdisciplinary approaches to program organization and (2) favor motivational techniques that emphasize cooperation rather than competition (Henson, 2004). The view that young people in this age group need school programs uniquely suited to their needs has greatly increased middle schools' popularity. Today the middle school is the dominant school type for learners between the elementary and high school years.

School-Improvement Initiatives.   Beginning in the early 1980s, public worries about the quality of American education led to a period of intense scrutiny of school programs. There were concerns about the sophistication of thinking being developed by school programs, the readiness of graduates to assume jobs requiring ever-more-complex levels of technical proficiency, the general reading and writing abilities of learners, the scores on academic-achievement tests, and unfavorable comparisons between American learners and those in other nations.

A number of major themes appear regularly in recommendations to improve the schools that have been broadly circulated since the early 1980s. There has been a frequent call for school programs to become more rigorous. At the high school level, this recommendation has sometimes taken the form of a proposal to reduce the number of electives and to require all learners to take a common core of content drawn from the academic disciplines.

Recommendations have also addressed the issue of teacher quality. There have been suggestions of various ways to attract brighter, more-committed people to teaching and to improve the quality of their preparation (Holmes Group, 1986). There also has been a recognition that quality people will not remain in the profession unless there are improvements in teachers' working conditions (e.g., improving salaries and empowering teachers to make more decisions about how they discharge their responsibilities).

The issue of school administrative organization also has been addressed. There have been recommendations to decrease sizes of schools to allow for more personal attention to learners. There have also been suggestions that principals spend more time in their roles as instructional leaders than in their roles as business managers. Additionally, there have been proposals to lengthen the school year to make it conform more to those in countries where learners are doing better on content achievement tests than their U.S. counterparts.

For the past 15 years, discussion of educational improvement has been stimulated by reports of interested national groups and federal-government action, as well as by increased local interest in providing parents with more choices regarding how and where their children are educated. National efforts have included the work of members of the Education Commission of the States and the National Governors' Association. They have focused attention on such issues as the kinds of school programming that should be provided for students not going on to colleges and universities, improvements needed in technological literacy of graduates of American schools, and enhancements in student learning of traditional academic subjects.

These efforts have spawned public interest in (1) various approaches to school choice, including voucher plans, open enrollment plans, magnet schools, and charter schools; (2) increased interest in school–business partnerships; and (3) recognition that it may be necessary to establish full-service schools to respond to the varied needs many learners bring with them to school. A theme running through all of these proposals is that reform needs to be systemic. As you will recall from Chapter 3, "Challenges of School Reform," *systemic reform* presumes that the problems schools face are multiple and diverse and no single difficulty can be solved without careful attention to the entire spectrum of problems.

Testing and Curriculum Standards.   You probably are well familiar with two key elements of systemic-reform initiatives: (1) the increased focus on the content learners are taught and (2) the reliance on test results to provide evidence about what learners have achieved. Over the past decade and a half, the general public has looked increasingly to standardized test scores as measures of educational quality. As interest in making place-to-place comparisons has increased, there has been a greater tendency to use test scores to compare performance levels of learners who may not have been exposed to the same kinds of content. As a result, schools increasingly have been pressured not only to introduce learners to rigorous content but also to provide the same *kinds* of content to similar groups of learners in all schools (Armstrong, 2003). Actions of federal and state governments and of subject-specialty groups (organizations interested in promoting better teaching in English, mathematics, science, social studies, and so forth) to identify **curriculum standards** accelerated during the 1990s. These standards identified specific content to be taught in individual grades and courses and often also identified expected levels of proficiency for learners.

At the federal level, much interest in promoting curriculum standards began in 1989, when President George H. Bush joined with the nation's governors to host an educational summit. Following this event, the **National Educational Goals Panel** and the **National Council on Education Standards and Testing** were formed. These two groups sought responses to questions about (1) what schools should teach, (2) kinds of testing that should be used, and (3) standards of student performance. In 1994, Congress passed the **Goals 2000—Educate America Act,** Public Law 103-227. This legislation called for massive efforts to improve the quality of the nation's schools. It provided for the establishment of a **National Education Standards and Improvement Council,** a group charged with overseeing the development of national content standards.

This development had two immediate effects. On the one hand, it stimulated a heated debate among conservative members of the U.S. Senate and the House of Representatives about the appropriateness of interfering with local control of education by imposing national curriculum standards on schools. The net result was a continuation of the idea that the federal government would support the idea of curriculum standards but that state and local officials should develop the standards.

A second result of discussions surrounding the Goals 2000 legislation was a great increase in subject-matter specialty groups' interest in developing curriculum standards related to their discipline areas. Beginning in the 1990s, many of these groups produced curriculum standards that featured content recommendations and, sometimes, teaching suggestions for individual elementary school grades and middle school and high school courses. (For more information about the work of these groups, see Chapter 7, "The Curriculum.") Interest in the importance of curriculum standards was reinforced by the passage of the No Child Left Behind Act of 2001 (2002). This legislation requires all states to have rigorous curriculum standards in place, to develop programs to assess learners' performance on tests related to these standards, and to provide interventions to help learners whose achievement levels fall below certain standards.

SELECTED NON-EUROPEAN INFLUENCES

Influences other than those originating in Europe may shape the views and priorities of some of the young people you will teach. Because these learners and their families live in a country where many European practices are commonplaces of everyday life, their perspectives probably will represent a blend of ancestral non-European worldviews and Euro-American worldviews.

This kind of mixing and accommodation somewhat parallels modifications many Americans make when they move from one state to another. Although many basic patterns and problems of living remain the same, there are subtle differences that must be accommodated. For example, if you move from a state that does not require stores to collect deposits on plastic bottles to one that does, you probably will become much more interested in saving used bottles in your new state so you can return them to regain your deposit. You may also have to make minor driving adjustments related to differences in regulations regarding turning right on a red light after coming to a complete stop, speed limits in school zones, and observed state holidays.

The sections that follow introduce you to some non-European educational perspectives. This information can be helpful if you recognize that these descriptions reference general patterns. You do not want to assume that every member of each of these groups sees the world in the same way. People in all groups are individuals who, although they often share some common commitments, also vary in important ways. Think about these descriptions as broad summary sketches that hint at certain characteristics you may find among young people whose personal histories tie to these traditions. You should see this information as a starting point as you begin the important responsibility of focusing on individuals and determining the unique perspectives each brings to the world of education.

Legacies from Africa

You may wonder about the wisdom of describing perspectives from a continent as large and diverse as Africa. This huge landmass is more than three times as large as the United States, cuts through numerous climatic zones, and includes people from diverse racial, religious, and language groups. Despite these differences, there are some commonalities among people living in widely separated parts of the continent. This situation parallels situations in Europe, where people living in the islands off southern Greece and people living hundreds of miles to the north in Norway share enough values for both to be regarded as members of a common European culture.

Throughout much of the African continent, education historically was viewed as a function of the community. Although there were people who functioned as official "teachers," the lines of responsibility between most African communities' teachers and learners and those among other members of the community and learners were not sharply defined. A key purpose of traditional African education was helping young people understand how solidly their own interests were rooted to the more-general interest of their society. Many African groups had a strong oral tradition, and knowledge passed to the young through riddles, anecdotes, tales, and verbal games of various kinds.

As you think about working effectively with learners from families with an African heritage, you might find some of them to be receptive to instruction featuring

- Frequent opportunities for group work
- Lessons that make clear that new information will benefit the larger community, not just learners in your classroom
- Information that helps members of your class play a meaningful role in the larger community
- Opportunities to engage in word play and other activities that emphasize oral learning

WEB EXTENSION 12–3

Traditional Education

At this Web site you will find information related to the traditional educational practices of the Yoruba, one of the largest cultural groups within Africa's most populous country, Nigeria. You will find discussions of the important emphasis on character development, moral development, and the importance of hard work. There also is an interesting description of how the arrival of Europeans affected educational practices.

http://www.yorubanation.org/yoruba/Education.htm

Legacies from Islam

Islam is one of the world's great religions. Though there are followers of Islam in Europe, it is fair to say that followers are concentrated in other parts of the world, particularly in the Middle East, Africa, Southern Asia, and the East Indies. Today, "Islam is the third largest U.S. religion, and by the year 2010 it is expected to be the second largest . . . " (Reagan, 2000; p. 182).

The religion traces to a date sometime after the year 600 C.E. when, followers believe, the angel Gabriel appeared to the Prophet Muhammad and informed him that God had chosen him to spread his message to all people in the world. Muhammad was instructed to listen and recite what he was told. These words comprise the *Qur'an*, a book that followers of Islam believe to be an exact transcription of God's words as spoken to Muhammad. These words were recited in Arabic. Because any change would, in effect, be an attempt to change God's words, followers of Islam reject the idea that the *Qur'an* can be translated. They refer to any such attempts, not as translations, but as less-important "interpretations" of the *Qur'an* (Reagan, 2000). Followers of Islam are taught to memorize and recite passages from the *Qur'an* in Arabic, even though many adherents do not understand the language. Believers do this in their daily prayers out of a conviction they are speaking God's words. The need to speak these words imparts a great oral tradition to Islam. The existence of these words in a written form in the *Qur'an* also provides an incentive to become literate.

The goal of education for a follower of Islam is an integrated personality that features a sound mind and a sound body that develop from actions grounded in the *Qur'an*. Human beings do have reason, which they use to learn skills required for making a living, for working cooperatively with others, and for interpreting God's plans as embedded in the *Qur'an*.

As you think about working effectively with learners from families with an Islamic heritage, you might find some of them to be receptive to instruction featuring:

- Opportunities to sharpen learners' memorization abilities
- Lessons involving opportunities to share memorized information
- Learning experiences designed to enhance class members' reading skills
- Opportunities for class members to evaluate action opportunities in light of their own moral code

Legacies from China's Confucian Tradition

For centuries, China had an examination system that was used to identify potential employees with the educational skills needed to work as government employees. Only male children took these tests. High scorers on local-level tests went on to take regional-level exams. High scorers on the regional tests competed at the national level. A small number from this group took palace-level exams, and the high scorers received important roles in the inner circle of the imperial government.

Preparation for these tests required candidates to memorize specific texts, many of them from the thoughts of **Confucius** (551–478 B.C.E.), a philosopher who emphasized the importance in status differences among people because of the roles they played in life. Each candidate studied exactly the same material. Grading placed no priority on interpretational ability. Instead, graders looked for examinees who were best able to conform to a prescribed style of presenting their information.

The examination system of ancient China no longer exists. However, because the examination tradition lasted for centuries, some patterns of thinking associated both with the system itself and with the Confucian texts that candidates studied may influence some individuals with ties to traditional Chinese culture. As you think about working effectively with learners from families with a Chinese heritage, you might consider how their perspectives may interact with lessons that have characteristics such as these:

- Information suggesting that human relationships should be based more on equality of participants rather than on the basis of some participants standing in positions that are either superior or inferior to others
- Lessons requiring students to use creativity in their responses
- Learning experiences that assign different work to different members of the class

Legacies from Hinduism

Many followers of Hinduism live in India, but, because of the high numbers of people immigrating to this country from India, many learners of Hindu heritage are now in the public schools. Hinduism, a highly decentralized religion, lacks a rigidly defined creed. However, many Hindus accept these ideas: (1) a Supreme Being exists; (2) a system of reincarnation involves people in a continuous death-and-rebirth cycle; (3) over time, the souls of all people evolve in the direction of a final end that will liberate them from this cycle; and (4) life of all kinds is sacred and must be protected.

Hindus see ignorance as a critically important problem. This is true because ignorance is an obstacle to the knowledge needed to free the soul from the death-rebirth cycle. In an effort to overcome ignorance, Hindu thinkers have embraced many approaches to obtaining knowledge. Timothy Reagan (2000), who has made an extensive study of Hindu and other non-Western educational traditions, explains that traditional Hindu education was provided only to males. It featured instruction that began with a teacher providing information to a learner orally. Next, the learner was asked to think about the new information. Finally, the teacher required the learner to use the results of this thinking during a time of personal meditation. The personal-meditation step was designed to help the learner develop a greater appreciation for the Supreme Being.

Hinduism features complexities that go beyond the scope of this discussion. However, these brief comments highlight two important points. First, Hinduism values multiple approaches to learning. Second, education in the Hindu tradition emphasizes self-knowledge, particularly as self-knowledge helps a person to grow toward a relationship with the Supreme Being. As you think about working effectively with learners from families with a Hindu heritage, you might consider how their perspectives may interact with lessons that have characteristics such as these:

- Lessons that feature extensive use of group work
- Instruction requiring the use of social science research skills
- Learning experiences that suggest the scientific method is "the best" method of acquiring knowledge

Today, much professional writing is available that focuses on non-European educational traditions. You can find articles on the Internet, in professional journals, and in books. One title we particularly like is Timothy Reagan's *Non-Western Educational Traditions: Alternative Approaches to Educational Thought and Practice*—2nd edition (2000).

Critical Incident

Why Study in High School?

"I grant you, we've tried hard to accommodate every group in the country. Our intentions have been good. We've developed this really complex system of elementary schools, middle schools, junior high schools, senior high schools, community colleges, and four-year colleges and universities. We've had experts look at every imaginable educational question. But, something is still wrong. Some of our best kids just aren't responding in the right ways. It's really frustrating." Eric Blanton, having delivered himself of this pronouncement, slumped wearily into one of the old vinyl-covered chairs in the Ryerson High School faculty lounge.

From across the room, Suyanna Muyami, the head of the English department, looked up. "OK, Eric, what is it today—taxes, our corrupt politicians, or one of the students?"

"Oh, I'll be all right, but I've been going round and round again with Roy Flynn. Flynn is so bright, but he's just doing nothing, absolutely nothing. He gives things a nice once-over-lightly before the tests and manages to get grades just high enough to squeak by. He'll graduate, but just barely. What really gets to me is that he could be a contender for top academic honors if he would just care."

"If school doesn't turn him on, what does?" asked Suyanna. "Is it the usual love affair with a car?"

"That's exactly it," replied Eric. "He's working 20 and more hours a week to keep it in gasoline."

Suyanna gave Eric a wry smile and said, "And I suppose you've been trying to point out the error of his ways, the tragedy of wasting his God-given brains—all the usual arguments we trot out. Right?"

"Well, yes," responded Eric. "And it makes me mad that he's got all this talent and he's just tossing it away. Just a few minutes ago I sat him down and tried to have a heart-to-heart with him about his future. Roy's sharp. He has an answer for every argument. What makes me mad is that we've set up a system in this country that encourages insightful kids like Roy to see high school as play time."

"What do you mean?" Suyanna asked.

"Well, I gave him the usual pitch about not preparing himself for college and that his grades are going to make it difficult for him to be admitted to many four-year colleges and universities. He had an answer for that one all figured out. He knows that any community college in the state will take him, no questions asked, once he finishes high school. He says he'll dig into the academics, get grades, and transfer to a good four-year school. And, you know, the system will allow him to do just that."

Suyanna followed Eric's thoughts with interest. "And just what do you make of all this?"

"I conclude," Eric replied, "that we have a system that sends bad signals to some of our brightest kids. We want them to study hard in high school. But why should they? Today, it almost makes sense for these kids to see high school as goof-off time. I mean, we've arranged things so they can always get their academic act together later on.

"Fine, but what's the answer?" Suyanna asked. "Do we get rid of community colleges? Just a hint, Eric—that's not going to happen. So, what's your next move?"

• • •

What does Eric see as the problem here? What alternatives does he see? What assumptions does he have about what high school students should value? How does he respond to this situation in light of these assumptions? Are there other responses that might have made sense? Which alternatives might you recommend, and why? How would your suggestions "connect" to what Roy Flynn believes is important in life?

Can you think of examples of incentives in our system that encourage learners to behave in ways you think are inappropriate? What historical situations might have led to the adoption of policies and practices that resulted in these incentives?

 To respond to this Critical Incident online, go to the Critical Incidents *module for this chapter of the Companion Website.*

Key Ideas in Summary   ░░░

- The history of American education, as is the case with all history, reflects the values and biases of those who have written it. Because the majority of Americans are white and of European descent, it is not surprising that much educational history fails to question the appropriateness for *all* American children of educational practices rooted in traditions from Europe. In times past, some instruction in American schools failed to provide positive models for learners from minority cultures. Educators today are increasingly sensitive to this issue.

- Among educational practices and assumptions that trace their origins to Europe are (1) the idea that content should be organized under major headings, (2) the practice of dividing knowledge into separate subjects, (3) the tradition of dividing schools into an ordered sequence of grades, (4) the view that teachers should develop instructional plans that take learners' individual differences into account, (5) the idea that as many people as possible should be educated, (6) the practice of providing special training for teachers, and (7) the vision of schooling as a preparation for effective citizenship.

- In the American colonial period, practices in early New England were influenced heavily by views of Puritan leaders. Schools there developed a strong tradition of local control and placed heavy emphases on teaching children to read and learn from the Bible. Schools in the middle colonies, which were less tied to perspectives of religious leaders than those in New England, featured varied emphases. There was special interest in developing schools that taught practical subjects to learners, and the first secondary-level *academies* appeared here. Great distances separated many families in the southern colonies. In many places no schools existed, and wealthy families hired resident tutors to teach their children. Sons of the upper classes often were sent to school in England.

- Settlers in the middle colonies came from more-diverse backgrounds than early residents of New England. In New York, many early private schools sought to prepare young people for commercial careers. In Pennsylvania, Quakers established schools that were open to all children.

- The first high school was established in Boston in 1821. Unlike academies, which were mostly private institutions, most high schools were publicly supported. At first, the growth of high schools proceeded slowly. In 1860, for example, there were only 40 high schools in the entire country.

- Horace Mann championed the common school in the 1820s and 1830s. He believed that it was in the taxpayers' interest to support a strong system of public education. He saw schools as vehicles for equalizing differences among people from different social classes and as engines for the future economic growth of the nation. Mann also supported the development of normal schools—formal institutions dedicated to the preparation of teachers.

- The post–Civil War period witnessed many changes in education. The famous *Kalamazoo case* established a legal precedent for public support of secondary as well as elementary education. Teachers began to form professional organizations. The large number of immigrants entering the country challenged educators to develop programs responsive to their needs and to the needs of American employers. Toward the end of the 19th century, there was interest in narrowing the focus of the school curriculum to place more emphasis on knowledge students would need to succeed in colleges and universities.

- During the first 20 years of the 20th century, the conflict regarding the purpose of the American high school was resolved with the development of the *comprehensive high school,* an institution that had multiple objectives. Comprehensive high schools, in theory at least, offered programs designed to serve the *Cardinal Principles of Secondary Education,* which included (1) health, (2) command of fundamental processes, (3) worthy home membership, (4) vocational preparation, (5) citizenship, (6) worthy use of leisure time, and (7) ethical character.

- John Dewey had a significant influence on 20th-century American education. Dewey believed that education should primarily focus on the development of the individual. He was especially interested in providing learners with the kinds of problem-solving abilities they would need to successfully confront the challenges they would face throughout their lives.

- By the second and third decades of the 20th century the *testing movement,* which originated in France and developed rapidly during World War I, led to the extensive use of intelligence testing of learners in American schools. In recent years, much skepticism has been generated regarding the idea that an IQ score represents an accurate measure of something as complex and sophisticated as human intelligence.

- After World War II, there was interest in *life-adjustment education.* Critics felt that this view of education encouraged learners to do only what pleased them and that school programs lacked needed intellectual substance. By the 1950s, much enthusiasm for life-adjustment education had faded.

- In the late 1950s, following the launch of the earth satellite *Sputnik* and continuing into the very early 1960s, there was a push to place heavier emphasis in schools on challenging academic content. Particular efforts were made to strengthen programs in mathematics and the sciences. As public dissatisfaction with the nation's fight in Vietnam increased, suspicions began to be directed at leaders of many public institutions, including the schools. In time, these suspicions led to widespread rejection of narrow school programs with strong focuses on traditional academic subjects; increasingly, young people questioned the relevance of such programs.

- Beginning in the 1960s, concerns about junior high schools prompted a great deal of interest in middle schools. This interest continues to the present time. Supporters of middle schools believe that their programs tend to be more responsive than junior high school programs to the special needs of learners ages 10 to 15.

- Beginning in the 1980s, a large number of proposals to reform the schools were made. These were prompted by concerns about the intellectual levels of school graduates, unfavorable achievement comparisons between American and foreign learners, and perceived learner deficiencies in such key areas as reading and writing.

- In recent years, there has been a great expansion in the establishment of *state curriculum standards* that specify content to be covered in individual elementary school grades and in middle school and high school courses. Increasingly, standardized tests are tying to content referenced in these standards. Adoption of state curriculum standards has been supported and, in some cases, mandated by federal legislation. In addition, the movement has been encouraged by many subject-matter specialty organizations that have developed standards pertaining to their own disciplines.

- Learners who come to school bring personal cultural histories with them that act as filters when they take in experiences provided by the school. Legacies from such diverse sources as the culture of Africa, Islamic beliefs, traditional Chinese examination practices, and Hinduism often affect how learners with ties to these influences perceive and react to the school programs.

Chapter 12 Self-Test

 To review terms and concepts in this chapter, go to the Companion Website and take the Chapter 12 Self-Test. Feedback for the self-test is immediate. You can keep track of your self-test scores yourself, or you can submit them to your instructor via e-mail.

Preparing for Praxis

 To learn more about the Praxis test and complete this activity online, go to the Preparing for Praxis *module for this chapter of the Companion Website.*

You may be required to pass Educational Testing Service's Praxis II exam as you seek formal authorization to teach in the public schools. The *Principles of Learning and Teaching* component of Praxis II seeks to assess your knowledge about these topics: (1) Students as Learners, (2) Instruction and Assessment, (3) Communication Techniques, and (4) Profession and Community.

You may wish to relate the educational history content from this chapter to several of these categories. For example, historical influences may influence students' receptivity to certain learning approaches, may affect choices you make in planning and implementing instructional strategies, may have some impact on patterns of communication within your classroom, and may suggest areas of new concern as you reflect on what it means to become an effective teacher. As you think about content from the chapter, look carefully at categories in the chart here that describe major focus categories for the Praxis II exam. Consider making a chart of your own with these categories and use it to jot down ideas as you consider implications of content related to educational history.

Students as Learners	**Instruction and Assessment**
• Student Development and the Learning Process	• Instructional Strategies
• Students as Diverse Learners	• Planning Instruction
• Student Motivation and the Learning Environment	• Assessment Strategies
Communication Techniques	**Profession and Community**
• Basic, Effective, Verbal and Nonverbal Communication Techniques	• The Reflective Practitioner
• Effect of Cultural and Gender Differences on Communications in the Classroom	• The Larger Community
• Types of Questions That Can Stimulate Discussion in Different Ways for Particular Purposes	

For Your Initial-Development Portfolio

 To complete this activity and submit your response online, go to the For Your Initial-Development Portfolio *module for this chapter of the Companion Website.*

1. What materials and ideas that you learned in this chapter about educational history will you include as "evidence" in your portfolio? Select up to three separate items of information. Number them 1, 2, and 3.

2. Think about why you selected these materials. As you do so, consider these issues:
   - Specific uses you might make of this information as you plan, deliver, and assess the impact of your teaching
   - The compatibility of the information with your own priorities and values
   - Any contributions this information can make to your development as a teacher
   - Factors that led you to include this information, as opposed to some alternatives you considered but rejected
3. Place a check in the chart here to indicate to which INTASC standard(s) each of your items of information relates. (You may wish to refer to Chapter 1 for more-detailed information about INTASC.)

INTASC Standard Number

ITEM OF EVIDENCE NUMBER	S1	S2	S3	S4	S5	S6	S7	S8	S9	S10
1										
2										
3										

4. Prepare a written reflection in which you analyze the decision-making process you followed. In your comments, mention the INTASC standard(s) to which your selected material relates.

Reflections

 To respond to these comments online, go to the Reflections *module for this chapter of the Companion Website.*

1. Has American schooling been designed to benefit individuals of European descent more than others? What evidence do you have to support your views? Should schools try to develop both a common and shared set of values and an appreciation for values of individual cultural groups that might differ from those common and shared values? Why or why not?

2. Some people allege that certain school programs and instructional materials have demeaned learners from some groups. Do you think this continues to be a problem? What might you do in your own classroom to help each learner develop a positive self-concept?

3. You were introduced in this chapter to a number of commonplace educational practices that were adopted by American educators from European precedents. (Recall such things as the practice of dividing knowledge into separate subjects, division of schools into grades, and so forth.) Suppose early on we had decided not to do these things. How might our schools be different? Why

do you think they might be more effective or less effective than they are today?

4. Today, some critics argue that curricula in our schools should place more emphasis on specific technical skills high school graduates will need when they enter the job market. How do you think John Dewey would have reacted to this proposal? What differences do you see between Dewey's values and those favoring more technical-skills training? What do you think about this issue, and how do your views reflect your personal values?

5. As a teacher, you have an obligation to help your learners make adjustments required for them to master certain content, get along with others, and prepare themselves for success either in a future academic environment or in the workplace. Some of your learners will come to you with personal histories tied to traditions that may have values and priorities that differ from your own. How will you discharge your responsibilities to help these learners develop competencies that, in your professional judgment, they should acquire while, at the same time, respecting the unique perspectives they bring to the classroom?

Field Experiences, Projects, and Enrichment

1. In the Middle Ages, many people in charge of teaching the young felt that certain kinds of information had to be kept secret. For example, information about the religious practices of the ancient Greeks and Romans was considered particularly dangerous. Do we face any similar situations in education today? Together with several other people from your class, organize a symposium on the topic, "What Learners Should *Not* Be Taught in School."

2. Many lingering influences from European precedents remain in our schools today. As you look ahead to schools during the next two decades, which of these influences will weaken? Which will grow stronger? Who stands to benefit from any changes you foresee? Prepare a chart that summarizes your ideas, and share it with your class as you briefly summarize your position.

3. Some people argue that the comprehensive high school has outlived its usefulness. They suggest that it would be better to have separate schools for separate purposes. Organize a debate on this topic: "Has the Comprehensive High School Outlived Its Usefulness?"

4. This chapter includes some examples of how legacies from the histories of particular groups can affect their receptivity to certain kinds of content and particular instructional practices. Are there fairly large numbers of learners from certain ethnic, religious, or cultural minority groups in the schools in your local area (or in an area where you might like to teach)? Your professor may be able to provide you with this information. Select one of these groups as a focus. Then, use Google (http://www.google.com) or another Web search engine to locate links to articles containing information about this group. Follow some links that interest you, and take notes you will use as the basis for a brief oral presentation to your class. In your presentation, emphasize specific perspectives of this group that may affect how its younger members view their school experiences.

5. Interview several teachers in an area where you might seek employment as a teacher once you complete your university program. Ask these individuals to tell you how their professional lives have been affected by the increased interest in state curriculum standards and related tests. Do they think these changes have acted to improve education? Share their reactions with others in your class.

References

Armstrong, D. G. (2003). *Curriculum today*. Upper Saddle River, NJ: Merrill/Prentice Hall.

Barry, T. N. (1961). *Origin and development of the American public high school in the 19th century*. Unpublished doctoral dissertation, Stanford University.

Bowen, J. A. (1981). *A history of Western education: Vol. 3. The modern West, Europe, and the New World*. New York: St. Martin's Press.

Coleman, M. (1993). *American Indian children at school, 1850–1930*. Jackson: University of Mississippi Press.

Commissioner of Indian Affairs. (1888). *Annual report*. Washington, DC: U.S. Government Printing Office.

Fischer, D. H. (1989). *Albion's seed*. New York: Oxford University Press.

Goals 2000—Educate America Act, Public Law 103-227, 114 Stat. 2763 (1994).

Gordon, P., & Szreter, R. (Eds.). (1989). *History of education: The making of a discipline*. London: Woburn Press.

Henson, K. T. (2004). *Constructivist teaching strategies for diverse middle level classrooms*. Boston: Allyn & Bacon.

Holmes Group. (1986). *Tomorrow's teachers*. East Lansing, MI: Author.

Lounsbury, J. H., & Vars, G. E. (1978). *Curriculum for the middle years*. New York: Harper and Row.

Nieto, S. (1992). *Affirming diversity: The sociopolitical context of multicultural education*. New York: Longman.

No Child Left Behind Act of 2001, Public Law 107-110, 115 Stat. 1425 (2002).

Popper, S. H. (1967). *The American middle school*. Waltham, MA: Blaisdell.

Reagan, T. (2000). *Non-Western educational traditions: Alternative approaches to educational thought and practice* (2nd ed.). Mahwah, NJ: Lawrence Erlbaum Associates.

Stuart v. School District No. 1 of the Village of Kalamazoo, 30 Mich. 69 (1874).

U.S. Department of Commerce. (1975). *Historical statistics of the United States, colonial times to 1970: Part I*. Washington, DC: Bureau of the Census.

13 *Influences of Technology*

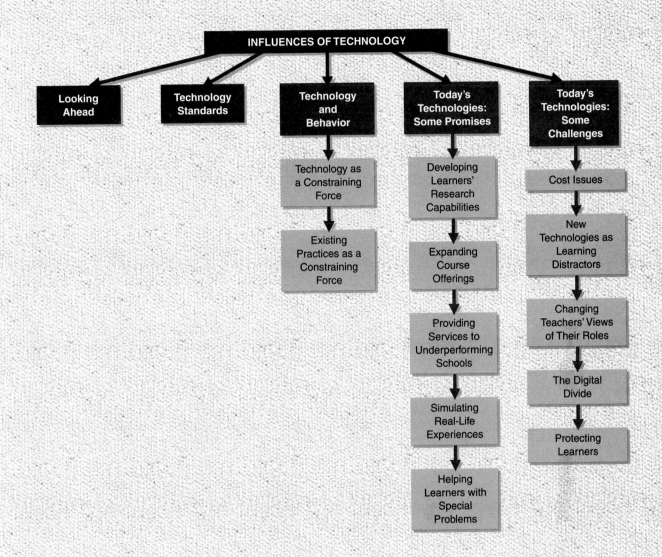

OBJECTIVES

This chapter will help you to

- recognize that effective use of technology requires (1) an understanding of the basic characteristics of available alternatives and (2) a willingness to fit and adapt them to meet the special needs of your own learners and circumstances.

- describe competencies included in technology standards that have been recommended for learners and teachers.

- point out how changes associated with modifications in technologies depend both on the nature of the new technologies and the force of tradition.

- cite examples of ways that today's digital-communication technologies are being used to help learners.

- point out examples of challenges that have accompanied the introduction of new technologies into schools.

- explain provisions of important federal laws that seek to shield learners from dangers that might result from introductions of new technologies into the schools.

LOOKING AHEAD

Project ahead a few years. As you look out over your classroom, you see that most members of your class have chosen to come to school today. Others are working at home. Some of your at-home learners may contact you during the day via e-mail, videophone, or other electronic means if they have questions.

Students in class cluster in small groups in areas you have created by arranging movable visual and sound barriers. A few individuals are working alone. Within each space, sufficient electronic equipment is in place to serve learners' needs. Computers are small and portable. They link to an advanced version of the Internet via satellite connections. Hence, little wiring is in sight.

As part of your social studies program, individuals and groups in your class are involved in the following activities:

- Using computers linked to the World Wide Web to participate in a virtual archaeological dig in cooperation with learners from other schools
- Engaging in a videoconference with learners in schools in other parts of the country focusing on similarities and differences of their home communities
- Organizing a multimedia presentation using video clips, music, and audio clips to contrast some differences in the lives of young people growing up in an urban part of the United Kingdom, such as London, and a rural section such as the Shetland Islands
- Preparing a recordable CD focusing on important issues facing the state that will feature (1) selected digital-camera pictures taken during a field trip to the state capital to meet with legislative leaders, (2) information gathered by using personal digital assistants to connect to Internet Web sites featuring state news, and (3) learners' own verbal comments
- Using a computer to write an article titled "Life in the World War I Trenches" based on information accessed from libraries and other Internet sites and from e-mail and, perhaps, videophone exchanges with directors of museums around the world with collections focusing on World War I

How realistic is this picture? This question is difficult to answer. There are places where learners are engaging in these kinds of experiences today. In other locations, classroom organizational patterns and teaching practices look little different than they did 50 or more years ago. Change produces tensions between opportunities to do things differently and the abiding appeal of familiar practices. As an educator, you will be challenged throughout your career to think about issues associated with **technology.**

Technology is the application of scientific processes to resources for the purpose of extending our capabilities to meet our needs and wants. What can technology do, and what are its limits? Thomas Glennan and Arthur Melmed (1996), in a report prepared for the Rand Corporation, point out that technology is a means to an end, not an instructional activity.

This distinction is not always understood, and sometimes you may even hear a question such as "Are computers in school good or bad for learners?" The question makes no more sense than one focused on an earlier technology such as textbooks. Nobody would think of asking, "Are textbooks good or bad for learners?" The only answer you logically can give is, "It depends on the quality of the texts and how they are used." Making appropriate use of technologies requires you to go beyond a basic understanding of how they work. You need to think about how their capabilities can be exploited to help a particular

Inexpensive video cameras have opened new opportunities for student creativity.

group of learners accomplish particular instructional ends. Even when learners have access to excellent technological aids, they still need your guidance to maximize benefits associated with their use.

During your years as a classroom teacher, you will be involved in making numerous decisions related to technology and its relationship to instruction and learning. As background for making responsible decisions, you may find it useful to think about these questions:

- What technological knowledge and skills do you expect your students to acquire as a result of your instruction?
- What happens when there is technological change?
- What are some promises of today's new technologies?
- What challenges do new technologies pose for teachers?
- What possible dangers do new technologies pose for learners?

TECHNOLOGY STANDARDS

You are entering education at a time when numerous forces press schools to make more-aggressive use of new digital-communication technologies. Proponents suggest that, properly integrated into the school program, these electronic innovations can engage young people in highly motivating learning activities that will support the development of sophisticated thinking abilities. In addition, government officials, business leaders, and many parents and guardians see technology as such a pervasive feature of life that schools must develop the technological capacities of young people to prepare them for advanced education and the world of work (Cuban, 2001).

In response to this interest, states and local communities increasingly are including components in school programs that are designed to develop learners' levels of **technological literacy.** Technological literacy implies a basic understanding of important technologies, a willingness to accept and adapt to new technological innovations, and an ability to employ technologies at an acceptable level of proficiency.

1. TECHNOLOGY OPERATIONS AND CONCEPTS
   Teachers demonstrate a sound understanding of technology operations and concepts. Teachers:

   - demonstrate introductory knowledge, skills, and understanding of concepts related to technology (as described in **ISTE NETS** for Students).
   - demonstrate continual growth in technology knowledge and skills to stay abreast of current and emerging technologies.

2. PLANNING AND DESIGNING LEARNING ENVIRONMENTS AND EXPERIENCES
   Teachers plan and design effective learning environments and experiences supported by technology. Teachers:

   - design developmentally appropriate learning opportunities that apply technology-enhanced instructional strategies to support the diverse needs of learners.
   - apply current research on teaching and learning with technology when planning learning environments and experiences.
   - identify and locate technology resources and evaluate them for accuracy and suitability.
   - plan for the management of technology resources within the context of learning activities.
   - plan strategies to manage student learning in a technology-enhanced environment.

3. TEACHING, LEARNING, AND THE CURRICULUM
   Teachers implement curriculum plans that include methods and strategies for applying technology to maximize student learning. Teachers:

   - facilitate technology-enhanced experiences that address content standards and student technology standards.
   - use technology to support learner-centered strategies that address the diverse needs of students.
   - apply technology to develop students' higher-order skills and creativity.
   - manage student learning activities in a technology-enhanced environment.

4. ASSESSMENT AND EVALUATION
   Teachers apply technology to facilitate a variety of effective assessment and evaluation strategies. Teachers:

   - apply technology in assessing student learning of subject matter using a variety of assessment techniques.
   - use technology resources to collect and analyze data, interpret results, and communicate findings to improve instructional practice and maximize student learning.
   - apply multiple methods of evaluation to determine students' appropriate use of technology resources for learning, communication, and productivity.

5. PRODUCTIVITY AND PROFESSIONAL PRACTICE
   Teachers use technology to enhance their productivity and professional practice. Teachers:

   - use technology resources to engage in ongoing professional development and lifelong learning.
   - continually evaluate and reflect on professional practice to make informed decisions regarding the use of technology in support of student learning.
   - apply technology to increase productivity.
   - use technology to communicate and collaborate with peers, parents, and the larger community in order to nurture student learning.

6. SOCIAL, ETHICAL, LEGAL, AND HUMAN ISSUES
   Teachers understand the social, ethical, legal, and human issues surrounding the use of technology in PK-12 schools and apply that understanding in practice. Teachers:

   - model and teach legal and ethical practice related to technology use.
   - apply technology resources to enable and empower learners with diverse backgrounds, characteristics, and abilities.
   - identify and use technology resources that affirm diversity.
   - promote safe and healthy uses of technology resources.
   - facilitate equitable access to technology resources for all students.

FIGURE 13.1   ISTE's National Educational Technology Standards (NETS) for Teachers

Promotion of more emphasis on technology in school is the primary mission of the **International Society for Technology in Education (ISTE).** ISTE has produced lists of national educational standards both for learners and teachers. ISTE's *National Educational Technology Standards for Students: Connecting Curriculum and Technology* (2000) has influenced the contents of many state-level technology standards for school learners. Similarly, large numbers of university teacher-preparation programs now require prospective teachers to meet standards identical or similar to ISTE's *National Educational Technology Standards for Teachers: Preparing Teachers to Use Technology* (2002). ISTE's standards for teachers (with accompanying performance indicators) and for students (with accompanying performance indicators) are listed in Figures 13.1 and 13.2, respectively.

As you prepare for your work as a classroom teacher, you need to be aware of technology standards for students in the state where you wish to teach. Often Web sites maintained by state departments of education provide this information. You might be interested in finding out how your technological preparation compares with the ISTE standards. Once you begin teaching, you need to review existing standards periodically. Because of the rapid rate of technological change, today's standards are certain to undergo frequent revision.

---

1. **BASIC OPERATIONS AND CONCEPTS**

   - Students demonstrate a sound understanding of the nature and operation of technology systems.
   - Students are proficient in the use of technologies.

2. **SOCIAL, ETHICAL, AND HUMAN ISSUES**

   - Students understand the ethical, cultural, and societal issues related to technology.
   - Students practice responsible use of technology systems, information, and software.
   - Students develop positive attitudes toward technology uses that support lifelong learning, collaboration, personal pursuits, and productivity.

3. **TECHNOLOGY PRODUCTIVITY TOOLS**

   - Students use technology tools to enhance learning, increase productivity, and promote creativity.
   - Students use productivity tools to collaborate in constructing technology-enhanced models, prepare publications, and produce other creative works.

4. **TECHNOLOGY COMMUNICATION TOOLS**

   - Students use telecommunications to collaborate, publish, and interact with peers, experts, and other audiences.
   - Students use a variety of media and formats to communicate information and ideas effectively to multiple audiences.

5. **TECHNOLOGY RESEARCH TOOLS**

   - Students use technology to locate, evaluate, and collect information from a variety of sources.
   - Students use technology tools to process data and report results.
   - Students evaluate and select new information resources and technological innovations based on their appropriateness for specific tasks.

6. **TECHNOLOGY PROBLEM-SOLVING AND DECISION-MAKING TOOLS**

   - Students use technology resources for solving problems and making informed decisions.
   - Students employ technology in the development of strategies for solving problems in the real world.

FIGURE 13.2 ISTE's National Educational Technology Standards (NETS) for Student

Source: Reprinted with permission from *National Educational Technology Standards for Students: Connecting Curriculum and Technology,* pp. 14–15, copyright © 2003, ISTE (International Society for Technology in Education), 800.336.5191 (U.S. & Canada) or 541.302.3777 (Int'l), iste@iste.org. All rights reserved. Permission does not constitute an endorsement by ISTE. For more information about the NETS Project, contact Lajeane Thomas, *Director, NETS Project,* 318.257.3923, lthomas@latech.edu.

WEB EXTENSION 13–1

International Society for Technology in Education (ISTE)

ISTE is the leading professional organization for educators interested in promoting the use of technology in school programs. At this site, you will find excellent links to information related to topics such as integrating technology in school curriculums, technology standards, promoting technological equity, policies related to technology and schools, and conferences and meetings focusing on technology and education.

http://www.iste.org/

TECHNOLOGY AND BEHAVIOR

When you look at today's classrooms and see that some teachers use many new technologies to support their instruction while others continue to operate much as teachers did decades ago, this point becomes abundantly clear: *Technology alters the limits of what can be done, but it does not ensure progress.* In other words, even though a new technology affords you the opportunity to do something, it by no means guarantees that you will decide to do it. Your decision to change requires understanding that the advantages of the change are significant enough for you to abandon the comfort of the familiar. Supporters of wider use of new technologies in school programs battle constantly to convince reluctant adopters of new technologies that the benefits of proposed changes are worth the psychological adjustments that accompany a break with traditional ways of doing things.

VIDEO VIEWPOINTS

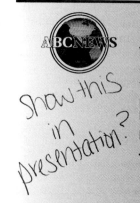

What Is the Impact of Computers in the Classroom?

WATCH: This ABC video segment focuses on the impact of computers in the classroom. It points out that school districts have increased dollar allocations for computers while reducing the budget for other things. However, research does not seem to indicate that computers have had much impact on student achievement. One of the reasons given is that teachers have not been educated on how to use computers. What is not covered in the segment is a discussion of some of the other problems associated with the widespread use of computers in the classroom.

THINK: Discuss with your classmates, or in your teaching journal, the following questions:

1. Do you think that student achievement is the only thing that should be considered when measuring the impact of computers in the classrooms?
2. What are some of the problems with using computers in the classroom that were not discussed in the video?
3. What should be the priorities when allocating scarce resources to technology?

LINK: How might widespread use of technology fundamentally change the way schools operate?

Complete this activity and submit your responses online in the Video Viewpoints *module for this chapter of the* Companion Website.

Technology as a Constraining Force

Let's return a moment to the idea that existing technology establishes the limits of what is possible. How has this principle affected what teachers and schools do? Consider pencils. Large-scale manufacture of these tools began only in the late 1860s. Initially pencils were expensive, and schools could not afford to buy them. If you had been teaching in the 1880s, you would have had your learners write on slates. Slates are difficult to write on, do not have much capacity, and are unsuited for lengthy responses. How would you have tested members of your class? Because of the limitations of slates, you probably would most often have used oral exams. The existing technology would have encouraged you to place great emphasis on helping learners develop well-organized oral-presentation skills.

Occasionally, you may have wanted members of your class to write essays. In the 1880s, straight steel pens were available in schools, and you could have assigned learners to write their essays in ink. Paper was expensive, and ink does not allow for easy correction. These limitations would have encouraged you to help learners carefully organize their ideas in their heads before beginning to write.

When inexpensive pencils featuring built-in erasers made their appearance after 1900, some teachers were concerned. Existing technologies had conditioned them to expect learners to do their revisions mentally before committing thoughts to paper. Pencils with erasers allowed young people to make on-the-fly corrections, something that many teachers initially felt resulted in sloppy preparatory thinking. In time, teachers came to appreciate that the multiple revisions made possible by erasers gave learners more opportunities to think about what they wrote than the old revising-in-the-head strategy that was necessary when ink was the only medium available for essay writing.

Over time, many technological changes have raised the limits of what is possible in the classroom. For example, equipment to score tests electronically provided teachers with the possibility of a timesaving correction process. This feature encouraged time-stressed educators to use test types that could be scored using this equipment (multiple-choice, true–false, and other so-called objective tests) rather than essays. Development of technologies such as films, television, personal computers, and the Internet gave learners opportunities to gather information from sources much wider and more diverse than traditional books and teacher presentations.

Existing Practices as a Constraining Force

Though new technologies present opportunities for the education profession to change many traditional organizational and instructional practices, you cannot be sure that education will experience the kinds of radical transformation sometimes envisioned by strong supporters of new technologies. Existing practices are preserved not only by technologies that allow no alternatives but also by tradition. For example, consider the traditional school year.

It has been decades since large numbers of children were needed for summer farm work; yet, with some exceptions, the long summer break remains a fixture of school calendars. Why is this so? The answer lies in the large number of developments and customs that have evolved over the years under the assumption that schools will not be in session during a good portion of the summer months. Among these are the following:

- Development of a large and sophisticated textbook-and-educational-materials industry that has huge inventories of products designed for use over a 9- to 10-month school year

- Assumptions by parents and guardians that children will be free to go on family vacations during the summer months
- School-district schedules that presume painting, repair work, and other activities associated with building maintenance will occur during the summer months when buildings are vacant
- College and university budgets that assume that large numbers of teachers will pay tuition and attend classes during the summer months
- Summer programs offered by school districts to assist learners who need to retake courses or receive other kinds of help if they are to "keep up" with others in their group when regular school classes begin in the fall

You may be interested in other examples of new or better technologies that, for various reasons, failed to win broad-based support. Everett M. Rogers (1995), who has studied innovations for years, points out that the common QWERTY layout of typewriter and computer keyboards is an arrangement that was designed to force people to type slowly. Early typewriters jammed when typists struck keys too rapidly. The QWERTY keyboard positioned letters so that frequently used letters such as e, i, and o required moving fingers off the "home keys"—an action that slowed the typing process.

In the 1930s when improved typewriters did not require typists to type slowly, August Dvorak developed a keyboard featuring an arrangement whereby frequently used letters were all "home keys." Typists who mastered Dvorak's arrangement were able to type faster and experience less fatigue than users of the QWERTY keyboard. Despite these advantages, the older, less-efficient placement of keys on the QWERTY keyboard continues to dominate, even in the first years of the 21st century.

What explains the persistence of this older technology? For one thing, when the Dvorak keyboard was introduced, manufacturers of typewriters had large numbers of models available with QWERTY keyboards. They were reluctant to take on the expense of producing machines with Dvorak layouts, given uncertainties regarding the numbers of users who would buy the machines. Also, by the time Dvorak's keyboard became available, huge numbers of people had mastered the QWERTY keyboard. They felt high levels of comfort with the QWERTY arrangement, and, as touch typists, did not feel it worth their time to learn the new Dvorak key arrangement.

To summarize, new technologies provide opportunities, but not mandates, for change. The "build it and they will come" perspective from the Kevin Costner film *Field of Dreams* might more properly be stated: "Build it and they *may* come." As you think about possibly adopting practices associated with a new technology, you need to weigh potential benefits against such "costs" as (1) time needed to master the new technologies, (2) impact on resources you have available to support other aspects of your instructional program, and (3) the effects on other practices that existing technologies have sustained.

TODAY'S TECHNOLOGIES: SOME PROMISES

Today's communication technologies make it possible for you to arrange for individuals or small groups of learners to work on assignments that vary according to their particular needs. In the past, this kind of individualized teaching was hard to implement. Hence, the practice was to organize learners into groups of 20 to 35 (sometimes more) and house them in a single large space called a classroom. Information basically came from two sources: the teacher and the textbook. Content presented was cut into manageable chunks, and to accommodate this pattern of division, the school day was divided into periods. These learning divisions were gathered together into large entities called units, and

"There aren't any icons to click. It's a chalk board."

textbook authors and teachers developed schemes to cover certain numbers of them during major divisions of the school year.

Newer technologies have overcome some of the constraints that supported these traditional arrangements. In addition to traditional interactions with classroom teachers, learners now have the possibility of gaining information from many other sources. For example, they may receive Web-based instruction from a teacher located hundreds of miles away from the learner's location. Although learners can continue to receive this instruction in a traditional classroom setting, there is no absolute necessity for them to do so. The technological capability is available for the information to be delivered to learners at home or in numerous other settings (Chou, McClintock, Moretti, & Nix, 1993).

Textbooks increasingly represent just one content source. Further, large numbers of texts, in addition to serving as self-contained knowledge sources, now also function as guides to wider information sources such as the World Wide Web of the Internet. Possibilities are increasing for learners in the years ahead to spend more time in front of computer screens than reading texts.

As a teacher, technology now gives you the ability to function more as an instructional guide than as a primary source of information. You may spend much of your time diagnosing individual learners' needs and helping them develop programs of study that use technologies appropriate for their own learning styles and interests. Ideally, members of your class will engage in considerable self-guided learning.

New technologies also relieve the need for school days and time to be organized so rigidly. In the future, you may find your students spending more time at home. When students are electronically linked to information sources that are located in various world time zones, they may need to access this information at various times during the school day. Increasingly, members of your class may spend part of their days at home or, perhaps, in neighborhood centers where computers are available that will allow them to connect to locations that have information they need (Rector, 2002).

Today, teachers are using digital-communication technologies for many purposes, including (1) reteaching and reinforcing content, (2) providing enrichment experiences for talented learners, (3) individualizing assignments, (4) promoting global perspectives (using World Wide Web sites, encouraging international e-mail pen pals, and so forth), (5) and desktop publishing. Let's briefly turn our attention to several more-complete descriptions of other present-day applications of newer communication technologies. These examples relate to

- Developing learners' research capabilities,
- Expanding course offerings,
- Providing services to underperforming schools,
- Simulating real-life experiences, and
- Helping learners with special problems.

PROFILING A TEACHER

THE TECHNOLOGY ENTHUSIAST

Lorene Boileau, a sixth-grade language arts teacher, has a reputation as an enthusiastic user of instructional technology. Though Ms. Boileau is known to be a savvy user of computers, the Internet, and other electronic wonders, she recognizes that her increased use of technology presents her with challenges as well as opportunities.

Ms. Boileau realizes that she now spends much more time planning lessons than she did in her pretechnology days. Among other things, she must carefully review Web sites she wishes students to use for her lessons. This must be done every time she wants to use a given site because site addresses often change. Also, computers and other equipment students will use must be tested. She also must preview software she wants learners to use to ensure an appropriate fit with her lesson objectives.

Ms. Boileau reports that she must carefully monitor learners when they use computers, particularly when the computers are connected to the Internet. If even a single learner, either accidentally or purposefully, contacts a pornographic site during a class period and a parent or guardian hears of it, complaints to school administrators are almost certain. Such parental and guardian concerns can prompt school leaders to impose restrictive conditions on student use of the World Wide Web—a circumstance that Ms. Boileau believes has the potential to deny students instructional benefits that can accrue when the Web is appropriately used to support instruction.

Despite these challenges, Ms. Boileau remains convinced that today's technologies allow students to get experiences they simply cannot get from traditional modes of instruction. She also points out that young people come to school accustomed to music, animation, and other sensory backups from years of watching electronically enhanced films, MTV, and other sophisticated audio/visual productions. They take naturally to learning that engages multiple senses.

For Ms. Boileau, the major attraction of technology-enhanced teaching is that it has the potential to place responsibility for learning in students' own hands. In technology-rich classrooms, learners are taught under conditions that engage them actively and promote development of the adult thinking skills of (1) accessing information, (2) processing information, and (3) applying information. Activities that help them develop these proficiencies also prepare them for the demands of a technologically oriented workplace that expects employees to know how to locate information, communicate, and work productively with others.

Developing Learners' Research Capabilities

Helping learners to become more-sophisticated thinkers has long been an aim of educators. As early as 1910, John Dewey, a famous educational philosopher, in his influential book, *How We Think,* suggested that learners' thinking skills should be developed by requiring them to follow a series of steps leading from consideration of specific information to formulation of conclusions supported by evidence.

An orientation to teaching that requires learners to engage content personally, think about it carefully, and draw conclusions is constructivism. Constructivism, derived from the work of learning theorists Jean Piaget (Piaget & Inhelder, 1958) and Lev Vygotsky (1962), holds that learners are not passive responders to the environment. Rather, they actively engage the environment and seek to derive personal meaning from this involvement. If you operate in a manner consistent with the constructivist perspective, you will favor lessons that involve your learners in constructing and understanding their own knowledge. New technologies can help you accomplish this.

Inquiry teaching, sometimes called **inductive teaching,** is one approach teachers use to actively engage learners with content they can use as they strive for meaningful and supportable conclusions. Many inquiry or inductive techniques require learners to follow these steps:

1. Describe the essential features of a problem or situation.
2. Suggest possible solutions or explanations.
3. Gather evidence to test the accuracy of these solutions or explanations.
4. Evaluate the solutions or explanations in light of this evidence.
5. Develop a conclusion that is supported by the best evidence.

Though inquiry and inductive techniques have been promoted for many years, new technologies give you options in implementing these approaches that were unavailable to teachers as recently as a decade ago. These techniques require learners to have access to large quantities of specific information. In years gone by, you would have had to assemble this information yourself and make it available to your learners in your own classroom or at some other location within your school building.

Today, the World Wide Web provides opportunities for your learners to access information available at locations throughout the globe. With proper training, they can engage in incredibly diverse activities. For example, you can involve learners in reading diaries of Civil War veterans, looking at paintings housed in the world's finest museums, downloading photographic and other images from famous repositories of these materials, noting how newspapers around the world are covering a common event, and downloading voice and music files. When you engage learners in inquiry activities in this new environment, you do not act as an assembler and presenter of information. Rather, your roles are (1) to guide learners to places they might productively search for information using tools such as computers connected to the Internet and (2) to monitor their progress, keeping them on task and providing assistance, as needed.

When you use new technologies to develop learners' capacities as researchers, you have opportunities to accommodate their individual learning styles and preferences. For example, you can provide alternative suggestions to individuals in your class who, respectively, prefer to learn (1) by reading prose materials, (2) by looking at photographs and other visuals, or (3) by hearing the spoken word. By teaming learners, you can encourage their use of individual strengths in final projects and reports that require them to develop technology-based multimedia presentations. Using new technologies to investigate problems, identify and weigh evidence, and draw conclusions involves members of your class in the generation of knowledge. Educational specialists who advocate using new technology for this purpose point out that learners find this kind of intellectual engagement motivating (Merrow, 2001).

Expanding Course Offerings

Schools in many parts of the country today use modern communication technologies to bring instruction to learners that, in prior years, could not be delivered. For example, electronic video and audio connections make it possible for courses in such specialized subjects as advanced calculus to be delivered to learners attending small schools where such subjects are not available. Individual small schools often cannot provide classes in specialty areas that would draw only small numbers of enrollees. Today, an instructor from a single location can serve many learners in isolated locations by electronically linking them together using modern video and audio technologies.

One variant of electronically based distance learning features complete courses that are offered over the World Wide Web. In many designs of this type, learners may "log on" to the courses they are taking whenever they are free to do so. In addition to promoting wide geographic dispersion of instruction, Web-based courses allow learners to do assignments at times that are convenient for them. In some places, learners take Web-based courses after normal school hours. Individuals who have worked with Web-based courses caution that such courses function well when the purpose is to transmit basic information but that they function less effectively when objectives call for individuals to work with others in group activities that require them to engage in higher-level thinking and decision making (Vallecorsa, 2001). Design of Web-based instruction is still in its formative years, and these difficulties eventually may be resolved.

Providing Services to Underperforming Schools

Over the past 10 years, many states have used test scores and other means to identify schools whose learners have not been performing at acceptable levels. In some places, legislators have adopted policies requiring states to provide young people in these schools with exemplary instruction as a means of improving learner performance. Although legislative mandates of this kind have been well-intentioned, state education leaders have found it difficult to comply. Schools in need of assistance often are dispersed in multiple locations throughout the state, and the numbers of expert teachers available to help are limited. With passage of the No Child Left Behind Act of 2001 (2002) this problem has broadened from one affecting some of the states to a difficulty facing educational leaders throughout the entire country.

The No Child Left Behind Act of 2001 requires schools that have failed to produce acceptable learner-achievement scores for three consecutive years to provide additional instructional services such as after-school tutoring if parents request them. Federal funds are available to help schools pay for communication technologies to provide these services.

With the encouragement of the Secretary of the U.S. Department of Education, schools are making plans to deliver these services to learners using the Web and other electronic means (Murray, 2002). John Bailey, Director of Education Technology for the U.S. Department of Education, comments that ". . . the Internet offers . . . the ability to tap into literally the best instructors, the best tutors from all around the country, and all around the world" (quoted in Murray, 2002).

Simulating Real-Life Experiences

Simulations have been used in school classrooms for many years. You have participated in examples during your own years as a public-school learner. Simulations give young people opportunities for learning experiences that allow them to experience reality in ways that provide quite a credible illusion of a real-life experience. Learners make decisions that have consequences, but the simulated environment always acts to preserve their personal safety. Simulations also provide opportunities for teachers to allow learners to vicariously experience conditions experienced by people in past times.

New digital technologies have greatly expanded the range of simulations available for use by public-school learners. These range in complexity from relatively simple gamelike experiences that are presented to learners on computer disks to hugely ambitious, multiple-day experiences that may require use of Web sites, CD-ROMs, DVDs, televisions, e-mail, and other technologies. Simulations supported by digital technology are now available for virtually all subject areas.

Some technology-based simulations are extraordinarily sophisticated. For example, the Quest Channel, a subscription service, makes available to subscribing school districts and teachers complex "explorations" that link multiple schools and learners with a team of individuals who go to interesting world places in search of answers to intriguing questions. Participating learners use the Web and e-mail to perform background work, to exchange information with "experts" and with other young people (in their own school and in other participating schools), and to see video images provided by the field team. These simulations also provide ways for involved teachers to communicate electronically and share information about learner progress on other issues. During the fall of 2002, the focus was on Christopher Columbus, and learners were involved in such activities as comparing historical accounts of Columbus's voyages with observations of the field team, studying the history of exploration and navigation, learning about cultural groups of the Caribbean, and reading reports in both Spanish and English.

Complex simulations, such as those provided by the Quest channel, highlight another advantage of technology-supported simulations. They provide a cost-effective way for learners to engage interesting and motivating content. Few, if any, public schools could afford to send an entire class on a trip replicating Columbus's route to the New World. Many can find the money to support a Quest Channel subscription that will allow young people to participate on a highly engaging simulated version of the journey.

Helping Learners with Special Problems

Various technologies have long been used to provide assistance to learners who have characteristics that can interfere with their ability to learn. For example, for many years devices called **braillers** or **braille-writers** that allow users to take notes and produce other prose materials in Braille have been available to learners with severe visual limitations. Learners who are not proficient readers sometimes have had access to audio recordings of important sections of course texts. In some places, enrichment experiences have been provided to bright young people through videocassettes and special computer software available for checking out and working with at home.

Until recently, educators have followed this general sequence in identifying support technologies to use: (1) the general demands of the existing curriculum were examined to identify potential problems that certain categories of learners might face, and (2) technologies were identified that might allow those learners to interact with program

*Applications of a wide variety of technologies has
opened new opportunities for student learning.*

materials and profit from them. In other words, the existing curriculum was considered as a "given," and technology was used to accommodate specific learner characteristics to it.

This approach places heavy demands on teachers. For example, in your class you might have learners with conditions requiring you to use a variety of technologies in your efforts to help them learn. One learner might have a physical condition that prevents any movement of arms or legs. Computer-based reading material would help this person, but you would need to develop a system that would allow screen changes to be made by striking a bar with the chin. Another person with very limited vision may require a computer with hugely oversized keys that will "speak" when they are pressed. Other learners may have additional needs to which you must respond. Although technologies are available to assist these learners, the process of getting together needed equipment, making certain that it is being used in ways that relate to the adopted curriculum, and familiarizing learners with use of new equipment can be frustrating and time-consuming.

Today, educational leaders are beginning to challenge this approach of using technologies to help learners cope with a preestablished curriculum. In part, suggestions for a better way have been prompted by revolutionary developments in digital technology over the past decade. Bart Pasha, the research director of the Center for Applied Special Technology (CAST), declares that these changes may affect learning and dissemination of information as much as the invention of the printing press (McHenry, 2002). These technologies make it possible for the initial design of school programs to build in features that will allow learners to access content in ways consistent with their own needs. In working with programs designed in this way, you will no longer need to think about technologies you might need to make it possible for learners with special needs (motor impairments, deafness, profound reading difficulties, visual impairments, and so forth) to succeed. The original design of the program will have access channels built in that learners with various needs can use as they seek to master program content.

WEB EXTENSION 13–2

Center for Applied Special Technology (CAST)

The Center for Applied Special Technology (CAST) is a not-for-profit organization dedicated to widening opportunities for people with disabilities through innovative uses of technology. You will find much useful information at this site, particularly topics related to using technologies to assist learners in your class who may have disabilities of various kinds. You may find the CAST Newsletter, which is electronically accessible, to be particularly helpful. This newsletter discusses innovative uses of technology in the classroom.

http://www.cast.org/

The term applied to efforts to develop curricula that include built-in access channels for different learners is **universal design for learning (UDL).** School programs that follow UDL principles seek to do the following (Rose & Meyer, 2002):

- Represent information in multiple formats and media
- Provide multiple pathways for learners' actions and expressions
- Provide multiple ways to engage learners' interest and motivation

School programs that are based on UDL principles try to eliminate barriers embedded within curricula that present problems for learners with certain characteristics. Ways to assist these young people will be incorporated as part of the basic design, and you will receive the information you need as part of your initial orientation to the program.

TODAY'S TECHNOLOGIES: SOME CHALLENGES

According to Tyack & Cuban (1995), most Americans embrace technology because of the potential it offers for solving learning problems. Given this reality, you should not be surprised if you hear or read that today's digital innovations have the power to "transform the school." In part, this hope is based on tangible evidence that teachers, in the past, have incorporated new technologies into their daily instructional routines. Such commonplaces as whiteboards, textbooks for every learner, overhead projectors, and ballpoint pens are examples. It is interesting to note that many of these innovations failed to completely displace earlier technologies. For example, if you visit a school you may well find both whiteboards and chalkboards. Older video playback units continue to coexist with DVD players.

When teachers have seen legitimate benefits of innovations, they have gradually accepted them as legitimate aids to instruction. On the other hand, sometimes, without input from educators, outsiders have zealously promoted "sure-fire cures" for educational problems (Cuban, 2001; Tyack & Cuban, 1995). These efforts have not always produced the results that promoters of these innovations promised.

Educational-policy specialist Larry Cuban (2001) has studied the history of educational innovations. He notes that attempts to install innovations in the school often have featured a cycle including these phases:

1. **Overblown-description-of-potential-benefits phase.** During this phase, supporters of the innovation go public with claims about how the innovative technology will transform education.
2. **Disappointing-research-results phase.** During this phase, reports emerge showing that the innovation has produced fewer beneficial results than its promoters had promised.
3. **Investigate-causes-for-failure phase.** During this phase, further investigation reveals that relatively few teachers have implemented the innovation or that they have implemented it in ways that deviated from its basic design.
4. **Place-the-blame phase.** This phase often features criticism of teachers who sometimes are described as human barriers to the installation of a new technology that, absent their resistance, would do wonderful things for young people.

Cuban (2001) notes that there is little evidence that teachers resist new technological innovations because they fear or dislike technology. Their decisions to use or not use a novel technology are grounded on their perceptions of its utility in helping them discharge their responsibilities. Before embracing a new technology, they want to know how much time they must commit to learn about it. They want assurances that the technology will be applicable to a variety of situations. They need information about how the technology will help them teach content for which they will be held accountable. They want assurances that the needed equipment will work as designed and that immediate help will be available to deal with breakdowns. They want to know whether use of the innovation will undermine their ability to maintain good order in the classroom. Cuban argues that concerns about these issues have often contributed to teachers' disinclination to embrace new technologies enthusiastically.

WEB EXTENSION 13–3

FNO—From Now On: The Educational Technology Journal

FNO is a monthly electronic journal that publishes articles related to school and teacher uses of technology. You may sign up for a free subscription. Individual issues include descriptions of classroom applications of technology, reviews of books related to technology and education, and other information you may find helpful as you think about integrating technology into your own instructional program.

http://www.fno.org

Given these concerns, in the long run will teachers embrace computer-based instruction? It is too early to give a definitive answer to this question. However, school leaders are working hard to encourage teachers to embrace computer technology. For example, there is increasing evidence that even less-affluent schools are investing substantial sums of money in high-tech hardware and software. Interests of governmental and business leaders at all levels have acted as an important influence on state legislatures to allocate funds for these kinds of purchases. These funds also increasingly are used to employ technicians to service equipment and to respond to problems teachers have when using it. Although few schools have all the technicians they need, clearly much more help of this kind is available than when technologies associated with films, radio, and television were being actively promoted as agents to improve the schools. Increasingly, too, school leaders are recognizing the need to provide funds to familiarize teachers with new hardware and software and to respond to general concerns related to issues such as classroom management, content accountability, and flexibility of use.

Removable storage media and ever-increasing numbers of schools with connections to the Internet make it possible for you and your learners to access digital information when you need it. The time-flexibility feature of today's new technology stands in marked contrast to characteristics of certain earlier innovations. Finally, if your teacher-preparation program is typical, you will receive instruction regarding how new technologies can be used to support your teaching activities. Ever-growing numbers of teachers have received formal training focused on making good use of new technologies. This situation is in marked contrast to the lack of attention that was given to preparing teachers to work effectively with certain earlier technological innovations.

Cost Issues

Costs associated with embedding new technologies, particularly computers, into school programs strain school budgets. Today, funds to support educational technology in the nation's schools total multiple billions annually. In seeking these funds, school leaders have struggled to maintain existing operations, while also responding to demands for computer purchases, equipment replacement, new software purchases and upgrades, Internet connections, teacher training, and maintenance services for computer equipment and networks.

If you discuss this situation with central-office administrators, you are likely to learn that, because of voter resistance to increased taxes to support school operations, new funds from state legislatures and local taxing authorities have been hard to obtain. In many school districts, financial support for technology comes from multiple sources, including donations from parent–teacher organizations and other school-based groups, private foundations, federal agencies, and grant competitions that award technology-dollars to successful applicants.

In recent years, the role of the federal government has assumed more importance as a provider of support for school technology programs. Though the amount of federal money used to support educational technology varies from state to state, on average federal funds now account for about 25% of the total dollars spent each year for this purpose (*T.H.E. Journal*, 2001). This figure represents a much higher level of federal support for school technology than for other expenses associated with maintaining public education. On average, federal expenditures account for only around 7% of the total annual costs of running our public schools. States and local governments pay virtually all of the remaining expenses.

One particularly important piece of legislation, the **Telecommunications Act of 1996** has been especially helpful to school leaders seeking to expand the numbers of Internet-connected computers in their districts. This law establishes a system whereby individual school districts can apply for funds that are used to support a special **e-rate** that makes them eligible for discounts that can run as high as 90 percent on telecommunications and Internet services (Wired News, 2000). This program has made it possible for at least some computers to be tied to the Internet in even our least-affluent schools and school districts.

In general, school districts have found ways to purchase large numbers of computers and to connect them to the Internet. Today, 99% of schools have computers. A national survey completed in 2000 revealed that 84% of teachers had at least one computer in their own classroom. Thirty-eight percent of teachers had two to five computers in their classroom, and 10% of respondents had five or more (National Center for Education Statistics, 2000).

Caution is needed when interpreting the impact of the increase in computers in schools. Simply because computers have become almost-universal features of the school environment does not suggest that everybody has equal access to up-to-date computer technology. Some school computers are too old to accommodate the demands of the latest software. Individual classrooms vary greatly in the numbers of computers available for learners to use. Some learners have access to computers only at school; others, typically from more-affluent families, also have computers to use at home. (You will learn more about differences in access to computer technology in the discussion of the digital divide that appears later in the chapter.) In some schools, sufficient funds have been found to purchase computers but not to train teachers and learners to use them.

The money issue is important virtually everywhere. School leaders are challenged to find funds for technology-related expenditures in areas not associated with initial hardware and software purchases and connections to networks. In particular, they must work hard to find money to

- Replace outdated hardware and software at regular intervals,
- Train teachers to make effective use of new technologies,
- Provide hardware and software to teachers experiencing difficulty, and
- Support technicians to make needed repairs quickly.

One way school systems have responded to the high cost of replacing hardware and software is to lengthen the expected use cycle. In the private sector, computers are replaced, on average, once every three years. Schools have stretched this average to once every five years (Fitzgerald, 1999). This can mean that, toward the end of the replacement cycle, you may be using equipment that limits what you and your learners can do.

If you are expected to use equipment and software that is unfamiliar to you, at the very least, the time required for you to become an effective user will increase. Using computer-based technology to involve learners in sophisticated lessons requires you to have high levels of comfort with both hardware and software. Funding problems that fail to pay for adequate training of teachers can undermine the potential effectiveness of even the best-designed instructional-support technologies. In some districts where funds have been insufficient to train all teachers, money has been used to prepare a few teacher experts to help others who have difficulties (Fitzgerald, 1999). In the long run, this is not a good option. Trained teachers who come to the assistance of others divert their time to working with teachers, rather than learners.

When you work with a book or other traditional print material, you can be reasonably confident that nothing will happen to make the information unusable. Computers and programs do not provide this assurance. Occasionally things go wrong. When difficulties arise, immediate help is needed to remedy the situation to minimize interference with your instructional program. Ideally, technicians should be available to provide this kind of help.

Technicians are expensive. Even when they can be found, their turnover rates are high because usually they can command higher salaries from private-sector employers. In response to these circumstances, learners—often individuals who are self-taught "techies"—handle chores associated with troubleshooting computers, networks, and software. A report provided to teachers attending the National Education Computing Conference found that today learners, themselves, provide technical support in over half of the nation's school districts (Dean, 2002). Although many young people are quite capable, their tenure within individual schools is limited. Hence, this arrangement provides no year-to-year continuity. In addition, critics wonder whether learners who engage in this kind of technological assistance are doing so at the expense of time they otherwise might be spending in activities more clearly tied to their educational needs.

Rapid adoption of new technologies, such as cell phones, provides both potential advantages and potential problems for teachers.

New Technologies as Learning Distractors

Should young people be permitted to bring electronic pagers, cell phones, portable CD players, MP3 players, personal digital assistants (PDAs), and laptop computers to school? In some places, school districts have adopted policies requiring learners to leave these devices at home. Other school districts are discussing this issue.

Supporters of bans tend to be most concerned about electronic devices that have little potential to be used as an integral part of instructional programs. If you have ever heard a group of teachers discussing pagers and cell phones, you know that some of them are adamantly opposed to learners bringing these devices to class. Among other things, they argue that teachers have worked for years to prevent unnecessary interruptions from school public-address systems. Pagers and cell phones divert learners' attention from their work much the same as voices blaring from public-address-system speakers. Even when buzzers and ringers are turned off and the devices are switched to vibrate mode, learners are distracted when a vibration signals an incoming call. Such interruptions break their concentration and interfere with the learning process (Should Cell Phones and Pagers Be Allowed in School?, 2001).

Views of teachers who want to keep pagers and cell phones out of their classrooms frequently are at odds with some parents and guardians who argue strongly that their children should be permitted to take these devices with them to school. Among other things, parents and guardians contend that their sons and daughters should have a means of contacting people outside the school when emergencies arise. Sometimes parents and guardians have had difficulty in getting messages passed to their children when they have called the central school office. This situation can be avoided when learners have cell phones or, at least, pagers. Increasing numbers of schoolchildren are raised in homes with a single parent or guardian. Communicating frequently with sons and daughters via cell phones provides these adults with assurances that their children are safe and secure (Should Cell Phones and Pagers Be Allowed in School?, 2001).

Although electronic pagers and cell phones have been the most-frequent targets of school attempts to keep learners from bringing digital-communication devices to school, some teachers believe that the bans should extend to personal digital assistants and laptop computers (School Board Weighs Ban on Student Laptops, PDAs, 2002). Many modern PDAs allow two or more users to engage in electronic conversations. Laptops can be used to exchange e-mail messages. Though these uses do pose the possibility that learners' attention will be diverted from assigned school tasks, both PDAs and laptops can be used for legitimate academic purposes. For example, young people can use these devices to take notes, gather data from Web sites, and organize information for presentations. Newer PDAs and laptops incorporate features that, collectively, are expanding their potential for integration into the instructional program. For this reason, opposition to learners' use of these devices in school may be diminishing.

When you begin teaching, you may find issues related to banning specific kinds of digital-communication devices becoming more complex. Today there are reasonably obvious distinctions among devices such as digital telephones and personal digital assistants, but these differences may be less clear in the future. There is a trend to blend functions of numerous one-purpose devices into single multiple-function devices. For example, some cell phones now function as personal digital assistants and are capable of establishing wireless connections with the Internet. As these devices become common, you and your colleagues will need to weigh their potential educational benefits against their capacity for disrupting the educational process.

Changing Teachers' Views of Their Roles

How are teachers using technologies today? The picture is mixed. Many educational leaders who promote these technologies as levers that can transform schools and engage learners in sophisticated thinking processes despair that many teachers are using computers as little more than electronic replacements for traditional worksheets and drill-and-practice exercises (Foa, Schwab, & Johnson, 1998; Merrow, 2001). On the other hand, in some places these technologies are leading teachers to individualize instruction, tailor programs to particular learner aptitudes and interests, and engage learners in doing highly motivating and important work (Rector, 2002; Roblyer, 2003).

Preparing learners to take advantage of multiple information sources places huge new demands on teachers. For example, if you wish to develop technology-intensive learning, you must commit considerable time to becoming informed about available options and going about the business of organizing learning programs that differ based on individual characteristics of members of your class. The work required to prepare for and deliver this kind of instruction can be daunting. In response to this situation, many school districts provide in-service training to help teachers become more comfortable as they think about and prepare for increasingly technologically based instructional roles.

Researchers have identified some measures school districts can take to assist teachers in adapting to and making effective use of newer communication technologies (Foa, Schwab, & Johnson, 1998):

- Providing support for teachers who are early adopters of innovations
- Providing training in how to use new technologies (which is as important as purchasing hardware and software)
- Training and building enthusiasm for technological change among administrators (which is critical if teachers are to receive needed administrative support when they begin using new technologies)

- Providing specific teacher training in the project-based, problem-solving, and constructivist approaches to teaching and schemes for managing classrooms so that individual learners may pursue different instructional ends

The Digital Divide

New technologies, to have any impact at all, must be accessible. Though the past two decades have witnessed dramatic advances in digital communication, different groups of people have responded differently to these developments. Experts who have studied new technologies have discovered enormous differences in the extent to which different categories of people use them. High percentages of people within some groups now actively work with these technologies, and high percentages of other groups scarcely use them at all. The term **digital divide** has been coined to describe this disparity.

The digital divide operates internationally as well as within the United States. For example, one recent study reported that 41% of all Internet users in the world live in Canada and the United States. Though Asia has a much larger total population than the combined total of Canada and the United States, people living on this continent account for only 20% of Internet users. South American Internet users comprise only 4% of the world's total (Digital Divide Network, 2002).

The United Nations, the World Bank, and other organizations interested in promoting more use of technology worldwide are taking steps to make these technologies more accessible to countries with limited numbers of digital technology users. These efforts are taken out of a conviction that countries need technologically literate populations to compete effectively in today's competitive economies. Similarly, the new communication technologies are thought to promote democracies. Because of the capacity it offers to link people, ideas, and government leaders, "the Internet has become both the fuel and the vehicle for a dramatic spread in democracy . . ."(Brown, October 9, 2001).

In the United States, a digital divide has been found between people who, collectively, tend to be (1) frequent and extensive users and those who are (2) less-frequent and more-limited users of newer digital technologies. See Figure 13.3 for a chart illustrating some of these differences.

MORE FREQUENCY OF USE	**LESS FREQUENCY OF USE**
• People with high incomes	• People with low incomes
• People who have had at least some college-level work	• People who did not graduate from high school
• Whites, Asian Americans, and Pacific Islanders	• African Americans and Latinos
• Younger people, especially those aged 10 to 25	• Older people, especially those over 60
• People living in rural areas	• People living in urban areas
• People who are employed	• People who are unemployed

FIGURE 13.3 Differences in Levels of Digital-Technology Use

Source: A Nation Online: How Americans Are Expanding Their Use of the Internet, by the National Telecommunications and Information Administration, 2002, Washington, DC: U.S. Department of Commerce, Economics, and Statistics Administration.

For educators, these trends present both positive news and continuing challenges. On the positive side, the growing presence of technologies in school is reflected in data that indicate that young people ages 10 to 25 use computers and access the Internet more frequently than do any other age group (National Telecommunications and Information Administration, 2002). This finding attests to the impact on learners of school systems' efforts to place more and more computers in schools, link them to the Internet, and encourage teachers to integrate their use into the regular instructional program. There is evidence, too, that some groups who, a decade ago, were infrequent users of advanced communication technologies now use them routinely. For example, until the late 1990s, fewer females than males used computers and the Internet. Today, these sex-based differences have disappeared (National Telecommunications and Information Administration).

WEB EXTENSION 13–4

Digital Divide Network

The Digital Divide Network brings together an electronically linked community of people interested in ensuring access to new technologies to groups that include Native Americans, females, economically impoverished Americans, the homeless, and many others. In addition to feature articles, the Digital Divide Network sponsors an electronic discussion group you can join if you would like to discuss equity and technology issues with others.

http://www.digitaldividenetwork.org

There are also interesting, and positive, developments that indicate that the technology-usage gap is closing between (1) whites and Asian Americans/Pacific Islanders and (2) African Americans and Latinos. In one recent three-year period, Internet use by African Americans grew at the annual rate of 31%, and Internet use by Latinos grew at an annual rate of 26% (National Telecommunications and Information Administration, 2002). Use among whites and Asian Americans/Pacific Islanders has continued to grow, but at a slower rate. Educators and others interested in promoting more use of digital technology hope this trend will continue. If it does, differences in computer use among racial and ethnic groups will greatly narrow in the years ahead.

One aspect of the digital divide that greatly concerns educational leaders is the disparity between the availability of technological equipment in high-poverty schools and affluent schools. One recent study reported that, on average, 16 learners shared a single computer in high-poverty schools. The comparable figure for affluent schools was seven learners (National PTA, 2001–2002). Large numbers of learners per computer in high-poverty schools may limit the types of computer-based learning teachers assign. There also is evidence that computers are used more often in high-poverty than in affluent schools to engage learners in unchallenging drill-and-practice activities (Merrow, 2001).

In thinking about how computer technology relates to families' economic conditions, consider the consequences of some learners having opportunities to use computers at home and others being limited to using them at school. Learners whose parents or guardians have limited incomes have few opportunities to take advantage of digital technologies once they leave the school building. To deal with this problem, some school districts are keeping school computer labs open during the evening so learners can use them if they need to do so. Many public libraries now make Internet-connected computers available for patrons, including students, to use. The private sector also has established some programs to address this issue. For example, Intel's Computer Clubhouse program, which is now in place in 50 locations throughout the country, establishes centers in underprivileged neighborhoods. These centers are designed to help learners from impoverished families develop their computer skills (Goot, 2002).

In times past, educators worked hard to provide textbooks for every learner. The idea was to provide every child with the basic tools needed to achieve academic success. If new technologies require learners to have access to specialized technological equipment, then the same equity principle that drove the effort to provide all learners with texts will support efforts to ensure that learners, regardless of family income or personal background, have access to these necessary learning tools. Developing ways to diminish and, it is hoped, to eliminate the digital divide may be among the most important tasks you and your colleagues confront in the decades ahead.

Protecting Learners

Digital-communication technologies such as those supporting e-mail and the World Wide Web make it possible for information from almost limitless numbers of sources to be directed to computers that are linked to the Internet. If you use e-mail, you probably are familiar with the problem of dealing with large numbers of unsolicited messages, many of them coming from individuals and firms pushing dubious financial schemes, encouraging you to participate in online gambling, or soliciting your interest in sites that feature pornographic material. When you use the Web, pages you view may feature pop-up ads directing your attention to sites that, in some cases, may not be suitable for learners. Certainly, any search engine can quickly identify dozens of sites featuring content that many parents and guardians consider unsuitable for young people. In addition, many online chat rooms feature exchanges of obscenities and discussions of topics that responsible adults believe are inappropriate for school-age learners.

In addition to concerns about learners' access to inappropriate material, school leaders also fear that some learners may use Internet-linked computers illegally or unethically. As a teacher, for example, you do not want members of your class to violate copyright laws nor to find completed term papers that they can copy and submit as their own work. Professional educators also sometimes worry that older learners will use taxpayer-supported electronic equipment and networks to engage in business transactions, for example through the use of Web-based auction sites.

In response to concerns about possible misuse of digital-communication technology, schools around the country have worked hard in recent years to develop **acceptable-use policies (AUPs).** Such policies typically make clear distinctions between acceptable and unacceptable learner uses of technology. Often, too, they contain information about sanctions that will be applied to learners who fail to follow established acceptable-use guidelines. These guidelines often differ according to variables including (1) whether learners have completed a class in computer responsibility, (2) learners' grade levels, and (3) whether online work is being done as part of a class assignment. Many lists of unacceptable uses include (1) participation in chat rooms, (2) sending and receiving personal e-mail (unless this is part of an assigned class activity), and (3) posting personal Web pages (unless this is part of an assigned class activity).

AUPs often include lists of the kinds of Web sites learners are forbidden to visit using school computers with Internet connections. Typical examples include Web sites that

- Promote violence or illegal behavior
- Feature sexually explicit information

- Provide entry to chat rooms
- Sell term papers
- Allow for copyright infringement or plagiarism
- Permit users to engage in commercial transactions (National Education Association, 1998)

Interest in protecting young people from certain kinds of Internet content helped win support for two important pieces of federal legislation you should know. These are the **Children's Internet Protection Act (CIPA)** and the **Neighborhood Children's Internet Protection Act (N-CIPA)**. Both laws are part of Public Law 105-554, a large federal appropriations measure passed in December 2000. Provisions of these acts have important implications for schools.

WHAT DO YOU THINK?

ARE SCHOOL RULES LIMITING LEARNER USE OF THE INTERNET TOO RESTRICTIVE?

In a report titled *The Digital Disconnect: The Widening Gap Between Internet-Savvy Students and Their Schools*, investigators Douglas Levin and Sousan Arafeh (2002) report that over three quarters of young people between the ages of 12 and 17 go online. Thirty percent to forty percent of teenagers fall into a technologically savvy category of elite Internet users. The numbers of young people in this group are growing. These sophisticated users regularly go to the Internet to do school-related work, including locating resources, downloading source materials, collaborating with other class members, and storing papers and notes. Many students in this group express frustration with school policies that are designed to

- Limit their access to the Internet to specific time periods during the school day.
- Limit their access to the Internet to only a few school computers located in particular rooms (often a computer laboratory).
- Impose content filters that are so restrictive that many legitimate information sources cannot be accessed from school-based computers.

WHAT DO YOU THINK?

1. Many school policies regarding limitation of learner access to the Internet are driven by state and federal legislation. Should such legislation exist at all? If yes, what kinds of limitations should schools be required to impose on learner Internet access?
2. Complaints of learners surveyed to gather information for *The Digital Disconnect* report centered on the idea that school policies were preventing them from accessing important Internet content. Are these concerns justified? Why or why not?
3. Suppose there were no federal or state regulations requiring schools to limit learner access to the Internet. If you were charged with putting together an Internet use policy for learners in your school, what might its provisions be? How would you reconcile (1) the need to maximize the potential for young people to learn from the Internet and (2) the need to prevent harm from coming to learners from Internet content?

 To respond to these questions online, go to the What Do You Think? *module for this chapter of the Companion Website.*

The CIPA requires schools and school libraries to install filters on all computers accessing the Internet that will block materials that (1) are obscene, (2) feature child pornography, or (3) are harmful to minors. School districts must have mechanisms in place that ensure that these provisions are enforced. The law also requires each school to have an adopted **Internet safety policy.** In addition, public meetings must be held to discuss the contents of this policy.

CIPA's companion law, the N-CIPA, focuses on the kinds of information that must be included in the Internet Safety Policy. The policy must include details regarding:

- Access by minors to inappropriate matter on the Internet and Web,
- The safety and security of minors when using e-mail, chat rooms, and other forms of direct electronic communications,
- Unauthorized access, including so-called "hacking," and other unlawful activities by minors online,
- Unauthorized disclosure, use, and dissemination of minors' personal-identification information, and
- Measures designed to restrict minors' access to harmful materials.

Failure to comply with CIPA and N-CIPA can produce negative financial consequences for school districts. Among other things, they may lose their access to the e-rate.

Because you may wish to make considerable use of Web-based technologies in your own work with learners, you need to learn about specific provisions of your district's acceptable-use policy. You may also have opportunities to participate in periodic revisions of the Internet safety policy. Concerns about protecting learners from potentially harmful Internet content and ensuring that they use the capabilities of the technology responsibly show little signs of abating. It is likely that you, other professionals, parents, guardians, community representatives, and political leaders will devote great attention to these concerns in the years ahead.

WEB EXTENSION 13–5

Pew Internet and American Life Project

This is the home page of the Pew Internet Project, an initiative funded by the Pew Charitable Trusts. Recent project reports focus on issues as diverse as divergences between Internet use at school and the interests of technologically savvy learners, the effects of broadband access on home-based Internet users, and the criteria Internet users apply when considering health care information provided by Internet sites.

http://www.pewinternet.org/

WEB EXTENSION 13–6

Electronic Portfolios

At this site, Dr. Helen Barrett provides numerous links that feature content about maintaining electronic portfolios. You may be interested in following links to content about (1) teacher education and professional-development portfolios, (2) high school graduation portfolios, and (3) family involvement in early childhood portfolios.

http://helenbarrett.com/

Key Ideas in Summary

- Technology has become such a pervasive feature of our national life that schools are being pressured by business leaders, political authorities, parents, guardians, and other citizens to incorporate more use of today's digital communication technologies into school programs.
- The leading professional organization advocating on behalf of technology in the schools, the International Society for Technology in Education (ISTE), has developed technology standards for learners and teachers. Increasing numbers of states and school districts are establishing technology standards, many of which are derived from those ISTE developed.
- Technology is not a single instructional methodology. It is a means to an end. Successful applications of technology require you to have a clear instructional purpose in mind and to select a technological alternative that is well suited to the particular needs of your students and instructional setting.
- Change does not automatically result when new technologies become available. Existing technologies place some restraints on what educators and learners can do. However, traditional practices also act as restraints. As a result, new technologies, although they offer the potential for change, do not always produce change.
- Today's newer digital-communication technologies are being applied in schools to achieve many purposes. Examples include (1) developing learners' research capabilities, (2) supporting expanded course offerings, (3) providing high-quality instructional services to underperforming schools, (4) allowing learners to simulate real-life experiences, and (5) matching instructional practices to characteristics of learners with special needs.
- Teachers rejected some technological innovations in the past because they failed to respond to teachers' needs or created new problems. Though the jury is still out on the fate of newer digital-communication technologies, there are hopes these innovations may take firm root in our nation's schools. These expectations result from the broad societal support for many of these innovations, the willingness of schools to invest in needed equipment, and in the increasing realization that resources to prepare teachers to take advantage of the capabilities offered by these technologies are needed.
- New technologies present some educators with ongoing challenges. Among them are (1) the high costs associated with technology-related equipment and instructional materials, maintenance and replacement of equipment and support materials, and teacher training; (2) within-the-classroom distractions occasioned by learner use and misuse of cell phones, PDAs, and other high-tech equipment; (3) changing the role conceptions of teachers trained before today's digital-technology revolution; and (4) differences in access to computers, the Internet, and the Web outside of school by learners from impoverished backgrounds.
- Concern about possible dangers that can come to learners who have access to the World Wide Web, the Internet, and other modern communication technologies has resulted in the passage of several important laws. These include the Children's Internet Protection Act and the Neighborhood Children's Internet Protection Act. Concerns about learner safety have prompted school districts to adopt acceptable-use policies that spell out acceptable and unacceptable kinds of learner uses of technology.

Chapter 13 Self-Test

To review terms and concepts in this chapter, go to the Companion Website and take the Chapter 13 Self-Test. Feedback for the self-test is immediate. You can keep track of your self-test scores, or you can submit them to your professor via e-mail.

Preparing for Praxis

To learn about the Praxis test and complete this activity online, go to the Preparing for Praxis *module for this chapter of the Companion Website.*

You may be required to pass Educational Testing Service's Praxis II exam as you seek formal authorization to teach in the public schools. The *Principles of Learning and Teaching* component of Praxis II seeks to assess your knowledge about these topics: (1) Students as Learners, (2) Instruction and Assessment, (3) Communication Techniques, and (4) Profession and Community.

Information presented in this chapter may be especially relevant as you prepare for questions related to the categories of Students as Learners, Instruction and Assessment, and Communication Techniques. Some content may also deal with issues having logical ties to the Profession and Community category. You may find it useful to prepare a chart similar to the one provided here. As you encounter information related to individual categories, you can enter it into the chart. A completed chart of this kind will be useful as you prepare to take the Praxis II exam.

Students as Learners	**Instruction and Assessment**
• Student Development and the Learning Process	• Instructional Strategies
• Students as Diverse Learners	• Planning Instruction
• Student Motivation and the Learning Environment	• Assessment Strategies
Communication Techniques	**Profession and Community**
• Basic, Effective, Verbal and Nonverbal Communication Techniques	• The Reflective Practitioner
• Effect of Cultural and Gender Differences on Communications in the Classroom	• The Larger Community
• Types of Questions That Can Stimulate Discussion in Different Ways for Particular Purposes	

For Your Initial-Development Portfolio

To complete this activity and submit your response online, go to the For Your Initial-Development Portfolio *module for this chapter of the Companion Website.*

1. What materials and ideas that you learned in this chapter about *influences of technology* will you include as "evidence" in your portfolio? Select up to three separate items of information. Number them 1, 2, and 3.
2. Think about why you selected these materials. As you do so, consider these issues:
   • Specific uses you might make of this information as you plan, deliver, and assess the impact of your teaching
   • The compatibility of the information with your own priorities and values
   • Any contributions this information can make to your development as a teacher
   • Factors that led you to include this information, as opposed to some alternatives you considered but rejected

3. Place a check in the chart here to indicate the INTASC standard(s) to which each of your items of information relates. (You may wish to refer to Chapter 1 for more-detailed information about INTASC.)

INTASC Standard Number

ITEM OF EVIDENCE NUMBER	S1	S2	S3	S4	S5	S6	S7	S8	S9	S10
1										
2										
3										

4. Prepare a written reflection in which you analyze the decision-making process you followed. In your comments, mention the INTASC standard(s) to which your selected material relates.

Reflections

 To respond to these questions online, go to the Reflections *module for this chapter of the* Companion Website.

1. Today's digital technologies make it possible for students to engage in simulated experiences of complex realities. Critic Bill Rukeyser (Philipkoski, 2000) points out that sometimes schools have taken advantage of these capabilities to substitute computer-based simulations for learning experiences that students could experience directly. For example, instead of having students do hands-on work in chemistry labs, some students simply use software to perform simulated versions of experiments. Rukeyser argues that discouraging students from directly interacting with the real world denies them valuable learning experiences. He claims that overuse of computers in schools substitutes artificial learning experiences for ones that have a stronger reality base. Do you agree? If so, how will you decide whether to use computer technology in your own classroom?

2. How might your own initial assumptions about your role as a teacher be influenced by newer developments in digital-communication technology? How do you feel about changes you may have to make in your approach to working with learners? How will you begin preparing for these changes?

3. Bart Pasha, the Center for Applied Special Technology's director of research, suggests that new technologies may have as profound an influence on teaching and learning as the invention of the printing press. Do you agree or disagree? On what do you base your own views about technology's potential impact on school classrooms?

4. Some teachers are excited about new technologies' abilities to help learners. Others are confounded by classroom disruptions that occur when pagers, cell phones, portable computers, and other technological devices interfere with the learning process. In the main, are benefits of newer technologies worth the problems that sometimes accompany them? Why, or why not?

5. As part of your teacher-preparation program, you probably will receive considerable instruction related to incorporating newer technologies into your routine instructional practices. Based on what you know, what, specifically, do you think you need to learn about making effective uses of these technologies as you implement them with your own students? What other sources might you consult in addition to your professors?

Field Experiences, Projects, and Enrichment

1. Interview someone who teaches a grade level and subject area that interest you. Ask how this teacher incorporates technology into the instructional program. What advantages do uses of this technology provide learners? What difficulties, problems, and challenges has this person encountered when incorporating newer technologies into the instructional program?

2. Invite a school principal or central-office administrator to come to your class to discuss issues associated with incorporating more use of technology into instructional programs. What has been the impact on budgets? What kind of an equipment-replacement cycle has been adopted? What provisions have been made to ensure that help is available to teachers when equipment breaks down or software fails to function as designed? Have special arrangements been made to instruct teachers on appropriate uses of new technologies?

3. Visit a professional who has expertise in the area of special education. What kinds of technological aids are now being used to help learners with disabilities and other unique conditions achieve? To what extent are these aids being used in regular classrooms to help learners with disabilities? How are regular-classroom teachers being prepared to use and manage this equipment effectively?

4. Look again at the ISTE technology standards for teachers and students. To what extent is your own preparation program preparing you to meet ISTE's teacher standards? Do your state and local school district have technology standards for students? How do they compare with those ISTE developed?

References

Brown, M. M. (2001, October 9). Democracy and the information revolution. *Digital Divide Network.* [http://www.digitaldividenetwork.org/content/stories/index.cfm?key=192]

Children's Internet Protection Act. [http://www.ifea.net/cipa.html]

Chou, L., McClintock, R., Morett, F., & Nix, D. H. (1993). *Technology and education: New wine in new bottles—Choosing pasts and imagining educational futures.* New York: New Lab for Teaching and Learning.

Cuban, L. (2001). *Oversold & underused: Computers in the classroom.* Cambridge, MA: Harvard University Press.

Dean, K. (2002, June 19). Schools' tech support: Students. *Wired News.* [http://www.wired.com/news/school/0,1383,53278,00.html]

Dewey, J. (1910). *How we think.* Boston: D. C. Heath.

Digital Divide Network. (2002). Digital divide basics fact sheet. [http://www.digitaldividenetwork.org/content/stories/index.cfm?key=168]

Fitzgerald, S. (1999). Technology's real cost. www.electronic-school.com. [http://www.electronic-school.com/199909/0999sbot.html]

Foa, L., Schwab, R., & Johnson, M. (1998). Introducing technologies into the schools: Triumph or train wreck? *Technology Briefs.* [http://www.nea.org/cet/briefs/13.html]

Glennan, T. K., & Melmed, A. (1996). *Fostering the use of educational technology: Elements of a national strategy.* Santa Monica, CA: Rand Corporation.

Goot, D. (2002, July 15). Divide is more than digital. *Wired News.* [http://www.wired.com/news/print/0,1294,53849,00.html]

International Society for Technology in Education. (2000). *National educational technology standards for students: Connecting curriculum and technology.* Eugene, OR: Author.

International Society for Technology in Education. (2002). *National educational technology standards for teachers: Preparing teachers to use technology.* Eugene, OR: Author.

Levin, D., & Arafeh, S. (2002, August 14). *The digital disconnect: The widening gap between Internet-savvy students and their schools.* Washington, DC: Pew Internet & American Life Project.

McHenry, E. (2002, June 1). The digital revolution's new bounty. *HGSE News.* [http://www.gse.harvard.edu/news/features/cast06012002.html]

Merrow, J. (2001). *Choosing excellence: 'Good enough' schools are not good enough.* Landham, MD: Scarecrow Press.

Murray, C. (2002, August 1). ED: Online courses key to boosting achievement. *eSCHOOL NEWSonline.* [http://www.eschoolnews.com/news/showStory.cfm?ArticleID=3870]

National Center for Education Statistics. (2000). *Teachers' tools for the 21st century*. Washington, DC: U.S. Department of Education, Office of Educational Research and Improvement.

National Education Association. (1998). Development of student acceptable use policies. *Technology Briefs*. [http://www.nea.org/cet/BRIEFS/brief12.html]

National PTA. (2001–2002). Education technology. [http://www.pta.org/ptawashington/issues/ed_tech.asp]

National Telecommunications and Information Administration. (2002). *A nation online: How Americans are expanding their use of the Internet*. Washington, DC: U.S. Department of Commerce, Economics, and Statistics Administration.

Neighborhood Children's Internet Protection Act (Bill S 1545 IS) [http://www.ifea.net/cipa.html]

No Child Left Behind Act of 2001, Public Law 107-110, 115 Stat. 1425 (2002).

Philipkoski, K. (2000, August 17). Costs do not compute. *Wired News*. [http://www.wired.com/news/school/0,1383,38079,00.html]

Piaget, J., & Inhelder, B. (1958). *The growth of logical thinking from childhood to adolescence: An essay on the construction of formal operational structures* (A. Parsons and S. Milgram, Trans.). New York: Basic Books.

Rector, L. (2002). A classroom without walls. [http://www.time.com/time/teach/class.html]

Roblyer, M. D. (2003). *Integrating educational technology into teaching* (3rd ed.). Upper Saddle River, NJ: Merrill/Prentice Hall.

Rogers, E. M. (1995). *Diffusion of innovations* (4th ed.). New York: Free Press.

Rose, D. H., & Meyer, A. (2002). *Teaching every student in the digital age: Universal design for learning*. Alexandria, VA: Association for Supervision and Curriculum Development.

School board weighs ban on student laptops, PDAs. (2002, June 30). *eSCHOOL NEWSonline*. [http://www.eschoolnews.com/news/showStory.cfm?ArticleID=2943&ref=wo.]

Should cell phones and pagers be allowed in school? (2001, March). *NEAToday Online*. [http://www.nea.org/neatoday/0103/debate.html]

Telecommunications Communications Act of 1996. http://www.fcc.gov/telecom.html

T.H.E. Journal. (2001, May). *First annual state-of-the-states survey*. [http://www.thejournal.com/magazine/stateofthestates]

Tyack, D., & Cuban, L. (1995). *Tinkering toward utopia: A century of public school reform*. Cambridge, MA: Harvard University Press.

Vallecorsa, A. (2001, March 21). Personal interview. Greensboro, NC: University of North Carolina at Greensboro.

Vygotsky, L. (1962). *Thought and language*. Cambridge, MA: MIT Press.

Wired News. (2000, September 12). Feds elated with e-rate. [http://wired.com/news/school/0,1383,38729,00.html]

CHAPTER

14

Legal Issues Affecting Learners and Teachers

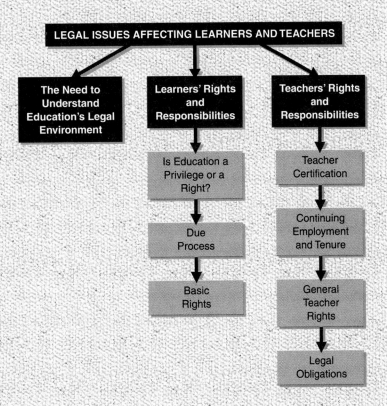

OBJECTIVES

This chapter will help you to

- recognize why today's teachers need to be familiar with the legal context within which they work.

- describe due process protections that students enjoy.

- describe some laws that have extended many constitutional rights of citizens to students.

- recognize the importance of legal issues associated with such issues as teacher certification, continuing employment, and tenure.

- describe some general patterns of court decisions regarding teachers' constitutional rights.

- point out examples of teachers' basic legal obligations.

THE NEED TO UNDERSTAND EDUCATION'S LEGAL ENVIRONMENT

As a prospective teacher, have you ever thought about how laws, regulations, and court decisions will affect your work? Many newcomers to education are unaware of how legal issues help define and, in some cases, can constrain what teachers can do. A lack of appreciation of these issues is widespread. For example, a popular talk show host recently recommended wholesale expulsion of students who cause discipline problems in school—a perspective revealing total ignorance of the legal protections today's learners enjoy. A newspaper columnist seriously recommended that a local school district simply pass a rule requiring every student to wear a prescribed uniform without as much as hinting that such an action probably would precipitate legal proceedings against the school district.

You will be entering a profession in which your actions will be greatly influenced by the legal environment within which today's schools operate. You have a professional responsibility to know the basics of the law and the implications they hold for your role, your relationship to students, your need to follow an adopted curriculum, and your professional and personal life. Without such information, you might take actions that have serious legal consequences.

As you begin learning about the general legal environment of education, you need to keep in mind that you are unlikely to find information that tells you exactly how a law will be applied to a particular set of circumstances. Each situation has unique features that may influence how the courts apply laws and previous legal precedents. However, you will find it useful to know and consider some general patterns as you seek to make informed decisions about situations that have possible legal implications.

WEB EXTENSION 14–1

Thomas: Legislative Information on the Internet

This site provides many links to sites with information related to education and the law in the United States. You will be able to locate education codes for individual states, summaries of court decisions, and many other topics.

<u>thomas.loc.gov</u>

LEARNERS' RIGHTS AND RESPONSIBILITIES

A few decades ago, you would have felt little need to understand the legal principles and issues related to your students. Rules and regulations governing teachers and teaching were not complex, and litigation was rare. A legal doctrine known as **in loco parentis** governed relationships between teachers and learners.

According to *in loco parentis,* the school and the teacher acted "in the place of the parent." This meant that school administrators and teachers were assumed to be agents who would promote the best interests of students and who would not harm them. Essentially, school authorities could deal with learners with little fear of legal complaints. This situation began to erode about four decades ago, when learners and parents and guardians acting for learners began to bring legal actions that questioned the basic assumptions underlying the *in loco parentis* doctrine. Over time, various court decisions increasingly have extended to students the same kinds of legal protections that adult citizens enjoy. As a teacher today, you can arm yourself against potentially unpleasant legal consequences by becoming acquainted with the legal context that currently governs relationships between educators and students.

Is Education a Privilege or a Right?

At the heart of the relationship between legal principles and education is the question of whether education is a right or a privilege. If education is a privilege, then those provisions of the U.S. Constitution protecting the rights of citizens are of minor concern. In fact, for most of its history, education was viewed as a privilege. When legal actions were taken, courts did not refer to the Bill of Rights for guidance. Rather, they based decisions on whether there was a reasonable relationship between the school policy and an educational purpose (Fischer, Schimmel, & Steelman, 2002).

Even if a school policy invaded learners' privacy or deprived them of an opportunity to receive an education, the courts generally were reluctant to substitute their judgments for those of school officials, and school officials had great latitude in making and implementing school policies and rules. If learners were removed from school for violating a school rule or regulation, they had little legal recourse. For example, in 1915 a young person was expelled because he refused to apologize for a speech he made during a school assembly that was critical of school officials. The state courts upheld his expulsion on the grounds that it was necessary in order to maintain discipline (Fischer, Schimmel, & Steelman, 2002).

The view of schooling as a privilege rather than a right began to unravel in the last half of the 20th century. Several factors led to this fundamental change. For one thing, it became apparent during the latter part of the century that literacy and education had become critical to individuals' economic well-being. Increasingly, denying a person an education was seen as denying that individual the right to economic and social advancement. Thus it was argued that education should be considered as a "substantial right" to which all citizens were entitled.

Social circumstances also had an impact. During the course of the fighting in Vietnam, many individuals questioned the wisdom of governmental officials, including those charged with managing the schools. One landmark case brought together the issue of schooling as a right and the wisdom of school officials: ***Tinker v. Des Moines Independent School District (1969).*** In this case, a group of learners in the Des Moines, Iowa, public schools wore black armbands to protest the U.S. involvement in Vietnam. School officials passed a rule prohibiting the wearing of the armbands. When students refused to remove them, they were suspended. They challenged this action, and the case eventually reached the U.S. Supreme Court. The Supreme Court ruled that once states establish public schools, individuals have a property right to the educational services the schools provide. The Court pointed out that neither students nor teachers leave their constitutional rights at the schoolhouse door.

This ruling established that individuals have a right to a public education and that learners enjoy the constitutional protections of any citizen. These rights cannot be abridged unless the specific process of due process as defined in the Constitution is followed. This ruling placed legal issues in schools in a whole new context and opened to question many traditional policies and actions of teachers and school officials.

Due Process

The Fourteenth Amendment to the U.S. Constitution outlines the principles of due process. Due process requires that certain procedures be followed in any action that might put a citizen's rights in jeopardy.

Do Learners Have Too Many Rights?

During earlier periods in our history, schooling was legally regarded as a *privilege*. Accordingly, professional educators were free to impose rules and enforce sanctions, including expulsion, without much concern for the legal rights of learners. Over the past few decades, schooling has been redefined as a *right*, and the full protection of the Constitution has been extended to students.

Some people see this extension of rights as reasonable. They point out that, in the past, school officials have acted capriciously to remove young people for arbitrary reasons that had little to do with the safe and orderly operation of the schools. Because education has such a powerful influence on a person's future, they argue that expulsion cannot be left to the whim of an administrator. They contend that this extension of rights has made schools better places.

Recent incidents of violence in schools across America have led others to believe that young people have too many rights and that school officials need more authority to protect the health and safety of students. Some claim that poor discipline in schools is rooted in the loss of authority of school officials. Proposed remedies often include reducing the number of students' legal rights.

What Do You Think?

1. Should schooling be defined as a privilege so that professional educators can more aggressively respond to problems without being so concerned about their legal rights?
2. How do you respond to the contention that poor discipline is related to the erosion of the authority of teachers and administrators?

 To respond to these questions online, go to the What Do You Think? *module for this chapter of the Companion Website.*

To be entitled to due process individuals must show that they have been deprived of either a **liberty right** or a **property right.** A liberty right refers to the right of people to be free from all restraints except those imposed by law. As applied to schools, liberty rights mean that decisions affecting learners cannot be arbitrary. They must be supported by relevant rules and regulations. A property right is the right to a specific tangible or intangible property.

The issue of property rights needs more clarification. Most importantly, you should know that these rights do not always refer to tangible assets. There also can be property rights to names, likenesses, and other kinds of intangibles. People interested in expanding the application of property rights to education have argued that a good education represents a kind of personal property and, hence, it should be regarded as a property right. In recent years, various court decisions have supported the idea that individuals have a property right to education.

Due process procedures that embed a respect for both property rights and liberty rights seek to ensure that people receive fair treatment in an adversarial situation. Due process imposes requirements such as the following:

- Individuals are not to be disciplined on the basis of unwritten rules or laws.
- Rules and laws are not to be vague.
- Individuals are entitled to a hearing before an impartial body.

- The identity of witnesses must be revealed.
- Decisions must be supported by substantial evidence.

What this means for teachers and schools is that

- Rules governing learner behavior must be distributed in writing to learners and their parents.
- Whenever a learner is accused of a rules infraction that might result in the loss of a right, the charges must be provided in writing.
- Notice must be given in sufficient time for the learner and his or her representative to prepare a defense.
- A hearing must be held in a timely manner, usually within two weeks.
- Individuals have a right to present a defense and to introduce evidence. An individual may have a right to legal counsel and to confront witnesses. These provisions have been applied differently according to the circumstances and the seriousness of situations. (Fischer, Schimmel, & Steelman, 2002).
- Decisions must be based on the evidence presented and must be given within a reasonable period of time.
- Individuals have a right to appeal.

These due process provisions have resulted in significant changes in school practice. Rules must be written. They must be clear. Evidence needs to be gathered, and a formal hearing must be held. All school districts now have specific procedures in place, based on due process. Simply suspending or expelling students based on the judgment of a school administrator or teacher is no longer permissible.

There are a few circumstances in which rigorous due process is not required. If a discipline situation does not involve a basic right, then due process is not required. For example, expulsion is a serious matter because it denies a learner a right to access educational services. Hence, rigorous due process procedures must be followed in cases that can lead to expulsion. On the other hand, if suspension of a student is for less than 10 days, a less-complex version of due process is required. This involves providing an oral or written notice of the offense and an explanation of the evidence and giving the accused an opportunity to present his or her view (Zirkel & Richardson, 1988).

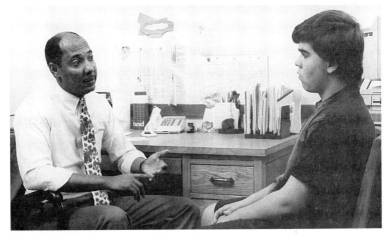

Students accused of serious violations of school rules must be informed of their rights and the nature of their offense.

WEB EXTENSION 14–2

Summary of Due Process Procedures

You will find information at this site about guidelines that are applied in cases that may result in a student's (a) immediate removal from school, (b) short-term suspension, or (c) long-term suspension/expulsion. There also is material on appeals.

www.wcpss.net/student-dueprocess/policies.html

Basic Rights

The following are examples of rights that now generally are extended to students:

- Freedom of expression
- Freedom of conscience
- Freedom from unreasonable search
- Freedom from harassment
- Right to privacy
- Special rights for learners with disabilities

Freedom of Expression.   The First Amendment to the U.S. Constitution provides citizens with a guarantee of **freedom of expression.** This right guarantees that citizens, except in a small number of highly specialized situations, face no governmental restrictions on what they can say. It is one of the most fundamental rights of citizens. Many court cases have focused on the extent to which schools can regulate freedom of expression.

Though the Supreme Court in the previously discussed *Tinker* case struck down arbitrary school rules that limited learners' freedom of expression, the ruling did not extend unrestricted freedom-of-expression rights to school learners. In many subsequent court cases, judges have wrestled with the question of when some limitations might legally be placed on learners' freedom of expression. Court decisions in individual cases have weighed carefully the expression rights of individual learners and the school authorities to discharge such responsibilities as providing safe and orderly learning environments.

In general, the courts have ruled that student expression cannot be prohibited simply to avoid discomfort or unpopular viewpoints that might be contrary to those of school officials. However, expression can be limited if it results in material or substantial interference with the work of a school or the rights of others. For example, limits on freedom of expression have been upheld when articles of clothing or symbols have led to fights or when the exercise of free speech has acted to disrupt classes. In addition, school officials have the right to punish learners who use lewd and offensive speech or who incite others to fight.

One case that came before the Supreme Court involved a student who, in a nominating speech for a friend, used language filled with sexual innuendo even after being warned by two teachers not to do so. The Court upheld the school district and stated that the public school, as an instrument of the state, may establish standards of civil and mature conduct (*Bethel School District No. 403 v. Fraser,* 1986). In general, the First Amendment does not protect behaviors of learners who engage in threats of violence (*Deskbook Encyclopedia of American School Law,* 2002). Learners who face legal action after making threats involving shooting, bombing, or otherwise rendering serious harm to others are likely to find little sympathy in the courts.

Censorship, another interesting freedom-of-expression issue, was the focus of the *Hazelwood School District v. Kuhlmeier* (1988) case. This case centered on the actions of a school principal who censored a school paper article that dealt with teenage pregnancy. The students involved with writing and publishing the article claimed that the principal's action illegally limited their freedom of expression. The Supreme Court ruled that such activities as theatrical presentations and student publications are a part of the curriculum and carry the implicit endorsement of the school. Therefore, administrative leaders responsible for the operation of the school and its programs can legally control expression occurring in this situation. The principal's actions were upheld.

Another area relating to freedom of expression involves actions schools have taken to regulate clothing that learners can wear to school. Sometimes dress codes specify the kinds of clothing that are acceptable. In other instances, school districts have decided to deal with the problem by prescribing a school uniform for students. There have been legal challenges both to dress codes and to school-uniform policies.

Let's first of all look at why school districts have adopted dress codes and uniform policies. Sometimes, school leaders have argued that certain kinds of clothing compromise learners' safety or threaten the health of others. On other occasions, they have contended that certain kinds of learner dress have the potential to disrupt the learning process. These disruptions sometimes relate to clothing being too revealing and sometimes to gang-related symbols that have the potential to generate conflicts among members of different gangs.

In considering general learner dress codes, the courts have wrestled with the question of whether a learner's choice of dress involves a constitutionally protected liberty right. Decisions generally have supported school dress codes when representatives of the districts have successfully demonstrated that their codes featured guidelines that preserved learners' health and safety and reduced discipline problems.

Debates about school dress codes continue to rage. During the 1990s, proponents of school uniforms pushed them as a solution to important educational problems, and many states rushed to pass legislation encouraging local schools to implement policies requiring learners to wear them. School districts that adopted these policies often found that they cause unanticipated, new problems. For example, in some places, parents provided their children with waivers to the uniform policy as presents and rewards for good grades. In other locations, more-affluent parents allowed their children to opt out. This action led to situations in which only racially diverse groups of less-affluent learners had to wear the prescribed uniforms. Finally, school administrators found that an inordinate amount of their time was being spent with paperwork associated with monitoring who did or did not have authorization to opt out of the uniform policy (Zernike, 2002). As a result of these difficulties, many school districts that once had mandatory uniform policies have abandoned them. Some state authorities, realizing that many problems have resulted from opt-out provisions in legislation, are working to remove those provisions.

The courts have considered a number of cases related to school-uniform policies. In a recent federal decision, judges in the Fifth Circuit ruled that mandatory uniforms are constitutional if: (1) they further a substantial government interest, (2) the interest is unrelated to the suppression of learner expression, and (3) incidental restrictions of First Amendment activities are not required to facilitate that interest (Fischer, Schimmel, & Steelman, 2002). Mandatory uniform policies that have avoided legal difficulties tend to have two basic characteristics. First, there has been heavy parental involvement at the school level when the policies have been proposed, debated, and adopted. Second, these successful policies tend to have an opt-out provision that allows parents and guardians to exempt their own children from the official dress code policy.

In addition to school regulations related to learners' clothing, some schools and school districts have attempted to impose regulations related to various aspects of personal appearance, particularly hairstyles. Critics have attacked these rules as invasions of liberty rights. Generally, the courts have viewed restrictions on hairstyles as more of an invasion of privacy than regulations related to clothing. Typically, judges in these cases have held that hairstyle is fundamental to personal appearance and restrictions on hairstyle can have important impacts on individuals. In addition, it has been difficult for school authorities to prove that hairstyle relates to issues of morality or that particular hairstyles substantially disturb the educational environment (Fischer, Schimmel, & Steelman, 2002).

Freedom of Conscience.   Controversies related to **freedom of conscience** have centered on several key issues. Among them are concerns related to the teaching of certain content, participation in ceremonies involving saluting the flag, and the free exercise of religion.

In recent years critics of reading materials have contended that certain books advance secular humanism and promote Satanism and witchcraft. The courts have generally upheld the rights of schools to use books that have a legitimate educational purpose. Decisions have reflected the ideas that required books are not advancing some poorly defined religion and that works of fantasy and fiction by well-known authors promote legitimate educational objectives (Fischer, Schimmel, & Steelman, 2002).

Another area relating to freedom of conscience that generates controversy involves saluting the U.S. flag. Supporters of the practice see saluting as a loyalty issue and believe that because the government supports the school, learners should give their allegiance willingly. Some religious groups object to the flag salute, along with others who object on other reasons of conscience. In general, the courts have ruled that learners can refuse to salute the flag on the basis of legal or moral convictions. Taken together, these decisions suggest that a learner's failure to salute the flag does not constitute a serious threat to the welfare of the state. In the absence of a compelling state interest, the courts give precedence to citizens' religious and moral convictions. They have also ruled that learners cannot be required to stand or leave a room while others participate in the flag-salute ceremony (*Lipp v. Morris,* 1978).

Federal-court decisions have decreed that students cannot be forced to participate in flag-saluting ceremonies.

The courts have determined that learners can be excused from certain segments of curriculum based on religious or moral grounds. Two principles have guided these decisions. The first relates to whether the subject being objected to is essential to some compelling state interest. The second refers to the degree to which school districts have the right to enforce regulations that ensure the efficient and effective operation of the schools. To understand how the first of these principles works, let's look at several issues that have come before the courts.

Although sex education courses are voluntary in many schools, in some schools they are not. It is these required sex education courses that often have drawn criticism. In adjudicating complaints about such policies, the courts have had to weigh arguments about how important the state's interest is in having citizens who have adequate knowledge of matters related to sexual relationships. Proponents of required sex education courses often point to the threat of AIDS and the social costs of teenage pregnancy as evidence of compelling state interests in this issue. Opponents contend that issues related to sexual understanding are personal and, sometimes, religious matters, not issues that should concern the state. Court decisions have varied somewhat. The courts have generally supported required sex education programs if there is a provision that allows individual families to remove their children from these classes if they wish to do so.

The courts have found it difficult to accept arguments that the state has a compelling interest in dancing in physical education classes or in assuring that learners watch particular films. As a result, judicial decisions generally have gone in favor of critics of these practices who have objected to them on religious grounds. It is possible, though, that in a future case school authorities might argue that a particular film presents curriculum content in a way that cannot be easily duplicated. In such a hypothetical case, the court might decide in favor of the film on the grounds that the state has a compelling interest in exposing learners to the content.

As noted earlier, in addition to the issue of whether the state has a compelling interest in some required school experience, courts also consider whether excusing some individuals from required program components of the school program might disrupt the educational process. School leaders often argue that accommodations that must be made for individuals who object to certain requirements create a disruption, require special accommodations for the involved learners, and place a hardship on the schools to find alternative materials and methods. For example, learners who are excused from reading a particular book or passage in an English class must be taken out of the classroom, taught individually, and provided with suitable alternative reading material.

Freedom from Unreasonable Search and Seizure.   The Fourth Amendment to the U.S. Constitution protects individuals against **unreasonable search and seizure.** This means that citizens can only be subjected to search when there is probable cause. **Probable cause** is a legal standard that requires that search actions, including issuing of warrants, must be justified by extraordinarily strong evidence that supports the view that someone is guilty of illegal behavior. Recent concerns about drug abuse and violence in schools have generated new interest in what kinds of searches school authorities legally can conduct.

School officials have a responsibility to maintain a safe educational environment. What is the balance between individual rights and the rights of school officials? Should school officials be required to meet the stringent test of probable cause? Probable cause requires a high standard of evidence to be met before certain actions can be taken. Could the less-stringent test of reasonable suspicion be used instead? Reasonable suspicion requires only evidence that is sufficiently compelling to convince a prudent and cautious individual that some criminal or illegal activity has occurred.

Typically, reasonable suspicion is the standard that has been applied to school searches. Two additional guidelines are applied. These relate to (1) the expectation of privacy and (2) the intrusiveness of the search. When a search will invade places where an individual has an expectation of privacy, or when it is potentially intrusive, then school officials need to have strong justification that approaches the probable cause test. For example, searching a student's desk is searching an area where there is little expectation of privacy. However, searching a personal possession such as a purse, where there is a higher expectation of privacy, requires more evidence and justification. **Intrusiveness** concerns the degree to which a search might come into close contact with the individual's body. The most intrusive of all is a strip search of learners, an action that some states prohibit.

When considering the appropriateness of a search, four tests need to be applied. These relate to

- The target of the search,
- The quality of information that has led to the search,
- The nature of the place to be searched, and
- The nature of the search itself.

There is more justification for a search when the targeted person or object poses significant potential danger to the learner population. Using this guideline, school authorities have more justification to initiate a search for a gun, bomb, or a controlled substance than for a missing CD player.

Before beginning a search, school authorities must assess the quality of the information they have that leads them to consider initiating this activity. They must weigh the reliability of the information using such criteria as the credibility of the person or persons who gave it to them. For example, if several identified individuals give school authorities similar information, officials have more-defensible grounds for launching a search than if information comes from a telephone message from an anonymous caller.

The third test concerns the nature of the place to be searched. If this is an area where there is a high expectation of privacy or where a search is potentially intrusive, then exceptionally solid information is required to justify a search. On the other hand, a proposed search of an area such as a school locker, where there is a low expectation of privacy, can be justified by less-rigorous evidence.

The fourth test focuses on the nature of the search itself. If searches of individuals are to be conducted, substantial evidence must be available to justify these actions. In making search decisions, school authorities also have to consider the ages and genders of individuals who may be searched.

The landmark case of *New Jersey v. T.L.O.* (1985) focused on several issues relating to school searches. In this case a female teacher entered a girl's restroom and found T.L.O. (the initials of the student) and another girl holding lighted cigarettes. Because smoking was against the school rules, she took both girls to the school office. When T.L.O. was asked to open her purse, she did so. Her open purse revealed additional cigarettes, drug paraphernalia, and other evidence suggesting she was engaged in selling drugs. T.L.O. claimed that the evidence could not be used against her because her purse was searched illegally. The Supreme Court ruled in favor of the school, rejecting the argument that probable cause was required to initiate this kind of a search. In their decision, the justices argued that school officials met the standard of reasonable suspicion and that this legal standard was sufficient if the case at issue involved a potential violation of either a school rule or a statute law. Because T.L.O. was observed smoking, a clear violation of a school rule, school officials were deemed to have sufficient legal grounds for their search. The fact that cigarettes were easily observable in her purse provided additional justification for the search.

Other questions have arisen when searches involved metal detectors, school lockers, school desks, and student cars. Although there have been no Supreme Court rulings, lower courts have generally applied the principle of reasonable suspicion established in *T.L.O.* The only exception seems to be if a search invades areas where learners have a high expectation of privacy. As a general rule, the courts have upheld searches of school lockers on the grounds that they are loaned to the students and young people have no expectation of privacy in these assigned spaces. In fact, school officials may have a duty to search lockers if they have a suspicion that something illegal or dangerous is being stored in them.

Case law in the area of search and seizure provides school officials with the right to search if there is a reasonable suspicion of wrongful activity. However, given the uncertainty in the applications of these standards, if you find yourself confronted with a situation that might lead you or others to conduct a search, you need to present the situation to a school administrator before acting. This person typically will check with the school district's legal counsel to get some assurance that there is a strong legal basis for the proposed search.

Freedom from Harassment.   School leaders are responsible for maintaining a safe and orderly educational environment. This means that if people's behaviors create a hostile environment, they need to be stopped. Among other things, learners should enjoy **freedom from harassment** when attending school. The courts have been especially severe in supporting learners and their families in documented cases in which teachers or administrators have engaged in harassment, particularly sexual harassment, of young people in the schools.

More recently, the issue of learner-to-learner harassment has become an issue. Although this is an emerging area of concern, the courts have generally ruled that the schools have a responsibility to take appropriate action if they know or should have known of the harassment. In other words, school officials cannot simply dismiss complaints of harassment or bullying as the problems of all young people. They must ensure that learners do not find schools to be hostile, even dangerous personal environments.

Right to Privacy.   In recent years concerns about potential misuses of many kinds of records, including school records, have prompted much interest in a learner's **right to privacy.** For example, some people have worried that a learner who has difficulty with a teacher in the early elementary grades might be stigmatized throughout his or her entire career by records suggesting that he or she is a troublemaker. Worries about possible misuses of records helped win passage of the **Family Educational Rights and Privacy Act** in 1974.

This act requires schools to provide parents and guardians free access to their children's school records. Furthermore, individuals over the age of 18 and those in postsecondary schools have a right to view their records. The law also restricts how schools can distribute those records. Before passage of this law, schools customarily released records to government agencies, law enforcement agencies, and others. Since adoption of the Family Educational Rights and Privacy Act, school records can be released only after strict guidelines have been followed. Access to records is restricted to personnel within the school and to those who have a "legitimate educational interest."

An implication for you as a teacher is that you need to choose your words carefully when writing comments about learners. Written notes or written comments might become a part of a learner's records that can be viewed by parents and by students who are 18 years of age or older. Parents and adult students can challenge material included in records if they believe it is inaccurate or unfair. Unsubstantiated or derogatory comments that label a student unfairly can lead to legal action. Negative comments about learners must be educationally relevant and have factual support.

You should also be sensitive to other, more-subtle ways that learners' privacy might be compromised. Such things as plotting learners' progress on charts that can be viewed by others can be a violation of privacy. You need to handle learner papers carefully and discreetly so that others do not have access to them. Faculty lounges are notorious as places where teachers complain about learners and even parents. You need to guard against this practice. You may find yourself involved in a legal action if parents or guardians suspect you have knowingly spread false gossip that harms a child's reputation.

The Family Educational Rights and Privacy Act also has implications for you when you seek a teaching position. Usually when you prepare your teacher-placement papers with your campus career center, you will be asked whether you prefer an **open file** or a **closed file.** If you choose an open file, the Family Educational Rights and Privacy Act allows you to retain the right to read everything that goes into it. If you chose a closed file, you waive that right. There are arguments for both open and closed files. Some people claim that school district personnel view open files negatively, believing that recommendations will be couched only in highly favorable terms to avoid any possible reaction from the person the file concerns. Others argue that you should not give up the right to an open file because, at some point, you may find it necessary to remove an unfairly negative recommendation that might hinder your employment opportunities. You will need to carefully weigh these issues and make your own decision about whether an open file or a closed file is best for you.

Special Rights for Learners with Disabilities.

Before the middle 1970s, many learners with disabilities were excluded from school or were placed in special classrooms. As a result of challenges from parents and guardians of children with disabilities, a series of state and federal laws addressed the needs of learners with disabilities. This legislation brought thousands of learners with disabilities into regular school classrooms for all or part of the school day. (For more information about learners with disabilities and specific legislation related to school services for these young people, see Chapter 6, "Meeting the Needs of Exceptional Learners.")

Provisions of this legislation require school districts to bear the cost of providing educational services to young people with disabilities. To establish compliance, school districts must do more than simply enroll these learners as members of regular school classrooms. They also must provide special equipment and services that will enable learners to derive educational benefits from their school experiences. If the school districts are unable to provide the services needed, they must pay for private facilities. In addition, attorney fees and costs must be paid by a school district if parents have to go to court to remedy an inappropriate placement.

A controversial part of legislation related to learners with disabilities concerns a legal requirement that school districts pay for related services that help support the education of these young people. Related services include developmental, corrective, and other support services and transportation required to help the learner to derive maximum benefits from an education.

The meaning of the term "related service" has been interpreted in different ways. For example, the actual dividing line between a related service and an unrelated "medical service" is unclear. Litigation sometimes has resulted from varying opinions about services that, legitimately, fall within the related-service category. In one case, the Supreme Court declared that providing a full-time nurse for a student paralyzed from the neck down was a related service that must be paid by a district (*Cedar Rapids Community School District v. Garret F.,* 1999).

In another case, parents of a hearing-impaired learner argued that their child was entitled to the services of a sign language interpreter in order to gain the maximum from her education. Because there was evidence that this learner was receiving some personalized instruction and that her achievement was above average, the Supreme Court ruled that her education was adequate and this related service was not required (*Board of Education v. Rowley*, 1982).

Considerable legal ambiguity continues to surround the related-services issue. It is probable that there will be future court cases as interested parties continue to seek legal clarification.

WEB EXTENSION 14–3

Internet Legal Resources about Special Education and Disabilities

This Web site, maintained by the Curry School of Education at the University of Virginia, includes links to sites containing laws and regulations relating to the rights of special education students.

http://aace.virginia.edu/go/specialed/resources/legal.html

TEACHERS' RIGHTS AND RESPONSIBILITIES

What protections will you enjoy as a classroom teacher? What legal responsibilities will you be expected to discharge? In general, how will the general legal environment where you work affect what you do? You need answers to these questions as you think about how you will deal with issues involving

- Teacher certification,
- Continuing employment and tenure,
- General teacher rights, and
- Teacher obligations.

Teacher Certification

One set of legal regulations that you will encounter as you prepare to enter the teaching profession relates to teacher certificates, licenses, and credentials. A teaching certificate, teaching license, or teaching credential confers on the holder the legal right to be hired as a teacher in the state that issues it.

Each state has the right to establish regulations concerning the qualifications of those who will be allowed to teach in its schools. As a result, each state has its own set of requirements. If you are enrolled in a teacher-preparation program in a state other than the one where you wish to teach, you will need to meet the requirements of the state where you wish to be employed. You should contact the Department of Education in the state that interests you and get information regarding requirements for teachers in that state. By obtaining this information now, you will find the process of getting the necessary certificate, license, or credential easier when the time comes for you to file the required paperwork. Today, some states have agreements with others that allow a person with a certificate, license, or credential in one state to easily obtain them in the other states that participate in these reciprocity arrangements.

A person has no basic right to hold or obtain a certificate, license, or credential without meeting governing state regulations. Once such a document is issued, the state still retains the right to change requirements through new regulations. Although many states do exempt teachers who already have certificates from new requirements, there is no legal obligation for them to do so.

Teaching certificates, licenses, and credentials grant specific benefits to those who hold them. For example, holders of valid documents have the right to apply for teaching jobs in their areas of specialization and to be issued a **teaching contract,** or **contract.** A teaching contract is an official employment agreement between a teacher and a school district that includes information related to issues such as conditions of employment, salary, sick-leave policies, insurance provisions, and complaint procedures. A teaching certificate, license, or credential gives a "presumption of competence." This presumption protects the holder by requiring that compelling evidence back any charges of incompetence.

State authorities, not your college or university, will issue your teaching certificate, license, or credential. Although your college or university will hold you responsible for meeting certain requirements, your institution of higher learning acts only to "recommend" you for certification, licensure, or credentialing. State authorities make the final decision and issue the documents.

You must hold a valid teaching certificate, license, or credential to accept employment as a public-school teacher. The courts have ruled that people who contract to teach with a school district without having a valid teaching certificate, license, or credential are volunteers who have no right to compensation or other employment privileges. In essence, if you sign a contract of employment as a teacher without having a certificate, license, or credential, the terms of your contract are invalid.

This teacher is supervising learners who are boarding a school bus. Sometimes this kind of responsibility is included in a teacher's contract; sometimes it is not. If you have questions about nonteaching duties, you need to ask them before you sign your contract.

In addition, even though you have an initial teaching certificate, license, or credential, you may need to meet additional requirements to keep this authorization in force. For example, you may be required to take additional course work within a prescribed period of time to qualify for a renewal of the authority your certificate, license, or credential confers. If your authority expires and you have not qualified for renewal, you lose your legal right to sign a teaching contract.

Continuing Employment and Tenure

Once you have signed a contract, your next concern is continuing employment. You may have been partly attracted to a career in teaching because teaching offers a high degree of job security. This view of security is tied to a feature of educational employment called **tenure.** The tenure principle assures that an employed teacher has a right to reemployment each year if certain stipulated conditions are met. Not all states and not all districts require or allow the issuance of tenure contracts. There is considerable misunderstanding of tenure and how it functions.

Typically, beginning teachers are issued a **yearly contract.** This contract guarantees the holder employment for a single academic year. The contract is not automatically renewable. Either party can terminate it at the end of the academic year. Typically, school districts inform holders of yearly contracts about mid-April whether they will be rehired for the next academic year. Generally, a school district has no obligation to explain its reasons for terminating yearly contract employees. The major exception to this pattern can occur when a holder of a yearly contract has reason to believe a refusal to rehire was based on a school-district objection to a constitutionally protected teacher behavior. For example, teachers who hold yearly contracts might have a legal case if they could demonstrate that the district's refusal to rehire was based on their religious affiliation or their decision to become an active member of a teachers' association.

Districts that issue tenure contracts typically do not issue them to all teachers. Often, there is a probationary period during which teachers who are new to the district are first issued a series of yearly contracts. When this probationary period is completed and a contract is given for the coming year, a person then has tenure.

If you are in a district that awards tenure, have completed your probationary period, and have been given a tenure contract, then you have a right to expect employment for an indefinite period of time. You can be dismissed only for reasons specified by law and only after a specified process has been followed.

Tenure was created because of a belief that an open exchange of information and free discussion of ideas are at the heart of our free society. Teachers are in a unique position relative to these values. More than any other professionals, they are in a position to facilitate the exchange and discussion of ideas. However, teachers' roles in helping learners to commit to free-speech values can be compromised if they hesitate to discuss politically unpopular views because they fear losing their jobs. Tenure was intended to protect teachers from this possibility. Before tenure laws were enacted, teachers in some places were dismissed for such offenses as involvement in a political campaign, active participation in union activities, using teaching approaches not popular with the school administration, and membership in particular religious bodies.

Another argument has also been advanced for tenure. Teachers' salaries generally are low relative to other professionals with equivalent levels of education. As a trade-off for modest pay levels, tenure laws promise teachers continued employment, even when economic times are not good and states and local communities face severe financial challenges. Supporters of tenure argue that the promise of employment security helps attract people to the teaching profession who, without this feature, might be reluctant to enter a field in which salaries tend to be lower than those in many competing occupations.

In recent years, some state legislatures have discussed eliminating or modifying tenure laws. Some opponents of tenure argue that the system guarantees lifetime employment and, therefore, protects incompetent teachers. Although school officials in districts with tenure policies must follow challenging procedures to remove a tenured teacher, the claim that tenure guarantees lifetime employment is not true. Tenure laws spell out circumstances in which a tenured teacher can be terminated. These conditions usually include incompetence, immorality, insubordination, conduct unbecoming of a teacher, and physical or mental incapacity. A school district must prove at least one of these allegations in order to remove a tenured teacher. Making a convincing case can be a time-consuming and costly process that requires the systematic collection of data to support the action. In one California case, it took eight years and over $300,000 in legal fees to remove a tenured teacher. Critics of tenure point out that some school districts lack the will to engage the processes needed to remove a tenured teacher.

General Teacher Rights

In the *Tinker* case cited earlier, the Supreme Court stated that neither teachers nor students leave their rights at the classroom door. However, as is true in the case of learners, rights of teachers must be balanced with the rights of the general public and the responsibilities of the school system (Valente, 1994). Because of the important role that teachers play in the education of impressionable youths, some people believe that teachers should be held to higher standards of behavior and conduct than the typical citizen. In one case that supported this view, a court declared that certain professions, such as teaching, impose limitations on personal actions that are not imposed on people engaged in other occupations (*Board of Trustees of Compton Junior College District v. Stubblefield*, 1971).

As you prepare for a career in teaching, you need to know something about the nature of teachers' rights as they pertain to

- Academic freedom,
- Freedom of religion, and
- Teachers' freedom and lifestyles outside of school.

Academic Freedom.   One of the most important and controversial aspects of teacher freedom relates to the concept of **academic freedom.** This refers to your right as a teacher to speak freely about the subjects you teach, to experiment with new ideas, to select the material used in the classroom, and to decide on teaching methods. Courts have held that academic freedom is based on First Amendment rights and is fundamental to a democratic society. Academic freedom protects your rights to evaluate and criticize existing practices in order to promote political, social, and scientific progress (Fischer, Schimmel, & Steelman, 2002).

Because a school board has an obligation to make sure that the adopted curriculum is taught, there is great potential for conflicts between teachers' rights and the obligations of the school board. Generally the courts have ruled in favor of teachers when school boards have tried to prescribe how they will teach. Court decisions have also supported giving teachers wide discretion in the selection of instructional materials.

In one case school administrators asked an 11th-grade English teacher to stop using a literary work they described as "literary garbage." The teacher defended the selection as an example of literature that was important for learners to read. When she refused to stop using the selection, she was dismissed. The teacher challenged the decision in court as a violation of academic freedom, and the court agreed. The judge ruled that the school district had failed to demonstrate that the use of the material would result in "material and substantial disruption of discipline," so it could not be banned. The opinion further pointed out that teachers have an obligation to defend the selection of materials in light of educational objectives and the age and maturity of their students (*Parducci v. Rutland*, 1970).

Cases related to academic freedom have not always been decided in favor of teachers. For example, the courts have also upheld the rights of a school district to select and eliminate textbooks. In one case, books were removed from a high school reading list because of sexual content and vulgar language. When this action was challenged, the court upheld the right of school district leaders to delete titles from a reading list if their action was based on a legitimate educational concern (*Virgil v. School Board of Columbia County, Florida*, 1989).

The *Virgil* case and others generally have laid down guidelines that require school districts to follow certain processes before rejecting or removing books. Removal decisions must be reached in a constitutional manner, and books cannot be removed simply because school authorities disagree with the ideas they present. In addition, books cannot be taken off the shelves because they are inconsistent with a particular political or religious view, because authorities wish to prevent certain ideas from being discussed, or because they contain content that fails to adopt a particular position on an issue such as racial discrimination (Fischer, Schimmel, & Steelman, 2002).

The academic freedom you enjoy as a teacher does not give you the right to ignore the course of study for the subject you teach. The material included in the classroom must be relevant to the course and appropriate for the age and maturity of your learners. You might be interested in knowing that teachers have lost academic-freedom cases in situations such as:

- A teacher continued to teach sex-related content in a health class because he believed it was of high interest to learners.
- A teacher showed an R-rated film to 9th- through 11th-grade students on a nonacademic day.
- A math teacher encouraged learners to protest the presence of military recruiters on campus.

Academic freedom also extends to the instructional methods you choose. In one case, a social studies teacher used a simulation exercise that evoked strong student responses on racial issues. The teacher was told to stop using the exercise. When she continued, the school board chose not to renew her contract. She took the issue to court, and the court ruled that the district had violated her First Amendment rights and ordered her reinstated (*Kingsville Independent School District v. Cooper*, 1980).

In another case, a high school psychology teacher was fired for using a survey from a periodical titled *Psychology Today*. The court upheld the teacher's contention that her firing violated her constitutional right to "engage in a teaching method of her choosing even though the subject matter might be controversial." The school district failed to show that the use of this method caused substantial disruption or that there was a clear regulation prohibiting it (*Dean v. Timpson Independent School District*, 1979).

In summary, though decisions related to academic freedom tend to be situation specific, there are some general patterns. These decisions suggest that as a teacher you have a right to address controversial issues that are relevant to the topic you are teaching. You are also free to choose methods and materials that are appropriate to the age and maturity of your students. However, the materials or methods you select must not be banned by clear school-district regulations, and their use must not result in substantial disruption of the learning process or contribute to a breakdown of discipline.

Awarding of grades is an issue that ties to academic freedom. In a litigious society such as ours, learners or their parents or guardians occasionally threaten legal action when they are dissatisfied with the grade a teacher has awarded. The courts have usually considered school officials to be uniquely qualified to judge the academic achievement of learners. As a result, they have been reluctant to overturn grading decisions unless there is overwhelming evidence that the grades were given for arbitrary, capricious, or bad-faith reasons. This means you need to have clear grading standards, keep accurate records, and make sure grades are awarded for academic reasons and not as punishment for inappropriate behavior.

School officials may prescribe guidelines for the administration of a grading system. However, the courts have ruled that guidelines may violate teacher rights if they are too prescriptive. In a Minnesota case, the courts ruled as inappropriate a policy stating that an individual teacher could not give grades that deviated more than 2% from the grade distribution of similar classes (*In re Termination of James Johnson*, 1990).

VIDEO VIEWPOINTS

Cheating Teachers

WATCH: This *Nightline* segment focuses on the issue of teachers helping students perform better on high-stakes tests. A teacher is interviewed who claims that her school principal told her to cheat to "help students get higher test scores." The segment places a great deal of emphasis on the stress that is created on administrators and teachers when their salaries and even their jobs are dependent on students doing well on a high-stakes test.

THINK: Discuss with your classmates, or in your teaching journal the following questions:

1. Do you think teacher cheating is a widespread problem? Why or why not?
2. What would you, as a new teacher, do if you were directed by an administrator to cheat to help students obtain higher scores?
3. What are some other indicators that might be used to hold schools accountable for student achievement?

LINK: How is the emphasis on high-stakes testing influencing education? Is it a positive influence?

 Complete this activity and submit your responses online in the Video Viewpoints *module for this chapter of the Companion Website.*

Freedom of Religion.   Teachers sometimes face important freedom-of-religion issues. Here are some questions for you to think about that relate to freedom of religion:

- What rights do you have in refusing to teach content that might conflict with your religious beliefs?
- Do you have to lead the pledge of allegiance to the flag if doing so is contrary to your religious beliefs?
- Do you have the right to wear distinctive religious clothing when you teach?
- Can you be absent from school in order to observe religious holidays?
- What restrictions can be imposed on you that limit what you can say to learners about your religious convictions?

Many court cases have dealt with questions such as these. In one case a teacher belonged to a religious group that opposed all references to patriotism and national symbols.

She informed her principal that she would not teach any curriculum content related to these topics, nor would she acknowledge national holidays such as Washington's birthday. The school district challenged her right to take this position. Ultimately a federal court ruled that the First Amendment does not provide license for a teacher to teach a curriculum that deviates from the one prescribed by the state. The court went on to point out that although the teacher had a right to her own beliefs, she had no right to require others to submit to her views. To do so would be to deprive students of an expected part of their educational experience (*Palmer v. Board of Education of the City of Chicago*, 1980).

In many places, teachers are required to start the school day with a ceremony that involves the pledge of allegiance. Some teachers have objected to participating in these ceremonies because of religious convictions. In one case, the court upheld the right of the teacher not to participate in the pledge of allegiance (*Russo v. Central School District No. 1*, 1972).

Other freedom-of-conscience cases have focused on the wearing of religious dress by teachers. The courts have usually supported the right of a school district to establish a dress code for teachers that may prohibit the wearing of distinctive religious clothing. Courts have reasoned that such clothing may give students the impression that the school supports a particular religion.

Courts have generally upheld a teacher's rights to take leave for religious holidays so long as two important conditions are met. First, the teacher's absence cannot create an undue hardship on the school district. Second, the amount of time taken off cannot be excessive.

In summary, your religious beliefs enjoy some legal protection, and you cannot be terminated because of your religious convictions or be required to sign an oath or take a pledge that violates your religious beliefs. However, the actions you can take in a school setting that relate to your religious beliefs can be limited if those actions interfere in important ways with the state's interest in educating children.

Lifestyle and Conduct Outside School.   When you are employed as a teacher, can your employing school district place restrictions on your out-of-school behavior? Many court cases have focused on issues such as teachers' sexual orientation, live-in arrangements with unmarried partners, and criminal conduct. In one decision, the court noted that people in certain professions, including teaching, have limitations placed on them that are not imposed on those of other callings (*Board of Trustees of Compton Junior College District v. Stubblefield*, 1971). This case established the point that certain kinds of out-of-class conduct by teachers can be used as grounds for dismissal.

Criminal conduct is usually recognized as a legal basis for revoking a teaching certificate, license, or credential. In most states teacher candidates must reveal if they have been convicted of a felony. Even conviction of a misdemeanor may be cause for dismissal. Criminal activity of any sort is likely to lead to serious difficulties for any teacher.

As noted earlier, many tenure laws include immorality as a legal ground for dismissing a teacher. In recent years, the courts have developed more-careful definitions of the kinds of immoral conduct that are serious enough to warrant dismissal. Recent decisions have required there to be evidence of a tight connection between the private behavior of a teacher and his or her work as a professional.

The courts have generally upheld that out-of-school behavior of teachers may be used for dismissal if their conduct poses a danger to learners or in some way interferes with their effectiveness in the classroom. Situations that result in widespread negative publicity throughout the community are more likely to be seen as interfering with the effectiveness of a teacher than those that receive little or no publicity. Charges of immorality that involve a minor are highly likely to result in dismissal decisions.

Legal Obligations

Teachers have legal responsibilities that include reporting cases of suspected child abuse and acting in a professional manner.

Reporting Child Abuse.   In recent years, there has been much public concern regarding child abuse. As a result, all 50 states and the District of Columbia have laws requiring mandatory reporting of suspected child abuse by certain professionals. Because, as a teacher, you are in prolonged contact with young people, you are considered to be in a particularly good position to spot child abuse.

Mandatory reporting places legal obligations on you to inform authorities when you see instances of suspected child abuse. Failure to do so can lead to both criminal and civil penalties. A high level of suspicion is not necessary before reporting suspected child abuse. Legal terms often used to describe the grounds for suspected child abuse include "reasonable grounds," "cause to believe," or "reasonable cause to believe."

You need not fear retribution as a consequence of reporting. All states provide some form of protection from lawsuits for mandatory reporters who report their observations in good faith. In most instances, the identity of the person reporting the suspected abuse is not revealed.

Negligence.   Teachers have a responsibility to act in a professional manner. Failure to do so may lead to charges of **negligence.** Negligence is defined as a failure to use reasonable care and/or to take prudent actions to prevent harm from coming to someone. There are three types of negligence:

- Misfeasance,
- Nonfeasance, and
- Malfeasance

Misfeasance occurs when a teacher acts unwisely or without taking proper safeguards. In these situations, the teacher might have a good motive but acts unwisely. For example, if you ask a very young child to carry a glass container, the child might fall and be cut by broken glass. Although you did not intend harm, a court might decide that you were guilty of misfeasance because you unwisely asked an immature learner to perform this type of a task. As a professional knowledgeable about child growth and development, you are expected to know that there is a high probability that a young child will drop a container.

Nonfeasance occurs when a teacher fails to act when there is a duty to do so. For example, if two members of your class begin to fight, you have a duty to protect these learners from injury. If you make no attempt to stop the fight, you could be found guilty of nonfeasance. One of the common reasons for charges of nonfeasance is when injury occurs when teachers are away from their areas of responsibility. For example, if you are unnecessarily out of the classroom when learners are present and an injury occurs, you could be charged with nonfeasance.

Malfeasance involves actions that are taken to deliberately and knowingly harm someone. To avoid charges of malfeasance, you want to be wary of imposing any forms of discipline that might bring harm to the learner.

To avoid problems associated with negligence you have to act as a professional. In deciding cases in this area, courts often test your behavior against what a person with similar professional preparation might do. The fact that you have completed a professional-preparation program and have a teaching certificate, license, or credential means that you should have the knowledge you need to make responsible decisions.

Critical Incident

How Free Is a Teacher to Choose a Teaching Method?

Todd Allenby teaches ninth graders. One of his classes is not motivated, and students' written work has been abysmal. Often, all he gets is a page with the student's name and one or two barely coherent sentences. At the end of last week, he discussed this problem with Darcie Schwarts, another English teacher.

Darcie listened carefully and asked, "Are you letting them write what they want? I find most of my students won't give me much unless they have a personal interest in the topic."

Todd thought about this idea over the weekend. On Monday he began the class with some general comments about how people can become frustrated when they have something to say and nobody listens. Then he announced that the next writing assignment was going to give class members an opportunity to write what they wanted about any subject. He promised that these essays would reach an audience because he would see that every one would be distributed to the entire class. After a few questions, most of the students began to write. Todd collected the papers at the end of the class. He was pleased to note that most were longer than those he usually received.

Todd began reading the papers that night at home. About halfway through, his initial pleasure turned to despair. Although several of the papers gave evidence of serious thinking, a number of them included sexually explicit language. As his stomach began knotting, Todd reflected on his promise to share all of the papers with the entire class. Despite his misgivings, Todd decided that he had to do what he had promised or he would have no credibility. He copied all the papers and circulated them to the class. Two days later, he received a call to report to Dwayne Clark, the school principal. When he arrived at the office, he noticed that several of the essays were spread across the top of the principal's desk.

"Todd," began Mr. Clark. "What in the world were you thinking about? It's bad enough that the students use this language, but to make copies and distribute them in class is too much. Can you imagine what some parents are going to say when they see these?"

"Look," replied Todd. "I'm not thrilled about the content of some of these papers. But, these kids did write something for the first time this year. The public is on our case about not teaching students to write, so we need to figure out how to get the students to do it. I made a commitment to distribute the papers and felt I had to follow through to keep my credibility intact and to continue to get them to write."

"That's a commitment you had no right to make," Mr. Clark replied. "It put you in a position of agreeing to distribute anything, even obscene material. That's not professional. In fact, we cannot tolerate this type of behavior in our district. You need to know that it is a serious matter and that I am going to file a formal complaint to the central office. This situation could lead to an official dismissal hearing."

• • •

What are the basic issues involved in this situation? Do you think Todd did the right thing? Do you think his approach was reasonable given the class and his past experience with them? What might he have done differently? How much professional freedom should a teacher have? What would you do if you were Todd? We do not know if Todd is tenured or untenured. How might this make a difference in what happens to Todd?

 To respond to this Critical Incident online, go to the Critical Incidents *module of this chapter of the Companion Website.*

- When you begin your teaching career, you will be entering a profession in which your behavior will be greatly influenced by the legal environment within which today's schools operate. As a professional, you have a need and a responsibility to be familiar with rules, regulations, and laws that govern your actions in the classroom.

- In the past, relationships between teachers and learners were governed by the *in loco parentis* doctrine, which held that school authorities, including teachers, acted "in place of the parent." Under this doctrine, school authorities had few limitations on their authority to make decisions about individual learners. Over time, the *in loco parentis* doctrine has been successfully challenged in the courts. The result is that, today, learners generally enjoy the same constitutional protections that adult citizens possess.

- An important right today's learners have is the right to *due process.* For example, learners cannot be denied access to education unless strict due process guidelines are followed. Due process guidelines also apply, in a slightly altered form, to special education students and parents. Among other things, due process protections assure that (1) learners cannot be disciplined on the basis of unwritten rules, (2) adopted school rules and regulations cannot be vaguely worded, (3) learners subject to a disciplinary action are entitled to request a hearing before an impartial body, (4) the identity of witnesses must be revealed, and (5) decisions must be supported by substantial evidence.

- Contemporary students' rights include (1) freedom of expression, (2) freedom of conscience, (3) freedom from unreasonable search, (4) freedom from harassment, and (5) the right to privacy.

- Teachers and school administrators must be aware of the rights of learners with disabilities. Laws require that learners with disabilities have an appropriate placement, that a plan is established that is carefully assessed, and that the schools supply needed related services to help these learners benefit from their educational experiences.

- *Teaching certificates, licenses,* and *credentials* are documents that allow an individual to contract for services as a teacher with a school district. State governments issue these documents. States can change the requirements for obtaining and renewing certificates, licenses, and credentials whenever they wish to do so.

- *Teaching contracts* are binding documents that spell out employment conditions for teachers and that give holders of teaching certificates, licenses, and credentials a "presumption of competence." Typically, teaching contracts clarify responsibilities both of the teacher and of the hiring school district.

- *Tenure* laws have been established to protect teachers from arbitrary dismissal because they have promoted discussions of controversial and debatable ideas. Tenure does not provide a lifetime guarantee of employment. Rather, it specifies the grounds that can be used to dismiss a teacher and places the burden of proof on the school district.

- Teachers enjoy substantial *academic freedom.* Among other things, they have the right to include course materials and teach methods relevant to the content of the course of study. However, academic freedom is also balanced with the state's right to deliver the prescribed curriculum to learners in the schools. Thus, school districts retain a legal power to place limits on material that is used in class.

- In *freedom of religion* cases, the courts generally have upheld the rights of teachers to refrain from participating in the pledge of allegiance, to take religious holidays, to be free from punishment for their religious convictions, and to be under no obligation to sign an oath that violates their religious beliefs.

- Because of their special relationship with impressionable young people, teachers' rights as individuals are weighed against the right of the state to provide a proper education. Therefore, teachers can be held to a higher level of personal conduct than that expected of the general population.
- Teachers and school officials have a responsibility to report suspected incidents of child abuse, and teachers who fail to do so may face both civil and criminal penalties.
- Teachers sometimes face charges of *negligence,* a failure to act in a professional manner. The three major categories of negligence are (1) *misfeasance,* (2) *nonfeasance,* and (3) *malfeasance.* Misfeasance occurs when a teacher acts unwisely or fails to implement proper safeguards. Nonfeasance occurs when a teacher fails to act when having a duty to do so. Malfeasance occurs when a teacher acts deliberately and knowingly to harm someone.

Chapter 14 Self-Test

 To review terms and concepts in this chapter, go to the Companion Website and take the Chapter 14 Self-Test. Feedback for the self-test is immediate. You can keep track of your self-test scores, or you can submit them to your instructor via e-mail.

Preparing for Praxis

To learn more about the Praxis test and complete this activity online, go to the Preparing for Praxis *module for this chapter of the Companion Website.*

You may be required to pass Educational Testing Service's Praxis II exam as you seek formal authorization to teach in the public schools. The *Principles of Learning and Teaching* component of Praxis II seeks to assess your knowledge about these topics: (1) Students as Learners, (2) Instruction and Assessment, (3) Communication Techniques, and (4) Profession and Community. Material presented in this chapter potentially relates to several of these categories.

You may find it useful to prepare a chart for your own use similar to the one provided here. As you encounter information related to individual categories, you can enter it into the chart. A completed chart of this kind will be useful as you prepare to take the Praxis II exam.

Students as Learners	Instruction and Assessment
• Student Development and the Learning Process	• Instructional Strategies
• Students as Diverse Learners	• Planning Instruction
• Student Motivation and the Learning Environment	• Assessment Strategies
Communication Techniques	**Profession and Community**
• Basic, Effective, Verbal and Nonverbal Communication Techniques	• The Reflective Practitioner
• Effect of Cultural and Gender Differences on Communications in the Classroom	• The Larger Community
• Types of Questions That Can Stimulate Discussion in Different Ways for Particular Purposes	

░░░░░░░░ **For Your Initial-Development Portfolio** ░░░░░░░░░░░░░░░░░░

 To complete this activity and submit your response online, go to the For Your Initial-Development Portfolio *module for this chapter of the Companian Website.*

1. What materials and ideas that you learned in this chapter about the legal environment within which you will discharge your duties might you include as "evidence" in your portfolio? Select up to three separate items of information. Number them 1, 2, and 3.
2. Think about why you selected these materials. As you do so, consider these issues:
    - Specific uses you might make of this information as you plan, deliver, and assess the impact of your teaching
    - The compatibility of the information with your own priorities and values
    - Any contributions this information can make to your development as a teacher
    - Factors that led you to include this information, as opposed to some alternatives you considered, but rejected
3. Place a check in the chart here to indicate the INTASC standard(s) to which each of your items of information relates.

INTASC Standard Number

ITEM OF EVIDENCE NUMBER	SI	S2	S3	S4	S5	S6	S7	S8	S9	S10
1										
2										
3										

4. Prepare a written reflection in which you analyze the decision-making process you followed. In your comments, mention the INTASC standard(s) to which your selected material relates.

░░░░░░░░ **Reflections** ░░

 To respond to these questions online, go to the Reflections *module for this chapter of the Companion Website.*

1. Review material in the chapter related to *in loco parentis* and the erosion of this doctrine over the years in favor of viewing learners as individuals enjoying the legal protections adult citizens enjoy. Has this change had a positive or negative impact on American education? What evidence and values support your position?
2. Due process requirements place limits on the nature of the rules you will develop for learners in your classroom. Develop a set of classroom rules that references explicit behaviors (a) that you wish to encourage in your classroom and (b) that you will not allow in your classroom. Think about what you would say to others who might ask about particular difficulties you encountered in attempting to meet the due process requirement that rules be written, clear, and specific.
3. The issue of tenure continues to be hotly debated. Opponents argue that tenure regulations make it extremely difficult for school districts to remove tenured teachers who are not performing up to expected standards. Proponents contend

that tenure laws make it possible for teachers to act in a professional way in the classroom without fear that they will lose their jobs if they teach information that may not be popular with administrators, certain groups of parents, or school policy makers. How do you assess the merits of arguments for and against tenure? What is your personal position on the issue, and what led you to this view?

4. Is your own private life your personal business? Do you believe school authorities have a right to hold you professionally accountable (e.g., to threaten you with job loss) if you behave in certain ways outside of normal school hours? How do you react to some court decisions that have supported actions of school districts that dismissed teachers for certain things they did on their own time? Have these decisions been justified? If not, are there *any* circumstances that you might imagine that would justify a school district's decision to fire a teacher for behavior outside of normal school hours?

5. Some people believe (and some courts have supported the idea) that teachers should be held to higher personal and moral standards than other adult citizens. Is this position justified? What arguments can you think of that support this view, and what arguments might you marshal against it?

Field Experiences, Projects, and Enrichment

1. Review copies of professional education journals such as *Phi Delta Kappan* or *Educational Leadership*. Look for articles and features dealing with legal issues in education. Take notes on several articles you read. Summarize this information, and share it with others in your class. Be sure to mention court decisions that may have implications for teachers as they work with learners in school classrooms.

2. Obtain a copy or a summary of the education code for your state. Your professor may be able to help you locate this information. Codes of many states are now available on the Internet. Many state departments of education maintain Web sites. When you locate your state's code, you may be surprised to find that it is quite a lengthy document. Look through the material until you find any existing rules related to such areas as corporal punishment, expulsion, mandatory attendance, teacher tenure, state curriculum, and selection of classroom material. Summarize your findings in a short paper or present your information in another manner as your professor directs.

3. Use a good search engine such as Google (http://www.google.com). Enter the phrase "teaching and the law." You will find many links to books that feature information on this topic.

Prepare a list of at least seven titles (author, title, publisher, place of publication, and date of publication). Make copies of your list to share with others in your class. You may find information in these books to be of interest as you seek to learn more about schools' legal environment.

4. Investigate the requirements for a teaching credential in your state. State departments of education often provide this information online at their Web sites. Seek answers to these questions: What are the basic requirements? How long is a credential valid? What needs to be done to keep it in process? What is the process for getting a credential?

5. Invite a school administrator or local teacher-association representative to your class to answer these questions:

   - What provisions are included in the school district's teaching contracts?
   - Specifically, what do contracts say about teachers' rights and responsibilities?
   - Does the school district operate under a tenure policy? If so, what does a teacher have to do to qualify for tenure?
   - If there is a tenure policy in place, what procedures must school district officials follow to seek removal of a tenured teacher?

References

Bethel School Dist. No. 403 v. Fraser, 478 U.S. 675, 106 S. Ct. 3159, 92 L. Ed. 2d 549 (1986).

Board of Education v. Rowley, 458 U.S. 176 (1982).

Board of Trustees of Compton Junior College District v. Stubblefield, 94 Cal. Rptr. 318, 321 (Cal. Ct. App. 1971).

Cedar Rapids Community School District v. Garret F., 526 U.S. 66 (1999).

Dean v. Timpson Independent School District, 486 F. Supp. 302 (E.D. Tex. 1979).

Deskbook encyclopedia of American school law. (2002). Birmingham, AL: Oakstone Legal and Business Publishing.

Family Educational Rights and Privacy Act (FERPA). [http// www.ed.gov/policy/gen/guid/fpco/ferpa/index.html]

Fischer, L., Schimmel, D., & Steelman, L. (2002). *Teachers and the law* (6th ed.) Boston, MA: Allyn & Bacon.

Hazelwood School District v. Kuhlmeier. 484 U.S. 260 (1988).

In re Termination of James Johnson, 451 N.W. 2d 343 (Minn. Ct. App.1990).

Kingsville Independent School District v. Cooper, 611 F. 2d 1109 (5th Cir. 1980).

Lipp v. Morris, 579 F. 2nd 834 (3rd Cir. 1978).

New Jersey v. T.L.O. 105 S. Ct. 733 (1985).

Palmer v. Board of Education of the City of Chicago, 603 F. 2d 1271 (7th Cir. 1979), cert. denied, 444 U.S. 1026 (1980).

Parducci v. Rutland, 316 F. Supp. 352 (m.d. Ala. 1970).

Russo v. Central School District No. 1, 469 F. 2d 623 (2nd Cir. 1972) cert denied, 411 U.S. 932 (1973).

Tinker v. Des Moines Independent Community School District, 393 U.S. 503 (1969).

Valente, W. (1994). *Law and the schools, (3rd ed.).* New York: Macmillan.

Virgil v. School Board of Columbia County, Florida, 862 F. 2d 1517 (11th Cir. 1989).

Zernike, K. (2002, Sept. 13). Plaids out again, as schools give up requiring uniforms. *New York Times on the Web.* [http://query.nytimes.com/gst/abstract.html?res= F50712FF3A550C708DDDA00894DA404482].

Zirkel, P., & Richardson, S. (1988). *A digest of Supreme Court decisions affecting education.* Bloomington, IN: Phi Delta Kappa Educational Foundation.

Glossary

Academic Freedom A right of teachers based on First Amendment rights that refers to teachers' rights to speak freely about their subjects, experiment with new ideas, select some materials used in their classrooms, and decide on teaching methods.

Academic-Subjects Orientation A perspective on curriculum that holds that school programs should be organized around clearly identified academic subjects, for example mathematics, science, and English. *See also:* Learner-Centered Orientation, Needs-of Society Orientation.

Academies Private secondary schools, first established in the 18th century, that were the primary form of secondary education in the years before a legal basis was established for public support of high schools.

Acceleration Programs Programs for gifted learners that increase the pace at which they complete their schooling. There is no attempt to keep gifted learners in classes with other learners of the same age. *See also:* Enrichment Programs.

Acceptable-Use Policy (AUP) Term applied to policies school districts adopt that specify acceptable and unacceptable learner uses of technology.

Accomodation A term introduced by Piaget meaning altering schemata to be consistent with the environment.

Accountability The idea that teachers and schools should be held directly responsible for teaching specific information to specific learners.

Achievement Gap A term used to describe the achievement discrepancy, for example as reflected on standardized test scores, between white learners and learners who are members of certain minority groups.

Active Teaching A term referring to teaching practices characterized by direct teacher leadership and by teachers acting as (1) presenters of new information, (2) monitors of learner progress, (3) planners of opportunities for learners to apply new knowledge, and (4) reteachers of content that has been poorly understood.

ADD *See:* Attention Deficit Disorder.

Advance Organizer A label or term a teacher presents to learners that succinctly describes the nature of a large and important body of knowledge that learners are about to study.

Affective Domain A category of learning that includes attitudes, feelings, interests, and values. *See also:* Cognitive Domain, Psychomotor Domain.

AFT *See:* American Federation of Teachers.

Ambiguous Designations A term used to describe vague references in lessons that include words such as "somehow," "somewhere," and "someone." Instruction featuring too many of them lacks clarity.

American Society for Training and Development (ASTD) A professional organization for trainers and educators who work in the private sector, in government agencies, and in other nonschool settings.

American Federation of Teachers (AFT) A national organization for teachers that is affiliated with organized labor. *See also:* National Education Association.

Americans with Disabilities Act Federal legislation that extends civil rights of individuals with disabilities to (a) private-sector employment, (b) all public services, (c) transportation, and (d) telecommunications.

Appropriate Education A principle associated with federal regulations for services to learners with disabilities that requires schools to devise educational programs that are responsive to the unique educational needs of each learner with a disability.

ASCD *See:* Association for Supervision and Curriculum Development.

Assessment   The purposeful collection of data from a variety of sources for the purpose of rendering a judgment. *See also:* Measurement, Evaluation.

Assessment Plan   A plan that features identification of sources of data that are relevant to a specified set of learning outcomes. *See also:* Assessment.

Assistive Technology   Technology that involves the use of individual pieces of equipment or complex systems of equipment to maintain or increase the functional capabilities of learners with disabilities.

Association for Supervision and Curriculum Development (ASCD)   A large professional organization for school administrators and university professors that is dedicated to developing better instructional programs for the schools.

ASTD   *See:* American Society for Training and Development.

Attendance Zone   A term used to describe the geographic area learners must live in to attend a particular school.

Attention Deficit Disorder (ADD)   A disorder characterized by impairments to one or more of the psychological processes associated with understanding and using language.

AUP   *See:* Acceptable-Use Policy.

Authentic Assessment   A category of assessment that attempts to make judgments about an individual's performance in settings that parallel as closely as possible "real world" conditions. *See also:* Assessment.

Automaticity   A person's ability to quickly turn new solutions into routine procedures.

Axiology   An area of philosophical thought that focuses on ethics, morality, and right conduct. *See also:* Epistemology, Logic, Metaphysics, Postmodern Philosophy.

Bacon, Francis   An educational thinker who lived in the late 16th and early 17th centuries who established the idea that truth could be found, challenged, and modified through systematic observation. He is regarded as the father of the scientific method.

Behavior Contract   A document developed with a misbehaving learner that specifies what he or she is to do to correct the situation.

Behavioral Setting   A space that influences the behavior of the individual or individuals who occupy it.

Bell-Shaped Curve   A symmetrical curve derived from a mathematical formula that assumes that any given trait or ability is found in the total population of interest in a distribution that roughly takes the shape of an outline of a bell. *See also:* Evaluation, Norm-Referenced Evaluation, Norms.

Bilingual Education   A term used to describe school programs in which learners are taught in their native language for at least part of the day until they become proficient in English.

Bloom's Taxonomy   Popular way of referring to an influential book titled *Taxonomy of Educational Objectives: Handbook 1, Cognitive Domain,* a work written by Benjamin Bloom and others. *See also:* Taxonomy.

Bodily Kinesthetic Intelligence   A category of intelligence identified by Howard Gardner that involves processes associated with the use of muscular and other body systems to respond to situations and solve problems. *See also:* Multiple Intelligences.

Boston English Classical School   The first public high school in the United States; it opened in Boston in 1821.

Boston Latin Grammar School   A private secondary school that opened in Boston in 1635 for the purpose of preparing boys for Harvard.

Braille   A system of touch reading developed for blind people that employs embossed dots that represent letters and words that trained users can read.

Brailler   A device used by blind or severely visually handicapped people to take notes or produce other prose materials in Braille.

Braille-Writer   *See:* Brailler.

Broad-Fields Curriculum   A variant of curricula developed according to an academic-subjects orientation that combines content from several separate academic subjects and uses them to focus learners' attention on various aspects of an organizing focus theme. *See also:* Academic-Subjects Orientation.

Cardinal Principles   A set of principles or goals developed by the National Education Association's Committee of the Reorganization of Secondary

Education in 1918 that were designed to embrace the multiple purposes of secondary education. These principles focus on (1) health, (2) command of fundamental processes, (3) worthy home membership, (4) vocational preparation, (5) citizenship, (6) worthy use of leisure time, and (7) ethical character. *See also:* Comprehensive High School.

Carl D. Perkins Vocational and Applied Technology Act   1990 federal legislation that supports establishment of tech-prep programs. *See also:* Tech-Prep Program.

Certificate   *See:* Teaching Certificate.

Charter School   A semiautonomous school, freed from many regulations imposed on other public schools, that can be established by groups including parents, teachers, or independent operators. *See also:* School Choice.

Charter School Demonstration Program   A U.S. Department of Education program that seeks to generate and disseminate knowledge about charter schools. *See also:* Charter School.

Checklist   A data-gathering tool that provides information about the presence or absence of targeted behaviors. This is done by using a sheet with a list of target behaviors and placing a check mark by each one that is found to occur during the observation.

Child Protective Services (CPS)   An organization based with state, county, or other governmental agencies that is charged with protecting the well-being of children who live within its area of responsibility.

Children's Internet Protection Act (CIPA)   This part of Public Law 105-554, passed in December 2000, requires schools to take actions to block content from the Internet that students could use that is obscene, features child pornography, or is harmful to minors. It also requires each school to set up an Internet safety policy. *See also:* Internet Safety Policy; Neighborhood Children's Internet Protection Act.

CIPA   *See:* Children's Internet Protection Act.

Citizenship Development   A school-program variety falling within the more-general needs-of-society category that seeks to help learners develop competencies that will make them successful, contributing adults when they mature. *See also:* Needs-of-Society Orientation.

Class History   A term that refers to prior patterns of teacher–learner interaction as producing a kind of mini-culture that affects future behaviors of both the teacher and learners.

Classroom Floor Plan   A plan for utilization of space in a classroom that includes information about locations of such items as desks, tables, and other objects that rest on the floor.

Classroom Management   All actions teachers take to maintain a smooth, focused flow of activity for the purpose of nurturing learners' academic and personal development.

Closed File   A category of placement file that denies the person creating the file an opportunity to see, comment on, or remove comments submitted to the file by others. *See also:* Open File.

Code of Ethics of the Education Profession   A code of ethics for educators adopted by the Representatives Assembly of the National Education Association in 1975.

Coding Systems   These classroom-observation schemes require the use of codes or symbols to represent behaviors that are of interest to the observer.

Coercive Power   Power that people wield because of their authority to administer punishment. *See also:* Expert Power, Legitimate Power, Referent Power, Reward Power.

Cognitive Domain   A category of thinking associated with remembering and processing information. *See also:* Affective Domain, Psychomotor Domain.

Comenius, John Amos   A 17th-century educational thinker who believed that education should prepare people for happiness. He proposed a compulsory system of schooling and advocated teaching practices that would provide instruction to learners in a humane manner.

Common School   The term given to Horace Mann's concept of a school for the average America. *See also:* Mann, Horace.

Communication-Process Position   A now generally rejected explanation for the failure of many minority-group children to do well in school that contended that their poor performance resulted from their parents' failure to provide intellectually stimulating home atmospheres. *See also:* Cultural-Deficit View.

Componential Intelligence   A component of Sternberg's Triarchic Theory of Intelligence that refers to the ability to acquire information by separating the relevant from the irrelevant, thinking abstractly, and determining what needs to be done. *See also:* Triarchic Theory of Intelligence.

Comprehensive High School   Term used to describe high schools pursuing programs consistent with the Cardinal Principles of Secondary Education. This kind of school sought to provide a broad range of programs to students, including those with both academic and world-of-work orientations. *See also:* Cardinal Principles.

Comprehensive School Reform Demonstration Program (CSRD)   A federal program established by 1997 legislation that seeks to promote school-wide educational reform. *See also:* Systemic Reform.

Conflict Perspective   Individuals who hold this perspective see changes in education as a result of conflict between different groups who are striving for power and dominance.

Confucius   A Chinese philosopher (551–478 B.C.E.) who emphasized the importance in status differences among people that result because of specific roles they play in life. For centuries, tests based on his thought were used in China to select new members of the civil service.

Connected Discourse   Verbal communication that features smooth, point-by-point development of ideas.

Constructivism   A perspective on teaching that holds that learners are not passive responders to the environment but rather individuals who engage it purposefully as they seek to extract personal meaning.

Content Standards   A category that includes standards that describe what teachers are supposed to teach and what young people in their classrooms are expected to learn. *See also:* Performance Standards; Standards-Based Education.

Contextual Intelligence   A component of Sternberg's Triarchic Theory of Intelligence that refers to the ability to adapt to new experiences and to solve problems in a specific situation or context. *See also:* Triarchic Theory of Intelligence.

Continuing-Growth Phase   Term used to describe process of professional growth that occurs continuously throughout a teacher's career in the classroom. *See also:* Formal-Preparation Phase, Induction-Years Phase, In-Service Education, Pretraining Phase, Staff Development.

Contract   *See:* Teaching Contract.

Controlled-Choice Plan   A type of open-enrollment plan that allows school district authorities to maintain some control over school choices made by parents and guardians for purposes such as maintaining appropriate racial balances at individual schools. *See also:* Open-Enrollment Plan.

Core-Studies Component   A part of the Formal-Preparation Phase of a teacher's professional development that provides a background in the general kind of information that educated adults are expected to know. *See also:* Formal-Preparation Phase.

Corrective Action Plan   A document prepared as a result of a multiperson conference that focuses on misbehavior problems of a single learner and that specifies proposed actions to be taken.

CPS   *See:* Child Protective Services.

Credential   *See:* Teaching Credential.

Criterion-Referenced Evaluation   An approach to evaluation that bases judgments of individual performance on how well a performance compares to a preestablished standard. *See also:* Evaluation, Norm-Referenced Evaluation.

CSRD   *See:* Comprehensive School Reform Demonstration Program.

Cultural Bias   A feature that gives advantage to people coming from particular cultural backgrounds and disadvantage to people coming from other cultural backgrounds.

Cultural-Deficit View   A now generally rejected explanation for the failure of many minority-group children to do well in school that contended that their poor performance was attributable to their failure to develop language skills sufficiently sophisticated for them to derive maximum benefits from school instruction. *See also:* Communication-Process Position.

Culturally Responsive Environment A classroom environment that is comfortable for students and their teachers and that enables learners to make acceptable academic progress.

Curriculum A term that embraces decisions relating to (1) selection of specific items of content to be included in instructional programs, (2) establishment of priorities among these items, and (3) recommendations related to instructional sequences that promise to promote learning. *See also:* Instruction.

Curriculum Coordinator *See*: Curriculum Leader.

Curriculum Director *See:* Curriculum Leader.

Curriculum Foundations Foundations of education that draw insights from studies of the curriculum. *See also:* Curriculum; Foundations of Education.

Curriculum Leader A school-district professional who is responsible for leadership in such areas as curriculum planning, in-service planning, and instructional-support planning.

Curriculum Standards Standards that reference content to be included in programs in every elementary grade and in every middle school and high school course that often also suggest expected performance levels and implementation approaches. Federal law now requires all states to have standards. Standards also have been developed by individual subject-matter specialty organizations. *See also:* No Child Left Behind Act of 2001.

Curriculum Supervisor *See:* Curriculum Leader.

Deductive Logic A pattern of logical thinking that begins with a general conclusion and then uses examples to illustrate and elaborate on the conclusion. *See also:* Logic, Inductive Logic.

Department Chair A teacher in a middle school, junior high school, or high school who is responsible for leading other teachers in his or her academic department. *See also:* Grade-Level Chair.

Derived Scores *See:* Norms. *See also:* Raw Score.

Dewey, John A leading educational philosopher who worked from the late 19th century to the middle of the 20th century. Dewey promoted

learner-centered education designed to respond to learners' individual needs as they developed the capability to fully participate in their society. He favored instruction that centered on teaching learners.

Diagnostic Assessment A category of assessment that strives to provide information that will explain causes of learners' problems and failures. *See also:* Assessment.

Digital Divide The term used to describe disparities in access to modern communication technologies of people in different groups—for example, members of affluent and impoverished families.

Direct Assessment *See:* Performance Assessment.

Distractors A term used to describe incorrect answers that appear among a list of alternatives on a multiple-choice item. *See also:* Multiple-Choice Tests.

Due Process A guarantee provided to U.S. citizens by the Fourteenth Amendment to the Constitution that requires certain procedures to be followed in any action that might put a citizen's rights at risk. *See also:* Liberty Right, Property Right.

Eclectic Philosophy A philosophy created by blending parts of two or more existing philosophies.

Education for All Handicapped Children Act Also often known as Public Law 94-142, this 1975 federal legislation required public schools to provide certain kinds of services to learners with disabilities.

Education-Related Systems of Philosophy Patterns of thought that focus on basic philosophical questions and their applications to education. *See also:* Essentialism, Existentialism, Perennialism, Progressivism, Reconstructionists.

Emergency Teaching Certificates Documents that enable the holder to accept a teaching position even though he or she has not met all normally required qualifications. *See also:* Teaching Certificate.

Emotional Intelligence A term referring to a person's ability to exercise self-control, remain persistent, and be self-motivating.

Empathy A component of emotional intelligence identified by Daniel Goleman that refers to a person's ability to recognize verbal and nonverbal cues of others and to be sensitive to their feelings. *See also:* Emotional Intelligence.

End-of-the-Instructional-Sequence Motivation
Motivational action taken by a teacher at the end of
an instructional sequence to reinforce learners'
interest in what they have learned and to help them
consolidate their understanding of new information.
See also: Initial Motivation, Motivational Activities,
Within-the-Lesson-Motivation.

Enrichment Programs   Programs for gifted
learners that provide enriched learning experiences
for these young people, but that maintain them as
members of regular school classes. *See also:* Acceleration Programs.

Epistemology   An area of philosophical thought
that focuses on the nature of knowledge. *See also:*
Axiology, Logic, Metaphysics, Postmodern Philosophy.

E-Rate   A special, highly discounted rate that the
Telecommunications Act of 1996 makes available to
schools that makes it possible for them to save
money on telecommunications and Internet services.
See also: Telecommunications Act of 1996.

Essentialism   An educational philosophy that
views the purpose of education as sound practical
and intellectual training. This philosophy holds that
all learners should master subjects that are viewed as
essential for preparing them to function as
contributing members of society. *See also:* Existentialism, Perennialism, Progressivism, Reconstructionists.

Evaluation   The process of making a judgment
about the worth or value of something. *See also:*
Assessment, Measurement.

Event Sampling   An approach to classroom observations in which the observer selects a particular
category of classroom events and gathers information only about classroom happenings related to the
identified category.

Exceptional Learners   Individuals who have characteristics that differentiate them from learners with
characteristics more commonly found among the
general population of young people.

Existential Intelligence   A category of intelligence
identified by Howard Gardner that involves seeking
insights regarding ultimate issues such as the
meaning of life and how a person's own existence
fits or should fit into this scheme. *See also:* Multiple
Intelligences.

Existentialism   A philosophy with a basic theme
that all individuals must confront only one
constraint: the inevitability of their own death. In all
other areas, individuals should have freedom to
make choices and identify their own reasons for
existence. *See also:* Essentialism; Perennialism;
Progressivism; Reconstructionists, Sudbury Model.

Experiential Intelligence   A component of
Sternberg's Triarchic Theory of Intelligence that
refers to coping with new experiences by formulating new ideas and combining unrelated ideas to
solve new problems. *See also:* Triarchic Theory of
Intelligence.

Expert Power   A kind of power that comes to a
person as a result of possessing specialized
knowledge. *See also:* Coercive Power, Legitimate
Power, Referent Power, Reward Power.

Family Educational Rights and Privacy Act   This
1974 legislation requires schools to provide parents
and guardians (and learners who are 18 years of age
and older) with free access to school records. Further,
this legislation restricts access to these records by
unauthorized persons. *See also:* Right to Privacy.

Family Partnership for Education (FAPE)   A
partnership funded by the Office of Special
Education Programs that promotes high-quality
school programs for learners with disabilities.

Formal-Preparation Phase   Term used to
describe the academic-training part of a program
designed to prepare new teachers. *See also:*
Continuing-Growth Phase, Core-Studies Component,
Induction-Years Phase, Pretraining Phase,
Professional-Education Component, Teaching
Specializations/Academic Majors.

Formative Assessment   Assessment that takes
place as a teaching sequence occurs and that
provides a teacher with information he or she can
use to modify instruction to better meet learners'
needs. *See also:* Assessment, Placement Assessment,
Summative Assessment.

Foundations of Education   The set of historical,
philosophical, social, legal, and cultural assumptions
that form a logical base for decisions about schools
and schooling.

Franklin Academy   An institution established in
1751 by Benjamin Franklin that was nonsectarian

and offered practical subjects, including mathematics, astronomy, navigation, and bookkeeping. *See also: Proposals Relating to the Youth of Pennsylvania.*

Freedom from Harassment An expression related to the idea that learners and citizens should not be expected to live or learn in an environment where they are subjected to the hostile or demeaning behaviors of others.

Freedom of Conscience A constitutional guarantee that relates to rights of citizens in the areas of personal belief and religion.

Freedom of Expression A legal guarantee that protects citizens, except in a small number of special situations, from facing governmental restrictions on what they can say.

Free-Response Measures A term used to describe tests that require learners to generate responses of their own rather than selecting from among a list of provided alternative answers. *See also:* Selected-Response Measures.

Frequency Counts A category of classroom observation in which the observer identifies a number of focus categories and maintains a record indicating how frequently each occurs.

Froebel, Friedrich German educator working in the first half of the 19th century who is best remembered as the "father of the kindergarten."

Full Inclusion The practice of placing challenged children in regular classrooms throughout the day and providing them special help, such as an Individualized Education Plan.

Full-Service School A school that, in addition to providing instruction to young people, attempts to provide learners and their families with a full range of human-support services (health services, legal services, counseling services, and so forth). *See also:* Human-Support-Service Profession.

Functionalist Perspective A sociological perspective that views present arrangements in society to be good and sees schools as institutions designed to prepare individuals to contribute to society and keep it functioning in a smooth, harmonious way.

Goals 2000—Educate America Act This 1994 legislation called for massive efforts to improve the quality of America's schools.

Grade-Level Chair A teacher in an elementary school who has responsibilities for leading other teachers in the building who teach the same grade. *See also:* Department Chair.

Hard Subjects A term used to describe subjects or disciplines in which there is heavy reliance on scientific observation as a means of determining truth. *See also:* Soft Subjects.

Hedonism A philosophical perspective that views the highest good as that of seeking immediate pleasure and living for the moment.

Herbart, Johann Friedrich An educational philosopher who did most of his work in the first half of the 19th century and who proposed a theory of learning. One of his lasting influences is the framework he developed for lesson plans. Many present-day lesson plans include categories similar to those he developed.

Hidden Curriculum A term used to describe "messages" sent to learners because of what they observe happening in schools. These are not always intentional and, often, are not consistent with the adopted curriculum.

High-Stakes Testing A term used to describe testing situations in which scores individuals receive may have significant consequences of various kinds.

Higher-Level Questions Questions that are designed to require sophisticated thinking, for example, thinking requiring application, analysis, synthesis, and evaluation. *See also:* Lower-Level Questions.

Historical Foundations Foundations of education that draw insights from political science. *See also:* Foundations of Education.

Homebound Setting As applied to learners with disabilities, this term refers to a home where a learner with a disability lives and is taught.

Hospital Setting As applied to learners with disabilities, this term refers to a hospital where a learner with a disability lives and is taught.

HRD *See:* Human Resource Development.

Human Resource Development (HRD) Term used to describe the education-and-training function of a private-sector, governmental, or other nonschool employer.

Human-Support-Service Profession   A profession that is dedicated to providing services that enhance the educational, health, emotional, and legal-protection levels of human beings.

IDEA   *See:* Individuals with Disabilities Education Act.

IEP   *See:* Individualized Educational Program.

Imaginary Audience   A term that learning-development theorist David Elkind uses to describe a propensity of many adolescents to assume that unseen groups of people are constantly scrutinizing everything these adolescents do. *See also:* Personal Fable.

Immediacy   A characteristic of teaching that refers to teachers' need to respond at once to situations that may arise in the classroom.

In-Class Isolation   An approach to improving learner behavior that features isolation of a misbehaving individual in an area of the classroom where his or her ability to interact with others is minimized.

Inclusion   A principle associated with federal regulations for services to learners with disabilities that requires schools to provide learners with disabilities education within a regular school classroom where special aids, supports, and instructional accommodations are made to respond to their needs and where such learners are welcomed as class members.

Individualized Education Program (IEP)   A requirement of federal education policy that requires schools to develop and implement a plan for instruction of each learner with a disability that is suited to the individual's unique needs.

Individuals with Disabilities Education Act (IDEA)   A modification and update of the Education for All Handicapped Children Act, this legislation and its accompanying frequent updates lay out federal guidelines for services to learners with disabilities. *See also:* Education for All Handicapped Children Act.

Induction-Years Phase   Term used to describe the first few years in a new teacher's career, a time when the newcomer must come to terms with new settings, new coworkers, and new responsibilities. *See also:* Continuing-Growth Phase, Formal-Preparation Phase, Pretraining Phase.

Inductive Logic   A pattern of logical thinking that begins with a study of particulars and uses this information to develop broad, explanatory conclusions. *See also:* Deductive Logic, Logic.

Inductive Teaching   Teaching that first engages learners in considerations of isolated pieces of information and then involves them in thinking processes that lead them to develop broad, explanatory generalizations. *See also:* Inquiry Teaching.

Initial-Development Portfolio   A portfolio type that focuses on information prospective teachers gather that they will find helpful as they begin reflecting on information and skills they will need to become effective beginning teachers. *See also:* Portfolio.

Initial Motivation   Motivational action taken by a teacher at the beginning of an instructional sequence to engage learners' interest and encourage them to want to learn the new material. *See also:* End-of-the-Instructional-Sequence Motivation, Motivational Activities, Within-the-Lesson-Motivation.

In Loco Parentis   A legal doctrine that formerly governed the legal relationship between school authorities (including teachers) and learners. It held that school authorities had a legal relationship with learners similar to that of parents. Hence, learners enjoyed a right to custody, but not full rights of citizenship allowing them to seek recourse in the courts in cases when they had grievances.

Inner Curriculum   A term used to describe the nature of learning that occurs within individuals as they process new information in light of their own past experiences.

Input Goals   A category of goals that focus on variables associated with teaching and learning which, when present, are thought to facilitate learner achievement.

Inquiry Teaching   An approach based on inductive logic that presents learners with isolated bits of information and engages them in processes designed to help them develop broad, explanatory generalizations. *See also:* Inductive Teaching.

In-Service Education   A term used to describe staff-development activities provided by or encouraged by school districts to improve the job-related expertise of teachers and other employees. *See also:* Staff Development.

Instruction   A term used to describe means or approaches used to achieve aims specified in the curriculum. *See also:* Curriculum.

Instructional Foundations   Foundations of education that draw insights from decisions made regarding appropriate instructional processes. *See also:* Foundations of Education, Instruction.

INTASC Model Core Standards   Standards developed by the Interstate New Teacher Assessment and Support Consortium that describe competencies needed by new teachers. *See also:* New Teacher Assessment and Support Consortium.

Intelligence Quotient (IQ) Test   A test designed to yield a score thought to be representative of the test-taker's general intelligence. This test is based on the idea that intelligence is a single measurable trait.

Internal Summaries   Pause points within lessons that teachers use to help learners stop, take stock, and reflect on what information has been presented to these points in a lesson's overall development.

International Society for Technology in Education (ISTE)   A leading national organization of professionals interested in promoting more and better use of technology in the schools.

Internet Safety Policy   A policy that is mandated by the Children's Internet Protection Act that seeks to protect children from harmful and illegal uses of technology by specifying kinds of learner access to these technologies that are authorized and unauthorized. *See also:* Children's Internet Protection Act, Neighborhood Children's Internet Protection Act.

Interpersonal Intelligence   A category of intelligence identified by Howard Gardner that involves recognizing and responding to feelings and motivations of others. *See also:* Multiple Intelligences.

Interstate New Teacher Assessment and Support Consortium (INTASC)   A group dedicated to identifying competencies new teachers should be able to demonstrate and to encouraging colleges and universities to emphasize development of identified knowledge and skill abilities in their teacher-preparation programs. *See also:* INTASC Model Core Standards.

Intrapersonal Intelligence   A category of intelligence identified by Howard Gardner that involves people drawing heavily on their own personal capacities and attitudes when determining which course of action to follow in a given situation. *See also:* Multiple Intelligences.

Intrusiveness   A term having to do with the degree to which a search can come into close contact with an individual or his/her personal possessions.

IQ Test   *See:* Intelligence Quotient (IQ) Test.

ISTE   *See:* International Society for Technology in Education.

Jacob K. Javits Gifted and Talented Students Education Act of 1994   Important federal legislation that allocated federal funds to school districts to support development of improved programs for bright learners.

Junior High School   A school type first introduced in Berkeley, California, in 1909 (often including grades 7, 8, and 9), that was designed to provide academic experiences that would smooth the transition from elementary-level to high school–level education. *See also:* Middle School.

Kalamazoo Case   An 1874 legal case that established the principle that a state legislature had the right to pass laws levying taxes to pay for secondary as well as elementary education.

Kappa Delta Pi   An honorary society for educators.

Knowledge- and Skills-Based Pay (KSBP)   An approach to establishing teachers' salaries that considers variables associated with their preparation to deliver high-quality instruction and their demonstrated abilities to positively affect learners' achievement levels. *See also:* Merit Pay.

Krathwohl's Taxonomy   Popular way of referring to an influential book titled *Taxonomy of Educational Objectives: The Classification of Educational Goals. Handbook II: Affective Domain,* a work written by David Krathwohl and others. *See also:* Taxonomy.

KSBP   *See:* Knowledge- and Skills-Based Pay.

Learner-Centered Orientation   A perspective on curriculum that holds that school programs should be organized around the interests and self-perceived needs of individual learners. *See also:* Academic-Subjects Orientation, Needs-of-Society Orientation.

Learner Portfolio   A purposeful collection of products and performances that tells a story about its creator's effort, progress, or achievement. *See also:* Record-Keeping Learner Portfolio, Showcase Learner Portfolio, Working Learner Portfolio.

Learning Intention   A statement that identifies what learners should know or be able to do as a result of mastering a related body of content.

Learning Styles   Preferred modes individuals have of learning new content. Individuals are thought to find the process of mastering new information easier when it is presented to them in a way consistent with their own preferred learning style.

Least-Restrictive Environment   A principle associated with federal regulations for services to learners with disabilities that requires schools to place learners in environments that enable them to take advantage of school experiences in ways that do not restrict or limit their access to experiences provided to so-called "normal" learners.

Legal Foundations   Foundations of education that refer to laws, regulations, and other legal mandates relating to all aspects of the operation of schools. *See also:* Foundations of Education.

Legitimate Power   Power that derives from a particular position a person holds. *See also:* Coercive Power, Expert Power, Referent Power, Reward Power.

Lesson Objective   *See:* Learning Intention.

Lesson Pacing   *See:* Pacing.

Lesson-Presentation Structure   The framework a teacher uses to organize and sequence delivery of learning experiences that are embedded in a given lesson.

Lesson Summary   A recapitulation of major ideas at the end of a lesson that helps learners draw new information into a coherent, understandable whole.

Liberty Right   A right of people to be free from all restraints except those imposed by law. *See also:* Due Process.

License   *See:* Teaching License.

Life-Adjustment Education   An outgrowth of the progressive movement that enjoyed brief popularity among some school leaders in the years following World War II that placed great amounts of control in the hands of learners in the hope that they would select learning experiences that would help them accommodate to their world. The approach drew many critics and, by 1950, had fallen into general disfavor.

Linguistic Intelligence   A category of intelligence identified by Howard Gardner that involves processes associated with seeking meaning through language. *See also:* Multiple Intelligences.

Local Control   A principle of school governance that holds that authority over schools and school programs should be vested at the local level rather than in the hands of state-level or federal-level leaders.

Logic   A subfield of philosophy that is concerned with the nature of exact thought. *See also:* Axiology, Epistemology, Metaphysics, Postmodern Philosophy.

Logical-Mathematical Intelligence   A category of intelligence identified by Howard Gardner that involves processes associated with seeking meaning through the use of abstract symbols. *See also:* Multiple Intelligences.

Lower-Level Questions   Questions that seek answers that require use of simple mental processes, involving recall of basic information. *See also:* Higher-Level Questions.

Magnet School   A school that features a particular theme and that accepts learners from all areas of a school district who meet entry requirements. *See also:* School Choice.

Mainstreaming   A principle associated with federal regulations for services to learners with disabilities that suggests that learners with disabilities should spend at least part of each instructional day in a regular school classroom.

Malfeasance   A category of behavior involving actions that are taken to deliberately and knowingly harm someone. *See also:* Misfeasance, Negligence, Nonfeasance.

Managing Relationships   A component of emotional intelligence identified by Daniel Goleman that refers to a person's ability to work productively with others to resolve conflicts, maintain open lines of communication, and negotiate compromises. *See also:* Emotional Intelligence.

Mann, Horace   A key educational leader of the first half of the 19th century who promoted the idea of the common school and worked hard to convince taxpayers of the merits of a publicly supported system of education. *See also:* Common School.

Marker Expressions   Teacher statements that underline, highlight, or otherwise draw attention to the importance of something that has been said.

Massachusetts School Law of 1642   The first law in America that attempted to make school attendance compulsory, it charged local magistrates with responsibility for assuring that parents did not neglect their children's education. *See also:* "Old Deluder Satan Act" of 1647.

Matching Test   A test type that requires individuals to look at items in a list and correctly match them to definitions appearing in a second list.

Measurement   The process of quantifying the presence or absence of a quality, trait, or attribute. *See also:* Assessment, Evaluation.

Mental Retardation   A term applied to people whose intellectual development (1) lags significantly behind that of their age-mates and (2) whose potential for academic achievement has been found to be markedly lower than that of so-called "normal" people.

Merit Pay   A general term used to describe approaches to establishing teachers' salary levels that focus on measures of their performance, particularly on information related to their ability to enhance learners' achievement levels.

Metacognitive Powers   A term referring to individuals' ability to become aware of their own thinking processes and to determine their relevancy for responding to a particular problem or set of conditions. *See also:* Constructivism.

Metaphysics   A philosophical category that deals with the nature of reality. Associated questions go beyond the physical and material and cannot be studied scientifically. *See also:* Axiology, Epistemology, Logic, Postmodern Philosophy.

Middle School   A school type featuring grade arrangements serving some learners between the ages of 10 and 15. It started to become popular in the 1960s and, today, has evolved to be the dominant school type (displacing the junior high school) for learners between their elementary and high school years. Middle schools seek to provide programs that are particularly sensitive to the emotional and developmental needs of early adolescents. *See also:* Junior High School.

Misfeasance   A category of behavior characterized by a person's failure to take proper safeguards to prevent harm from coming to someone. *See also:* Malfeasance, Negligence, Nonfeasance.

Modification   Altering tasks for children who are challenged to make the assignment possible for them to successfully complete.

Monitoring   Actions teachers take to keep themselves apprised about how well members of a class understand instruction and how well they are performing assigned tasks.

Mood Management   A component of emotional intelligence identified by Daniel Goleman that refers to a person's ability to handle feelings in ways that are appropriate to a situation. *See also:* Emotional Intelligence.

Motivational Activities   Activities a teacher uses to stimulate and maintain interest in what is being taught. *See also:* End-of-the-Instructional-Sequence Motivation, Initial Motivation, Within-the-Lesson-Motivation.

Multicultural Education   A perspective on education that holds that school programs should present learners with instruction that honors and respects the contributions that many individual cultures have made to our nation and world. It promotes equity of educational treatment to all learners who come to school.

Multidimensionality   A characteristic of teaching that refers to the idea that teachers' responsibilities range across a broad range of duties.

Multiple-Choice Tests   Tests that require learners to select an answer from among three or more options. *See also:* Distractors.

Multiple Intelligences   A perspective that holds that intelligence is not a unitary trait but, instead, consists of many separate categories.

Musical Intelligence   A category of intelligence identified by Howard Gardner that involves processes associated with seeking meaning by attending carefully to sound. *See also:* Multiple Intelligences.

NAEP *See:* National Assessment of Educational Progress.

NAEYC *See:* National Association for the Education of Young Children.

Narrative Approach A kind of classroom observation in which the observer tries to establish a record of what happens by trying to write down everything that occurs.

National Assessment of Educational Progress (NAEP) A program administered by the U.S. Department of Education that periodically tests the nation's learners to ascertain their levels of knowledge of various school subjects.

National Association for the Education of Young Children (NAEYC) A large, national professional group dedicated to promoting the education and general interests of young children.

National Center for Children Exposed to Violence An organization dedicated to sharing information and promoting policies that seek to reduce children's exposure to violence.

National Clearinghouse on Child Abuse and Neglect A service of the U.S. Department of Health and Human Services that gathers information and promotes services related to responding to and preventing child abuse and neglect.

National Council for Accreditation of Teacher Education (NCATE) A national organization that evaluates and accredits colleges, schools, and departments of teacher education.

National Council for the Social Studies (NCSS) A leading national professional organization for educators interested in improving the teaching of the social studies in the schools.

National Council of Teachers of English (NCTE) A leading national professional organization for educators interested in improving the teaching of English in the schools.

National Council of Teachers of Mathematics (NCTM) A leading national professional organization for educators interested in improving the teaching of mathematics in the schools.

National Council on Education Standards and Testing A group formed following a national "Education Summit" in 1989 that was one of two groups charged with seeking responses to questions about what (1) schools should teach, (2) kinds of testing should be used, and (3) standards of performance learners should be held to. *See also:* National Education Goals Panel.

National Defense Education Act This 1958 legislation, passed as a response to concerns about educational quality following the launch of *Sputnik,* provided federal funds to support curriculum reform, teacher training, and other initiatives to improve the quality of American education. *See also: Sputnik.*

National Education Association (NEA) The nation's largest professional organization for teachers. *See also:* American Federation of Teachers.

National Education Standards and Improvement Council A group authorized by the 1994 Goals 2000—Educate America Act that was charged with overseeing the development of national content standards. Responsibility for developing these standards was later delegated to individual states. *See also:* Goals 2000—Educate America Act.

National Educational Goals Panel A group formed following a national "Education Summit" in 1989 that was one of two groups charged with seeking responses to questions about what (1) schools should teach, (2) kinds of testing should be used, and (3) standards of performance learners should be held to. *See also:* National Council on Education Standards and Testing.

National Middle School Association (NMSA) The nation's leading professional organization for educators and others who are interested in promoting the development and support of high-quality middle schools and middle school learners.

National Science Teachers Association (NSTA) A leading national professional organization for educators interested in improving the teaching of science in the schools.

Naturalist Intelligence A category of intelligence identified by Howard Gardner that involves heavy reliance on making inferences that are based on classifications and other analyses of the physical world. *See also:* Multiple Intelligences.

N-CIPA *See:* Neighborhood Children's Internet Protection Act.

NCSS *See:* National Council for the Social Studies.

NCTE *See:* National Council of Teachers of English.

NCTM *See:* National Council of Teachers of Mathematics.

NEA *See:* National Education Association.

Needs-of-Society Orientation A perspective on curriculum that holds that school programs should be organized around widely recognized needs of society—for example, such objectives as preparing learners to move smoothly into the workplace. *See also:* Academic-Subjects Orientation, Learner-Centered Orientation.

Negligence A failure to use reasonable care and/or to take prudent actions to prevent harm from coming to someone. *See also:* Malfeasance, Misfeasance, Nonfeasance.

Neighborhood Children's Internet Protection Act (N-CIPA) This part of Public Law 105-554, passed in December 2000, focuses on kinds of information that must be included in a school's Internet safety policy. *See also:* Children's Internet Protection Act, Internet Safety Policy.

NMSA *See:* National Middle School Association.

No Child Left Behind Act of 2001 This 2002 legislation encompasses numerous initiatives designed to ensure that all learners derive maximum benefits from their experiences in schools. Among other things, it requires states to have rigorous curriculum standards, to develop plans to assess learners' performance on tests related to these standards, and to intervene to help learners whose achievement falls below certain levels. It holds schools accountable for the annual progress of learners in all subgroups of the school population, including learners with disabilities.

Nondiscriminatory Testing A principle associated with federal regulations for services to learners with disabilities that requires schools to use multiple indicators to determine whether a learner has a disability and whether special services are needed.

Nonfeasance A failure of a person to act in circumstances when he or she had an obligation to act. *See also:* Malfeasance, Misfeasance, Negligence.

Nonverbal Behaviors Gestures and other behaviors that communicate meaning but that do not involve the use of the voice.

Nonverbal Responses Reactions reflected in facial expressions and body language.

Normal School An institution specifically designed to educate future school teachers.

Norming Group The group whose scores are used to establish expected scores for individuals who take a standardized test. *See also:* Norms.

Norm-Referenced Evaluation An evaluation type in which judgments about individual learner performance are made based on how well the performance compares to scores of other, similar learners. *See also:* Bell-Shaped Curve, Criterion-Referenced Evaluation, Evaluation, Norms.

Norms Expected range of scores for individuals in an identified group. *See also:* Bell-Shaped Curve, Evaluation, Norm-Referenced Evaluation.

NSTA *See:* National Science Teachers Association.

Null Curriculum The messages and lessons that students receive as a result of what is ignored or left out of the school curriculum.

Office of Gifted and Talented A federal office concerned with the educational development of gifted and talented learners.

Office of Special Education Programs (OSEP) A component of the U.S. Department of Education that oversees programs for learners with disabilities.

"Old Deluder Satan Act" of 1647 Legislation that extended the Massachusetts School Law of 1642. The law required every town of 50 or more families to hire a teacher of reading or writing. It represented an early attempt to establish the principle of public responsibility for education. *See also:* Massachusetts School Law of 1642.

Ontology *See:* Metaphysics.

Open-Enrollment Plan A plan that allows a parent or guardian to send his or her son or daughter to any existing school within a school district. In a few places, it is possible for parents to select a school located in a school district other than their own. *See also:* School Choice.

Open File A category of a placement file that allows the person who is the subject of the file to view paperwork submitted by others and, at his or her discretion, to remove any material he or she deems inappropriate. *See also:* Closed File.

OSEP   *See:* Office of Special Education Programs.

Outcome Goals   A category of goals that emphasize the results or effects of instruction.

Pacing   A term that refers to the rate at which a teacher proceeds through steps involved in teaching a particular lesson.

Paraeducator   An individual a school district hires to work with and assist teachers in the classroom.

Paralanguage   A term that includes voice intonation, variations in articulation of individual words, and rates of speaking that act as an overlay on words that affect listeners' understandings of what is said.

Paraprofessional   *See:* Paraeducator.

Parent/Guardian Participation   A principle associated with federal regulations for services to learners with disabilities that requires schools to allow parents/guardians to play substantive roles in making decisions about educational experiences provided to their sons and daughters.

Peer-Evaluation System   A practice that uses peers (in schools, other teachers) to evaluate performance, as opposed to administrative officials.

Peer Group   A term used to describe individuals who are similar in age and interests.

Perennialism   An educational philosophy that emphasizes the search for and the dissemination of unchanging principles and enduring truths and that views knowledge as consisting of unified and unchanging principles. Learners should be taught truths that have been discovered throughout history. *See also:* Essentialism, Existentialism, Progressivism, Reconstructionists.

Performance Assessment   A category of assessment that attempts to make judgments about an individual's performance in settings that parallel as closely as possible real-world conditions. *See also:* Assessment.

Performance Standards   A category of standards that describe levels of proficiency that a given group of learners is expected to attain as a result of their exposure to a particular body of content. *See also:* Content Standards, Standards-Based Education.

Personal Fable   A term that learning-development theorist David Elkind uses to describe a tendency of many adolescents to believe they are experiencing a unique life story that features feelings and reactions no one has ever before experienced. *See also:* Imaginary Audience.

Personal Filter   A psychological screen, based on experiences, that everyone unwittingly uses to interpret information and events.

Pestalozzi, Johann Heinrich   A Swiss educational philosopher of the late 18th and early 19th centuries who believed education should be provided to children in a warm, nurturing atmosphere and that one of its important purposes was improvement of society.

Phi Delta Kappa   An honorary society for eductors.

Philosophical Perspectives   Clusters of values and attitudes that individuals use to screen alternative action options and make decisions regarding which ones to adopt. *See also:* Axiology, Epistemology, Logic, Metaphysics, Postmodern Philosophy.

Placement Assessment   Assessment that is designed to provide information a teacher can use to determine an appropriate entry point for instruction. *See also:* Assessment, Formative Assessment, Pretest, Summative Assessment.

Political Foundations   Foundations of education that draw insights from history. *See also:* Foundations of Education.

Portfolio   A set of organized information that helps the person who prepared it to synthesize what he or she knows in ways that allow for easy retrieval of information. *See also:* Learner Portfolio, Teaching Portfolio.

Postmodern Philosophy   A philosophical position that holds that individuals create knowledge in ways that free them from considering any boundaries, limits, or thought guidelines. *See also:* Axiology, Epistemology, Logic, Metaphysics.

Praxis I   A component of the Praxis Series that tests prospective teacher candidates' proficiencies in reading, writing, and mathematics. *See also:* Praxis Series.

Praxis II   A component of the Praxis Series, often used to determine qualification for certification, licensure, or credentialing, that assesses teacher candidates' knowledge of the subjects they wish to teach and their knowledge of important pedagogical principles. *See also:* Praxis Series.

Praxis III   A component of the Praxis Series that is administered during the first year of teaching and that seeks to judge the quality of performance and provide a basis for professional-improvement plans. *See also:* Praxis Series.

Praxis Series   A sequence of tests, developed by the Educational Testing Service, that are widely used for the purposes of (1) screening prospective candidates for admission to professional teacher education; (2) ascertaining prospective teachers' eligibility for certification, licensure or credentialing; and (3) evaluating teachers during their first year on the job. *See also:* Praxis I, Praxis II, Praxis III.

Prereferral Intervention Process   A process developed to prevent excessive numbers of minority learners from being classified as learners with disabilities. The process encourages school professionals to determine whether the individual in question might be better served by being provided with better-designed classroom instruction, thereby avoiding the necessity of classifying him or her as someone who needs special-education services.

Pretest   A test designed to provide information about what a learner may already know or think about content that is to be introduced. *See also:* Placement Assessment.

Pretraining Phase   Term used to describe processes and experiences to which prospective teachers may have been exposed prior to beginning a formal preparation program that may influence their views of teaching and teachers. *See also:* Continuing-Growth Phase, Formal-Preparation Phase, Induction-Years Phase.

Private Residential Setting   As related to learners with disabilities, this term refers to a privately supported facility where learners live and are taught.

Probability Statements   Statements that sometimes confuse learners because they lack precision. Examples include words such as frequently, generally, and often may be defined differently by individual learners.

Probable Cause   A rigorous legal standard that requires that actions of governmental authorities such as issuing warrants must be justified by exceptionally strong evidence pointing to the possible guilt of someone suspected of illegal behavior.

Probing Questions   Questions teachers ask that seek to challenge learners' judgments when they have arrived at premature conclusions about complex issues.

Problems Approach   A school-program variety falling within the more-general needs-of-society category that seeks to help learners develop competencies they will need to successfully confront pressing social problems. *See also:* Needs-of-Society Orientation.

Product Assessment   *See:* Performance Assessment.

Professional-Education Component   A part of the Formal-Preparation Phase of a teacher's professional development that provides teacher candidates with the background they will need to deliver instruction and manage learners. *See also:* Formal-Preparation Phase.

Progressive Education Movement   An approach to education that was especially popular in the 1920s and 1930s that drew inspiration from John Dewey's work and emphasized the need of schools to respond to needs and interests of individual learners. *See also:* Dewey, John.

Progressivism   As applied to education, a philosophical position that emphasizes change as the essence of reality and that sees educated persons as people who have developed the insights and problem-solving skills they need to adapt to change. *See also:* Dewey, John; Essentialism; Existentialism; Perennialism; Reconstructionists.

Property Right   A right to a specific tangible or intangible property. *See also:* Due Process, Liberty Right.

Proposals Relating to the Youth of Pennsylvania In this 1749 work, Benjamin Franklin proposed a new kind of school, oriented to the real world, that would be free of all religious ties. *See also:* Franklin Academy.

Proximity Control   Control over learner behavior that occurs when the teacher's position in the classroom is close to that of an individual learner.

Psychomotor Domain   A learning category that focuses on muscular coordination, manipulation, and motor skills. *See also:* Affective Domain, Cognitive Domain.

Public Law 94-142   *See:* Education for All Handicapped Children Act.

Publicly Supported Residential Facility   A facility that serves learners with disabilities that is publicly supported and where learners live and are taught.

Publicness   A characteristic of teaching that refers to teachers' work occurring in a setting where their actions are open to continual scrutiny by others.

Rating Scales   Data-gathering tools that allow observers to make judgments about the quality of observed behaviors by using descriptors of rating points such as "unacceptable," "acceptable," "above average," "greatly above average."

Raw Score   A student's score, based on the number of correct answers, that has not been subjected to any kind of mathematical adjustment. *See also:* Derived Scores.

Reconstructionists   People who believe in an educational philosophy that holds that society is not organized appropriately and that schools should serve as a catalyst in the effort to improve the human condition by producing graduates who are capable of promoting social reform. *See also:* Essentialism, Existentialism, Perennialism, Progressivism.

Record-Keeping Learner Portfolio   A portfolio that one teacher keeps and passes on to another to help the new teacher better understand a learner's state of development and better prepare an instructional program to meet this individual's needs. *See also:* Learner Portfolio, Showcase Learner Portfolio, Working Learner Portfolio.

Reference Group   A group of learners within a class that the teacher uses to sample levels of learner understanding of ongoing instruction.

Referent Power   Power that results from a warm, positive relationship. *See also:* Coercive Power, Expert Power, Legitimate Power, Reward Power.

Reliability   A concept that refers to the degree to which an evaluation process is designed to ensure that different evaluators will arrive at similar conclusions when making judgments about the performance of the same individual. *See also:* Validity.

Reteaching   A process that involves a teacher in renewed presentation of material provided in a given lesson, often involving use of different examples. The purpose is to clear up misunderstandings and help learners who failed to grasp the material when it was introduced.

Reward Power   Power that comes to individuals as a result of their ability to provide something other people see as desirable. *See also:* Coercive Power, Expert Power, Legitimate Power, Referent Power.

Right to Privacy   This term refers to learners' legal rights to privacy, particularly as those rights are protected by the Family Educational Rights and Privacy Act. *See also:* Family Educational Rights and Privacy Act.

Rigorous Assessment   A term used to describe assessment procedures that require learners to demonstrate their abilities to use sophisticated thinking processes. *See also:* Assessment.

Risk Factors   A term used to describe characteristics or conditions of learners that diminish their probability of achieving success at school.

Rubric   *See:* Scoring Rubric.

Salary Schedule   *See:* Teacher-Salary Schedule.

SAT   *See:* Scholastic Achievement Test.

Scholastic Achievement Test (SAT)   A widely used college entrance examination.

School–Business Partnership   A term used to describe the relationship between a business and a school for the purpose of enhancing the quality of educational programs.

School-Busing Policies   Policies that seek to achieve an appropriate mixture of learners in all schools by transporting learners from various groups to schools outside of their neighborhoods to achieve an appropriate racial, cultural, and ethnic mix in each building.

School Choice   A term used to describe a policy that allows parents and guardians to choose the school their children attend, irrespective of its location. *See also:* Attendance Zone.

School Climate   A term used to describe the general atmosphere within which instruction, learning, and person-to-person interactions occur within a school.

School-to-Work Opportunities Act   Federal legislation that provides grants to states and communities to develop arrangements that prepare young people for additional education and careers. *See also:* Tech-Prep Program.

Scientific Problem-Solving   A systematic approach to solving problems, much admired by John Dewey, that features (1) identification of a problem, (2) gathering of information relevant to its solution, (3) development of a tentative solution, and (4) testing of the solution in the light of additional evidence. *See also:* Dewey, John.

Scoring Rubric   A set of guidelines that provides clear definitions for performances and evidences required for specific ratings to be awarded.

Scripting   *See:* Narrative Approach.

Search and Seizure   *See:* Unreasonable Search and Seizure.

Seating-Chart Systems   Observation instruments that allow for the gathering of information about behaviors of individual members of an observed class.

Selected-Response Measures   A term used to refer to tests that require learners to select responses from among several provided choices. *See also:* Free-Response Measures.

Selective Verbatim   An approach to classroom observation in which the observer identifies a particular dimension of classroom verbal interaction as a focus and records all that happens that falls within the identified category.

Self-Awareness   A component of emotional intelligence identified by Daniel Goleman that refers to a person's ability to know feelings he or she is sensing and to discriminate among them in meaningful ways. *See also:* Emotional Intelligence.

Self-Motivation   A component of emotional intelligence identified by Daniel Goleman that refers to a person's ability to organize feelings in ways that allow self-directed activity on behalf of a goal to go forward, even in the face of self-doubts and distracting temptations. *See also:* Emotional Intelligence.

Sense of Efficacy   A feeling that a person's existence "matters" and that he or she is a competent individual who has important contributions to make to his or her world.

Separate Private-School Facility   A facility designed to serve learners with disabilities that a private firm or organization operates and that is located at a site away from a regular school.

Separate Public-School Facility   A facility designed to serve learners with disabilities that a school district operates and that is located at a site away from a regular school.

Showcase Learner Portfolio   A portfolio type that is designed to highlight a learner's most significant accomplishments. *See also:* Learner Portfolio, Record-Keeping Learner Portfolio, Working Learner Portfolio.

Simultaneity   A characteristic of teaching that refers to teachers' need to operate in an environment where many things occur at the same time.

Social and Philosophical Foundations   Foundations of education that draw insights from sociology and philosophy. *See also:* Foundations of Education.

Social Cohesion   A sense of communal belonging and caring that binds together members of society.

Socialization   The process that teaches people how to function in society.

Society for the History of Children and Youth   A professional organization whose members are interested in historical views of children and their development.

Soft Subjects   A term used to describe subjects or disciplines in which there is heavy reliance on intuition, feeling, and reason, as opposed to scientific observation, to determine truth. *See also:* Hard Subjects.

Spatial Intelligence   A category of intelligence identified by Howard Gardner that involves processes associated with seeking meaning by perceiving, transforming, and re-creating visual images. *See also:* Multiple Intelligences.

Special Class   As related to learners with disabilities, this term refers to a class that consists exclusively of learners with disabilities.

Special Education Teachers   Teachers who have received special academic preparation to teach learners with varying kinds of disabilities.

Sputnik   The name of an earth satellite put into orbit in 1957 by the Soviet Union. Its launch stimulated a wide range of concerns in the United States about the adequacy of educational programming, particularly with a focus on school courses in mathematics and the sciences. This concern prompted a decade-long wave of curriculum reform.

Staff Development   Term used to describe efforts of employing organizations to provide additional education and training to employees, for example teachers, to improve their knowledge, skills, and general job-related expertise. *See also:* In-Service Education.

Standardized Tests   Tests that report learner scores in terms of how they compare with expected scores of similar kinds of learners. *See also:* Assessments, Norms.

Standards-Based Education   A movement that seeks to develop clear, measurable descriptions of what learners should know and be able to do as a result of their exposure to instruction in the schools.

State Curriculum Standards   Summaries of actions taken by individual states that specify elements of content that must be taught in individual elementary school grades and in specific middle school and high school courses.

Stem   In the area of testing, this term refers to the first, or cueing, portion of a multiple-choice item that precedes the three or more answer options. *See also:* Distractors.

Structure-of-the-Disciplines Emphasis   A variant of the academic-subject orientation that focuses learners' attention on how specialists in academic disciplines go about their work rather than on the findings resulting from efforts of these academic specialists. *See also:* Academic-Subjects Orientation.

Sudbury Model   A school program followed by a few schools in the United States that is based on principles associated with existentialism. *See also:* Existentialism.

Summative Assessment   Assessment that takes place at the conclusion of an instructional sequence to ascertain what knowledge and skills learners have acquired as a result of their exposure to this set of learning experiences. *See also:* Assessment, Formative Assessment, Placement Assessment.

Systemic Reform   The idea that school reform cannot be achieved by improving only a single variable associated with education and schooling. The term implies that true reform can occur only when there is simultaneous improvement of all factors that contribute to educational and school quality.

Task-Analysis Activities   Actions teachers take to (1) break a given body of content into smaller components or subtasks and (2) identify a good beginning point for instruction.

Taxonomy   A term that refers to a classification scheme. *See also:* Bloom's Taxonomy, Krathwohl's Taxonomy.

Teacher's Aide   *See:* Paraeducator.

Teacher-Salary Schedule   A document produced by a school district that describes salary levels for teachers with varying characteristics (e.g., academic degrees, numbers of credits earned, years of experience, and so forth).

Teacher's Assistant   *See:* Paraeducator.

Teachers' Dispositons   Perceptions and attitudes of teachers that influence the character of their interactions with learners and the overall nature of their performance in the classroom.

Teaching Certificate   A document that makes it legally possible for a person to teach in a state's schools. *See also:* Teaching Credential, Teaching License.

Teaching Contract   An official employment agreement between a teacher and a school district that includes information related to such issues as conditions of employment, salary, sick leave policies, insurance provisions, and complaint procedures.

Teaching Credential   A document that makes it legally possible for a person to teach in a state's schools. *See also:* Teaching Certificate, Teaching License.

Teaching License   A document that makes it legally possible for a person to teach in a state's schools. *See also:* Teaching Certificate, Teaching Credential.

Teaching Portfolio   A portfolio that includes evidence a teacher gathers to document what he or she has accomplished with a given group of learners over a period of time, perhaps a grading term, a semester, or an academic year.

Teaching Specializations/Academic Majors A part of the Formal-Preparation Phase of a teacher's professional development that provides teacher candidates with the content background they will need to prepare lessons for their learners. *See also:* Formal-Preparation Phase.

Teaching Team A group of teachers who cooperate and collaborate in various ways to assure that learners are receiving instruction that is appropriate to their individual needs.

Technological Literacy A capability of people who have a basic understanding of important technologies, a willingness to accept and adapt to new technological innovations, and an ability to employ technologies at an acceptable level of proficiency. *See also:* Technology.

Technology The application of scientific processes to resources for the purpose of extending our capabilities to meet our needs and wants.

Tech-Prep Demonstration Program A U.S. Department of Education grant competition that results in allocations of funds to groups operating Tech-Prep programs. *See also:* Tech-Prep Program.

Tech-Prep Program A term used to describe programs that seek to provide practical training to help students prepare for the world of work with integrated school experiences that feature two years of high school work and two additional years of training, often at community or junior colleges.

Telecommunications Act of 1996 Federal legislation that included provisions designed to make funds available to schools to support costs associated with integrating modern communication technologies into instructional programs. *See also:* E-Rate.

Tenure A principle guaranteed by law in some places and as policy by school districts in some others that assures an employed teacher of reemployment each year provided certain stipulated conditions are met. *See also:* Yearly Contract.

Terms of Approximation Terms or short phrases including "kind of," "sort of," and "about" that provide only vague descriptions of events and circumstances.

Theism A belief that the universe was created by God.

Thinking Aloud An instructional approach that features a teacher talking about thinking processes that might be appropriate for learners to use in responding to a specific assignment.

Time Sampling An approach to classroom observation in which the observer records what is happening in the classroom at selected time intervals, for example once every 15 seconds.

Tinker v. Des Moines Independent School District (1969) A famous legal case that helped establish the point that students and teachers both enjoy the constitutional protections accorded to citizens. The case involved a free speech issue centering on whether a school district could prohibit students from wearing black armbands to protest U.S. involvement in the Vietnam war.

Total Immersion A category of school program that attempts to help nonnative speakers of English acquire English by involving them in instructional programs that surround them with English-language usage.

Transitions Points within lessons or between lessons that feature a shift from one activity to another.

Triarchic Theory of Intelligence A multiple-intelligences framework developed by Robert Sternberg that includes componential intelligence, experiential intelligence, and contextual intelligence. *See also:* Componential Intelligence, Experiential Intelligence, Contextual Intelligence.

Two-Response Tests Tests that that require learners to select the correct response by deciding between two provided alternatives.

UDL *See:* Universal Design for Learning.

Universal Design for Learning (UDL) Term applied to efforts to design curricula that provide built-in access channels for learners with varying needs, for example for deaf learners and blind learners.

Unpredictability A characteristic of teaching that refers to the fact that teachers work in an environment where learners' behaviors often vary from day to day and where other unexpected occurrences often disrupt typical patterns.

Unreasonable Search and Seizure   A constitutional guarantee that protects citizens from searches and seizure of their property unless rigorous evidentiary conditions are met.

Validity   A measurement concept that focuses on the degree to which a measurement tool measures what it is supposed to measure. *See also:* Reliability.

Visualizing Thinking   An instructional approach that encourages learners to use diagrams that (1) help them understand the demands of an assigned task, (2) prompt them to consider the kinds of thinking they will need to apply, and (3) help them to identify the specific information they will need to achieve success.

Voucher Plans   An approach to school choice that gives parents tax money they can turn over to a school of their choice to support the education of their children. *See also:* School Choice.

Wait Time   The interval between the time when a teacher asks a question and when a learner responds.

Whole Language   An approach to language teaching that features lessons in which reading, writing, speaking, and listening are taught as a single, integrated process.

Within-Individual-School Segregation   A pattern that can occur within a school that may have a total learner population that is highly diverse but that has individual classes where members of some groups are overrepresented and members of some groups are underrepresented. This pattern can occur when members of particular groups are thought to have more aptitude for certain subjects than members of other groups.

Within-Lesson Checks for Understanding   Actions, often short questions, a teacher takes while teaching a lesson to determine whether learners are grasping the new material.

Within-the-Lesson Motivation   Motivational action taken by a teacher during an instructional sequence to sustain students' levels of interest in material being presented. *See also:* End-of-the-Instructional-Sequence Motivation, Initial Motivation, Motivational Activities.

Working Learner Portfolio   A portfolio that shows a learner's growth over time and reveals both strengths and weaknesses. *See also:* Learner Portfolio, Record-Keeping Learner Portfolio, Showcase Learner Portfolio.

Yearly Contract   A contract type that offers a position to a teacher one year at a time with no guarantees or legal obligations to renew the agreement at the end of each year. *See also:* Tenure.

Zero Rejects   A principle associated with federal regulations for services to learners with disabilities that requires schools to enroll every child, regardless of his or her disability.

Name Index

Subject Index

A

A Nation at Risk: The Imperative for Educational Reform, 59
Abused and neglected learners, 96–97, 392, 395
Academic freedom, 388–90, 394, 399
Academic learning time, 234–35
Academic majors, 35, 52, 416
Academic-subjects curricula, 179, 182–86, 191
Academic-subjects orientation, 399
Academies, 320, 335, 399
Acceleration programs, 161, 164, 399
Acceptable-use policies (AUPs), 363, 399
Accepting disabilities, preparing others for, 150
Accommodation, 145, 163
Accountability, 19, 20–22, 73, 399
Achievement gap, 92, 399
Achievement levels, concerns about, 121–23
Active teaching, 199–204, 222, 399
    lesson preparation, 200
    monitoring, 201
    pacing lessons, 203
    program planning, 200
    sequencing instruction, 202–3
    specifying objectives, 200
    stimulating and maintaining interest, 201
    task analysis, 200
    within-lesson questioning, 201–2
Addressing Over-Representation of African American Students in Special Education, 156, 157
Administration/administrators, 48–49, 329
Advance organizer, 210, 399
Affective domain, 265, 399
Affluence, 321
AFL-CIO, 40
Africa, educational legacies from, 331
African Americans
    busing and neighborhood schools, 293
    diversity issues, 120, 121, 122
    intelligence tests and, 326
    learner profiles, 91–92
    learners with disabilities, 155–57

Quaker schools and, 320
technology and, 362
Alaska Native, 156
All can learn, 124
Alliance for Technology Access, 155
Alternative certification, 22
Ambiguous designations, 211, 399
American education history, 318
    Civil War to 1900, 323
    colonial period to independence, 319–21
    independence to Civil War, 321–23
    1900 to World War II, 323–27
    World War II to 21st century, 327–30
American Evaluation Association, 259
American Federation of Teachers (AFT), 34, 38–39, 40, 52, 323, 399
American Indians, 91, 156, 320
American Society for Supervision and Curriculum Development, 173
American Society for Training and Development (ASTD), 50, 399
Americans with Disabilities Act (ADA), 141, 399
Analysis, 266
Anchorage School Business Partnership program, 76
Anticipatory set, 203
Antisocial behavior, 93
Application, 203, 265
Appropriate education, 142, 399
Approximation, terms of, 211, 417
Arthur and Elizabeth Schlesinger Library on the History of Women in America, 129
Artifacts, 25
Arts, 303
Asian Americans, 91–92, 156, 362
Assessment, 15, 257, 277
    authentic, 62, 273, 278, 400
    bell-shaped curve, 259
    checklists, 273
    criterion-referenced evaluation, 260–61
    definition of, 399
    derived scores, 259
    direct, 273
    evaluation, 259–61
    formative, 263–64
    instructional process and, 263–64

IQ tests, 325–26
key terms, 257–63
measurement, 257–58
measurement options, 268–75
norm-referenced evaluation, 259–60
norming group, 260
performance, 273, 276–77, 278, 412
placement, 263
planning for, 264–68
product, 273
purposes of, 256–57
rating scales, 273
raw scores, 259
rigorous, 62, 414
Scholastic Achievement Test, 258–59
standardized testing, 258–59
summative, 264
teaching portfolios, 44–45
testing movement, 325–26
understanding, 256
Assessment plan, 257, 400
Assignments
    learners with disabilities and, 146
    teaching, 186
Assistance, providing, 236
Assistive technology, 154–55, 164, 400
Association, 203
Association for Supervision and Curriculum Development (ASCD), 187, 205, 400
At-risk learners, 97, 107
Attendance, 327
Attendance zone, 63, 400
Attention, of learners, 243
Attention deficit disorder (ADD), 143, 151, 153, 164, 400
Attitude of public toward schools, 4, 230
Attitudes of parents toward standardized tests, 173
Attitudes of teachers toward technology, 356, 360–61
Augments opposing inclusion, 148
Augments supporting inclusion, 148
Authentic assessment, 62, 273, 278, 400
Automaticity, 17, 400
Axiology, 298–99, 308, 400